S0-AUR-327

Discovering Computers 2004

A Gateway to Information
Web Enhanced

Brief

Discovering Computers 2004
A Gateway to Information
Web Enhanced

Brief

Gary B. Shelly
Thomas J. Cashman
Misty E. Vermaat

Contributing Authors
Jeffrey J. Quasney
Susan L. Sebok
Timothy J. Walker
Jeffrey J. Webb

THOMSON
COURSE TECHNOLOGY

COURSE TECHNOLOGY
25 THOMSON PLACE
BOSTON MA 02210

SHELLY
CASHMAN
SERIES®

Australia • Canada • Denmark • Japan • Mexico • New Zealand • Philippines • Puerto Rico • Singapore
South Africa • Spain • United Kingdom • United States

Discovering Computers 2004
A Gateway to Information
Web Enhanced

Gary B. Shelly
Thomas J. Cashman
Misty E. Vermaat

Managing Editor:
Cheryl Ouellette

Marketing Manager:
Katie McAllister

Senior Product Manager:
Alexandra Arnold

Product Manager:
Erin Runyon

Associate Product Manager:
Reed Cotter

Editorial Assistant:
Emilie Perreault

Print Buyer:
Denise Powers

Signing Representative:
Cheryl Ouellette

Director of Production:
Becky Herrington

Production Manager:
Doug Cowley

Developmental Editor:
Ginny Harvey

Copy Editor:
Ginny Harvey

Proofreaders:
Nancy Lamm
Lori Silfen
Kim Kosmatka

Interior Design:
Hector Arvizu

Cover Design:
Kenny Tran

Illustrators:
Hector Arvizu
Kenny Tran

Photo Researchers:
Abby Reip
Rachel Lucas
Sarah Evertson

Compositors:
Hector Arvizu
Betty Hopkins
Kenny Tran
Kellee LaVars

Indexer:
Cristina Haley

Printer:
Banta Company

COPYRIGHT © 2003
Course Technology, a division of Thomson Learning, Inc. Thomson Learning ™ is a trademark used herein under license.

Printed in the United States of America

2 3 4 5 6 7 8 9 10 BC 07 06 05 04 03

For more information, contact
Course Technology
25 Thomson Place
Boston, Massachusetts, 02210

Or find us on the World Wide Web at:
www.course.com

ALL RIGHTS RESERVED. No part of this work covered by the copyright hereon may be reproduced or used in any form or by any means — graphic, electronic, or mechanical, including photocopying, recording, taping, Web distribution, or information storage and retrieval systems — without the written permission of the publisher.

For permission to use material from this text or product, contact us by
Tel (800) 730-2214
Fax (800) 730-2215
www.thomsonrights.com

Course Technology reserves the right to revise this publication and make changes from time to time in its content without notice.

Course Technology, the Course Technology logo, the Shelly Cashman Series® and **Custom Edition**® are registered trademarks used under license. All other names used herein are for identification purposes only and are trademarks of their respective owners.

ISBN 0-7895-6702-4

Discovering Computers 2004
A Gateway to Information
Web Enhanced

Brief

Contents

SPECIAL FEATURE

Guide to World Wide Web Sites and Searching Techniques

CHAPTER 3

Application Software

CHAPTER 4

The Components of the System Unit

CHAPTER 5
Input

SPECIAL FEATURE
PDA Application Software

CHAPTER 6
Output

SPECIAL FEATURE
Digital Imaging and Video Technology

Preface

The Shelly Cashman Series® offers the finest textbooks in computer education. We are proud of the fact that the previous eight editions of this textbook have been runaway best-sellers. As with previous editions, *Discovering Computers 2004: A Gateway to Information, Web Enhanced* is intended for use as a stand-alone textbook or in combination with an applications, Internet, or programming textbook in a one-quarter or one-semester introductory computer course. No experience with computers is assumed. The material presented provides an in-depth treatment of introductory computer subjects. Students will finish the course with a solid understanding of computers, how to use computers, and how to access information on the World Wide Web. The objectives of this book are as follows:

- Teach the fundamentals of computers and computer nomenclature, particularly with respect to personal computer hardware and software, the World Wide Web, and enterprise computing

- Present the most-up-to-date technology in an ever-changing discipline

- Give students an in-depth understanding of why computers are essential components in business and society

- Present the material in a visually appealing and exciting manner that motivates students to learn

- Offer distance-education providers a textbook with a meaningful and exercise-rich companion Web site.

- Provide exercises and lab assignments that allow students to interact with a computer and learn by actually using the computer and the World Wide Web

- Offer alternative learning techniques and reinforcement via the Web

- Present strategies for purchasing, installing, and maintaining a desktop computer, a notebook computer, a Tablet PC, and a PDA

- Assist students in planning a career and getting certified in the computer field

WHAT'S NEW IN THIS EDITION

Each of the previous eight editions of this book included learning innovations such as integration of the World Wide Web, WebCT, Blackboard, Interactive Labs, online learning games, MyCourse.com, and Teaching Tools that set it apart from its competitors. *Discovering Computers 2004: A Gateway to Information, Web Enhanced* continues with the innovation, quality, timeliness, and reliability that you have come to expect from the Shelly Cashman Series. This latest edition of *Discovering Computers* includes these enhancements:

- Companion Web site redesigned and enhanced to provide much more reinforcement and F currency.

- Two new special features titled PDA Application Software and Digital Imaging and Video Technology present cutting-edge technologies.

- New two-column, easy-to-read flow of text and figures.

- New set of end-of-chapter exercises titled Web Research includes a dozen exercises to help students improve their oral and written communication skills.

- New 32-page appendix titled Making Use of the Web introduces students to the major Web applications, such as finance, travel, arts, education, auctions, entertainment, and much more.

- New appendix titled Computer Acronyms provides students with a quick reference with page numbers for the hundreds of computer-related acronyms included throughout the book.

- New two-page chapter openers include a Picture Yourself article, a list of the chapter objectives, and the chapter table of contents to set the mood and help students focus on the chapter content.

- Three Quiz Yourself boxes placed throughout each chapter refer students to the companion Web site to take a short quiz, which helps ensure they know the material just read and are ready to move on in the chapter.

- Buyer's Guide 2004 completely updated and expanded to include Tablet PCs and PDAs.

- Expanded pencil-and-paper and small-group exercises.

- Latest hardware, technology, and trends, including enterprise computing, smart display, digital imaging and video technology, Tablet PC, and much more.

- All figures replaced with updated screens, art, and photographs.

- Nearly 100 new computer terms and their definitions added to this latest edition.

- High-Tech Talk articles at the end of each chapter offer a more technical discussion of information related to a topic presented in the chapter.

- Looking Ahead boxes give students a glimpse at the latest advances in computer technology that will be available within the next five to ten years.

- Issue boxes updated to include the latest controversial topics in the computer field.

- Additional step figures present the more complex computer concepts using a step-by-step pedagogy.

- FAQ boxes offer common questions and answers about subjects related to the topic at hand.

- All questions in the 3,500-question test bank are new and identified by objective and, if term based, whether it is a primary or secondary term.

- New and improved one-click-per-slide PowerPoint presentation lecture tool for each chapter.

DISTINGUISHING FEATURES

The Brief edition of *Discovering Computers 2004: A Gateway to Information, Web Enhanced* includes the following distinguishing features.

A Proven Book

More than 5.5 million students have learned about computers using Shelly and Cashman computer fundamentals textbooks. With the additional World Wide Web integration and interactivity, streaming up-to-date audio and video, extraordinary step-by-step visual drawings and photographs, unprecedented currency, and the Shelly and Cashman touch, this book will make your computer concepts course exciting and dynamic.

World Wide Web Enhanced

This book uses the World Wide Web as a major supplement. The purpose of integrating the World Wide Web into the book is to (1) offer students additional information and currency on important topics; (2) use its interactive capabilities to offer creative reinforcement and online quizzes; (3) make available alternative learning techniques with Web-based learning games, practice tests, and interactive labs; (4) underscore the relevance of the World Wide Web as a basic information tool that can be used in all facets of society; (5) introduce students to doing research on the Web; and (5) offer instructors the opportunity to organize and administer their traditional campus-based or distance-education-based courses on the Web using WebCT, Blackboard, or My Course 2.0.

This textbook, however, does not depend on Web access to be used successfully. The Web access adds to the already complete treatment of topics within the book. The World Wide Web is integrated into the book in the following ways:

- Streaming audio that speaks the end-of-chapter Chapter Review sections to students.

- End-of-chapter pages, glossary index, and three of the special features in the book are stored as Web pages on the World Wide Web.

- Web-based quizzes are interspersed throughout the chapters; each chapter includes a chapter-ending Web-based practice test, which randomly selects questions from a pool, so students can take a chapter practice test as often as they want.

- All Issue boxes, Apply It boxes, Looking Ahead boxes, FAQ boxes, Career Corner boxes, High-Tech Talk articles, Technology Trailblazers articles, and Companies on the Cutting Edge articles include suggested Web sites that contain information beyond that presented.

- Streaming computer-related videos on the Web are in the end-of-chapter Learn It Online section.

- Throughout the text, marginal annotations titled Web Links provide suggestions on how to obtain additional information via the Web about an important topic covered on the page.

- Interactive Labs on the Web in the end-of-chapter Learn It Online sections help students gain a better understanding of a specific subject.

- WebCT and Blackboard offer Web-based course management systems for use in a traditional classroom setting or in a distance education environment.

- MyCourse 2.0 offers instructors and students an opportunity to supplement classroom learning with additional content on the Web.

A Visually Appealing Book that Maintains Student Interest

The latest technology, pictures, drawings, and text are combined artfully to produce a visually appealing and easy-to-understand book. Many of the figures show a step-by-step pedagogy, which simplifies the more complex computer concepts. Pictures and drawings reflect the latest trends in computer technology. Finally, the text is set in two columns, which instructors and reviewers say their students prefer. This combination of pictures, step-by-step drawings, and easy-to-read text layout sets a new standard for computer textbook design.

High-Tech Talk

Each chapter ends with a page titled High-Tech Talk. Students who are technically inclined will enjoy these articles that expand on information related to a topic presented in the chapter. Topics include IP addresses, How Viruses Work, How Memory Works, Wireless Communications, Sound Cards, and much more.

Companies on the Cutting Edge and Technology Trailblazers

All students graduating from an institution of higher education should be aware of the major companies and leaders in the field of computers. Thus, a two-page spread at the end of each chapter introduces students to two companies on the cutting edge and two technology trailblazers. The Companies on the Cutting Edge articles present the major computer companies, such as Microsoft, Intel, AOL, Network Associates, Red Hat, EMC, and others. The Technology Trailblazers articles present people who have made a difference in the field of computing, such as Bill Gates, Gordon Moore, Donna Dubinsky, Linus Torvalds, Carly Fiorina, Tim Berners-Lee, and others.

Latest Technologies and Terms

The technologies and terms your students see in this book are those they will encounter when they start using computers. This book covers nearly 100 topics and terms new to this edition of the book, such as modular computer, customer relationship management (CRM), enterprise computing, Athlon™ MP, Hyper-Threading (HT) Technology, ovonic memory chips, holographic storage, Windows XP Tablet PC Edition, Palladium, and much more.

End-of-Chapter Exercises

The Shelly Cashman Series authors and team dedicate as many resources to create the end-of-chapter material as we do to develop the chapter content. We believe strongly in offering exciting, rich, and thorough end-of-chapter material to reinforce the chapter objectives and assist you in making your course the finest ever offered. As indicated earlier, each of the end-of-chapter pages is stored as a Web page on the World Wide Web to provide your students in-depth information and alternative methods of preparing for examinations. Each chapter ends with the following:

- **Chapter Review** This section summarizes the chapter material in the form of questions and answers. Each question addresses a specific chapter objective, making this section invaluable in reviewing and preparing for examinations. Quiz Yourself boxes offer students the opportunity to take Web-based quizzes as they step through the Chapter Review. Links on the Web page provide additional current information. With a single-click on the Web page, the Chapter Review section is spoken to students using streaming audio.

- **Key Terms** This list of the key terms found in the chapter together with the page numbers on which the terms are defined will aid students in mastering the chapter material. The key terms in this book are divided into two categories — Primary and Secondary. The Primary Terms are terms students should know after reading the chapter. They are shown in bold black characters in the book and on the Key Terms page. The Secondary Terms are terms students should be familiar with after reading the chapter. They are shown in italics in the book and on the Key Terms page. A complete summary of all key terms in the book, together with their definitions, appears in the

Glossary Index at the end of the book. All computer acronyms with their meanings are listed in Appendix C. On the corresponding Key Terms Web page, students can click any term to view a definition and a picture and then click a link to visit a Web page that offers additional information.

- **Checkpoint**   These pencil-and-paper exercises are presented on three pages. Exercises include Label the Figure, True/False, Multiple Choice, Matching, Short Answer, and Working Together (small-group exercises). Students accessing the Checkpoint Web page can answer the questions in an interactive forum.

- **Learn It Online**   These Web-based exercises include exciting activities and reinforcement that maintain student interest. Exercises include watching streaming video, a scavenger hunt, search sleuth, Interactive Labs, practice tests, and learning games. Other exercises in this section, such as working with newsgroups and reviewing the latest news in technology, also use the World Wide Web.

- **Lab Exercises**   A series of lab assignments using Windows XP/2000/98 procedures begins with the simplest exercises within Windows. Students then are led through additional activities that, by the end of the book, enable them to be proficient using Windows.

- **Web Research**   Students need to improve their oral and written communication skills. To this end we have included a dozen Web research projects at the end of each chapter. These exercises require students to do research on the Web and write a short article about their findings or share their findings with the class by means of a formal presentation.

Ideal Book for Distance Education

Because of the companion Web site, this book is ideal for a distance education environment. Not only do students have access to the book's Web site to view movies, take practice quizzes and tests, use the learning games, complete Web research, and visit the recommended Web sites, but tests can be delivered over the Web using the test generator, ExamView.

Timeline 2004: Milestones in Computer History

A colorful, highly informative 14-page timeline following Chapter 1 steps students through the major computer technology developments during the past 60 years, including the most recent advances, as well as expectations for 2003.

Guide to World Wide Web Sites and Searching Techniques

More than 150 popular up-to-date Web sites are listed and described in this guide to Web sites that follows Chapter 2. This guide also introduces students to basic searching techniques.

PDA Application Software

This special feature following Chapter 5 offers a detailed presentation of PDA operating systems, built-in PDA software, and PDA software related to synchronization, business, communications, corporate/government, medical, scientific, travel, education, multimedia, and entertainment. Also included is a discussion about how to obtain and install PDA software.

Digital Imaging and Video Technology

This special feature following Chapter 6 introduces students to using a personal computer, digital camera, and video camera to manipulate photographs and video.

Buyer's Guide 2004: How to Purchase, Install, and Maintain a Personal Computer

The Buyer's Guide following Chapter 8 has been expanded from 15 pages to 23 pages. The guide introduces students to purchasing, installing, and maintaining a desktop computer, notebook computer, Tablet PC, and PDA.

Shelly Cashman Series Interactive Labs

A total of 18 Interactive Labs, each of which takes 10 to 15 minutes to step through, help students gain a better understanding of subjects covered in the chapters.

SHELLY CASHMAN SERIES INSTRUCTOR RESOURCES

Four ancillaries accompany this textbook: (1) Instructor Resources (ISBN 0-7895-6706-7); (2) Course Presenter (ISBN 0-7895-6707-5); (3) My Course 2.0; and (4) Blackboard and WebCT Online Content. These ancillaries are available to adopters through your Course Technology representative or by calling one of the following telephone numbers: Colleges and Universities, 1-800-648-7450; High Schools, 1-800-824-5179; Private Career Colleges, 1-800-347-7707; Canada, 1-800-268-2222; Corporations with IT Training Centers, 1-800-648-7450; and Government Agencies, Health-Care Organizations, and Correctional Facilities, 1-800-477-3692.

Instructor Resources

The Instructor Resources for this textbook include both teaching and testing aids. The contents of the Instructor Resources CD-ROM are listed below.

- **Instructor's Manual**   The Instructor's Manual is made up of Microsoft Word files. The Instructor's Manual includes detailed lesson plans with page number references, lecture notes, teaching tips, classroom activities, discussion topics, projects to assign, and transparency references. The transparencies are available through the Figure Files described on the next page.

- **Syllabus**   Any instructor who has been assigned a course at the last minute knows how difficult it is to come up with a course syllabus. For this reason, sample syllabi are included that can be customized easily to a course.

- **Figure Files**   Illustrations for every figure in the textbook are available in electronic form. Use this ancillary to present a slide show in lecture or to print transparencies for use in lecture with an overhead projector. If you have a personal computer and LCD device, this ancillary can be an effective tool for presenting lectures.

- **Solutions to Exercises**   Solutions are included for the end-of-chapter exercises.

- **Test Bank & Test Engine**   The test bank includes 220 questions for every chapter (50 multiple-choice, 100 true/false, and 70 fill-in-the-blank) with page number references, and when appropriate, figure references. Each question also is identified by objective and type of term (primary or secondary). A version of the test bank you can print also is included. The test bank comes with a copy of the test engine, ExamView. ExamView is a state-of-the-art test builder that is easy to use. ExamView enables you quickly to create printed tests, Internet tests, and computer (LAN-based) tests. You can enter your own test questions or use the test bank that accompanies ExamView.

- **Pretest/Posttest** Use these carefully prepared tests at the beginning and the end of the semester to measure student progress. A master student answer sheet is included. See the Test Bank & Test Engine menu item on the Instructor Resources CD-ROM.

- **Test Out/Final Exam** Use this objective-based test to test students out of your course, or use it as a final examination. The recommended passing score is 75 percent. A master student answer sheet is included. See the Test Bank & Test Engine menu item on the Instructor Resources CD-ROM.

- **Data Files for Students** All the files that are required by students to complete the exercises are included. You can distribute the files on the Instructor Resources CD-ROM to your students over a network, or you can have them follow the instructions on the inside back cover of this book to obtain a copy of the Discovering Computers 2004 Data Disk.

- **Study Guide Sampler** The *Study Guide Sampler* consists of Word documents of the preface and first three chapters of the *Study Guide for Discovering Computers 2004* that is described in the Supplements section on the next page. See the Instructor's Manual menu item on the Instructor Resources CD-ROM.

- **Interactive Labs** These are the nonaudio versions of the 18 hands-on Interactive Labs exercises. Students can step through each Lab in about 15 minutes to solidify and reinforce computer concepts. Assessment requires students to answer questions about the contents of the Interactive Labs. See the Software menu item on the Instructor Resources CD-ROM.

Course Presenter with Figures, Animations, and CNN Video Clips

Course Presenter is a one-click-per-slide presentation system on CD-ROM that provides PowerPoint slides for every subject in each chapter. Use this presentation system to give interesting, well-organized, and knowledge-based lectures. More than 30 two- to three-minute, up-to-date CNN computer-related video clips are available for optional presentation. Course Presenter provides consistent coverage for multiple lecturers.

MyCourse 2.0 – Course Management Made Easy

MyCourse 2.0 is a flexible, easy-to-use course management tool that gives you true customization over the online components of your course. MyCourse 2.0 allows you to personalize your course home page, schedule your course activities and assignments, post messages, administer tests, and file the results in a grade book. You also can use text-specific preloaded content for this book, add your own content, select from a pool of test bank questions, or create questions yourself. MyCourse 2.0 is hosted by Thomson Learning, allowing you hassle-free maintenance and student access at all times. For more information, visit course.com/onlinecontent.

Blackboard and WebCT Online Content

Course Technology offers you options for online content. For those who want online testing, we provide a Blackboard test bank and a WebCT test bank, available for download in the Instructor Resources section on course.com. For those who desire more content, we offer course management and access to a Web site that is fully populated with content for this book. Also see Blackboard and WebCT Online Content in the Supplements section. For more information, visit course.com/onlinecontent.

SUPPLEMENTS

Two supplements can be used in combination with *Discovering Computers 2004: A Gateway to Information, Web Enhanced*.

Shelly Cashman Series Interactive Labs with Audio on CD-ROM

The Shelly Cashman Series Interactive Labs with Audio on CD-ROM (ISBN 0-7895-6111-5) may be used in combination with this textbook to augment your students' learning process. See page xxiv for a description of each Lab. These Interactive Labs also are available at no cost on the Web by clicking the appropriate button on the Learn It Online exercise pages (see page 1.46) and as a nonaudio version on the Instructor Resources CD-ROM. A companion student guide for the Interactive Labs, titled *A Record of Discovery for Exploring Computers, Fourth Edition* (ISBN 0-7895-6372-X), enhances the Interactive Labs presentation, reinforces concepts, shows relationships, and provides additional facts.

Study Guide

This highly popular *Study Guide* (ISBN 0-7895-6705-9) includes a variety of activities that help students recall, review, and master introductory computer concepts. The *Study Guide* complements the end-of-chapter material with a guided chapter outline; a self-test consisting of true/false, multiple-choice, short answer, fill-in, and matching questions; an entertaining puzzle; and other challenging exercises. See the *Study Guide Sampler* through the Instructor's Manual menu item on the Instructor Resources CD-ROM.

ACKNOWLEDGMENTS

The Shelly Cashman Series would not be the leading computer education series without the contributions of outstanding publishing professionals. First, and foremost, among them is Becky Herrington, director of production and designer. She is the heart and soul of the Shelly Cashman Series, and it is only through her leadership, dedication, and tireless efforts that superior products are made possible.

Under Becky's direction, the following individuals made significant contributions to these books: Doug Cowley, production manager; Ken Russo, senior Web and graphic designer; Kenny Tran, cover designer; Hector Arvizu, Kenny Tran, Ken Russo, and Michelle French illustrators; Hector Arvizu, book designer; Hector Arvizu, Jeanne Black, Betty Hopkins, Michelle French, and Kellee LeVars, QuarkXPress compositors; Ginny Harvey, developmental/ copy editor; Nancy Lamm, Lori Silfen, and Kim Kosmatka, proofreaders; Cristina Haley, indexer; and Abby Reip, Rachel Lucas, Sarah Evertson, and Jennifer Quiambao, photo researchers. Additional thanks go to William Vermaat, researcher and photographer, and to Jeffrey Quasney, Susan Sebok, Timothy Walker, and Jeffrey Webb for their exceptional efforts as contributing authors.

We also would like to thank Kristen Duerr, senior vice president and publisher; Cheryl Ouellette, managing editor; Jim Quasney, series consulting editor; Alexandra Arnold, senior product manager; Erin Runyon, product manager; Katie McAllister, marketing manager; Reed Cotter, associate product manager; and Emilie Perreault, editorial assistant.

Finally, we were fortunate to have a truly dedicated group of reviewers whose critical evaluations of the initial manuscript were of great value during the preparation of this book. Special thanks goes to the following:

Dr. Nazih Abdallah, University of Central Florida
Ann Allen, Mid Michigan Community College
Paul Bartolomeo, Community College of Rhode Island
Brenda Britt, Fayetteville Technical Community College
Kristen Callahan, Mercer County Community College
Sandy Campbell, Brevard Community College
Wilbur P. Dershimer, Jr., Ed.D., Seminole Community College
Larry Farrer, Guilford Tech Community College
L. Marshall Ford, Temple University
Nichol Free, Computer Learning Network
Dr. Homa Ghajar, Oklahoma State University
Sherry Green, Purdue University Calumet
Ann Hammer, Tulsa Community College
Jerry Humphrey, Tulsa Community College
Emily Ketcham, Baylor University
Leigh McGregor, Mid Michigan Community College
Pat Ormond, Utah Valley State College
Erhan Uskup, Houston Community College
Barbara Wells, Central Carolina Technical College

Gary B. Shelly
Thomas J. Cashman
Misty E. Vermaat

Discovering Computers 2004
A Gateway to Information
Web Enhanced

To the Student
Getting the Most Out of Your Book

Welcome to *Discovering Computers 2004: A Gateway to Information, Web Enhanced*. You can save yourself a lot of time and gain a better understanding of the computer concepts presented in this book if you spend a few minutes reviewing this section.

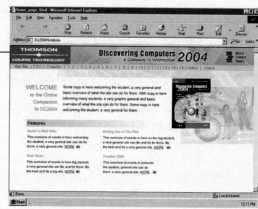

1 Companion Web Site

Use the companion Web site at scsite.com/dc2004, which includes additional information about important topics and provides unparalleled currency; and make use of online learning games, practice tests, and additional reinforcement.

2 Picture Yourself

Picture yourself using the concepts presented in the chapter you are about to read. This section at the beginning of each chapter is intended to help you see how the specific material might apply to your everyday life using computers.

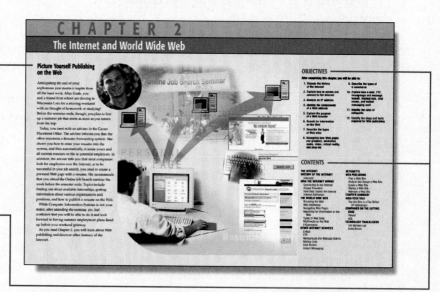

3 Chapter Objectives and Table of Contents

Before you read the chapter, carefully step through the Objectives and Contents so that you know what you should learn from the chapter.

4 Initial Chapter Figure

Carefully study the first figure in each chapter because it will give you an easy-to-follow overview of the major purpose of the chapter.

5 Web Link

Obtain current information and a different perspective about key terms and concepts by visiting the Web addresses in the Web Links found in the margins throughout the book.

6 Step Figures

Each chapter includes numerous step figures that present the more complex computer concepts using a step-by-step pedagogy.

7 Apply It

The Apply It boxes illustrate how the material presented in the chapter can be applied to everyday life.

8 Issue

Issue boxes provide you with computer-related controversial topics of the day and stimulating questions that offer insight into the general concerns of computers in society.

9 Looking Ahead

The Looking Ahead boxes offer you a glimpse at the latest advances in computer technology that will be available, usually within five years.

10 FAQ

FAQ (frequently asked questions) boxes offer common questions and answers about subjects related to the topic at hand.

11 Quiz Yourself

Three Quiz Yourself boxes per chapter help ensure that you know the material you just read and are ready to move on in the chapter. You take these quizzes on the Web for interactivity and easy use.

12 Career Corner

Each chapter ends with a Career Corner feature that introduces you to a computer-career opportunity relating to a topic covered in the chapter.

13 High-Tech Talk

If you are technically inclined, you will enjoy the High-Tech Talk article at the end of each chapter. These presentations expand on a topic covered in the chapter and present a more technical discussion.

14 Companies on the Cutting Edge

Each chapter includes a profile about two key computer-related companies of which you should be aware, especially if you plan to major in the computer field.

15 Technology Trailblazers

The Technology Trailblazers page in each chapter offers a glimpse into the life and times of the more famous leaders of the computer industry.

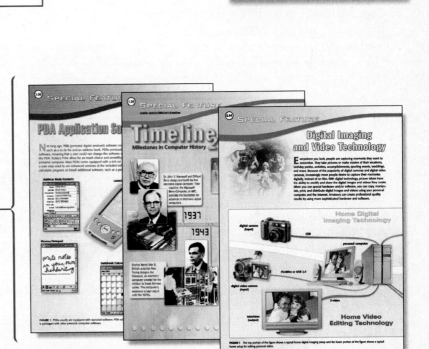

16 Guide to World Wide Web Sites and Searching Techniques

To ensure your skills using the World Wide Web are up to date, this special feature following Chapter 2 provides three resources: (1) a list of useful Web sites, (2) an introduction to searching techniques, and (3) a guide to popular search engines.

17 Buyer's Guide 2004

Do not buy a computer without reading the highly regarded Buyer's Guide that follows Chapter 8. This unique feature introduces you to purchasing, installing, and maintaining a desktop computer, notebook computer, Tablet PC, and PDA.

18 Other Special Features

Several additional special features follow chapters that will add value to your learning experience: Timeline 2004 (Chapter 1); PDA Application Software (Chapter 5); and Digital Imaging and Video Technology (Chapter 6).

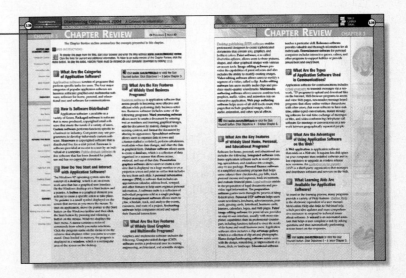

19 Chapter Review

Use the two-page Chapter Review before you take an examination to ensure that you are familiar with the computer concepts presented. This section includes each objective, followed by a one- or two-paragraph summary. Visit a Chapter Review page on the Web, and click the Audio button to listen to the Chapter Review.

20 Primary and Secondary Key Terms

Before you take a test, use the Key Terms page as a checklist of terms you should know. In the text, primary key terms appear in bold font and secondary key terms appear in italic font. Ask your instructor whether you are responsible for knowing only the primary key terms or all the key terms. Visit a Key Terms page on the Web and click any term for additional information.

21 Checkpoint

Use these three pages of exercises to reinforce your understanding of the topics presented in the chapter.

22 Learn It Online

If you prefer online reinforcement, then the Learn It Online exercises are for you. The exercises include online videos, practice tests, Interactive Labs, learning games, and Web-based activities.

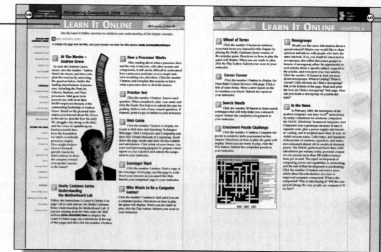

23 Lab Exercises

If you want to become proficient with the Windows operating system while you are taking your computer concepts course, then you should step through these carefully designed Windows exercises. Many of them take only a few minutes to complete.

24 Web Research

If you enjoy doing research on the Web, then you will like the Web Research exercises. Each exercise in this section references an element in the book and suggests you write a short article or do a class presentation on your findings.

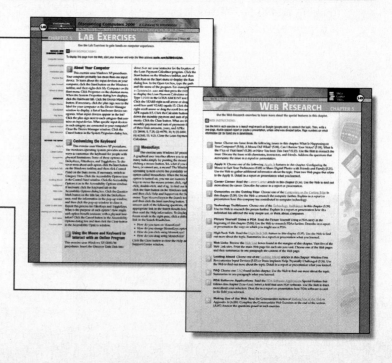

25 Making Use of the Web

Use this appendix to learn about the major Web applications: finance, travel, arts, learning, auctions, entertainment, and much more, and then test your knowledge by completing the Web Exercises.

26 Computer Acronyms

When you have trouble remembering the meaning of an abbreviation for a term, look it up in the Computer Acronyms list.

27 Glossary Index

The Glossary Index at the back of the book not only provides page references, it also offers definitions of all the primary and secondary key terms included in the text and special boxed features.

SHELLY CASHMAN SERIES INTERACTIVE LABS WITH AUDIO

Each of the 8 chapters in this textbook includes the Learn It Online exercises, which utilize the World Wide Web. The Shelly Cashman Series Interactive Labs described below are included as exercises in the Learn It Online section. These Interactive Labs are available on the Web (see page 1.46) or on CD-ROM. The audio version on CD-ROM (ISBN 0-7895-6111-5) is available at an additional cost. A nonaudio version also is available on the Instructor Resources CD-ROM that is available free to adopters.

A student guide for the Interactive Labs is available at an additional cost. The student guide is titled *A Record of Discovery for Exploring Computers, Fourth Edition* (ISBN 0-7895-6372-X), which reviews the Interactive Labs content, shows relationships, and provides additional facts.

Each Lab takes approximately 15 minutes to complete using a personal computer and helps the reader gain a better understanding of a specific subject covered in the chapter. Assessment is available within each Lab.

Shelly Cashman Series Interactive Labs with Audio

Lab	Function	Page
Using the Mouse	Master how to use a mouse. The Lab includes exercises on pointing, clicking, double-clicking, and dragging.	1.46
Using the Keyboard	Learn how to use the keyboard. The Lab discusses different categories of keys, including the edit keys, function keys, ESC, CTRL, and ALT keys and how to press keys simultaneously.	1.47
Connecting to the Internet	Learn how a computer is connected to the Internet. The Lab presents using the Internet to access information.	2.46
The World Wide Web	Understand the significance of the World Wide Web and how to use Web browser software and search tools.	2.46
Word Processing	Gain a basic understanding of word processing concepts, from creating a document to printing and saving the final result.	3.44
Working with Spreadsheets	Learn how to create and utilize spreadsheets, including entering formulas, creating graphs, and performing what-if analysis.	3.44
Understanding the Motherboard	Step through the components of a motherboard. The Lab shows how different motherboard configurations affect the overall speed of a computer.	4.46
Scanning Documents	Understand how document scanners work.	5.46
Setting Up to Print	See how information flows from the system unit to the printer and how drivers, fonts, and physical connections play a role in generating a printout.	6.40
Configuring Your Display	Recognize the different monitor configurations available, including screen size, display cards, and number of colors.	6.40
Maintaining Your Hard Drive	Understand how files are stored on disk, what causes fragmentation, and how to maintain an efficient hard drive.	7.40
Evaluating Operating Systems	Evaluate the advantages and disadvantages of different categories of operating systems.	8.40
Working at Your Computer	Learn the basic ergonomic principles that prevent back and neck pain, eye strain, and other computer-related physical ailments.	8.40

Discovering Computers 2004

Introduction to Computers

Picture Yourself Using Computers

After thanking the loan officer for her time, you leave the bank and imagine driving down the highway in a red Ford Mustang. When your friend bought the car ten years ago, you were first to ride in it. Just last week, he told you it is for sale. You want that car!

This is your lucky day. Your local bank is offering a zero percent interest, no money down, five-year car loan to students with at least a 3.0 grade point average. After dropping off the application, you anxiously await the results. The loan officer said she would place a message on the Internet letting you know if the loan is approved.

The next morning, you access the Internet from your home computer … no message about the loan. Later, when you meet your brother for lunch, he takes a small computer from his briefcase and uses it to access the Internet. Still no message. While visiting a friend that afternoon, you ask if he has Internet access. He pulls a cellular telephone out of his coat pocket and uses it to connect to the Internet. Your account has a message from the bank. You cross your fingers and then slowly read the message. Yes! You are going to own an awesome red Ford Mustang. Life is good.

As you read Chapter 1, you will learn about Internet access and discover other practical uses of computers.

0% Interest

0$ Dow

OBJECTIVES

After completing this chapter, you will be able to:

1. Recognize the importance of computer literacy
2. Define the term computer and identify its components
3. Explain why a computer is a powerful tool
4. Recognize the purpose of a network
5. Discuss the uses of the Internet and World Wide Web
6. Recognize the difference between installing and running a program
7. Identify the types of software
8. Describe the categories of computers
9. Determine how the elements of an information system interact
10. Identify the types of computer users
11. Discuss various computer applications in society

CONTENTS

A WORLD OF COMPUTERS

Computers are everywhere: at home, at work, and at school. Many daily activities either involve the use of or depend on information from a computer. As shown in Figure 1-1, people use all types and sizes of computers for numerous reasons and in various places. Some computers sit on top of a desk or on the floor; others are small enough to carry.

Computers are a primary means of communications for all types of people. Employees correspond with clients, students with teachers, and family with friends and other family members. In addition to corresponding via text messages, people send each other pictures, diagrams, drawings, music, and videos. Today's technology provides the ability to see or hear others personally while you chat with them.

Through computers, society has instant access to information from around the globe. Local and national news, weather reports, sports scores, airline schedules, job listings, your credit report, and countless forms of educational material always are accessible. From the computer, you can meet new friends, shop, fill prescriptions, file taxes, or take a course.

At home or while on the road, people use computers to manage schedules, balance a checkbook, pay bills, track personal income and expenses, transfer funds, and buy or sell stocks. Banks place automated teller machines (ATMs) all over the world, making it easy to deposit or withdraw funds at anytime with a small plastic card. At the grocery store, a computer tracks purchases, calculates the amount of money due, and often generates

FIGURE 1-1   People use computers in their daily activities.

coupons customized to buying patterns. Vehicles include onboard navigation systems that provide directions, call for emergency services, and track the vehicle if it is stolen.

In the workplace, employees use computers to create correspondence such as memos and letters, calculate payroll, track inventory, and generate invoices. Some applications such as automotive design and weather forecasting use computers to perform complex mathematical calculations. At school, teachers use computers to assist with classroom instruction. Students complete assignments and do research on computers in lab rooms and at home.

People also spend hours of leisure time on the computer. They play games, listen to music, create music, watch a video or a movie, read a book or magazine, build a family tree, compose a video, retouch a photograph, make reservations, or plan a vacation.

As technology continues to advance, computers are becoming more a part of daily living. Thus, many people believe that computer literacy is vital to success. **Computer literacy** entails having knowledge and understanding of computers and their uses.

This book presents the knowledge you need to be computer literate. As you read this first chapter, keep in mind it is an overview. Many of the terms and concepts introduced in this chapter will be discussed in more depth later in the book.

Wireless Trends
Spanning the Globe

March 6 and 7
San Francisco, CA

WHAT IS A COMPUTER?

A **computer** is an electronic device, operating under the control of instructions stored in its own memory, that can accept data, manipulate the data according to specified rules, produce results, and store the results for future use.

Data and Information

Data is a collection of unprocessed items, which can include text, numbers, images, audio, and video. **Information** conveys meaning and is useful to one or more people. For example, when data such as course codes, course credit hours, and grades are arranged in the form of a grade report, a student has information.

Computers process data into information. In a grocery store, computers process several data items to print information in the form of a grocery receipt (Figure 1-2). To produce a paycheck (information), a computer processes the employee's name, number of hours worked, and the hourly rate of pay (data).

Information Processing Cycle

Computers process input (data) into output (information). A computer often holds data, information, and instructions in storage for future use. *Instructions* are the steps that tell the computer how to perform a particular task. Some people refer to the series of input, process, output, and storage activities as the *information processing cycle*.

Most computers today can communicate with other computers. As a result, communications also has become an essential element of the information processing cycle.

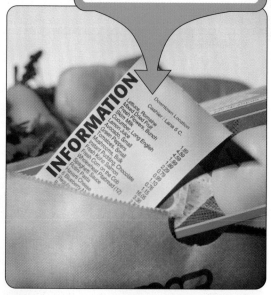

Lettuce **Napkins** **$1.99 per gallon** **$1.89 each** **Lane** **$1.89 a head** **Spaghetti Sauce** **Milk** **DATA** **$2.99 per jar**

PROCESSES
- Adds each item cost together
- Organizes data
- Computes sales tax
- Computes total due

INFORMATION

FIGURE 1-2 A computer processes data into information. In this example, the cashier name, grocery item, and cost per unit each represent data. The computer processes the data to produce the grocery receipt (information).

⁇ FAQ 1-1

Is data a singular or plural word?

With respect to computers, it is accepted and common practice to use the word data in both the singular and plural context.

For more information about data, visit the Discovering Computers 2004 FAQ Web page (**scsite.com/dc2004/faq**). Click Data below Chapter 1.

An **FAQ** (frequently asked questions) list helps you find answers to commonly asked questions. Web sites often post an FAQ section, and each chapter in this book includes FAQ boxes related to topics in the text.

THE COMPONENTS OF A COMPUTER

A computer contains many electric, electronic, and mechanical components known as **hardware**. These components include input devices, output devices, a system unit, storage devices, and communications devices. Figure 1-3 shows some common computer hardware components.

Input Devices

An **input device** is any hardware component that allows you to enter data or instructions into a computer. Six widely used input devices are the keyboard, mouse, microphone, scanner, digital camera, and PC video camera (Figure 1-3).

A computer keyboard contains keys you press to enter data into the computer. A mouse is a small handheld device. With the mouse, you control movement of a small symbol on the screen, called the pointer, and you make selections from the screen.

Handwritten note:
Hardware:
- electric c.
- electronic c.
- mechanical components

Handwritten note:
Components:
- input devices
- output devices
- a system unit
- storage devices
- communication devices

drive (storage)

drive

PC video camera (input)

monitor (output)

screen

pointer

speaker (output)

system unit (processor, memory, and storage)

keyboard (input)

mouse (input)

scanner (input)

printer (output)

card reader (storage)

microphone (input)

digital camera (input)

FIGURE 1-3 Common computer hardware components include the keyboard, mouse, microphone, scanner, digital camera, PC camera, printer, monitor, speakers, system unit, disk drives, card reader, and modem.

A microphone allows a user to speak into the computer to enter data and instructions. A scanner converts printed material (such as text and pictures) into a form the computer can use. For example, you can scan a picture and then include the picture in invitations you create on the computer.

With a digital camera, you take pictures and then transfer the photographed images to the computer or printer instead of storing the images on traditional film. A PC video camera is a digital video camera that allows users to create a movie or take still photographs electronically. With the PC video camera attached to the computer, users can make a video telephone call — during which both parties see each other as they talk.

Output Devices

An **output device** is any hardware component that conveys information to one or more people. Three commonly used output devices are a printer, a monitor, and speakers (Figure 1-3 on the previous page).

A printer produces text and graphics on a physical medium such as paper. A monitor displays text, graphics, and videos on a screen. Many monitors look similar to a television. Speakers allow you to hear music, voice, and other audio (sounds).

System Unit

The **system unit** is a box-like case that contains electronic components of the computer that are used to process data (Figure 1-3). The circuitry of the system unit usually is part of or is connected to a circuit board called the motherboard.

Two main components on the motherboard are the processor and memory. The *processor* is the electronic component that interprets and carries out the basic instructions that operate the computer. *Memory* consists of electronic components that store instructions waiting to be executed and data needed by those instructions. Most memory keeps data and instructions temporarily, although some forms of memory are permanent.

WEB LINK 1-1

Input Devices

Visit the Discovering Computers 2004 WEB LINK page (**scsite.com/dc2004/weblink**). Click Input Devices below Chapter 1.

WEB LINK 1-2

Output Devices

Visit the Discovering Computers 2004 WEB LINK page (**scsite.com/dc2004/weblink**). Click Output Devices below Chapter 1.

? FAQ 1-2

What is a CPU?

The processor. Most people in the computer industry use the terms *CPU* (*central processing unit*) and processor to mean the same.

For more information about processors, visit the Discovering Computers 2004 FAQ Web page (**scsite.com/dc2004/faq**). Click Processor below Chapter 1.

Storage Devices

Storage holds data, instructions, and information for future use. For example, computers can store hundreds or millions of customer names and addresses. Storage holds these items permanently.

A computer keeps data, instructions, and information on **storage media**. Examples of storage media are floppy disks, Zip® disks, hard disks, CDs, DVDs, and memory cards. A **storage device** records (writes) and/or retrieves (reads) items to and from storage media. Drives and readers, which are types of storage devices, accept a certain kind of storage media. For example, a CD drive (storage device) accepts a CD (storage media). Storage devices often function as a source of input because they transfer items from storage into memory.

A floppy disk consists of a thin, circular, flexible disk enclosed in a square-shaped plastic shell. You insert a floppy disk and remove it from a floppy disk drive (Figure 1-4). A Zip disk looks similar to a floppy disk but has much greater storage capabilities — up to the equivalent of 170 standard floppy disks. As with floppy disks, you insert Zip disks and remove them from Zip drives.

FIGURE 1-4 A floppy disk is inserted in and removed from a floppy disk drive.

A hard disk provides much greater storage capacity than a floppy disk or Zip disk. The average hard disk can hold more than 40,000 times that of a standard floppy disk. Although some hard disks are removable, most are enclosed in an airtight, sealed case housed inside the system unit (Figure 1-5).

A compact disc is a flat, round, portable metal disc. One type of compact disc is a CD-ROM, which you can access using most CD and DVD drives. Another type of compact disc is a DVD-ROM, which has tremendous storage capacities — enough for a full-length movie. To use a DVD-ROM, you need a DVD drive (Figure 1-6).

Some portable devices, such as digital cameras, use memory cards or other types of miniature storage media. You then can use a card reader (Figure 1-3 on page 1.05) to transfer the stored items, such as the electronic photographs, from the memory card to a computer or printer.

FIGURE 1-5 Most hard disks are self contained devices housed inside the system unit. The hard disk shown here must be installed into the system unit before it can be used.

Communications Devices

A **communications device** is a hardware component that enables a computer to send (transmit) and receive data, instructions, and information to and from one or more computers. A widely used communications device is the modem (Figure 1-3).

Communications occur over cables, telephone lines, cellular radio networks, satellites, or other transmission media. Some transmission media, such as satellites and cellular radio networks, are wireless, which means they have no physical lines or wires. People around the world communicate with each other using transmission media. Read Issue 1-1 for a related discussion.

？FAQ 1-3

What kind of drive do I need to burn a CD or DVD?

Burning is the process of writing (erasing or recording) on a compact disc. With a CD-RW (rewritable) drive, you can burn CD-RW and CD-R (recordable) discs. With a DVD+RW drive, you can burn DVD+RW and DVD-R discs and usually CD-RW discs too.

For more information about burning discs, visit the Discovering Computers 2004 FAQ Web page (**scsite.com/dc2004/faq**). Click Burning Discs below Chapter 1.

◆ WEB LINK 1-3

Communications Devices

Visit the Discovering Computers 2004 WEB LINK page (**scsite.com/dc2004/weblink**). Click Communications Devices below Chapter 1.

▓ ISSUE 1-1

Does Technology Discriminate?

Educated people. Higher-income families. Urbanites. Industrially developed nations. Upper-class neighborhoods. Individuals without disabilities. Statistics show that people in these groups have more access to technology than uneducated people, lower-income families, those living in rural areas, less industrially developed nations, middle-class neighborhoods, and individuals with disabilities. One study claims that those with less access to technology are at least a generation behind with respect to education. Another study alleges that those with less access to technology are less successful. Do you agree that access to technology such as a computer, the Internet, television, and telephone makes you more successful? Why? Are students who do not have computers at home facing an academic disadvantage in competing for good grades? Does the student with a computer at home have an unfair advantage? Are job seekers who have a computer more likely to find a job than those without a computer? What can be done to ensure that all members of society have access to technology?

For more information about technology discrimination, visit the Discovering Computers 2004 Issues Web page (**scsite.com/dc2004/issues**). Click Issue #1 below Chapter 1.

FIGURE 1-6 To use a DVD-ROM, you need a DVD drive.

Why is a computer so powerful?
- speed
- reliability & consistency
- accuracy
- storage
- communications

WHY IS A COMPUTER SO POWERFUL?

Computers are powerful for a variety of reasons. They perform the information processing cycle operations (input, process, output, and storage) with amazing speed, reliability, consistency, and accuracy. Computers can store huge amounts of data and information. Also, computers allow users to communicate with other users or computers. A **user** is anyone who communicates with a computer or utilizes the information it generates.

Speed

In the system unit, operations occur through electronic circuits. When data, instructions, and information flow along these circuits, they travel at incredibly fast speeds. Most computers carry out billions of operations in a single second. The world's fastest computer can perform trillions of operations in one second.

Reliability and Consistency

The electronic components in modern computers are dependable because they have a low failure rate. The high reliability of components enables the computer to produce consistent results.

Accuracy

Computers process large amounts of data and generate error-free results, provided the data is input correctly and the instructions work properly. If data is inaccurate, the resulting output will be incorrect. A computing phrase — known as *garbage in, garbage out* — points out that the accuracy of a computer's output depends on the accuracy of the input.

Storage

With current storage devices, the computer can transfer data quickly from storage to memory, process it, and then store it again for future use. Many computers store enormous amounts of data and make this data available for processing anytime it is needed.

Communications

Most computers today can communicate with other computers. Computers with this capability can share any of the four information processing cycle operations — input, process, output, and storage — with another computer. For example, two computers connected by a communications device, such as a modem, can share stored data, instructions, and information. These two computers can be located in the same room or thousands of miles away from each other in two different countries. For a more technical discussion about how data transfers among computers and devices, read the High-Tech Talk article on page 1.37.

QUIZ YOURSELF 1-1

To check your knowledge of computer literacy, computers and their components, and why a computer is powerful, visit the Discovering Computers 2004 Quiz Yourself Web page (**scsite.com/dc2004/quiz**). Click Objectives 1 – 3 below Chapter 1.

NETWORKS AND THE INTERNET

A **network** is a collection of computers and devices connected together via communications devices and transmission media. Networks allow computers to share *resources*, such as hardware, software, data, and information. Sharing resources saves time and money. For example, instead of purchasing one printer for every computer in a business, school, or home, you can connect all computers to a single printer via a network. This enables all connected computers to access the same printer. When a computer connects to a network, it is **online**.

In many networks, one or more computers act as a server. The *server* controls access to the resources on a network. The other computers on the network, each called a *client* or *workstation*, request resources from the server (Figure 1-7). The major differences between the server and client computers are that the server ordinarily has more power, more storage space, and is more reliable.

Many homes and most businesses and schools network their computers together. Home networks usually are small, existing within a single structure. Business and school networks can be small or quite widespread. A network can connect computers in a school laboratory, an office building, a group of buildings, or across a city, country, or the globe. The world's largest network is the Internet.

The Internet

The **Internet** is a worldwide collection of networks that connects millions of businesses, government agencies, educational institutions, and individuals (Figure 1-8).

Users can make well-informed decisions because they have instant access to information stored all over the world (read Apply It 1-1 for more information).

FIGURE 1-7   A server manages the resources on a network and clients access the resources on the server. This network enables three separate computers to share the same printer.

☑ APPLY IT 1-1

Directory Storage Power at Your Fingertips

When you need the telephone number of the neighborhood pizza restaurant or directions to tomorrow's job interview, try accessing Switchboard.com on the Internet. Switchboard.com connects you to a plethora of merchants, advertisers, and consumers.

This online directory of names, telephone numbers, and street addresses demonstrates the power of computers, as Internet users easily can look up millions of stored records instantly. Mobile computer users can communicate with the Switchboard.com network via their wireless computer or device.

For more information about Switchboard.com, visit the Discovering Computers 2004 Apply It Web page (**scsite.com/dc2004/apply**). Click Apply It #1 below Chapter 1.

FIGURE 1-8   The Internet is the largest network, connecting millions of computers around the world.

More than one-half billion people around the world use the Internet daily for a variety of reasons, including the following purposes:

- Communicate with and meet other people around the world
- Access a wealth of information, news, and research findings
- Shop for goods and services
- Bank and invest
- Take a class
- Access sources of entertainment and leisure, such as online games, music, videos, books, and magazines

Figure 1-9 shows examples in each of these areas.

Figure 1-9a (communications)

Figure 1-9b (access information)

Figure 1-9c (shop)

Figure 1-9d (bank and invest)

Figure 1-9e (take a class)

Figure 1-9f (entertainment)

FIGURE 1-9 Users access the Internet for a variety of reasons: to communicate with others, to access a wealth of information, to shop for goods and services, to bank and invest, to take a class, and for entertainment.

The **Web**, short for World Wide Web, is one of the more popular services on the Internet. Think of the Web as a global library of information available to anyone connected to the Internet. The Web contains billions of documents called Web pages. A Web page can contain text, graphics, audio, and video. The six screens shown in Figure 1-9 are examples of Web pages.

Web pages often have built-in connections, or links, to other documents, graphics, other Web pages, or Web sites. A Web site is a collection of related Web pages. For example, Wal-Mart has a Web site that contains many Web pages. Some of the Web pages at the Wal-Mart Web site display products for sale, other pages allow you to shop the Wal-Mart store, and yet other pages provide information about Wal-Mart.

People also connect to the Internet to exchange information with others around the world. E-mail allows you to send messages to other users. With instant messaging, you can have a live conversation with another connected user. In a chat room, you can communicate with multiple users at the same time — much like a group discussion. Some Web sites offer online calendars and address books so you can share appointments and contacts with others.

In addition to accessing and using information on the Web, many people use the Web as a means to share personal information, photographs, videos, or artwork with the world. Anyone can create a Web page and then make it available, or *publish* it, on the Internet for others to see (read Issue 1-2 for a related discussion). As an alternative, some Web sites provide publishing services free. At a **photo community** Web site, for example, users can create an online photo album and store their electronic photographs free (Figure 1-10).

Several companies offer access to the Internet. By paying a small monthly fee to this type of company, you can use your computer and a modem to connect to the many services of the Internet.

For more information about using the Web, read Making Use of the Web in Appendix A at the back of the book.

ISSUE 1-2

Is Everything You Read True?

It is against the law for Americans to contact space aliens. An ingredient in many popular shampoos has been proven to cause cancer. Chicken feet were discovered in the nuggets meal of a national fast-food chain. None of these statements is true, but each has appeared on a World Wide Web page. In today's society, many people think that anything in print is true. Yet, authors with a wide range of expertise, authority, and biases create Web pages. Web pages can be as accurate as the most scholarly journal, or no truer than the most disreputable supermarket tabloid. The Web makes it easy to obtain information, but Web page readers must make an extra effort to determine the quality of that information. In evaluating a Web page, experts suggest that you consider such factors as the purpose, scope, sponsor, timeliness, presentation, author, and permanence of the page. Ultimately, who is responsible for the accuracy of information on the Web? Why? What factors are most important in evaluating the accuracy of a Web page? Why?

For more information about Web page accuracy, visit the Discovering Computers 2004 Issues Web page (**scsite.com/dc2004/issues**). Click Issue #2 below Chapter 1.

WEB LINK 1-4

The Internet

Visit the Discovering Computers 2004 WEB LINK page (**scsite.com/dc2004/weblink**). Click The Internet below Chapter 1.

FIGURE 1-10 This happy student posted graduation pictures at a photo community.

COMPUTER SOFTWARE

Software, also called a program, is a series of instructions that tells the computer what to do and how to do it. A program exists on storage media such as a floppy disk or compact disc. When purchasing software from a computer store, you typically receive a box that includes a CD(s) or DVD(s) that contains the program (Figure 1-11). You also may receive a manual or printed instructions explaining how to install, execute, and use the software.

Installing is the process of setting up the software to work with the computer, printer, and other hardware components. To begin installing the software from a CD or DVD, a user inserts the program disc into a CD or DVD drive. The computer then copies all or part of the program from the disc to the computer's hard disk.

During installation, the program may ask you to register or activate the software online. If your computer has an Internet connection, this online procedure saves the time of telephoning the vendor or completing a paper registration card and mailing it. If requested, it is important to register and/or activate software. Some vendors make the software so it does not function or has limited functionality until you register or activate it.

When you buy a computer, it usually has some software preinstalled on its hard disk. This enables you to use the computer the first time you turn it on.

Once software is installed, you can use it. Some software requires you to insert the program disc into the drive while you use, or run, the software. Others do not, because the installation process copies the entire program to the hard disk. When a user tells the computer to start the program, the computer places, or loads, the program into its memory from storage (either the hard disk or the program disc). Once in memory, the computer can carry out, or execute, the instructions in a program. Figure 1-12 illustrates the steps that occur when a user installs and runs an encyclopedia program.

You interact with a program through its user interface. The user interface controls how you enter data and instructions and how information displays on the screen. Software today often has a graphical user interface. With a **graphical user interface** (**GUI** pronounced gooey), you interact with the software using text, graphics, and visual images such as icons (Figure 1-13). An icon is a small image that represents a program, an instruction, or some other object. You can use the mouse to select icons that perform operations such as starting a program.

Software is the key to productive use of computers. With the proper software, a computer can be a valuable tool. The two categories of software are system software and application software. The following sections describe these categories of software.

WEB LINK 1-5

Computer Programs

Visit the Discovering Computers 2004 WEB LINK page (**scsite.com/dc2004/ weblink**). Click Computer Programs below Chapter 1.

software box

program discs

FIGURE 1-11   When buying software, you receive media such as a CD(s) or DVD(s) that contains the program.

FAQ 1-4

Which spelling is correct, disk or disc?

Both are correct, depending on usage. When referring to CD, DVD, and other optical (laser) storage, computer professionals typically use the term disc. Floppy disks, Zip® disks, hard disks, and other nonoptical storage media normally use the term disk.

For more information about disks and discs, visit the Discovering Computers 2004 FAQ Web page (**scsite.com/dc2004/faq**). Click Disk or Disc below Chapter 1.

FIGURE 1-12 INSTALLING AND RUNNING A COMPUTER PROGRAM

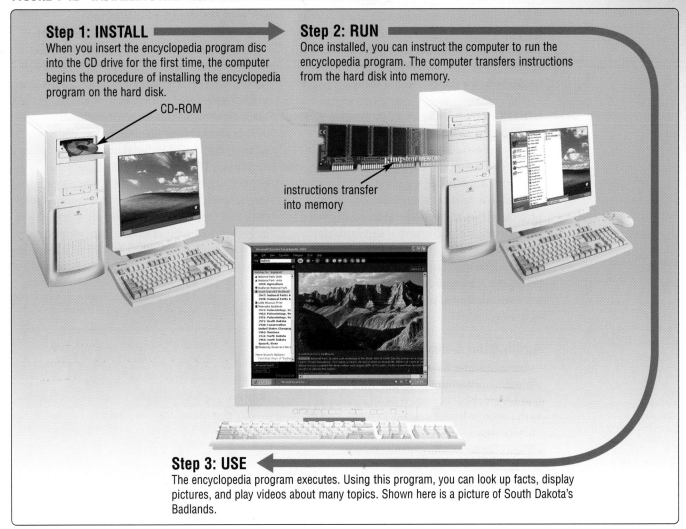

Step 1: INSTALL
When you insert the encyclopedia program disc into the CD drive for the first time, the computer begins the procedure of installing the encyclopedia program on the hard disk.

CD-ROM

Step 2: RUN
Once installed, you can instruct the computer to run the encyclopedia program. The computer transfers instructions from the hard disk into memory.

instructions transfer into memory

Step 3: USE
The encyclopedia program executes. Using this program, you can look up facts, display pictures, and play videos about many topics. Shown here is a picture of South Dakota's Badlands.

System Software

System software consists of the programs that control or maintain the operations of the computer and its devices. System software serves as the interface between the user, the application software, and the computer's hardware.

Two types of system software are the operating system and utility programs.

OPERATING SYSTEM An *operating system* is a set of programs that coordinates all the activities among computer hardware devices. The operating system also contains instructions that allow users to run application software. Many of today's computers use Microsoft's operating system, called Windows XP (Figure 1-13).

FIGURE 1-13 The graphical user interface of Windows XP.

When a user starts a computer, portions of the operating system load into memory from the computer's hard disk. It remains in memory while the computer is on. The operating system provides a means for users to communicate with the computer and other software.

UTILITY PROGRAMS A *utility program* allows a user to perform maintenance-type tasks usually related to managing a computer, its devices, or its programs. For example, one type of utility program can examine a floppy disk or hard disk to determine if it contains any physical flaws such as a scratch. Most operating systems include several utility programs for managing disk drives, printers, and other devices. You also can buy utility programs, which allow you to perform additional computer management functions.

Application Software

Application software consists of programs that perform specific tasks for users. A widely used type of application software related to communications is a Web browser, which allows users with an Internet connection to access and view Web pages. Other popular application software includes word processing software, spreadsheet software, database software, and presentation graphics software.

Word processing software allows users to create documents such as letters, memos, and brochures. Spreadsheet software calculates numbers arranged in rows and columns and allows users to perform financial tasks such as budgeting and forecasting. Database software provides a way to store data in an organized fashion, as well as retrieve, manipulate, and display that data in a variety of formats. With presentation graphics software, users create visual aids for a presentation.

Software vendors often bundle and sell word processing, spreadsheet, database, and presentation graphics application software together as a single unit. This bundle, called a suite, costs much less than if you purchased the application software individually. Microsoft's Office XP is a very popular suite.

Many other types of application software exist that enable users to perform a variety of tasks. Some widely used application software includes personal information manager, project management, accounting, computer-aided design, desktop publishing, paint/image editing, audio and video editing, multimedia authoring, Web page authoring, personal finance, legal, tax preparation, home design/landscaping, educational, reference, and entertainment (games, simulations, etc.). As shown in Figure 1-14, you often purchase application software from a store that sells computer products. Read Issue 1-3 for a related discussion.

WEB LINK 1-6

Application Software
Visit the Discovering Computers 2004 WEB LINK page (**scsite.com/dc2004/ weblink**). Click Application Software below Chapter 1.

FIGURE 1-14 Stores that sell computer products have shelves stocked with software for sale.

ISSUE 1-3

Does Software Promote Violence?

One of today's more popular computer games is Grand Theft Auto. In the game, players advance through the mafia by conveying secret packages, following alleged snitches, and other similar activities. Since its release, buyers have purchased more than three million copies of Grand Theft Auto. Proponents praise the game's vivid graphics, edgy characters, and wide range of allowable behaviors. Critics condemn the game's explicit violence and the rewards it gives players for partaking in illegal acts. Grand Theft Auto is rated M (for Mature, meaning it is suitable for ages 17 and older), but children as young as 12 are familiar with it. Even worse, opponents fear that the game's popularity may influence future developers of computer games aimed at younger children. What impact do violent computer games or games that promote unacceptable acts have on individual behavior? Do these games desensitize players to violence or increase aggression? Why or why not? Should restrictions be placed on sales of computer games?

For more information about computer entertainment and video games, visit the Discovering Computers 2004 Issues Web page (**scsite.com/dc2004/issues**). Click Issue #3 below Chapter 1.

Software Development

A *programmer* is someone who develops application or system software. Programmers develop programs or write the instructions that direct the computer to process data into information. When writing instructions, a programmer must be sure the program works properly so the computer generates the desired results. Complex programs can require thousands to millions of instructions.

Programmers use a programming language or program development tool to create computer programs. Popular programming languages include C++, C#, Visual Basic .NET, and JavaScript. Figure 1-15 shows some of the instructions a programmer may write to create an Internet application.

QUIZ YOURSELF 1-2

To check your knowledge of networks, the Internet and Web, installing and running programs, and types of software, visit the Discovering Computers 2004 Quiz Yourself Web page (**scsite.com/dc2004/quiz**). Click Objectives 4 – 7 below Chapter 1.

Figure 1-15a (JavaScript program)

Figure 1-15b (resulting Internet application)

FIGURE 1-15 The top figure illustrates some of the instructions a programmer writes in JavaScript to create the application that runs on the Internet, shown in the bottom figure.

CATEGORIES OF COMPUTERS

Industry experts typically classify computers in five categories: personal computers, mobile computers and mobile devices, midrange servers, mainframes, and supercomputers. A computer's size, speed, processing power, and price typically determine the category it best fits. Due to rapidly changing technology, however, the distinction among categories is not always clear-cut. For example, the speed that defines a mainframe computer today may define a midrange server next year. Some characteristics may overlap categories. Still, many people refer to these categories when discussing computers.

Figure 1-16 summarizes the five categories of computers (read Looking Ahead 1-1 for a look at the next generation of computers). The following pages discuss computers and devices that fall into each category.

PERSONAL COMPUTERS

A **personal computer** is a computer that can perform all of its input, processing, output, and storage activities by itself. A personal computer contains a processor, memory, and one or more input, output, and storage devices.

CATEGORIES OF COMPUTERS

Category	Physical Size	Number of Simultaneously Connected Users	General Price Range
Personal computers (desktop)	Fits on a desk	Usually one (can be more if networked)	Several thousand dollars or less
Mobile computers and mobile devices	Fits on your lap or in your hand	Usually one	Several thousand dollars or less
Midrange servers	Small cabinet	Two to thousands	$5,000 to $850,000
Mainframe computers	Partial room to a full room of equipment	Hundreds to thousands	$300,000 to several million dollars
Supercomputers	Full room of equipment	Hundreds to thousands	$500,000 to more than $85 million dollars

FIGURE 1-16 This table summarizes some of the differences among the categories of computers. These should be considered general guidelines only because of rapid changes in technology.

LOOKING AHEAD 1-1

Wearable Computers Serve Practical Purposes

When FedEx aircraft mechanics access detailed schematics, they consult their new wearable computers. Ticket vendors at the Toronto Blue Jays stadium can print tickets at mobile kiosks using these computers, too. Indeed, wearable computers are finding a home in classrooms, power plants, and manufacturing facilities.

Experts predict that this hardware will be a trillion-dollar business in the next few years. Hundreds of companies currently are testing devices that use headsets and eyeglasses for input and output.

For a look at the next generation of wearable computers, visit the Discovering Computers 2004 Looking Ahead Web page (**scsite.com/dc2004/ looking**). Click Looking Ahead #1 below Chapter 1.

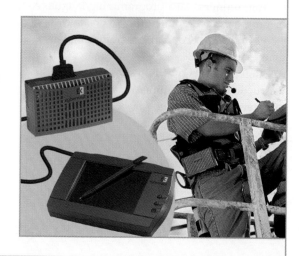

Two popular types of personal computers are the PC (Figure 1-17) and the Apple (Figure 1-18). The term, *PC-compatible*, refers to any personal computer based on the original IBM personal computer design. Companies such as Dell, Gateway, and Toshiba sell PC-compatible computers. PC and PC-compatible computers have processors with different architectures than processors in Apple computers. These two types of computers also use different operating systems. PC and PC-compatible computers use the Windows operating system. Apple computers use the Macintosh operating system (Mac OS).

Two types of personal computers are desktop computers and notebook computers. The next section discusses desktop personal computers. Notebook computers are discussed in the mobile computers section.

Desktop Computers

A **desktop computer** is designed so the system unit, input devices, output devices, and any other devices fit entirely on or under a desk or table (Figure 1-19). In some models, the monitor sits on top of the system unit, which is placed on top of the desk. The more popular style of system unit is the tall and narrow *tower*, which can sit on the floor vertically — if desktop space is limited. Towers are available in a variety of heights. A tower is at least 24 inches tall, a mid-tower is about 16 inches tall, and a minitower is usually 13 inches tall. The desktop computer design you choose often depends on the layout of your work area.

WEB LINK 1-7

Personal Computers
Visit the Discovering Computers 2004 WEB LINK page (**scsite.com/dc2004/weblink**). Click Personal Computers below Chapter 1.

FIGURE 1-17   The PC and compatible computers use the Windows operating system.

FIGURE 1-18   Apple computers, such as the iMac, use the Macintosh operating system.

Figure 1-19b
(system unit sitting below desk)

Figure 1-19a
(monitor sitting on system unit)

system unit

tower system unit

FIGURE 1-19   Components of a desktop computer fit entirely on or under a desk or table. On some models, the system unit sits on top of the desk below the monitor. A tower system unit can sit below the desk.

Some desktop computers are powerful enough to function as a server on a network. These high-end computers cost much more than the basic desktop computer.

Another expensive, powerful desktop computer is the workstation, which is geared for work that requires intense calculations and graphics capabilities. Fields such as engineering, desktop publishing, and graphic art require the power of a workstation. An architect uses a workstation to view and create maps. A graphic artist uses a workstation to create computer-animated special effects for full-length motion pictures and video games.

?FAQ 1-5

Does the term workstation have two meanings?

Yes. In the computer industry, a *workstation* can be a high-powered computer or a client computer.

For more information about workstations, visit the Discovering Computers 2004 FAQ Web page (**scsite.com/dc2004/faq**). Click Workstation below Chapter 1.

MOBILE COMPUTERS AND MOBILE DEVICES

A **mobile computer** is a personal computer that you can carry from place to place. Similarly, a **mobile device** is a computing device small enough to hold in your hand.

The most popular type of mobile computer is the notebook computer. The following sections discuss the notebook computer and widely used mobile devices.

Notebook Computers

A **notebook computer**, also called a **laptop computer**, is a portable, personal computer small enough to fit on your lap. Today's notebook computers are thin and lightweight, yet they can be as powerful as the average desktop computer. Notebook computers generally are more expensive than desktop computers with equal capabilities.

On a typical notebook computer, the keyboard is on top of the system unit and the monitor attaches to the system unit with

WEB LINK 1-8

Notebook Computers

Visit the Discovering Computers 2004 WEB LINK page (**scsite.com/dc2004/ weblink**). Click Notebook Computers below Chapter 1.

hinges (Figure 1-20). Weighing on average between 2.5 and 8 pounds, users easily can transport these computers from place to place. Most notebook computers can operate on batteries or a power supply or both.

CD and DVD drives

FIGURE 1-20 On a typical notebook computer, the keyboard is on top of the system unit and the monitor attaches to the system unit with hinges.

TABLET PC Resembling a letter-sized slate, the **Tablet PC** is a special type of notebook computer that allows you to write on the screen using a digital pen (Figure 1-21). With a *digital pen*, users write on the screen or issue instructions to the Tablet PC, for example, by tapping on the screen. For users who prefer typing instead of handwriting, you can attach a keyboard to these computers. Most Tablet PC applications run with or without a keyboard. Tablet PCs also support voice input so users can enter text and issue instructions by speaking into the computer.

Tablet PCs are useful especially for taking notes in lectures, at meetings, conferences, and other forums where the standard notebook computer is not practical. With a cost of about only $1,000, some users may find Tablet PCs more appropriate for their needs than traditional notebook computers. An even smaller version of a Tablet PC is the *modular computer*, which fits in the palm of your hand (Figure 1-22).

digital pen

FIGURE 1-21 The Tablet PC combines the features of a traditional notebook computer with the simplicity of pencil and paper.

FIGURE 1-22 A modular computer weighs less than nine ounces.

Mobile Devices

Some mobile devices are **Web-enabled**, meaning they can connect to the Internet wirelessly. Mobile devices usually do not have disk drives. Instead, these devices store programs and data permanently on memory inside the system unit or on small storage media such as memory cards. You typically connect a mobile device to a personal computer to exchange information between the computer and the mobile device.

Three popular types of mobile devices are handheld computers, PDAs, and smart phones. Some combination mobile devices also are available, for example, a PDA/smart phone.

HANDHELD COMPUTER   A **handheld computer** is a computer small enough to fit in one hand while you operate it with the other hand. Because of their reduced size, the screens on handheld computers are quite small. The primary input device on a handheld computer is a small keyboard. A business traveler might prefer this type of handheld computer to a notebook computer.

Some handheld computers have a specialized keyboard. These industry-specific computers serve mobile employees, such as meter readers and parcel delivery people, whose jobs require them to move from place to place.

PDA   The PDA is one of the more popular lightweight mobile devices in use today. A **PDA** (*personal digital assistant*) provides personal organizer functions such as a calendar, appointment book, address book, calculator, and notepad (Figure 1-23). Most PDAs also offer a variety of other application software such as word processing, spreadsheet, personal finance, and games. Some even include software that enables users to read a book on the device's screen.

PDA
Personal Digital Assistant

stylus —→

FIGURE 1-23   PDAs are a widely used mobile device, providing personal information management functions as well as Internet access and telephone capabilities.

Many PDAs are Web-enabled so users can check e-mail and access the Internet. Some also provide telephone capabilities. Because of all the added features, increasingly more people are replacing their pocket-sized appointment books with PDAs (read Apply It 1-2 for more information).

The primary input device of a PDA is the stylus (Figure 1-23 on the previous page). A *stylus* looks like a small ballpoint pen, but uses pressure instead of ink to write and draw. If you prefer to type, you can insert PDAs without keyboards into a special keyboard. Some PDAs also support voice input.

SMART PHONES Offering the convenience of one-handed operation, a **smart phone** is a Web-enabled telephone (Figure 1-24). In addition to basic phone capabilities, a smart phone allows you to send and receive e-mail and access the Internet. Some higher-priced models have color screens and play music.

MIDRANGE SERVERS

A **midrange server** is more powerful and larger than a workstation computer (Figure 1-25). Midrange servers typically support several hundred and sometimes up to a few thousand connected computers at the same time. In the past, midrange servers were known as *minicomputers*.

Midrange servers store data and programs. In many cases, one server accesses data on another server. In other cases, people use personal computers or terminals to access programs on a server. A terminal is a device with a monitor and keyboard. Some terminals have no processing power and must connect to a server to operate. Others have the capability of functioning when not connected to the server.

FIGURE 1-24 In addition to basic telephone functionality, smart phones allow you to check e-mail and access the Internet.

☑ **APPLY IT 1-2**

Prescription for Saving Doctors' Time

In doctors' hectic schedules, time is precious. Locating lab test reports, prescribed medications, and medical notes quickly at patients' bedsides during rounds can be challenging.

This task has been simplified with a wireless system that allows doctors to obtain patients' records on a PDA. The doctors can move from room to room and have this data available at their fingertips. This wireless PDA system helps reduce errors and increase patient satisfaction.

For more information about PDAs, visit the Discovering Computers 2004 Apply It Web page (**scsite.com/dc2004/apply**). Click Apply It #2 below Chapter 1.

FIGURE 1-25 A midrange server is more powerful than a workstation, but less powerful than a mainframe.

MAINFRAMES

A **mainframe** is a large, expensive, very powerful computer that can handle hundreds or thousands of connected users simultaneously (Figure 1-26). Mainframes store tremendous amounts of data, instructions, and information. Large companies such as banks, airlines, and insurance companies use mainframes.

Mainframes also can act as servers on a network environment. Midrange servers and other mainframes can access data and information from a mainframe. People also can access programs on the mainframe with terminals or personal computers.

SUPERCOMPUTERS

A **supercomputer** is the fastest, most powerful computer — and the most expensive (Figure 1-27). The fastest supercomputers are capable of processing more than 100 trillion instructions in a single second. With weights that exceed 100 tons, these computers can store more than 16,000 times the data and information than an average desktop computer. Supercomputers often are built using thousands of personal computer processors.

Applications requiring complex, sophisticated mathematical calculations use supercomputers. For example, applications in medicine, aerospace, automotive design, online banking, weather forecasting, nuclear energy research, and petroleum exploration use a supercomputer.

FIGURE 1-26 Mainframe computers are large, expensive, powerful computers that can handle thousands of connected computers and process millions of instructions per second.

ASCI White
Lawrence Livermore National Laboratory

FIGURE 1-27 This IBM supercomputer requires an area the size of two basketball courts to house its more than 2,000 miles of wiring (enough wiring to connect Washington, D.C., to Phoenix, Arizona).

WEB LINK 1-9

Women in Technology

Visit the Discovering
Computers 2004
WEB LINK page
(**scsite.com/dc2004/
weblink**). Click
Women in Technology
below Chapter 1.

WEB LINK 1-10

**Minorities
in Technology**

Visit the Discovering
Computers 2004
WEB LINK page
(**scsite.com/dc2004/
weblink**). Click
Minorities in Technology
below Chapter 1.

ELEMENTS OF AN INFORMATION SYSTEM

Obtaining timely and useful information from a computer requires more than the hardware and software discussed thus far. Other elements include accurate data, trained information technology staff and knowledgeable users (people), and documented procedures. Together, these elements (hardware, software, data, people, and procedures) comprise an *information system.* Figure 1-28 shows how each of the elements of an information system might interact.

The hardware must be reliable and capable of handling the expected workload. The software must be developed carefully and tested thoroughly. The data input into the computer must be accurate. Incorrect data generates incorrect information.

Most companies with mid-sized and large computers have an IT (information technology) department. Staff in the IT department should be highly skilled and up to date on the latest technology. IT staff also should train users so they understand how to use the computer properly. Today's users also work closely with IT staff in the development of computer applications that relate to their areas of work.

Finally, all the IT applications should have readily available documented procedures. These procedures should address starting, operating, and using the computer.

FIGURE 1-28   HOW THE ELEMENTS OF AN INFORMATION SYSTEM MIGHT INTERACT

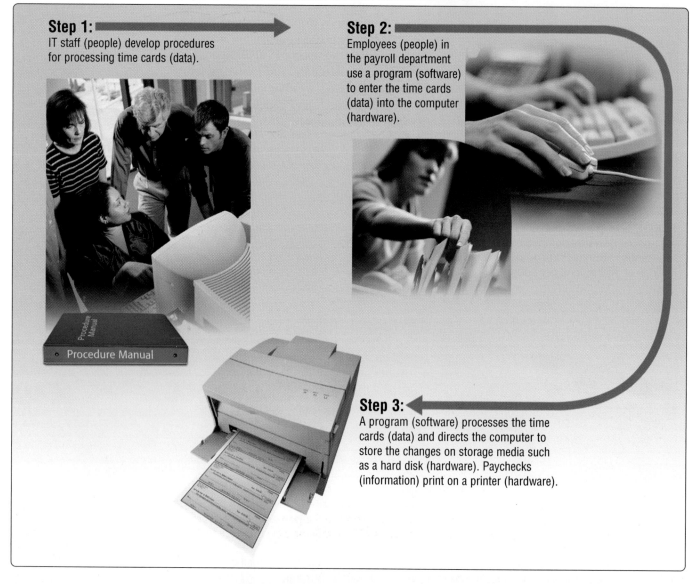

Step 1: IT staff (people) develop procedures for processing time cards (data).

Step 2: Employees (people) in the payroll department use a program (software) to enter the time cards (data) into the computer (hardware).

Step 3: A program (software) processes the time cards (data) and directs the computer to store the changes on storage media such as a hard disk (hardware). Paychecks (information) print on a printer (hardware).

Procedure Manual

EXAMPLES OF COMPUTER USAGE

Every day, numerous users rely on different types of computers for a variety of applications. To illustrate the variety of uses for computers, this section takes you on a visual and narrative tour of five categories of users: a home user, a small office/home office (SOHO) user, a mobile user, a large business user, and a power user.

The table in Figure 1-29 identifies some hardware and software that each user may require. The following pages discuss the items listed in the table. For a history of hardware and software developments, read the Timeline 2004 that follows this chapter.

CATEGORIES OF USERS

User	Hardware	Software
Home	• Desktop computer • PDA	• Business (e.g., word processing) • Personal information manager • Personal finance, online banking, tax preparation • Web browser • E-mail, instant messaging, and chat rooms • Reference (e.g., encyclopedias, medical dictionaries, road atlas) • Entertainment (e.g., games, music composition, greeting cards) • Educational (e.g., tutorials, children's math and reading software)
Small Office/Home Office	• Desktop computer • PDA • Shared network printer	• Business (e.g., word processing, spreadsheet, database) • Personal information manager • Company specific (e.g., accounting, legal reference) • Network management • Web browser • E-mail
Mobile	• Notebook computer equipped with a modem, or a Tablet PC • Video projector • Web-enabled PDA/smart phone	• Business (e.g., word processing, spreadsheet, presentation graphics) • Personal information manager • Web browser • E-mail
Large Business	• Midrange server or mainframe • Desktop or notebook computer • Industry specific handheld computer • PDA • Kiosk	• Business (e.g., word processing, spreadsheet, database, presentation graphics) • Personal information manager • Accounting • Network management • Web browser • E-mail
Power	• Workstation or other powerful computer with multimedia capabilities • PDA	• Desktop publishing • Multimedia authoring • Computer-aided design • Photo, audio, and video editing • Personal information manager • Web browser • E-mail

FIGURE 1-29 Today, computers are used by millions of people to support work tasks, school assignments, and leisure activities. Different computer users require different kinds of hardware and software to meet their needs effectively.

Home User

In an increasing number of homes, the computer no longer is a convenience. Instead, it is a basic necessity. Each family member, or **home user**, spends time on the computer for different reasons. These include budgeting and personal financial management, Web access, communications, and entertainment (Figure 1-30).

On the Internet, home users access a huge amount of information, take college classes, pay bills, manage investments, shop, listen to the radio, watch a movie, read a book, play games, file taxes, and make airline reservations. They also communicate with others around the world through e-mail, instant messaging, and chat rooms. Their communications are not limited to text. Today's technology provides users with the means to send graphics, audio, and video. With a digital camera, you can take a photograph and then send the electronic image to anyone. Using a

Figure 1-30a (personal financial management)

Figure 1-30b (Web access)

Figure 1-30c (communications)

Figure 1-30d (entertainment)

FIGURE 1-30 The home user spends time on a computer for a variety of reasons.

PC video camera, which costs less than $100, home users easily have live video calls with friends and family members (Figure 1-31).

Today's homes typically have one or more desktop computers. Many are available in a variety of stylish colors and sleek designs, so the computer complements a room décor and the user's lifestyle. Some home users network multiple desktop computers throughout the house. These small networks allow family members to access each other's data, information, programs, printers, and other devices.

Home users sometimes have PDAs to maintain daily schedules and address lists. Special-purpose handheld computers can manage and monitor the health condition of a family member.

Some families have an **Internet appliance**, which is a special type of computer whose sole function is to connect to the Internet from home. The set-top box is an example of an Internet appliance. A *set-top box* sits on top of or next to a television set and allows the home user to access the Internet and navigate Web pages with a device that resembles a remote control (Figure 1-32).

To meet their needs, home users have a variety of software. They type letters, homework assignments, and other documents with word processing software. Personal finance software helps the home user with personal finances, investments, and family budgets. Other software assists with preparing taxes, keeping a household inventory, and setting up maintenance schedules.

Reference software, such as encyclopedias, medical dictionaries, or a road atlas, provides valuable information for everyone in the family. With entertainment software, the home user can play games such as solitaire, chess, and Monopoly™; compose music; make a family tree; or create a greeting card. Educational software helps adults learn to speak a foreign language and youngsters to read, write, count, and spell. These forms of software are available on CD, DVD, and also on the Web.

⁇FAQ 1-6

Can I listen to an audio CD on my computer?

Yes, in most cases. Simply insert the CD into the computer's CD or DVD drive. Within a few seconds, you should hear music from the computer's speakers or in your headset. If no music plays, it is likely the music company configured the CD so it will not play on a computer.

For more information about listening to music on the computer, visit the Discovering Computers 2004 FAQ Web page (**scsite.com/dc2004/faq**). Click Listen to Music below Chapter 1.

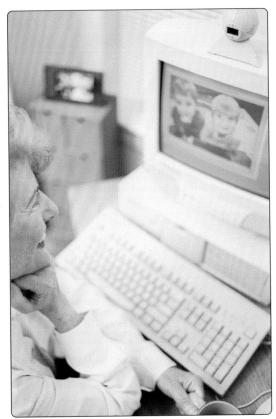

FIGURE 1-31 A grandmother uses a PC video camera to talk to and see her grandchildren on the computer.

FIGURE 1-32 With a set-top box, home users can access the Internet from the comfort of their family room or any other room that has television access.

Small Office/Home Office User

Computers assist small business and home office users in managing their resources effectively. A **small office/home office** (*SOHO*) includes any company with fewer than 50 employees, as well as the self-employed who work from home. Small offices include local law practices, accounting firms, travel agencies, and florists. SOHO users typically have a desktop computer to perform some or all of their duties (Figure 1-33). Many also have PDAs to manage appointments and contact information.

Figure 1-33a (Web access)

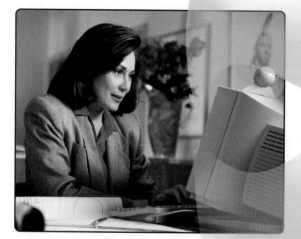

Figure 1-33b (spreadsheet)

FIGURE 1-33 People with a home office and employees in small offices typically use a desktop personal computer for some or all of their duties.

SOHO users access the Web to look up information such as addresses, postal codes, flights, and package shipping rates. Nearly all SOHO users communicate with others through e-mail. Many are entering the *e-commerce* arena and conduct business on the Web (Figure 1-34). Their Web sites advertise products and services and may provide a means for taking orders. Small business Web sites sometimes use a *Web cam*, which is a video camera that displays its output on a Web page. A Web cam allows SOHO users to show the world a live view of some aspect of their business.

To save money on hardware and software, small offices often network their computers together. For example, the small office connects one printer to a network for all employees to share. Many companies also purchase network versions of their software. A network version usually costs less than purchasing a separate software package for each desktop or notebook computer. Employees then access the software on a server, as needed.

SOHO users often have basic business software such as word processing and spreadsheet software to assist with document preparation and finances. They also may use other industry-specific types of software. A florist, for example, will have software that allows for taking orders, updating inventory, billing customers, and paying vendors.

Mobile User

Today, businesses and schools are expanding to serve people across the country and around the world. Thus, increasingly more employees and students are **mobile users**, working on a computer while away from a main office or school (Figure 1-35). Examples of mobile users are sales representatives, real estate agents, insurance agents, meter readers, package delivery people, journalists, consultants, and students.

Mobile users often have a notebook computer, Web-enabled PDA, or smart phone. With these computers and devices, the mobile user can connect to other computers on a network or the Internet. Often, mobile users transfer information between their mobile device and another computer, such as one at the main office or school.

FIGURE 1-34 Many small businesses, such as this local florist, have a Web site to promote their products and services.

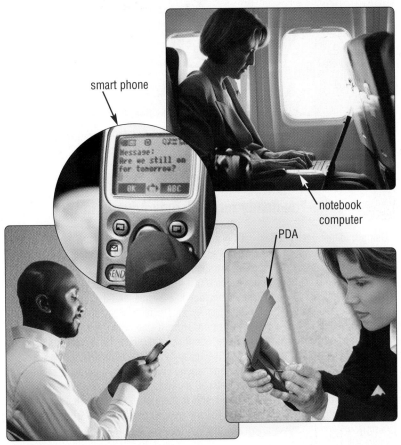

FIGURE 1-35 Mobile users have notebook computers, PDAs, and smart phones so they can work, do homework, send messages, or access the Internet while away from the office, home, or school.

The mobile user works with basic business software such as word processing and spreadsheet software. With presentation graphics software, the mobile user can create and deliver presentations to a large audience by connecting a mobile computer or device to a video projector that displays the presentation on a full screen (Figure 1-36). Many scaled down programs are available for mobile devices such as PDAs and smart phones. Read Issue 1-4 for a related discussion.

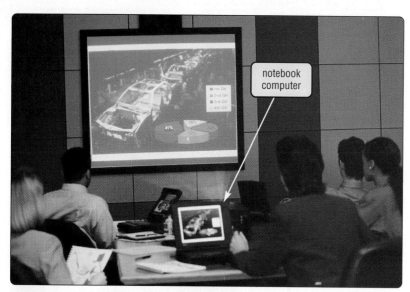

notebook computer

FIGURE 1-36   A mobile user often connects a notebook computer to a video projector to make a presentation.

Large Business User

A large business has hundreds or thousands of employees in offices across the country or around the world. Each employee who uses a computer in the large business is a **large business user** (Figure 1-37).

Many large companies use the term, *enterprise computing,* to refer to the huge network of computers that meets their diverse computing needs. The network facilitates communications among employees at all locations. Users access the network through desktop computers, handheld computers, and PDAs. Mainframes often act as servers in the large business network.

Large businesses use computers and the computer network to process high volumes of transactions in a single day. Although they may differ in size and in the products or services offered, all generally use computers for basic business activities. For example, they bill millions of customers or prepare payroll for thousands of employees.

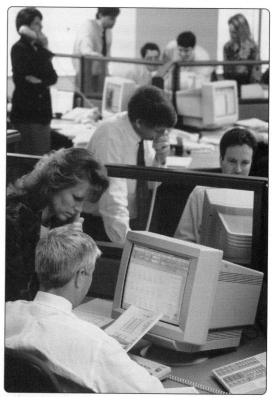

FIGURE 1-37   A large business can have hundreds or thousands of users in offices across a region, the country, or the world. Throughout the business, computers help employees perform a variety of job-related tasks.

ISSUE 1-4

Are You Ready for Real-Time Advertising?

Using traditional telephones, calls dialed to 911 or other emergency numbers can be traced to the caller's exact location. This allows emergency crews quickly to ascertain the whereabouts of someone in need. Despite a Federal Communications Commission (FCC) mandate, this is not the case with cellular telephones. The tracking technology is available, and the FCC has begged the cellular telephone industry to implement it. The technology can trace a user's position whenever the device is turned on. Thus, it also could be used for nonemergency purposes. Advertisements, coupons, and other messages could be sent to users' cellular telephones as they pass by a place of business. Imagine driving by a Dairy Queen® and hearing the following message from your cellular telephone: Hungry for ice cream? Get a 20 percent discount for the next 10 minutes. Some people fear that if a carrier knows their location, they will be bombarded with this type of advertising. Privacy-minded consumers worry that the companies and the government will use the technology to monitor their every move. Should cellular telephone carriers be required to implement this tracking technology? If advertisers use the technology, do customers have the right to know they are being tracked? How might this technology violate a user's privacy?

For more information about tracking technology and location-based advertising, visit the Discovering Computers 2004 Issues Web page (**scsite.com/dc2004/issues**). Click Issue #4 below Chapter 1.

In a large business, an automated telephone system routes telephone calls to the proper department or person. By telephone, fax, or e-mail, order-entry clerks process millions of customer orders daily using a desktop computer. Some companies have inside sales representatives who handle customer telephone orders. Outside sales representatives — the mobile users in the firm — conduct business while on the road with mobile computers or devices.

Large businesses typically have e-commerce Web sites, allowing customers and vendors to make transactions online. The Web site showcases products, services, and other company information (Figure 1-38). Thousands of customers, vendors, and any other interested parties can access this information on the Web. Once an order is placed, computers update inventory records to reflect goods sold and goods purchased.

The marketing department in the large business uses desktop publishing software to prepare marketing literature such as newsletters, product brochures, and advertising material. The accounting department uses software for accounts receivable, accounts payable, billing, general ledger, and payroll activities. Computers process thousands of customer payments, generate checks to pay vendors, print invoices to send to customers, and balance all book records. Additionally,

computers handle the payroll and taxes, ensuring that thousands of employees receive paychecks on time.

The employees in the *information technology (IT) department* keep the computers and the network running. They also determine when and if the company requires new hardware or software. Large business users access networked versions of word processing, spreadsheet, database, and presentation graphics software. They also may use calendar programs to post their schedules on the network. And, they might use PDAs to maintain contact information. E-mail and Web browsers enable communications among employees, vendors, and customers. Many large businesses have *customer relationship management (CRM)* software, which allows the company to provide a personalized touch and customized service to its customers.

Some large businesses place kiosks in public locations. A *kiosk* is a freestanding computer, usually with a touch screen (Figure 1-39). Certain kiosks simply provide information to the public. More advanced kiosks allow customers to place orders, make payments, and access the Web. Some stores, for example, have Web kiosks to save a sale, allowing a customer to purchase items not in stock in the store.

WEB LINK 1-11

Enterprise Computing

Visit the Discovering Computers 2004 WEB LINK page (**scsite.com/dc2004/ weblink**). Click Enterprise Computing below Chapter 1.

FIGURE 1-38 Large businesses, such as Boeing, usually have their own Web sites to showcase products, services, and company information.

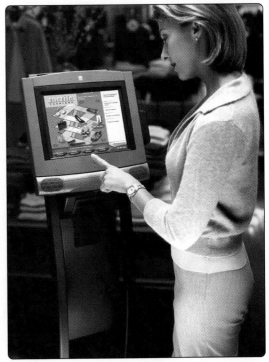

FIGURE 1-39 A kiosk is a freestanding computer that often has a touch screen.

Many employees of large businesses today telecommute (Figure 1-40). **Telecommuting** is a work arrangement in which employees work away from a company's standard workplace, and often communicate with the office through the computer. Employees who telecommute have flexible work schedules so they can combine work and personal responsibilities, such as child care. For those individuals with disabilities or those recovering from injury or illness, telecommuting provides a convenient, comfortable work environment.

Power User

Another category of user, called a **power user**, requires the capabilities of a workstation or other powerful computer. Examples of power users include engineers, scientists, architects, desktop publishers, and graphic artists. Power users typically work with *multimedia*, combining text, graphics, audio, and video into one application. These users need computers with extremely fast processors because of the nature of their work.

The power user's workstation contains industry-specific software. For example, engineers and architects use software to draft and design floor plans, mechanical assemblies, or vehicles. A desktop publisher uses software to prepare marketing literature such as newsletters, brochures, and annual reports. A geologist uses software to study the earth's surface (Figure 1-41). This software usually is quite expensive because of its specialized design.

Power users exist in all types of businesses, both large and small. Some also work at home. Depending on where they work, power users might fit into one of the previously discussed categories, as well. Their computers typically have network connections and Internet access.

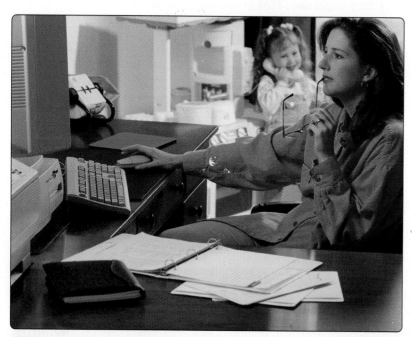

FIGURE 1-40 Many employees of large businesses often telecommute, which allows them to combine work and other responsibilities such as child care.

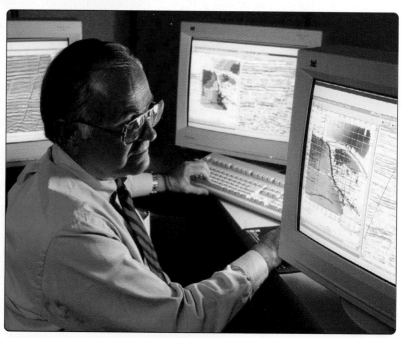

FIGURE 1-41 Power users require the capabilities of a powerful computer.

COMPUTER APPLICATIONS IN SOCIETY

The computer has changed society today as much as the industrial revolution changed society in the eighteenth and nineteenth centuries. In a recent report, the United States government attributed one-third of the country's economic growth to digital technologies, resulting in tremendous increases in productivity.

You may interact directly with computers in fields such as education, finance, government, health care, science, publishing, travel, and industry. Or, you may reap the benefits from breakthroughs and advances in these fields. The following pages describe how computers have made a difference in people's interactions with these disciplines. Read Looking Ahead 1-2 for a look at the next generation of computer applications in society.

LOOKING AHEAD 1-2

Robots Perform Real-World Tasks

Cleaning your house may become less of a chore when your new robot arrives. So will guarding hazardous production plants, teaching children new vocabulary words, and performing daily inventory checks.

Robotic pets also may serve as companions for nursing home residents, although they are not replacing the relationship between families and the elderly.

Sophisticated robots soon will be commonplace as these products become easier and less expensive to manufacture. Robot developer kits include controls for mobility, speech recognition and synthesis, decision making, and vision. Some even include emotions and personalities. The robots can be trained to detect specific colors and search for objects.

For a look at the next generation of robots, visit the Discovering Computers 2004 Looking Ahead Web page (**scsite.com/dc2004/looking**). Click Looking Ahead #2 below Chapter 1.

Education

Education is the process of acquiring knowledge. In the traditional model, people learn from other people such as parents, teachers, and employers. Many forms of printed material such as books and manuals are used as learning tools. Today, educators also are turning to computers to assist with education.

As the cost of computers drops, many schools and companies can afford to equip labs and classrooms with computers (Figure 1-42). Some schools even require students to have a notebook computer or PDA, along with textbooks and other supplies.

Students use software to assist with learning or to complete assignments. To promote education by computer, many vendors offer substantial student discounts on software.

Sometimes, the delivery of education occurs at one place while the learning occurs at other locations. For example, students can take a class on the Web. Some classes are blended, that is, part of the learning occurs in a classroom and the other part occurs on the Web. More than 70 percent of colleges offer some type of distance learning classes. A few even offer entire degrees online.

A concern of society is the digital divide. The *digital divide* is the idea that you can split people of the world into two distinct groups: (1) those who have access to technology and (2) those who do not. In this definition, technology includes telephones, television, computers, and the Internet. The concern is that some of the less fortunate people in the world may not be able to take advantage of the technology that makes much of society prosper and grow. For example, a recent study shows that the 20 largest cities in the United States receive 86 percent of Internet delivery.

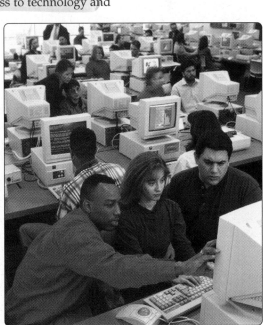

FIGURE 1-42 Many schools and businesses have computer labs to provide an environment conducive for students and employees to learn.

Computer Applications
In Society:
- education
- finance
- government
- health care
- science
- publishing

- travel
- industry

To help close the gap in the digital divide, the United States government and many organizations have efforts in progress. They are setting up community training centers and supplying teachers and students with necessary technology. For example, Microsoft and hardware partners such as Toshiba and IBM are part of the *Anytime Anywhere Learning program* that provides teachers and students with notebook computers ready with Microsoft applications and Internet access.

Finance

Many people and companies use computers to help manage their finances. Some use finance software to balance checkbooks, pay bills, track personal income and expenses, manage investments, and evaluate financial plans. This software usually includes a variety of online services. For example, computer users can track investments, compare insurance rates from leading insurance companies, and do online banking. With **online banking**, users access account balances, pay bills, and copy monthly transactions from the bank's computer right into their computers.

Many financial institutions' Web sites also offer online banking. When using a Web site instead of finance software on your computer, all your account information is stored on the bank's computer. The advantage is you can access your financial records from anywhere in the world (Figure 1-43). Web-based financial institutions often allow you to transfer cash from a credit card, debit card, or checking account to another person's credit card or bank account. Some people use this service for monetary gifts. Companies use it for rebates and refunds.

Investors often use **online investing** to buy and sell stocks and bonds — without using a broker. With online investing, the transaction fee for each trade usually is much less than when trading through a broker.

Government

A government provides society with direction by making and administering policies. Many people associate government with executive, judicial, and legislative offices. The United States government also includes areas such as law enforcement, employment, military, national security, taxes, and state and local agencies. To provide citizens with up-to-date information, most government offices have Web sites (Figure 1-44). A recent survey estimated that about 62 percent of people in the United States access government Web sites. They file taxes, apply for permits and licenses, pay parking tickets, buy stamps, report crimes, apply for financial aid, and renew vehicle registrations and driver's licenses.

Employees of government agencies use computers as part of their daily routine. North American 911 call centers use computers to dispatch calls for fire, police, and medical assistance. Law enforcement officers have online

FIGURE 1-43 Many financial institutions' Web sites offer online banking.

FIGURE 1-44 The United States government has many Web sites that provide official information.

access to the FBI's National Crime Information Center (NCIC) in police cars that have computers and fingerprint scanners. The NCIC contains more than 39 million criminal records, including names, fingerprints, parole/probation records, mug shots, and other information.

Health Care

Nearly every area of health care uses computers. Whether you are visiting a family doctor for a regular checkup, having lab work or an outpatient test, or being rushed in for emergency surgery, the medical staff around you will be using computers for various purposes:

- Hospitals and doctors use computers to maintain patient records.
- Computers monitor patients' vital signs in hospital rooms and at home.
- Computers and computerized devices assist doctors, nurses, and technicians with medical tests (Figure 1-45).
- Doctors use the Web and medical software to assist with researching and diagnosing health conditions.
- Doctors use e-mail to correspond with patients.
- Pharmacists use computers to file insurance claims.
- Surgeons implant computerized devices, such as pacemakers, that allow patients to live longer.
- Surgeons use computer-controlled devices to provide them with greater precision during operations, such as for laser eye surgery and robot-assisted heart surgery

Many times, you leave a doctor's office or hospital with a diagnosis and a prescription in hand. On the way home, you stop at the pharmacy to fill the prescription. For more information about your diagnosis, you could read a medical dictionary or attend a seminar. You might find it preferable to use the Web. Many Web sites provide up-to-date medical, fitness, nutrition, or exercise information. These Web sites also maintain lists of doctors and dentists to help you find the one that suits your needs. They have chat rooms, so you can talk to others diagnosed with similar conditions. Some Web sites even allow you to order prescriptions online.

Much of society today is fitness conscious. Diet and exercise are a part of daily life. Doctors often recommend some type of physical activity along with proper nutrition to maintain a healthy lifestyle. Whether you exercise at the local health club or at home in your basement, the equipment often has a computer built into it to track your progress. These computers monitor physical conditions, such as heart rate and pulse, to be sure you are exercising within safe limits.

An exciting development in health care is telemedicine, which is a form of long-distance health care. Through *telemedicine*, health-care professionals in separate locations have live conferences on the computer. For example, a doctor at one location can have a conference with a doctor at another location to discuss a bone x-ray. Live images of each doctor, along with the x-ray, are displayed on each doctor's computer.

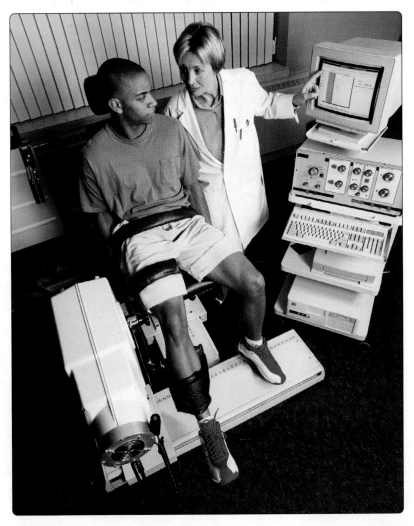

FIGURE 1-45 Dentists, doctors, nurses, technicians, and other medical staff use computers to perform tests on patients.

Science

All branches of science, from biology to astronomy to meteorology, use computers to assist them with collecting, analyzing, and modeling data. Scientists also use the Internet to communicate with colleagues around the world.

Breakthroughs in surgery, medicine, and treatments often result from scientists' use of computers. Tiny computers now imitate functions of the central nervous system, retina of the eye, and cochlea of the ear. A cochlear implant allows a deaf person to listen. Electrodes implanted in the brain stop tremors associated with Parkinson's disease. Cameras small enough to swallow take pictures inside your body to detect polyps, cancer, and other abnormalities (Figure 1-46).

The capability of the computer to recognize spoken words is a result of scientific experimentation with neural networks. A *neural network* is a system that attempts to imitate the behavior of the human brain. Scientists create neural networks by connecting thousands of processors together much like the neurons in the brain are connected.

Publishing

Publishing is the process of making work available to the public. These works include books, magazines, and newspapers. Special software assists publishers in designing pages that include text, graphics, and photographs. Journalists carry notebook computers, mobile devices, and digital cameras to capture and record news as it occurs.

In addition to printing materials, many publishers make the content of magazines and newspapers available online (Figure 1-47). Some Web sites allow you to copy an entire book to your desktop computer, handheld computer, or PDA. Handheld devices specially designed for reading electronic books also are available.

FIGURE 1-47 Many magazine and newspaper publishers make the content of their publications available online.

FIGURE 1-46 HOW A CAMERA PILL WORKS

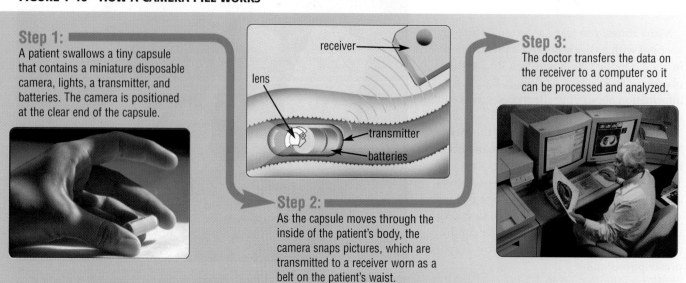

Step 1:
A patient swallows a tiny capsule that contains a miniature disposable camera, lights, a transmitter, and batteries. The camera is positioned at the clear end of the capsule.

Step 2:
As the capsule moves through the inside of the patient's body, the camera snaps pictures, which are transmitted to a receiver worn as a belt on the patient's waist.

Step 3:
The doctor transfers the data on the receiver to a computer so it can be processed and analyzed.

Travel

Whether traveling by car or airplane, your goal is to arrive safely at your destination. As you make the journey, you may interact with some of the latest technology.

Many vehicles manufactured today include some type of **onboard navigation facility** (Figure 1-48). Depending on the one you choose, these communications systems offer the consumer many worthwhile features:

- Provide directions
- Automatically call for help if the airbag deploys and you do not respond to voice contact
- Provide emergency services as soon as you press the emergency button
- Dispatch roadside assistance
- Perform remote diagnostics if a warning light appears on the dashboard
- Unlock the driver's side door if you lock the keys in the car
- Track the vehicle if it is stolen
- Honk the horn to help you locate the car in a parking lot

Many vehicles today also include options such as screens with e-mail and Internet access, printers, and fax capability. Airlines also provide online access. Airplanes equipped with Internet connections allow passengers to connect their mobile computer or device to the Web. Some airlines even provide passengers with Web-enabled devices during flights.

In preparing for a trip, you may need to reserve a car, hotel, or flight. Many Web sites offer these services to the public. For example, you can order airline tickets on the Web and have the tickets waiting for you at the airport or delivered directly to your door. If you plan to drive somewhere and are unsure of the road to take to your destination, you can print directions and a map from the Web. By entering the starting address and ending address, the Web site generates the best route for your trip.

FIGURE 1-48 Many vehicles made by General Motors are equipped with an onboard navigation facility called OnStar. By pushing the OnStar button, you immediately connect to an OnStar advisor.

Industry

Industries that manufacture products usually have large numbers of employees and high capital expenditures. Capital includes factories, warehouses, machinery, and computers. **Computer-aided manufacturing** (*CAM*) refers to the use of computers to assist with manufacturing processes such as fabrication and assembly. Industries use CAM to reduce product development costs, shorten a product's time to market, and stay ahead of the competition.

Often, robots carry out processes in a CAM environment. CAM is used by a variety of industries, including drilling for oil, generating power, and the manufacture of foodstuffs and automobiles. Automobile plants,

for example, have an entire line of industrial robots that assemble a car (Figure 1-49).

Special computers on the shop floor record actual labor, material, machine, and computer time used to manufacture a particular product. The computers process this data and automatically update inventory, production, payroll, and accounting records on the company's network.

> **QUIZ YOURSELF 1-3**
>
> To check your knowledge of categories of computers, elements of an information system, types of computer users, and computer applications in society, visit the Discovering Computers 2004 Quiz Yourself Web page (**scsite.com/dc2004/quiz**). Click Objectives 8 – 11 below Chapter 1.

FIGURE 1-49   Automotive factories use industrial robots to weld car bodies.

CHAPTER SUMMARY

Chapter 1 introduced you to basic computer concepts such as what a computer is, how it works, and what makes it a powerful tool. You learned about the components of a computer. Next, the chapter discussed networks, the Internet, and computer software. The many different categories of computers, computer users, and computer applications in society also were presented. This chapter was an overview. Many of the terms and concepts introduced will be discussed further in later chapters.

Career Corner

Personal Computer Salesperson

When you decide to buy or upgrade a personal computer, the most important person with whom you interact probably will be a personal computer salesperson. This individual will be a valuable resource to you in providing the information and expertise you need to select a computer that meets your requirements.

Computer manufacturers, and retailers that sell several types of personal computers, need competent salespeople. A *personal computer salesperson* must be computer literate and have a specific knowledge of the computers he or she sells. In addition, a successful salesperson has a friendly, outgoing personality that helps customers feel comfortable. Through open-ended questions, the salesperson can determine a customer's needs and level of experience. With this information, the salesperson can choose the best computer for the customer and explain the features of the computer in language the customer will understand.

Most computer salespeople have at least a high school diploma. Before reaching the sales floor, however, salespeople usually complete extensive company training programs. These programs often consist of self-directed, self-paced Web-training classes. Most salespeople also participate in training updates, often on a monthly basis.

Personal computer salespeople generally earn a guaranteed amount plus a commission for each sale. A computer salesperson can earn about $40,000 a year. Top salespeople can be among a company's most highly compensated employees, earning more than $70,000.

To learn more about the field of personal computer salesperson as a career, visit the Discovering Computers 2004 Careers Web page (**scsite.com/dc2004/careers**). Click Personal Computer Salesperson.

HIGH-TECH TALK

Analog versus Digital: Making the Conversion

Data is processed in one of two ways: analog or digital. People generally process *analog* data — that is, continuous wave patterns. The sight and sound of a traveling subway car transmits to your eyes and ears as light and sound waves, or smooth up-and-down patterns (Figure 1-50a). A computer, by contrast, is *digital*, which means computers process data in two discrete states: positive (on or 1) and nonpositive (off or 0) as shown in Figure 1-50b.

If sound and light waves are analog and a computer is digital, how does a computer record audio clips, play music, or show a movie? How can a digital computer use an analog telephone line to dial up to access the Internet?

The key lies in analog-to-digital and digital-to-analog conversions. The computer's sound card, for example, performs these conversions to record a digital audio clip of your analog voice. The sound card connects to the microphone, which is an analog input source. The diaphragm in the microphone converts the analog sound waves into an electrical signal. This signal flows to the sound card's *analog-to-digital-converter* (*ADC*), which converts the signal into digital data. The digital data flows to the *digital signal processor* (*DSP*), compressing the data to save space. Finally, the DSP sends the compressed data to the processor, which stores the data in an audio file format.

To play a recorded sound, the computer reverses the process. The processor retrieves and sends the digital data to the DSP to be decompressed. The DSP sends the decompressed, digital data to the sound

card's *digital-to-analog converter* (*DAC*), which converts the digital data back to an analog voltage for output via a speaker or headset.

Similarly, a video card allows you to record a video or play a movie on a DVD. A camera and microphone capture and send the analog picture and sound signals to a video card. The video card's ADC converts the signals into digital data. The digital data is compressed and saved in a file format such as AVI (audio/video interleave) or MPEG. When playing a movie, the computer decompresses and separates the video and audio data. It then sends the signals to the video card's DAC. The DAC translates the digital data into analog signals and sends them to the monitor and speakers, where they display as your movie.

The modem in a computer also links the analog and digital worlds. When using a dial-up modem, the computer does not transmit digital data directly across analog telephone lines. Instead, the modem converts the computer's digital signals to analog signals (called *modulation*) to be sent over telephone lines. When the analog signal reaches its destination, another modem recreates the original digital signal (*demodulation*). This allows the receiving computer to process the data. The next time you dial up using a modem, pick up the telephone. The loud, screeching noise you hear is the sound of digital data after being converted to analog sound waves.

For more information about analog versus digital, visit the Discovering Computers 2004 High-Tech Talk Web page (**scsite.com/dc2004/tech**) and click Analog versus Digital.

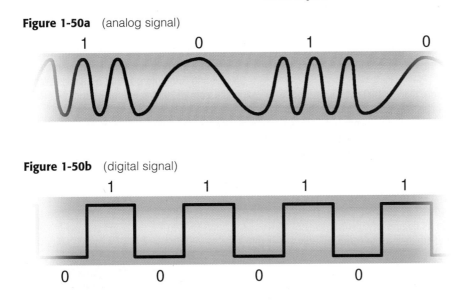

Figure 1-50a (analog signal)

1   0   1   0

Figure 1-50b (digital signal)

1   1   1   1

0   0   0   0

FIGURE 1-50 Analog versus digital signals.

COMPANIES ON THE CUTTING EDGE

Dell
Computers Your Way

"Dude, you're gettin' a Dell!" With this euphoric phrase, Dell's popular spokesperson tells another friend that he is about to acquire one of the world's favorite computers. The friend is not alone. Last year, Dell Computer Corporation earned revenues exceeding $31 billion.

Founded by Michael Dell in 1984, the largest private employer in Austin, Texas has millions of square feet of office and manufacturing space at its corporate headquarters. Along with its other U.S. location in Nashville, Tennessee, Dell has offices in Japan, Malaysia, Ireland, China, and Brazil.

Dell Computer Corporation prides itself on its direct approach to sales. The company deals openly with customers, one at a time. The direct approach allows Dell to build every computer to order and offer complete systems at competitive prices. The approach also eliminates retailers that add time and cost, increases awareness of customer expectations, and allows faster introduction of new technologies.

Dell uses the Internet to enhance the advantages of direct marketing. In 1997, Dell became the first company to reach $1 million a day in online sales. Today, Dell hosts one of the world's largest volume e-commerce Web sites, where customers can configure and price computers, order systems, and track their orders.

Dell employs more than 34,000 people worldwide. Employees work in an environment that recognizes their diversity and skills. The Dell corporate philosophy fosters the creativity generated by a workforce composed of individuals with varied backgrounds and experiences. Workers have the opportunity to contribute fully to corporate goals and can achieve their professional goals through the company's virtual university, The Dell Learning Center. Dell also takes pride in its community involvement. Through The Dell Foundation, the company offers targeted grant programs with a focus on technology education.

For more information about Dell Computer Corporation, visit the Discovering Computers 2004 Companies Web page (**scsite.com/dc2004/companies**) and click Dell Computer Corporation.

Palm
Ubiquitous Palm Is a Phenomenon

When Michael Jordan announced his return to the National Basketball Association to play for the Washington Wizards, he endorsed his line of two special-edition Palm PDAs, software, and accessories. He is one of 14 million people worldwide who have a Palm PDA in their pocket or purse or briefcase to help them manage and organize their professional and personal lives.

Palm is a leading provider of PDAs and a pioneer in the field of mobile and wireless Internet communications. The Palm PDA, manufactured by Palm, Inc., commands nearly 70 percent of the PDA market worldwide. More than 13,000 types of application software are available for this versatile and stylish product. Currently, software for Palm PDAs enables users to perform a multitude of tasks, including read e-books, record golf scores, and play games.

Palm emphasizes that PDAs are different from notebook or desktop computers. PDAs are designed to manage and access information, rather than create and edit documents. With this in mind, Palm PDAs are intended to be simple so that you easily can retrieve information, wearable so that you can carry it anywhere, expandable so that you can add functionality, and mobile so that you can access information anywhere.

Palm was founded in 1992 and acquired by U.S. Robotics in 1995. One year later, the company introduced the Pilot 1000 and 5000 products, which blazed a trail for the PDA market. In 1997, 3Com acquired U.S. Robotics and made Palm a subsidiary of the corporation. Two years later, 3Com made Palm an independent, publicly traded company. In 2002, Palm formed a subsidiary, called PalmSource, Inc., to separate the company's device and operating systems businesses.

For more information about Palm, visit the Discovering Computers 2004 Companies Web page (**scsite.com/dc2004/companies**) and click Palm.

TECHNOLOGY TRAILBLAZERS

Bill Gates
Microsoft's Founder

What advice does one of the richest men in the world have for students? Get the best education you can. Take advantage of high school and college. Learn how to learn.

As Microsoft's founder and former CEO, *Bill Gates* receives hundreds of e-mail messages from students asking for insight on education. He emphasizes that college graduates know about a multitude of subjects and group dynamics. Gates dropped out of Harvard during his junior year, but he stresses that students should not quit going to school unless they are facing extraordinary prospects.

Gates began programming computers when he was 13. Early in his career, he developed the BASIC programming language for the MITS Altair, one of the first microcomputers. He founded Microsoft in 1975 with Paul Allen, and five years later they provided the first operating system for the IBM PC, called MS-DOS. Under Gates's leadership, Microsoft continued to update MS-DOS and then develop Windows, Internet Explorer, and the MSNBC cable television news network and corresponding Web site. Today, Bill Gates's official title at Microsoft is Chief Software Architect, which allows him a greater role in program design and development. He still is regarded as the most powerful person in the computer industry.

Gates has written two books: *Business @ The Speed of Thought* and *The Road Ahead*. All proceeds have been donated to nonprofit organizations. Bill Gates is a devoted father and claims that his children "make things fun all the time." The feeling for children has spilled over into his charitable contributions. Together with his wife, Gates has endowed the Bill & Melinda Gates Foundation, which supports global health and learning, with more than $24 billion.

For more information about Bill Gates, visit the Discovering Computers 2004 People Web page (**scsite.com/dc2004/people**) and click Bill Gates.

Carly Fiorina
CEO of Hewlett-Packard

Although seemingly improbable that a shipping department secretary someday would return to become the company's chairman of the board and chief executive officer, it is a true story for *Carly Fiorina*. As Hewlett-Packard's leader, she is focusing on improving profitability, innovation, customer service, and Internet applications.

Fiorina credits her liberal arts undergraduate studies at Stanford University, where she majored in philosophy and medieval history, with helping her learn how to think and make choices. She urges college graduates to love what they do and not to make decisions based on the desires of others.

After a brief stint in law school, she became a sales representative for AT&T. That short-term job eventually grew into leading and guiding the AT&T spin-off, Lucent Technologies, Inc., to one of the more successful initial public offering (IPO) stock offerings. Fiorina says leadership involves influencing others and mastering change. It also empowers people to reach their full potential and make decisions.

In 1999, Fiorina became CEO of Hewlett-Packard, one of the oldest companies in Silicon Valley. Many people felt that the company, once known for its innovations, had become stagnant and slow to embrace new ideas. To combat this, Fiorina engineered a merger between Hewlett-Packard and inventive, but struggling, Compaq Computer Corporation. Certain employees and retirees, and even children of Hewlett-Packard's founders, opposed the merger. But, after a nine-month struggle that included court appearances and some personal animosity, the merger was completed. "There's no question that there were a lot of unfortunate consequences…" Fiorina admits, "but I think it's also true that employees are ready to move on." In fact, the theme of the meeting that finally announced the merger was, "We are ready." And so is Fiorina, promising that Hewlett-Packard again will compete with the giants in technology.

For more information about Carly Fiorina, visit the Discovering Computers 2004 People Web page (**scsite.com/dc2004/people**) and click Carly Fiorina.

CHAPTER 1   CHAPTER REVIEW

◀● Previous | Next ●▶

The Chapter Review section summarizes the concepts presented in this chapter.

WEB INSTRUCTIONS:

To display this page from the Web, start your browser and enter the Web address **scsite.com/dc2004/ch1/review**. Click the links for current and additional information. To listen to an audio version of this Chapter Review, click the Audio button.

1 Why Is Computer Literacy Important?

Computer literacy entails having knowledge and understanding of computers and their uses. As computers become an increasingly important part of daily living, many people believe that computer literacy is vital to success.

2 What Is a Computer and What Are Its Components?

A **computer** is an electronic device, operating under the control of instructions stored in its own memory, that can accept data, manipulate the data according to specified rules, produce results, and store the results for future use. The electric, electronic, and mechanical components of a computer, or **hardware**, include input devices, output devices, a system unit, storage devices, and communications devices. An **input device** allows you to enter data or instructions into a computer. An **output device** conveys information to one or more people. The **system unit** is a box-like case that contains electronic components of a computer that are used to process data. A **storage device** records and/or retrieves items to and from storage media. A **communications device** enables a computer to send and receive data, instructions, and information to and from one or more computers.

3 Why Is a Computer a Powerful Tool?

A computer is a powerful tool because it performs the information processing cycle operations (input, process, output, and storage) with amazing speed, reliability, consistency, and accuracy. Computers also can store huge amounts of data and information.

Visit **scsite.com/dc2004/quiz** or click the Quiz Yourself button. Click Objectives 1 – 3 below Chapter 1.

4 What Is the Purpose of a Network?

A **network** is a collection of computers and devices connected together via communications devices and transmission media. Networks allow computers to share *resources*, such as hardware, software, data, and information.

5 How Are the Internet and the World Wide Web Used?

The **Internet** is a worldwide collection of networks that connects millions of businesses, government agencies, educational institutions, and individuals. People use the Internet to communicate with and meet other people, to access news and information, to shop for goods and services, to bank and invest, to take classes, and to access sources of entertainment and leisure. The **Web**, short for World Wide Web, is a global library of documents containing information that is available to anyone connected to the Internet.

6 How Is Installing a Program Different from Running a Program?

Software, also called a **program**, is a series of instructions that tells the computer what to do and how to do it. **Installing** a program is the process of setting up the program to work with a computer, printer, and other hardware components. To **run** a program means to use it. Running a program happens when a user instructs the computer to start the program, either by inserting a disc or by issuing a command. The computer *loads*, or places, the program into its memory from storage and then *executes*, or carries out, the program instructions.

7 What Are the Types of Software?

The two categories of software are system software and application software. **System software** consists of the programs that control or maintain the operations of a computer and its devices. Two types of system software are the *operating system*, which coordinates activities

CHAPTER REVIEW

CHAPTER 1

among computer hardware devices, and *utility programs*, which perform maintenance-type tasks usually related to a computer, its devices, or its programs. **Application software** consists of programs that perform specific tasks for users. Popular application software includes Web browser, word processing software, spreadsheet software, database software, and presentation graphics software.

> Visit **scsite.com/dc2004/quiz** or click the Quiz Yourself button. Click Objectives 4 – 7 below Chapter 1.

8 What Are the Categories of Computers?

Industry experts typically classify computers into five categories: personal computers, mobile computers and mobile devices, midrange servers, mainframes, and supercomputers. A **personal computer** is a computer that can perform all of its input, processing, output, and storage activities by itself. A **mobile computer** is a personal computer that you can carry from place to place, and a **mobile device** is a computing device small enough to hold in your hand. A **midrange server** is a large and powerful computer that typically supports several hundred and sometimes up to a few thousand networked computers at the same time. A **mainframe** is a large, very expensive, very powerful computer that can handle hundreds or thousands of connected users simultaneously and can store tremendous amounts of data, instructions, and information. A **supercomputer** is the fastest, most powerful, and most expensive computer and is used for applications requiring complex, sophisticated mathematical calculations.

9 How Do the Elements of an Information System Interact?

An *information system* combines hardware, software, data, people, and procedures to produce timely and useful information. People in an information technology department develop procedures for processing data. Following these procedures, people use hardware and software to enter the data into a computer. Software processes the data and directs the computer hardware to store changes on storage media and produce information in a desired form.

10 What Are the Types of Computer Users?

Computer users can be separated into five categories: home users, small office/home office users, mobile users, large business users, and power users. A **home user** is a family member who uses a computer for a variety of reasons, such as budgeting and personal financial management, Web access, communications, and entertainment. A **small office/home office** (*SOHO*) user is a small company or self-employed individual who works from home and uses basic business software and sometimes industry-specific software. Mobile users are employees and students who work on a computer while away from a main office or school. A **large business user** works in a company with many employees and uses a computer and computer network to process high volumes of transactions. **Power users** are employed in all types of businesses and use powerful computers to work with industry-specific software.

11 What Computer Applications Are Used in Society?

You may interact directly with computers in fields such as education, finance, government, health care, science, publishing, travel, and industry. In education, students use computers and software to assist with learning or take distance learning classes. In finance, people use computers for **online banking** to access information and **online investing** to buy and sell stocks and bonds. Government offices have Web sites to provide citizens with up-to-date information, and government employees use computers as part of their daily routines. In medicine, computers are used to maintain patient records, assist doctors with medical tests and research, file insurance claims, provide greater precision during operations, and as implants. All branches of science use computers to assist with collecting, analyzing, and modeling data and to communicate with scientists around the world. Publishers use computers to assist in designing pages and make the content of their publications available online. Many vehicles use some type of **online navigation facility** to help people travel more quickly and safely. Industries use **computer-aided manufacturing** (*CAM*) to assist with the manufacturing process.

> Visit **scsite.com/dc2004/quiz** or click the Quiz Yourself button. Click Objectives 8 – 11 below Chapter 1.

CHAPTER 1 · KEY TERMS

◄● Previous | Next ●►

You should know the Primary Terms and be familiar with the Secondary Terms.

WEB INSTRUCTIONS:

To display this page from the Web, start your browser and enter the Web address **scsite.com/dc2004/ch1/terms**. Click a term to display its definition and a picture. When the picture displays, click the more info button for current and additional information about the term from the Web.

>> Primary Terms
(shown in bold-black characters in the chapter)

application software (1.14)
communications device (1.07)
computer (1.04)
computer literacy (1.03)
computer-aided manufacturing (1.36)
data (1.04)
desktop computer (1.17)
graphical user interface (GUI) (1.12)
handheld computer (1.19)
hardware (1.05)
home user (1.24)
information (1.04)
input device (1.05)
installing (1.12)
Internet (1.09)
Internet appliance (1.25)
laptop computer (1.18)
large business user (1.28)
mainframe (1.21)
midrange server (1.20)
mobile computer (1.18)

mobile device (1.18)
mobile users (1.27)
network (1.08)
notebook computer (1.18)
onboard navigation facility (1.35)
online (1.08)
online banking (1.32)
online investing (1.32)
output device (1.06)
PDA (1.19)
personal computer (1.16)
photo community (1.11)
power user (1.30)
program (1.12)
run (1.12)
small office/home office (1.26)
smart phone (1.20)
software (1.12)
storage device (1.06)
storage media (1.06)
supercomputer (1.21)
system software (1.13)
system unit (1.06)
Tablet PC (1.18)
telecommuting (1.30)
Web (1.11)
Web-enabled (1.19)

>> Secondary Terms
(shown in italic characters in the chapter)

Anytime Anywhere Learning program (1.32)
CAM (1.36)
client (1.08)
customer relationship management (CRM) (1.29)
digital divide (1.31)
digital pen (1.18)
e-commerce (1.27)
enterprise computing (1.28)
execute (1.12)
garbage in, garbage out (1.08)
icon (1.12)
information processing cycle (1.04)
information system (1.22)
information technology (IT) department (1.29)
instructions (1.04)

kiosk (1.29)
loads (1.12)
memory (1.06)
minicomputers (1.20)
modular computer (1.18)
multimedia (1.30)
neural network (1.34)
operating system (1.13)
PC-compatible (1.17)
personal digital assistant (1.19)
processor (1.06)
programmer (1.15)
publish (1.11)
resources (1.08)
server (1.08)
set-top box (1.25)
SOHO (1.26)
stylus (1.20)
telemedicine (1.33)
tower (1.17)
utility program (1.14)
Web cam (1.27)

CHECKPOINT CHAPTER 1

Use the Checkpoint exercises to check your knowledge level of the chapter.

WEB INSTRUCTIONS:

To display this page from the Web, start your browser and enter the Web address **scsite.com/dc2004/ch1/check**. Click the links for current and additional information.

LABEL THE FIGURE   Identify these common computer hardware components.

- a. card reader (storage)
- b. CD/DVD drive (storage)
- c. digital camera (input)
- d. floppy disk drive (storage)
- e. hard disk drive (storage)
- f. keyboard (input)
- g. microphone (input)
- h. modem (communications)
- i. monitor (output)
- j. mouse (input)
- k. PC video camera (input)
- l. printer (output)
- m. scanner (input)
- n. speaker (output)
- o. system unit (processor, memory, storage)

TRUE/FALSE   Mark T for True and F for False. (See page numbers in parentheses.)

F   1. <u>Computer literacy</u> entails knowing how to program computers. (1.03) *(compt. & their usage)*

T   2. <u>Data</u> is a collection of unprocessed items. (1.04)

T   3. A <u>user</u> is anyone who communicates with a computer. (1.08)

F   4. The client controls access to the resources on a <u>network</u>. (1.08) *(server)*

F   5. The <u>Internet</u> is a worldwide collection of servers. (1.09) *network*

T   6. Software is a series of <u>instructions</u> that tells the computer what to do. (1.12)

T   7. <u>System software</u> is a set of programs that coordinates all the activities among computer hardware devices. (1.13)

T   8. A <u>notebook computer</u> is a portable, personal computer small enough to fit on your lap. (1.18)

T   9. A power user requires the capabilities of a <u>workstation</u> or other powerful computer. (1.30)

T   10. Few <u>publishers</u> make the content of magazines and newspapers available online. (1.34)

CHAPTER 1 CHECKPOINT

MULTIPLE CHOICE   Select the best answer. (See page numbers in parentheses.)

1. As <u>technology</u> continues to advance, many people believe that ___ is vital to success. (1.03)
   a. computer animation
   b. computer programming
   c. computer crime
   d. computer literacy

2. Three commonly used ___ are a printer, a <u>monitor</u>, and speakers. (1.06)
   a. input devices
   b. output devices
   c. storage devices
   d. communications devices

3. A computing phrase known as <u>garbage in, garbage out</u> points out that the ___ of a computer's output depends on the accuracy of the input. (1.08)
   a. speed
   b. accuracy
   c. storage
   d. consistency

4. In a network, the major differences between the <u>server</u> and client computers are that the server ordinarily has ___ . (1.08)
   a. less power, less storage, and is less reliable
   b. less power, more storage, but is less reliable
   c. more power, less storage, but is more reliable
   d. more power, more storage, and is more reliable

5. ___ allows people connected to the Internet to communicate with multiple users at the same time — much like a <u>group discussion</u>. (1.11)
   a. A chat room   c. A Web page
   b. E-mail   d. Instant messaging

6. During ___, a <u>program</u> may ask you to register or activate the software online. (1.12)
   a. execution
   b. loading
   c. installation
   d. running

7. Some widely used ___ include(s) <u>personal information manager</u>, desktop publishing, and Web page authoring. (1.14)
   a. system software
   b. operating systems
   c. application software
   d. utility programs

8. The term, <u>PC-compatible</u>, refers to any personal computer ___ (1.17)
   a. with processors having the same architecture as processors in Apple computers
   b. based on the original IBM personal computer design
   c. that uses the Macintosh operating system (Mac OS)
   d. all of the above

9. Two types of ___ are <u>desktop computers</u> and notebook computers. (1.17)
   a. personal computers
   b. midrange servers
   c. mainframe computers
   d. supercomputers

10. Three popular types of ___ are handheld computers, <u>PDAs</u>, and smart phones. (1.19)
    a. mobile devices
    b. notebook computers
    c. desktop computers
    d. tower computers

11. In addition to <u>hardware</u> and software, an information system includes ___ (1.22)
    a. accurate data
    b. trained information technology staff and knowledgeable users
    c. document procedures
    d. all of the above

12. ___ have employees in the <u>information technology (IT) department</u> who keep the computers and the network running. (1.29)
    a. Home users
    b. Small office/home office users
    c. Large business users
    d. Power users

13. ___ is the idea that you can split people of the world into two distinct groups: those who have access to <u>technology</u> and those who do not. (1.31)
    a. Computer-aided manufacturing
    b. The digital divide
    c. E-commerce
    d. Anytime Anywhere Learning

14. Many vehicles manufactured today include some type of ___ that can provide directions and dispatch <u>roadside assistance</u>. (1.35)
    a. onboard navigation system
    b. personal digital assistant
    c. digital signal processor
    d. analog-to-digital converter

CHECKPOINT CHAPTER 1

MATCHING   Match the terms with their definitions. (See page numbers in parentheses.)

_____ 1. instructions (1.04)
_____ 2. hardware (1.05)
_____ 3. network (1.08)
_____ 4. server (1.08)
_____ 5. publish (1.11)
_____ 6. software (1.12)
_____ 7. icon (1.12)
_____ 8. modular computer (1.18)
_____ 9. Web-enabled (1.19)
_____ 10. kiosk (1.29)

a. computer's electric, electronic, and mechanical components
b. mobile devices that can connect to the Internet wirelessly
c. computer that controls access to network resources
d. someone who develops application or system programs
e. small image that represents a program, an instruction, or some other object
f. freestanding computer usually with a touch screen
g. collection of computers connected together that allows sharing of resources
h. small version of a Tablet PC that fits in the palm of your hand
i. make a Web page available on the Internet for others to see
j. system that attempts to illustrate the behavior of the human brain
k. steps that tell a computer how to perform a particular task
l. series of instructions that tells a computer what to do and how to do it

SHORT ANSWER   Write a brief answer to each of the following questions.

1. What are some ways people use computers in the home, at work, and at school? _____ What does it mean to be computer literate? _____
2. How is hardware different from software? _____ What is installing? _____
3. How is an input device different from an output device? _____ What are commonly used input and output devices? _____
4. What are six common storage devices? _____ How are they different? _____
5. Why do people use the Internet? _____ How do most users connect to the Internet? _____

1. Six commonly used input devices are listed in this chapter. These devices include a keyboard,

WORKING TOGETHER   Working with a group of your classmates, complete the following team exercises.

mouse, microphone, scanner, PC video camera, and digital camera. Using the Internet or other resources, prepare a report about each one of these devices. Discuss how and when you would use one device instead of another. What are some of the different features available in each device? How would you determine which keyboard, mouse, and so on is the best for your particular needs? Share your reports with the class.

2. Choose one Issue from the following issues in this chapter: Does Technology Discriminate? (1.07), Is Everything You Read True? (1.11), Does Software Promote Violence? (1.15), or Are You Ready for Real-Time Advertising? (1.28). Use the Web and/or print media to research the issue. Then, present a debate for the class, with different members of your team supporting different responses to the questions that accompany the issue.

3. Computers are everywhere. Watching television, driving a car, using a charge card, ordering fast food, and the more obvious activity of typing a term paper on a personal computer, all involve interaction with computers. For one day, have each member of your team make a list of every computer he or she encounters (be careful not to limit yourselves just to the computers you see). Meet with the members of your team and combine your lists. Consider how each computer is used. How were the tasks the computers perform done before computers? Use PowerPoint to create a group presentation and share your findings with the class.

CHAPTER 1 LEARN IT ONLINE

‹● Previous | Next ●›

Use the Learn It Online exercises to reinforce your understanding of the chapter concepts.

☐ **WEB INSTRUCTIONS:**

To display this page from the Web, start your browser and enter the Web address **scsite.com/dc2004/ch1/learn**.

1 At The Movies – Computer Takeaways

To view the Computer Takeaways movie, click the number 1 button. Watch the movie and then complete the exercise by answering the questions below. ZapMe!, an innovative marketing firm, originally provided 2,000 cash-strapped schools across the country with *free* computers for student use. The catch was that the students would be exposed to advertising messages flashing across their computer screens. ZapMe! provided the computers free, and made their money by selling screen-space to advertisers. Consumer groups, however, quickly began a campaign claiming it was not politically correct (PC) to do that. Under this pressure, most advertisers quit ZapMe!. Without sales, ZapMe! was forced to demand that the schools pay for the computers, or they would be taken away. What was not PC about this seemingly clever way of getting computers and Internet access in the hands of students who otherwise might not have this technology? Is this acceptable or not? Do you agree with this?

b. Running from a CD-ROM: Insert the Shelly Cashman Series Labs with Audio CD-ROM in your CD-ROM drive.

c. Running the No-Audio Version from a hard disk or network: Click the Start button on the Windows taskbar, point to Shelly Cashman Series Labs on the All Programs submenu, and then click Interactive Labs.

2. When the Shelly Cashman Series IN THE LAB screen shown in the figure below is displayed, follow the instructions on the screen to start the Using the Mouse Lab.

3. When the Using the Mouse screen displays, read the objectives.

4. If assigned, follow the instructions on the screen to print the questions associated with the Lab.

5. Follow the instructions on the screen to continue in the Lab.

6. When completed, follow the instructions on the screen to quit the Lab.

7. If assigned, submit your answers for the printed questions to your instructor.

2 Shelly Cashman Series Using the Mouse Lab

1. To start the Shelly Cashman Series Using the Mouse Lab, complete the step that applies to you.

a. Running from the World Wide Web: Enter the Web address **scsite.com/sclabs/menu** or display the Learn It Online page (see instructions at the top of this page) and then click the number 2 button.

LEARN IT ONLINE — CHAPTER 1

3 Shelly Cashman Series Using the Keyboard Lab

Follow the appropriate instructions in Learn It Online exercise 2 to start and use the Shelly Cashman Series Using the Keyboard Lab. If you are running from the Web, enter the Web address **scsite.com/sclabs/menu**; or display the Learn It Online page (see instructions at the top of page 1.46) and then click the number 3 button.

4 Practice Test

Click the number 4 button. Answer each question. When completed, enter your name and click the Grade Test button to submit the quiz for grading. Make a note of any missed questions. If required, print a copy to submit to your instructor.

5 Web Guide

Click the number 5 button to display the Guide to Web Sites and Searching Techniques Web page. Click Reference and then click Ask Jeeves. Ask Jeeves about computer science. Click an answer of your choice. Use your word processing program to prepare a brief report on what you learned and submit your assignment to your instructor.

6 Scavenger Hunt

Click the number 6 button. Print a copy of the Scavenger Hunt page; use this page to write down your answers as you search the Web. Submit your completed page to your instructor.

7 Who Wants to Be a Computer Genius?

Click the number 7 button to find out if you are a computer genius. Directions on how to play the game will display. When you are ready to play, click the Play button. Submit your score to your instructor.

8 Wheel of Terms

Click the number 8 button to reinforce important terms you learned in this chapter by playing the Shelly Cashman Series version of this popular game. Directions on how to play

the game will display. When you are ready to play, click the Play button. Submit your score to your instructor.

9 Career Corner

Click the number 9 button to display the Quintessential Careers page. Search for jobs in your state. Write a brief report about the jobs you found. Submit the report to your instructor.

10 Search Sleuth

Click the number 10 button to learn search techniques that will help make you a research expert. Submit the completed assignment to your instructor.

11 Crossword Puzzle Challenge

Click the number 11 button. Complete the puzzle to reinforce skills you learned in this chapter. Directions on how to play the game will display. When you are ready to play, click the Play button. Submit the completed puzzle to your instructor.

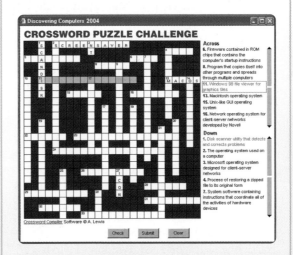

12 Learn the Net

No matter how much computer experience you have, navigating the Net for the first time can be intimidating. How do you get started? Click the number 12 button and click the links to discover how you can find out everything you want to know about the Internet.

CHAPTER 1 LAB EXERCISES

◀● Previous | Next ●▶

Use the Lab Exercises to gain hands-on computer experience.

WEB INSTRUCTIONS:

To display this page from the Web, start your browser and enter the Web address **scsite.com/dc2004/ch1/lab**.

1 Using Windows XP Help and Support

Windows XP Help and Support brings together the Help features that were available in previous versions of Windows (Search, Index, and Favorites) with the online Help features found on the Microsoft Web site. Help and Support also allows you to see the differences among Windows XP and earlier versions of Windows. Click the Start button on the Windows taskbar and then click Help and Support on the Start menu. Click the What's new in Windows XP link and then click the What's new topics link. Click a topic in which you are interested. If necessary, scroll through and read the information. How is this version of Windows better than previous versions of Windows? Will the improvement make your work more efficient? Why or why not? What improvement, if any, would you still like to see? The Help and Support Center includes a Search text box below the Help toolbar. When would you use the Search text box to find Help? Click the Index button on the Help toolbar. What do you see? When would you use the Index sheet to find Help? Click the Favorites button on the Help toolbar. What do you see? When would you use the Favorites sheet to find Help? Close the Help and Support Center window.

2 Using Windows 2000/98 Help

In the past, when you purchased computer software, you also received large printed manuals that attempted to answer any questions you might have. Today, Help usually is offered directly on the computer. To make it easy to find exactly the Help you need, Windows Help is arranged on three sheets: Contents, Index, and Search. Windows 2000 includes a fourth sheet, Favorites. Click the Start button on the Windows taskbar and then click Help on the Start menu. Click the Contents tab in the Windows Help window. What do you see? When would you use the Contents sheet to find Help? Click the Index tab. What do you see? When would you use the Index sheet to find Help? Click the Search tab. What do you see? When would you use the Search sheet to find Help? If you are using Windows 2000, click

the Favorites tab. What do you see? When would you use the Favorites sheet to find Help? Close the Windows Help window.

3 Improving Mouse Skills

This exercise uses Windows XP procedures. Click the Start button on the Windows taskbar. Point to All Programs on the Start menu, point to Games on the All Programs submenu, and then click Solitaire on the Games submenu. When the Solitaire window displays, click the Maximize button. Click Help on the Solitaire menu bar, and then click Contents. Click the Contents tab. Click the Solitaire overview topic and read the information. Click the Play Solitaire topic. Read and print the information by clicking the Solitaire Help window's Options button, clicking Print, and then clicking the OK button. Click the Close button in the Solitaire Help window. Play the game of Solitaire. Close the Solitaire window.

4 Learning About Your Computer

This exercise uses Windows XP/2000/98 procedures. You can learn some important information about your computer by studying the system properties. Click the Start button on the Windows taskbar. Click Control Panel on the Start menu. If necessary, click the Switch to Classic View link in the Control Panel area in the left pane of the Control Panel window. In Windows 2000/98, point to Settings on the Start menu, and then click Control Panel on the Settings submenu. Double-click the System icon in the Control Panel window. Click the General tab in the System Properties dialog box. Use the General sheet to find the answers to these questions:

• What operating system does your computer use?
• To whom is your computer registered?
• What type of processor does your computer have?
• How much memory (RAM) does your computer have?

Close the System Properties dialog box. Close the Control Panel window.

WEB RESEARCH CHAPTER 1

Use the Web Research exercises to learn more about the special features in this chapter.

◻ WEB INSTRUCTIONS:

Use the link in each exercise or a search engine such as Google (google.com) to research the topic. Then, write a one-page, double-spaced report or create a presentation, unless otherwise directed below. Page numbers on which information can be found are in parentheses.

1. Issue Choose one Issue from the following issues in this chapter: Does Technology Discriminate? (1.07), Is Everything You Read True? (1.11), Does Software Promote Violence? (1.15), or Are You Ready for Real-Time Advertising? (1.28). Use the Web to research the issue. Discuss the issue with classmates, instructors, and friends. Address the questions that accompany the issue in a report or presentation.

2. Apply It Choose one of the following Apply It features in this chapter: Directory Storage Power at Your Fingertips (1.09) or Prescription for Saving Doctors' Time (1.20). Use the Web to gather additional information about the topic. Print two Web pages that relate to the Apply It. Detail in a report or presentation what you learned.

3. Career Corner Read the Career Corner article in this chapter (1.36). Use the Web to find out more about the career. Describe the career in a report or presentation.

4. Companies on the Cutting Edge Choose one of the Companies on the Cutting Edge in this chapter (1.38). Use the Web to research the company further. Explain in a report or presentation how this company has contributed to computer technology.

5. Technology Trailblazers Choose one of the Technology Trailblazers in this chapter (1.39). Use the Web to research the person further. Explain in a report or presentation how this individual has affected the way people use, or think about, computers.

6. Picture Yourself Using Computers Read the Picture Yourself Using Computers story at the beginning of this chapter (1.00). Use the Web to research the uses of computers further. Describe in a report or presentation the ways in which you might use a computer.

7. High-Tech Talk Read the High-Tech Talk feature in this chapter (1.37). Use the Web to find out more about the topic. Summarize in a report or presentation what you learned.

8. Web Link Review the Web Link boxes found in the margins of this chapter. Visit five of the Web Link sites. Print the main Web page for each site you visit. Choose one of the Web pages and then summarize in one paragraph the content of the Web page.

9. Looking Ahead Choose one of the Looking Ahead articles in this chapter: Wearable Computers Serve Practical Purposes (1.16) or Robots Perform Real-World Tasks (1.31). Use the Web to find out more about the topic. Detail in a report or presentation what you learned.

10. FAQ Choose one FAQ found in this chapter. Use the Web to find out more about the topic. Summarize in one paragraph what you learned.

11. History of Computers Read the Timeline 2004 Special Feature that follows this chapter (1.50–1.62). Select an individual, product, or event presented in the Timeline 2004. Use the Web to learn more about your selection. Explain in a report or presentation why your selection is a milestone in computer history.

12. Making Use of the Web Read the Fun and Entertainment section of Making Use of the Web in Appendix A (A.02). Complete the Fun and Entertainment Web Exercises at the end of the section (A.03). Answer the questions posed in each exercise.

SPECIAL FEATURE

scsite.com/dc2004/ch1/timeline

Timeline 2004

Milestones in Computer History

Dr. John V. Atanasoff and Clifford Berry design and build the first electronic digital computer. Their machine, the Atanasoff-Berry-Computer, or ABC, provides the foundation for advances in electronic digital computers.

Dr. John von Neumann writes a brilliant paper describing the stored program concept. His breakthrough idea, where memory holds both data and stored programs, lays the foundation for all digital computers that have since been built.

1937

1945

1943

1946

During World War II, British scientist Alan Turing designs the Colossus, an electronic computer created for the military to break German codes. The computer's existence is kept secret until the 1970s.

Dr. John W. Mauchly and J. Presper Eckert, Jr. complete work on the first large-scale electronic, general-purpose digital computer. The ENIAC (Electronic Numerical Integrator And Computer) weighs thirty tons, contains 18,000 vacuum tubes, occupies a thirty-by-fifty-foot space, and consumes 160 kilowatts of power. The first time it is turned on, lights dim in an entire section of Philadelphia.

William Shockley, John Bardeen, and Walter Brattain invent the transfer resistance device, eventually called the transistor. The transistor would revolutionize computers, proving much more reliable than vacuum tubes.

Dr. Grace Hopper considers the concept of reusable software in her paper, "The Education of a Computer." The paper describes how to program a computer with symbolic notation instead of the detailed machine language that had been used.

1952

1947

FORTRAN (FORmula TRANslation), an efficient, easy-to-use programming language, is introduced by John Backus.

1957

1951

1953

The IBM model 650 is one of the first widely used computer systems. Originally planning to produce only 50 machines, the system is so successful that eventually IBM manufactures more than 1,000. With the IBM 700 series of machines, the company will dominate the mainframe market for the next decade.

Core memory, developed in the early 1950s, provides much larger storage capacity than vacuum tube memory.

The first commercially available electronic digital computer, the UNIVAC I (UNIVersal Automatic Computer), is introduced by Remington Rand. Public awareness of computers increases when the UNIVAC I, after analyzing only five percent of the popular vote, correctly predicts that Dwight D. Eisenhower will win the presidential election.

The IBM 305 RAMAC system is the first to use magnetic disk for external storage. The system provides storage capacity similar to magnetic tape that previously was used, but offers the advantage of semi-random access capability.

Jack Kilby of Texas Instruments invents the integrated circuit, which lays the foundation for high-speed computers and large-capacity memories. Computers built with transistors mark the beginning of the second generation of computer hardware.

1958

Computer Science Corporation becomes the first software company listed on the New York Stock Exchange.

1960

COBOL, a high-level business application language, is developed by a committee headed by Dr. Grace Hopper. COBOL uses English-like phrases and runs on most business computers, making it one of the more widely used programming languages.

Alan Shugart at IBM demonstrates the first regular use of an 8-inch floppy (magnetic storage) disk.

In a letter to the editor titled, "GO TO Statements Considered Harmful," Dr. Edsger Dijsktra introduces the concept of structured programming, developing standards for constructing computer programs.

1968

1959

More than 200 programming languages have been created.

IBM introduces two smaller, desk-sized computers: the IBM 1401 for business and the IBM 1620 for scientists. The IBM 1620 initially is called the CADET, but IBM drops the name when campus wags claim it is an acronym for, Can't Add, Doesn't Even Try.

The number of computers has grown to 18,000.

Third-generation computers, with their controlling circuitry stored on chips, are introduced. The IBM System/360 computer is the first family of compatible machines, merging science and business lines.

1964

1965

Dr. John Kemeny of Dartmouth leads the development of the BASIC programming language. BASIC will be widely used on personal computers.

BASIC

Digital Equipment Corporation (DEC) introduces the first mini-computer, the PDP-8. The machine is used extensively as an interface for time-sharing systems.

IBM

Under pressure from the industry, IBM announces that some of its software will be priced separately from the computer hardware. This unbundling allows software firms to emerge in the industry.

MITS, Inc. advertises one of the first microcomputers, the Altair. Named for the destination in an episode of Star Trek, the Altair is sold in kits for less than $400. Although initially it has no keyboard, no monitor, no permanent memory, and no software, 4,000 orders are taken within the first three months.

ARPANET

The ARPANET network, a predecessor of the Internet, is established.

Ethernet, the first local area network (LAN), is developed at Xerox PARC (Palo Alto Research Center) by Robert Metcalf. The LAN allows computers to communicate and share software, data, and peripherals. Initially designed to link minicomputers, Ethernet will be extended to personal computers.

1969

1975

1970

1971

1976

Fourth-generation computers, built with chips that use LSI (large-scale integration) arrive. While the chips used in 1965 contained as many as 1,000 circuits, the LSI chip contains as many as 15,000.

Dr. Ted Hoff of Intel Corporation develops a microprocessor, or micro-programmable computer chip, the Intel 4004.

Steve Jobs and Steve Wozniak build the first Apple computer. A subsequent version, the Apple II, is an immediate success. Adopted by elementary schools, high schools, and colleges, for many students the Apple II is their first contact with the world of computers.

VisiCalc, a spreadsheet program written by Bob Frankston and Dan Bricklin, is introduced. Originally written to run on Apple II computers, VisiCalc will be seen as the most important reason for the acceptance of personal computers in the business world.

3,275,000 personal computers are sold, almost 3,000,000 more than in 1981.

Instead of choosing a person for its annual award, TIME magazine names the computer Machine of the Year for 1982, acknowledging the impact of computers on society.

Compaq, Inc. is founded to develop and market IBM-compatible PCs.

1979

The first public online information services, CompuServe and the Source, are founded.

Hayes introduces the 300 bps smart modem. The modem is an immediate success.

1982

1983

IBM offers Microsoft Corporation co-founder, Bill Gates, the opportunity to develop the operating system for the soon-to-be announced IBM personal computer. With the development of MS-DOS, Microsoft achieves tremendous growth and success.

1980

1981

Lotus Development Corporation is founded. Its spreadsheet software, Lotus 1-2-3, which combines spreadsheet, graphics, and database programs in one package, becomes the best-selling program for IBM personal computers.

Alan Shugart presents the Winchester hard drive, revolutionizing storage for personal computers.

The IBM PC is introduced, signaling IBM's entrance into the personal computer marketplace. The IBM PC quickly garners the largest share of the personal computer market and becomes the personal computer of choice in business.

Apple introduces the Macintosh computer, which incorporates a unique, easy-to-learn, graphical user interface.

Hewlett-Packard announces the first LaserJet printer for personal computers.

Several personal computers utilizing the powerful Intel 80386 microprocessor are introduced. These machines perform processing that once only large systems could handle.

Microsoft surpasses Lotus Development Corporation to become the world's top software vendor.

1987

1988

1984

1989

The Intel 486 becomes the world's first 1,000,000 transistor microprocessor. It crams 1.2 million transistors on a .4" x .6" sliver of silicon and executes 15,000,000 instructions per second — four times as fast as its predecessor, the 80386 chip.

IBM introduces a personal computer, called the PC AT, that uses the Intel 80286 microprocessor.

While working at CERN, Switzerland, Tim Berners-Lee invents an Internet-based hypermedia enterprise for information sharing. Berners-Lee will call this innovation the World Wide Web.

Several companies introduce computer systems using the Pentium® processor from Intel. The Pentium® chip is the successor to the Intel 486 processor. It contains 3.1 million transistors and is capable of performing 112,000,000 instructions per second.

World Wide Web Consortium releases standards that describe a framework for linking documents on different computers.

Jim Clark and Marc Andreessen found Netscape and launch Netscape Navigator 1.0, a browser for the World Wide Web.

1991

1993

1994

1992

Microsoft releases Windows 3.1, the latest version of its Windows operating system. Windows 3.1 offers improvements such as TrueType fonts, multimedia capability, and object linking and embedding (OLE). In two months, 3,000,000 copies of Windows 3.1 are sold.

Marc Andreessen creates a graphical Web browser called Mosaic. This success leads to the organization of Netscape Communications Corporation.

The White House launches its Web site, which includes an interactive citizens' handbook and White House history and tours.

Linus Torvalds creates the Linux kernel, a UNIX-like operating system that he releases free across the Internet for further enhancement by other programmers.

U.S. Robotics introduces PalmPilot, a handheld personal organizer. The PalmPilot's user friendliness and low price make it a standout next to more expensive personal digital assistants (PDAs).

JAVA™

Sun Microsystems launches Java, an object-oriented programming language that allows users to write one application for a variety of computer platforms. Java becomes one of the hotter Internet technologies.

The Summer Olympics in Atlanta makes extensive use of computer technology, using an IBM network of 7,000 personal computers, 2,000 pagers and wireless devices, and 90 industrial-strength computers to share information with more than 150,000 athletes, coaches, journalists, and Olympics staff members, and millions of Web users.

Microsoft Windows NT Server

Microsoft releases Windows NT 4.0, an operating system for client-server networks. Windows NT's management tools and wizards make it easier for developers to build and deploy business applications.

1995

1996

An innovative technology called webtv combines television and the Internet by providing viewers with tools to navigate the Web.

Microsoft releases Windows 95, a major upgrade to its Windows operating system. Windows 95 consists of more than 10,000,000 lines of computer instructions developed by 300 person-years of effort. More than 50,000 individuals and companies test the software before it is released.

Two out of three employees in the United States have access to a personal computer, and one out of every three homes has a personal computer. Fifty million personal computers are sold worldwide and more than 250,000,000 are in use.

Intel introduces the Pentium® II processor with 7.5 million transistors. The new processor, which incorporates MMX™ technology, processes video, audio, and graphics data more efficiently and supports applications such as movie-editing, gaming, and more.

More than 10,000,000 people take up telecommuting, which is the capability of working at home and communicating with an office via computer. Increasingly more firms embrace telecommuting to help increase productivity, reduce absenteeism, and provide greater job satisfaction.

Deep Blue, an IBM supercomputer, defeats world chess champion Gary Kasparov in a six-game chess competition. Millions of people follow the nine-day long rematch on IBM's Web site.

Fifty million users are connected to the Internet and World Wide Web.

1997   1998

Microsoft releases Internet Explorer 4.0 and seizes a key place in the Internet arena. This new Web browser is greeted with tremendous customer demand.

Apple and Microsoft sign a joint technology development agreement. Microsoft buys $150,000,000 of Apple stock.

E-commerce, or electronic commerce — the marketing of goods and services over the Internet — booms. Companies such as Dell, E*TRADE, and Amazon.com spur online shopping, allowing buyers to obtain everything from hardware and software to financial and travel services, insurance, automobiles, books, and more.

DVD, the next generation of optical disc storage technology, is introduced. DVD can store computer, audio, and video data in a single format, with the capability of producing near-studio quality. By year's end, 500,000 DVD players are shipped worldwide.

Microsoft ships Windows 98, an upgrade to Windows 95. Windows 98 offers improved Internet access, better system performance, and support for a new generation of hardware and software. In six months, more than 10,000,000 copies of Windows 98 are sold worldwide.

Intel releases its Pentium® III processor, which provides enhanced multimedia capabilities.

Governments and businesses frantically work to make their computer systems Y2K (Year 2000) compliant, spending more than $500 billion worldwide. Y2K non-compliant computers cannot distinguish whether 01/01/00 refers to 1900 or 2000, and thus may operate using a wrong date. This Y2K bug can affect any application that relies on computer chips, such as ATMs, airplanes, energy companies, and the telephone system.

The Department of Justice's broad antitrust lawsuit asks that Microsoft offer Windows 98 without the Internet Explorer browser or that it bundle the competing Netscape Navigator browser with the operating system.

U.S. District Judge Thomas Penfield Jackson rules in the antitrust lawsuit brought by the Department of Justice and 19 states that Microsoft used its monopoly power to stifle competition.

Y2K COMPLIANT

1998   1999

Compaq Computer, the United States' leading personal computer manufacturer, buys Digital Equipment Corporation in the biggest take-over in the history of the computer industry. Compaq becomes the world's second largest computer firm, behind IBM.

Microsoft introduces Office 2000, its premier productivity suite, offering new tools for users to create content and save it directly to a Web site without any file conversion or special steps.

Apple Computer introduces the iMac, the next version of its popular Macintosh computer. The iMac abandons such conventional features as a floppy disk drive but wins customers with its futuristic design, see-through case, and easy setup. Consumer demand outstrips Apple's production capabilities, and some vendors are forced to begin waiting lists.

Open Source Code software, such as the Linux operating system and the Apache Web server created by unpaid volunteers, begin to gain wide acceptance among computer users.

Microsoft ships Windows 2000 and Windows Me. Windows 2000 offers improved behind-the-scene security and reliability. Windows Me is designed for home users and lets them edit home movies, share digital photos, index music, and create a home network.

Shawn Fanning, 19, and his company, Napster, turn the music industry upside down by developing software that allows computer users to swap music files with one another without going through a centralized file server. The Recording Industry of America, on behalf of five media companies, sues Napster for copyright infringement.

According to the U.S. Department of Commerce, Internet traffic is doubling every 100 days, resulting in an annual growth rate of more than 700 percent. It has taken radio and television 30 years and 15 years, respectively, to reach 60 million people. The Internet has achieved the same audience base in three years.

2000

Intel® unveils its Pentium® 4 chip with clock speeds starting at 1.4 GHz. The Pentium 4 includes 42 million transistors, nearly twice as many contained on its predecessor, the Pentium III.

Dot.com companies (Internet based) go out of business at a record pace — nearly one per day — as financial investors withhold funding due to the companies' unprofitability.

E-commerce achieves mainstream acceptance. Annual e-commerce sales exceed $100 billion, and Internet advertising expenditures reach more than $5 billion.

Microsoft introduces Office XP, the next version of the world's leading suite of productivity software. Features include speech and handwriting recognition, smart tags, and task panes.

Telemedicine uses satellite technology and videoconferencing to broadcast consultations and to perform distant surgeries. Robots are used for complex and precise tasks. Computer-aided surgery uses virtual reality to assist with training and planning procedures.

More than 25 million computer users subscribe to America Online and take advantage of its AOL Anywhere features, including Instant Messenger, e-mail, and customized news and information pages. AOL's merger with Time Warner combines the strengths of the Internet, entertainment, and communications industries.

TIME WARNER

2001

Application service providers offer a return to a centralized computing environment, in which large megaservers warehouse data, information, and software, so it is accessible using a variety of devices from any location.

Microsoft releases major operating system updates with Windows XP for the desktop and servers, and Pocket PC 2002 for handheld computers. Windows XP is significantly more reliable than previous versions, features a 32-bit computing architecture, and offers a new look and feel. Pocket PC 2002 offers the handheld computer user a familiar Windows interface and consistent functionality.

Avid readers enjoy e-books, which are digital texts read on compact computer screens. E-books can hold the equivalent of 10 traditional books containing text and graphics. Readers can search, highlight text, and add notes.

Microsoft launches its .NET strategy, which is a new environment for developing and running software applications featuring ease of development of Web-based services. Users of applications immediately see the benefit of .NET as instant access to data and services in the context of their current task.

U.S. District Judge Colleen Kollar-Kotelly rules against the nine states appealing the antitrust settlement reached between Microsoft and the Justice Department. The nine states were seeking tougher sanctions against the software giant for abusing its monopoly power. Two of the nine states, Massachusetts and West Virginia, plan to appeal the latest ruling to the U.S. District Court of Appeals.

Handspring begins shipping the Treo™ communicator, a handheld computer with cellular telephone, e-mail, text messaging, and wireless Web capabilities.

2002

Intel® ships its revamped Pentium® 4 chip with the 0.13 micron processor and Hyper-Threading (HT) Technology, operating at speeds of 3.06 GHz. This new development eventually will enable processors with a billion transistors to operate at 20 GHz.

DVD writers (DVD+RW) begin to replace CD writers (CD-RW). DVDs can store up to eight times as much data as CDs. Uses include storing home movies, music, photos, and backups. Digital cameras and video editors help the average user develop quality video to store on DVDs.

Digital video cameras, DVD writers, easy-to-use video editing software, and improvements in storage capabilities allow the average computer user to create Hollywood-like videos with introductions, conclusions, scenes rearranged, music, and voice-over.

After several years of negligible sales, the Tablet PC is reintroduced as the next-generation mobile PC. The lightweight device, the size of a three-ring notebook, is ideal for people on the go. It runs Windows XP Tablet PC Edition, has wireless capabilities, and features natural input capabilities including pen and speech technologies.

Computer manufacturers and software companies integrate high-end PCs and entertainment devices. The result is PCs with great entertainment functions that let you watch and record TV, burn CDs and DVDs, play games, and more.

Wireless computers and devices, such as keyboards, mouse devices, home networks, and public Internet access points become commonplace. Latest operating systems include support for both the Wi-Fi (wireless fidelity) and Bluetooth standards. Wireless capabilities are standard on many PDAs and Tablet PCs.

2003

Computer manufacturers begin shipping the smart display. Smart displays are lightweight touch screen monitors that let you use your PC wirelessly from anywhere in your home. Check your e-mail from the couch, surf the Web on the patio, or share digital pictures in the rec room.

IBM puts its weight behind On Demand computing. Its intention is to invest up to $10 billion in hardware and software, and then sell computing time and the use of applications to businesses in a manner similar to an electric utility company.

Microsoft ships the latest version of its flagship Office suite. New features include a consistent user interface, an overhauled Outlook, increased emphasis on task panes, improved collaboration, enhanced XML functionality, and a new application called OneNote for organizing your notes.

The Internet and World Wide Web

Picture Yourself Publishing on the Web

Anticipating the end of your sophomore year means a respite from all the hard work. After finals, you and a friend from school are driving to Wisconsin Lake for a relaxing weekend with no thought of homework or studying! Before the semester ends, though, you plan to line up a summer job that starts as soon as you return from the trip.

Today, you meet with an adviser in the Career Placement Office. The adviser informs you that the office maintains a Resume Forwarding system. She shows you how to enter your resume into the system, and then automatically, it sends yours and all current resumes on file to potential employers. In addition, the adviser tells you that most companies look for employees over the Internet, so to be successful in your job search, you need to create a personal Web page with a resume. She recommends that you attend the Online Job Search seminar the week before the semester ends. Topics include finding out about available internships, getting information about various organizations and positions, and how to publish a resume on the Web.

While Computer Information Systems is not your major, after attending the seminar, you feel confident that you will be able to do it and look forward to having summer employment plans lined up before your weekend getaway.

As you read Chapter 2, you will learn about Web publishing and discover other features of the Internet.

OBJECTIVES

After completing this chapter, you will be able to:

1. Discuss the history of the Internet

2. Explain how to access and connect to the Internet

3. Analyze an IP address

4. Identify the components of a Web address

5. Explain the purpose of a Web browser

6. Search for information on the Web

7. Describe the types of Web sites

8. Recognize how Web pages use graphics, animation, audio, video, virtual reality, and plug-ins

9. Describe the types of e-commerce

10. Explain how e-mail, FTP, newsgroups and message boards, mailing lists, chat rooms, and instant messaging work

11. Identify the rules of netiquette

12. Identify the steps and tools required for Web publishing

CONTENTS

THE INTERNET

One of the major reasons business, home, and other users purchase computers is for Internet access. Through the Internet, society has access to global information and instant communications. Further, access to the Internet can occur anytime from a computer anywhere: at home, at work, at school, in a restaurant, on an airplane, and even at the beach.

The **Internet**, also called the *Net*, is a worldwide collection of networks that links millions of businesses, government agencies, educational institutions, and individuals. Each of the networks on the Internet provides resources that add to the abundance of goods, services, and information accessible via the Internet.

Today, more than one-half billion users around the world connect to the Internet for a variety of reasons, some of which are shown in Figure 2-1. The World Wide Web and e-mail are two of the more widely accessed Internet services. Other services include file transfer, newsgroups and message boards, mailing lists, chat rooms, and instant messaging. This chapter explains each of these services. To enhance understanding of these services, the chapter begins by discussing the history of the Internet and how the Internet works.

HISTORY OF THE INTERNET

The Internet has its roots in a networking project started by the Pentagon's *Advanced Research Projects Agency* (*ARPA*), an agency of the U.S. Department of Defense. ARPA's goal

Figure 2-1b   (e-mail)

Figure 2-1c   (file transfer)

Figure 2-1a   (Web)

FIGURE 2-1   Users around the world connect to the Internet to access the Web, send e-mail messages, transfer documents and photographs, post messages, chat with a group, or have a private conversation with an online friend or family member.

was to build a network that (1) allowed scientists at different locations to share information and work together on military and scientific projects and (2) could function even if part of the network were disabled or destroyed by a disaster such as a nuclear attack. That network, called *ARPANET*, became functional in September 1969, linking scientific and academic researchers across the United States.

The original ARPANET consisted of four main computers, one each located at the University of California at Los Angeles, the University of California at Santa Barbara, the Stanford Research Institute, and the University of Utah. Each computer served as a host on the network. A *host* is any computer that directly connects to a network. Hosts typically use high-speed communications to transfer data and messages over a network. They also provide network connections for other computers.

As researchers and others realized the great benefit of using ARPANET's e-mail to share data and information, ARPANET underwent phenomenal growth. By 1984, ARPANET had more than 1,000 individual computers linked as hosts. (Today, more than 150 million hosts connect to the Internet.)

Some organizations connected entire networks to ARPANET to take advantage of the high-speed communications it offered. In 1986, the National Science Foundation (NSF) connected its huge network of five supercomputer centers, called *NSFnet*, to ARPANET. This configuration of complex networks and hosts became known as the Internet.

Until 1995, NSFnet handled the bulk of the communications activity, or *traffic*, on the Internet. In 1995, NSFnet terminated its network on the Internet and returned its status to a research network.

Figure 2-1d (message board)   **Figure 2-1e** (chat)

Figure 2-1f (instant messaging)

Today, the Internet consists of many local, regional, national, and international networks. Numerous corporations, commercial firms, and other companies provide networks to handle the Internet traffic. Both public and private organizations own networks on the Internet. These networks, along with telephone companies, cable and satellite companies, and the government, all contribute toward the internal structure of the Internet.

Even as the Internet grows, it remains a public, cooperative, and independent network. Each organization on the Internet is responsible only for maintaining its own network. No single person, company, institution, or government agency controls or owns the Internet (read Issue 2-1 for a related discussion). The *World Wide Web Consortium* (*W3C*), however, oversees research and sets standards and guidelines for many areas of the Internet. The mission of the W3C is to contribute to the growth of the Web. More than 500 organizations from around the world are members of the W3C. They advise, define standards, and address other issues.

ISSUE 2-1

Who Controls the Internet?

Who owns and controls the Internet? No one? Everyone? Ownership of the Internet is a complicated issue. In theory, everyone who uses the Internet owns it. Before 1995, the National Science Foundation primarily financed and controlled the Internet. Today, large corporations and political organizations wield the most influence over regulation of the Internet. Media conglomerates, for example, control most of the heavily accessed news and political Web sites. Because of its worldwide scope, many people maintain that the Internet simply is too massive for regulation. If the Internet is not restricted, however, it also may be a forum for covert and illegal activities. Modern terrorist organizations have established sophisticated communications by creating Web sites, using e-mail, and secretly coding pictures on Web pages. Should the Internet be regulated? If so, by whom or what entity? Does the public have the power to maintain control of the Internet? Why or why not?

For more information about Internet control and Internet access, visit the Discovering Computers 2004 Issues Web page (**scsite.com/dc2004/issues**). Click Issue #1 below Chapter 2.

Internet2

Internet2 is a not-for-profit Internet-related research and development project. The focus is to improve on the inefficiencies of the Internet, such as relieving bottlenecks in the current architecture. Thus, the intent of Internet2 is not to replace the current Internet but to enhance tomorrow's Internet with advanced technologies and capabilities. Members of Internet2 include more than 190 universities in the United States, along with more than 60 companies and the U.S. government. Various companies have invested more than $200 million in Internet2 technology.

Internet2 develops and tests advanced Internet technologies for research, teaching, and learning. These applications require an extremely high speed network that exceeds the capabilities of today's Internet. A current Internet2 project that will benefit a large number of Internet users in the future involves digital video applications, such as video conferencing and remote control of microscopes and other instruments.

Once this Internet2 technology reaches the mainstream Internet, many applications will reap its benefits. In the operating room, surgeons will consult other surgeons thousands of miles away over the Internet – during an operation. A professional musician, while on a concert tour, will check a student's finger position during an online lesson. Those working with Internet2 expect this type of high-quality video conferencing to be available on the current Internet within the next few years.

HOW THE INTERNET WORKS

Data sent over the Internet travels via networks and communications media owned and operated by many companies. The following sections present various ways to connect to these networks on the Internet.

Connecting to the Internet

Employees and students often connect to the Internet through a business or school network. In this case, the computers usually are part of a network that connects to an access provider through a high-speed connection line leased from the local telephone company.

Many homes and some small businesses use dial-up access to connect to the Internet. **Dial-up access** takes place when the modem in your computer uses a standard telephone line to connect to the Internet. This type of access is an easy and inexpensive way for users to connect to the Internet. A dial-up connection, however, is slow-speed technology.

As an alternative, some home and small business users are opting for higher-speed connections such as DSL, ISDN, or cable television Internet services. **DSL** (*digital subscriber line*) and **ISDN** (*Integrated Services Digital Network*) are technologies that provide higher-speed Internet connections using regular copper telephone lines. Some experts predict DSL eventually will replace ISDN because it is much easier to install and can provide faster data transfer speeds than ISDN. A **cable modem** provides high-speed Internet connections through the cable television network. These services cost about twice as much as dial-up access. Read Apply It 2-1 for more information.

In most cases, higher-speed Internet access, such as through DSL, ISDN, and cable television, is always on. That is, it is connected to the Internet the entire time the computer is running. With a dial-up access, by contrast, you must establish the connection to the Internet. Usually a modem dials the telephone number to the access provider.

Many hotels and airports provide dial-up or broadband Internet connections for mobile users, which allows them to connect to the Internet while on the road. Some mobile users, however, access the Internet without wires. Wireless Internet access technologies enable mobile users to connect easily to the Internet with notebook computers, PDAs, and smart phones while away from a telephone, cable, or other wired connection. A variety of wireless Internet technologies exists, including satellite connections and cellular radio network connections. Most wireless Internet connections transfer data at speeds comparable to dial-up access, but some are much faster.

FAQ 2-1

What does bandwidth have to do with Internet access?

Bandwidth is a measure of how fast data and information travel over transmission media. Thus, higher-speed broadband Internet connections have a higher bandwidth than dial-up connections.

For more information about bandwidth, visit the Discovering Computers 2004 FAQ Web page (**scsite.com/dc2004/faq**). Click Bandwidth below Chapter 2.

APPLY IT 2-1

Connect to the Internet at High Speeds

If you want a high-speed Internet connection, then DSL and cable television (CATV) Internet services are two feasible options. Referred to as *broadband* Internet connections, both DSL and CATV Internet services offer constant connections, so you can be online 24 hours a day.

Which should you choose: DSL or CATV Internet service? The answer may depend on which service is available in your area. For a CATV Internet connection, your local CATV company must service your area. Likewise, DSL service is available only in certain regions.

If both are available, consider these factors. CATV Internet connections are shared with other users in the neighborhood, whereas DSL is a dedicated line that is not shared. DSL transfers data at slightly faster speeds, but CATV Internet connections are a little less costly.

For more information about DSL versus CATV Internet service, visit the Discovering Computers 2004 Apply It Web page (**scsite.com/dc2004/ apply**). Click Apply It #1 below Chapter 2.

Access Providers

An **access provider** is a business that provides individuals and companies access to the Internet free or for a fee. The most common fee arrangement for an individual account is a fixed amount, usually about $10 to $25 per month for dial-up access and $40 to $55 for higher-speed access. For this fee, many providers offer unlimited Internet access. Others specify a set number of access hours per month. With the latter arrangement, the provider charges extra for each hour of connection time that exceeds an allotted number of access hours. To attract more customers, some access providers also offer Web publishing services. Web publishing is discussed later in this chapter.

With dial-up Internet access, the telephone number you dial connects you to an access point on the Internet, called a *point of presence* (*POP*). When selecting an access provider, ensure it provides at least one local POP telephone number. Otherwise, long-distance telephone charges will apply for the time you connect to the Internet.

Users access the Internet through regional or national ISPs, online service providers, and wireless service providers (Figure 2-2). An **ISP** (**Internet service provider**) is a regional or national access provider. A *regional ISP* usually provides Internet access to a specific geographic area. A *national ISP* is a larger business that provides Internet access in several major cities and towns nationwide. For dial-up access, some national ISPs provide both local and toll-free telephone numbers. Due to their larger size, national ISPs usually offer more services and have a larger technical support staff than regional ISPs. Examples of national ISPs are AT&T WorldNet and EarthLink™.

In addition to providing Internet access, an **online service provider (OSP)** also has many members-only features. These features include special content and services such as news, weather, legal information, financial data, hardware and software guides, games, travel guides, e-mail, photo communities, online calendars, and instant messaging. Some even have their own built-in Web browser. The fees for using an OSP sometimes are slightly higher than fees for an ISP. The two more popular OSPs are AOL (America Online) and MSN (The Microsoft Network). AOL differs from many OSPs in that it provides gateway functionality to the Internet, meaning it regulates the Internet services to which members have access.

A **wireless service provider** (*WSP*) is a company that provides wireless Internet access to users with wireless modems or Web-enabled mobile devices. Notebook computers, for example, can use wireless modems. Web-enabled mobile devices include PDAs, smart phones, and hands-free (voice activated) Internet devices in

FIGURE 2-2 Common ways to access the Internet are through a regional or national Internet service provider, an online service provider, or a wireless service provider.

automobiles. An antenna on the wireless modem or Web-enabled device typically sends signals through the airwaves to communicate with a wireless service provider. Examples of wireless service providers include AT&T Wireless, GoAmerica, and Verizon Wireless.

How Data Travels the Internet

Computers connected to the Internet work together to transfer data and information around the world using servers and clients. On the Internet, your computer is a client that can access data, information, and services on a variety of servers.

The inner structure of the Internet works much like a transportation system. Just as interstate highways connect major cities and carry the bulk of the automotive traffic across

the country, several main transmission media carry the heaviest amount of traffic on the Internet. These major carriers of network traffic are known collectively as the *Internet backbone*.

In the United States, the transmission media that make up the Internet backbone exchange data at several different major cities across the country. The high-speed equipment in these major cities functions similarly to a highway interchange. That is, they transfer data from one network to another until it reaches its final destination (Figure 2-3).

? FAQ 2-2

How do I find the right access provider?

The Web has many comprehensive lists of access providers. These lists often use the terms ISP and OSP interchangeably. One of the more popular lists on the Web is called The List™.

For more information about access providers, visit the Discovering Computers 2004 FAQ Web page (**scsite.com/dc2004/faq**). Click Access Providers below Chapter 2.

WEB LINK 2-1

Internet Backbone
Visit the Discovering Computers 2004 WEB LINK page (**scsite.com/dc2004/weblink**). Click Internet Backbone below Chapter 2.

FIGURE 2-3   HOW DATA MIGHT TRAVEL THE INTERNET USING A DIAL-UP CONNECTION

Step 1:
You initiate an action to request data from the Internet. For example, you request to display a Web page on your computer screen.

Step 2:
A modem converts the digital signals from the computer into analog signals, which are carried by telephone lines.

Step 3:
Data (request) travels through telephone lines to a regional ISP.

ROUTER

Step 4:
Data may pass through one or more routers before reaching its final destination.

Step 5:
The regional ISP uses lines, leased from a telephone company, to send data to a national ISP.

REGIONAL ISP

NATIONAL ISP

Step 6:
A national ISP routes data through the Internet backbone to another national ISP.

INTERNET BACKBONE

REGIONAL ISP

Step 7:
Data moves from a national ISP to a regional ISP and then to a destination server (in this example, the server that contains the requested Web site).

NATIONAL ISP

Step 8:
The server retrieves the requested data (a Web page), and sends it back through the Internet backbone to your computer.

Internet Addresses

The Internet relies on an addressing system much like the postal service to send data to a computer at a specific destination. An **IP address**, short for *Internet Protocol address*, is a number that uniquely identifies each computer or device connected to the Internet. The IP address usually consists of four groups of numbers, each separated by a period. The number in each group is between 0 and 255. For example, the numbers 198.80.146.30 are an IP address. In general, the first portion of each IP address identifies the network and the last portion identifies the specific computer.

These all-numeric IP addresses are difficult to remember and use. Thus, the Internet supports the use of a text name that represents one or more IP addresses. A **domain name** is the text version of an IP address. Figure 2-4 shows an IP address and its associated domain name. As with an IP address, the components of a domain name are separated by periods.

In Figure 2-4, the com portion of the domain name is called the top-level domain. Every domain name contains a *top-level domain*, which identifies the type of organization associated with the domain. *Dot-com* is the term sometimes used to describe organizations with a top-level domain of com.

The group that assigns and controls top-level domains is the *Internet Corporation for Assigned Names and Numbers (ICANN* pronounced EYE-can). Figure 2-5 lists current top-level domains. For international Web sites outside the United States, the domain name also includes a country code. In these cases, the domain name ends with the country code, such as au for Australia or fr for France.

The *domain name system (DNS)* is the method that the Internet uses to store domain names and their corresponding IP addresses. When you specify a domain name, a *DNS server* translates the domain name into its associated IP address so data can route to the correct computer. A DNS server is an Internet server that usually is associated with an Internet access provider.

For a more technical discussion about Internet addresses, read the High-Tech Talk article on page 2.37.

QUIZ YOURSELF 2-1

To check your knowledge of Internet history, accessing and connecting to the Internet, and Internet addresses, visit the Discovering Computers 2004 Quiz Yourself Web page (**scsite.com/dc2004/quiz**). Click Objectives 1 – 3 below Chapter 2.

FAQ 2-3

How does a person or company get a domain name?

You register for a domain name from a *registrar*, which is an organization that maintains a master list of names for a particular top-level domain. In addition to determining prices and policies for a domain name registration, a registrar may offer additional services such as Web site hosting.

For more information about registering domain names, visit the Discovering Computers 2004 FAQ Web page (**scsite.com/dc2004/faq**). Click Registering Domain Names below Chapter 2.

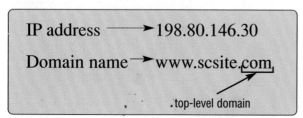

IP address ⟶ 198.80.146.30

Domain name ⟶ www.scsite.com

.top-level domain

FIGURE 2-4 The IP address and domain name for the Shelly Cashman Series® Instructional Web site.

TOP-LEVEL DOMAINS

Original Top-Level Domains	Type of Domain
com	Commercial organizations, businesses, and companies
edu	Educational institutions
gov	Government agencies
mil	Military organizations
net	Network providers
org	Nonprofit organizations

Newer Top-Level Domains	Type of Domain
museum	Accredited museums
biz	Businesses of all sizes
info	Businesses, organizations, or individuals providing general information
name	Individuals or families
pro	Certified professionals such as doctors, lawyers, and accountants
aero	Aviation community members
coop	Business cooperatives such as credit unions and rural electric coops

FIGURE 2-5 With the dramatic growth of the Internet during the last few years, the Internet Corporation for Assigned Names and Numbers (ICANN) recently adopted seven new top-level domains.

THE WORLD WIDE WEB

Although many people use the terms World Wide Web and Internet interchangeably, the World Wide Web actually is a newer service of the Internet. While the Internet was developed in the late 1960s, the World Wide Web emerged three decades later — in the early 1990s. Since then, however, it has grown phenomenally to become one of the more widely used services on the Internet.

The **World Wide Web** (*WWW*), or **Web**, consists of a worldwide collection of electronic documents. Each electronic document on the Web is called a **Web page**, which can contain text, graphics, audio (sound), and video. Additionally, Web pages usually have built-in connections to other documents. A **Web site** is a collection of related Web pages and associated items, such as documents and pictures, stored on a Web server.

The following pages discuss how to browse the Web, use a Web address, search for information on the Web, and recognize types of Web sites. Also discussed are multimedia on the Web and e-commerce (business on the Web).

Browsing the Web

A **Web browser**, or **browser**, is application software that allows users to access and view Web pages. To browse the Web, you need a computer that is connected to the Internet and that has a Web browser.

With the Internet connection established, you can use the mouse to start a Web browser. The browser retrieves and displays a starting Web page, sometimes called the browser's home page. The initial home page that is displayed is one selected by your Web browser. You can change your browser's home page at anytime.

The more widely used Web browsers for personal computers are Microsoft Internet Explorer, Netscape, and Mozilla. Figure 2-6 shows the steps a user may follow to start the Internet Explorer Web browser.

FIGURE 2-6 ONE METHOD OF STARTING A WEB BROWSER

Step 1:
Click the Web browser program name.

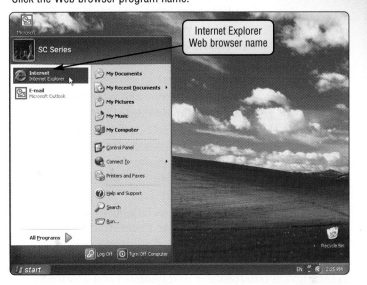

Internet Explorer Web browser name

Step 2:
If you use dial-up Internet access and are not connected to the Internet already, your computer attempts to establish a connection with your access provider. In this case, click the Dial button.

Dial button

Step 3:
The Internet Explorer Web browser starts and displays its home page. Shown here is The Microsoft Network (MSN) home page. In your browser, you can customize (change) the home page that displays.

The more common usage of the term, **home page**, refers to the first page that a Web site displays (see Figure 2-1a on page 2.02 for an example). Similar to a book cover or a table of contents for a Web site, the home page provides information about the Web site's purpose and content. Often it provides connections to other documents, Web pages, or Web sites. Many Web sites allow you to personalize the home page so it contains areas of interest to you.

Web-enabled mobile devices such as PDAs and cellular telephones use a special type of browser, called a *microbrowser*, which is designed for their small screens and limited computing power (Figure 2-7). Many Web sites design Web pages specifically for display on a microbrowser.

Downloading is the process of a computer receiving information, such as a Web page, from a server on the Internet. While a browser downloads a Web page, it typically displays an animated logo or icon in the top-right corner of the browser window. The animation stops when the download is complete.

Depending on the speed of your Internet connection and the amount of graphics involved, a Web page download can take from a few seconds to several minutes. To speed up the display of Web pages, most Web browsers allow users to turn off the graphics and display only text.

? FAQ 2-4

How do I change my Web browser's home page and graphics settings?

To change the home page in Internet Explorer, click Tools on the menu bar, click Internet Options, click the General tab, type the desired Web address, and then click the OK button. To turn off pictures from displaying, click the Advanced tab and remove the check mark from the Show pictures check box.

For more information about Internet Explorer, visit the Discovering Computers 2004 FAQ Web page (**scsite.com/dc2004/faq**). Click Internet Explorer below Chapter 2.

Web Addresses

A Web page has a unique address, called a **URL** (*Uniform Resource Locator*) or **Web address**. For example, the home page for the Johnson & Johnson Web site has a Web address of http://www.jnj.com. A Web browser retrieves a Web page, such as Johnson & Johnson's home page, using its Web address.

Many companies and organizations use the Web as an alternate or supplemental means of advertising or publicizing information. They assume the public is familiar with Web addresses. Television, radio broadcasts, printed newspapers, and magazines, for example, often refer viewers or readers to Web addresses for additional information.

Figure 2-7a
(microbrowser for a Web-enabled PDA)

Figure 2-7b
(microbrowser for a smart phone)

FIGURE 2-7   Sample microbrowser screens.

If you know the Web address of a Web page, you can type it into the Address text box at the top of the browser window. If you type the Web address http://www.jnj.com/careers/index.html in the Address text box and then press the ENTER key, the browser downloads and displays a Web page about careers at Johnson & Johnson (Figure 2-8).

As shown in Figure 2-8, a Web address consists of a protocol, domain name, and sometimes the path to a specific Web page or location on a Web page. Many Web page Web addresses begin with http://. The *http*, which stands for *Hypertext Transfer Protocol*, is a set of rules that defines how pages transfer on the Web.

If you do not enter a Web address correctly, your browser will not locate the Web site or Web page you want to visit (view). To help minimize errors, most current browsers and Web sites do not require the http://and www portions of the Web address. For example, typing jnj.com/careers/index.html instead of the entire address http://www.jnj.com/careers/index.html still accesses the Web site. If you enter an incorrect Web address, a list of similar addresses from which you can select may display in the browser window. Many Web sites also allow users to eliminate the .htm or .html from the Web page name.

A **Web server** is a computer that delivers requested Web pages to your computer. For example, when you enter the Web address, jnj.com/careers/index.html in the Web browser, it sends a request to the server that stores the www.jnj.com Web site. The server then retrieves the Web page named index.html in the careers path and sends it to your browser.

The same Web server can store multiple Web sites. For example, many Internet service providers grant their subscribers free storage space on a Web server for personal or company Web sites.

When you enter a Web address, you request, or *pull*, information from a Web server. Some Web servers also can *push* content to your computer at regular intervals or whenever updates are made to the site. For example, some Web servers provide the capability of displaying current sporting event scores or weather reports on your computer screen.

For a list of widely used Web sites and their associated Web addresses, read the Searching Techniques and Guide to Web Sites feature that follows this chapter and Making Use of the Web in Appendix A at the back of the book.

Navigating Web Pages

Most Web pages contain links. A **link**, short for *hyperlink*, is a built-in connection to another related Web page or part of a Web page. Links allow you to obtain information in a nonlinear way. That is, instead of accessing topics in a specified order, you move directly to a topic of interest. Reading a book from cover to cover is a linear way of learning. Branching off and researching related topics as you encounter them can be a different and very effective nonlinear way of learning.

WEB LINK 2-2

Web Addresses
Visit the Discovering Computers 2004 WEB LINK page (**scsite.com/dc2004/weblink**). Click Web Addresses below Chapter 2.

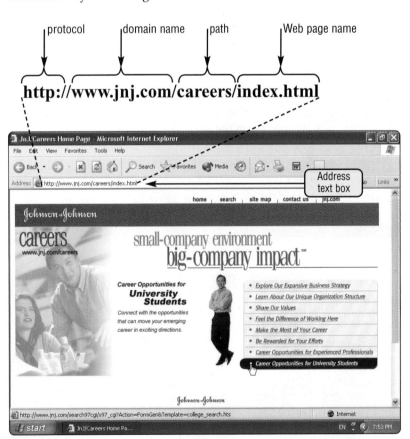

FIGURE 2-8 After entering the Web address www.jnj.com/careers/index.html in the Address text box, this Johnson & Johnson careers Web page displays.

While reading an article on the Web about nutrition, you might want to learn more about counting calories. Having linked to and read information about counting calories, you might want to find low-fat, low-calorie recipes. Reading these might inspire you to learn about a chef who specializes in healthy but tasty food preparation. Branching from one related topic to another in a nonlinear fashion is what makes links so powerful. Some people use the phrase, **surfing the Web**, to refer to the activity of using links to explore the Web.

On the Web, a link can be text or an image. You often identify text links by looking at the Web page. Text links usually are underlined and are in a color different from other text on the Web page. Pointing to, or positioning the pointer on, a link on the screen, typically changes the shape of the pointer to a small hand with a pointing index finger. The Web page shown in Figure 2-9 contains a variety of link types, with the pointer on one of the links.

Each link on a Web page corresponds to another Web address. To activate a link, you *click* it, that is, point to the link and then press the left mouse button. Clicking a link causes the Web address associated with the link to display on the screen. The linked object might be on the same Web page, a different Web page

at the same Web site, or a separate Web page at a different Web site in another city or country. To remind you visually that you have clicked a link, a text link often changes color after you click it.

Searching for Information on the Web

No single organization controls additions, deletions, and changes to Web sites. This means no central menu or catalog of Web site content and addresses exists. Several companies, however, maintain organized directories of Web sites to help people find information on specific topics.

A **search engine** is a software program that finds Web sites and Web pages. Search engines are particularly helpful in locating Web pages about certain topics or in locating specific pages for which you do not know the exact Web address. Thousands of search engines exist. Some search on any topic and others are restricted to certain subjects, such as finding people, job hunting, or locating real estate. The table in Figure 2-10 lists the Web addresses of several popular general-purpose Internet search engines. For example, to use the Google search engine, you enter google.com in the Address text box in the browser window.

FIGURE 2-9 This Web page contains various types of links: text that is underlined, text in a different color, and images.

WIDELY USED SEARCH ENGINES

Search Engine	Web Address
AllTheWeb	alltheweb.com
AltaVista	altavista.com
Ask Jeeves®	askjeeves.com
Excite	excite.com
Google	google.com
HotBot	hotbot.com
LookSmart	looksmart.com
Lycos	lycos.com
Overture	overture.com
WebCrawler™	webcrawler.com
Yahoo!	yahoo.com

FIGURE 2-10 Many widely used search engines allow searching about any topic on the Web.

From a search engine, you easily can find Web pages. Simply enter a word or phrase, called **search text** or *keywords*, in the search engine's text box. For example, to display a list of retailers in Denver that sell Yamaha portable music keyboards, you could enter Yamaha portable music keyboards Denver retailer as your search text. The search engine displays a list of *hits*, or Web page names, that contain the search text (Figure 2-11). Each hit in the list has a link that, when clicked, displays the associated Web site or Web page.

FIGURE 2-11 HOW TO DISPLAY AND USE A SEARCH ENGINE

When you enter search text that contains multiple keywords, the search engine usually locates Web sites that contain all or most of the words. For example, a search with the search text, Yamaha retailer, displays more than 15,000 hits that contain the word Yamaha and the word retailer. To reduce the number of hits, be more specific in the search. The more specific search text, Yamaha portable music keyboards Denver retailer, reduces the number of hits to about 40.

Many search engines use a program, called a *spider*, to build and maintain lists of words found on Web sites. When you enter search text, the search engine scans this prebuilt list for hits. The more sophisticated the search engine combined with sophisticated search criteria, the more rapid the response and effective the search.

Most search engines also have subject directories of Web sites. On the Web, a **subject directory** classifies Web pages into an organized set of categories, such as sports or shopping, and related subcategories (Figure 2-12). If you want information about television programs, you could use a directory to click the subcategory television in the entertainment category.

Read Looking Ahead 2-1 for a look at the next generation of searching techniques. For more information about search engines, subject directories, and searching techniques, read the Searching Techniques and Guide to Web Sites feature that follows this chapter.

LOOKING AHEAD 2-1

Let the Bot Shop for You

Driving from store to store in search of the perfect gift in your price range can be a daunting task. This chore can be simplified, however, by using shopping bots, intelligent agents, and network agents. *Shopping bots* search many online stores for prices on thousands of items. *Network agents* are sophisticated intelligent agents that perform specific tasks on remote computers and send the results to users, such as notifying consumers when the price of a particular item has been reduced.

These intelligent software applications are becoming increasingly sophisticated. They are being programmed to adapt to the consumers' preferences for brands and prices and then evaluate products and services based on the perceived value to buyers. Some may even manage grocery lists, purchase goods, and then schedule deliveries without the shoppers' immediate approval. They will provide product reviews and possibly suggest alternative products.

For a look at the next generation of shopping bots and intelligent and network agents, visit the Discovering Computers 2004 Looking Ahead Web page (**scsite.com/dc2004/looking**). Click Looking Ahead #1 below Chapter 2.

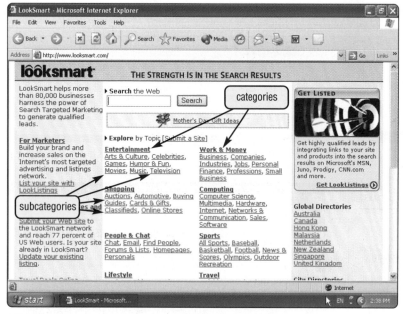

FIGURE 2-12 An example of a directory Web page.

Types of Web Sites

Eight types of Web sites are portal, news, informational, business/marketing, educational, entertainment, advocacy, and personal (Figure 2-13). Many Web sites fall into more than one of these categories. The following pages discuss each of these types of Web sites.

Figure 2-13a (portal)

Figure 2-13b (news)

Figure 2-13d (business/marketing)

Figure 2-13c (informational)

Figure 2-13e (educational)

Figure 2-13f (entertainment)

Figure 2-13h (personal)

Figure 2-13g (advocacy)

FIGURE 2-13 Types of Web sites.

PORTAL A **portal** is a Web site that offers a variety of Internet services from a single, convenient location (Figure 2-13a on the previous page). Most portals offer the following free services: search engine and/or subject directory; news; sports and weather; free Web publishing services; reference tools such as yellow pages, stock quotes, and maps; shopping malls and auctions; and e-mail and other forms of online communications. Some portals are for the general population, while others focus on a particular audience, such as gardeners or investors. Companies often create their own portals for use by employees, vendors, and customers.

Many portals have Web communities. A **Web community** is a Web site that joins a specific group of people with similar interests or relationships. These communities may offer online photo albums, chat rooms, and other services to facilitate communications among members.

When you connect to the Internet, the first Web page that is displayed often is a portal. Popular portals include AltaVista, America Online, Excite, GO.com, HotBot, LookSmart, Lycos, The Microsoft Network, Netscape, and Yahoo! You may notice that many of these portals are popular search engines or subject directories. Some also are Internet access providers.

A *wireless portal* is a portal specifically designed for Web-enabled mobile devices. Wireless portals attempt to provide all information a wireless user might require. These portals offer services geared to the mobile user such as search engines, news, stock quotes, weather, maps, e-mail, calendar, instant messaging, and shopping.

NEWS A news Web site contains newsworthy material including stories and articles relating to current events, life, money, sports, and the weather (Figure 2-13b). Many magazines and newspapers sponsor Web sites that provide summaries of printed articles, as well as articles not included in the printed versions. Newspapers and television and radio stations are some of the media that maintain news Web sites.

INFORMATIONAL An informational Web site contains factual information (Figure 2-13c). Many United States government agencies have informational Web sites providing information such as census data, tax codes, and the congressional budget. Other organizations provide information such as public transportation schedules and published research findings.

BUSINESS/MARKETING A business/marketing Web site contains content that promotes or sells products or services (Figure 2-13d). Nearly every business has a business/marketing Web site. Allstate Insurance Company, Dell Computer Corporation, General Motors Corporation, Kraft Foods Inc., and Walt Disney Company all have business/marketing Web sites. Many of these companies also allow you to purchase their products or services online.

EDUCATIONAL An educational Web site offers exciting, challenging avenues for formal and informal teaching and learning (Figure 2-13e). On the Web, you can learn how airplanes fly or how to cook a meal. For a more structured learning experience, companies provide online training to employees; colleges offer online classes and degrees (read Issue 2-2 for a related discussion). Instructors often use the Web to

ISSUE 2-2

Can You Learn It Online?

College can be a rewarding experience, both personally and professionally. Some people, however, do not have the opportunity, time, or money needed to attend a traditional college. Today, many schools address this obstacle with online learning. Online learning allows students to learn whenever and wherever they can access a course's Web page, often more economically than traditional tuitions. A student might be able to complete an entire degree program without ever physically attending a class. Many online classes present material using captivating simulations, real-life case studies, and interactive tools. Yet, even the best online classes lack some of the most important features of the campus experience, such as casual talks with professors, informal study groups in the dorm or library, or enthusiastic discussions in the campus coffee shop. What are the more important advantages and disadvantages of online classes? Why? What type of student is best, and least, suited for online classes? Why? Would you be interested in taking a class online? Why or why not? Should it be possible to obtain a four-year college degree without attending a single class on a college campus? Why?

For more information about online learning, visit the Discovering Computers 2004 Issues Web page (**scsite.com/dc2004/issues**). Click Issue #2 below Chapter 2.

enhance classroom teaching by publishing course materials, grades, and other pertinent class information.

ENTERTAINMENT   An entertainment Web site offers an interactive and engaging environment (Figure 2-13f). Popular entertainment Web sites offer music, videos, sports, games, ongoing Web episodes, sweepstakes, chats, and more. Sophisticated entertainment Web sites often partner with other technologies. For example, you can cast your vote about a topic on a television show.

ADVOCACY   An advocacy Web site contains content that describes a cause, opinion, or idea (Figure 2-13g). The purpose of an advocacy Web site is to convince the reader of the validity of the cause, opinion, or idea. These Web sites usually present views of a particular group or association. Sponsors of advocacy Web sites include the Democratic National Committee, the Republican National Committee, the Society for the Prevention of Cruelty to Animals, and the Society to Protect Human Rights.

PERSONAL   A private individual or family who normally is not associated with any organization may maintain a personal Web site or just a single Web page (Figure 2-13h). People publish personal Web pages for a variety of reasons. Some are job hunting. Others simply want to share life experiences with the world. Publishing Web pages is discussed in more depth at the end of this chapter.

EVALUATING A WEB SITE   Do not assume that information presented on the Web is correct or accurate. Any person, company, or organization can publish a Web page on the Internet. No one oversees the content of these Web pages. Figure 2-14 lists guidelines for assessing the value of a Web site or Web page before relying on its content.

Multimedia on the Web

Most Web pages include more than formatted text and links. In fact, some of the more exciting Web pages use multimedia. **Multimedia** refers to any application that combines text with graphics, animation, audio, video, and/or virtual reality. A Web page that uses multimedia has much more appeal than one with only text on a gray background. Multimedia brings a Web page to life, increases the types of information available on the Web, expands the Web's potential uses, and makes the Internet a more entertaining place to explore. Multimedia Web pages often require proper hardware and software and take more time to download because they contain large graphics files and video or audio clips.

? FAQ 2-5

What is a file?

A *file* is a unit of storage. When you want the computer to store items (e.g., data, information, programs, graphics, an audio clip, or a video clip), it places them into files on storage media such as a hard disk. File sizes vary depending on items being stored. For example, graphics files usually consume more storage space than data files.

For more information about files, visit the Discovering Computers 2004 FAQ Web page (**scsite.com/dc2004/faq**). Click Files below Chapter 2.

GUIDELINES FOR EVALUATING THE VALUE OF A WEB SITE

Evaluation Criteria	Reliable Web Sites
Affiliation	A reputable institution should support the Web site without bias in the information.
Audience	The Web site should be written at an appropriate level.
Authority	The Web site should list the author and the appropriate credentials.
Content	The Web site should be well organized and the links should work.
Currency	The information on the Web page should be current.
Design	The pages at the Web site should download quickly and be visually pleasing and easy to navigate.
Objectivity	The Web site should contain little advertising and be free of preconceptions.

FIGURE 2-14   Criteria for evaluating a Web site's content.

Read Looking Ahead 2-2 for a look at the next generation of sharing multimedia files. The sections that follow discuss how the Web uses graphics, animation, audio, video, and virtual reality.

GRAPHICS A **graphic**, or *graphical image*, is a digital representation of nontext information such as a drawing, chart, or photograph. Graphics were the first media used to enhance the text-based Internet. The introduction of graphical Web browsers allowed Web page developers to incorporate illustrations, logos, and other images into Web pages. Today, many Web pages use colorful graphical designs and images to convey messages (Figure 2-15).

The Web contains countless images on a variety of subjects. You can download many of these images at no cost and use them for noncommercial purposes. Recall that downloading is the process of transferring an object from the Web to your computer. For example, you can incorporate images into greeting cards, announcements, and other documents.

Of the graphics formats that exist on the Web (Figure 2-16), the two more common are JPEG and GIF formats. *JPEG* is a format that compresses graphics to reduce their file size, which means the file takes up less storage space. Smaller file sizes result in faster downloading of Web pages because small files transmit faster than large files. The more compressed the file, the smaller the image, but the lower the quality. The goal with JPEG graphics is to reach a balance between image quality and file size.

GRAPHICS FORMATS USED ON THE WEB

Acronym	Name
BMP	Bit Map
GIF (pronounced JIFF)	Graphics Interchange Format
JPEG (pronounced JAY-peg)	Joint Photographic Experts Group
PCX	PC Paintbrush
PNG (pronounced ping)	Portable Network Graphics
TIFF	Tagged Image File Format

FIGURE 2-16 The Web uses graphics file formats for images.

LOOKING AHEAD 2-2

Share Multimedia Files Easily

Your new Web site is nearly complete, but you want to add a song from your brother's band and video taken by a friend who lives 1,000 miles away. How can you obtain these multimedia files quickly and simply? File sharing software allows users to receive and distribute files across the Internet. Many college network administrators, however, have blocked access completely to these programs to avoid overloading computer resources and violating copyright laws.

As the entertainment industry cases lawsuits against colleges, more schools are expected to lift the limitations. Some schools may ease these restrictions by allowing students to download multimedia files at off-peak network traffic times. In time, they also will post Internet usage policies and emphasize that unauthorized sharing of music and movie files may violate federal copyright law. Network administrators will install monitoring software that identifies students who are not complying with these rules.

For a look at the next generation of sharing multimedia files, visit the Discovering Computers 2004 Looking Ahead Web page (**scsite.com/dc2004/looking**). Click Looking Ahead #2 below Chapter 2.

FIGURE 2-15 Many Web pages use colorful graphical designs and images to convey their messages.

GIF graphics also use compression techniques to reduce file sizes. The GIF format works best for images that have only a few distinct colors, such as line drawings, single-color borders, and simple cartoons. The newer *PNG format* improves upon the GIF format, and thus is expected eventually to replace the GIF format.

The BMP, PCX, and TIFF formats listed in Figure 2-16 have larger file sizes, may require special viewer software, and thus are not used on the Web as frequently as JPEG and GIF.

Some Web sites use thumbnails on their pages because graphics can be time-consuming to display. A **thumbnail** is a small version of a larger graphic. You usually click a thumbnail to display a larger image (Figure 2-17).

ANIMATION   Many Web pages use **animation**, which is the appearance of motion created by displaying a series of still images in sequence. Animation can make Web pages more visually interesting or draw attention to important information or links. For example, text that animates by scrolling across the screen can serve as a ticker to display stock updates, news, sports scores, weather, or other information. Web-based games often use animation. Some animations even contain links to a different Web page.

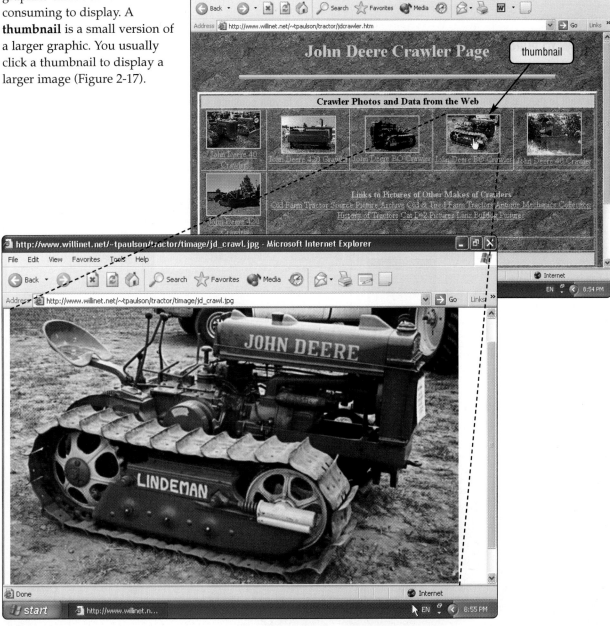

FIGURE 2-17   Clicking the thumbnail of a vintage John Deere crawler in the top screen displays a larger image in a separate window.

A popular type of animation, called an *animated GIF*, uses computer animation and graphics software to combine several images into a single GIF file. Web page developers often find animated GIFs easier to create than using a programming language to create animations.

AUDIO On the Web, you can listen to audio clips and live audio. **Audio** includes music, speech, or any other sound.

Simple audio applications on the Web consist of individual sound files available for downloading to a computer. Once downloaded, you can play (listen to) the contents of these files.

As with graphics files, audio files exist in a variety of formats. Some common Web audio file formats are MP3, WAV, WMA (Windows Media Audio), MPEG, RealAudio, and QuickTime. Audio files are compressed to reduce their file sizes. For example, the **MP3** format reduces an audio file to about one-tenth of its original size, while preserving much of the original quality of the sound.

Some music publishers have Web sites that allow users to download sample tracks free to persuade them to buy the entire CD. Other Web sites allow a user to purchase and download an entire CD of music tracks to the hard disk (Figure 2-18). Keep in mind that it is legal

FIGURE 2-18   HOW TO PURCHASE AND DOWNLOAD MUSIC

Step 1:
Display the music Web site on the screen. Search for, select, and pay for the music you want to purchase from the music Web site.

Step 2:
Download the music from the Web site's server to your computer's hard disk.

Step 3:
Listen to the music from your computer's hard disk.

to download copyrighted music only if the song's copyright holder has granted permission for users to download and play the song.

To listen to an audio file on your computer, you need special software called a **player**. Most current operating systems contain a player. Windows Media Player and RealOne Player are two popular players. If your player will not play a particular audio format, you can download the necessary player free from the Web.

Some applications on the Web use streaming audio. **Streaming** is the process of transferring data in a continuous and even flow. Streaming allows users to access and use a file while it is transmitting. For example, *streaming audio* enables you to listen to music as it downloads to your computer. Many radio and television stations use streaming audio to broadcast

music, interviews, talk shows, sporting events, music videos, news, live concerts, and other segments (Figure 2-19).

Accepted standards supported by most Web browsers for transmitting streaming audio data on the Internet are MP3, QuickTime, Windows Media Format, and RealAudio. RealAudio is a component of RealOne Player.

WEB LINK 2-3

Streaming Media
Visit the Discovering Computers 2004 WEB LINK page (**scsite.com/dc2004/ weblink**). Click Streaming Media below Chapter 2.

? FAQ 2-6

How long does it take to download a single song from a music Web site?

Depending on the speed of your Internet connection and the size of the file, a single song can take from one to eight minutes to download.

For more information about downloading audio files, visit the Discovering Computers 2004 FAQ Web page (**scsite.com/dc2004/faq**). Click Downloading Audio Files below Chapter 2.

FIGURE 2-19 Many radio and television stations use streaming audio. An NPR (National Public Radio) news report is broadcast in Windows Media Player in this illustration.

VIDEO **Video** consists of full-motion images that are played back at various speeds. Most video also has accompanying audio. As with audio, many Web sites include video to enhance your understanding or for entertainment purposes. Instead of turning on the television, you can watch live and pre-recorded coverage of your favorite programs (Figure 2-20) or enjoy a live performance of your favorite vocalist right on the computer.

Like audio, simple video applications on the Web consist of individual video files, such as movie or television clips, that you must download completely before you can play them on the computer. Video files often are compressed because they are quite large in size. These clips also are quite short in length, usually less than 10 minutes, because they can take a long time to download. The *Moving Pictures Experts Group (MPEG)* defines a popular video compression standard, the current one being called *MPEG-4*.

As with streaming audio, *streaming video* allows you to view longer or live video images as they download to your computer. Widely used standards supported by most Web browsers for transmitting streaming video data on the Internet are AVI (Audio Video Interleaved), QuickTime, Windows Media Format, and RealVideo. Like RealAudio, RealVideo is a component of RealOne Player.

VIRTUAL REALITY **Virtual reality (VR)** is the use of computers to simulate a real or imagined environment that appears as a three-dimensional (3-D) space. On the Web, VR involves the display of 3-D images that users explore and manipulate interactively.

Using special VR software, a Web developer creates an entire 3-D Web site that contains infinite space and depth, called a *VR world*. A VR world, for example, might show a room with furniture. Users walk through such a VR room by moving an input device forward, backward, or to the side.

Games often use VR. Many practical applications of VR also exist. Science educators create VR models of molecules, organisms, and other structures for students to examine (Figure 2-21). Companies use VR to showcase products or create advertisements. Architects create VR models of buildings and rooms so clients can see how a completed construction project will look before it is built.

FIGURE 2-20 A video broadcast from the Animal Planet television channel Web site.

FIGURE 2-21 This Web site uses VR to illustrate the functionality of the Hubble Space Telescope.

PLUG-INS Most Web browsers have the capability of displaying basic multimedia elements on a Web page. Sometimes, a browser might need an additional program, called a plug-in. A **plug-in** is a program that extends the capability of a browser. You can download many plug-ins at no cost from various Web sites (Figure 2-22). Some plug-ins run on all sizes of personal computers and mobile devices. Others have special versions for mobile devices.

> **WEB LINK 2-4**
>
> **Plug-Ins**
>
> Visit the Discovering Computers 2004 WEB LINK page (**scsite.com/dc2004/ weblink**). Click Plug-Ins below Chapter 2.

POPULAR PLUG-IN APPLICATIONS

	Plug-In Application	Description	Web Address
▶ Get Acrobat Reader free!	**Acrobat Reader**	View, navigate, and print Portable Document Format (PDF) files — documents formatted to look just as they look in print	www.adobe.com
INSTALL NOW	**Flash Player**	View dazzling graphics and animation, hear outstanding sound and music, display Web pages across an entire screen	macromedia.com
Liquid Player Six	**Liquid Player**	Listen to and purchase CD-quality music tracks and audio CDs over the Internet; burn CDs; access MP3 files	liquidaudio.com
	QuickTime	View animation, music, audio, video, and VR panoramas and objects directly in a Web page	apple.com
realONe PLAYER	**RealOne Player**	Listen to live and on-demand near-CD-quality audio and newscast-quality video; stream audio and video content for faster viewing; play MP3 files; create music CDs	real.com
INSTALL NOW	**Shockwave Player**	Experience dynamic interactive multimedia, 3-D graphics, and streaming audio	macromedia.com
Windows Media Player	**Windows Media Player**	Listen to live and on-demand audio; play or edit WMA and MP3 files; burn CDs; watch DVD movies	microsoft.com

FIGURE 2-22 Most plug-ins can be downloaded free from the Web.

E-Commerce

E-commerce, short for *electronic commerce*, is a business transaction that occurs over an electronic network such as the Internet. Anyone with access to a computer, an Internet connection, and a means to pay for purchased goods or services can participate in e-commerce (Figure 2-23).

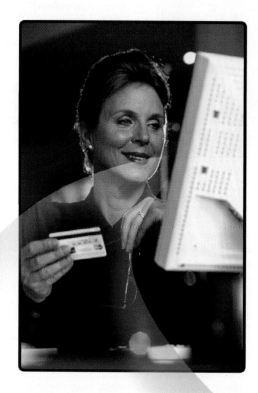

In the past, e-commerce transactions were conducted primarily using desktop computers. Today, many mobile computers and devices, such as PDAs and smart phones, also access the Web wirelessly. Some people use the term *m-commerce* (mobile commerce) to identify e-commerce that takes place using mobile devices.

E-commerce has changed the way people conduct business. It virtually eliminates the barriers of time and distance that slow traditional transactions. Now, with e-commerce, transactions occur instantaneously and globally. This saves time for participants on both ends.

Popular uses of e-commerce by consumers include shopping, investing, and banking. Users can purchase just about any product or service on the Web. Some examples include flowers, books, computers, prescription drugs, music, movies, cars, airline tickets, and concert tickets. Through online investing, individuals buy and sell stocks or bonds without using a broker.

Three types of e-commerce are business-to-consumer, consumer-to-consumer, and business-to-business. *Business-to-consumer (B2C) e-commerce* consists of the sale of goods and services to the general public. For example, Dell Computer Corporation has a B2C Web site. Instead of visiting a computer store to purchase a computer, customers can order one that meets their specifications directly from the Dell Web site.

A customer (consumer) visits an online business through an **electronic storefront**, which contains product descriptions, graphics, and a shopping cart. The **shopping cart** allows the customer to collect purchases. When ready to complete the sale, the customer enters personal data and the method of payment, preferably through a secure Internet connection (read Issue 2-3 for a related discussion).

FIGURE 2-23   E-commerce activities include shopping for goods at an online auction.

WEB LINK 2-5

E-Commerce
Visit the Discovering Computers 2004 WEB LINK page (**scsite.com/dc2004/ weblink**). Click E-Commerce below Chapter 2.

ISSUE 2-3

To Tax or Not to Tax Internet Purchases?

The Supreme Court has ruled that buyers must pay state and local sales taxes only when merchants have a physical presence, such as a store or office building, in the buyer's state. Many Internet purchases usually are sales-tax free because the Internet merchants do not have a physical presence in a buyer's state. Some believe this tax-free status has a negative impact on local businesses that must charge sales tax and lower-income families who are less likely to buy online. A new study predicts that by 2011, online sales will cost state and local governments more than $54 billion in sales tax revenues, forcing governments either to raise taxes or cut services. Yet, many feel any tax on e-commerce would be unmanageable (forcing vendors to adjust to varying sales tax rates) and unjustified. Should a sales tax be applied to Internet purchases? Why or why not? How can the problems of taxing, or not taxing, Internet purchases be addressed?

For more information about e-commerce and taxing issues, visit the Discovering Computers 2004 Issues Web page (**scsite.com/dc2004/issues**). Click Issue #3 below Chapter 2.

Often, merchants ship goods to a specified location such as your house. As an alternative, merchants potentially can deliver some items directly to your mobile computer or device. For example, you could purchase a movie ticket on the Web and store the ticket on your PDA. When you want to see the movie, a device at the movie theater wirelessly collects the ticket from your PDA.

Instead of purchasing from a business, consumers can purchase from each other. For example, with an **online auction**, users bid on an item being sold by someone else. The highest bidder at the end of the bidding period purchases the item. *Consumer-to-consumer (C2C) e-commerce* occurs when one consumer sells directly to another, such as in an online auction. eBay is one of the more popular Web sites that provide a means for C2C e-commerce through online auctions (Figure 2-23).

Most e-commerce, though, actually takes place between businesses, which is called *business-to-business (B2B) e-commerce*. Businesses often provide goods and services to other businesses, such as online advertising, recruiting, credit, sales, market research, technical support, and training. For example, some MasterCard

and Visa credit card companies provide corporations with Web-based purchasing, tracking, and transaction downloading capabilities.

QUIZ YOURSELF 2-2

To check your knowledge of Web addresses, Web browsers, searching, types of Web sites, elements of a Web page, and e-commerce, visit the Discovering Computers 2004 Quiz Yourself Web page (**scsite .com/dc2004/quiz**). Click Objectives 4 – 9 below Chapter 2.

OTHER INTERNET SERVICES

The World Wide Web is only one of the many services on the Internet. Other Internet services include e-mail, FTP, newsgroups and message boards, mailing lists, chat rooms, and instant messaging. The following pages discuss each of these services.

E-Mail

E-mail (short for *electronic mail*) is the transmission of messages and files via a computer network. E-mail was one of the original services on the Internet, enabling scientists and researchers working on government-sponsored projects to communicate with colleagues at other locations. Today, e-mail is a primary communications method for both personal and business use. Read Issue 2-4 for a related discussion.

ISSUE 2-4

How Expensive Is E-Mail and Internet Privacy?

With security a major concern in the aftermath of terrorist attacks, law enforcement agencies have sought greater leeway in monitoring a suspect's computer activities such as e-mail communications. Investigators would like to expand their use of a software program that can be set up on an Internet service provider or local area network. The surveillance software can track e-mail exchanges, reconstruct e-mail messages, or recreate downloaded files and Web pages visited from a suspect's computer. Law enforcement agencies insist that this program is a valuable weapon in the fight for national security. Yet, privacy advocates maintain that no evidence exists proving that surveillance software increases national security, and it may provide access to information outside the limit of legitimate surveillance. Should government be allowed to use surveillance software to monitor computer use? Why or why not? Some analysts maintain that, to combat terrorism justifiably, surveillance tools must be restricted to terrorism investigations and be established for a limited period. Are these legitimate restrictions? Why or why not?

For more information about government monitoring, visit the Discovering Computers 2004 Issues Web page (**scsite.com/dc2004/issues**). Click Issue #4 below Chapter 2.

You use an **e-mail program** to create, send, receive, forward, store, print, and delete e-mail messages. Microsoft Outlook and Outlook Express are two popular e-mail programs. The steps in Figure 2-24 illustrate how to send an e-mail message using Microsoft Outlook. The message can be simple text or can include an attachment such as a word processing document, a graphic, an audio clip, or a video clip.

FIGURE 2-24   HOW TO SEND AN E-MAIL MESSAGE

Step 1:
Start an e-mail program and point to the New Mail Message button.

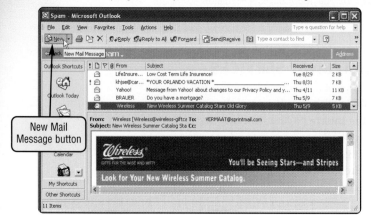

Step 2:
Click the New Mail Message button to display the Message window.

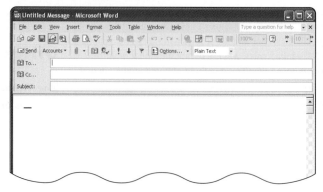

Step 3:
Enter the recipient's e-mail address, the subject, and the message in the Message window.

Step 4:
Click the Insert file button to attach a JPEG file containing a picture to the message. Click the Send button to send the message.

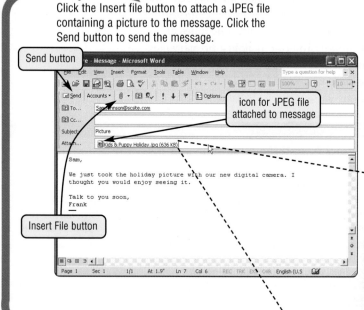

Step 5:
When Sam receives the e-mail message, he opens the JPEG file to view the picture.

Just as you address a letter when using the postal system, you must address an e-mail message with the e-mail address of your intended recipient. To receive messages, you need to have an e-mail address. Likewise, when someone sends you a message, they must have your e-mail address. An **e-mail address** is a combination of a user name and a domain name that identifies a user so he or she can receive Internet e-mail (Figure 2-25).

Internet access providers typically supply an e-mail program as a standard part of their Internet access services. Some Web sites, such as MSN Hotmail and Yahoo!, provide free e-mail services. To use these Web-based e-mail programs, you connect to the Web site and set up an e-mail account, which typically includes an e-mail address and a password.

A **user name** is a unique combination of characters, such as letters of the alphabet and/or numbers, that identifies a specific user. Your user name must be different from the other user names in the same domain. For example, a user named Sam Johnson whose server has a domain name of scsite.com might select SJohnson as his user name. If scsite.com already has an SJohnson (for Sheila Johnson), Sam will have to select a different user name, such as SamJohnson or Sam_Johnson.

Sometimes, companies decide user names for employees. In many cases, however, users select their own user names, often selecting a nickname or any other combination of characters for their user name. Many users select a combination of their first and last names so others can remember it easily.

In an Internet e-mail address, an @ (pronounced at) symbol separates the user name from the domain name. Your service provider supplies the domain name. Using the example in Figure 2-25, a possible e-mail address for Sam would be SamJohnson@scsite .com, which would be read as follows: Sam Johnson at s c site dot com. Most e-mail programs allow you to create an **address book**, which contains a list of names and e-mail addresses.

Although no complete listing of Internet e-mail addresses exists, several Web sites such as Yahoo! and Switchboard.com list addresses collected from public sources. Some of these Web sites allow you to list your e-mail address voluntarily so others can find it. The Web site also might ask for other information, such as your high school or college so others can determine if you are the person they want to reach.

When you send an e-mail message, an outgoing mail server that is operated by your Internet access provider determines how to route the message through the Internet and then sends the message. *SMTP (simple mail transfer protocol)* is a communications technology used by some outgoing mail servers.

As you receive e-mail messages, an incoming mail server — also operated by your Internet access provider — holds the messages in your mailbox. The incoming mail server holds the message until you use your e-mail software to retrieve it. *POP3* is the latest version of POP (*Post Office Protocol*), which is a communications technology used by some incoming mail servers. Most e-mail programs

FIGURE 2-25   An e-mail address is a combination of a user name and a domain name.

WEB LINK 2-6

E-Mail

Visit the Discovering
Computers 2004
WEB LINK page
(**scsite.com/dc2004/
weblink**). Click E-Mail
below Chapter 2.

have a mail notification alert
that informs you via a message
or sound when you receive new
mail, even if you are working in
another application. Figure
2-26 illustrates how an e-mail
message may travel from a
sender to a receiver.

FAQ 2-7

Can my computer get a virus through e-mail?

Yes. A *virus* is a potentially damaging computer program. Once in
your computer, a virus can damage files and the operating system.
One way that virus authors attempt to spread a virus is by sending
virus-infected e-mail attachments. If you receive an e-mail attachment,
you should use an antivirus program to verify that it is virus free.

For more information about viruses and antivirus programs, read
the High-Tech Talk page at the end of Chapter 3, the section on
viruses and antivirus programs in Chapter 8, and visit the Discovering
Computers 2004 FAQ Web page (**scsite.com/dc2004/faq**). Click
Viruses below Chapter 2.

FIGURE 2-26   HOW AN E-MAIL MESSAGE MAY TRAVEL FROM A SENDER TO A RECEIVER

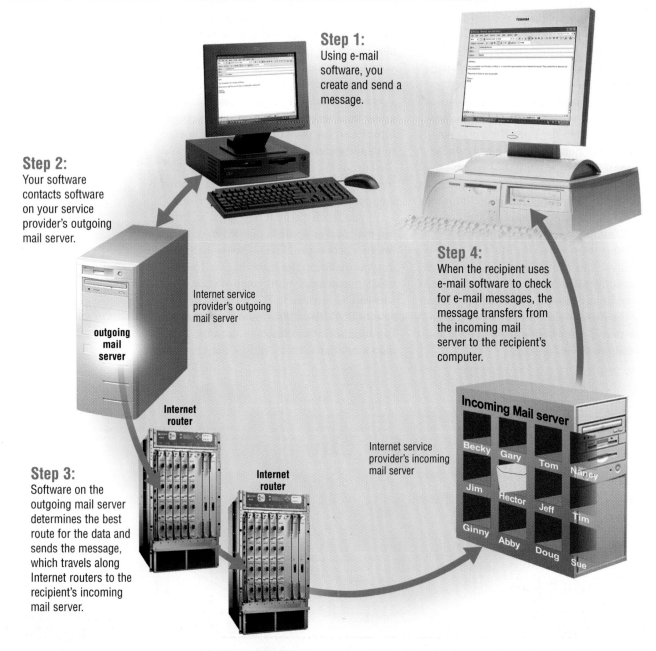

Step 1:
Using e-mail
software, you
create and send a
message.

Step 2:
Your software
contacts software
on your service
provider's outgoing
mail server.

Internet service
provider's outgoing
mail server

outgoing
mail
server

Internet
router

Step 3:
Software on the
outgoing mail server
determines the best
route for the data and
sends the message,
which travels along
Internet routers to the
recipient's incoming
mail server.

Internet
router

Step 4:
When the recipient uses
e-mail software to check
for e-mail messages, the
message transfers from
the incoming mail
server to the recipient's
computer.

Internet service
provider's incoming
mail server

Incoming Mail server

Becky   Gary   Tom   Nancy
Jim   Hector   Jeff   Tim
Ginny   Abby   Doug   Sue

FTP

FTP (*File Transfer Protocol*) is an Internet standard that permits file uploading and downloading with other computers on the Internet. Uploading is the opposite of downloading; that is, **uploading** is the process of transferring documents, graphics, and other objects from your computer to a server on the Internet.

Many operating systems include FTP capabilities (Figure 2-27). If yours does not, you can download FTP programs from the Web, usually for a small fee.

An *FTP server* is a computer that allows users to upload and download files using FTP. An FTP site is a collection of files including text, graphics, audio clips, video clips, and program files that reside on an FTP server. Many FTP sites have *anonymous FTP*, whereby anyone can transfer some, if not all, available files. Some FTP sites restrict file transfers to those who have authorized accounts (user names and passwords) on the FTP server.

Large files on FTP sites often are compressed to reduce storage space and download time. Before you can use a compressed (zipped) file, you must uncompress (unzip) it. Chapter 8 discusses utilities that zip and unzip files.

Newsgroups and Message Boards

A **newsgroup** is an online area in which users have written discussions about a particular subject. To participate in a discussion, a user sends a message to the newsgroup, and other users in the newsgroup read and reply to the message. The entire collection of Internet newsgroups is called *Usenet*, which contains thousands of newsgroups on a multitude of topics. Some major topic areas include news, recreation, society, business, science, and computers.

A computer that stores and distributes newsgroup messages is called a *news server*. Many universities, corporations, Internet access providers, and other large organizations have a news server. Some newsgroups require you to enter a user name and password to participate in the discussion. Only authorized members can use this type of newsgroup. For example, a newsgroup for students taking a college course may require a user name and password to access the newsgroup. This ensures that only students in the course participate in the discussion.

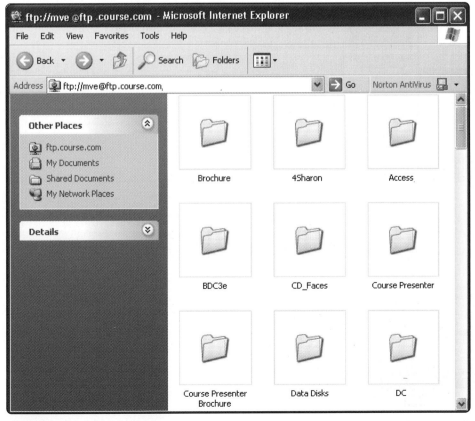

FIGURE 2-27 Many operating systems, such as Windows XP, have built-in FTP capabilities.

WEB LINK 2-7

FTP

Visit the Discovering Computers 2004 WEB LINK page (**scsite.com/dc2004/ weblink**). Click FTP below Chapter 2.

To participate in a newsgroup, typically you use a program called a newsreader. Most browsers have newsreaders. Instead of using your own newsreader, some Web sites that sponsor newsgroups have a built-in newsreader. A newsreader enables you to access a newsgroup to read previously entered messages, called *articles*. You can *post*, or add, articles of your own. The newsreader also keeps track of which articles you have and have not read.

Newsgroup members frequently post articles as a reply to another article — either to answer a question or to comment on material in the original article. These replies may cause the author of the original article, or others, to post additional articles related to the original article. A *thread* or *threaded discussion* consists of the original article and all subsequent related replies. A thread can be short-lived or continue for some time, depending on the nature of the topic and the interest of the participants.

Using a newsreader, you can search for newsgroups discussing a particular subject such as a type of musical instrument, brand of sports equipment, or employment opportunities. If you like the discussion in a particular newsgroup, you can *subscribe* to it, which means its location is saved in your newsreader for easy future access.

In some newsgroups, posted articles are sent to a moderator instead of immediately displaying on the newsgroup. The *moderator* reviews the contents of the article and then posts it, if appropriate. With a *moderated newsgroup*, the moderator decides if the article is relevant to the discussion. The moderator may choose to edit or discard inappropriate articles. For this reason, the content of a moderated newsgroup is considered more valuable.

A popular Web-based type of discussion group that does not require a newsreader is a **message board** (Figure 2-28). Many Web sites use message boards instead of newsgroups because they are easier to use.

WEB LINK 2-8

Newsgroups and Message Boards

Visit the Discovering Computers 2004 WEB LINK page (**scsite.com/dc2004/ weblink**). Click Newsgroups and Message Boards below Chapter 2.

FIGURE 2-28 On this message board, users discuss travel destinations.

Mailing Lists

A **mailing list** is a group of e-mail names and addresses given a single name. When a message is sent to a mailing list, every person on the list receives a copy of the message in his or her mailbox. To add your e-mail name and address to a mailing list, you **subscribe** to it (Figure 2-29). To remove your name, you **unsubscribe** from the mailing list. Some mailing lists are called *LISTSERVs*, named after a popular mailing list software product.

Thousands of mailing lists exist on a variety of topics in areas of entertainment, business, computers, society, culture, health, recreation, and education. To locate a mailing list dealing with a particular topic, you can search for the keywords, mailing list or LISTSERV, in a search engine. Many vendors use mailing lists to communicate with their customer base.

WEB LINK 2-9

Mailing Lists
Visit the Discovering Computers 2004 WEB LINK page (**scsite.com/dc2004/ weblink**). Click Mailing Lists below Chapter 2.

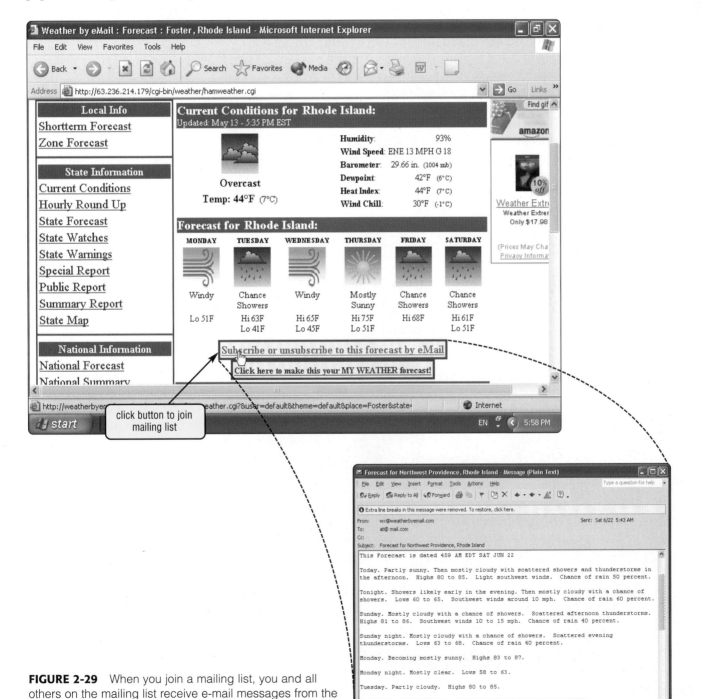

FIGURE 2-29 When you join a mailing list, you and all others on the mailing list receive e-mail messages from the Web site.

Chat Rooms

A **chat** is a real-time typed conversation that takes place on a computer. **Real time** means that you and the people with whom you are conversing are online at the same time. A **chat room** is a location on an Internet server that permits users to chat with each other. Anyone in the chat room can participate in the conversation, which usually is specific to a particular topic.

As you type on your keyboard, a line of characters and symbols is displayed on the computer screen. Others connected to the same chat room server also see what you have typed (Figure 2-30). In many chat rooms, you can click a button to see a profile of someone in the chat room.

Some chat rooms support voice chats and video chats, in which people hear or see each other as they chat (read Apply It 2-2 for more information about voice communications).

WEB LINK 2-10

Chat Rooms

Visit the Discovering Computers 2004 WEB LINK page (**scsite.com/dc2004/weblink**). Click Chat Rooms below Chapter 2.

APPLY IT 2-2

Send Voice Messages Via the Internet

Talk is cheap, according to an old saying. It is particularly cheap — and effective — when using Internet services. You can add voice message attachments to e-mail messages, talk in chat rooms, and send voice instant messages. You also can make relatively inexpensive online calls to another computer or to a telephone, although the audio quality generally is no match for a home telephone line.

To accomplish this task, you need a computer with a sound card, speakers, and a microphone, and you must install the appropriate software. Many of these programs are free, and they offer volume control and compression, which reduces the size of the speech files.

For more information about voice messages, visit the Discovering Computers 2004 Apply It Web page (**scsite.com/dc2004/apply**). Click Apply It #2 below Chapter 2.

To start a chat session, you connect to a chat server through a chat client. A chat client is a program on your computer. Today's browsers usually include a chat client. If yours does not, you can download a chat client from the Web. Once you have installed a *chat client*, you can create or join a conversation on the chat server to which you are connected. The chat room should indicate the discussion topic. The person who creates a chat room acts as the operator and has responsibility for monitoring the conversation and disconnecting anyone who becomes disruptive. Operator status can be shared or transferred to someone else.

Instant Messaging

Instant messaging (IM) is a real-time Internet communications service that notifies you when one or more people are online and then allows you to exchange messages or files or join a private chat room with them (Figure 2-31). Many IM services also can alert you to information such as calendar appointments, stock quotes, weather, or sports scores. They also allow you to send pictures or other documents to a recipient. For IM

FIGURE 2-30   As you type a line of text on your computer keyboard, the words and symbols you enter display on the computer screens of other people in the same chat room.

to work, both parties must be online at the same time. And, the receiver of a message must be willing to accept messages. Many businesses have found IM preferable to telephone tag for interoffice communications.

People use IM on all types of computers, including desktop computers and mobile computers and devices. To use IM, you may have to install *instant messenger* software onto the computer or device you plan to use IM. Some operating systems, such as Windows XP, include an instant messenger. No standards currently exist for IM. To ensure successful communications, all individuals on the notification list need to use the same or a compatible instant messenger.

WEB LINK 2-11

Instant Messaging
Visit the Discovering Computers 2004 WEB LINK page (**scsite.com/dc2004/ weblink**). Click Instant Messaging below Chapter 2.

FIGURE 2-31 AN EXAMPLE OF INSTANT MESSAGING

Step 1:
Log in to the IM server.

Step 2:
The server determines if any of your established friends, family, or coworkers, called *buddies*, are online.

IM server

Step 3:
You send instant messages to an online buddy.

messaging server

Step 4:
Your instant message travels through a messaging server and then to the online buddy.

NETIQUETTE

Netiquette, which is short for Internet etiquette, is the code of acceptable behaviors users should follow while on the Internet; that is, it is the conduct expected of individuals while online. Netiquette includes rules for all aspects of the Internet, including the World Wide Web, e-mail, FTP, newsgroups and message boards, chat rooms, and instant messaging. Figure 2-32 outlines some of the rules of netiquette.

Netiquette

Golden Rule: Treat others as you would like them to treat you.

1. In e-mail, newsgroups, and chat rooms:
   - Keep messages brief and use proper grammar and spelling.
   - Be careful when using sarcasm and humor, as it might be misinterpreted.
   - Be polite. Avoid offensive language.
   - Avoid sending or posting *flames*, which are abusive or insulting messages. Do not participate in *flame wars*, which are exchanges of flames.
   - Avoid sending spam, which is the Internet's version of junk mail. *Spam* is an unsolicited e-mail message or newsgroup posting sent to many recipients or newsgroups at once.
   - Do not use all capital letters, which is the equivalent of SHOUTING!
   - Use **emoticons** to express emotion. Popular emoticons include
:)	Smile	:\	Undecided
:(	Frown	:o	Surprised
:|	Indifference		
   - Use abbreviations and acronyms for phrases:
BTW	by the way
FYI	for your information
FWIW	for what it's worth
IMHO	in my humble opinion
TTFN	ta ta for now
TYVM	thank you very much
   - Clearly identify a *spoiler*, which is a message that reveals a solution to a game or ending to a movie or program.
2. Read the *FAQ* (frequently asked questions), if one exists. Many newsgroups and Web pages have an FAQ.
3. Do not assume material is accurate or up to date. Be forgiving of others' mistakes.
4. Never read someone's private e-mail.

FIGURE 2-32 Some of the rules of netiquette.

WEB PUBLISHING

Before the World Wide Web, the means to share opinions and ideas with others easily and inexpensively was limited to the media, classroom, work, or social environments. Generating an advertisement or publication that could reach a massive audience required much expense. Today, businesses and individuals convey information to millions of people by creating their own Web pages.

Web publishing is the development and maintenance of Web pages. To develop a Web page, you do not have to be a computer programmer. For the small business or home user, Web publishing is fairly easy as long as you have the proper tools.

The five major steps to Web publishing are as follows:

1. Plan a Web site
2. Analyze and design a Web site
3. Create a Web site
4. Deploy a Web site
5. Maintain a Web site

Figure 2-33 illustrates these steps with respect to a personal Web site. The following paragraphs describe these steps in more depth.

Plan a Web Site

Planning a personal Web site involves thinking about issues that could affect the design of the Web site. Identify the purpose of the Web site and the characteristics of the people whom you want to visit the Web site. Determine ways to differentiate your Web site from similar ones.

Analyze and Design a Web Site

A Web site can be simple or complex. In this step, determine specific ways to meet the goals identified in the previous step. Design the layout of elements of the Web site such as text, graphics, audio, video, and virtual reality. Decide if you have the means to include all the elements of the design into the Web site.

Required hardware may include a digital camera, scanner, sound card, microphone, and PC video camera. To incorporate pictures in your Web pages, you can take digital photographs with a digital camera, have pictures developed on a CD or DVD, or scan existing photographs and other graphics into a digital format with a scanner. You also can download images from the Web or purchase a CD or DVD that contains a collection of images. With a sound card, you can add sounds to your Web pages. A microphone allows you to include your voice in a Web page. To incorporate videos, you could use a PC video camera or purchase special hardware that captures still photographs from videos.

Create a Web Site

Creating a Web site, sometimes called *Web page authoring*, involves working on the computer to compose the Web site. Many current word processing packages include Web page authoring features so you can create basic Web pages that contain text and graphics.

To create more sophisticated Web pages that include video, sound, animation, and other special effects, you can use *Web page authoring software*, which is software specifically designed to help you create Web pages. Both new and experienced users can create fascinating Web sites with this software. Popular Web page authoring software packages include Microsoft FrontPage, Adobe GoLive, Lotus FastSite, Macromedia Dreamweaver, and Macromedia Flash.

FIGURE 2-33   HOW TO PUBLISH YOUR RESUME ON THE WEB

Step 1:
Plan a Web site.
Think about issues that could
affect the design of the Web site.

Step 2:
Analyze and design a Web site.
Design the layout of the elements of the Web site.

Step 3:
Create a Web site.
Use word processing or Web page authoring
software to create the Web site.

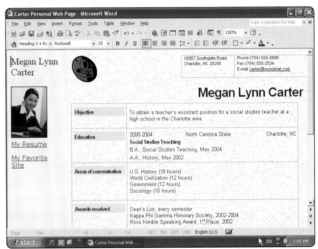

Step 4:
Deploy a Web site.
Copy the Web site from your hard disk to a Web server.

Step 5:
Maintain a Web site.
Visit your Web site
regularly to be sure it is
working and current.

Deploy a Web Site

After the Web pages are created, you store them on a Web server. Many Internet access providers offer their customers storage space on a Web server for a personal Web site at no additional cost. If your access provider does not include this service, companies called *Web hosting services* provide storage for your Web pages for a reasonable monthly fee.

If your access provider does not supply a Web address or if you want to obtain a different domain name, you apply to an official registrar for a specific domain name. You then pay a small annual fee to continue using the domain name.

Once you have created a Web site and located a Web server to store it, you need to upload the Web site from your computer to the Web server. One way to upload files is with FTP.

To help others locate your Web site, you should register it with various search engines. Doing so ensures your site will appear in the hit lists for searches on related keywords. Many search engines allow you to register your Web address and keywords at no cost. Registering your site with the various search engines, however, can be an extremely time-consuming task. Instead, you can use a *submission service*, which is a Web-based business that registers your Web site with hundreds of search engines for a fee.

Maintain a Web Site

A successful Web site's contents must be up to date and its links must work properly at all times. Ensure currency and suitability by reviewing and updating the Web site frequently.

A **Webmaster** is the individual responsible for maintaining a Web site and developing Web pages. Webmasters and other Web developers maintain Web sites using software products. Most Web page authoring software packages provide basic Web site management tools, allowing you to add and modify Web pages within the Web site. For more advanced features such as managing users, passwords, chat rooms, and e-mail, you need to purchase specialized Web site management software, if your Internet access provider does not provide the software.

QUIZ YOURSELF 2-3

To check your knowledge of e-mail, FTP, newsgroups and message boards, mailing lists, chat rooms, instant messaging, netiquette, and Web publishing, visit the Discovering Computers 2004 Quiz Yourself Web page (**scsite.com/dc2004/quiz**). Click Objectives 10 – 12 below Chapter 2.

CHAPTER SUMMARY

This chapter presented the history and structure of the Internet. It discussed the World Wide Web at length, including topics such as browsing, navigating, searching, and e-commerce. It also introduced other services available on the Internet, such as e-mail, FTP, newsgroups and message boards, chat rooms, and instant messaging. Finally, the chapter listed rules of netiquette and discussed Web publishing.

Career Corner

Web Developer

If you are looking for a job working with the latest Internet technology, then Web developer could be the career for you. *Web developers* analyze, design, develop, implement, and support Web applications and functionality. Specialized programming skills required include HTML, JavaScript, Java, Perl, C++, and VBScript. Developers also may need multimedia knowledge, including Adobe Photoshop and Macromedia Flash and Macromedia Director. Developers must be aware of emerging technologies and know how they can be used to enhance a Web presence.

A Web developer must be able to appreciate a client's needs, recognize the technologies involved to meet those needs, and explain those technologies to the client. For example, if the client is a large corporation seeking to set up an online store, a Web developer must understand e-commerce and be able to explain what is required, probable costs, and possible outcomes in a way that the client can understand.

Educational requirements vary from company to company and can range from a high school education to a four-year degree. Many companies place heavy emphasis on certifications. Two of the more popular certifications are available through the International Webmasters Association (IWA) and the World Organization of Webmasters (WOW). A wide salary range exists — from $25,000 to $65,000 — depending on educational background and location.

To learn more about the field of Web Developer as a career, visit the Discovering Computers 2004 Careers Web page (**scsite.com/dc2004/careers**). Click Web Developer.

HIGH-TECH TALK

You Are One in a Few Billion (IP Addresses)

Every computer on the Internet has a unique address, called an IP address, that distinguishes it from other computers on the Internet. An IP address has two parts that identify a specific computer: one part to identify the network where that computer resides and a second part to pinpoint the specific computer or host within that network.

A typical IP address — such as 207.46.197.113 — has four groups of numbers that range from 0 through 255. This form of the IP address is sometimes called a *dotted decimal number* or *dotted quad*. The four groups of numbers in the dotted quad are called octets, because they each have 8 bits when viewed in binary form for a total of 32 bits in the IP address. For instance, the binary form of 207.46.197.113 is 11001111.00101110.11000101.01110001 (Figure 2-34). For more information about how the binary system works, see Appendix A.

Because each of the 8 bits can be 1 or 0, the total possible combinations per octet are 2^8, or 256. Combining the four octets of an IP address provides a possible 2^{32} or 4,294,967,296 unique values. The actual number of available addresses is about 3 billion, because some values are reserved for special use or are off limits.

To request data such as a Web page from a computer on the Internet, you really need only an IP address. For instance, if you type the Web address, http://207.46.197.113, your browser will display the home page on the machine hosting the Microsoft Web site. Of course, remembering one IP address out of billions is a little overwhelming — so you probably would just type the domain name, www.microsoft.com, into your browser. Your browser then contacts a domain name server (DNS) to resolve the human-readable domain name into a machine-readable IP address. Each domain name server houses a simple database that maps domain names to IP addresses. The DNS would resolve the human-readable domain name, www.microsoft.com, into a machine-readable IP address, 207.46.197.113.

Domain names are helpful because they are easier for people to remember than IP addresses. You can learn more about a domain using the whois form at the Network Solutions Web site (www.netsol.com and then click whois link). If you type in a domain name, such as scsite.com, the form displays the registration information for that domain, including its IP address.

Like all others, your computer must have an IP address to connect to the Internet or another computer that has an IP address. Servers generally have *static IP addresses*, because they usually are connected to the Internet and their IP addresses do not change often. When you dial up to the Internet using your home computer, you most likely are using a temporary or *dynamic IP address*. Your access provider uses the *Dynamic Host Configuration Protocol (DHCP)* to assign your computer a temporary dynamic IP address from a pool of IP addresses. The dynamic IP address is unique only for that session. Once you disconnect, the DHCP server puts that IP address back into the IP address pool so it can assign it to the next requesting computer. Even if you immediately reconnect, the DHCP server might not assign you the same IP address. Using DHCP and dynamic IP addresses means an Internet service provider needs only one IP address for each modem it supports, rather than one for each of its millions of customers.

FIGURE 2-34
Components of an IP address.

Billions of IP addresses sounds like a lot. But, because so many computers connected to the Internet need unique IP addresses, a growing shortage of IP addresses exists. A new IP addressing scheme, called *IPv6* or *IPng (IP Next Generation)* will lengthen IP addresses from 32 bits to 128 bits and increase the number of available IP addresses to a whopping 3.4×10^{38}, or 340,000,000,000,000,000,000,000,000,000,000,000,000.

Do you want to know the IP address currently assigned to your computer?

- With Windows 2000/XP, click the Start button on the taskbar and then click Run. Type cmd to display the MS-DOS window. Type ipconfig and then press the ENTER key.
- With Windows 98, click Start on the menu bar and then click Run. Type winipcfg and then press the ENTER key.

If you are using an older version of AOL, the IP address might read 0.0.0.0 because AOL uses a proprietary method to assign IP addresses.

For more information about IP addresses, visit the Discovering Computers 2004 High-Tech Talk Web page (**scsite.com/dc2004/tech**) and click IP Addresses.

COMPANIES ON THE CUTTING EDGE

Yahoo!
Indexing the World Wide Web

One of the more popular sites on the World Wide Web has one of the more unusual names. *Yahoo!*, an online navigational guide, is visited by millions of people every day. Yahoo!'s cofounders, Jerry Yang and David Filo, claim they named their creation Yahoo! because they considered themselves two tough guys, or yahoos. For millions of grateful users, however, the name is the cry of joy they utter when Yahoo! guides them to an elusive Web site.

Yang and Filo started creating lists in 1994 at Stanford University to organize their favorite Web sites. Before they knew it, they had developed a tree-style database and a method of searching for specific Web pages. Yang maintained the lists on his student workstation, and Filo kept the search engine on his computer. The machines were dubbed "Akebono" and "Konishiki" in honor of two celebrated sumo wrestlers. Grappling with the Web went from part-time pursuit to full-time fixation. Yang and Filo shared their creation with thousands of information seekers and continued to add new categories and sites. In 1995, they moved their operation to large computers at Netscape Communications Corporation.

What makes Yahoo! unique is that people build the directory. Every Web site is visited and evaluated by a Yahoo! staff member. Site creators suggest the category under which a site belongs, but Yahoo! staff members ultimately decide where each site is placed by assuming the role of a typical user.

At Yahoo!, more than 200 million visitors access 1.2 billion pages daily, including the network's e-mail, chat rooms, shopping site, and personal Web pages. These services, which are supported by more than 3,000 advertisers, are free to users.

For more information about Yahoo!, visit the Discovering Computers 2004 Companies Web page (**scsite.com/dc2004/companies**) and click Yahoo!

AOL
Interacting Anywhere

Meg Ryan and Tom Hanks fostered an online relationship in their hit movie, *You've Got Mail*. Worldwide, more than 34 million users likewise cultivate associations by using *America Online (AOL)*, a division of AOL Time Warner, for their interactive requirements.

AOL's corporate mission is "to build a global medium as central to people's lives as the telephone or television …and even more valuable." With a strategy of AOL Anywhere, the company is the world's leading online service provider, with features such as e-mail, software, computer support services, and access to many other Internet services. Members use AOL more than 1 billion hours each month. Every day members send 228 million e-mail messages, seek 245 million stock quotes, and browse 11.1 billion Web pages. At any given time, nearly 2.2 million users can be online simultaneously. AOL International operates in 17 countries and 8 different languages.

Stephen M. Case founded the company in 1985 as Quantum Computer Services Corporation with a vision of simplifying the Internet for people other than computer scholars and specialists. He partnered with a series of companies, including Commodore International, Ltd., Tandy Corporation, and Apple Computer. Case changed the company name to America Online in 1991.

AOL is renowned for providing a convenient and easy-to-use interactive service. The company pioneered technologies such as Keywords to simplify navigation and the Buddy List feature to enable instant messaging by displaying contacts who are online. Throughout the 1990s, AOL experienced tremendous growth, partly due to its aggressive marketing campaign using direct mail, membership kits, and magazine inserts. It acquired Netscape Communications in 1998 and, in a $172 billion pact, merged with Time Warner, one of the world's leading media conglomerates, in 2001.

For more information about America Online, visit the Discovering Computers 2004 Companies Web page (**scsite.com/dc2004/companies**) and click AOL.

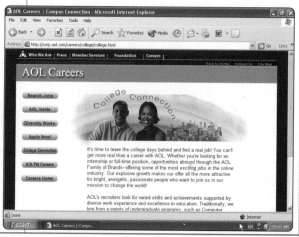

TECHNOLOGY TRAILBLAZERS

Tim Berners-Lee
Creator of the World Wide Web

WWW: three simple letters that have transformed the way people use computers and obtain information. Thanks to the innovation of *Tim Berners-Lee,* the World Wide Web has become the most popular service on the Internet. Many wonder why Berners-Lee refuses to step into the limelight to profit from his invention. In his words, commercializing his brainchild would suggest that people would be respecting him "as a function of [my] net worth. That's not an assumption I was brought up with."

Berners-Lee's parents, who met while working with one of the first commercially sold computers, instilled his values and sparked his interest in electronics and mathematics. After graduating from Queen's College at Oxford University with a degree in physics, Berners-Lee worked with various types of computer programs. He found that although computers could store and process information, "one of the things computers have not done… [is] store random associations between disparate things, although this is something the brain has always done relatively well." So, Berners-Lee developed a program called Enquire that stored both information and random associations in the form of links that pointed to related documents. Enquire's associations were limited, but Berners-Lee suggested a universal system using links that could point to any document — primitive or polished, personal or public, everyday or exotic. As a name for the project, the World Wide Web (WWW) was chosen as both descriptive and memorable. The World Wide Web debuted on the Internet in 1991, and its popularity exploded.

Today, Berners-Lee works quietly in academia as director of the World Wide Web Consortium (W3C) at the Massachusetts Institute of Technology. This organization consists of hundreds of representatives from the world's leading Internet companies, including IBM, Microsoft, and Hewlett-Packard. W3C considers issues in the Web's evolution and hopes to realize the Web's full potential and ensure its reliability.

For more information about Tim Berners-Lee, visit the Discovering Computers 2004 People Web page (**scsite.com/dc2004/people**) and click Tim Berners-Lee.

Anita Brown
Miss DC

She is known affectionately as Miss DC among the Internet community. As founder and chair of the Washington, D.C.-based Black Geeks Online, *Anita Brown* is guiding online participation among the African-American community.

Black Geeks Online is not just a Web site. "We are a network that HAS a website." Brown writes that, "Our objective has been to connect people of color from around the world — both on and off-line — to share our talents and time to make others aware of the potential and pitfalls of information technology." Originally having 18 members in 1995, today more than 30,000 technical professionals, teachers, students, parents, and community leaders belong to Anita Brown's nonprofit virtual community. These

volunteers impart their talents by educating others about the Internet, promoting computer literacy, and providing information regarding professional opportunities in the information technology field.

For more than 30 years, Brown has been developing a variety of businesses, including running a desktop publishing service and a T-shirt company and managing a help desk on America Online. She uses her experiences to tap resources and bring computers and professionals into the city's neighborhoods. At AOL, Brown served as "SistahGeek," translating confusing terms into language people could understand and supporting African-Americans, especially women, who were cautious of or puzzled by the growth of information technology.

Brown's honors include being named one of the 50 Most Important African-Americans in Technology and voted one of the Top 25 Women on the Web by the San Francisco Women on the Web. THE CONDUIT™ *the definitive technological guide for the African in America* voted Black Geeks Online seventh on its list of Top 20 Black Tech Companies.

For more information about Anita Brown, visit the Discovering Computers 2004 People Web page (**scsite.com/dc2004/people**) and click Anita Brown.

CHAPTER 2 CHAPTER REVIEW

◀● Previous | Next ●▶

The Chapter Review section summarizes the concepts presented in this chapter.

■WEB INSTRUCTIONS:

To display this page from the Web, start your browser and enter the Web address **scsite.com/dc2004/ch2/review**. Click the links for current and additional information. To listen to an audio version of this Chapter Review, click the Audio button.

1 What Is the History of the Internet?

The **Internet** is a worldwide collection of networks that links millions of businesses, government agencies, educational institutions, and individuals. The Internet has its roots in *ARPANET*, a network started in 1969 by an agency of the U.S. Department of Defense to link scientific and academic researchers across the United States. In 1986, the National Science Foundation (NSF) connected its huge network, called *NSFnet*, to ARPANET, creating a configuration of complex networks and hosts that became known as the Internet. Today, the Internet consists of many local, regional, national, and international networks.

2 How Can You Access and Connect to the Internet?

Employees and students often connect to the Internet through a business or school network. The networks usually use a high-speed line leased from a local telephone company to connect to an access provider. Many home and small businesses connect to the Internet with **dial-up access**, which uses a modem in the computer and a standard telephone line. Some home and small business users opt for higher-speed connections, such as DSL, ISDN, or cable television Internet services. **DSL** and **ISDN** are technologies that provide Internet connections using regular copper telephone lines. A **cable modem** provides high-speed Internet connections through the cable television network. An **access provider** is a business that provides access to the Internet free or for a fee. An **ISP** (**Internet service provider**) is a regional or national access provider. An **online service provider** (**OSP**) provides Internet access in addition to members-only features. A **wireless service provider** (*WSP*) is a company that provides wireless Internet access to users with wireless modems or Web-enabled mobile devices.

3 What Is an IP Address?

An **IP address** (*Internet Protocol address*) is a number that uniquely identifies each computer or device connected to the Internet. The Internet relies on IP addresses to send data to computers at specific locations. A **domain name** is the text version of an IP address. As with an IP address, the components of a domain name are separated by periods. A <u>DNS</u> (*domain name system*) **server** translates a domain name into its associated IP address so data can route to the correct computer.

 Visit **scsite.com/dc2004/quiz** or click the Quiz Yourself button. Click Objectives 1 – 3 below Chapter 2.

4 What Are the Components of a Web Address?

The **World Wide Web** (*WWW*), or **Web**, consists of a worldwide collection of electronic documents. Each document is called a **Web page**. A <u>Web address</u>, or **URL** (*Uniform Resource Locator*), is a unique address for a Web page. A Web address consists of a protocol that defines how the page transfers on the Web, a domain name, and sometimes the path to a specific Web page or location on a Web page and the Web page name.

5 What Is the Purpose of a Web Browser?

A **Web browser**, or **browser**, is application software that allows users to access and view Web pages. When you type a Web address in the Address text box at the top of the browser window, a computer called a <u>Web server</u> delivers the requested Web page to your computer. Most Web pages contain links. A **link** is a built-in connection to a related Web page or part of a Web page.

6 How Can You Search for Information on the Web?

A **search engine** is a software program that finds Web pages and Web sites. A **Web site** is a collection of related Web pages and associated items. To display a search engine, enter the search engine

CHAPTER REVIEW   CHAPTER 2

Web address into your Web browser. From the search engine, enter a word or phrase, called **search text**, or *keywords*, in the search engine's text box. The search engine displays a list of *hits*, or Web page names, that contain the search text. Click the desired link to display the Web page.

7 What Are the Types of Web Sites?

A **portal** is a Web site that offers a variety of Internet services from a single location. A news Web site contains newsworthy material. An informational Web site contains factual information. A business/marketing Web site contains content that promotes or sells products or services. An educational Web site offers avenues for formal and informal teaching and learning. An entertainment Web site offers an interactive and engaging environment. An advocacy Web site contains content that describes a cause, opinion, or idea. A personal Web site is maintained by a private individual or family.

8 How Do Web Pages Use Graphics, Animation, Audio, Video, Virtual Reality, and Plug-Ins?

Some Web pages use **multimedia**, which combines text with graphics, animation, audio, video, and/or virtual reality. A **graphic** is a digital representation of nontext information such as a drawing, chart, or photograph. **Animation** is the appearance of motion created by displaying a series of still images in sequence. **Audio** includes music, speech, or any other sound. **Video** consists of full-motion images that are played back at various speeds. Virtual reality (**VR**) is the use of computers to simulate a real or imagined environment that appears as three-dimensional space.

9 What Are the Types of E-Commerce?

E-commerce, short for *electronic commerce*, is a business transaction that occurs over an electronic network such as the Internet. Business-to-consumer (B2C) e-commerce consists of the sale of goods and services to the general public. Consumer-to-consumer (C2C) e-commerce occurs when one consumer sells directly to another, such as an online auction. Business-to-business (B2B) e-commerce, which is the most

common form of e-commerce, takes place between businesses that exchange goods and services.

 Visit **scsite.com/dc2004/quiz** or click the Quiz Yourself button. Click Objectives 4 – 9 below Chapter 2.

10 How Do E-Mail, FTP, Newsgroups and Message Boards, Mailing Lists, Chat Rooms, and Instant Messaging Work?

E-mail (short for *electronic mail*) is the transmission of messages and files via a computer network. **FTP** (*File Transfer Protocol*) is an Internet standard that permits file uploading and downloading with other computers on the Internet. A **newsgroup** is an online area in which users have written about a particular subject. A **message board** is a popular Web-based type of discussion group that is easier to use than a newsgroup. A **mailing list** is a group of e-mail names and addresses given a single name, so that everyone on the list receives a message sent to the list. A **chat room** is a location on an Internet server that permits users to **chat**, or conduct real-time typed conversations. **Instant messaging** (**IM**) is a real-time Internet communications service that notifies you when one or more people are online.

11 What Are the Rules of Netiquette?

Netiquette, which is short for Internet etiquette, is the code of acceptable behaviors users should follow while on the Internet. Keep messages short. Be polite. Read the FAQ if one exists. Do not assume material is accurate or up to date, and never read someone's private e-mail.

12 What Are the Steps and Tools Required for Web Publishing?

Web publishing is the development and maintenance of Web pages. The five major steps to Web publishing are: (1) plan a Web site, (2) analyze and design a Web site, (3) create a Web site, (4) deploy a Web site, and (5) maintain a Web site. You can use *Web page authoring software* to create sophisticated Web pages with special effects. A **Webmaster** or Web developer maintains a Web site using software products.

 Visit **scsite.com/dc2004/quiz** or click the Quiz Yourself button. Click Objectives 10 – 12 below Chapter 2.

CHAPTER 2 KEY TERMS

◀● Previous | Next ●▶

You should know the Primary Terms and be familiar with the Secondary Terms.

WEB INSTRUCTIONS:

To display this page from the Web, start your browser and enter the Web address **scsite.com/dc2004/ch2/terms**. Click a term to display its definition and a picture. When the picture displays, click the more info button for current and additional information about the term from the Web.

>> Primary Terms
(shown in bold-black characters in the chapter)

>> Secondary Terms
(shown in italic characters in the chapter)

QUIZZES AND
LEARNING GAMES

Computer Genius

Crossword Puzzle

Interactive Labs

Practice Test

Quiz Yourself

Wheel of Terms

EXERCISES

Chapter Review

Checkpoint

Key Terms

Lab Exercises

Learn It Online

Web Research

BEYOND THE BOOK

Apply It

Career Corner

Companies

FAQ

High-Tech Talk

Issues

Looking Ahead

Trailblazers

Web Links

FEATURES

Guide to Web Sites

Making Use of the Web

Tech News

Timeline 2004

Primary Terms:

access provider (2.05)
address book (2.27)
animation (2.19)
audio (2.20)
browser (2.09)
cable modem (2.05)
chat (2.32)
chat room (2.32)
dial-up access (2.04)
domain name (2.08)
downloading (2.10)
DSL (2.05)
e-commerce (2.24)
e-mail (2.25)
e-mail address (2.27)
e-mail program (2.26)
electronic storefront (2.24)
emoticons (2.34)
FTP (2.29)
graphic (2.18)
home page (2.10)
instant messaging (IM) (2.32)
Internet (2.02)
IP address (2.08)
ISDN (2.05)
ISP (Internet service provider) (2.06)
link (2.11)
mailing list (2.31)
message board (2.30)
MP3 (2.20)
multimedia (2.17)
netiquette (2.34)
newsgroup (2.29)
online auction (2.25)

online service provider (OSP) (2.06)
player (2.21)
plug-in (2.23)
portal (2.16)
real time (2.32)
search engine (2.12)
search text (2.13)
shopping cart (2.24)
streaming (2.21)
subject directory (2.14)
subscribe (mailing list) (2.31)
surfing the Web (2.12)
thumbnail (2.19)
traffic (2.03)
unsubscribe (2.31)
uploading (2.29)
URL (2.10)
user name (2.27)
video (2.22)
virtual reality (VR) (2.22)
Web (2.09)
Web address (2.10)
Web browser (2.09)
Web community (2.16)
Web page (2.09)
Web publishing (2.34)
Web server (2.11)
Web site (2.09)
Webmaster (2.36)
wireless service provider (2.06)
World Wide Web (2.09)

Secondary Terms:

Advanced Research Projects Agency (ARPA) (2.02)
animated GIF (2.20)
anonymous FTP (2.29)
ARPANET (2.03)
articles (2.30)
buddies (2.33)
business-to-business (B2B) e-commerce (2.25)
business-to-consumer (B2C) e-commerce (2.24)
chat client (2.32)
click (2.12)
consumer-to-consumer (C2C) e-commerce (2.25)
digital subscriber line (2.05)
DNS server (2.08)
domain name system (DNS) (2.08)
dot-com (2.08)
electronic commerce (2.24)
electronic mail (2.25)
FAQ (frequently asked questions) (2.34)
File Transfer Protocol (2.29)
flame wars (2.34)
flames (2.34)
FTP server (2.29)
GIF (2.19)
graphical image (2.18)
hits (2.13)
host (2.03)
http (2.11)
hyperlink (2.11)
Hypertext Transfer Protocol (2.11)
instant messenging (IM) (2.32)
Integrated Services Digital Network (2.05)
Internet backbone (2.07)
Internet Corporation for Assigned Names and Numbers (ICANN) (2.08)
Internet Protocol address (2.08)
Internet2 (2.04)
JPEG (2.18)
keywords (2.13)

LISTSERVs (2.31)
m-commerce (2.24)
microbrowser (2.10)
moderated newsgroup (2.30)
moderator (2.30)
Moving Pictures Experts Group (MPEG) (2.22)
MPEG-4 (2.22)
national ISP (2.06)
Net (2.02)
news server (2.29)
NSFnet (2.03)
PNG format (2.19)
point of presence (POP) (2.05)
POP3 (2.27)
post (2.30)
Post Office Protocol (2.27)
pull (2.11)
push (2.11)
regional ISP (2.06)
shopping bots (2.14)
SMTP (simple mail transfer protocol) (2.27)
spam (2.34)
spider (2.14)
spoiler (2.34)
streaming audio (2.21)
streaming video (2.22)
submission service (2.36)
subscribe (newsgroup) (2.30)
thread (2.30)
threaded discussion (2.30)
top-level domain (2.08)
Uniform Resource Locator (2.10)
Usenet (2.29)
VR world (2.22)
Web hosting services (2.36)
Web page authoring (2.34)
Web page authoring software (2.34)
wireless portal (2.16)
World Wide Web Consortium (W3C) (2.04)
WSP (2.06)
WWW (2.09)

CHECKPOINT CHAPTER 2

Use the Checkpoint exercises to check your knowledge level of the chapter.

 WEB INSTRUCTIONS:

To display this page from the Web, start your browser and enter the Web address **scsite.com/dc2004/ch2/check**. Click the links for current and additional information.

LABEL THE FIGURE   Identify each part of the Web address and e-mail address.

a. domain name
b. path
c. protocol
d. user name
e. Web page name
f. domain name

TRUE/FALSE   Mark T for True and F for False. (See page numbers in parentheses.)

_____ 1. The <u>World Wide Web Consortium</u> (W3C) oversees research and sets standards and guidelines for many areas of the Internet. (2.04)

_____ 2. An <u>access provider</u> is a business that provides access to the Internet for a fee. (2.05)

_____ 3. A <u>domain name</u> is the text version of an IP address. (2.08)

_____ 4. Each electronic document on the Web is called a <u>Web site</u>. (2.09)

_____ 5. <u>Downloading</u> is the process of sending information to a server on the Internet. (2.10)

_____ 6. A <u>search engine</u> is a software program that finds Web sites and Web pages. (2.12)

_____ 7. An <u>educational Web site</u> contains content that describes a cause, opinion, or idea. (2.16)

_____ 8. <u>Streaming</u> is the process of transferring data in a continuous and even flow. (2.21)

_____ 9. <u>Consumer-to-consumer (C2C) e-commerce</u> consists of the sale of goods and services to the general public. (2.25)

_____ 10. <u>Instant messaging</u> (IM) is a location on an Internet server that permits users to chat with each other. (2.32)

CHAPTER 2 CHECKPOINT

◄● Previous | Next ●►

MULTIPLE CHOICE Select the best answer. (See page numbers in parentheses.)

1. _____ oversees research and sets standards and guidelines for many areas of the Internet. (2.04)
   a. The World Wide Web Consortium (W3C)
   b. Internet2
   c. The National Science Foundation (NSF)
   d. The Advanced Research Projects Agency (ARPA)

2. With dial-up Internet access, the telephone number you dial connects to an access point called a _____ . (2.05)
   a. DSL (digital subscriber line)
   b. WSP (wireless service provider)
   c. URL (Uniform Resource Locator)
   d. POP (point of presence)

3. An IP address usually consists of _____ . (2.08)
   a. two groups of numbers separated by commas
   b. two groups of numbers separated by periods
   c. four groups of numbers separated by commas
   d. four groups of numbers separated by periods

4. Web-enabled mobile devices use a _____ , which is designed for small screens and limited computing power. (2.10)
   a. unibrowser
   b. microbrowser
   c. demibrowser
   d. minibrowser

5. Many Web addresses begin with http, which is the _____ . (2.11)
   a. path
   b. domain name
   c. protocol
   d. page name

6. Many search engines use a program called a _____ to build and maintain lists of words found on Web sites. (2.14)
   a. bug
   b. caterpillar
   c. spider
   d. worm

7. Many _____ have Web communities that join a specific group of people with similar interests or relationships. (2.16)
   a. portals
   b. news Web sites
   c. informational Web sites
   d. entertainment Web sites

8. The purpose of an advocacy Web site is to _____ . (2.17)
   a. present newsworthy material related to current events
   b. contain factual information of public interest
   c. promote or sell products or services
   d. convince the reader of the validity of the cause, opinion, or idea

9. _____ format reduces the size of an audio file to about one-tenth its original size, while preserving the quality of the sound. (2.20)
   a. JPEG
   b. MP3
   c. BMP
   d. GIF

10. In _____ e-commerce, a customer visits an online business through an electronic storefront. (2.24)
   a. consumer-to-consumer
   b. business-to-business
   c. consumer-to-business
   d. business-to-consumer

11. A computer that stores and distributes newsgroup messages is called a(n) _____ . (2.29)
   a. news server
   b. moderator
   c. newsreader
   d. article

12. In a newsgroup, a thread or threaded discussion consists of the original article and all _____ . (2.30)
   a. previous related antecedents
   b. previous unrelated antecedents
   c. subsequent related replies
   d. subsequent unrelated replies

13. _____ is a rule of netiquette. (2.34)
   a. Use all capital letters
   b. Avoid offensive language
   c. Participate in flame wars
   d. Assume material is accurate

14. A submission service helps in _____ a Web site. (2.36)
   a. planning
   b. analyzing
   c. deploying
   d. creating

CHECKPOINT   CHAPTER 2

MATCHING   Match the terms with their definitions. (See page numbers in parentheses.)

_____ 1. traffic (2.03)

_____ 2. home page (2.10)

_____ 3. downloading (2.10)

_____ 4. thumbnail (2.19)

_____ 5. player (2.21)

_____ 6. streaming (2.21)

_____ 7. shopping cart (2.24)

_____ 8. e-mail program (2.26)

_____ 9. e-mail address (2.27)

_____ 10. uploading (2.29)

a. special software needed to listen to an audio file on a computer

b. communications activity on the Internet

c. combination of a user name and a domain name that identifies an Internet user

d. process of transferring data in a continuous and even flow

e. first page that a Web site displays

f. built-in connection to a related Web page or part of a Web page

g. allows an e-commerce customer to collect purchases

h. process of a computer receiving information from a server on the Internet

i. software that extends the multimedia capabilities of a browser

j. software used to create, send, receive, forward, store, print, and delete e-mail messages

k. small version of a larger graphic

l. process of transferring documents, graphics, and other objects from your computer to an Internet server

SHORT ANSWER   Write a brief answer to each of the following questions.

1. How is a regional ISP different from a national ISP? _____ How are an ISP, OSP, and WSP different? _____

2. How is a Web page different from a Web site? _____ How can you use a Web address to display a Web page? _____

3. What is a search engine? _____ How can you reduce the number of hits a search engine returns? _____

4. What is an FTP server? _____ What is anonymous FTP? _____

5. What happens when you subscribe to, or unsubscribe from, a mailing list? _____ How can you locate a mailing list on a particular topic? _____

WORKING TOGETHER   Working with a group of your classmates, complete the following team exercises.

1. This chapter lists eight types of Web sites: portal, news, informational, business/marketing, educational, entertainment, advocacy, and personal. Working as a team, use the Internet to find at least two examples of each type of Web site. For each Web site, identify the Web address, the multimedia elements used, the purpose of the Web site, and the type of Web site. Explain why you classified each site as you did. Then, keeping in mind the purpose of each Web site, rank the sites in terms of their effectiveness. Share your findings in a report and/or a PowerPoint presentation with the class.

2. Choose one Issue from the following issues in this chapter: Who Controls the Internet? (2.04), Can You Learn It Online? (2.16), To Tax or Not to Tax Internet Purchases? (2.25), or How Expensive Is E-Mail and Internet Privacy? (2.25). Use the Web and/or print media to research the issue. Then, present a debate for the class, with different members of your team supporting different responses to the questions that accompany the issue.

3. The Internet has had a tremendous impact on business. For some businesses, that influence has not been positive. For example, surveys suggest that as a growing number of people make their own travel plans online, travel agents are seeing fewer customers. Have each member of your team interview a businessperson who is or has been affected negatively by the Internet. What effect has the Internet had? How has the Internet changed business in positive ways? How can the business compete with the Internet? Meet with your team to discuss the results of your interviews. Create a group PowerPoint presentation and share your findings with the class.

CHAPTER 2 LEARN IT ONLINE

◀● Previous | Next ●▶

Use the Learn It Online exercises to reinforce your understanding of the chapter concepts.

WEB INSTRUCTIONS:

To display this page from the Web, start your browser and enter the Web address **scsite.com/dc2004/ch2/learn**.

1 At the Movies – Chat Room Lawsuit

To view the Chat Room Lawsuit movie, click the number 1 button. Watch the movie and then complete the exercise by answering the questions below. Many companies are fed up with being trashed online and are fighting back with lawsuits. Most chat room posters offer legitimate criticisms and warnings, but instances of outright lies and intentional sabotage are a reality. In some cases, unsubstantiated comments have caused a company's stock to nose-dive and even have caused bankruptcy. Tracking down the anonymous posters (by filing subpoenas against Internet providers, such as Yahoo! or America Online) raises free speech issues and threatens the free flow of information on the Web. Who deserves greater protection: the companies and their products or individuals and the free flow of information on the Web? What agency should be the judge?

2 Shelly Cashman Series Connecting to the Internet Lab

Follow the instructions in Learn It Online 2 on page 1.46 to start and use the Shelly Cashman Series Connecting to the Internet Lab. If you are running from the Web, enter the Web address **scsite.com/sclabs/menu** or display the Learn It Online page (see instructions at the top of this page) and then click the number 2 button.

3 Shelly Cashman Series The World Wide Web Lab

Follow the instructions in Learn It Online 2 on page 1.46 to start and use the Shelly Cashman Series The World Wide Web Lab. If you are running from the Web, enter the Web address **scsite.com/sclabs/menu** or display the Learn It Online page (see instructions at the top of this page) and then click the number 3 button.

4 Practice Test

Click the number 4 button. Answer each question. When completed, enter your name and click the Grade Test button to submit the quiz for grading. Make a note of any missed questions. If required, print a copy to submit to your instructor.

5 Web Guide

Click the number 5 button to display the Guide to Web Sites and Searching Techniques Web page. Click Reference and then click AskERIC. Click ERIC Database and search for Internet History. Click search results link of your choice. Use your word processing program to prepare a brief report on what you learned and submit your assignment to your instructor.

GUIDE TO WWW WORLD WIDE WEB SITES	
CATEGORY	COMMENTS
Animation	
Animation World Network	Cool animations
RGB Gallery	Art animations
Shockwave	Cool Shockwave animations
Art	
Fine Art Forum	Art and technology net news
Leonardo da Vinci	Works of the famous Italian artist and thinker
Louvre Museum	Web version of Louvre Museum, Paris
The Andy Warhol Museum	Famous American pop artist
World Wide Arts Resources	Links to many art sites
Business and Finance	
All Business Network	Links to Web business information
FinanCenter.com	Personal finance information
Morningstar, Inc.	Mutual fund site
MSN MoneyCentral	Microsoft's Financial portal
PC Quote	Free delayed stock quotes
Quicken	Personal financial advice
Raging Bull	Real-time stock quotes
SiliconInvestor	Stock chat for technology investors
SmartMoney	Live snapshot of the stock market
Stockgroup Research	Investment information

Categories shown in left column of guide: ANIMATION, ART, BUSINESS AND FINANCE, CAREERS AND EMPLOYMENT, COMPUTERS AND COMPUTING, DIGITAL MUSIC, EDUCATION, ENTERTAINMENT, ENVIRONMENT, FITNESS, GOVERNMENT & POLITICS, HEALTH AND MEDICINE, HISTORY, HUMOR, INTERNET, INTERNET SECURITY, LAW, MUSEUMS, NEWS SOURCES, REFERENCE, ROBOTICS, SCIENCE, SHOPPING, SOCIETY, SPORTS, TRAVEL, UNCLASSIFIED, WEATHER, ZINES

BACK TO TOP

SHELLY CASHMAN SERIES.

2.47

LEARN IT ONLINE   CHAPTER 2

6 Scavenger Hunt

Click the number 6 button. Print a copy of the Scavenger Hunt page; use this page to write down your answers as you search the Web. Submit your completed page to your instructor.

7 Who Wants to Be a Computer Genius?

Click the number 7 button to find out if you are a computer genius. Directions on how to play the game will display. When you are ready to play, click the Play button. Submit your score to your instructor.

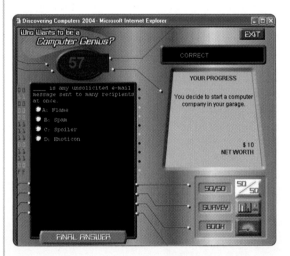

8 Wheel of Terms

Click the number 8 button to reinforce important terms you learned in this chapter by playing the Shelly Cashman Series version of this popular game. Directions on how to play the game will display. When you are ready to play, click the Play button. Submit your score to your instructor.

9 Career Corner

Click the number 9 button to display the Quintessential Careers page. Search for jobs in your state. Write a brief report on the jobs you found. Submit the report to your instructor.

10 Search Sleuth

Click the number 10 button to learn search techniques that will help make you a research expert. Submit the completed assignment to your instructor.

11 Crossword Puzzle Challenge

Click the number 11 button. Complete the puzzle to reinforce skills you learned in this chapter. Directions on how to play the game will display. When you are ready to play, click the Play button. Submit the completed puzzle to your instructor.

12 Internet Newsgroups

One of the more popular topics for Internet newsgroups is the Internet. Click the number 12 button for a list of newsgroups. Find one or more newsgroups that discuss something about the Internet. Read the newsgroup postings and briefly summarize the topic under discussion. If you like, post a reply to a message.

13 In the News

In her book, Caught in the Net, Kimberly S. Young contends that the Internet can be addictive. Young's methodology and conclusions have been questioned by several critics, but Young remains resolute. She points out that at one time, no one admitted the existence of alcoholism. Click the number 13 button and read a news article about the impact of Internet use on human behavior. What effect did the Internet have? Why? In your opinion, is the Internet's influence positive or negative? Why?

CHAPTER 2 LAB EXERCISES

◄● Previous | Next ●►

Use the Lab Exercises to gain hands-on computer experience.

■ WEB INSTRUCTIONS:

To display this page from the Web, start your browser and enter the Web address **scsite.com/dc2004/ch2/lab**.

1 Online Services

This exercise uses Windows XP procedures. Right-click the Online Services icon on the desktop and then click Open on the shortcut menu. If the Online Services icon does not exist on your desktop, locate it by clicking the Search command on the Start menu. Click the All files and folders link. Type Online Services in the All or part of the file name text box. Click the Search button and then click the Stop button when Online Services is displayed in the Search window. What online services have shortcut icons in the Online Services window? Right-click each icon and then click Properties on each shortcut menu. Click the General tab. When was each icon created? Close the dialog box and then click the Close button to close the Online Services window and, if necessary, the Search Results window.

2 Understanding Internet Properties

This exercise uses Windows XP/2000/98 procedures. Right-click an icon for a Web browser that is displayed on your desktop. Click Properties on the shortcut menu. When the Internet Properties dialog box or Netscape Properties dialog box is displayed, if necessary, click the General tab. Click the Question Mark button on the title bar and then click one of the buttons. Read the information in the pop-up window and then click the pop-up window to close it. Repeat the process for other areas of the dialog box. What new information did you learn? Click the Cancel button in the Internet Properties or Netscape Properties dialog box.

3 Dial-Up Networking Connections

This exercise uses Windows XP procedures. Click the Start button on the Windows taskbar and then click Help and Support on the Start menu. Click the Networking and the Web link in the Pick a Help topic area in the table of contents. In the Help navigation pane on the left, click Networking, and then click Dial-up

connections. In the Help topics pane on the right, click Make a dial-up connection to your workplace using a phone line. What steps are necessary to make a dial-up connection by phone line? Click the Network Connections link. What topics are listed in the Network Tasks area? Close the Network Connections window. Close the Help and Support Center window.

4 Using Help to Understand the Internet

This exercise uses Windows 2000/98 procedures. Click the Start button on the Windows taskbar and then click Help on the Start menu. Click the Contents tab. Click the Exploring the Internet book and then click the Explore the Internet topic. Click the Click here link to find out more about Internet Explorer. Answer the following questions:

- How can you update your favorite Web sites and view them at your leisure?
- How can you move around the Web faster and easier with the Explorer bar?
- How can you browse the Web safely?
- How can you view Web pages in other languages?

Close the Microsoft Internet Explorer Help window and the Windows Help window.

WEB RESEARCH CHAPTER 2

Use the Web Research exercises to learn more about the special features in this chapter.

WEB INSTRUCTIONS:

Use the link in each exercise or a search engine such as Google (google.com) to research the topic. Then, write a one-page, double-spaced report or create a presentation, unless otherwise directed below. Page numbers on which information can be found are in parentheses.

1 **Issue**   Choose one Issue from the following issues in this chapter: Who Controls the Internet? (2.04), Can You Learn It Online? (2.16), To Tax or Not to Tax Internet Purchases? (2.25), or How Expensive Is E-Mail and Internet Privacy? (2.25). Use the Web to research the issue. Discuss the issue with classmates, instructors, and friends. Address the questions that accompany the issue in a report or presentation.

2 **Apply It**   Choose one of the following Apply It features in this chapter: Connect to the Internet at High Speeds (2.05) or Send Voice Messages Via the Internet (2.32). Use the Web to gather additional information about the topic. Print two Web pages that relate to the Apply It. Detail in a report or presentation what you learned.

3 **Career Corner**   Read the Career Corner article in this chapter (2.36). Use the Web to find out more about the career. Describe the career in a report or presentation.

4 **Companies on the Cutting Edge**   Choose one of the Companies on the Cutting Edge in this chapter (2.38). Use the Web to research the company further. Explain in a report or presentation how this company has contributed to computer technology.

5 **Technology Trailblazers**   Choose one of the Technology Trailblazers in this chapter (2.39). Use the Web to research the person further. Explain in a report or presentation how this individual has affected the way people use, or think about, computers.

6 **Picture Yourself Publishing on the Web**   Read the Picture Yourself Publishing on the Web story at the beginning of this chapter (2.00). Use the Web to research publishing further. Describe in a report or presentation the ways in which you might publish on the Web.

7 **High-Tech Talk**   Read the High-Tech Talk feature in this chapter (2.37). Use the Web to find out more about the topic. Summarize in a report or presentation what you learned.

8 **Web Links**   Review the Web Link boxes found in the margins of this chapter. Visit five of the Web Link sites. Print the main Web page for each site you visit. Choose one of the Web pages and then summarize in one paragraph the content of the Web page.

9 **Looking Ahead**   Choose one of the Looking Ahead articles in this chapter: Let the Bot Shop for You (2.14) or Share Multimedia Files Easily (2.18). Use the Web to find out more about the topic. Detail in a report or presentation what you learned.

10 **FAQ**   Choose one FAQ found in this chapter. Use the Web to find out more about the topic. Summarize in one paragraph what you learned.

11 **Searching the Web**   Read the Searching Techniques and Guide to Web Sites Special Feature that follows this chapter (2.50–2.63). Select at least two sites from the list of popular Web sites and use the location given to visit the site. Use the searching techniques presented to locate and visit at least two additional Web sites on a topic of interest. Describe in a report or presentation each Web site you visited and the searching techniques you used.

12 **Making Use of the Web**   Read the Travel section of Making Use of the Web in Appendix A (A.04). Complete the Travel Web Exercises at the end of the section (A.05). Answer the questions posed in each exercise.

"Knowledge is of two kinds: we know a subject ourselves, or we know where we can find information upon it."

Samuel Johnson
(1709 – 1794)

Guide to World Wide Web Sites and Searching Techniques

The World Wide Web is an exciting and highly dynamic medium that has revolutionized the way people access information. You can display information about virtually any topic you can imagine if you know the Web address, or URL. If you do not know the URL, you must use a search tool because the Web has no bibliographic control. The Internet consists of an estimated 10 billion Web pages with dozens being added every second. Given this, finding the information you want can be a massive chore if you do not know the URL or how to use Web search tools.

To help you locate information, this special feature provides three resources: a topical list of some of the more popular Web sites, an introduction to searching techniques, and a list of popular search engines and their URLs.

Web Instructions: *To gain World Wide Web access to additional and up-to-date information regarding this special feature, start your browser and enter the Web address shown at the top of this page.*

CATEGORIES

Animation	Genealogy	Reference
Art	Government and Politics	Robotics
Business and Finance	Health and Medicine	Science
Careers and Employment	History	Shopping
Computers and Computing	Humor	Society
Digital Music	Internet	Sports
Directories	Internet Security	Travel
Education	Kid-Safe Sites	Unclassified
Entertainment	Law	Weather
Environment	Museums	Zines
Fitness	News Sources	

CATEGORY/SITE NAME	LOCATION	COMMENT
Animation		
Animation World Network	awn.com	Animation-related publishing group pertaining to all aspects of animation
RGB Gallery	hotwired.lycos.com/rgb	Art animations
Shockwave.com	shockwave.com	Cool Shockwave animations
Art		
fineArt forum	msstate.edu/fineart_online/home.html	Art plus technology net news
Louvre Museum	www.louvre.fr/louvrea.htm	Web version of Louvre Museum in Paris
The Andy Warhol Museum	Warhol.org	Famous American pop artist
WebMuseum: Leonardo da Vinci	ibiblio.org/wm/paint/auth/vinci	Works of the famous Italian artist and thinker
World Wide Arts Resources	wwar.com	Links to many art Web sites
Business and Finance		
All-Biz.com – Small Business Network	all-biz.com	Links to Web business information
BusinessWeek Online	businessweek.com	Online investing
FinanCenter®	financenter.com	Personal finance information
Lycos Finance	ragingbull.lycos.com	Lycos's financial portal
Morningstar.com	www.morningstar.com	Mutual fund Web site
MSN Money	money.msn.com	Microsoft's financial portal
PCQuote.com	pcquote.com	Free delayed stock quotes
Quicken.com	quicken.com	Personal financial advice
SiliconInvestor®	siliconinvestor.com	Stock chat for technology investors
SmartMoney	smartmoney.com	Live snapshot of the stock market
Stockgroup	stockgroup.com	Investment information and technology solutions
The Wall Street Journal Online	online.wsj.com	Financial news page
Yahoo! Finance	quote.yahoo.com	Free real-time stock quotes
Careers and Employment		
CareerBuilder	careerpath.com	Job listings from U.S. newspapers
Careermag.com	vertical.worklife.com/onlines/careermag/	Career articles and information
Job Options	joboptions.com	Searchable job database
Monster.com	monster.com	Job finder

For an updated list: scsite.com/dc2004/ch2/websites

CATEGORY/SITE NAME	LOCATION	COMMENT
Computers and Computing		
Computer companies	Insert name or initials of most computer companies before .com to find their Web sites. Examples: ibm.com, microsoft.com, dell.com	
Computer History Museum	computerhistory.org	Exhibits and history of computing
Expertcity®	expertcity.com	Live experts offer technical support
Internet.com	internet.com	E-business and technology network
MIT Media Lab	www.media.mit.edu	Information on computer trends
The Apple Museum	theapplemuseum.com	The history of the Apple computer
The PC Guide	pcguide.com	PC reference information
The Virtual Museum of Computing	vlmp.museophile.com/computing	History of computing and online computer-based exhibits
Virtual Computer Library	www.utexas.edu/computer/vcl	Information on computers and computing
ZDNet	zdnet.com	Downloads and product reviews
Digital Music		
Live Concerts	liveconcerts.com	RealMedia streamed concerts
MP3.com	mp3.com	Music files
Sonique	sonique.com	MP3 player and media products
This American Life	thislife.org	Public radio program
Directories		
555-1212.com®	555-1212.com	Online directory information service
InfoSpace	infospace.com	Directory and search engine
SuperPages.com	superpages.com	Verizon Information Services
Switchboard.com	switchboard.com	Variety of directories
WhoWhere?	whowhere.lycos.com	Lycos directory
Yahoo! People Search	people.yahoo.com	Yahoo! directory
Education		
CollegeNET	www.collegenet.com	Searchable database of thousands of colleges and universities
EdLinks	webpages.marshall.edu/~jmullens/ edlinks.html	Links to many educational Web sites
The Open University	www.open.ac.uk	Independent study courses from the U.K.
UMUC Distance Education	umuc.edu/distance	University of Maryland distance education
WiredScholar	www.wiredscholar.com	Information on financing an education

For an updated list: scsite.com/dc2004/ch2/websites

CATEGORY/SITE NAME	LOCATION	COMMENT
Entertainment		
CDNOW	cdnow.com	Search for and buy all types of music
Internet Movie Database (IMDb)	imdb.com	Movies
IUMA (Music Archive)	iuma.com	Underground music database
Mr. Showbiz	abcnews.go.com/sections/entertainment/	ABC's entertainment page
Online Classics	www.onlineclassics.com	Classical music information
Playbill® On-Line™	playbill.com	Theater news
Rock and Roll Hall of Fame	rockhall.com	Cleveland museum Web site
Environment		
EnviroLink Network	envirolink.com	Environmental information
Greenpeace	greenpeace.org	Environmental activism
EPA	epa.gov	U.S. government environmental news
Fitness		
24 Hour Fitness	24hourfitness.com	A health and fitness community
GlobalFitness.com	global-fitness.com	Health and fitness
Genealogy		
Cyndi's List	cyndislist.com	List of genealogy sites
Mormon Church	familysearch.org	Renowned Internet genealogy service
National Genealogical Society	ngsgenealogy.org	Genealogical information
Government and Politics		
CIA	cia.gov	International information about countries
Democratic National Committee	democrats.org	Democratic party news
FedWorld	fedworld.gov	Links to U.S. government Web sites
PoliSci.com	polisci.com	Politics on the Web
Republican National Committee	rnc.org	GOP party news
The Library of Congress	www.loc.gov	Variety of U.S. government information
The White House	www.whitehouse.gov	Take a tour and learn about the occupants
U.S. Census Bureau	www.census.gov	Population and other statistics
United Nations	www.un.org	Latest UN projects and information
Health and Medicine		
Centers for Disease Control and Prevention (CDC)	www.cdc.gov	How to prevent and control disease
Cornucopia of Disability Information (CODI)	codi.buffalo.edu	Resource for disability products and services
Mayo Clinic	mayoclinic.com	Diseases and conditions reference
Women's Medical Health Page	cbull.com/health.htm	Articles and links to other Web sites

For an updated list: scsite.com/dc2004/ch2/websites

CATEGORY/SITE NAME	LOCATION	COMMENT
History		
American Memory	rs6.loc.gov/amhome.html	American history
The History Channel	historychannel.com	Search any topic in history
Virtual Library History	www.ukans.edu/history/VL	Organized links to history Web sites
World History Archives	www.hartford-hwp.com/archives	Links to history Web sites
Humor		
Comedy Central	comcentral.com	Comedy TV network online
Late Show with David Letterman	cbs.com/latenight/lateshow/	Letterman's nightly show including archived Top 10 lists
Dilbert.com	dilbert.com	Humorous insights about the workplace
Ucomics.com	ucomics.com	Comic strip gallery
Internet		
Beginners' Central	northernwebs.com/bc	Beginners' guide to the Internet
Glossary of Internet Terms	matisse.net/files/glossary.html	Matisse Enzer's definitions of Internet terms
WWW Frequently Asked Questions	www.boutell.com/faq/oldfaq/index.html	Common Web questions and answers
Internet Security		
F-Secure Security Information Center	f-secure.com/virus-info/	Industry standard information source for new virus hoaxes and false alerts
Internet Security Alliance	www.isalliance.org	A Public-Private Partnership for Information Sharing and E-Security Issues
Kid-Safe Sites		
CartoonNetwork.com	cartoonnetwork.com	Interactive site for the cable network
Disney Online	disney.com	Disney's interactive site
FoxKids	foxkids.com	The Fox network's interactive site for children
Nick.com	nick.com	Nickelodeon's site for fun and games
Law		
American Bar Association	www.abanet.org	Source for legal information
Copyright Website	benedict.com	Provides copyright information
FindLaw	findlaw.com	Law resource portal
KuesterLaw	kuesterlaw.com	Technology law resource
Legal Information Institute	www.law.cornell.edu	Cornell Law School legal information

For an updated list: scsite.com/dc2004/ch2/websites

CATEGORY/SITE NAME	LOCATION	COMMENT
Museums		
Smithsonian Institution	www.si.edu	Information and links to Smithsonian museums
The National Gallery of Art, Washington, D.C.	nga.gov	Plan a visit or take an online tour
U.S. Holocaust Memorial Museum	ushmm.org	Dedicated to World War II victims
University of California Museum of Paleontology	www.ucmp.berkeley.edu	Information about dinosaurs and other exhibits
News Sources		
Cable News Network	cnn.com	CNN all-news network
CNET	cnet.com	Technology news
Newsday.com	newsday.com	All the latest information
TIME.com	time.com	Excerpts from Time-Warner magazines
USA TODAY	usatoday.com	Latest U.S. and international news
Wired News	wired.com	Wired magazine online and HotWired network
Reference		
AskERIC Virtual Library	askeric.org/Virtual	Educational resources
Ask Jeeves®	askjeeves.com	Search engine
Bartleby	bartleby.com	Reference books online
Internet Public Library	ipl.org	Literature and reference works
The New York Public Library	www.nypl.org	Extensive reference and research material
Webopedia	webopedia.com	Online dictionary and search engine
What You Need to Know About™	about.com	Search engine and portal
Robotics		
Remotebot.net	remotebot.net	Control a robot with your Netscape Web browser; interactive Robotic Museum
Robotics and Intelligent Machines Laboratory	robotics.eecs.berkeley.edu	Robotics and mechanical and electrical engineering
University of Massachusetts Robotics Information	www-robotics.cs.umass.edu/robotics.html	Robotics resource index page
Science		
American Institute of Physics	www.aip.org	Physics research information
Exploratorium	exploratorium.edu	Interactive science exhibits
Chemistry Information Service	chemie.de	List of chemistry information Web sites
Molecular Expressions: Science, Optics and You	www.micro.magnet.fsu.edu/primer/java/scienceopticsu/powersof10/index.html	Examine the Milky Way at 10 million light years from the Earth; travel space and more
National Institute for Discovery Science (NIDS)	www.nidsci.org	Research of anomalous phenomena
Solar System Simulator	space.jpl.nasa.gov	JPL's spyglass on the cosmos
The NASA Homepage	www.nasa.gov	Information about U.S. space program
The Nine Planets	www.nineplanets.org	Tour the solar system's nine planets

For an updated list: scsite.com/dc2004/ch2/websites

SPECIAL FEATURE

CATEGORY/SITE NAME	LOCATION	COMMENT
Shopping		
ActivePlaza	activeplaza.com	Online shopping mall
Amazon.com	amazon.com	Books and gifts
Barnes & Noble	bn.com	Online bookstore
BizRate	bizrate.com	Rates e-commerce Web sites
BizWeb	bizweb.com	Search for products from more than 46,000 companies
CNET Shopper	shopper.cnet.com	Computer and electronic products
CommerceNet	www.commerce.net	Nonprofit with focus on B2B e-commerce
Consumer World	consumerworld.org	Consumer information
Ebay	ebay.com	Online auctions
CarsDirect.com	www.carsdirect.com/home	Automobile buying Web site
Internet Bookshop	www.bookshop.co.uk	1.4 million titles about more than 2,000 subjects
Lands' End	landsend.com	Classic clothing for the family
Society		
Association for Computing Machinery (ACM)	acm.org	World's first educational and scientific computing society
Center for Applied Ethics	www.ethics.ubc.ca/resources/computer	Computer and information ethics resources
Center for Computing and Social Responsibility	www.ccsr.cse.dmu.ac.uk/index.html	Social and ethical impacts of information and communications technologies
Computer Professionals for Social Responsibility	cpsr.org	A public-interest alliance of computer scientists and others concerned about the impact of computer technology on society
Computers and Society	acm.org/sigcas	Special interest group within Association for Computing Machinery (ACM)
Electronic Frontier Foundation	eff.org	Protecting rights and promoting freedom
Electronic Privacy Information Center	epic.org	Links to latest news regarding privacy issues
International Center for Information Ethics (ICIE)	icie.zkm.de	An academic Web site about information ethics
International Federation for Information Processing (IFIP)	www.ifip.or.at/	Computers and social accountability
ISWorld Net Professional Ethics	http://www.iscityu.edu.hk/Research/Resources/ethics/ethics.htm	Practice of ethics in the information systems profession
Privacy.Org	privacy.org	Current privacy issues

For an updated list: scsite.com/dc2004/ch2/websites

CATEGORY/SITE NAME	LOCATION	COMMENT
Sports		
ESPN SportsZone	msn.espn.go.com/main.html	Latest sports news
NBA Basketball	nba.com	Information and links to team Web sites
NFL Football	nfl.com	Information and links to team Web sites
Sports Illustrated	sportsillustrated.cnn.com	Leading sports magazine
Travel		
CitySearch	citysearch.com	United States and international city guides
InfoHub Specialty Travel Guide	infohub.com	Worldwide travel information
Lonely Planet Online	www.lonelyplanet.com	Budget travel guides and stories
Expedia.com	expedia.com	Complete travel resource
Travelocity.com	www.travelocity.com	Online travel agency
TravelWebSM	travelweb.com	Places to stay
Unclassified		
American Singles™.com	americansingles.com	Links to dating resources
Cool Site of the Day	cool.infi.net	Different Web site each day
Famous Name Changes	www.famousnamechanges.com	Names of stars before they were stars
WebPhotos	webphotos.com	Online photo community
Where's George?	wheresgeorge.com	The Great American Dollar Bill Locator
Weather		
Intellicast	intellicast.com	International weather and skiing information
The Weather Channel	weather.com	National and local forecasts
Weather Underground	wunderground.com	Weather maps
Zines		
Rock School™	rockschool.com	Everything you need to know about being in a rock band
The AFU & Urban Legends Archive	urbanlegends.com	Urban legends
TruthOrFiction.com	truthorfiction.com	Check out the latest rumors circulating on the Web

For an updated list: scsite.com/dc2004/ch2/websites

World Wide Web Search Tools

Successful Searching

Successful searching of the Web involves two key steps:

1. Briefly describe the information you are seeking. Start by identifying the main idea or concept in your topic and determine any synonyms, alternate spellings, or variant word forms for the concept.

2. Use the brief description with a search tool to display links to pages containing the desired information.

The two most common search tools are subject directories and search engines. You use a **subject directory** by clicking through its collection of categories and subcategories until you reach the information you want. You use a **search engine** to search for a keyword. The following sections describe how to use a subject directory and a search engine.

Using a Subject Directory

A subject directory provides categorized lists of links. These categorized lists are arranged by subject and then displayed in a series of menus. Using this type of search tool, you can locate a particular topic by starting from the top and clicking links through the different levels, going from the general to the specific. Each time you click a category link, the search tool displays a page of subcategory links from which you again choose. You continue in this fashion until the search tool displays a list of Web pages on the desired topic. Browsing a subject directory requires that you make assumptions about the topic's hierarchical placement within the categorized list.

For the following example, assume you have been assigned the task of writing a research paper about Stephen King's background. The assignment requires that you include at least one Web page citation. This example uses the Yahoo! (yahoo.com) directory to locate information about Stephen King's background.

Start your browser and enter the URL yahoo.com in the Address box. When the Yahoo! home page is displayed, point to the scroll bar on the right side of the screen as shown in Figure 1.

FIGURE 1 Yahoo! home page.

Scroll down to display the Web Site Directory. Point to the Literature link below Arts & Humanities as shown in Figure 2. You point to Literature because that is the category in which Stephen King made his contributions.

FIGURE 2 Web site directory.

 Click the Literature link. When the Literature page is displayed, scroll down and point to the Authors link as shown in Figure 2. You point to Authors because Stephen King is an author. Each time you click a category link, you move closer to the topic.

FIGURE 3 Literature categories.

 Click the Authors link. When the Authors page is displayed, scroll down and point to the Horror link as shown in Figure 4. You point to Horror because that is the area of literature in which Stephen King specializes.

FIGURE 4 Authors categories.

 Scroll down and point to the King, Stephen link as shown in Figure 5.

FIGURE 5 Alphabetical listing for K.

Click the King, Stephen link. When the King, Stephen page is displayed, point to the Official Stephen King Web Presence, The link as shown in Figure 6.

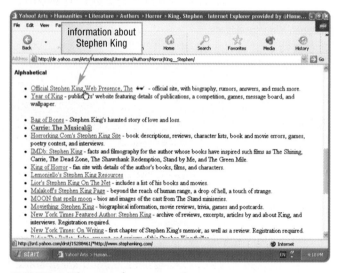

FIGURE 6 King, Stephen categories.

Click the Official Stephen King Web Presence, The link. When The Official Stephen King Web Presence page is displayed (Figure 7), one at a time, click the links. Use the browser's Back button to return to The Official Stephen King Web Presence page after viewing each page associated with a link.

FIGURE 7 The Official Stephen King Web Presence Web page.

With just a few clicks, the Yahoo! subject directory displays information about Stephen King's background. The Stephen King page in Figure 7 shows several links to pages describing his life.

The major problem with a subject directory is deciding which categories to choose as you work through the menus of links presented. For additional information about how to use the Yahoo! subject directory, click the Help link in the upper-right corner of its home page (Figure 1 on page 2.58).

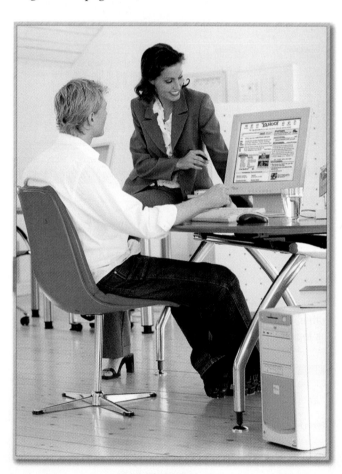

Using a Search Engine

Search engines require that you enter search text or keywords (single word, words, or phrase) that define what you are looking for, rather than clicking through menus of links. Search engines often respond with results that include thousands of links to Web pages, many of which have little or no bearing on the information you are seeking. You can eliminate the superfluous pages by carefully crafting a keyword that limits the search. The following example uses the Google search engine to search for the phrase, Stephen King quotations.

Start your browser and enter the URL `google.com` in the Address box. When the Google home page is displayed, type `stephen king quotations` in the Search text box and then point to the Google Search button as shown in Figure 8.

FIGURE 8 Google home page.

 Click the Google Search button. When the results of the search are displayed, scroll through the links and read the descriptions. Point to the Stephen King Quotations link as shown in Figure 9.

FIGURE 9 Google search results.

 Click the Stephen King Quotations link. A Web page is displayed containing links to quotations, special features awards, and other resources about Stephen King (Figure 10).

FIGURE 10 Web page containing links to information about Stephen King.

The results shown in Figure 9 include about 24,600 links to Web pages that reference Stephen King's quotations. Most search engines sequence the results based on how close the words in the keyword are to one another in the Web page titles and their descriptions. Thus, the first few links probably contain more relevant information. For additional information about how to use the Google search engine, click the Search Tips link in the upper-right corner of the results page (Figure 9).

Guidelines to Successful Searching

You can improve your Web searches by following these guidelines.

1. Use nouns as keywords, and put the most important terms first in your keyword.

2. Use the asterisk (*) to find plurals of words. For example: retriev* returns retrieves, retrieval, retriever, and any other variation.

3. Type keywords in lowercase to find both lowercase and uppercase variations.

4. Use quotation marks to create phrases so the search engine finds the exact sequence of words.

5. Use a hyphen alternative. For example, use email, e-mail.

6. Limit the search by language.

7. Use uppercase characters for Boolean operators in your search statements to differentiate between the words and operators.

8. Before you use a search engine, read its Help.

9. The Internet contains many search engines. If your search is unsuccessful with one search engine, try another.

Limiting the Search

If you enter a phrase with spaces between the keywords, most search engines return links to pages that include all of the words. Figure 11 lists some common operators, commands, and special characters you can use to refine your search.

CATEGORY OF OPERATOR	OPERATOR	KEYWORD EXAMPLES	DESCRIPTION
Boolean	AND (+)	art AND music smoking health hazards fish +pollutants +runoff	Requires both words to be in the page. No operator between words or the plus sign (+) are shortcuts for the Boolean operator AND.
	OR	mental illness OR insane canine OR dog OR puppy flight attendant OR stewardess OR steward	Requires only one of the words to be in the page.
	AND NOT (–)	auto AND NOT SUV AND NOT convertible computers–programming shakespeare–hamlet	Excludes page with the word following AND NOT. The minus sign (–) is a shortcut for the Boolean operator AND NOT.
Parentheses	( )	physics AND (relativity OR einstein) –(romeo+juliet)	Parentheses group portions of Boolean operators together.
Phrase Searching	" "	"harry potter" "19th century literature"	Requires the exact phrase within quotation marks to be in the page.
Wildcard	*	writ* clou*	The asterisk (*) at the end of words substitutes for any combination of characters.

FIGURE 11 Search engine keyword operators, commands, and special characters.

Popular Search Sites

Figure 12 contains a list of popular search sites, their URLs, and their usage in a recent study. Most of these search sites have both a search engine and subject directory. For additional information on search sites, visit searchenginewatch.com.

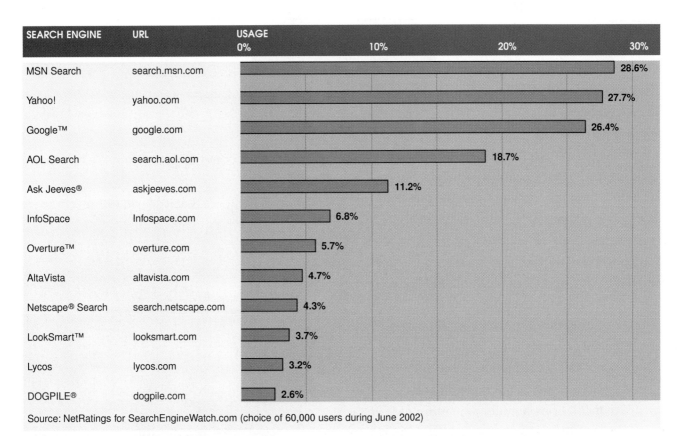

SEARCH ENGINE	URL	USAGE
MSN Search	search.msn.com	28.6%
Yahoo!	yahoo.com	27.7%
Google™	google.com	26.4%
AOL Search	search.aol.com	18.7%
Ask Jeeves®	askjeeves.com	11.2%
InfoSpace	Infospace.com	6.8%
Overture™	overture.com	5.7%
AltaVista	altavista.com	4.7%
Netscape® Search	search.netscape.com	4.3%
LookSmart™	looksmart.com	3.7%
Lycos	lycos.com	3.2%
DOGPILE®	dogpile.com	2.6%

Source: NetRatings for SearchEngineWatch.com (choice of 60,000 users during June 2002)

FIGURE 12 Popular search sites, their URLs, and a summary of their usage in a recent study. Because a Web surfer may visit more than one service, the combined totals in the search site usage study exceed 100 percent. Also, several of the search engines listed use other search engines in the list for some or all searches.

Application Software

Picture Yourself Using Software

With the morning coffee brewing, you start the computer and check e-mail. As you begin deleting the unwanted junk e-mail messages, you notice a message from your bank. This one could be important — probably related to your online banking. As you open the message, you think back when it took hours to balance a bank statement.

Today, checkbook registers are a thing of the past. Once a week, you connect to the bank and copy your personal account transactions from the bank's computer to your computer. Your computerized checkbook balance always is up to date. It shows cleared checks, ATM withdrawals, debit card transactions, and automatic payments. Bank statement reconciliations literally take minutes. The online payment feature also saves you time. Your bank automatically transfers the specified funds on a specified date from your checking account to the payees' accounts.

This e-mail message from your bank is offering an opportunity to prepare and file your taxes online. Having just received your W2, you immediately click the link in the message and sign up for the service. Next, you complete an online tax preparation form and answer some tax-related questions. As soon as you click the File Taxes button, a message displays indicating that the refund will be in your checking account within two weeks!

As you read Chapter 3, you will learn about personal finance and Web-based tax preparation software and discover other types of application software.

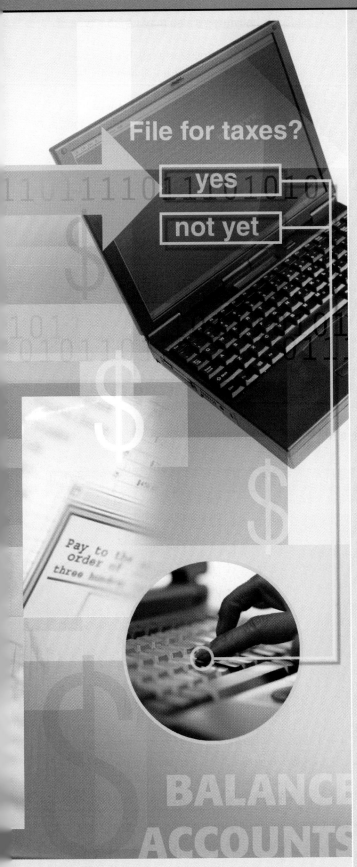

File for taxes?

yes

not yet

OBJECTIVES

After completing this chapter, you will be able to:

1. Identify the categories of application software

2. Explain ways software is distributed

3. Explain how to start and interact with application software

4. Identify the key features of widely used business programs

5. Identify the key features of widely used graphics and multimedia programs

6. Identify the key features of widely used home, personal, and educational programs

7. Identify the types of application software used in communications

8. Discuss the advantages of using application software on the Web

9. Describe the learning aids available for application software

CONTENTS

APPLICATION SOFTWARE

Application software consists of programs that perform specific tasks for users. Application software is used for a variety of reasons:

1. As a business tool
2. To assist with graphics and multimedia projects
3. To support home, personal, and educational activities
4. To facilitate communications

The table in Figure 3-1 categorizes popular types of application software by their general use. Although many types of communications software exist, the ones listed in Figure 3-1 are application software oriented. Many of these communications software are included as a part of other application or system software.

As you become proficient in your understanding of application software, it is likely that you will find yourself using software from more than one of the categories in Figure 3-1. The four categories are not mutually exclusive. That is, software listed in one category may be used in other categories. For example, software suites (business) often include e-mail

(communications) and Web page authoring software (graphics and multimedia). Although home users have educational and reference software, businesses also may use this type of software.

Application software is available in a variety of forms: packaged, custom, shareware, freeware, and public domain.

- **Packaged software** is mass produced, copyrighted retail software that meets the needs of a wide variety of users, not just a single user or company. Word processing and spreadsheet software are examples of packaged software. Packaged software is available in retail stores or on the Web. Figure 3-2 shows packaged software for purchase at one online retailer.

- **Custom software** performs functions specific to a business or industry. Sometimes a company cannot find packaged software that meets its unique requirements. In this case, the company may use a programmer to develop tailor-made custom software, which usually costs more than packaged software.

- **Shareware** is copyrighted software that is distributed free for a trial period. To use a shareware program beyond that period, you

CATEGORIES OF APPLICATION SOFTWARE

① Business	② Graphics and Multimedia	③ Home/Personal/Educational
• Word Processing	• Computer-Aided Design (CAD)	• Integrated Software (e.g., word processing, spreadsheet, database)
• Spreadsheet	• Desktop Publishing (for the Professional)	• Personal Finance
• Database	• Paint/Image Editing (for the Professional)	• Legal
• Presentation Graphics	• Video and Audio Editing	• Tax Preparation
• Personal Information Manager (PIM)	• Multimedia Authoring	• Desktop Publishing (for Personal Use)
• PDA Software	• Web Page Authoring	• Paint/Image Editing (for Personal Use)
• Software Suite (e.g., word processing, spreadsheet, presentation graphics, PIM)		• Clip Art/Image Gallery
• Project Management		• Home Design/Landscaping
• Accounting		• Educational
		• Reference
		• Entertainment

④ C o m m u n i c a t i o n s
• E-Mail • FTP • Web Browser • Newsgroup/Message Board
• Chat Room • Instant Messaging • Video Conferencing/ Telephone Calls

FIGURE 3-1 The four major categories of popular application software are outlined in this table. Many types of communications software are application software oriented. The communications software usually is bundled with other application or system software.

send a payment to the person or company who developed the program. Developers of shareware rely on the honor system, trusting users to send payment if software use extends beyond the stated trial period. In some cases, the shareware is a scaled-down version of the software, and payment entitles the user to a fully functional product.

• **Freeware** is software provided at no cost to a user by an individual or a company. Freeware is copyrighted. Thus, programmers cannot incorporate freeware into applications they intend to sell.

• **Public-domain software** also is free software, but it has been donated for public use and has no copyright restrictions. Anyone can copy or distribute public-domain software to others.

Thousands of shareware, freeware, and public-domain programs are available on the Web for users to download. Other ways to obtain copies of these programs are from the developer, a coworker, or a friend. Shareware, freeware, and public-domain programs usually have fewer capabilities than retail programs. Examples of shareware, freeware, and public-domain programs include communications programs, graphics programs, and games.

The Role of System Software

System software serves as the interface between the user, the application software, and the computer's hardware (Figure 3-3). To use application software, such as a word processing program, your computer must be running system software, specifically, an operating system. Two popular personal computer operating systems are Microsoft's Windows XP and Apple's Mac OS X.

FIGURE 3-2 Many online retailers, such as BUY.COM, have packaged software available for sale.

FIGURE 3-3 A user does not communicate directly with the computer hardware. Instead, system software is the interface between the user, the application software, and the hardware. For example, when a user instructs the application software to print, the application software sends the print instruction to the system software, which in turn sends the print instruction to the hardware.

Each time you start a computer, the operating system *loads* (copies) from the computer's hard disk into memory. Once the operating system loads, it coordinates all the activities of the computer. This includes starting application programs and transferring data among input and output devices and memory. While the computer is running, the operating system remains in memory.

Starting and Interacting with Application Software

To use application software, you must instruct the operating system to start the program. The steps in Figure 3-4 illustrate how to start and interact with the Paint program. The following paragraphs explain the steps in Figure 3-4.

FIGURE 3-4 HOW TO START AN APPLICATION

Step 1:
When you turn on a PC-compatible computer, Windows XP loads into memory and displays the desktop on the screen.

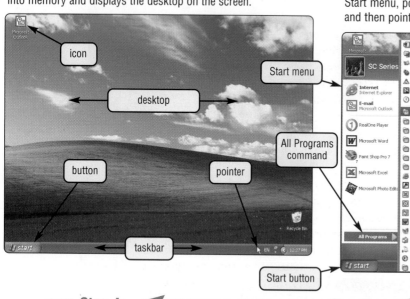

Step 2:
Click the Start button on the taskbar, point to All Programs on the Start menu, point to Accessories on the All Programs submenu, and then point to Paint on the Accessories submenu.

Step 4:
Instruct the Paint program to open a picture that is stored on the hard disk.

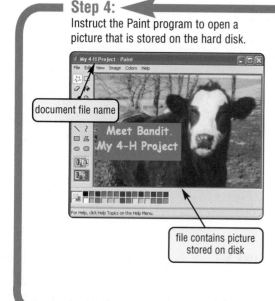

Step 3:
Click Paint. The Paint window is displayed on the desktop.

Step 5:
Instruct the Paint program to print the picture. When the Print dialog box is displayed, click the Print button.

Both the Windows XP and the Mac OS X operating systems use the concept of a desktop to make the computer easier to use. The **desktop** is an on-screen work area that has a graphical user interface. Step 1 of Figure 3-4 shows icons, buttons, and a pointer on the Windows XP desktop. An **icon** is a small image displayed on the screen that represents a program, a document, or some other object. A **button** is a graphical element that you activate to cause a specific action to take place. For example, activating a button may cause a program to start. Buttons usually are rectangular or square shapes.

One way to activate a button is to click it. To **click** a button on the screen requires moving the pointer to the button and then pressing and releasing a button on the mouse (usually the left mouse button). The **pointer** is a small symbol displayed on the screen that moves as you move the mouse. Common pointer shapes are an I-beam (I), a block arrow ( ), and a pointing hand ( ).

The Windows XP desktop contains a Start button in its lower-left corner. Using the Start button starts an application. When you click the Start button, the Start menu is displayed on the desktop. A **menu** contains a series of commands from which you make selections. A **command** is an instruction that causes a program to perform a specific action.

The arrowhead symbol at the right edge of some menu commands indicates a submenu of additional commands is available. A *submenu* is a menu that is displayed when you point to a command on a previous menu. As illustrated in Step 2 of Figure 3-4, when you click the Start button and point to the All Programs command on the Start menu, the All Programs submenu is displayed. Pointing to the Accessories command on the All Programs submenu displays the Accessories submenu. Notice that the Accessories submenu contains several programs such as Calculator, Paint, and WordPad.

Programs sometimes display shortcut menus. A *shortcut menu* is a list of commonly used commands for completing a task related to the current activity or selected item. To display a shortcut menu in Windows applications, for example, you click the right mouse button.

To start a program, you can click its program name on a menu or submenu. This action instructs the operating system to start the application, which means the program's instructions load from a storage medium (such as a hard disk) into memory. For example, when you click Paint on the Accessories submenu, Windows loads the Paint program instructions from the computer's hard disk into memory.

Once loaded in memory, a program is displayed in a window on the desktop (Step 3 of Figure 3-4). A **window** is a rectangular area of the screen that displays a program, data, and/or information. The top of a window has a **title bar**, which is a horizontal space that contains the window's name.

With the program loaded, you can create a new file or open an existing one. A *file* is a named collection of stored data, instructions, or information. A file can contain text, images, audio, and video. To distinguish among various files, each file has a file name. A *file name* is a unique combination of letters of the alphabet, numbers, and other characters that identifies a file. For example, the picture of a 4-H member's steer may have the file name My 4-H Project. The title bar of the document window usually displays a document's file name. Step 4 of Figure 3-4 shows the contents of the file, My 4-H Project, displaying in the Paint window. The file contains an image photographed with a digital camera and edited to contain text.

In some cases, when you instruct a program to perform an activity such as printing, the program displays a dialog box. A *dialog box* is a special window that provides information, presents available options, or requests a response. For example, a Print dialog box includes many printing options such as specifying a different printer, printing all or part of a document, or printing multiple copies. Dialog boxes, such as the one in Step 5 of Figure 3-4, often contain option buttons, text boxes, check boxes, and command buttons. Clicking the Print button, for example, instructs the computer to print the picture.

FAQ 3-1

Will a document print like it looks on a screen?

Yes, because most current application software is *WYSIWYG* (*what you see is what you get*). The application software embeds invisible codes around the text and graphics, which instructs the computer how to present the information.

For more information about WYSIWYG, visit the Discovering Computers 2004 FAQ Web page (**scsite.com/dc2004/faq**). Click WYSIWYG below Chapter 3.

QUIZ YOURSELF 3-1

To check your knowledge of application software categories, ways software is distributed, and starting and interacting with application software, visit the Discovering Computers 2004 Quiz Yourself Web page (**scsite.com/dc2004/quiz**). Click Objectives 1 – 3 below Chapter 3.

BUSINESS SOFTWARE

Business software is application software that assists people in becoming more effective and efficient while performing their daily business activities. Business software includes programs such as word processing, spreadsheet, database, presentation graphics, personal information manager, PDA software, software suite, project management, and accounting. Figure 3-5 lists popular programs for each of these categories. Read Issue 3-1 for a related discussion.

The following sections discuss the features and functions of business software. Word processing and spreadsheet software have a heavier emphasis because of their predominant use.

ISSUE 3-1

Is It Ethical to Copy Software?

With purchased software, users typically are allowed to install the program on one computer and legally make one copy of the software for backup purposes. Despite the law, many people make several copies, either to share or to sell. In a recent survey, more than 50 percent of respondents admitted that they had illegally copied, or would illegally copy, software. Microsoft, a leading software manufacturer, estimates that almost 25 percent of software in the United States has been copied illegally. Illegally copied software costs the software industry more than $10 billion a year in lost revenues. Some of the reasons that people give for copying software illegally include: software prices are too high, copying software harms no one, software often is copied for educational or other altruistic purposes, you can do whatever you want with software you have purchased, and everyone copies software. Do you think it is ethical to copy purchased software and install it on your computer and also a friend's computer? Why or why not? Can you counter the reasons people give for copying software illegally? How? Would you copy software illegally? Why or why not?

For more information about illegally copying software, visit the Discovering Computers 2004 Issues Web page (**scsite.com/dc2004/issues**). Click Issue #1 below Chapter 3.

BUSINESS SOFTWARE

Application Software	Popular Programs
Word Processing	• Microsoft® Word • Sun StarOffice™ Writer • Corel® WordPerfect®
Spreadsheet	• Microsoft® Excel • Sun StarOffice™ Calc • Corel® Quattro® Pro
Database	• Microsoft® Access • Sun StarOffice™ Base • Corel® Paradox® • Microsoft® Visual FoxPro • Oracle • MySQL™
Presentation Graphics	• Microsoft® PowerPoint • Sun StarOffice™ Impress • Corel® Presentations™
Personal Information Manager (PIM)	• Microsoft® Outlook • Corel®CENTRAL™ • Lotus Organizer • Microsoft® Pocket Outlook • Palm Desktop
PDA Software	• Microsoft® Pocket Word • Microsoft® Pocket Excel • Microsoft® Pocket Outlook • Ultrasoft™ Money • QuickNotes®
Software Suite	• Microsoft® Office • Sun StarOffice™ • OpenOffice.org • Corel® WordPerfect® Office • Lotus SmartSuite
Project Management	• Microsoft® Project • Primavera® SureTrak Project Manager • Macromedia Sitespring™
Accounting	• Intuit QuickBooks® • Peachtree Complete® Accounting

FIGURE 3-5 Popular business software programs.

WEB LINK 3-1

Sun StarOffice™

Visit the Discovering Computers 2004 WEB LINK page (**scsite.com/dc2004/weblink**). Click Sun StarOffice™ below Chapter 3.

Word Processing Software

Word processing software is one of the more widely used types of application software. **Word processing software**, sometimes called a *word processor*, allows users to create and manipulate documents containing mostly text and sometimes graphics (Figure 3-6). Millions of people use word processing software every day to develop documents such as letters, memos, reports, fax cover sheets, mailing labels, newsletters, and Web pages.

Word processing software has many features to make documents look professional and visually appealing. Some of these features include the capability of changing the shape and size of characters in headlines and headings, changing the color of characters, and organizing text into newspaper-style columns. When using colors for characters, however, they will print as black or gray unless you have a color printer.

Most word processing software allows users to incorporate many types of graphical images into documents. One popular type of graphical image is clip art. **Clip art** is a collection of drawings, diagrams, maps, and photographs that you can insert into documents. In Figure 3-6, a user inserted a clip art image of flowers into the document. Word processing software usually includes public-domain clip art. You can find additional public-domain and proprietary images on the Web or purchase them on CD or DVD.

All word processing software provides at least some basic capabilities to help users create and modify documents. Defining the size of the paper on which to print and specifying the *margins*, that is, the portion of the page outside the main body of text, including the top, the bottom, and both sides of the paper, are examples of some of these capabilities. If you type text that extends beyond the right page margin, the word processing software automatically positions text at the beginning of the next line. This feature, called *wordwrap*, allows users to type words in a paragraph continually without pressing the ENTER key at the end of each line. When you modify paper size or margins, the word processing software automatically re-wraps text so it fits within the adjusted paper size and margins.

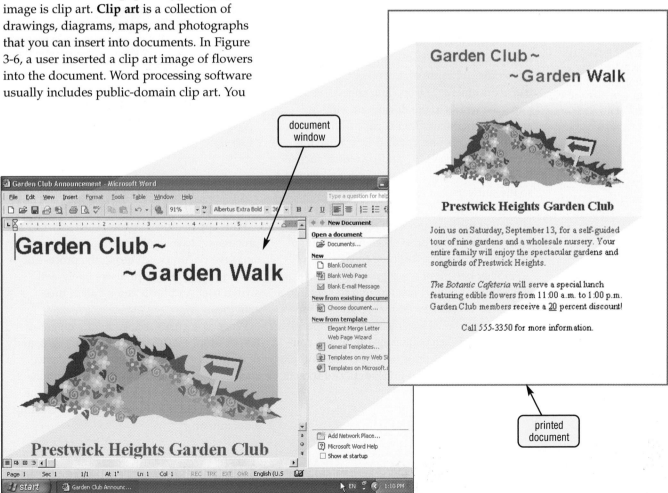

FIGURE 3-6 Word processing software enables users to create professional and visually appealing documents.

As you type more lines of text than can display on the screen, the top portion of the document moves upward, or scrolls, off the screen. *Scrolling* is the process of moving different portions of the document on the screen into view.

A major advantage of using word processing software is that users easily can change what they have written. For example, a user can insert, delete, or rearrange words, sentences, paragraphs, or entire sections. The find or *search* feature allows you to locate all occurrences of a certain character, word, or phrase. This feature in combination with the *replace* feature allows you to substitute existing characters or words with new ones. For example, the word processing software can locate the word, spectacular, in an announcement and replace it with the word, stunning.

Current word processing programs also have a feature that automatically corrects errors and makes word substitutions as users type text. For instance, when you type the abbreviation asap, the word processing software replaces the abbreviation with the phrase, as soon as possible.

Word processing software includes a *spelling checker*, which reviews the spelling of individual words, sections of a document, or the entire document. The spelling checker compares the words in the document with an electronic dictionary that is part of the word processing software. You can customize the electronic dictionary by adding words such as companies, streets, cities, and personal names, so the software can check the spelling of those words too. Many word processing programs allow you to check the spelling of a whole document at one time, or to check the spelling of individual words as you type them.

Another benefit of word processing software is the ability to insert headers and footers into a document. A *header* is text that appears at the top of each page, and a *footer* is text that appears at the bottom of each page. Page numbers, company names, report titles, and dates are examples of items often included in headers and footers.

In addition to these basic features, most current word processing programs provide numerous additional features. The table in Figure 3-7 lists these additional features. Read Issue 3-2 for a related discussion.

▓ ISSUE 3-2

Personal or Processed?

Two schools of thought exist when it comes to composing and editing documents on the computer. Many people believe word processing software greatly improves the quality of written material by making it easier to create, modify, and print documents. Some word processing software even provides templates — patterns or blueprints for a document — that produce reports, memos, cover letters, resumes, legal pleadings, and even personal letters. Yet, other people argue word processing software has become a crutch, making it unnecessary for students to learn the rudiments and nuances of languages. These people feel that much of the work produced with word processing software is processed, lacking the beauty, artistry, and individuality of great literature. What effect do you think word processing software has on written communications? Does it result in better work or simply more correct mediocre work? What word processing features, if any, do you feel are particularly valuable to an author?

For more information about word processing and the writing process, visit the Discovering Computers 2004 Issues Web page (**scsite.com/dc2004/issues**). Click Issue #2 below Chapter 3.

Developing a Document

With application software, such as word processing, users create, edit, format, print, and save documents. During the process of developing a document, users likely will switch back and forth among all of these activities.

When you **create** a document, you enter text or numbers, insert graphical images, and perform other tasks using an input device such as a keyboard, mouse, or microphone. If you are using Microsoft Word to design an announcement, for example, you are creating a document.

ADDITIONAL WORD PROCESSING FEATURES

AutoCorrect	As you type words, the AutoCorrect feature corrects common spelling errors. AutoCorrect also corrects capitalization mistakes.
AutoFormat	As you type, the AutoFormat feature automatically applies formatting to the text. For example, it automatically numbers a list or converts a Web address to a hyperlink.
Collaboration	Collaboration includes discussions and online meetings. Discussions allow multiple users to enter comments in a document and read and reply to each other's comments. Through an online meeting, users share documents with others in real time and view changes as they are being made.
Columns	Most word processing software can arrange text in two or more columns to look like a newspaper or magazine. The text from the bottom of one column automatically flows to the top of the next column.
Grammar Checker	The grammar checker proofreads documents for grammar, writing style, sentence structure errors, and reading statistics.
Macros	A *macro* is a sequence of keystrokes and instructions that a user records and saves. When you want to execute the same series of instructions, execute the macro instead.
Mail Merge	Creates form letters, mailing labels, and envelopes.
Smart Tags	*Smart tags* automatically appear on the screen when you perform a certain action. For example, typing an address causes a smart tag to appear. Clicking this smart tag provides options to display a map of the address or driving directions to or from the address.
Tables	Tables organize information into rows and columns. In addition to evenly spaced rows and columns, some word processing programs allow you to draw tables of any size or shape.
Templates	A *template* is a document that contains the formatting necessary for a specific document type. Templates usually exist for memos, fax cover sheets, and letters.
Thesaurus	With a thesaurus, a user looks up a synonym (word with the same meaning) for a word in a document.
Tracking Changes	If multiple users work with a document, the word processing software highlights or color-codes changes made by various users.
Voice Recognition	With some word processing programs, users can speak into the computer's microphone and watch the spoken words display on the screen as they talk. With these programs, users edit and format the document by speaking or spelling an instruction.
Web Page Development	Most word processing software allows users to create, edit, format, and convert documents to display on the World Wide Web.

FIGURE 3-7   Many additional features are included with word processing software.

To **edit** a document means to make changes to its existing content. Common editing tasks include inserting, deleting, cutting, copying, and pasting. In Microsoft Word, inserting text indicates that you are adding text to a document, such as listing a facility's hours of operation. Deleting text means that you are removing text or other content.

To cut involves removing a portion of the document and storing it in a temporary storage location, sometimes called a *clipboard*.

A clipboard also contains items that you copy (duplicate) in a document. *Pasting* is the process of transferring an item from a clipboard to a specific location in a document.

When users **format** a document, they change its appearance. Formatting is important because the overall look of a document significantly can affect its ability to communicate clearly. Examples of formatting tasks are changing the font, font size, or font style of text.

A **font** is a name assigned to a specific design of characters. Two basic types of fonts are serif and sans serif. A *serif font* has short decorative lines at the upper and lower ends of the characters. Sans means without. Thus, a *sans serif font* does not have the short decorative lines at the upper and lower ends of the characters. Times New Roman is an example of a serif font. Arial is an example of a sans serif font.

Font size indicates the size of the characters in a particular font. Font size is gauged by a measurement system called points. A single *point* is about 1/72 of an inch in height. The text you are reading in this book is 10 point. Thus, each character is about 5/36 (10/72) of an inch in height. A *font style* adds emphasis to a font. Bold, italic, and underline are examples of font styles. Figure 3-8 illustrates fonts, font sizes, and font styles.

During the process of creating, editing, and formatting a document, the computer holds it in memory. To keep the document for future use requires that you save it. When you **save** a document, the computer transfers the document from memory to a storage medium such as a floppy disk, hard disk, or CD. Once saved, a document is permanently stored as a file on a storage medium.

It is a good practice to save frequently while working on documents. Saving at regular intervals ensures that the majority of your work will not be lost in case a power failure or other system failure occurs. Many programs have an optional AutoSave feature that automatically saves open documents at specified time intervals.

When you **print** a document, the computer sends a copy of the document to a medium such as paper. One of the benefits of word processing software is the ability to print the same document many times, with each copy looking just like the first. Instead of printing a document and physically distributing it, some users e-mail the document to others on a network such as the Internet. Either they include the document as part of an e-mail message, or they attach the electronic document (file) to an e-mail message.

?FAQ 3-2

How does the computer know which application software was used to save a file?

When the computer saves a file, it often appends an extension to the file name. The *extension* indicates the file type. For example, files saved in Microsoft Word have an extension of .doc and files saved in Paint have an extension of .bmp.

For more information about file types and extensions, visit the Discovering Computers 2004 FAQ Web page (**scsite.com/dc2004/faq**). Click File Types and Extensions below Chapter 3.

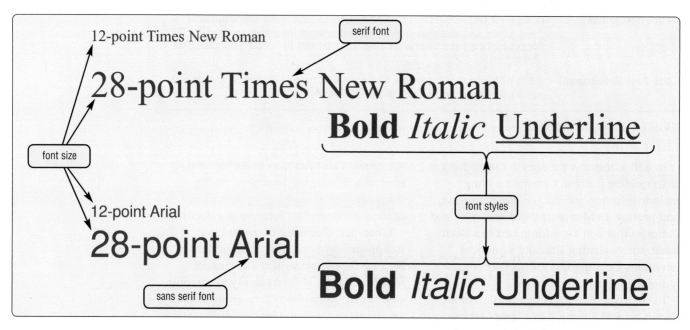

12-point Times New Roman

serif font

28-point Times New Roman

Bold *Italic* Underline

font size

12-point Arial

28-point Arial

sans serif font

font styles

Bold *Italic* Underline

FIGURE 3-8   The Times New Roman and Arial fonts are shown in two font sizes and a variety of font styles.

VOICE RECOGNITION Many programs support **voice recognition**, which is the computer's capability of distinguishing spoken words. Users can speak into the computer's microphone or into a headset attached to the computer and watch the spoken words display on the screen as they talk. This feature, also called *speech recognition*, allows users to edit and format a document by speaking or spelling instructions.

Figure 3-9 illustrates how Microsoft Word recognizes dictated words and voice commands.

Voice recognition programs available for purchase allow users to speak into their existing application software. Popular voice recognition programs include IBM ViaVoice and Dragon NaturallySpeaking. The voice input section of Chapter 5 discusses voice recognition in more depth.

WEB LINK 3-2

Voice Recognition Software

Visit the Discovering Computers 2004 WEB LINK page (**scsite.com/dc2004/weblink**). Click Voice Recognition below Chapter 3.

FIGURE 3-9   HOW TO DICTATE WORDS AND COMMANDS

Step 1:
Say, "dictation" to instruct the program you will be dictating and then say, "apartment for rent".

Step 2:
Say, "voice command" to instruct the program you will be issuing commands and then say, "center".

Step 3:
Say, "select line". Say "all caps" and then say, "font".

Step 4:
Say, "Impact" and then say, "font size".

Step 5:
Say, "forty eight" and then say, "font color".

Step 6:
Say, "blue" and then say, "end".

Spreadsheet Software

Spreadsheet software is another widely used type of application software. **Spreadsheet software** allows users to organize data in rows and columns and perform calculations on the data. These rows and columns collectively are called a *worksheet*. For years, people used pencil and gridded accounting paper to organize data and do calculations by hand. In an electronic worksheet, you organize data in the same manner, and the computer does the calculations more quickly and accurately (Figure 3-10). Because of the logical approach that spreadsheet software has for organizing data, many people use this software to organize and present non-financial data, as well as financial data.

As with word processing software, most spreadsheet software has basic features to help users create, edit, and format worksheets.

Spreadsheet software also incorporates many of the features found in word processing software such as macros, checking spelling, changing fonts and font sizes, adding colors, tracking changes, recognizing voice input, inserting audio and video clips, and converting an existing spreadsheet document into a format for the World Wide Web.

The following sections describe the features unique to most spreadsheet programs.

SPREADSHEET ORGANIZATION A spreadsheet file is similar to a notebook with up to 255 related individual worksheets. Data is organized vertically in columns and horizontally in rows on each worksheet. Each worksheet typically has 256 columns and 65,536 rows. One or more letters identify each column, and a number identifies each row. The column letters begin with A and end with IV. The row numbers begin with 1 and end with 65,536. Only a small fraction of these columns and rows are displayed on the screen at one time. As with word processing software, scrolling through the worksheet displays different parts of it on the screen.

A *cell* is the intersection of a column and row. Each worksheet has more than 16 million (256 × 65,536) cells in which you can enter data. The spreadsheet software identifies cells by the column and row in which they are located. For example, the intersection of column B and row 6 is referred to as cell B6. As shown in Figure 3-10, cell B6 contains the number, $72,631,781, which represents the electricity revenue for the first quarter.

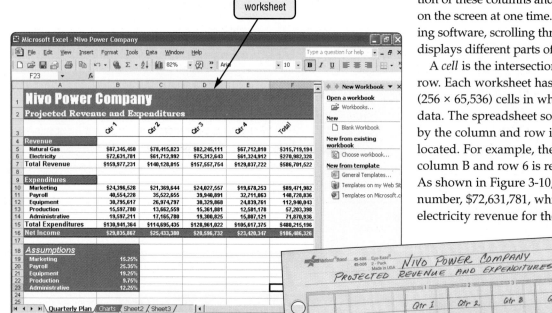

FIGURE 3-10 With spreadsheet software, you create worksheets that contain data arranged in rows and columns.

Cells may contain three types of data: labels, values, and formulas. The text, or *label*, entered in a cell identifies the worksheet data and helps organize the worksheet. Using descriptive labels, such as Total Revenue and Total Expenditures, helps make a worksheet more meaningful.

CALCULATIONS Many of the worksheet cells shown in Figure 3-10 contain a number that can be used in a calculation, called a *value*. Other cells, however, contain formulas that generate values. A *formula* performs calculations on the data in the worksheet and displays the resulting value in a cell, usually the cell containing the formula. When creating a worksheet, you can enter your own formulas. In Figure 3-10, for example, cell B15 could contain the formula =B10+B11+B12+B13+B14 to calculate the projected total expenditures for the first quarter. A much more efficient way to sum the contents of cells, however, is to use a function, which is built into the spreadsheet software.

A *function* is a predefined formula that performs common calculations such as adding the values in a group of cells or generating a value such as the time or date. For example, instead of using the formula =B10+B11+B12+B13+B14 to calculate the projected total expenditures for the first quarter, using the function =SUM(B10:B14) totals the contents of cells B10 through B14. Figure 3-11 lists functions commonly included in spreadsheet programs.

RECALCULATION One of the more powerful features of spreadsheet software is its capability of recalculating the rest of the worksheet when data in a worksheet changes. To appreciate this capability, consider what happens each time you change a value in a manual worksheet. You must erase the old value, write in a new value, erase any totals that contain calculations based on the changed value, and then recalculate these totals and enter the new results. When working with a manual worksheet, accurately making changes and updating the affected values can be time-consuming and may result in new errors.

Making changes in an electronic worksheet is much easier and faster. When you enter a new value to change data in a cell, any value affected

SPREADSHEET FUNCTIONS

Financial	
FV (rate, number of periods, payment)	Calculates the future value of an investment
NPV (rate, range)	Calculates the net present value of an investment
PMT (rate, number of periods, present value)	Calculates the periodic payment for an annuity
PV (rate, number of periods, payment)	Calculates the present value of an investment
RATE (number of periods, payment, present value)	Calculates the periodic interest rate of an annuity
Date and Time	
DATE	Returns the current date
NOW	Returns the current date and time
TIME	Returns the current time
Mathematical	
ABS (number)	Returns the absolute value of a number
INT (number)	Rounds a number down to the nearest integer
LN (number)	Calculates the natural logarithm of a number
LOG (number, base)	Calculates the logarithm of a number to a specified base
ROUND (number, number of digits)	Rounds a number to a specified number of digits
SQRT (number)	Calculates the square root of a number
SUM (range)	Calculates the total of a range of numbers
Statistical	
AVERAGE (range)	Calculates the average value of a range of numbers
COUNT (range)	Counts how many cells in the range have numeric entries
MAX (range)	Returns the maximum value in a range
MIN (range)	Returns the minimum value in a range
STDEV (range)	Calculates the standard deviation of a range of numbers
Logical	
IF (logical test, value if true, value if false)	Performs a test and returns one value if the result of the test is true and another value if the result is false

FIGURE 3-11 Functions typically found in spreadsheet software.

by the change is updated automatically and instantaneously. In Figure 3-10 on page 3.12, for example, if you change the electricity revenue for the first quarter from $72,631,781 to $77,631,781, the total revenue in cell B7 automatically changes from $159,977,231 to $164,977,231.

Spreadsheet software's capability of recalculating data also makes it a valuable budgeting, forecasting, and decision making tool. Most spreadsheet software includes a *what-if analysis* feature, where you change certain values in a spreadsheet to reveal the effects of those changes.

CHARTING　Another standard feature of spreadsheet software is *charting*, which depicts the data in graphical form. A visual representation of data through charts often makes it easier for users to see at a glance the relationship among the numbers.

Three popular chart types are line charts, column charts, and pie charts. Figure 3-12 shows examples of these charts that were plotted from the data in Figure 3-10 on page 3.12. A *line chart* shows a trend during a period of time, as indicated by a rising or falling line. For example, a line chart could show the expenditures for the four quarters. A *column chart*, also called a *bar chart*, displays bars of various lengths to show the relationship of data. The bars can be horizontal, vertical, or stacked on top of one another. For example, a column chart might show the expenditure breakdown by quarter, with each bar representing a different expenditure. A *pie chart*, which has the shape of a round pie cut into slices, shows the relationship of parts to a whole. For example, you might use a pie chart to show the percentage each expenditure category contributed to the total expenditure.

WEB LINK 3-3

Spreadsheet Software

Visit the Discovering Computers 2004 WEB LINK page (**scsite.com/dc2004/ weblink**). Click Spreadsheet Software below Chapter 3.

FIGURE 3-12　Three basic types of charts provided with spreadsheet software are line charts, column charts, and pie charts. The line chart, column chart, and pie chart shown here were created from the data in the worksheet in Figure 3-10 on page 3.12.

Database Software

A **database** is a collection of data organized in a manner that allows access, retrieval, and use of that data. In a manual database, you might record data on paper and store it in a filing cabinet. With a computerized database, such as the one shown in Figure 3-13, the computer stores the data in an electronic format on a storage medium such as a floppy disk or hard disk.

Database software is application software that allows users to create, access, and manage a database. Using database software, you can add, change, and delete data in a database; sort and retrieve data from the database; and create forms and reports using the data in the database.

With most popular personal computer database software programs, a database consists of a collection of tables, organized in rows and columns. Each row, called a *record*, contains data about a given person, product, object, or event. Each column, called a *field*, contains a specific category of data within a record.

The Condo Management database shown in Figure 3-13 consists of two tables: a Condo table and an Owner table. The Condo table contains ten records (rows), each storing data about one condo unit. The condo data is grouped into eight fields (columns): unit number, bedrooms, bathrooms, sleeps, powder room, linens, weekly rate, and owner id (identification). The bedrooms field, for instance, contains the number of bedrooms in the condo unit. The Condo and Owner table relate to one another through a common field, Owner Id.

Users run queries to retrieve data. A *query* is a request for specific data from the database. For example, a query might request a list of the condos that have two or more bathrooms. Database software can take the results of a query and present it in a window on the screen, called a *form*, or send it as a report to the printer.

FIGURE 3-13 This database contains two tables: one for Condo and one for Owner. The Condo table has 10 records and 8 fields; the Owner table has 4 records and 8 fields.

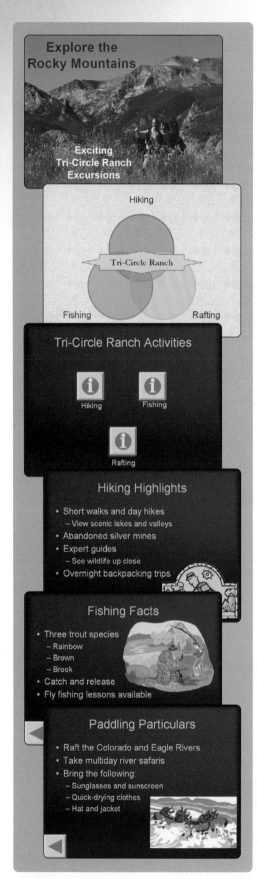

FIGURE 3-14 This presentation created with presentation graphics software consists of six slides.

Presentation Graphics Software

Presentation graphics software is application software that allows users to create visual aids for presentations to communicate ideas, messages, and other information to a group. The presentations can be viewed as slides, sometimes called a *slide show*, that display on a large monitor or on a projection screen (Figure 3-14).

Presentation graphics software typically provides a variety of predefined presentation formats that define complementary colors for backgrounds, text, and graphical accents on the slides. This software also provides a variety of layouts for each individual slide such as a title slide, a two-column slide, and a slide with clip art, a chart, a table, or animation. In addition, you can enhance any text, charts, and graphical images on a slide with 3-D and other special effects such as shading, shadows, and textures.

When building a presentation, users can set the slide timing so the presentation automatically displays the next slide after a preset delay. Presentation graphics software allows you to apply special effects to the transition between each slide. One slide, for example, might fade away slowly as the next slide is displayed.

To help organize the presentation, you can view thumbnail versions of all the slides in slide sorter view (Figure 3-15). *Slide sorter view* presents a screen view similar to how 35mm slides look on a photographer's light table. The slide sorter allows users to arrange the slides in any order.

Presentation graphics software typically includes a clip gallery that provides images, pictures, video clips, and audio clips to enhance multimedia presentations. Users with an artistic ability can create their own graphics using paint/image editing software (discussed later in the chapter) and then *import* (bring in) the graphics into the slide. Once clip art

FIGURE 3-15 Slide sorter view shows a thumbnail version of each slide. Using an input device, such as a mouse or keyboard, users can rearrange the slides to change the sequence of the presentation.

images or graphics are inserted or imported, they can be moved, resized, rotated, cropped, or altered in many ways.

You can view or print a finished presentation in a variety of formats. An *outline* includes only the text from each slide such as the slide title and the key points (Figure 3-16a). *Audience handouts* include images of two or more slides on a page, for distribution to audience members (Figure 3-16b). Speakers sometimes print a notes page to help them deliver the presentation. A *notes page* shows an image of the slide along with any additional notes a presenter wants to see while discussing a topic or slide (Figure 3-16c).

Presentation graphics software incorporates some of the features found in word processing software such as checking spelling, formatting, recognizing voice input, and converting an existing slide show into a format for the World Wide Web.

WEB LINK 3-4

Presentation Graphics Software

Visit the Discovering Computers 2004 WEB LINK page (**scsite.com/dc2004/ weblink**). Click Presentation Graphics Software below Chapter 3.

Figure 3-16a (outline)

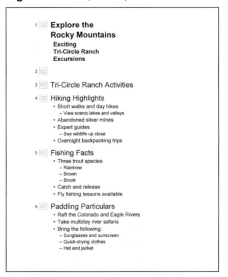

Figure 3-16b (audience handout)

Figure 3-16c (notes page)

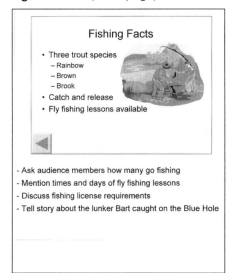

FIGURE 3-16 In addition to viewing the presentation as slides, presentation graphics software allows users to print the presentation as an outline, as audience handouts, or as notes pages for the speaker.

Personal Information Managers

A **personal information manager (PIM)** is application software that includes an appointment calendar, address book, notepad, and other features to help users organize personal information. The appointment calendar allows you to schedule activities for a particular day and time. With the address book, you can enter and maintain names, addresses, and telephone numbers of customers, coworkers, family members, and friends. Instead of writing notes on a piece of paper, you can use the notepad to record ideas, reminders, and other important information. With a PIM, you can take information previously tracked in a weekly or daily calendar, and organize and store it on your computer.

Most PDAs today include, among many other features, PIM functionality. Using a PDA, you can synchronize, or coordinate information so that both device and computer have the latest version of the information (Figure 3-17).

FIGURE 3-17 With most PDAs, you can synchronize or transfer PIM information from the PDA to a personal computer, so the updated list of appointments, addresses, and other important information always is available.

? FAQ 3-3

How does information transfer between a PDA and a personal computer?

Some transfer wirelessly; that is, you hold one end of the PDA near a specified area on the computer. With others, you insert the PDA into a cradle, which has a cable that plugs into the computer, or connect the PDA to the computer directly with a cable.

For more information about PDA synchronizing, visit the Discovering Computers 2004 FAQ Web page (**scsite.com/dc2004/faq**). Click PDA Synchronizing below Chapter 3.

PDA Software

In addition to PIM software, a huge variety of software is available for PDAs. Although some PDAs have software built in, most have the capability of accessing software on miniature storage media such as memory cards. The software on memory cards allows PDA users to create documents, take notes, manage budgets and finances, create slide shows, view and edit photographs, read electronic books, plan travel routes, and play games. For additional information about available software for PDAs, read the PDA Software feature that follows Chapter 5. Read Looking Ahead 3-1 for a look at the next generation of accessing software on PDAs and other mobile devices.

🔲 LOOKING AHEAD 3-1

3G Wireless Service Developing

Mobile communications service in the United States is undergoing a series of upgrades. The third-generation (*3G*) standard is available in Asia and parts of Europe, but U.S. service has been developing slowly.

3G service features enhanced data transfer capability so files download more quickly to handheld computers and PDAs. In Japan, consumers eagerly use 3G service to download songs and video clips, shop, bank, and share digital images.

In the United States, Verizon and AT&T Wireless are developing 3G networks and increasing their coverage. As hardware supporting the 3G standard is manufactured, demand for this service is expected to grow as an alternative method of remotely accessing the Internet and computer networks.

For a look at the next generation of accessing software on PDAs and other mobile devices, visit the Discovering Computers 2004 Looking Ahead Web page (**scsite.com/dc2004/looking**). Click Looking Ahead #1 below Chapter 3.

Software Suite

A **software suite** is a collection of individual programs sold as a single package. When installing the software suite, you install the entire collection of programs at once instead of installing each one individually. Business software suites typically include the following programs: word processing, spreadsheet, e-mail, and presentation graphics. Two of the more widely used software suites are Microsoft® Office XP and Sun StarOffice™.

Software suites offer two major advantages: lower cost and ease of use. Buying a collection of programs in a software suite usually costs significantly less than purchasing them individually. Software suites provide ease of use because the programs within a software suite normally use a similar interface and share features such as clip art and checking spelling. Once you learn how to use one program in the software suite, you are familiar with the interface of the other programs in the software suite. For example, once you learn how to print using the software suite's word processing program, you can apply the same skill to the spreadsheet and presentation graphics programs in the software suite.

Project Management Software

Project management software allows a user to plan, schedule, track, and analyze the events, resources, and costs of a project (Figure 3-18). Project management software helps users track, control, and manage project variables, allowing them to complete a project on time and within budget. A general contractor, for example, might use project management software to manage a home-remodeling job to schedule carpenters, electricians, painters, and other subcontractors. A publisher might use it to coordinate the production of a textbook.

Accounting Software

Accounting software helps companies record and report their financial transactions (Figure 3-19). With accounting software, business users perform accounting activities related to the general ledger, accounts receivable, accounts payable, purchasing, invoicing, and payroll functions. Accounting software also enables users to write and print checks, track checking account activity, and update and reconcile balances on demand.

? FAQ 3-4

What are the various Microsoft Office XP software suites?

All Office XP software suites include Word (word processing), Excel (spreadsheet), and Outlook (e-mail and PIM). Office XP Standard also includes PowerPoint (presentation graphics). Office XP Professional also includes PowerPoint and Access (database). Office XP Developer also includes PowerPoint, Access, FrontPage (Web publishing), and other developer tools. Office XP Small Business also includes Publisher.

For more information about Office XP Software Suites, visit the Discovering Computers 2004 FAQ Web page (**scsite.com/dc2004/faq**). Click Office XP Software Suites below Chapter 3.

FIGURE 3-18 Project management software allows users to track, control, and manage the events, resources, and costs of a project.

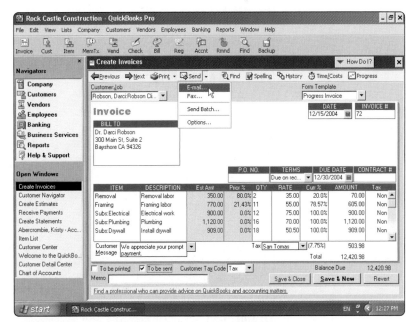

FIGURE 3-19 Accounting software helps companies record and report their financial transactions.

Newer accounting software packages support online credit checks, billing, direct deposit, and payroll services. For example, a company can deposit paychecks directly into employees' checking accounts and pay employee taxes electronically.

Some accounting software offers more complex features such as job costing and estimating, time tracking, multiple company reporting, foreign currency reporting, and forecasting the amount of raw materials needed for products. The cost of accounting software for small businesses ranges from less than one hundred to several thousand dollars. Accounting software for large businesses can cost several hundred thousand dollars.

GRAPHICS AND MULTIMEDIA SOFTWARE

In addition to business software, many people work with software designed specifically for their field of work. Power users such as engineers, architects, desktop publishers, and graphic artists often use sophisticated software that allows them to work with graphics and multimedia. This software includes computer-aided design, desktop publishing, paint/image editing, video and audio editing, animation, multimedia authoring, and Web page authoring. Figure 3-20 lists the more popular programs for each of these categories. Some of these programs incorporate user-friendly interfaces, or scaled-down versions, making it possible for the home and small business users to create documents in these programs. The following sections discuss the features and functions of this application software.

GRAPHICS AND MULTIMEDIA SOFTWARE

Application Software	Popular Programs
Computer Aided Design (CAD)	• Autodesk AutoCAD® • Quality Plans Chief Architect® • Microsoft® Visio Professional
Desktop Publishing (for the Professional)	• Adobe InDesign® • Adobe PageMaker® • Corel VENTURA™ • QuarkXPress
Paint/Image Editing (for the Professional)	• Adobe Illustrator® • Adobe Photoshop® • CorelDRAW® • Macromedia FreeHand® • Micrografx Picture Publisher® Professional • procreate™ Painter 7™
Video and Audio Editing	• Adobe Premiere® • Cakewalk® SONAR • Macromedia SoundEdit™ • Pinnacle Studio DV • Ulead MediaStudio® Pro
Multimedia Authoring	• click2learn.com ToolBook Instructor • Macromedia Authorware® • Macromedia Director® Shockwave® Studio
Web Page Authoring	• Adobe GoLive® • Adobe LiveMotion™ • Lotus FastSite • Macromedia Dreamweaver® • Macromedia Fireworks® • Macromedia Flash™ • Microsoft® FrontPage

FIGURE 3-20 Popular graphics and multimedia programs.

Computer-Aided Design

Computer-aided design (CAD) software is a sophisticated type of application software that assists a professional user in creating engineering, architectural, and scientific designs. For example, engineers create design plans for airplanes and security systems. Architects design building structures and floor plans (Figure 3-21). Scientists design drawings of molecular structures.

CAD software eliminates the laborious manual drafting that design processes can require. Using CAD software, designers make changes to a drawing or design and immediately view the results. Three-dimensional CAD programs allow designers to rotate designs of 3-D objects to view them from any angle. Some CAD software even can generate material lists for building designs.

Some manufacturers of CAD software sell a scaled-down product, designed specifically for the home user or small business user.

Desktop Publishing Software (for the Professional)

Desktop publishing (DTP) software enables professional designers to create sophisticated documents that contain text, graphics, and many colors. Professional DTP software is ideal for the production of high-quality color documents such as textbooks, corporate newsletters, marketing literature (Figure 3-22), product catalogs, and annual reports. In the past, documents of this type were created by slower, more expensive traditional publishing methods such as typesetting. Today's DTP software also allows designers to convert a color document into a format for use on the World Wide Web.

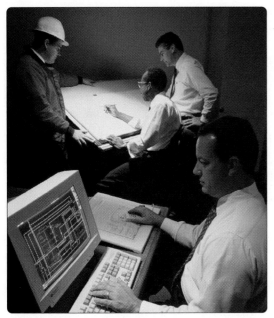

FIGURE 3-21 CAD software is sophisticated software that assists engineers, architects, and scientists in creating designs.

FIGURE 3-22 Professional designers and graphic artists use DTP software to produce sophisticated publications such as marketing literature.

❓FAQ 3-5

What prevents me from opening some files on the Web that contain company literature and brochures?

Some companies save documents on the Web, such as brochures, using the Adobe® PDF format. This is so readers do not need to have the same program the company used to create the document. To view and print a PDF file, simply download the free Adobe Acrobat® Reader® software from Adobe's Web site.

For more information about Adobe Acrobat Reader, visit the Discovering Computers 2004 FAQ Web page (**scsite.com/dc2004/faq**). Click Adobe Acrobat Reader below Chapter 3.

Although many word processing programs have some of the capabilities of DTP software, professional designers and graphic artists use DTP software because it supports page layout. *Page layout* is the process of arranging text and graphics in a document on a page-by-page basis. DTP software programs include color libraries to assist in color selections for text and graphics. A *color library* is a standard set of colors used by designers and printers to ensure that colors will print exactly as specified. Designers and graphic artists can print finished publications on a color printer, take them to a professional printer, or post them on the Web.

Paint/Image Editing Software (for the Professional)

Graphic artists, multimedia professionals, technical illustrators, and desktop publishers use paint software and image editing software to create and modify graphical images such as those used in DTP documents and Web pages. **Paint software**, also called *illustration software*, allows users to draw pictures, shapes, and other graphical images with various on-screen tools

such as a pen, brush, eyedropper, and paint bucket. **Image editing software** provides the capabilities of paint software and also includes the ability to modify existing images (Figure 3-23). Modifications can include adjusting or enhancing image colors, and adding special effects such as shadows and glows. This software often has photo editing tools, allowing users to retouch photographs. Read Issue 3-3 for a related discussion.

FIGURE 3-23   With image editing software, artists create and modify any type of graphic image.

ISSUE 3-3

Should What We See Be What We Get?

Today, many commercial artists, photojournalists, and creators of cartoons, book covers, and billboards use paint and image editing software. With this software, artists can convert photographs to a digital form that can be colorized, stretched, squeezed, texturized, or otherwise altered. They can import graphics files and manipulate the images in ways that previously were unachievable. For example, you can add clouds to a blue sky, manipulate a picture of a group of people so that it looks like they are standing in front of the Great Pyramids of Egypt, or even remove a person from a picture altogether. The National Press Photographers Association endorses the following: "As [photo] journalists we believe the guiding principle of our profession is accuracy; therefore, we believe it is wrong to alter the content of a photograph in any way, electronically or in the darkroom, that deceives the public." Do you agree with this guideline? Should professional graphic artists be able to alter photographs or other existing illustrations with paint and image editing software? Is it ethical? Is altering someone else's photograph a copyright issue?

For more information about paint and image editing software and photograph altering, visit the Discovering Computers 2004 Issues Web page (**scsite.com/dc2004/issues**). Click Issue #3 below Chapter 3.

Video and Audio Editing Software

Video editing software (Figure 3-24) allows users to modify a segment of a video, called a clip. For example, you can reduce the length of a video clip, reorder a series of clips, or add special effects such as words that move horizontally across the screen. Video editing software typically includes audio editing capabilities.

Audio editing software lets users modify audio clips and produce studio-quality soundtracks. Audio editing software usually includes *filters*, which are designed to enhance audio quality. For example, a filter might remove a distracting background noise from the audio clip.

Some operating systems include audio editing and video editing capabilities. These operating systems give the home user the ability to edit home movies and share clips on the Web.

FIGURE 3-24   With video editing software, users modify video images.

Multimedia Authoring Software

Multimedia authoring software allows users to combine text, graphics, audio, video, and animation into an interactive application (Figure 3-25). With this software, users control the placement of text and images and the duration of sounds, video, and animation. Once created, multimedia presentations often take the form of interactive computer-based presentations or Web-based presentations designed to facilitate learning, demonstrate product functionality, and elicit direct-user participation. Training centers, educational

FIGURE 3-25   Multimedia authoring software allows you to create dynamic presentations that include text, graphics, video, sound, and animation.

institutions, and online magazine publishers all use multimedia authoring software to develop interactive applications. These applications may be available on a CD or DVD, over a local area network, or via the Internet.

Web Page Authoring Software

Web page authoring software helps users of all skill levels create Web pages that include graphical images, video, audio, animation, and other special effects. In addition, many Web page authoring programs allow users to organize, manage, and maintain Web sites.

Application software programs, such as Microsoft Word and Excel, often include Web page authoring features. This allows home users to create basic Web pages using application software they already own. For more sophisticated Web pages, users work with Web page authoring software. Many Web page developers also use multimedia authoring software along with, or instead of, Web page authoring software for Web page development.

FAQ 3-6

How do I know which program to buy?

Many companies offer downloadable *trial versions* of their software that allow you to use the software free for a limited time. Try a few. Read computer magazines and Web sites for reviews of various products.

For more information about trial versions, visit the Discovering Computers 2004 FAQ Web page (**scsite.com/dc2004/faq**). Click Trial Versions below Chapter 3.

QUIZ YOURSELF 3-2

To check your knowledge of the types and features of business programs and graphics/multimedia programs, visit the Discovering Computers 2004 Quiz Yourself Web page (**scsite.com/dc2004/quiz**). Click Objectives 4 – 5 below Chapter 3.

SOFTWARE FOR HOME, PERSONAL, AND EDUCATIONAL USE

A large amount of application software is designed specifically for home, personal, and educational use. Most of the programs in this category are relatively inexpensive, often priced less than one hundred dollars. Figure 3-26 lists popular software programs for many of these categories. The following sections

PROGRAMS FOR HOME/PERSONAL/EDUCATIONAL USE

Application Software	Popular Programs
Integrated Software	• Microsoft® Works
Personal Finance	• Intuit Quicken® • Microsoft® Money
Legal	• Broderbund Family Lawyer® • Kiplinger's Home & Business Attorney • Kiplinger's WILLPower™ • Quicken Lawyer
Tax Preparation	• H&R Block Kiplinger TaxCut® • Quicken TurboTax®
Desktop Publishing (for Personal Use)	• Broderbund The Print Shop® Pro Publisher™ • Microsoft® Publisher
Paint/Image Editing (for Personal Use)	• Adobe PhotoDeluxe® • Broderbund PrintMaster® • Broderbund The Print Shop® • Corel PHOTO-PAINT® • Jasc® Paint Shop Pro® • Microsoft® Picture It! Photo • Micrografx Picture Publisher • Sun StarOffice™ Draw • Ulead PhotoImpact
Clip Art/Image Gallery	• Corel GALLERY™ • Nova Development Art Explosion®
Home Design/Landscaping	• Broderbund 3D Home Design Suite • Broderbund 3D Home Architect® • Broderbund 3D Home Landscape Designer • Quality Plans 3D Home Architect • Quality Plans Complete LandDesigner
Reference	• American Heritage Talking Dictionary Classic • Microsoft® Encarta® • Microsoft® Streets & Trips • Rand McNally StreetFinder • Rand McNally TripMaker

FIGURE 3-26 Many popular software programs are available for home, personal, and educational use.

discuss the features and functions of this application software.

Integrated Software

Integrated software combines application software such as word processing, spreadsheet, and database into a single, easy-to-use package. Many computer vendors install Microsoft Works, a widely used type of integrated software, on new computers sold to home users.

As with a software suite, the programs within integrated software use a similar interface and share some common features. Once you learn how to use one program in the integrated software, you are familiar with the interface in the other programs.

The programs in integrated software usually are available only through the integrated software; that is, you cannot purchase them individually. These programs typically do not have all the capabilities of business application software such as Microsoft Word and Microsoft Excel. Integrated software thus is less expensive than a more powerful software suite. For many home users, however, the capabilities of an integrated software program more than meet their needs. Word processing typically is the most widely used program in integrated software.

Personal Finance Software

Personal finance software is a simplified accounting program that helps home users and small office/home office users balance their checkbooks, pay bills, track personal income and expenses, track investments, and evaluate financial plans (Figure 3-27). Personal finance software helps determine where, and for what purpose, you are spending money so you can manage your finances. Reports can summarize transactions by category (such as dining), by payee (such as the electric company), or by time (such as the last two months).

Most of these programs offer a variety of online services, which require access to the Internet. For example, users can track investments online, compare insurance rates from leading insurance companies, and bank online. **Online banking** offers access to account balances, provides bill paying services, and includes copies of monthly transactions from the bank's computer into your computer. Additionally, you can download monthly transactions and statements from the Web directly into your computer.

Most personal finance software includes financial planning features, such as analyzing home and personal loans, preparing income taxes, and managing retirement savings. Other features include managing home inventory and setting up budgets.

WEB LINK 3-5

Personal Finance Software

Visit the Discovering Computers 2004 WEB LINK page (**scsite.com/dc2004/ weblink**). Click Personal Finance Software below Chapter 3.

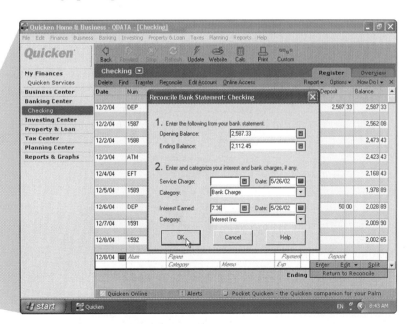

FIGURE 3-27 Many home users work with personal finance software to assist them with balancing their checkbooks and paying bills.

Legal Software

Legal software assists in the preparation of legal documents and provides legal information to individuals, families, and small businesses (Figure 3-28). Legal software provides standard contracts and documents associated with buying, selling, and renting property; estate planning; marriage and divorce; and preparing a will or living trust. By answering a series of questions or completing a form, the legal software tailors the legal document to specific needs.

Once the legal document is created, you can file the paperwork with the appropriate agency, court, or office; or take the document to your attorney for his or her review and signature. Before using one of these software programs to create a document, you may want to check with your local bar association for its legality.

FIGURE 3-28 Legal software provides legal information to individuals, families, and small businesses and assists in record keeping and the preparation of legal documents.

Tax Preparation Software

Tax preparation software guides individuals, families, or small businesses through the process of filing federal taxes (Figure 3-29). These software programs forecast tax liability

FIGURE 3-29 Tax preparation software guides individuals, families, or small businesses through the process of filing federal taxes.

and offer money-saving tax tips, designed to lower your tax bill. After you answer a series of questions and complete basic forms, the software creates and analyzes your tax forms to search for missed potential errors and deduction opportunities.

Once the forms are complete, you can print any necessary paperwork, and then they are ready for filing. Some tax preparation programs also allow you to file your tax forms electronically. Read Apply It 3-1 for more information.

APPLY IT 3-1

Easing a Taxing Part of Life

President Abraham Lincoln established the first U.S. income tax in 1862 to help fund Civil War expenses. Incomes between $600 and $10,000 were charged 3 percent, and incomes above $10,000 were charged 5 percent. Today, some individuals may pay 39 percent of their income to Uncle Sam.

This chore is somewhat more palatable by *e-filing*, or using tax software and the Internet to file federal and state returns electronically. More than one-third of all taxpayers use tax preparation Web sites, such as TurboTax for the Web, to guide them step by step through the process. With tax professionals available to answer questions in a chat room or via e-mail, many taxpayers use this easy-to-use and relatively inexpensive tax preparation service.

Some companies provide electronic W2 forms to employees, making e-filing even easier. The Internal Revenue Service (IRS) allows electronic transfer of funds from taxpayers' bank accounts if taxes are owed and for direct deposit of refunds, sometimes in as few as 10 days.

Data security and privacy are two e-filing concerns. Most IRS-approved tax preparation Web sites secretly code tax return data while it transmits to the IRS. These sites also have strict confidentiality policies regarding personal data privacy.

For more information about using the Internet to file taxes, visit the Discovering Computers 2004 Apply It Web page (**scsite.com/dc2004/apply**). Click Apply It #1 below Chapter 3.

Desktop Publishing Software (for Personal Use)

Instead of using professional DTP software (as discussed earlier in this chapter), many home and small business users utilize much simpler, easy-to-understand DTP software designed for smaller-scale desktop publishing projects (Figure 3-30). **Personal DTP software** helps users create newsletters, brochures, advertisements, postcards, greeting cards, letterhead, business cards, banners, calendars, logos, and Web pages.

Personal DTP software programs provide hundreds of thousands of graphical images. You also can import your own digital photographs into the documents. These programs typically guide you through the development of a document by asking a series of questions, offering numerous predefined layouts, and providing standard text you can add to documents. In some programs, as you enter text, the personal DTP software checks your spelling. Then, you can print a finished publication on a color printer or post it on the Web.

Many personal DTP programs also include paint/image editing software and photo editing software.

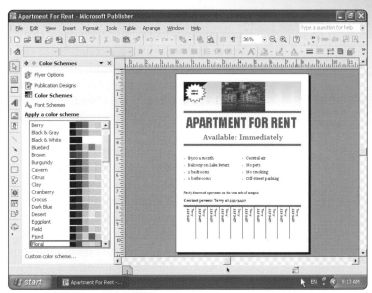

FIGURE 3-30 With Microsoft Publisher, home and small business users can create professional looking publications such as this flyer with tear-offs.

Paint/Image Editing Software (for Personal Use)

Personal paint/image editing software provides an easy-to-use interface, usually with more simplified capabilities than its professional counterpart, including functions tailored to meet the needs of the home and small business user.

As with the professional versions, personal paint software includes various simplified tools that allow you to draw pictures, shapes, and other images. Personal image editing software provides the capabilities of paint software and the ability to modify existing graphics. These products also include many templates to assist you in adding an image to documents such as greeting cards, banners, calendars, signs, labels, business cards, and letterhead (Figure 3-31).

One popular type of image editing software, called **photo editing software**, allows users to edit digital photographs by removing red-eye, erasing blemishes, restoring aged photos, adding special effects, or creating electronic photo albums. When you purchase a digital camera, it usually includes photo editing software. You can print edited photographs on labels, calendars, business cards, and banners; or post them on a Web page. Some photo editing software allows users to send digital photographs to an online print service, which will send high-resolution printed images through the postal service. Many online print services have a photo community where users can post photographs on the Web for others to view.

WEB LINK 3-6

Personal DTP Software

Visit the Discovering Computers 2004 WEB LINK page (**scsite.com/dc2004/ weblink**). Click Personal DTP Software below Chapter 3.

FAQ 3-7

How do pictures get into the computer from a digital camera?

Most digital cameras save pictures onto miniature storage media, such as a memory card. By inserting the memory card into a card reader attached to the computer, users can access images the same way they access files on a disk drive. With some cameras, pictures also can transfer along a cable that connects the camera to the computer.

For more information about digital imaging, visit the Discovering Computers 2004 FAQ Web page (**scsite.com/ dc2004/faq**). Click Digital Imaging below Chapter 3.

FIGURE 3-31 Home users can purchase affordable paint/image editing programs that enable them to include personal pictures and graphics in many different types of documents.

WEB LINK 3-7

Microsoft® Design Gallery Live

Visit the Discovering Computers 2004 WEB LINK page (**scsite.com/dc2004/ weblink**). Click Microsoft® Design Gallery Live below Chapter 3.

Clip Art/Image Gallery

Application software often includes a **clip art/image gallery**, which is a collection of clip art and photographs. Some applications have links to additional clips available on the Web (Figure 3-32). You also can purchase clip art/ image gallery software that contains thousands of images.

In addition to clip art, many clip art/image galleries provide fonts, animations, sounds, video clips, and audio clips. You can use the images, fonts, and other items from the clip art/image gallery in all types of documents, including word processing, desktop publishing, spreadsheet, and presentation graphics.

FIGURE 3-32 Application software often includes a built-in clip art/image gallery that has links to the Web for additional images.

FIGURE 3-33 Home design/ landscaping software helps users design or remodel a home, deck, or landscape.

Home Design/ Landscaping Software

Homeowners or potential homeowners can use **home design/landscaping software** to assist them with the design, remodeling, or improvement of a home, deck, or landscape (Figure 3-33). Home design/ landscaping software includes hundreds of predrawn plans that you can customize to meet your needs. Once designed, many home design/landscaping programs print a material list outlining costs and quantities for the entire project.

Educational and Reference Software

Educational software is software that teaches a particular skill. Educational software exists for just about any subject, from learning how to type to learning how to cook. Preschool to high school learners use educational software to assist them with subjects such as reading and math or to prepare them for class or college entry exams. Educational software often includes games and contents to make the learning experience more fun.

Many educational programs use a computer-based training approach. **Computer-based training (CBT)**, also called computer-aided instruction (CAI), is a type of education in which students learn by using and completing exercises with instructional software. CBT typically consists of self-directed, self-paced instruction on a topic. Athletes, for example use CBT programs to learn the intricacies of baseball, football, soccer, tennis, and golf. The military uses CBT simulations to train pilots to fly in various conditions and environments (Figure 3-34). Schools use CBT to teach students math, language, and software skills.

FIGURE 3-34 A soldier practices flight patterns using a CBT flight simulation program.

Reference software provides valuable and thorough information for all individuals (Figure 3-35). Popular reference software includes encyclopedias, dictionaries, health/medical guides, and travel directories. Read Looking Ahead 3-2 for a look at software for teachers.

FIGURE 3-35 Reference software provides valuable and thorough information for all types of users. This reference software shows text you can read about snakes and includes a variety of pictures, videos, and links to the Web.

LOOKING AHEAD 3-2

Plagiarism Software Detects Cheating

Term paper Web sites provide complete papers on a vast number of topics. Professors, however, have tools to help them detect these plagiarized papers easily and quickly.

A variety of Web sites, such as Plagiarism.org, have databases of papers found on the term paper Web sites.

Professors upload suspected papers to these Web sites, at which computers attempt to match the phrases and paragraphs with text in the database documents. The Web sites then return an originality report highlighting text that may have been copied.

As the plagiarism services become easier to use and less expensive, many professors are expected to submit every paper their students write to these Web services. The objective and reliable results ultimately are expected to help deter plagiarism.

For a look at the next generation of plagiarism-detection software, visit the Discovering Computers 2004 Looking Ahead Web page (**scsite.com/dc2004/looking**). Click Looking Ahead #2 below Chapter 3.

Entertainment Software

Entertainment software for personal computers includes interactive games, videos, and other programs designed to support a hobby or provide amusement and enjoyment. For example, you might use entertainment software to play games, make a family tree (Figure 3-36), compose music, or fly an aircraft.

FIGURE 3-36 Entertainment software, such as Family Tree Maker, can provide hours of recreation.

WEB LINK 3-8

Entertainment Software

Visit the Discovering Computers 2004 WEB LINK page (**scsite.com/dc2004/weblink**). Click Entertainment Software below Chapter 3.

APPLICATION SOFTWARE FOR COMMUNICATIONS

One of the main reasons people use computers is to communicate and share information with others. Some communications software is considered system software because it works with hardware and transmission media. Other communications software performs specific tasks for users, and thus, is considered application software. Chapter 2 presented a variety of application software for communications, which are summarized in the table in Figure 3-37. Read Issue 3-4 for a related discussion.

▨ ISSUE 3-4

Is Someone Watching You?

A recent survey indicates that more than 75 percent of Fortune 500 companies routinely monitor employees' e-mail and Web browsing habits. About one company in four has fired an employee based on its discoveries. Some companies even use automated software that searches e-mail messages for derogatory language. One unidentified woman, for example, was fired for using her office e-mail to complain about her boss. Although she felt her e-mail conversations were private and would not be monitored, she learned, to her chagrin, that she was wrong. Do you think that employers have the right to monitor e-mail? Why or why not? If you knew that a fellow employee criticized the company through the e-mail system, would you tell your boss? What if you heard the same employee planning a theft of company products? At what point do you refuse to get involved?

For more information about employee monitoring, visit the Discovering Computers 2004 Issues Web page (**scsite.com/dc2004/issues**). Click Issue #4 below Chapter 3.

APPLICATION SOFTWARE FOR COMMUNICATIONS

E-Mail
- Transmission of messages and files via a network such as the Internet
- Requires an e-mail program
  - Integrated in many software suites, integrated software, and operating systems
  - Available free at portals on the Web
  - Included with paid Internet access service
  - Can be purchased separately from retailers

FTP
- Method of uploading and downloading files with other computers and on the Internet
- Download may require an FTP program; upload usually requires an FTP program
  - Integrated in some operating systems
  - Available for download on the Web for a small fee
  - Can be purchased separately from retailers

Web Browser
- Allows users to access and view Web pages on the Internet
- Requires a Web browser program
  - Integrated in some operating systems
  - Available for download on the Web free or for a fee
  - Included with paid Internet access service

Newsgroup/Message Board
- Online area where users have written discussions
- Newsgroup may require a newsreader program
  - Integrated in some operating systems, e-mail programs, and Web browsers
  - Available for download on the Web, usually at no cost
  - Included with some paid Internet access services
  - Built into some Web sites

Chat Room
- Real-time, online typed conversation
- Requires chat client software
  - Integrated in some operating systems, e-mail programs, and Web browsers
  - Available for download on the Web, usually at no cost
  - Included with some paid Internet access services
  - Built into some Web sites

Instant Messaging
- Real-time exchange of messages or files with another online user
- Requires instant messenger software
  - Integrated in some operating systems
  - Available for download on the Web, usually at no cost
  - Included with some paid Internet access services

Video Conferencing/Telephone Calls
- Meeting/conversation between geographically separated people who use a network such as the Internet to transmit audio and video
- Requires a microphone, speakers, and a video camera attached to your computer
- Requires video conferencing software, which is included with some digital video cameras

FIGURE 3-37 A summary of application software for home and business communications.

APPLICATION SOFTWARE ON THE WEB

As discussed earlier in this chapter, users can purchase application software from a software vendor, retail store, or Web-based business. Users typically install purchased application software onto a computer before they run it. Installed software has two disadvantages: (1) it requires disk space on your computer and (2) it can be costly to upgrade as vendors release new versions. As an alternative, some home and business users opt to use products on the Web. Read Apply It 3-2 for more information.

A **Web application** is application software that exists on a Web site. These Web application sites often store personal data and information at their sites.

To access a Web application, a user simply visits the Web site that offers the program. Some Web sites provide free access to the program. For example, one site creates a map and driving directions when a user enters a starting and destination point (Figure 3-38).

Other Web sites allow you to use the program free and pay a fee when a certain action occurs. For example, you can prepare your tax return free using TurboTax for the Web, but if you elect to print it or file it electronically, you pay a minimal fee.

Some companies provide free software to use or download. Figure 3-39 shows OpenOffice.org, a free business software suite. Microsoft's Web applications, called *.NET*, enable users to access software created for the .NET platform from any type of device or computer that can connect to the Internet.

✓ APPLY IT 3-2

Obtaining Application Software

Shop until you drop is not necessarily the best method for acquiring application software. Rather than having software stacked on store shelves, today's marketplace offers options to suit differing needs and budgets.

Downloading software from the Internet is a convenient option that usually is less expensive than purchasing software from a store shelf. Downloading is a relatively easy process that only requires users to have Internet access. Users with higher-speed Internet connections, such as DSL and cable television Internet services, experience much faster download times than those with dial-up access. Occasionally, the service fails during the download. Some consumers do not use this option because vendors usually require buyers to enter personal (e.g., name and telephone number) and credit card information online.

Another alternative is subscribing to and using Web-based software, where the latest version of the software is available on the Web. Users access Web-based software anywhere from any computer or device, as long as it has an Internet connection. Web-based software is a convenient choice for the mobile user. Web-based businesses usually store users' data and information on their computer. For this reason, users concerned with data security may shy away from this option.

For more information about software purchasing, downloading, and subscribing, visit the Discovering Computers 2004 Apply It Web page (**scsite.com/dc2004/apply**). Click Apply It #2 below Chapter 3.

🖱 WEB LINK 3-9

Web Applications

Visit the Discovering Computers 2004 WEB LINK page (**scsite.com/dc2004/weblink**). Click Web Applications below Chapter 3.

FIGURE 3-38 This Web site creates a map and provides directions between a starting and destination point.

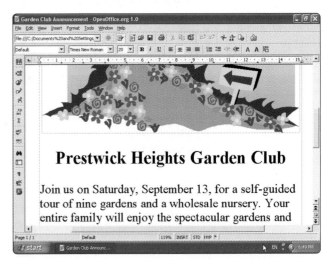

FIGURE 3-39 OpenOffice.org is a free suite that consists of word processing, spreadsheet, presentation graphics, and drawing programs.

Application Service Providers

Storing and maintaining programs can be a costly investment for businesses. Thus, some have elected to outsource one or more facets of their information technology (IT) needs to an application service provider. An *application service provider* (*ASP*) is a third-party organization that manages and distributes software and services on the Web. That is, instead of installing the software on your computer, you run the programs from the Internet.

The five categories of ASPs are:

1. *Enterprise ASP*: customizes and delivers high-end business applications, such as finance and database
2. *Local/Regional ASP*: offers a variety of software applications to a specific geographic region
3. *Specialist ASP*: delivers applications to meet a specific business need, such as human resources or project management
4. *Vertical Market ASP*: provides applications for a particular industry, such as construction, health care, or retail
5. *Volume Business ASP*: supplies prepackaged applications, such as accounting, to businesses

Despite the advantages, companies may wait to outsource to an ASP until they have faster Internet connections. A variety of payment schemes exist. Some rent use of the application on a monthly basis or charge based on the number of user accesses. Others charge a one-time fee.

Many Web sites offer WBT to the general public. Such training covers a wide range of topics, from how to change a flat tire to creating documents in Word (Figure 3-40). Many of these Web sites are free. Others require registration and payment to take the complete Web-based course.

WBT often is combined with other materials for distance learning courses. **Distance learning (DL)** is the delivery of education at one location while the learning takes place at other locations. DL courses provide time, distance, and place advantages for students who live far from a college campus or work full time. These courses enable students to attend class from anywhere in the world and at times that fit their schedules. Many national and international companies offer DL training. These training courses eliminate the costs of airfare, hotels, and meals for centralized training sessions.

WBT companies often specialize in providing instructors with the tools for preparation, distribution, and management of DL courses. These tools enable instructors to create rich, educational Web-based training sites and allow the students to interact with a powerful Web learning environment. Through the training site, students can check their progress, take practice tests, search for topics, send e-mail, and participate in discussions and chats. The appeal of these products is they generally are quite easy to learn and use for both the instructors and the students.

Web-Based Training

Web-based training (*WBT*) is a type of CBT (computer-based training) that uses Internet technology and consists of application software on the Web. Similar to CBT, WBT typically consists of self-directed, self-paced instruction on a topic. WBT is popular in business, industry, and schools for teaching new skills or enhancing existing skills of employees, teachers, or students. When using a WBT product, students actively become involved in the learning process instead of passive recipients of information.

WEB LINK 3-10

Web-Based Training
Visit the Discovering Computers 2004 WEB LINK page (**scsite.com/dc2004/ weblink**). Click Web-Based Training below Chapter 3.

FIGURE 3-40 Web-based training, such as the Training Online Manager™ (TOM), is designed so students can choose learning activities that complement their learning styles.

LEARNING AIDS AND SUPPORT TOOLS FOR APPLICATION SOFTWARE

Learning how to use application software effectively involves time and practice. To assist in the learning process, many programs provide online Help, Web-based Help, and wizards (Figure 3-41).

Online Help is the electronic equivalent of a user manual. It usually is integrated into a program. Online Help provides assistance that help users increase productivity and reduce frustrations by minimizing the time spent learning how to use application software.

In most programs, a function key or a button on the screen starts the Help feature. When using a program, you can use the Help feature to ask a question or access the Help topics in subject or alphabetical order. Often the Help is *context-sensitive*, meaning that the Help information relates to the current task being attempted.

Most online Help also links to Web sites that offer *Web-based help*, which provide updates and more comprehensive resources to respond to technical issues about software. These Web sites often have an *FAQ* (frequently asked questions) list to help you find answers to common questions. Some Web sites contain chat rooms, in which a user can talk directly with a technical support person or join a conversation with other users who may be able to answer questions or solve problems.

In many cases, online Help has replaced the user manual altogether. Most software developers no longer include user manuals with the software. If you want to learn more about the software program from a printed manual, however, many books are available to help you learn to use the features of personal computer application programs.

Figure 3-41a (online Help)

Figure 3-41b (Web-based Help)

Figure 3-41c (wizard)

FIGURE 3-41 Many programs include online Help, Web-based help, and wizards.

These books typically are available in bookstores and software stores (Figure 3-42).

A **wizard** is an automated assistant that helps a user complete a task by asking questions and then automatically performing actions based on the responses. Many software applications include wizards. For example, word processing software uses wizards to help you create memorandums, meeting agendas, fax cover sheets, flyers, letters, and resumes.

Spreadsheet software includes chart and function wizards. Database software has form and report wizards.

Many colleges and schools provide training on several of the applications discussed in this chapter. If you would like more direction than is provided in online Help, Web-based Help, wizards, and trade books, contact your local school for a list of class offerings.

FIGURE 3-42 Bookstores often sell trade books to help you learn to use the features of personal computer application software.

QUIZ YOURSELF 3-3

To check your knowledge of the types and features of home, personal, educational, and communications programs, Web applications, and software learning aids, visit the Discovering Computers 2004 Quiz Yourself Web page (**scsite.com/dc2004/quiz**). Click Objectives 6 – 9 below Chapter 3.

CHAPTER SUMMARY

This chapter illustrated how to start and use application software. It then presented an overview of a variety of business software, graphics and multimedia software, home/personal/educational software, and communications software. The chapter identified various Web applications. Finally, learning aids and support tools for application software programs were presented.

Help Desk Specialist

Career Corner

A Help Desk specialist position is an entryway into the information technology (IT) field. A *Help Desk specialist* deals with problems in hardware, software, or communications systems. Job requirements may include the following:

- Solve procedural and software questions both in person and over the telephone
- Develop and maintain Help Desk operations manuals
- Assist in training new Help Desk personnel

Usually, a Help Desk specialist must be knowledgeable about the major software packages in use. Entry-level positions primarily answer calls from people with questions. Other positions provide additional assistance and assume further responsibilities, often demanding greater knowledge and problem-solving skills that can lead to more advanced positions in the IT field. Help Desk specialist is an ideal position for people who must work irregular hours, because many companies need support people to work evenings, weekends, or part-time.

Educational requirements are less stringent than they are for other jobs in the computer field. In some cases, a high school diploma is sufficient. Advancement requires a minimum of a two-year degree, while management generally requires a bachelor's degree in IT or a related field. Certification is another way Help Desk specialists can increase their attractiveness in the marketplace. Entry-level salaries average $30,000 per year. Managers average between $42,000 and $50,000.

To learn more about the field of Help Desk specialist as a career, visit the Discovering Computers 2004 Careers Web page (**scsite.com/dc2004/careers**). Click Help Desk Specialist.

HIGH-TECH TALK

Infection and Delivery: How Computer Viruses Work

Melissa. Monkey. Concept. Nimda. Like the common cold, tons of variations of computer viruses exist. A *virus* is a potentially damaging program that affects a computer negatively by altering the way the computer works without a user's knowledge or permission. Unlike the biological viruses that cause the common cold, people create computer viruses. To create a virus, an unscrupulous programmer must code and then test the virus code to ensure the virus can replicate itself, conceal itself, monitor for certain events, and then deliver its *payload* — the destructive event or prank the virus was created to deliver. Despite the many variations of viruses, most have two phases to their execution: infection and delivery.

To start the infection phase, the virus must be activated. Today, the most common way viruses spread is by people running infected programs disguised as e-mail attachments. During the infection phase, viruses typically perform three actions:

1. First, a virus replicates by attaching itself to program files. A *macro virus* hides in the macro language of an application, such as Microsoft Word. A *boot sector virus* targets the master boot record and executes when the computer boots up. A *file virus* attaches itself to program files. The file virus, Win32.Hatred, for example, replicates by first infecting Windows executable files for the Calculator, Notepad, Help, and other applications on the hard disk. The virus then scans the computer to locate .exe files on other drives and stores this information in the system registry. The next time an infected file is run, the virus reads the registry and continues infecting another drive.

2. Viruses also conceal themselves to avoid detection. A *stealth virus* disguises itself by hiding in fake code sections, which it inserts within working code in a file. A *polymorphic virus* actually changes its code as it infects computers. Win32.Hatred uses both concealment techniques. The virus writes itself to the last file section, while modifying the file header to hide the increased file size. It also uses a polymorphic engine to scramble and encrypt the virus code as it infects files.

3. Finally, viruses watch for a certain condition or event and activate when that condition or event occurs. The event might be booting up the computer or hitting a date on the system clock. A *logic bomb* activates when it detects a specific condition (say, a name deleted from the employee list). A *time bomb* is a logic bomb that activates on a particular date or time. Win32.Hatred, for instance, unleashes its destruction when the computer clock hits the seventh day of any month. If the triggering condition does not exist, the virus simply replicates.

During the delivery phase, the virus unleashes its payload, which might be a harmless prank that displays a silly message — or it might be destructive, corrupting or deleting data and files. When Win32.Hatred triggers, it displays the author's message and then covers the screen with black dots. The virus also deletes several antivirus files as it infects the system. The most dangerous viruses do not have an obvious payload, instead quietly modifying files. A virus, for example, could randomly change numbers in an inventory program or introduce delays to slow a computer.

Other kinds of electronic annoyances exist, in addition to viruses. While often called viruses, worms and Trojan horse applications actually are part of a broader category called *malicious-logic programs.*

- A *worm*, such as the CodeRed or Sircam worm, resides in active memory and replicates itself over a network to infect machines, using up the system resources and possibly shutting the system down.

- A *Trojan horse* is a destructive program disguised as a real application, such as a screen saver. When a user runs a seemingly innocent program, a Trojan horse hiding inside can capture information, such as user names and passwords, from your system or open up a backdoor that allows a hacker remotely to control your computer. Unlike viruses, Trojan horses do not replicate themselves.

As with the common cold, every computer user is susceptible to a computer virus. In 1995, the chance that a virus would infect your computer was 1 in 1,000; by 2002, the odds were only 1 in 9. Even with better antivirus software, viruses are tough to avoid, as deceitful programmers craft new electronic maladies to infect your computer.

For more information about computer viruses, visit the Discovering Computers 2004 High-Tech Talk Web page (**scsite.com/dc2004/tech**) and click Computer Viruses.

COMPANIES ON THE CUTTING EDGE

Microsoft
Realizing Potential with Business Software

In 1975, *Microsoft* had three programmers, one product, and revenues of $16,000. Less than 30 years later, the software giant is one of the larger corporations in the world, employs nearly 49,000 people, offers scores of software titles, has offices in 60 countries, and has annual earnings of more than $27.5 billion. Microsoft's rapid ascent is an achievement unparalleled in the history of American business.

In 1980 Microsoft got its big break when IBM, a $30 billion dollar behemoth, asked Microsoft to provide an operating system for its new personal computer. Fortunately, Bill Gates, founder of Microsoft, was able to purchase and modify an operating system he later called MS-DOS. By 1984 Microsoft's sales rocketed to $97 million.

Microsoft did not rest. It began to develop and sell mouse units and keyboards that eventually sold by the millions. While updating its MS-DOS operating system it worked on its successor, Windows. Originally released in 1985, Windows did not take hold until Windows 3.0 was released in 1990. From that point on, Windows replaced MS-DOS as the standard operating system on personal computers. During this same period, Microsoft also developed its Office suite, which today dominates the application software market.

Considered to have a lock on the software industry, the company reinvented itself in 1995 in response to the growing Internet craze when it incorporated its newly created browser, Internet Explorer, in the Windows 95 operating system. Microsoft also invested heavily in the telecommunications area and an online service, called MSN. In less than two years, Microsoft moved from the peripheral to the vanguard of the information revolution.

Microsoft's recent efforts have focused on server operating systems for large companies, .NET software technologies for connectivity, and scaling down Windows to run on PDAs and Tablet PCs. Its most recent venture was developing the Xbox™ to compete against PlayStation 2 and GameCube™.

For more information about Microsoft, visit the Discovering Computers 2004 Companies Web page (**scsite.com/dc2004/companies**) and click Microsoft.

Apple Computer
Introducing Innovative Technologies

Apple Computer users share a fervent kind of loyalty. With a passion usually reserved for fans of musical groups or sports teams, millions of users in more than 120 countries extol the virtues of Apple's hardware and software.

Steven Jobs and Stephen Wozniak founded Apple in 1976 when they decided to market the Apple I, a circuit board they had developed in Jobs's garage. Jobs suggested the name Apple, but no one is sure why. "He doesn't always let on where ideas come from," Wozniak says, "or how they come into his head." Whatever the origin, Wozniak maintains that other names "all sounded boring compared to Apple." The company's logo is easier to explain – an apple with a bite (a play on byte) taken out of it. In 1977, Apple Computer incorporated and introduced the Apple II, the first mass-marketed personal computer. The machine helped generate more than $1 billion in annual sales and became a school standard. Apple's Macintosh computer and operating system, released in 1984, was one of the first commercially successful GUIs.

Apple discontinued the Apple II product line in 1993, and the following year introduced the high-performance Power Macintosh line. The Macintosh had a larger processor and more memory, but its greatest strengths were its stability, flexibility, creative capabilities, and user-friendliness. Advertised as "the computer for the rest of us," buyers enthusiastically embraced the Macintosh. Apple then licensed its Macintosh computer and operating system to other computer manufacturers. This decision was reversed later, however, as other manufacturers reduced Apple's market share and revenues dropped. After a series of personnel changes, Jobs became Apple's CEO. Under his direction, *Apple Computer* introduced the iMac, the iBook, the PowerMac G4, and Mac OS X, which includes applications that let users create desktop movies, rip MP3s, and burn CDs and DVDs.

For more information about Apple Computer, visit the Discovering Computers 2004 Companies Web page (**scsite.com/dc2004/companies**) and click Apple Computer.

TECHNOLOGY TRAILBLAZERS

Dan Bricklin
Developer of VisiCalc

The next time you use your calculator to balance your checkbook, think about *Dan Bricklin*. He used his Texas Instruments calculator constantly in the late 1970s and recognized a need to develop VisiCalc (Visible Calculator), the first electronic spreadsheet, in graduate school. He still owns that calculator, along with the original VisiCalc code.

Bricklin got the idea for VisiCalc at Harvard Business School. There, classes often asked students to calculate the effect of changing one value on a business balance or account sheet. "Creating VisiCalc involved figuring out how to make a calculating tool that was easier than the back of an envelope so people would do their first calculation on a computer spreadsheet so that their second one could be automatic." Bricklin and his friend, Bob Frankston, formed a company called Software Arts and programmed the VisiCalc prototype using Apple Basic on an Apple II computer. The small program included many of the features found in today's spreadsheet software. VisiCalc did not make Bricklin a great deal of money (the final version sold for $100), but it had an immediate impact, increasing computer sales and reducing business costs. "I'm not rich because of VisiCalc," Bricklin says, "but I feel that I've made a change in the world. That's a satisfaction money can't buy." VisiCalc still runs on personal computers, and Bricklin includes the program on his personal Web site.

Lotus Software purchased Software Arts in 1985. After serving as a consultant to Lotus, Bricklin turned his attention to starting a new company, Software Garden, Inc., and developing new software that focuses on pen-based computing and interactive video conferencing. His current venture, Trellix, lets people turn everyday documents into Web pages with colors, graphics, and links.

For more information about Dan Bricklin, visit the Discovering Computers 2004 People Web page (**scsite.com/dc2004/people**) and click Dan Bricklin.

Masayoshi Son
Japan's Bill Gates

Often called "the Bill Gates of Japan," *Masayoshi Son* has helped bring that country to the forefront of the digital age.

When he was 16 years old, the second-generation Korean-Japanese moved from Japan to California to learn English. At the University of California, Berkeley, Son majored in economics and also took some computer courses. He recalls being fascinated by a picture of a microchip in a magazine, realizing the microchip would change people's lives. Other students carried pictures of Elvis Presley, but in his book bag Son kept the picture of the microchip.

While in school, Son earned his first million dollars by importing arcade games from Japan for the campus, developing computer games, and selling a patent for a multilingual pocket translator to Sharp Corporation. In 1981, at age 23 he founded Softbank Corporation, a software distribution operation. Son predicted that the company would be worth $400 million in five years and $1 billion in ten. His first employees were less optimistic – both left after two weeks – but Son's forecasts proved uncannily accurate. By 1995, Softbank Corporation controlled one-half of the personal computer software in Japan. Profits from this company formed the basis for other profitable investments, including Yahoo!, Kingston Technology, Ziff Davis Media, and E*TRADE. Besides these software investments, Son has holdings in more than 50 international technology companies, including publishing, electronic banking, and broadcasting.

Son is a leading member of Japan's Prime Minister's IT Strategy Council. Though criticized for heavy investment in U.S. Internet companies, Son sees such alliances as helpful to both countries' economies. Today, Son is one of the world's wealthiest entrepreneurs, but that is not enough. "Some people make money just to make money…My satisfaction comes when I see people smile."

For more information about Masayoshi Son, visit the Discovering Computers 2004 People Web page (**scsite.com/dc2004/people**) and click Masayoshi Son.

CHAPTER 3 CHAPTER REVIEW ‹● Previous | Next ●›

The Chapter Review section summarizes the concepts presented in this chapter.

 WEB INSTRUCTIONS:

To display this page from the Web, start your browser and enter the Web address **scsite.com/dc2004/ch3/review**. Click the links for current and additional information.

1 What Are the Categories of Application Software?

Application software consists of programs that perform specific tasks for users. The four major categories of popular application software are business software; graphics and multimedia software; software for home, personal, and educational use; and software for communications.

2 How Is Software Distributed?

Application software is available in a variety of forms. **Packaged software** is mass produced, copyrighted retail software that meets the needs of a variety of users. **Custom software** performs functions specific to a business or industry. Companies may use programmers to develop tailor-made custom software. **Shareware** is copyrighted software that is distributed free for a trial period. **Freeware** is copyrighted software provided at no cost to a user by an individual or a company. Public-domain software is free software that has been donated for public use and has no copyright restrictions.

3 How Do You Start and Interact with Application Software?

The Windows XP operating system uses the concept of a **desktop**, which is an on-screen work area that has a graphical user interface. On the Windows desktop are a Start button and a pointer. A **button** is a graphical element you activate to cause a specific action to take place. The **pointer** is a small symbol displayed on the screen that moves as you move the mouse. To start an application, move the pointer to the Start button on the Windows taskbar and then **click** the Start button by pressing and releasing a button on the mouse. Windows displays the Start menu. A **menu** contains a series of commands from which you make selections. Click the program name on the menu or on the *submenu* that displays when you point to a command. Once loaded in memory, the program is displayed in a **window**, which is a rectangular area of the screen on the desktop.

Visit **scsite.com/dc2004/quiz** or click the Quiz Yourself button. Click Objectives 1 – 3 below Chapter 3.

4 What Are the Key Features of Widely Used Business Programs?

Business software is application software that assists people in becoming more effective and efficient while performing daily business activities. Business software includes the following programs. **Word processing software** allows users to **create** a document by entering text or numbers and inserting graphical images, **edit** the document by making changes to its existing content, and **format** the document by altering its appearance. **Spreadsheet software** allows users to organize data in rows and columns (called a *worksheet*), perform calculations, recalculate when data changes, and chart the data in graphical form. **Database software** allows users to create a **database**, which is a collection of data organized in a manner that allows access, retrieval, and use of that data. **Presentation graphics software** allows users to create a *slide show* that is displayed on a large monitor or on a projection screen and print an *outline* that includes the text from each slide. A **personal information manager (PIM)** is software that includes an appointment calendar, address book, notepad, and other features to help users organize personal information. A **software suite** is a collection of individual programs sold as a single package. **Project management software** allows users to plan, schedule, track, and analyze the events, resources, and costs of a project. **Accounting software** helps companies record and report their financial transactions.

5 What Are the Key Features of Widely Used Graphics and Multimedia Programs?

Graphics and multimedia software includes the following. **Computer-aided design (CAD) software** assists a professional user in creating engineering, architectural, and scientific designs.

CHAPTER REVIEW

Desktop publishing (DTP) software enables professional designers to create sophisticated documents that contain text, graphics, and brilliant colors. **Paint software**, also called *illustration software*, allows users to draw pictures, shapes, and other graphical images with various on-screen tools. **Image editing software** provides the capabilities of paint software and also includes the ability to modify existing images. **Video editing software** allows users to modify a segment of a video, called a clip. **Audio editing software** lets users modify audio clips and produce studio-quality soundtracks. **Multimedia authoring software** allows users to combine text, graphics, audio, video, and animation into an interactive application. **Web page authoring software** helps users of all skill levels create Web pages that include graphical images, video, audio, animation, and other special effects.

> **[STOP]** Visit **scsite.com/dc2004/quiz** or click the Quiz Yourself button. Click Objectives 4 – 5 below Chapter 3.

6 What Are the Key Features of Widely Used Home, Personal, and Educational Programs?

Software for home, personal, and educational use includes the following. **Integrated software** combines application software such as word processing, spreadsheet, and database into a single, easy-to-use package. **Personal finance software** is a simplified accounting program that helps users balance their checkbooks, pay bills, track personal income and expenses, track investments, and evaluate financial plans. **Legal software** assists in the preparation of legal documents and provides legal information. **Tax preparation software** guides users through the process of filing federal taxes. **Personal DTP software** helps users create newsletters, brochures, advertisements, postcards, greeting cards, letterhead, business cards, banners, calendars, logos, and Web pages. **Paint/ image editing software** for personal use provides an easy-to-use interface, usually with more simplified capabilities than its professional counterpart, including functions tailored to meet the needs of the home and small business users. Application software often includes a **clip art/image gallery**, which is a collection of clip art and photographs. **Home design/landscaping software** assists users with the design, remodeling, or improvement of a home, deck, or landscape. **Educational software**

teaches a particular skill. **Reference software** provides valuable and thorough information for all individuals. **Entertainment software** for personal computers includes interactive games, videos, and other programs to support hobbies or provide amusement and enjoyment.

7 What Are the Types of Application Software Used in Communications?

Application software for communications includes e-mail programs to transmit messages via a network, FTP programs to upload and download files on the Internet, Web browser programs to access and view Web pages, newsreader/message board programs that allow online written discussions with other users, chat room software to have real-time, online typed conversations, instant messaging software for real-time exchange of messages or files, and video conferencing/telephone call software for meetings or conversations on a network between geographically separated people.

8 What Are the Advantages of Using Application Software on the Web?

A **Web application** is application software that exists on a Web site. It requires less disk space on your computer than installed software and is less expensive to upgrade as vendors release new versions. An *application service provider (ASP)* is a third-party organization that manages and distributes software and services on the Web.

9 What Learning Aids Are Available for Application Software?

To assist in the learning process, many programs provide a variety of Help features. Online Help is the electronic equivalent of a user manual. Most online Help also links to *Web-based help*, which provides updates and more comprehensive resources to respond to technical issues about software. A **wizard** is an automated assistant that helps a user complete a task by asking questions and then automatically performing actions based on the responses.

> **[STOP]** Visit **scsite.com/dc2004/quiz** or click the Quiz Yourself button. Click Objectives 6 – 9 below Chapter 3.

CHAPTER 3 KEY TERMS

◀● Previous | Next ●▶

QUIZZES AND LEARNING GAMES

Computer Genius

Crossword Puzzle

Interactive Labs

Practice Test

Quiz Yourself

Wheel of Terms

EXERCISES

Chapter Review

Checkpoint

Key Terms

Lab Exercises

Learn It Online

Web Research

BEYOND THE BOOK

Apply It

Career Corner

Companies

FAQ

High-Tech Talk

Issues

Looking Ahead

Trailblazers

Web Links

FEATURES

Guide to Web Sites

Making Use of the Web

Tech News

Timeline 2004

You should know the Primary Terms and be familiar with the Secondary Terms.

■ **WEB INSTRUCTIONS:**

To display this page from the Web, start your browser and enter the Web address **scsite.com/dc2004/ch3/terms**. Click a term to display its definition and a picture. When the picture displays, click the more info button for current and additional information about the term from the Web.

>> Primary Terms
(shown in bold-black characters in the chapter)

accounting software (3.19)
application software (3.02)
audio editing software (3.23)
business software (3.06)
button (3.05)
click (3.05)
clip art (3.07)
clip art/image gallery (3.28)
command (3.05)
computer-aided design (CAD) software (3.21)
computer-based training (CBT) (3.28)
create (3.08)
custom software (3.02)
database (3.15)
database software (3.15)
desktop (3.05)
desktop publishing (DTP) software (3.21)
distance learning (DL) (3.32)
edit (3.09)
educational software (3.28)
entertainment software (3.29)
font (3.10)
font size (3.10)
format (3.09)
freeware (3.03)
home design/ landscaping software (3.28)
icon (3.05)
image editing software (3.22)
integrated software (3.25)
legal software (3.26)
menu (3.05)
multimedia authoring software (3.23)

online banking (3.25)
online Help (3.33)
packaged software (3.02)
paint software (3.22)
personal DTP software (3.27)
personal finance software (3.25)
personal information manager (PIM) (3.18)
personal paint/image editing software (3.27)
photo editing software (3.27)
pointer (3.05)
presentation graphics software (3.16)
print (3.10)
project management software (3.19)
public-domain software (3.03)
reference software (3.29)
save (3.10)
shareware (3.02)
software suite (3.19)
spreadsheet software (3.12)
tax preparation software (3.26)
title bar (3.05)
video editing software (3.23)
voice recognition (3.11)
voice recognition programs (3.11)
Web application (3.31)
Web page authoring software (3.24)
Web-based training (3.32)
window (3.05)
wizard (3.34)
word processing software (3.07)

>> Secondary Terms
(shown in italic characters in the chapter)

application service provider (ASP) (3.32)
audience handouts (3.17)
bar chart (3.14)
cell (3.12)
charting (3.14)
clipboard (3.09)
color library (3.22)
column chart (3.14)
context-sensitive (3.33)
dialog box (3.05)
enterprise ASP (3.32)
FAQ (3.33)
field (3.15)
file (3.05)
file name (3.05)
filters (3.23)
font style (3.10)
footer (3.08)
form (3.15)
formula (3.13)
function (3.13)
header (3.08)
illustration software (3.22)
import (3.16)
label (3.13)
line chart (3.14)
loads (3.04)
local/regional ASP (3.32)
macro (3.09)
margins (3.07)
.NET (3.31)
notes page (3.17)

outline (3.17)
page layout (3.22)
pasting (3.09)
pie chart (3.14)
point (3.10)
query (3.15)
record (3.15)
replace (3.08)
sans serif font (3.10)
scrolling (3.08)
search (3.08)
serif font (3.10)
shortcut menu (3.05)
slide show (3.16)
slide sorter view (3.16)
smart tags (3.09)
specialist ASP (3.32)
speech recognition (3.11)
spelling checker (3.08)
submenu (3.05)
system software (3.03)
template (3.09)
value (3.13)
vertical market ASP (3.32)
volume business ASP (3.32)
WBT (3.32)
Web-based help (3.33)
what-if analysis (3.14)
word processor (3.07)
wordwrap (3.07)
worksheet (3.12)

CHECKPOINT CHAPTER 3

Use the Checkpoint exercises to check your knowledge level of the chapter.

WEB INSTRUCTIONS:

To display this page from the Web, start your browser and enter the Web address **scsite.com/dc2004/ch3/check**. Click the links for current and additional information.

LABEL THE FIGURE   Identify these elements in the Windows XP graphical user interface.

a. All Programs command

b. All Programs submenu

c. Accessories command

d. Accessories submenu

e. Paint program command

f. Start menu

g. Start button

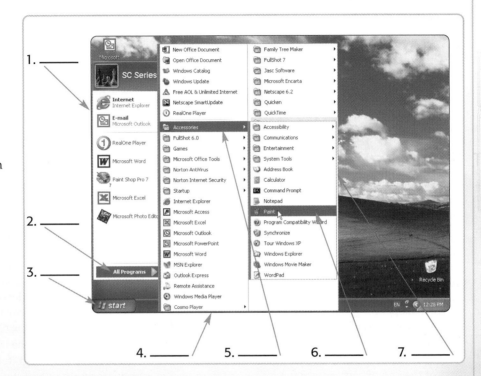

1. _____

2. _____

3. _____

4. _____   5. _____   6. _____   7. _____

TRUE/FALSE   Mark T for True and F for False. (See page numbers in parentheses.)

_____ 1. Public-domain software is mass produced, copyrighted retail software that meets the needs of a wide variety of users. (3.03)

_____ 2. Shareware, freeware, and public-domain programs are not usually available on the Web for users to download. (3.03)

_____ 3. The desktop is an on-screen work area that has a graphical user interface. (3.05)

_____ 4. A button is a small image displayed on the screen that represents a program, a document, or some other object. (3.05)

_____ 5. Business software includes programs such as word processing, spreadsheet, and presentation graphics. (3.06)

_____ 6. A font is a name assigned to a specific design of characters. (3.10)

_____ 7. Integrated software combines application software into a single package. (3.25)

_____ 8. Educational software is software that assists instructors in planning a course. (3.29)

_____ 9. A Web application is application software that helps you design a Web site. (3.31)

_____ 10. A wizard is an automated assistant that helps a user complete a task by asking questions and then automatically performing actions based on the responses. (3.34)

CHAPTER 3 CHECKPOINT

‹● Previous | Next ●›

MULTIPLE CHOICE Select the best answer. (See page numbers in parentheses.)

1. E-mail, Web browser, instant messaging, and FTP programs are examples of _____ software. (3.02)
   a. business
   b. graphics and multimedia
   c. home, personal, and educational
   d. communications

2. If a company cannot find software to meet its unique requirements, the company may use a programmer to develop tailor-made _____ . (3.02)
   a. freeware
   b. custom software
   c. shareware
   d. packaged software

3. The _____ at the right edge of some menu commands indicates that a submenu of additional commands is available. (3.05)
   a. I-beam
   b. block arrow
   c. pointing hand
   d. arrowhead

4. The title bar of a document window usually displays the document's _____ . (3.05)
   a. file name   b. file size
   c. file path   d. all of the above

5. A feature, called _____, allows users of word processing software to type words continually without pressing the ENTER key at the end of each line. (3.07)
   a. AutoCorrect   b. wordwrap
   c. AutoFormat   d. clipboard

6. When using spreadsheet software, a function _____ . (3.13)
   a. depicts data in graphical form
   b. changes certain values to reveal the effects of the changes
   c. is a predefined formula that performs common calculations
   d. contains the formatting necessary for a specific worksheet type

7. With database software, users can run a _____ to request specific data from the database. (3.15)
   a. query   b. record
   c. field   d. form

8. Page layout, which is a feature of DTP software, is the process of _____ . (3.22)
   a. drawing pictures, shapes, and other images with various on-screen tools
   b. modifying a segment of a video, called a page

   c. arranging text and graphics in a document on a page-by-page basis
   d. standardizing the colors on a page used by designers and printers

9. Training centers, educational institutions, and online magazine publishers all use _____ software to develop interactive applications. (3.24)
   a. multimedia authoring
   b. desktop publishing
   c. computer-aided design
   d. image editing

10. Integrated software _____ . (3.25)
    a. usually offers programs that can be purchased individually
    b. typically has all the capabilities of business application software
    c. is less expensive than a more powerful software suite
    d. all of the above

11. _____ typically consists of self-directed, self-paced instruction on a topic. (3.28)
    a. CBT (computer-based training)
    b. DTP (desktop publishing)
    c. CAD (computer-aided design)
    d. PIM (personal information manager)

12. A(n) _____ program, which allows messages and files to be transmitted via a network, is integrated in many software suites, integrated software, and operating systems. (3.30)
    a. FTP
    b. instant messenger
    c. Web browser
    d. e-mail

13. A Volume Business ASP _____ . (3.32)
    a. customizes and delivers high-end business applications
    b. supplies prepackaged applications
    c. offers a variety of applications to a specific geographic region
    d. provides applications for a particular industry

14. Online Help often is context-sensitive, meaning that the Help information _____ . (3.33)
    a. is available only to certain users
    b. lists answers to common questions
    c. provides updates and more comprehensive resources
    d. relates to the current task being attempted

CHECKPOINT

CHAPTER 3

MATCHING Match the terms with their definitions. (See page numbers in parentheses.)

_____ 1. clip art (3.07)

_____ 2. clipboard (3.09)

_____ 3. voice recognition (3.11)

_____ 4. cell (3.12)

_____ 5. record (3.15)

_____ 6. slide sorter view (3.16)

_____ 7. filters (3.23)

_____ 8. online banking (3.25)

_____ 9. specialist ASP (3.32)

_____ 10. distance learning (3.32)

a. capability of a computer to distinguish spoken words

b. row in a database table that contains data about a given item

c. column in a database table that contains a specific category of data

d. usually included in audio editing software to enhance audio quality

e. collection of drawings, diagrams, maps, and photographs

f. intersection of a row and column in a worksheet

g. delivers applications to meet a specific business need

h. offers access to account balances and provides bill paying services

i. temporary storage location that contains items cut or copied in a document

j. indicates the size of characters in a particular font

k. delivery of education at one location while learning takes place at another

l. presents a screen view that helps to organize presentations

SHORT ANSWER Write a brief answer to each of the following questions.

1. How is a serif font different from a sans serif font? _____ How is font size measured? _____

2. What is charting? _____ How are line charts, column charts, and pie charts different? _____

3. Why do professional designers and graphic artists use DTP software instead of word processing packages? _____ What is a color library? _____

4. What are two disadvantages of using installed software? _____ How can you access a Web application? _____

5. What is online Help? _____ How do FAQs and wizards help software users? _____

WORKING TOGETHER Working with a group of your classmates, complete the following team exercises.

1. A Web application is a software application that exists on a Web site. With your group, develop a report describing at least three Web applications and explaining how an individual could use these various applications effectively. Include in your report a description of each application, a short overview of any online Help or FAQs, and the Web address for each application within your report. Share your findings with your class.

2. Choose one Issue from the following issues in this chapter: Is It Ethical to Copy Software? (3.06), Personal or Processed? (3.08), Should What We See Be What We Get? (3.22), or Is Someone Watching You? (3.30). Use the Web and/or print media to research the issue. Then, present a debate for the class, with different members of your team supporting different responses to the questions that accompany the issue.

3. In any software application, each software package is not exactly the same. Different spreadsheet packages, for example, may have different methods to enter formulas, use functions, and draw charts. Have each member of your team interview someone who works with an application described in this chapter. What specific software package is used? Why? For what purpose is the package used? What does the interviewee like, or dislike, about the package? Would the interviewee recommend this software package? Why? Meet with the members of your team to discuss the results of your interviews. Then, use PowerPoint to create a group presentation and share your findings with the class.

CHAPTER 3 LEARN IT ONLINE

◀● Previous | Next ●▶

Use the Learn It Online exercises to reinforce your understanding of the chapter concepts.

WEB INSTRUCTIONS:

To display this page from the Web, start your browser and enter the Web address **scsite.com/dc2004/ch3/learn**.

1 At the Movies – What Is Microsoft?

To view the What Is Microsoft? movie, click the number 1 button. Watch the movie and then complete the exercise by answering the questions below. Founded in 1975, Microsoft is a $25 billion company. It is divided into three main business groups: operating systems, software products, and consumer products, which include games, Web browsers, and other home, personal, and educational products. With this exposure, Microsoft dominates in many markets. Nine out of ten personal computers run some version of the Microsoft Windows operating system. In addition, Microsoft has 90 percent of the office/spreadsheet/graphics software market. Its MSN Internet Explorer comprises more than 60 percent of the Web-browser market. And, because Microsoft bundles and interlocks its systems and programs, organizations with a network of computers are compelled to buy Microsoft products continually. What do you think should be done, if anything, and why?

2 Shelly Cashman Series Word Processing Lab

Follow the instructions in Learn It Online 2 on page 1.46 to start and use the Shelly Cashman Series Word Processing Lab. If you are running from the Web, enter the Web address **scsite.com/sclabs/menu** or display the Learn It Online page (see instructions at the top of this page) and then click the number 2 button.

3 Shelly Cashman Series Working with Spreadsheets Lab

Follow the instructions in Learn It Online 2 on page 1.46 to start and use the Shelly Cashman Series Working with Spreadsheets Lab. If you are running from the Web, enter the Web address **scsite.com/sclabs/menu** or display the Learn It Online page (see instructions at the top of this page) and then click the number 3 button.

4 Practice Test

Click the number 4 button. Answer each question. When completed, enter your name and click the Grade Test button to submit the quiz for grading. Make a note of any missed questions. If required, print a copy to submit to your instructor.

5 Web Guide

Click the number 5 button to display the Searching Techniques and Guide to Web Sites Web page. Click Shopping and then click eBay. Search for Software. Use your word processing program to prepare a brief report on the software programs you found. Submit your assignment to your instructor.

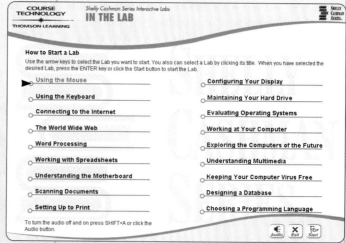

COURSE TECHNOLOGY
THOMSON LEARNING

Shelly Cashman Series Interactive Labs
IN THE LAB

SHELLY CASHMAN SERIES

How to Start a Lab
Use the arrow keys to select the Lab you want to start. You also can select a Lab by clicking its title. When you have selected the desired Lab, press the ENTER key or click the Start button to start the Lab.

▶ Using the Mouse
○ Using the Keyboard
○ Connecting to the Internet
○ The World Wide Web
○ Word Processing
○ Working with Spreadsheets
○ Understanding the Motherboard
○ Scanning Documents
○ Setting Up to Print

○ Configuring Your Display
○ Maintaining Your Hard Drive
○ Evaluating Operating Systems
○ Working at Your Computer
○ Exploring the Computers of the Future
○ Understanding Multimedia
○ Keeping Your Computer Virus Free
○ Designing a Database
○ Choosing a Programming Language

To turn the audio off and on press SHIFT+A or click the Audio button.

🔊 ✕ ▶
Audio Exit Start

LEARN IT ONLINE   CHAPTER 3

6 Scavenger Hunt

Click the number 6 button. Print a copy of the Scavenger Hunt page; use this page to write down your answers as you search the Web. Submit your completed page to your instructor.

7 Who Wants to Be a Computer Genius?

Click the number 7 button to find out if you are a computer genius. Directions on how to play the game will display. When you are ready to play, click the Play button. Submit your score to your instructor.

8 Wheel of Terms

Click the number 8 button to reinforce important terms you learned in this chapter by playing the Shelly Cashman Series version of this popular game. Directions on how to play the game will display. When you are ready to play, click the Play button. Submit your score to your instructor.

9 Career Corner

Click the number 9 button to display the Penn State's Career Services Web page. Click a link of your choice. Write a brief report on the information you found. Submit the report to your instructor.

10 Search Sleuth

Click the number 10 button to learn search techniques that will help make you a research expert. Submit the completed assignment to your instructor.

11 Crossword Puzzle Challenge

Click the number 11 button. Complete the puzzle to reinforce skills you learned in this chapter. Directions on how to play the game will display. When you are ready to play, click the Play button. Submit the completed puzzle to your instructor.

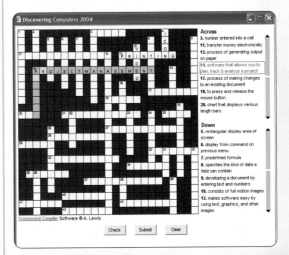

12 Setting Up an E-Mail Account

E-mail has become one of the more widespread ways of communication in today's society. Based on various 1999 estimates, 610 billion to 1,100 billion messages are sent each year. To set up a free e-mail account, click the number 12 button. Follow the online procedures to establish an e-mail account. When you are finished, send yourself an e-mail.

13 In the News

It is a computer user's worst fear — he or she opens an unfamiliar e-mail or uses a disk of unknown origin and a computer virus is released that damages and/or deletes files. Fortunately, specialized software prevents such things from happening to your computer. Click the number 13 button and read a news article about antivirus programs. Which program does the article recommend? What does it do? Who will benefit from using this software? Why? Where can the software be obtained? Would you be interested in this software? Why or why not?

CHAPTER 3 LAB EXERCISES

◄● Previous | Next ●►

Use the Lab Exercises to gain hands-on computer experience.

■ WEB INSTRUCTIONS:

To display this page from the Web, start your browser and enter the Web address **scsite.com/dc2004/ch3/lab**.

1 Working with Application Programs

This exercise uses Windows XP procedures. Windows is a multitasking operating system, meaning you can work on two or more applications that reside in memory at the same time. To find out how to work with multiple application programs, click the Start button on the Windows taskbar and then click Help and Support on the Start menu. Click the Windows basics link in the Pick a Help topic area. Click the plus sign to the left of Core Windows tasks and then click the Working with programs link. Click an appropriate topic to answer each of the following questions:

- How do you start a program?
- How do you switch between running programs?
- How do you add a program to your computer?
- How do you quit a program?

Close the Windows Help and Support Center window.

2 Creating a Word Processing Document

This exercise uses Windows XP/2000/98 procedures. WordPad is a simple word processing program included with the Windows operating system. To create a document with WordPad, click the Start button on the Windows taskbar, point to All Programs (Programs in Windows 2000/98) on the Start menu, point to Accessories on the All Programs submenu (Programs submenu in Windows 2000/98), and then click WordPad on the Accessories submenu. If necessary, when the WordPad window is displayed, click its Maximize button. Click View on the WordPad menu bar. If a check mark is not displayed to the left of the Toolbar command, click the Toolbar command. Type two paragraphs summarizing the features of one of the software packages in Figure 3-5 on page 3.06. Press the TAB key to indent the first line of each paragraph and the ENTER key to begin a new paragraph. To correct errors, press the BACKSPACE key to erase to the left of the insertion point or

press the DELETE key to erase to the right. To insert text, position the I-beam mouse pointer at the location where the text is to be inserted and then begin typing. At the end of the document, press the ENTER key twice and then type your name. When the document is complete, save it on a floppy disk inserted into drive A. Click the Save button on the WordPad toolbar, type `a:\lab3-2` in the File name text box and then click the Save button in the Save As dialog box. Click the Print button on the WordPad toolbar to print the document. Close the WordPad window.

3 Using WordPad Help

This exercise uses Windows XP procedures. Start WordPad as described in exercise 2 on this page. Click Help on the WordPad menu bar and then click Help Topics. When the WordPad Help window is displayed, if necessary, click the Index tab. Type `documents saving` in the Type in the keywords to find text box and then press the ENTER key. If necessary, click Create, open, or save a WordPad document in the Topics Found dialog box and then click the Display button.

- How can you save changes to a document?
- How can you save an existing document with a new name?

Close the WordPad Help window and quit WordPad.

4 Business Software Products

This exercise uses Windows XP/2000/98 procedures. What business software packages are on your computer? Click the Start button on the Windows taskbar and then point to All Programs (Programs in Windows 2000/98) on the Start menu. Scan the All Programs submenu (Programs submenu in Windows 2000/98) for the names of popular productivity packages (if necessary, point to the arrow at the top or bottom of the submenu to scroll the submenu up or down). Write the package name and type of application software (refer to Figure 3-5 on page 3.06). When you are finished, click an empty area of the desktop.

WEB RESEARCH CHAPTER 3

Use the Web Research exercises to learn more about the special features in this chapter.

WEB INSTRUCTIONS:

Use the link in each exercise or a search engine such as Google (google.com) to research the topic. Then, write a one-page, double-spaced report or create a presentation, unless otherwise directed below. Page numbers on which information can be found are in parentheses.

1 **Issue**   Choose one Issue from the following issues in this chapter: Is It Ethical to Copy Software? (3.06), Personal or Processed? (3.08), Should What We See Be What We Get? (3.22), or Is Someone Watching You? (3.30). Use the Web to research the issue. Discuss the issue with classmates, instructors, and friends. Address the questions that accompany the issue in a report or presentation.

2 **Apply It**   Choose one of the following Apply It features in this chapter: Easing a Taxing Part of Life (3.26) or Obtaining Application Software (3.31). Use the Web to gather additional information about the topic. Print two Web pages that relate to the Apply It. Detail in a report or presentation what you learned.

3 **Career Corner**   Read the Career Corner article in this chapter (3.34). Use the Web to find out more about the career. Describe the career in a report or presentation.

4 **Companies on the Cutting Edge**   Choose one of the Companies on the Cutting Edge in this chapter (3.36). Use the Web to research the company further. Explain in a report or presentation how this company has contributed to computer technology.

5 **Technology Trailblazers**   Choose one of the Technology Trailblazers in this chapter (3.37). Use the Web to research the person further. Explain in a report or presentation how this individual has affected the way people use, or think about, computers.

6 **Picture Yourself Using Software**   Read the Picture Yourself Using Software story at the beginning of this chapter (3.00). Use the Web to research software further. Describe in a report or presentation the ways in which you might use software.

7 **High-Tech Talk**   Read the High-Tech Talk feature in this chapter (3.35). Use the Web to find out more about the topic. Summarize in a report or presentation what you learned.

8 **Web Links**   Review the Web Link boxes found in the margins of this chapter. Visit five of the Web Link sites. Print the main Web page for each site you visit. Choose one of the Web pages and then summarize in one paragraph the content of the Web page.

9 **Looking Ahead**   Choose one of the Looking Ahead articles in this chapter: 3G Wireless Service Developing (3.18) or Plagiarism Software Detects Cheating (3.29). Use the Web to find out more about the topic. Detail in a report or presentation what you learned.

10 **FAQ**   Choose one FAQ found in this chapter. Use the Web to find out more about the topic. Summarize in one paragraph what you learned.

11 **Making Use of the Web**   Read the Finance section of Making Use of the Web in Appendix A (A.06). Complete the Finance Web Exercises at the end of the section (A.07). Answer the questions posed in each exercise.

Picture Yourself Upgrading a Computer

Cable television Internet access finally is available in your neighborhood! You immediately call the toll-free number to sign up for this high-speed broadband access. Great news… the service technician can be at your house one week from today. While taking your order, the customer service agent explains that your computer needs a network card to access the cable Internet service. Your computer is an older model and does not have a network card. She says the technician can install one for you, but it may be less expensive if you purchased one from a local computer store and installed it yourself.

You do not have the slightest idea how to install a network card, or any kind of adapter card for that matter, into a computer. What next? A visit to the computer store where you purchased the computer seems like the solution. After explaining the situation to a personal computer salesperson, he assures you the network card installation kit includes thorough instructions with detailed pictures. Then, he walks you to a disassembled computer and has you insert a sample network card into the computer. That was simple! While you make the purchase, the salesperson gives you advice to ensure that you work carefully inside the computer.

As you read Chapter 4, you will learn about various adapter cards and discover other components of the system unit.

processor

memory

audio

video

modem

OBJECTIVES

After completing this chapter, you will be able to:

1. Differentiate among various styles of system units

2. Identify chips, adapter cards, and other components of a motherboard

3. Describe the components of a processor and how they complete a machine cycle

4. Identify characteristics of various personal computer processors on the market today

5. Define a bit and describe how a series of bits represents data

6. Explain how programs transfer in and out of memory

7. Differentiate among the various types of memory

8. Describe the types of expansion slots and adapter cards

9. Explain the differences among a serial port, a parallel port, a USB port, and other ports

10. Describe how buses contribute to a computer's processing speed

11. Identify components in mobile computers and mobile devices

CONTENTS

THE SYSTEM UNIT

Whether you are a home user or a business user, you most likely will make the decision to purchase a new computer or upgrade an existing computer within the next several years. Thus, you should understand the purpose of each component in a computer. As Chapter 1 discussed, a computer includes devices used for input, processing, output, storage, and communications. Many of these components are part of the system unit.

The **system unit** is a case that contains electronic components of the computer used to process data. Although many system units resemble a box, they are available in many shapes and sizes. The case of the system unit, sometimes called the *chassis*, is made of metal or plastic and protects the internal electronic components from damage. All computers have a system unit (Figure 4-1).

On desktop personal computers, the electronic components and most storage devices are part of the system unit. Other devices, such as the keyboard, mouse, microphone, monitor, printer, scanner, PC video camera, and speakers, normally occupy space outside the system unit. On notebook computers, the keyboard and pointing device often occupy the area on the top of the system unit, and the display attaches to the system unit by hinges. The system unit on a PDA usually consumes the entire device. On these mobile devices, the display often is part of the system unit.

system unit

system unit

system unit

system unit

FIGURE 4-1 All sizes of computers have a system unit.

At some point, you might have to open the system unit on a desktop personal computer to replace or install a new electronic component. For this reason, you should be familiar with the electronic components of a system unit. Figure 4-2 identifies some of these components, which include the processor, memory, adapter cards, ports, drive bays, and the power supply.

The processor interprets and carries out the basic instructions that operate a computer. Memory typically holds data waiting to be processed and instructions waiting to be executed. The electronic components and circuitry of the system unit, such as the processor and memory, usually are part of or are connected to a circuit board called the motherboard.

Adapter cards are circuit boards that provide connections and functions not built into the motherboard. Four adapter cards found in some desktop personal computers today are a sound card, a video card, a modem card, and a network card. Devices outside the system unit often attach to ports on the system unit by a connector on a cable. These devices may include a keyboard, mouse, microphone, monitor, printer, scanner, card reader, PC video camera, and speakers. A drive bay holds a disk drive. The power supply allows electricity to travel through a power cord from a wall outlet into a computer.

FIGURE 4-2 The system unit on a typical personal computer consists of numerous electronic components, some of which are shown in this figure. The sound card, video card, modem card, and network card are four types of adapter cards.

The Motherboard

The **motherboard**, sometimes called a *system board*, is the main circuit board of the system unit. Many electronic components attach to the motherboard; others are built into it. Figure 4-3 shows a photograph of a desktop personal computer motherboard and identifies components attached to it, including adapter cards, the processor, and memory chips.

WEB LINK 4-1

Motherboards

Visit the Discovering Computers 2004 WEB LINK page (**scsite.com/ dc2004/weblink**). Click Motherboards below Chapter 4.

A computer **chip** is a small piece of semi-conducting material, usually silicon, on which integrated circuits are etched. An *integrated circuit* contains many microscopic pathways capable of carrying electrical current. Each integrated circuit can contain millions of elements such as resistors, capacitors, and transistors. A *transistor*, for example, can act as an electronic switch that opens or closes the circuit for electrical charges. Most chips are no bigger than one-half-inch square. Read Apply It 4-1 for information about a use of chips.

FIGURE 4-3 The motherboard in a desktop personal computer contains many electronic components, including adapter cards, a processor chip, memory chips, memory slots, and expansion slots. Memory slots hold memory cards (modules) and expansion slots hold adapter cards.

APPLY IT 4-1

Chip Identifies Pets and Valuables

The next time a beloved pet runs away from home, it can be traced back to its owner if it has been implanted with a tiny, permanent chip.

Veterinarians and animal breeders inject this programmed chip under the animal's skin. It contains a unique identification number that cannot be lost, intentionally removed, or altered. If the animal needs to be identified, a small, handheld scanning device is held close to the implant site and sends a radio signal to the chip. The chip transmits its number to the scanner, and then the breeder or veterinarian can telephone a central office to determine the pet owner's identity. The animal does not feel the chip, which has a useful life of more than 25 years. It does not require any care and does not move in or through the body.

The chip has many other uses, including protecting and studying grizzly bears, ferrets, tortoises, whales, elephants, birds, and snakes. Wildlife research communities implant the chips in endangered animals to guard and observe these animals humanely in their natural habitats. The technology also is used to identify valuable works of art and other priceless possessions.

For more information about injectable identification chips, visit the Discovering Computers 2004 Apply It Web page (**scsite.com/ dc2004/apply**). Click Apply It #1 below Chapter 4.

Manufacturers package chips so the chips can be attached to a circuit board, such as a motherboard or an adapter card. Two types of packaging for processor and memory chips in desktop personal computers are the DIP and PGA (Figure 4-4). A *DIP* (*dual inline package*) consists of two parallel rows of downward-pointing thin metal feet (pins) that attach to the circuit board. A *PGA* (*pin grid array*) holds a larger number of pins because the pins are mounted on the surface of the package. A variation of the PGA, called the *flip chip-PGA* (*FC-PGA*), places the chip on the opposite side (flip side) of the pins.

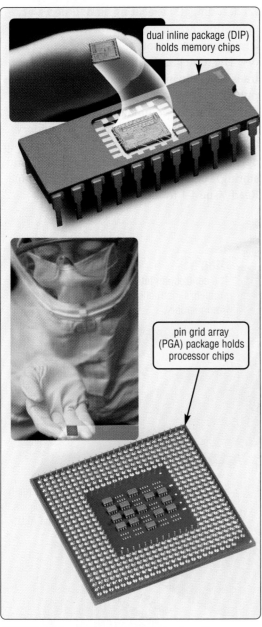

dual inline package (DIP) holds memory chips

pin grid array (PGA) package holds processor chips

FIGURE 4-4 Chips are packaged so they can be attached to a circuit board.

PROCESSOR

The **processor**, also called the **central processing unit (CPU)**, interprets and carries out the basic instructions that operate a computer. The processor significantly impacts overall computing power and manages most of a computer's operations. On larger computers, such as mainframes and supercomputers, the various functions performed by the processor extend over many separate chips and often multiple circuit boards. On a personal computer, all functions of the processor usually are on a single chip. Some computer and chip manufacturers use the term *microprocessor* to refer to a personal computer processor chip.

Processors contain a control unit and an arithmetic logic unit (ALU). These two components work together to perform processing operations. Figure 4-5 illustrates how other devices connected to the computer communicate with the processor to carry out a task.

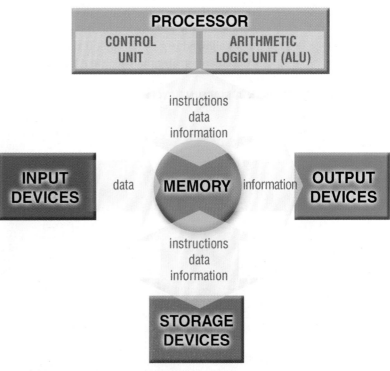

FIGURE 4-5 Most devices connected to the computer communicate with the processor to carry out a task. When a user starts a program, for example, its instructions transfer from a storage device to memory. Data needed by programs enters memory from either an input device or a storage device. The control unit interprets and executes instructions in memory and the ALU performs calculations on the data in memory. Resulting information is stored in memory, from which it can be sent to an output device or a storage device for future access, as needed.

The Control Unit

The **control unit** is the component of the processor that directs and coordinates most of the operations in the computer. The control unit has a role much like a traffic cop: it interprets each instruction issued by a program and then initiates the appropriate action to carry out the instruction.

The Arithmetic Logic Unit

The **arithmetic logic unit** (*ALU*), another component of the processor, performs arithmetic, comparison, and logical operations.

Arithmetic operations include basic calculations such as addition, subtraction, multiplication, and division. *Comparison operations* involve comparing one data item with another to determine whether the first item is greater than, equal to, or less than the other item. Depending on the result of the comparison, different actions may occur. For example, to determine if an employee should receive overtime pay, the software instructs the ALU to compare the number of hours an employee worked during the week with the regular time hours allowed (e.g., 40 hours). If the hours worked are greater than 40, the ALU calculates an overtime wage. If the hours worked are not greater than 40, the ALU does not calculate an overtime wage.

Logical operations include conditions along with logical operators such as AND, OR, and NOT. For example, if only employees paid hourly can receive overtime pay, the ALU must verify two conditions before computing an overtime wage: (1) the employee is paid hourly AND (2) the employee worked more than 40 hours.

Machine Cycle

For every instruction, a processor repeats a set of four basic operations: (1) fetching, (2) decoding, (3) executing, and, if necessary, (4) storing. *Fetching* is the process of obtaining a program instruction or data item from memory. The term *decoding* refers to the process of translating the instruction into signals the computer can execute. *Executing* is the process of carrying out the commands. *Storing*, in this context, means writing the result to memory (not to a storage medium). Together, these four operations (fetching, decoding, executing, and storing) comprise a *machine cycle* (Figure 4-6). Read Issue 4-1 for a related discussion.

FIGURE 4-6   THE STEPS IN A MACHINE CYCLE

A student enters a math problem into the memory of the computer.

Step 1:
The control unit fetches the math problem's instructions and data from memory.

Step 2:
The control unit decodes the math problem's instructions and sends the instructions and data to the ALU.

Step 3:
The ALU performs calculations on the data.

Step 4:
The results of the math problem are stored in memory.

The results in memory display on the screen of the monitor.

STORE 4   MEMORY   FETCH 1

EXECUTE 3   PROCESSOR   2 DECODE

ALU   CONTROL UNIT

100 x 52 = 5200   100 x 52

In some computers, the processor fetches, decodes, executes, and stores only one instruction at a time. In these computers, the processor waits until an instruction completes all four stages of the machine cycle (fetch, decode, execute, and store) before beginning work on the next instruction.

Most of today's personal computers support a concept called pipelining. With *pipelining*, the processor begins fetching a second instruction before it completes the machine cycle for the first instruction. Processors that use pipelining are faster because they do not have to wait for one instruction to complete the machine cycle before fetching the next. Think of a pipeline as an assembly line. By the time the first instruction is in the last stage of the machine cycle, three other instructions could have been fetched and started through the machine cycle (Figure 4-7).

MACHINE CYCLE (without pipelining):

FETCH	DECODE	EXECUTE	STORE	FETCH	DECODE	EXECUTE	STORE

INSTRUCTION 1   INSTRUCTION 2

MACHINE CYCLE (with pipelining):

	FETCH	DECODE	EXECUTE	STORE
INSTRUCTION 1				
INSTRUCTION 2				
INSTRUCTION 3				
INSTRUCTION 4				

FIGURE 4-7 Most modern personal computers support pipelining. With pipelining, the processor fetches a second instruction before the first instruction is completed. The result is faster processing.

Registers

A processor contains small high-speed storage locations, called *registers*, that temporarily hold data and instructions. Registers are part of the processor, not part of memory or a storage device. Processors have many different types of registers, each with a specific storage function. Register functions include storing the location from where an instruction was fetched, storing an instruction while the control unit decodes it, storing data while the ALU computes it, and storing the results of a calculation.

The System Clock

The processor relies on a small quartz crystal circuit called the **system clock** to control the timing of all computer operations. Just as your heart beats at a regular rate to keep your body functioning, the system clock generates regular electronic pulses, or ticks, that set the operating pace of components of the system unit.

Each tick equates to a *clock cycle*. In the past, processors used one or more clock cycles to execute each instruction. Processors today often are *superscalar*, which means they can execute more than one instruction per clock cycle.

ISSUE 4-1

Do People Perform the Machine Cycle?

The control unit's function is to direct and coordinate most of the operations in the computer. To do this, the control unit performs the machine cycle. For each instruction, the processor repeats a set of four operations: fetching, decoding, executing, and storing. These four operations may seem new to you, but in a sense you carry out these same operations each time you complete certain ordinary tasks. Through one of your five senses, you input data, you decode this data and change it into information, you execute the task in some way, and then you store this information for later retrieval. Do people solve all problems in the same way that a computer solves a problem? Why or why not? Describe a simple task in which you perform operations such as those in the machine cycle. What is different and why? If the human brain can perform all of these functions, are computers really necessary? Why?

For more information about the control unit versus the human brain, visit the Discovering Computers 2004 Issues Web page (**scsite.com/ dc2004/issues**). Click Issue #1 below Chapter 4.

WEB LINK 4-2

Clock Speed

Visit the Discovering Computers 2004 WEB LINK page (**scsite.com/dc2004/weblink**). Click Clock Speed below Chapter 4.

The pace of the system clock, called the **clock speed**, is measured by the number of ticks per second. Current personal computer processors have clock speeds in the gigahertz range. Giga is a prefix that stands for billion, and a *hertz* is one cycle per second. Thus, one **gigahertz (GHz)** equals one billion ticks of the system clock per second. A computer that operates at 1.7 GHz has 1.7 billion (giga) clock cycles in one second (hertz).

The system clock is one of the major factors that influence a computer's speed. The faster the clock speed, the more instructions the processor can execute per second. Given two otherwise equal processors, the one with a higher clock speed will process more instructions per second. For example, a 2.3 GHz processor is faster than a 1.3 GHz processor. The speed of the system clock has no effect on devices such as a printer or disk drive.

Some computer professionals measure a processor's speed according to the number of *MIPS* (*millions of instructions per second*) it can process. Current desktop personal computers, for example, can process more than 300 MIPS. No real standard for measuring MIPS exists, however, because different instructions require varying amounts of processing time.

Comparison of Personal Computer Processors

The leading processor chip manufacturers for personal computers are Intel®, AMD (Advanced Micro Devices), and Motorola. These manufacturers often identify their processor chips by a model name or model number. Figure 4-8 summarizes the historical development of the personal computer processor and documents the increases in clock speed and number of transistors in chips since 1982. The greater the number of transistors, the more complex and powerful the chip.

With its earlier processors, Intel used a model number to identify the various chips. After learning that processor model numbers could not be trademarked and protected from use by competitors, Intel began identifying its processors with names — thus emerged the series of processors known as the Pentium®. Most high-performance PCs use some type of **Pentium**® processor. Less expensive, basic PCs use a brand of Intel processor called the **Celeron**®. Two more brands, called the **Xeon**™ and **Itanium**® processors, are ideal for workstations and low-end servers. Read Issue 4-2 for a related discussion.

❓FAQ 4-1

Does the system clock also keep track of the current day and time?

No, a separate battery-backed chip, called the *real-time clock*, keeps track of the date and time in a computer. The battery continues to run the real-time clock even when the computer is off.

For more information about the system and real-time clocks, visit the Discovering Computers 2004 FAQ Web page (**scsite.com/dc2004/faq**). Click Computer Clocks below Chapter 4.

ISSUE 4-2

Perfection at What Price?

A glitch within a single computer chip can cause untold problems. A design flaw in Intel's Pentium® processor chip caused a rounding error once in nine billion division operations. For most users, this would result in a mistake only once in every 27,000 years, so Intel initially ignored the problem. After an unexpected public outcry, however, Intel eventually supplied replacements to anyone who wanted one, at a cost of almost $500 million. (Intel's costs were equivalent to half a year's research and development budget.) In 2000 and 2001, overheating, processing delays, and micro-code problems affected Intel's Pentium® III chips, resulting in a recall of the defective chips. Do people overreact to chip issues? Why? How much perfection do consumers have a right to expect? How serious should the problem be before a chip is recalled? Should the company be responsible for notifying all customers who have purchased defective chips?

For more information about processors and flaw issues, visit the Discovering Computers 2004 Issues Web page (**scsite.com/dc2004/issues**). Click Issue #2 below Chapter 4.

COMPARISON OF WIDELY USED PERSONAL COMPUTER PROCESSORS

Name	Date Introduced	Manufacturer	Clock Speed	Number of Transistors
Itanium® 2	2002	Intel	1 GHz and up	221 million
Xeon™	2001	Intel	1.4–2.8 GHz	140 million
Itanium®	2001	Intel	733–800 MHz	25.4–60 million
Pentium® 4	2000	Intel	1.4–3.06 GHz	42–55 million
Pentium® III Xeon™	1999	Intel	500–900 MHz	9.5–28 million
Pentium® III	1999	Intel	400 MHz–1.4 GHz	9.5–28 million
Celeron®	1998	Intel	266 MHz–2.20 GHz	7.5–19 million
Pentium® II Xeon	1998	Intel	400–450 MHz	7.5–27 million
Pentium® II	1997	Intel	234–450 MHz	7.5 million
Pentium® with MMX™ technology	1997	Intel	166–233 MHz	4.5 million
Pentium® Pro	1995	Intel	150–200 MHz	5.5 million
Pentium®	1993	Intel	75–200 MHz	3.3 million
80486DX	1989	Intel	25–100 MHz	1.2 million
80386DX	1985	Intel	16–33 MHz	275,000
80286	1982	Intel	6–12 MHz	134,000
Opteron™	2003	AMD	2–2.4 GHz	100 million
Athlon™ MP	2002	AMD	1.53–1.6 GHz	37.5 million
Athlon™ XP	2001	AMD	1.33–1.73 GHz	37.5 million
Athlon™	1999	AMD	500 MHz–1.4 GHz	22–38 million
Duron™	1999	AMD	600 MHz–1.4 GHz	18 million
AMD–K6® III	1999	AMD	400–450 MHz	21.3 million
AMD–K6®–2	1998	AMD	366–550 MHz	9.3 million
AMD–K6®	1998	AMD	300 MHz	8.8 million
PowerPC	1994	Motorola	50 MHz–1.25 GHz	Up to 50 million
68040	1989	Motorola	25–40 MHz	1.2 million
68030	1987	Motorola	16–50 MHz	270,000
68020	1984	Motorola	16–33 MHz	190,000

FIGURE 4-8   A comparison of some of the more widely used personal computer and server processors.

AMD is the leading manufacturer of **Intel-compatible processors**, which have a similar internal design as Intel processors and perform the same functions and can be as powerful, but often are less expensive. Intel and Intel-compatible processors are used in PCs.

Apple Macintosh and Power Macintosh computers use a *Motorola processor*, which has a design different from the Intel-style processor. For Apple's PowerPC, Motorola introduced a new processor architecture that increased the speed of the computer.

Many of Intel's latest processor chips contain *Hyper-Threading (HT) Technology*, which improves processing power and time by allowing the processor chip to mimic the power of two processors. Intel, AMD, and Motorola processors have built-in instructions to improve the performance of multimedia, the Web, and 3-D graphics. Their processors for notebook computers also include technology to optimize and extend battery life.

A new type of processor, called *system on a chip*, integrates the functions of a processor, memory, and a video card on a single chip. Lower priced personal computers, Tablet PCs, set-top boxes, networking devices, and consumer electronics such as music players and game consoles sometimes have a system-on-a-chip processor. The goal of system-on-a-chip manufacturers is to create processors that have faster clock speeds, consume less power, are small, and are cost effective.

If you are ready to buy a new computer, the processor you select should depend on how you plan to use the computer. If you purchase an IBM-compatible PC, you will choose an Intel processor or an Intel-compatible processor. Apple Macintosh and Power Macintosh users will choose a Motorola processor. Current models include the PowerPC G3 and PowerPC G4.

Your intended use also will determine the clock speed you need. A home user surfing the Web, for example, will not need as fast a processor as an artist working with graphics or applications requiring multimedia capabilities such as full-motion video. Figure 4-9 outlines guidelines for selecting an Intel processor. Remember, the higher the clock speed, the faster the processor, and the more expensive the computer.

Processor Installation and Upgrades

Instead of buying an entirely new computer, you might be able to upgrade your processor to increase the computer's performance. Be certain the processor you buy is compatible with your computer's motherboard; otherwise, you will have to replace the motherboard, too. Replacing a processor is a fairly simple process, whereas replacing a motherboard is much more complicated.

Processor upgrades fall into one of three types: chip for chip, piggyback, or daughterboard. A *chip-for-chip upgrade* requires you remove the existing processor chip and replace it with a new one. With a *piggyback upgrade*, you stack the new processor chip on top of the old one. In a *daughterboard upgrade*, the new

GUIDELINES FOR SELECTING AN INTEL PROCESSOR

Intel Processor	Desired Clock Speed	Use
Itanium® or Xeon™	1 GHz and up	Power users with workstations; low-end servers on a network
Pentium® family	2.5 GHz and up	Power users or users who design professional drawings; produce and edit videos; record and edit music; participate in video conferences; create professional Web sites; play graphic-intensive multiplayer Internet games
	1.7 GHz to 2.5 GHz	Users who design professional documents containing graphics such as newsletters or number-intensive spreadsheets; produce multimedia presentations; use the Web as an intensive research tool; send documents and graphics via the Web; watch videos; play graphic-intensive games on CD or DVD; create personal Web sites
	Up to 1.7 GHz	Home users who manage personal finances; create basic documents with word processing and spreadsheet software; edit photographs; communicate with others on the Web via e-mail, chat rooms, and discussions; shop on the Web; create basic Web pages
Celeron®	1.2 GHz and up	Home users who manage personal finances; create basic documents with word processing and spreadsheet software; edit photographs; make greeting cards and calendars; use educational or entertainment CDs; communicate with others on the Web via e-mail, chat rooms, and discussions

FIGURE 4-9 Determining which processor to obtain when you purchase a computer depends on computer usage.

processor chip is physically on an adapter card that plugs into the motherboard.

With some chip-for-chip upgrades, you insert the new processor chip into an opening, or *socket*, on the motherboard. Many PGA (pin grid array) chips use a zero-insertion force socket. A *zero-insertion force* (ZIF) socket has a small lever or screw that allows users to install and remove processor chips with no force (Figure 4-10). Some motherboards have a second ZIF socket that holds an upgrade chip. In this case, the existing processor chip remains on the motherboard, and you install the upgrade chip into the second ZIF socket.

FIGURE 4-10   HOW TO INSTALL A PROCESSOR CHIP IN A ZERO-INSERTION FORCE SOCKET

Step 1:
Lift the lever on the socket.

lever

Step 2:
Insert the chip.

Step 3:
Push the lever down.

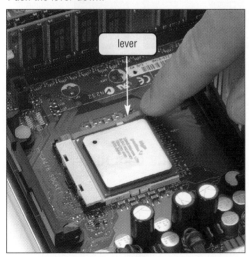
lever

⟨?⟩FAQ 4-2

Do I need to take any special precautions when I am working inside the computer case?

Turn off and unplug the computer before opening the case. For less than $10 from an electronics or computer store, buy an *antistatic wristband* to prevent static electricity from damaging the computer's circuitry while you replace components. Do not twist, bend, or force components into place. Gently work around existing cables.

For more information about replacing components in the system unit, visit the Discovering Computers 2004 FAQ Web page (**scsite.com/dc2004/faq**). Click Replacing Components below Chapter 4.

Heat Sinks and Heat Pipes

Newer processor chips generate a lot of heat, which could cause the chip to burn up. Although the computer's main fan generates airflow, today's processors require additional cooling. A *heat sink* is a small ceramic or metal component with fins on its surface that absorbs and ventilates heat produced by electrical components such as a processor (Figure 4-11). Some heat sinks are packaged as part of a processor chip. Others are installed on top or the side of the chip. Because a heat sink consumes a lot of space, a smaller device called a *heat pipe* cools processors in notebook computers.

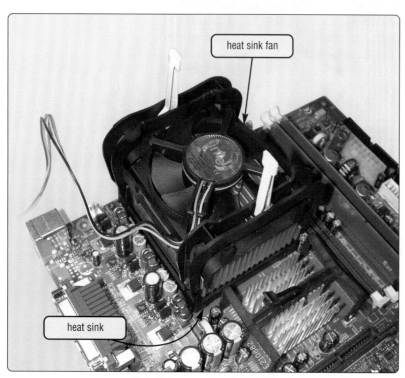

FIGURE 4-11 A heat sink, which is attached to the top of a processor below the fan, prevents the chip from overheating. The heat sink fan helps distribute air dissipated by the heat sink.

Coprocessors

A *coprocessor* is a special additional processor chip or circuit board that assists the processor in performing specific tasks and increases the performance of the computer. Users running engineering or scientific programs, for instance, will notice a dramatic increase in speed in applications that take advantage of a *floating-point coprocessor*. Floating-point coprocessors sometimes are called math or numeric coprocessors. Processors for personal computers today usually include floating-point processing capabilities.

Parallel Processing

Some computers use more than one processor to speed processing times. Known as *parallel processing*, this method uses multiple processors simultaneously to execute a program (Figure 4-12). Parallel processing divides up a problem so that multiple processors work on their assigned portion of the problem at the same time. As you might expect, parallel processing requires special software that recognizes how to divide up the problem and then bring the results back together again. Supercomputers use parallel processing for applications such as weather forecasting. Some applications draw on the idle time of home users' personal computers to achieve parallel processing. Read Apply It 4-2 for more information.

FIGURE 4-12 Parallel processing divides up a problem so that multiple processors work on their assigned portion of a problem at the same time. In this illustration, one processor, called the control processor, is managing the operations of four other processors.

☑ APPLY IT 4-2

Computers at Work While You Sleep

When you are napping, studying for a test, or going to class, your computer can be working to cure life-threatening diseases, thanks to a special Intel-sponsored PC philanthropy program.

The *Intel® Philanthropic Peer-to-Peer Program* researches cures and medicines for cancer, Alzheimer's disease, Type II diabetes, Mad Cow disease, and other medical conditions. The company has recorded more than 3 million users and is networking thousands of computers to perform complex calculations and run intricate programs during the computers' idle time, which has amounted to more than 1 million years of processing time.

The research expenses are reduced for these researchers because they are obtaining unlimited computational power for practically no cost. Instead of needing expensive supercomputers to perform these operations, they use this peer-to-peer computing network to process up to 1 zettaflop (10 followed by 21 zeros) per second, which is the largest computation ever performed. Intel estimates it has saved $500 million during the past 10 years utilizing this networking technology to develop new chips.

Medical science is not the only peer-to-peer application, however. The *SETI@home* screensaver program searches for extraterrestrial communications by processing radio telescope signals. Other applications have searched for unique prime numbers, mapped hydrogen gas in the Milky Way, looked for disappearing black holes, and investigated global climate changes.

A few companies pay home users to donate their spare computer time based on the computers' productivity, which usually amounts to a sum that defrays Internet access charges.

For more information about peer-to-peer philanthropy, visit the Discovering Computers 2004 Apply It Web page (**scsite.com/dc2004/apply**). Click Apply It #2 below Chapter 4.

☑ QUIZ YOURSELF 4-1

To check your knowledge of the system unit styles, motherboards, processor components and machine cycles, and characteristics of personal computer processors, visit the Discovering Computers 2004 Quiz Yourself Web page (**scsite.com/dc2004/quiz**). Click Objectives 1 – 4 below Chapter 4.

DATA REPRESENTATION

To understand fully the way a computer processes data, you should know how a computer represents data. People communicate through speech by combining words into sentences. Human speech is **analog** because it uses continuous (wave form) signals that vary in strength and quality. Most computers are **digital**. They recognize only two discrete states: on and off. This is because computers are electronic devices powered by electricity, which also has only two states: on and off.

The two digits, 0 and 1, easily can represent these two states (Figure 4-13). The digit 0 represents the electronic state of off (absence of an electronic charge). The digit 1 represents the electronic state of on (presence of an electronic charge).

When people count, they use the digits in the decimal system (0 through 9). The computer, by contrast, uses a binary system because it recognizes only two states. The **binary system** is a number system that has just two unique digits, 0 and 1, called bits. A **bit** (short for *binary digit*) is the smallest unit of data the computer can process. By itself, a bit is not very informative.

When 8 bits are grouped together as a unit, they form a **byte**. A byte is informative because it provides enough different combinations of 0s and 1s to represent 256 individual characters. These characters include numbers, uppercase and lowercase letters of the alphabet, punctuation marks, and others, such as the letters of the Greek alphabet.

BINARY DIGIT (BIT)	ELECTRONIC CHARGE	ELECTRONIC STATE
1		ON
0		OFF

FIGURE 4-13 A computer circuit represents the 0 or the 1 electronically by the presence or absence of an electronic charge.

The combinations of 0s and 1s that represent characters are defined by patterns called a coding scheme. In one coding scheme, the number 3 is represented as 00110011, the number 5 as 00110101, and the capital letter D as 01000100 (Figure 4-14). Two popular coding schemes are ASCII and EBCDIC (Figure 4-15). The *American Standard Code for Information Interchange* (*ASCII* pronounced ASK-ee) scheme is the most widely used coding system to represent data. Most personal computers and midrange servers use the ASCII coding scheme. The *Extended Binary Coded Decimal Interchange Code* (*EBCDIC* pronounced EB-see-dic) scheme is used primarily on mainframe computers and high-end servers.

The ASCII and EBCDIC coding schemes are sufficient for English and Western European languages but are not large enough for Asian and other languages that use different alphabets. *Unicode* is a coding scheme capable of representing all the world's current languages. Appendix B at the back of this book discusses the ASCII, EBCDIC, and Unicode schemes in more depth, along with the parity bit and number systems.

ASCII	SYMBOL	EBCDIC
00110000	0	11110000
00110001	1	11110001
00110010	2	11110010
00110011	3	11110011
00110100	4	11110100
00110101	5	11110101
00110110	6	11110110
00110111	7	11110111
00111000	8	11111000
00111001	9	11111001
01000001	A	11000001
01000010	B	11000010
01000011	C	11000011
01000100	D	11000100
01000101	E	11000101
01000110	F	11000110
01000111	G	11000111
01001000	H	11001000
01001001	I	11001001
01001010	J	11010001
01001011	K	11010010
01001100	L	11010011
01001101	M	11010100
01001110	N	11010101
01001111	O	11010110
01010000	P	11010111
01010001	Q	11011000
01010010	R	11011001
01010011	S	11100010
01010100	T	11100011
01010101	U	11100100
01010110	V	11100101
01010111	W	11100110
01011000	X	11100111
01011001	Y	11101000
01011010	Z	11101001
00100001	!	01011010
00100010	"	01111111
00100011	#	01111011
00100100	$	01011011
00100101	%	01101100
00100110	&	01010000
00101000	(	01001101
00101001	)	01011101
00101010	*	01011100
00101011	+	01001110

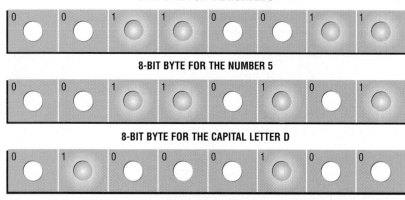

8-BIT BYTE FOR THE NUMBER 3

| 0 | 0 | 1 | 1 | 0 | 0 | 1 | 1 |

8-BIT BYTE FOR THE NUMBER 5

| 0 | 0 | 1 | 1 | 0 | 1 | 0 | 1 |

8-BIT BYTE FOR THE CAPITAL LETTER D

| 0 | 1 | 0 | 0 | 0 | 1 | 0 | 0 |

FIGURE 4-14 Eight bits grouped together as a unit are called a byte. A byte represents a single character in the computer.

FIGURE 4-15 Two popular coding schemes are ASCII and EBCDIC.

Coding schemes such as ASCII make it possible for humans to interact with a digital computer that processes only bits. When you press a key on a keyboard, the electronic signal is converted into a binary form the computer can process and is stored in memory. Every character is converted to its corresponding byte. The computer then processes the data as bytes, which actually is a series of on/off electrical states. When processing is finished, software converts the byte into a human-recognizable number, letter of the alphabet, or special character that is displayed on a screen or is printed (Figure 4-16). All of these conversions take place so quickly that you do not realize they are occurring.

Standards, such as those defined by ASCII and EBCDIC, also make it possible for components within computers to communicate with each other successfully. By following these and other standards, manufacturers can produce a component and be assured that it will operate correctly in a computer. Standards also enable consumers to purchase components that are compatible with their computer configurations.

MEMORY

Memory consists of electronic components that store instructions waiting to be executed by the processor, data needed by those instructions, and the results of processed data (information). Memory usually consists of one or more chips on the motherboard or some other circuit board in the computer.

FIGURE 4-16   HOW A LETTER IS CONVERTED TO BINARY FORM AND BACK

Step 1:
The user presses the capital letter **D** (SHIFT+D keys) on the keyboard.

Step 2:
An electronic signal for the capital letter **D** is sent to the system unit.

Step 3:
The signal for the capital letter **D** is converted to its ASCII binary code (01000100) and is stored in memory for processing.

Step 4:
After processing, the binary code for the capital letter **D** is converted to an image, and displayed on the output device.

Memory stores three basic categories of items: (1) the operating system and other system software that control or maintain the computer and its devices; (2) application programs that carry out a specific task such as word processing; and (3) the data being processed by the application programs and resulting information. This role of memory to store both data and programs is known as the *stored program concept*.

A byte (character) is the basic storage unit in memory. When application program instructions and data transfer into memory from storage devices, the instructions and data exist as bytes. Each byte resides temporarily in a location in memory, called an *address*. An address simply is a unique number that identifies the location of the byte in memory. The illustration in Figure 4-17 shows how seats on a long-distance passenger train are similar to addresses in memory: (1) a seat holds one person at a time and an address in memory holds a single byte, (2) both a seat and an address can be empty, and (3) a seat has a unique identifier and so does a memory address. To access data or instructions in memory, the computer references the addresses that contain bytes of data.

Manufacturers state the size of memory chips and storage devices in terms of the number of bytes the chip or device has available for storage (Figure 4-18). Recall that storage devices hold data, instructions, and information for future use, while most memory holds these items temporarily. A **kilobyte** (**KB** or **K**) is equal to exactly 1,024 bytes. To simplify memory and storage definitions, computer users often round a kilobyte down to 1,000 bytes. For example, if a memory chip can store 100 KB, it can hold approximately 100,000 bytes (characters). A **megabyte** (**MB**) is equal to approximately 1 million bytes. A **gigabyte** (**GB**) equals approximately 1 billion bytes.

The system unit contains two types of memory: volatile and nonvolatile. When the computer's power is turned off, *volatile memory* loses its contents. *Nonvolatile memory*, by contrast, does not lose its contents when power is removed from the computer; for example, when the computer is turned off or in case of a power failure or other loss of electricity to the computer. Thus, volatile memory is temporary and nonvolatile memory is permanent. RAM is the most common type of volatile memory. Examples of nonvolatile memory include ROM, flash memory, and CMOS. The following sections discuss these types of memory.

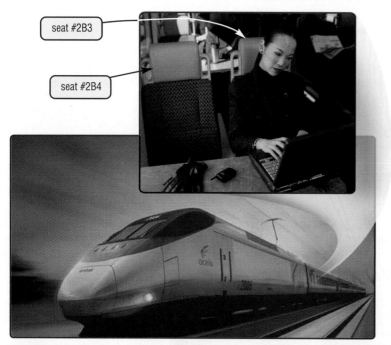

seat #2B3

seat #2B4

FIGURE 4-17 Seats in a long-distance passenger train are similar to addresses in memory in several ways: (1) a seat holds one person at a time and an address in memory holds a single byte; (2) both a seat and an address can be empty; and (3) a seat has a unique identifier and so does a memory address.

MEMORY AND STORAGE SIZES

Term	Abbreviation	Approximate Size	Exact Amount	Approximate Number of Pages of Text
Kilobyte	KB or K	1 thousand bytes	1,024 bytes	1/2
Megabyte	MB	1 million bytes	1,048,576 bytes	500
Gigabyte	GB	1 billion bytes	1,073,741,824 bytes	500,000
Terabyte	TB	1 trillion bytes	1,099,511,627,776 bytes	500,000,000

FIGURE 4-18 Terms commonly used to define memory and storage sizes.

RAM

Users typically are referring to RAM when discussing computer memory. **RAM** (*random access memory*), also called *main memory* or *primary storage*, consists of memory chips that can be read from and written to by the processor and other devices. When the computer is powered on, certain operating system files (such as the files that determine how the Windows XP desktop is displayed) load into RAM from a storage device such as a hard disk. These files remain in RAM as long as the computer has continuous power. As additional programs and data are requested, they also load into RAM from storage.

The processor interprets and executes a program's instructions while the program is in RAM. During this time, the contents of RAM may change (Figure 4-19). RAM can hold multiple programs simultaneously, provided the computer has enough RAM to accommodate all the programs. The program with which you are working usually is displayed on the screen.

FIGURE 4-19   HOW PROGRAM INSTRUCTIONS TRANSFER IN AND OUT OF RAM

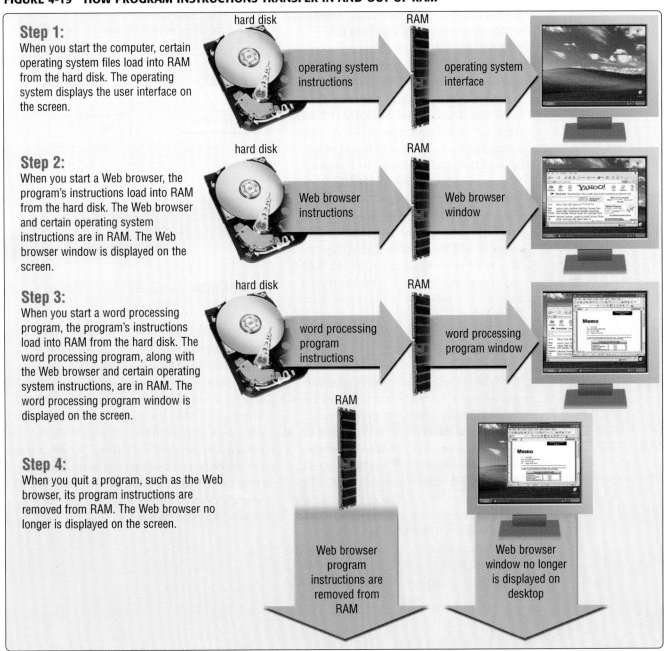

Step 1:
When you start the computer, certain operating system files load into RAM from the hard disk. The operating system displays the user interface on the screen.

hard disk — RAM
operating system instructions → operating system interface

Step 2:
When you start a Web browser, the program's instructions load into RAM from the hard disk. The Web browser and certain operating system instructions are in RAM. The Web browser window is displayed on the screen.

hard disk — RAM
Web browser instructions → Web browser window

Step 3:
When you start a word processing program, the program's instructions load into RAM from the hard disk. The word processing program, along with the Web browser and certain operating system instructions, are in RAM. The word processing program window is displayed on the screen.

hard disk — RAM
word processing program instructions → word processing program window

Step 4:
When you quit a program, such as the Web browser, its program instructions are removed from RAM. The Web browser no longer is displayed on the screen.

RAM
Web browser program instructions are removed from RAM

Web browser window no longer is displayed on desktop

WEB LINK 4-3

RAM

Visit the Discovering
Computers 2004 WEB
LINK page (**scsite.com/
dc2004/weblink**). Click
RAM below Chapter 4.

Most RAM is volatile, which means it loses
its contents when the power is removed from
the computer. For this reason, you must save
any items you may need in the future. Saving
is the process of copying items from RAM to a
storage device such as a hard disk.

Two basic types of RAM chips exist:
dynamic RAM and static RAM.

- *Dynamic RAM* (*DRAM* pronounced DEE-
ram) chips must be re-energized constantly
or they lose their contents. Many variations
of DRAM chips exist, most of which are
faster than the basic DRAM. *Synchronous
DRAM* (*SDRAM*) chips are much faster than
DRAM chips because they are synchronized
to the system clock. *Double Data Rate
SDRAM* (*DDR SDRAM*) chips are even
faster than SDRAM chips because they
transfer data twice for each clock cycle,
instead of just once, and DDR 2 is even
faster than DDR. *Rambus® DRAM* (*RDRAM®*)
chips are yet another type of DRAM chips
that are much faster than SDRAM chips
because they use pipelining techniques.
Most personal computers today use some
form of SDRAM chips or RDRAM chips.

- *Static RAM* (*SRAM* pronounced ESS-ram)
chips are faster and more reliable than any
variation of DRAM chips. These chips do not
have to be re-energized as often as DRAM
chips, thus, the term static. SRAM chips,
however, are much more expensive than
DRAM chips. Special applications such as
cache use SRAM chips. A later section in this
chapter discusses cache.

RAM chips often are smaller in size than
processor chips. RAM chips usually reside on a
memory module, which is a small circuit
board. **Memory slots** on the motherboard hold
memory modules (Figure 4-20). Three types of
memory modules are SIMMs, DIMMs, and
RIMMs. A *SIMM* (*single inline memory module*)
has pins on opposite sides of the circuit board
that connect together to form a single set of
contacts. With a *DIMM* (*dual inline memory
module*), by contrast, the pins on opposite sides
of the circuit board do not connect and thus
form two sets of contacts. SIMMs and DIMMs

typically hold SDRAM chips. A *RIMM*
(*Rambus® inline memory module*) houses
RDRAM chips. For a more technical discussion
about RAM, read the High-Tech Talk article on
page 4.37 at the end of this chapter.

dual inline
memory module

memory chip

memory slot

FIGURE 4-20 This photo shows a memory
module being inserted into a motherboard.

RAM CONFIGURATIONS The amount of
RAM necessary in a computer often depends
on the types of software you plan to use. A
computer executes programs that are in RAM.
Think of RAM as the workspace on the top of
your desk. Just as the top of your desk needs a
certain amount of space to hold papers, a computer needs a certain amount of memory to
store programs, data, and information. The
more RAM a computer has, the faster the
computer will respond.

A software package typically indicates the minimum amount of RAM it requires (Figure 4-21). If you want the application to perform optimally, usually you need more than the minimum specifications on the software package.

Generally, home users running Windows XP and using basic application software such as word processing should have at least 128 MB of RAM. Most business users who work with accounting, financial, or spreadsheet programs, voice recognition, and programs requiring multimedia capabilities should have a minimum of 256 MB of RAM. Users creating professional Web sites or using graphics-intensive applications will want at least 1 GB of RAM.

Figure 4-22a provides guidelines for the amount of RAM for various types of users. Figure 4-22b shows advertisements that match to each user requirement. Advertisements normally list the type of processor, the clock speed of the processor, and the amount of RAM in the computer. The amount of RAM in computers purchased today ranges from 128 MB to 2 GB.

System Requirements	Windows® 2000 Professional	Windows NT® Workstation	Windows® 98/Me
Windows® XP Home Edition/ Professional	• Intel Pentium processor at 133MHZ or higher	• Windows NT v4.0 Workstation operating system with service pack 6 or higher	• Intel Pentium processor at 133MHZ or higher
• Intel® Pentium® processor at 233MHZ or higher	• AMD K5™ Family processor at 133MHZ or higher	• Intel Pentium processor at 133MHZ or higher	• AMD K5 processor at 133MHZ or higher
• AMD K6®/Athlon™/Duron™ Family processor at 233MHZ or higher	• 64 MB of RAM	• AMD K5 processor at 133MHZ or higher	• 32 MB of RAM
• 64 MB of RAM		• 32MB of RAM	**REQUIRED FOR ALL INSTALLATIONS**
			• 50 MB of available hard disk space
			• CD-ROM or DVD-ROM drive

FIGURE 4-21 The minimum system requirements for a software product usually are printed on the box.

? FAQ 4-3

Can I add more RAM to my computer?

Check your computer documentation to see how much RAM you can add. RAM modules are relatively inexpensive and usually include easy-to-follow installation instructions. Be sure to purchase RAM compatible with your brand and model of computer.

For more information about upgrading RAM, visit the Discovering Computers 2004 FAQ Web page (**scsite.com/dc2004/faq**). Click Upgrading RAM below Chapter 4.

Figure 4-22a (RAM guidelines)

RAM	128 to 256 MB	256 to 1 GB	1 GB and up
Use	Home and business users managing personal finances; using standard application software such as word processing; using educational or entertainment CD-ROMs; communicating with others on the Web	Users requiring more advanced multimedia capabilities; running number-intensive accounting, financial, or spreadsheet programs; using voice recognition; working with videos, music, and digital imaging; creating Web sites; participating in video conferences; playing Internet games	Power users creating professional Web sites; running sophisticated CAD, 3-D design,or other graphics-intensive software

Figure 4-22b (computers for sale)

Model	C130	A1.4Q	A173	P2G	AI6M	P253R
Processor	1.3 GHz Celeron® processor	1.4 GHz Duron™ processor	1.73 GHz Athlon™ XP processor	2 GHz Pentium® 4 processor	1.6 Athlon™ MP processor	2.53 GHz Xeon™ processor
Memory	128 MB SDRAM	256 MB SDRAM	256 MB SDRAM	512 MB SDRAM	1 GB SDRAM	2 GB RDRAM

FIGURE 4-22 Determining how much RAM you need depends on the applications you intend to run on your computer. Advertisements for computers normally list the type of processor, the speed of the processor, and the amount of RAM installed.

Cache

Most of today's computers improve processing times with **cache** (pronounced cash). Two types of cache are memory cache and disk cache. This chapter discusses memory cache. Chapter 7 discusses disk cache.

Memory cache helps speed the processes of the computer because it stores frequently used instructions and data. Most personal computers today have two types of memory cache: L1 cache and L2 cache. Servers also may have L3 cache.

- *L1 cache* is built directly into the processor chip. L1 cache usually has a very small capacity, ranging from 8 KB to 128 KB. The most common size is 8 KB.

- *L2 cache* is slightly slower than L1 cache but has a much larger capacity, ranging from 64 KB to 4 MB. When discussing cache, most users are referring to L2 cache. On older computers, L2 cache consisted of high-speed SRAM chips on the motherboard or an adapter card of chips inserted into the motherboard. Current processors include *advanced transfer cache*, a type of L2 cache built directly on the processor chip. Processors that use advanced transfer cache perform at much faster rates than those that do not use it.

- *L3 cache* is a cache separate from the processor chip on the motherboard. L3 cache exists only on computers that use L2 advanced transfer cache.

Cache speeds up processing time because it stores frequently used instructions and data. When the processor needs an instruction or data, it searches memory in this order: L1 cache, then L2 cache, then L3 cache (if it exists), then RAM — with a greater delay in processing for each level of memory it must search. If the instruction or data is not found in memory, then it must search a slower speed storage medium such as a hard disk, CD, or DVD.

A computer with L2 cache usually performs at speeds 10- to 40-percent faster than those without cache. To realize the largest increase in performance, a personal computer should have at least 256 KB of L2 advanced transfer cache (Figure 4-23). Servers and workstations can have at least 2 MB of L2 or L3 cache.

Desktop 2500

- Intel® Pentium® 4 Processor 2 GHz with 256 KB built-in L2 cache
- 1 GB DDR SDRAM
- 19" Flat Panel Display
- 60 GB Ultra ATA Hard Disk
- 4 PCI Slots, 1 AGP Slot
- 4 USB Ports (2 in front)
- Front Audio Port
- 64 MB Video Card
- Microsoft Windows XP
- Microsoft Office XP Standard

L2 advanced transfer cache

FIGURE 4-23 This current computer advertisement shows that most new computers have at least 256 KB of L2 advanced transfer cache.

ROM

Read-only memory (**ROM** pronounced rahm) refers to memory chips storing permanent data and instructions. The data on most ROM chips cannot be modified — hence, the name read-only. ROM is nonvolatile. Its contents are not lost when power is removed from the computer. In addition to the computer, many devices contain ROM chips. For example, ROM chips in printers contain data for fonts.

Manufacturers of ROM chips often record data, instructions, or information on the chips when they manufacture the chip. These ROM chips, called **firmware**, contain permanently written data, instructions, or information. One type of firmware, for example, contains the computer's startup instructions.

A *PROM* (*programmable read-only memory*) chip is a blank ROM chip onto which a programmer can write permanently. Programmers use *microcode* instructions to program a PROM chip. Once a programmer writes the microcode onto the PROM chip, it functions like a regular ROM chip and cannot be erased or changed.

A variation of the PROM chip, called an *EEPROM* (*electrically erasable programmable read-only memory*) chip, allows a programmer to erase the microcode with an electric signal.

WEB LINK 4-4

Cache

Visit the Discovering Computers 2004 WEB LINK page (**scsite.com/ dc2004/weblink**). Click Cache below Chapter 4.

Flash Memory

Flash memory is a type of nonvolatile memory that can be erased electronically and reprogrammed, similar to EEPROM. Most computers use flash memory to hold their startup instructions because it allows the computer easily to update its contents. For example, when the computer changes from standard time to daylight savings time, the contents of a flash memory chip (and the real-time clock chip) change to reflect the new time. When you add new hardware devices to the computer, the flash memory chip changes the configuration information about the computer.

Flash memory chips also store data and programs on many mobile computers and devices, such as PDAs, digital cellular telephones, printers, set-top boxes, digital cameras, automotive devices, music players, digital voice recorders, and pagers. When you enter names and addresses into a PDA, a flash memory chip stores the data. The flash memory chip in a digital cellular telephone stores names and telephone numbers. Current MP3 players can play more than one hour of music stored on a flash memory chip (Figure 4-24). Read Looking Ahead 4-1 for a look at the next generation of computers and chips.

Another type of flash memory is the flash memory card. A later section in this chapter discusses flash memory cards, which store flash memory on a removable device instead of a chip.

WEB LINK 4-5

Flash Memory

Visit the Discovering Computers 2004 WEB LINK page (**scsite.com/ dc2004/weblink**). Click Flash Memory below Chapter 4.

FIGURE 4-24   HOW AN MP3 MUSIC PLAYER MIGHT STORE MUSIC

Step 1:
Purchase and download MP3 music tracks from a Web site. With one end of a special cable connected to the system unit, connect the other end into the MP3 player.

Step 2:
Instruct the computer to copy the MP3 music tracks to the flash memory chip in the MP3 player.

Step 3:
Plug the headphones into the MP3 player, push a button on the MP3 player, and listen to the music through the headphones.

to headphones

flash memory chip

from computer

flash memory card

MP3 player

LOOKING AHEAD 4-1

Next-Generation Computers and Chips: Faster and Smaller

When Intel cofounder Gordon Moore predicted in 1965 that the number of transistors and resistors placed on computer chips would double every year, he realized that the computer industry was in store for incredible growth and technological advances. Although he changed his prediction in 1975 to doubling every two years, the computer industry has continued to develop at breakneck speed.

Researchers and engineers have a variety of predictions for the next generation of computers. For example, *ovonic memory* chips store data virtually forever and are expected eventually to replace flash memory chips, which wear out over time. Scientists at Newcastle University in England are developing clock-free systems, called *asynchronous computers*, that would reduce heat and further shrink hardware sizes. These computers would be useful in complex systems demanding speedy performance, such as in global air traffic control.

Ovonic Memory Diagram

Top Electrode

Polycrystalline Chalcogenide

Programmable Volume

Heater

Bottom Electrode

For a look at next-generation computers and chips, visit the Discovering Computers 2004 Looking Ahead Web page (**scsite.com/dc2004/ looking**). Click Looking Ahead #1 below Chapter 4.

CMOS

Some RAM chips, flash memory chips, and other types of memory chips use **complementary metal-oxide semiconductor** (**CMOS** pronounced SEE-moss) technology because it provides high speeds and consumes little power. CMOS technology uses battery power to retain information even when the power to the computer is off. Battery-backed CMOS memory chips, for example, can keep the calendar, date, and time current even when the computer is off. The flash memory chips that store a computer's startup information often use CMOS technology.

FAQ 4-4

What should I do if my computer's date and time are wrong?

First, try resetting the date and time. To do this in Windows XP, double-click the time at the right edge of the taskbar. If the computer continues to lose time or display an incorrect date, you may need to replace the CMOS battery on the motherboard that powers the system clock.

For more information about the CMOS battery, visit the Discovering Computers 2004 FAQ Web page (**scsite.com/dc2004/faq**). Click CMOS Battery below Chapter 4.

Memory Access Times

Access time is the amount of time it takes the processor to read data, instructions, and information from memory. A computer's access time directly affects how fast the computer processes data. Today's manufacturers use a variety of terminology to state access times (Figure 4-25). Some use fractions of a second, which for memory occurs in nanoseconds. A **nanosecond** (abbreviated *ns*) is one billionth of a second. A nanosecond is extremely fast (Figure 4-26). In fact, electricity travels about one foot in a nanosecond.

Other manufacturers state access times in MHz; for example, 83 MHz SDRAM. If a manufacturer states access time in megahertz, you can convert it to nanoseconds by dividing the megahertz number into 1 billion ns. For example, 133 MHz equals approximately 7.5 ns (1,000,000,000/133,000,000).

The access time (speed) of memory contributes to the overall performance of the computer. Standard SDRAM chips can have access times up to 133 MHz (about 7.5 ns), and access times of the DDR SDRAM chips reach 333 MHz (about 3 ns). The faster RDRAM chips can have access times up to 800 MHz (about 1.25 ns). ROM access times range from 25 to 250 ns. Accessing data in memory can be more than 200,000 times faster than accessing data on a hard disk because of the mechanical motion of the hard disk.

While access times of memory greatly affect overall computer performance, manufacturers and retailers usually list a computer's memory in terms of its size, not its access time. Thus, an advertisement might describe a computer as having 128 MB of SDRAM expandable to 512 MB.

10 million operations = 1 blink

FIGURE 4-26 It takes about one-tenth of a second to blink your eye, which is the equivalent of 100 million nanoseconds. A computer can perform some operations in as few as 10 nanoseconds. In the time it takes to blink your eye, a computer can perform some operations 10 million times.

QUIZ YOURSELF 4-2

To check your knowledge of bits, bytes, data representation, and types of memory, visit the Discovering Computers 2004 Quiz Yourself Web page (**scsite.com/dc2004/quiz**). Click Objectives 5 – 7 below Chapter 4.

ACCESS TIME TERMINOLOGY

Term	Abbreviation	Speed
Millisecond	ms	One-thousandth of a second
Microsecond	µs	One-millionth of a second
Nanosecond	ns	One-billionth of a second
Picosecond	ps	One-trillionth of a second

FIGURE 4-25 Access times are measured in fractions of a second. This table lists the terms used to define access times.

EXPANSION SLOTS AND ADAPTER CARDS

An **expansion slot** is a socket on the motherboard that can hold an adapter card. An **adapter card**, sometimes called an *expansion card*, is a circuit board that enhances functions of a component of the system unit and/or provides connections to peripherals. A **peripheral** is a device that connects to the system unit and is controlled by the processor in the computer. Examples of peripherals are modems, disk drives, printers, scanners, and keyboards.

Figure 4-27 lists a variety of types of adapter cards. Sometimes, all functionality is built into the adapter card. With others, a cable connects the adapter card to a peripheral, such as a scanner, outside the system unit. Figure 4-28 shows an adapter card being inserted into an expansion slot on a personal computer motherboard.

FIGURE 4-28 Illustrated is an adapter card being inserted into an expansion slot on the motherboard of a personal computer.

TYPES OF ADAPTER CARDS

Adapter Card	Purpose
Accelerator	Increases the speed of the processor
Disk controller	Connects disk drives
Game	Connects a joystick
I/O	Connects input and output devices such as a printer or mouse; being phased out because newer motherboards support these connections
Interface	Connects other peripherals such as a mouse, CD, DVD, or scanner
MIDI	Connects musical instruments
Modem	Connects other computers through telephone or cable television lines
Network	Connects other computers and peripherals
PC-to-TV converter	Connects a television
Sound	Connects speakers or a microphone
TV tuner	Allows viewing of television channels on the monitor
USB 2.0	Connects USB 2.0 devices
Video	Connects a monitor
Video capture	Connects a camcorder

FIGURE 4-27 Various types of adapter cards and their functions.

Some motherboards include all necessary capabilities and do not require adapter cards. For example, sound and video functions may be built into a newer motherboard. Other motherboards may require adapter cards to provide sound, video, modem, and network capabilities. A **sound card** enhances the sound-generating capabilities of a personal computer by allowing sound to be input through a microphone and output through external speakers or headset. A **video card**, also called a *graphics card*, converts computer output into a video signal that travels through a cable to the monitor, which displays an image on the screen. A **modem card**, also called an *internal modem*, is a communications device that enables computers to communicate via telephone lines, cable television lines, or other media. A **network card** is a communications device that allows the computer to access a network. Read Issue 4-3 for a related discussion.

ISSUE 4-3

Does Lower Price Mean Less Value?

Today, you can buy a personal computer for less than $1,000 that can do more than one nearly twice its cost two years ago. Part of the plunge in prices is lower-cost components, but another factor is a growing demand for less expensive machines. Many consumers are looking for inexpensive computers that are adequate for basic tasks, such as word processing and Internet access. They feel that spending higher prices for faster processors, more memory, 3-D video cards, higher-quality sound cards, more hard disk space, and other extras is an unnecessary, frivolous expense. As one industry analyst asks, "Why buy a Porsche when you are going to drive only 55 miles per hour?" How might a greater availability of lower priced personal computers change the way people, schools, and businesses buy and use them? With respect to computers, does a higher price always mean greater usefulness? Why or why not? Who might be satisfied with less than the latest computer technology? Why?

For more information about personal computer prices, visit the Discovering Computers 2004 Issues Web page (**scsite.com/dc2004/issues**). Click Issue #3 below Chapter 4.

WEB LINK 4-6

Adapter Cards

Visit the Discovering Computers 2004 WEB LINK page (**scsite.com/ dc2004/weblink**). Click Adapter Cards below Chapter 4.

In the past, installing a card was not easy and required you to set switches and other elements on the motherboard. Many of today's computers support **Plug and Play**, which means the computer automatically can configure adapter cards and other peripherals as you install them. Having Plug and Play support means you can plug in a device, turn on the computer, and then immediately begin using the device.

PC Cards and Flash Memory Cards

Notebook and other mobile computers have at least one **PC Card slot**, which is a special type of expansion slot that holds PC Cards. A **PC Card** is a thin credit card-sized device that adds memory, storage, sound, fax/modem, communications, and other capabilities to mobile computers (Figure 4-29). Because of their small size and versatility, some consumer electronics products such as digital cameras and automobiles use PC Cards.

All PC Cards conform to standards developed by the *Personal Computer Memory Card International Association* (these cards originally were called *PCMCIA cards*). These standards help to ensure the interchangeability of PC Cards among mobile computers.

PC Cards are one type of **flash memory card**, or removable flash memory device, that allows users to transfer data and information

conveniently from mobile devices to their desktop computers. Figure 4-30 shows a variety of flash memory cards. Many mobile and consumer devices, such as PDAs, digital cameras, digital music players, and cellular telephones, use these memory cards. Some printers and computers have built-in card readers or slots. In addition, you can purchase an external card reader that attaches to any computer. The type of flash memory card you have will determine the type of card reader you need.

Unlike adapter cards that require you to open the system unit and install the card onto the motherboard, you can change a flash memory card, such as a PC Card, without having to open the system unit or restart the computer. For example, if you need to connect to the Internet, simply insert the modem card in the PC Card slot of your notebook computer while the computer is running. The operating system automatically recognizes the new PC Card and allows you to connect to the Internet.

This feature of PC Cards and other flash memory cards, called *hot plugging*, allows you to insert and remove the cards while the computer is running. Chapter 7 discusses flash memory cards in more depth.

WEB LINK 4-7

PC Cards

Visit the Discovering Computers 2004 WEB LINK page (**scsite.com/ dc2004/weblink**). Click PC Cards below Chapter 4.

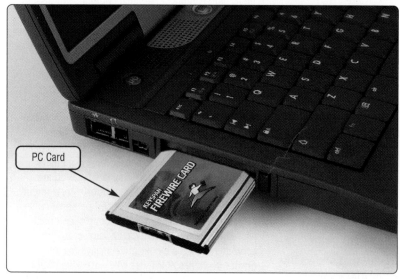

FIGURE 4-29   A PC card is sticking out of a PC Card slot on this notebook computer.

FIGURE 4-30   Flash memory cards are available in a wide range of sizes.

PORTS AND CONNECTORS

A **port** is the point at which a peripheral attaches to a system unit so it can send data or receive information from the computer. An external device, such as a keyboard, monitor, printer, mouse, and microphone, often attaches by a cable to a port on the system unit. Instead of port, the term *jack* sometimes is used to identify audio and video ports. The back of the system unit contains many ports; some newer personal computers also have ports on the front of the system unit (Figure 4-31).

Ports have different types of connectors. A **connector** joins a cable to a peripheral (Figure 4-32). One end of a cable attaches to the connector on the system unit and the other end of the cable attaches to a connector on the peripheral. Most connectors are available in one of two genders: male or female. *Male connectors* have one or more exposed pins, like the end of an electrical cord you plug into the wall. *Female connectors* have matching holes to accept the pins on a male connector, like an electrical wall outlet.

power cord
keyboard connector
serial connector
USB connector
monitor connector
FireWire connector
network connector
cable TV connector

mouse connector
printer connector
S-video connector
microphone connector
speaker connector
telephone line connectors
television audio connectors

FIGURE 4-32 A connector attaches an external peripheral to the system unit.

USB port   headphone port (or jack)

mouse port
keyboard port
serial port
USB port
monitor port
game port
FireWire ports
network port
FM reception port

printer port (parallel port)
USB port
S-video out port
microphone port
speaker port
telephone line in port

cable TV port

FIGURE 4-31 The back of a system unit has many ports. Some computers have ports on the front of the system unit, also.

WEB LINK 4-8

Ports and Connectors

Visit the Discovering Computers 2004 WEB LINK page (**scsite.com/dc2004/weblink**). Click Ports and Connectors below Chapter 4.

Sometimes, attaching a new peripheral to the computer is not possible because the connector on the system unit is the same gender as the connector on the cable. In this case, purchasing a gender changer solves this problem. A *gender changer* is a device that enables you to join two connectors that are both female or both male.

Manufacturers often identify the cables by their connector types to assist you with purchasing a cable to connect a computer to a peripheral. For example, a printer port might use any one of these connectors: 25-pin female, 36-pin female, 36-pin Centronics female, or

USB. Thus, you should understand the differences among connector types.

Figure 4-33 shows the different types of connectors on a system unit. Some system units include these connectors when you buy the computer. You add other connectors by inserting adapter cards onto the motherboard. Certain adapter cards have ports that allow you to attach a peripheral to the adapter card.

Most personal computers have at least one serial port, one parallel port, and two USB ports. The next section discusses these and other ports.

FIGURE 4-33 Examples of different types of connectors on a system unit.

Serial Ports

A **serial port** is a type of interface that connects a device to the system unit by transmitting data 1 bit at a time (Figure 4-34). Serial ports usually connect devices that do not require fast data transmission rates, such as a mouse, keyboard, or modem. The *COM port* (short for communications port) on the system unit is one type of serial port.

Some modems that connect the system unit to a telephone line use a serial port because the telephone line expects the data in a specific frequency. Serial ports conform to either the RS-232 or RS-422 standard, which specifies the number of pins used on the port's connector. Two common connectors for serial ports are a male 25-pin connector and a male 9-pin connector.

Parallel Ports

Unlike a serial port, a **parallel port** is an interface that connects devices by transferring more than 1 bit at a time (Figure 4-35). Parallel ports originally were developed as an alternative to the slower speed serial ports.

FIGURE 4-34 A serial port transmits data one bit at a time. One wire sends data, another receives data, and the remaining wires are used for other communications operations.

FIGURE 4-35 A parallel port is capable of transmitting more than one bit at a time. The port shown in this figure has eight wires that transmit data; the remaining wires are used for other communications operations.

Many printers connect to the system unit using a parallel port with a 25-pin female connector. This parallel port can transfer 8 bits of data (one byte) simultaneously through eight separate lines in a single cable. A parallel port sometimes is called a *Centronics interface*, after the company that first defined the standard for communications between the system unit and a printer.

USB Ports

A **USB port**, short for *universal serial bus port*, can connect up to 127 different peripherals together with a single connector type. Personal computers typically have two to four USB ports either on the front or back of the system unit (Figure 4-31 on page 4.25). To attach multiple peripherals using a single port, you can daisy chain the devices together outside the system unit. *Daisy chain* means the first USB device connects to the USB port on the computer, the second USB device connects to the first USB device, the third USB device connects to the second USB device, and so on. An alternative to daisy chaining is to use a USB hub. A **USB hub** is a device that plugs into a USB port on the system unit and contains multiple USB ports into which you plug cables from USB devices.

Some newer peripherals may attach only to a USB port. Others attach to either a serial or parallel port, as well as a USB port. When you connect a device to a USB port, you do not need to install an adapter card in the computer. Simply plug one end of the cable into the USB port and the other end into the device. Having a standard port and connector greatly simplifies the process of attaching devices to a personal computer.

USB also supports hot plugging and Plug and Play, which means you can attach peripherals while the computer is running. With serial and parallel port connections, by

contrast, you often must restart the computer after attaching the peripheral.

The latest version of USB, called *USB 2.0*, is a more advanced and faster USB, with speeds 40 times higher than that of its predecessor. A USB 2.0 port supports higher-powered devices than those of older USB ports. The USB 2.0 port is designed for devices that transfer a lot of data, such as MP3 music players, CDs, DVDs, and removable hard disks.

? FAQ 4-5

Can older USB devices plug into a USB 2.0 port?

Yes. USB 2.0 is *backward compatible*, which means that it supports older USB devices as well as new USB 2.0 devices. Keep in mind though, that older USB devices do not run any faster in a USB 2.0 port.

For more information about USB 2.0, visit the Discovering Computers 2004 FAQ Web page (**scsite.com/dc2004/faq**). Click USB 2.0 below Chapter 4.

Special-Purpose Ports

Five special-purpose ports are FireWire, MIDI, SCSI, IrDA, and Bluetooth™. The following sections discuss each of these ports.

FIREWIRE PORT   Previously called an *IEEE 1394 port*, a **FireWire port** is similar to a USB port in that it can connect multiple types of devices that require faster data transmission speeds, such as digital video cameras, digital VCRs, color printers, scanners, digital cameras, and DVD drives, to a single connector. Using a FireWire port allows you to connect up to 63 devices together. The FireWire port also supports Plug and Play.

Many computer professionals believe that ports such as USB and FireWire someday will replace all other types of ports (Figure 4-36).

FIGURE 4-36 Many computer professionals believe that ports such as USB and FireWire someday will replace all other ports completely.

MIDI PORT   A special type of serial port that connects the system unit to a musical instrument, such as an electronic keyboard, is called a **MIDI port**. Short for *Musical Instrument Digital Interface*, MIDI (pronounced MID-dee) is the electronic music industry's standard that defines how devices, such as sound cards and synthesizers, represent sounds electronically. A *synthesizer*, which can be a peripheral or a chip, creates sound from digital instructions.

A system unit with a MIDI port has the capability of recording sounds that have been created by a synthesizer and then processing the sounds (the data) to create new sounds. Just about every sound card supports the MIDI standard, so you can play and manipulate sounds on a computer that were created originally on another computer.

SCSI PORT   A special high-speed parallel port, called a **SCSI port**, allows you to attach SCSI (pronounced skuzzy) peripherals such as disk drives and printers. Depending on the type of *SCSI*, which stands for *small computer system interface*, you can daisy chain either up to 7 or 15 devices together. Some computers include a SCSI port. Others have a slot that supports a SCSI card.

IrDA PORT   Some devices can transmit data via infrared light waves. For these wireless devices to transmit signals to a computer, both the computer and the device must have an **IrDA port** (Figure 4-37). These ports conform to standards developed by the *IrDA* (*Infrared Data Association*).

FIGURE 4-37 Smart phones and other mobile devices have IrDA ports, allowing the device to communicate wirelessly with other devices and computers.

To ensure nothing obstructs the path of the infrared light wave, you must align the IrDA port on the device with the IrDA port on the computer, similarly to the way you operate a television remote control. Devices that use IrDA ports include a PDA, keyboard, mouse, printer, digital camera, digital telephone, and pager. Several of these devices use a high-speed IrDA port, sometimes called a *fast infrared port*.

BLUETOOTH™ PORTS   An alternative to IrDA, **Bluetooth™** technology uses radio waves to transmit data between two devices. Unlike IrDA, the Bluetooth devices do not have to be aligned with each other. Many computers, peripherals, PDAs, cellular telephones, cars, and other consumer electronics are Bluetooth-enabled, which means they contain a small chip that allows them to communicate with other Bluetooth-enabled computers and devices. If you have a computer that is not Bluetooth enabled, you can purchase a Bluetooth wireless port adapter that will convert an existing USB port or serial port into a Bluetooth port. Also available are Bluetooth PC Cards for notebook computers and Bluetooth cards for PDAs and cellular telephones.

BUSES

As explained earlier in this chapter, a computer processes and stores data as a series of electronic bits. These bits transfer internally within the circuitry of the computer along electrical channels. Each channel, called a **bus**, allows the various devices both inside and attached to the system unit to communicate with each other. Just as vehicles travel on a highway to move from one destination to another, bits travel on a bus (Figure 4-38).

Buses transfer bits from input devices to memory, from memory to the processor, from the processor to memory, and from memory to output or storage devices. Buses consist of two parts: a data bus and an address bus. The *data bus* transfers actual data and the *address bus* transfers information about where the data should reside in memory.

The size of a bus, called the *bus width*, determines the number of bits that the computer can transmit at one time. For example, a 32-bit bus can transmit 32 bits (4 bytes) at a time. On a 64-bit bus, bits transmit from one location to another 64 bits (8 bytes) at a time. The larger the number of bits handled by the bus, the faster the computer transfers data. Using the highway analogy again, assume that one lane on a highway can carry 1 bit. A 32-bit bus is like a 32-lane highway. A 64-bit bus is like a 64-lane highway.

processor

memory chips

FIGURE 4-38   Just as vehicles travel on a highway to move from one destination to another, bits travel on a bus. Buses transfer bits from input devices to memory, from memory to the processor, from the processor to memory, and from memory to output or storage devices.

If a number in memory occupies 8 bytes, or 64 bits, the computer must transmit it in two separate steps when using a 32-bit bus: once for the first 32 bits and once for the second 32 bits. Using a 64-bit bus, the computer can transmit the number in a single step, transferring all 64 bits at once. The wider the bus, the fewer number of transfer steps required and the faster the transfer of data. Most personal computers today use a 64-bit bus.

In conjunction with the bus width, many computer professionals refer to a computer's word size. **Word size** is the number of bits the processor can interpret and execute at a given time. That is, a 64-bit processor can manipulate 64 bits at a time. Computers with a larger word size can process more data in the same amount of time than computers with a smaller word size. In most computers, the word size is the same as the bus width.

Every bus also has a clock speed. Just like the processor, manufacturers state the clock speed for a bus in hertz. Recall that one megahertz (MHz) is equal to one million ticks per second. Most of today's processors have a bus clock speed of 100, 133, 266, or 400 MHz. The higher the bus clock speed, the faster the transmission of data, which results in applications running faster.

A computer has two basic types of buses: a system bus and an expansion bus. A *system bus* is part of the motherboard and connects the processor to main memory. An *expansion bus* allows the processor to communicate with peripherals. When computer professionals use the term bus by itself, they usually are referring to the system bus.

Expansion Bus

Some peripherals outside the system unit connect to a port on an adapter card, which is inserted into an expansion slot on the motherboard. This expansion slot connects to the expansion bus, which allows the processor to communicate with the peripheral attached to the adapter card. Data transmitted to memory or the processor travels from the expansion bus via the expansion bus and the system bus (Figure 4-39).

WEB LINK 4-9

Buses

Visit the Discovering Computers 2004 WEB LINK page (**scsite.com/dc2004/weblink**). Click Buses below Chapter 4.

FIGURE 4-39 Buses allow the various devices both inside and attached to the system unit to communicate with each other. The buses in order of speed from fastest to slowest are the system bus, the AGP bus, the PCI bus, and the ISA bus.

? FAQ 4-6

What is the chipset shown in Figure 4-39 on the previous page?

A *chipset* is a set of integrated circuits. These circuits work together to perform a common task. In this case, the chipset is a bus controller.

For more information about chipsets, visit the Discovering Computers 2004 FAQ Web page (scsite.com/dc2004/faq). Click Chipsets below Chapter 4.

The types of expansion buses on a motherboard determine the types of cards you can add to the computer. Thus, you should understand the following types of expansion buses: ISA bus, PCI bus, AGP bus, USB, FireWire bus, and PC Card bus.

- The most common and slowest expansion bus is the *ISA bus* (*Industry Standard Architecture bus*). A mouse, modem card, sound card, and low-speed network card are examples of devices that connect to the ISA bus directly or through an ISA bus expansion slot.

- A *local bus* is a high-speed expansion bus that connects higher speed devices such as hard disks. The first standard local bus was the *VESA local bus* (*Video Electronics Standards Association local bus*), which was used primarily for video cards. The current local bus standard is the *PCI bus* (*Peripheral Component Interconnect bus*) because it is more versatile than the VESA local bus. Types of cards you can insert into a PCI bus expansion slot include video cards, sound cards, SCSI cards, and high-speed network cards. The PCI bus transfers data about four times faster than the ISA bus. Most current personal computers have a PCI bus as well as an ISA bus.

- The *Accelerated Graphics Port* (*AGP*) is a bus designed by Intel to improve the speed with which 3-D graphics and video transmit. With an AGP video card in an AGP bus slot, the AGP bus provides a faster, dedicated interface between the video card and memory. Newer processors support AGP technology.

- The USB (universal serial bus) and *FireWire bus* are buses that eliminate the need to install cards into expansion slots. In a computer with a USB, for example, USB devices connect to each other outside the system unit and then a single cable attaches to the USB port. The USB port then connects to the USB, which connects to the PCI bus on the motherboard. The FireWire bus works in a similar fashion. With these buses, expansion slots are available for devices not compatible with USB or FireWire.

- The expansion bus for a PC Card is the *PC Card bus*. With a PC Card inserted into a PC Card slot, data travels on the PC Card bus to the PCI bus.

BAYS

After you purchase a computer, you may want to install an additional storage device such as a disk drive into the system unit. A **bay** is an opening inside the system unit in which you can install additional equipment. A bay is different from a slot, which is used for the installation of adapter cards. Rectangular openings, called **drive bays**, typically hold disk drives.

Two types of drive bays exist: internal and external. An *external drive bay* allows a user to access the drive from outside the system unit. Floppy disk drives, CD drives, DVD drives, Zip drives, and tape drives are examples of devices installed in external drive bays (Figure 4-40). An *internal drive bay* is concealed entirely within the system unit. Hard disk drives are installed in internal bays.

DVD drive

CD drive

floppy disk drive

Zip drive

FIGURE 4-40 External drive bays usually are located beside or on top of one another.

POWER SUPPLY

Many personal computers plug into standard wall outlets, which supply an alternating current (AC) of 115 to 120 volts. This type of power is unsuitable for use with a computer, which requires a direct current (DC) ranging from 5 to 12 volts. The **power supply** is the component of the system unit that converts the wall outlet AC power into DC power.

Near the power supply is a fan that keeps components of the system unit cool. This fan dissipates heat generated by the processor and other components of the system unit. Many newer computers have additional fans near certain components in the system unit such as the processor, hard disk, and ports.

Some external peripherals such as an external modem, speakers, or a tape drive have an **AC adapter**, which is an external power supply. One end of the AC adapter plugs into the wall outlet and the other end attaches to the peripheral. The AC adapter converts the AC power into DC power that the peripheral requires.

❓ FAQ 4-7

Can I disable the computer fan?

No. Without the fan, the electronics could overheat. For optimum performance, be sure the vents on the computer case are not blocked and keep the area around the system unit dust free. To reduce noise level, purchase a utility program that slows or stops the fan until the temperature reaches a certain level.

For more information about the computer fan, visit the Discovering Computers 2004 FAQ Web page (**scsite.com/dc2004/faq**). Click Computer Fan below Chapter 4.

MOBILE COMPUTERS AND DEVICES

As businesses and schools expand to serve people across the country and around the world, increasingly more people need to use a computer while traveling to and from a main office or school to conduct business, communicate, or do homework. As Chapter 1 discussed, users with such mobile computing needs — known as mobile users — often have a mobile computer such as a notebook computer or mobile device such as a PDA (Figure 4-41).

flash memory card

Figure 4-41b (PDA)

CD or DVD drive

PC Cards in PC Card slots

disk in floppy disk drive or Zip disk drive

battery

Figure 4-41a (notebook computer)

FIGURE 4-41 Users with mobile computing needs often have a notebook computer and/or PDA.

Weighing on average between 2.5 and 8 pounds, notebook computers can run either using batteries or using a standard power supply. Smaller PDAs run strictly on batteries.

Like their desktop counterparts, mobile computers and devices have a motherboard that contains electronic components that process data (Figure 4-42). The difference is many other devices also are part of the system unit. In addition to the motherboard, processor, memory, sound card, PC Card slot, and drive bay, the system unit also houses devices such as the keyboard, pointing device, speakers, and display.

A notebook computer usually is more expensive than a desktop computer with the same capabilities because it is more costly to miniaturize the components. PDAs are quite affordable, usually priced at a few hundred dollars or less.

The typical notebook computer often has a keyboard/mouse, IrDA, serial, parallel, video, and USB ports (Figure 4-43).

Tablet PCs usually include several slots and ports (Figure 4-44). PDAs often have an IrDA port or are Bluetooth enabled so users can communicate wirelessly with other computers or devices such as a printer. Many also include a serial port. Read Issue 4-4 for a discussion about another type of mobile computer.

FIGURE 4-42   The motherboard in notebook computers and PDAs contains electronic components that process data.

FIGURE 4-44   Ports on a Tablet PC.

FIGURE 4-43   A notebook computer often has parallel, serial, video, USB, speaker, microphone, and keyboard/mouse ports.

✦ **ISSUE 4-4**

Do You Want Air Conditioning?
Power Windows? A Car Computer?

About five years ago, Citroen unveiled the first car equipped with an onboard computer. Today, a number of automobiles incorporate a car computer that allows drivers to access e-mail, receive weather and traffic data, obtain navigation information, and even allow passengers to watch movies on DVD. Developing and producing car computers is expensive. Because of their special environment, they must be more durable than desktop computers and provide a simpler interface. Some manufacturers wonder if car computers offer buyers enough to justify the cost. Would you be interested in a car computer and, if so, how much would you be willing to spend for one? The state of New York recently passed a law mandating that automobile drivers not hold and talk on portable telephones while in motion. Should a similar law be enacted regarding the use of car computers? Why or why not? What activities performed on a car computer could, and could not, endanger drivers? Why?

For more information about car computers, visit the Discovering Computers 2004 Issues Web page (**scsite.com/dc2004/issues**). Click Issue #4 below Chapter 4.

PUTTING IT ALL TOGETHER

When you purchase a computer, it is important to understand how the components of the system unit work. Many components of the system unit influence the speed and power of a computer. These include the type of processor, the clock speed of the processor, the amount of RAM, and the clock speed of the bus. The configuration you require depends on your intended use.

The table in Figure 4-45 lists the suggested minimum processor, clock speed, and RAM requirements based on the needs of various types of computer users.

SUGGESTED MINIMUM CONFIGURATIONS BY USER

User	Processor and Clock Speed
Home	Pentium® 4 or Athlon™ XP 1.7 GHz or higher or Celeron® or Duron™ 1.2 GHz or higher Minimum RAM: 128 MB
Small Office/Home Office	Pentium® 4 or Athlon™ XP 2 GHz or higher Minimum RAM: 256 MB
Mobile 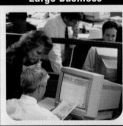	Pentium® 4 or Athlon™ XP 1.8 GHz or higher Minimum RAM: 256 MB
Large Business	Pentium® 4 or Athlon™ XP 3 GHz or higher Minimum RAM: 512 MB
Power	Xeon™ or Itanium® or Athlon™ MP 2.5 GHz or higher Minimum RAM: 1 GB

FIGURE 4-45 Suggested processor, clock speed, and RAM configurations by user.

For more detailed computer purchasing guidelines, read the Buyer's Guide 2004 feature that follows Chapter 8. Read Looking Ahead 4-2 for a look at the next generation of computers.

QUIZ YOURSELF 4-3

To check your knowledge of adapter cards, expansion slots, ports, buses, and components of mobile computers and devices, visit the Discovering Computers 2004 Quiz Yourself Web page (**scsite .com/dc2004/quiz**). Click Objectives 8 – 11 below Chapter 4.

CHAPTER SUMMARY

Chapter 4 presented the components of the system unit, described how memory stores data, instructions, and information, and discussed the sequence of operations that occur when a computer executes an instruction. The chapter included a comparison of various personal computer processors on the market today.

LOOKING AHEAD 4-2

Robotic Rats May Perform Rescue Missions

When people are trapped under piles of rubble from a collapsed building, emergency teams may have a new tool for their rescue operations: rats.

Researchers at the State University of New York Downstate Medical Center at Brooklyn have attached electrodes and battery-powered backpacks to five rats and have trained these rodents to dash in precise locations in response to radio signals sent from the scientists' computers. For example, signals to the left-whisker neurons command the rats to turn left. The researchers then send another signal to the rats' pleasure center in the brain when the assigned task is complete. The scientists hope their research will be used in search and rescue missions.

Research from these experiments has the potential for other uses, including helping paralyzed individuals use their brain signals to control artificial limbs. Electrodes implanted in the brain receive signals generated when paralyzed people think about moving their hands, tongue, or eyes; the electrodes then send feedback to the artificial hands or arms to perform such actions as hold a pencil or a cup or grasp a barbell.

For a look at the next generation of remotely controlled rodents, visit the Discovering Computers 2004 Looking Ahead Web page (**scsite.com/ dc2004/looking**). Click Looking Ahead #2 below Chapter 4.

Career Corner

Computer Engineer

A *computer engineer* designs and develops the electronic components found in computers and peripheral devices. Computer engineers work as researchers, theorists, and inventors. Computer engineers can work as part of a company's permanent staff or as consultants, with jobs that extend from a few months to a few years, depending on the project. Engineers in research and development often work on projects that will not be released to the general public for two years.

Responsibilities vary from company to company. All computer engineering work, however, demands problem solving skills and the ability to create and use new technologies. Computer engineers also must be able to handle multiple tasks and concentrate on detail. Computer engineers often function as part of a team. Therefore, computer engineers must be able to communicate clearly with both computer personnel and computer users, who may have little technical knowledge.

Before taking in-depth computer engineering design and development classes, students usually take mathematics, physics, and basic engineering. Computer engineering degrees include B.S., M.S., and Ph.D. Because computer engineers employed in private industry often advance into managerial positions, many computer engineering graduates obtain a master's degree in business administration (M.B.A.). Most computer engineers earn between $35,000 and $90,000 annually, depending on their experience and employer, but salaries can approach $115,000.

To learn more about the field of Computer Engineer as a career, visit the Discovering Computers 2004 Careers Web page (**scsite.com/ dc2004/careers**). Click Computer Engineer.

HIGH-TECH TALK

The Genius of Memory: Transistors, Capacitors, and Electricity

Inside your computer, RAM takes the form of separate microchip modules that plug into slots in the computer's motherboard. These slots connect through a line (bus) or set of electrical paths to the computer's processor. Before you turn on a computer, its RAM is a blank slate. As you start and use your computer, the operating system files, applications, and any data currently being used by the processor are written to and stored in RAM so the processor can access them quickly.

How is this data written to and stored in RAM? In the most common form of RAM, dynamic random access memory (DRAM), *transistors* (in this case, acting as switches) and a *capacitor* (as a data storage element) create a *memory cell*, which represents a single bit of data.

Memory cells are etched onto a silicon wafer in a series of columns (bitlines) and rows (wordlines), known as an *array*. The intersection of a column and row constitutes the *address* of the memory cell (Figure 4-46). Each memory cell has a unique address that can be found by counting across columns and then counting down by row. The address of a character consists of a series of memory cell addresses put together. Most DRAM chips actually have arrays that are 16 rows deep.

To write data to RAM, the processor sends the memory controller the address of a memory cell in which to store data. The *memory controller* organizes the request and sends the column and row address in an electrical charge along the appropriate address lines, which are very thin electrical lines etched into the RAM chip. This causes the transistors along those address lines to close.

These transistors act as a switch to control the flow of electrical current in an either closed or open circuit. While the transistors are closed, the software sends bursts of electricity along selected data lines. When the electrical charge traveling down the data line reaches an address line where a transistor is closed, the charge flows through the closed transistor and charges the capacitor.

A capacitor works as electronic storage that holds an electrical charge. Each charged capacitor along the address line represents a 1 bit. An uncharged capacitor represents a 0 bit. The combination of 1s and 0s from eight data lines forms a single byte of data.

The capacitors used in dynamic RAM, however, lose their electrical charge. The processor or memory controller continuously has to recharge all of the capacitors holding a charge (a 1 bit) before the capacitor discharges. During this *refresh operation*, which happens automatically thousands of times per second, the memory controller reads memory and then immediately rewrites it. This refresh operation is what gives dynamic RAM its name. Dynamic RAM has to be refreshed continually, or it loses the charges that represent bits of data. A specialized circuit called a counter

tracks the refresh sequence to ensure that all of the rows are refreshed.

The process of reading data from RAM uses a similar, but reverse, series of steps. When the processor gets the next instruction it is to perform, the instruction may contain the address of a memory cell from which to read data. This address is sent to the memory controller. To locate the memory cell, the memory controller sends the column and row address in an electrical charge down the appropriate address lines.

This electrical charge causes the transistors along the address line to close. At every point along the address line where a capacitor is holding a charge, the capacitor discharges through the circuit created by the closed transistors, sending electrical charges along the data lines.

A specialized circuit called a *sense amplifier* determines and amplifies the level of charge in the capacitor. A capacitor charge over a certain voltage level represents the binary value 1; a capacitor charge below that level represents a 0. The sensed and amplified value is sent back down the address line to the processor.

As long as a computer is running, data continuously is being written to and read from RAM. As soon as you shut down a computer, RAM loses its data. The next time you turn on a computer, operating system files and other data are again loaded into RAM and the read/write process starts all over.

For more information about memory, visit the Discovering Computers 2004 High-Tech Talk Web page (**scsite.com/dc2004/tech**) and click Memory.

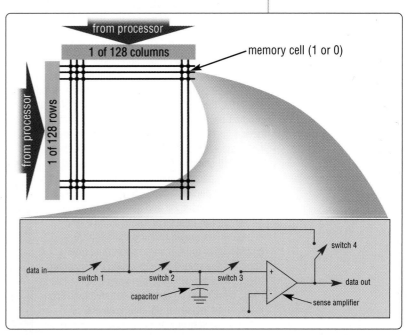

FIGURE 4-46   An illustration of one type of DRAM. When writing data, switches 1 and 2 in the circuit are closed and switches 3 and 4 are open. When reading data, switches 2, 3, and 4 in the circuit are closed and switch 1 is open.

COMPANIES ON THE CUTTING EDGE

Intel®
Chip Maker Dominates the Computer Market

On an August day in 1968, Robert Noyce was mowing his lawn when Gordon Moore, a coworker at Fairchild Semiconductor, stopped by to talk. The two shared gripes about work and, in a moment of inspiration, decided to start their own company. Noyce typed a one-page business plan, and a company called "Moore Noyce" was born. The name, unfortunately, sounded a lot like "More Noise" – hardly suitable for an electronics firm – so they incorporated as NM Electronics. Later, after they purchased rights from a motel chain, they adopted a new name – *Intel* (for integrated electronics).

From such humble beginnings came a company that today is the world's largest maker of computer chips. When Moore and Noyce started Intel, their goal was to build semiconductor memory to replace magnetic core memory. Critics maintained that even if semiconductors could be used for memory storage, they would cost too much to manufacture. Undismayed, Noyce and Moore, together with Andy Grove, another Fairchild expatriate, struggled to reduce production costs. They refined the process of placing thousands of tiny electronic devices on a silicon chip and, in 1970, successfully introduced the 1103, the first DRAM chip. One year later, this product became the world's best-selling semiconductor device. In 1971, Intel developed the 4004, the world's first processor. In 1980, when IBM chose the Intel 8088 chip for its new personal computer, Intel chips became standard for all IBM-compatible personal computers.

An innovative spirit and attention to detail remain part of Intel's corporate culture. The company has grown to more than 85,000 employees in more than 45 countries. Intel supports the values of responding to customer needs, working with discipline and quality, taking risks, working in an open and satisfying environment, and striving for optimum results.

For more information about Intel, visit the Discovering Computers 2004 Companies Webpage (**scsite.com/dc2004/companies**) and click Intel.

AMD
Intel-Compatible Processor Leader

In the eighteenth century, philosophers spoke of The Age of Enlightenment. Could today be The Age of Asparagus? In the early 1980s, *Advanced Micro Devices* (*AMD*) adopted the phrase to characterize its commitment to develop increasing numbers of proprietary products for the computer industry. Executives identified this goal with asparagus farming because the crop grows slowly, but it is very lucrative once it takes hold.

AMD's seeds sprouted and grew into the world's second-largest manufacturer of processors for Microsoft Windows-compatible personal computers. Along with the AMD-K6®-2 and Athlon™ processors, AMD also produces flash memory devices, embedded processors, and support circuitry for communications and networking applications. In 2002, AMD expanded its product line by acquiring Alchemy Semiconductor, a manufacturer of low-power, high-performance processors for personal connectivity devices such as PDAs.

A Fortune 500 company, AMD develops advanced process technologies at its Submicron Development Center (SDC) in Sunnyvale, California. The technologies are put into production at manufacturing facilities in the United States, Europe, Asia, and Japan. Today, AMD employs almost 14,000 people worldwide. More than one-half of the approximately $4 billion in annual company revenues is generated from sales outside the United States.

Cofounders Jerry Sanders and John Carey laid the foundation for AMD in Carey's living room in 1968. From the beginning, AMD guaranteed its microchips for every customer would meet or exceed stringent standards. More than three decades later, the company continues this commitment to "parametric superiority." A central tenet of AMD's corporate philosophy is that people are the ultimate source of its competitive advantage. "Our customer's success is our success."

For more information about AMD, visit the Discovering Computers 2004 Companies Web page (**scsite.com/dc2004/companies**) and click AMD.

TECHNOLOGY TRAILBLAZERS

Jack Kilby
Inventor of the Integrated Circuit

The National Inventors Hall of Fame honors inventors whose innovations have made progress possible. In 1982, *Jack Kilby* took his place in this elite group. His invention, the integrated circuit, is an essential part of the high-speed computers that form the foundation of today's information age.

Kilby started his work with miniature electrical components at Centralab, where he developed transistors for hearing aids. The transistors were made from germanium, but scientists at Bell Laboratories convinced Kilby that silicon was a better choice. Because Centralab seemed committed to germanium, Kilby went to Texas Instruments where he could be at the forefront of the effort to connect electrical components.

When he arrived in the summer of 1958, most of the staff was on vacation. Almost alone in the lab, Kilby examined prototypes that used wires to join stacks of components. He theorized that if the circuit elements were made from the same material (silicon) they could be placed on a single chip, eliminating the need for wire connections. With this thought in mind, Kilby developed a working model of the first integrated circuit, which was patented in 1959. Coincidentally, at about the same time, Robert Noyce of Fairchild Semiconductor filed for a patent on a similar integrated circuit produced with a different manufacturing process. Both Kilby and Noyce are given credit for inventing the integrated circuit.

Today, retired from Texas Instruments, Kilby works as a consultant and teacher and holds more than 60 patents. In 2000, Kilby was awarded the Nobel Prize in Physics for his invention of the integrated circuit, an innovation he believes will continue to change the world. "Every day [new crops of engineers are] pushing the limits of integrated circuits and making practical what was once considered impossible."

For more information about Jack Kilby, visit the Discovering Computers 2004 People Web page (**scsite.com/dc2004/people**) and click Jack Kilby.

Gordon Moore
Intel Cofounder

The name Intel has become synonymous with processors. From its inception, the name *Gordon Moore* has been synonymous with Intel.

Moore's life-long interest in technology was kindled at an early age by a neighbor's chemistry set. Even then, he displayed the passion for practical outcomes that has typified his work. "With the chemistry set," he says, "I had to get a good explosion at the end or I wasn't happy." Yet, Moore was hardly a science geek. In high school, he devoted more time to athletics than to homework, lettering in four different sports. Moore was the first member of his family to attend college, graduating from the California Institute of Technology with a Ph.D. in chemistry and physics.

Moore worked with Bill Shockley, inventor of the transistor, at Shockley Semiconductor. There, he met Robert Noyce, and eventually the two left to join Fairchild Semiconductor. At Fairchild in 1965, in an article for *Electronics* magazine, Moore made a startling prediction. The number of transistors and resistors placed on computer chips, he claimed, would double every year, with a proportional increase in computing power and decrease in cost. This bold forecast, now known as Moore's law, proved amazingly accurate for 10 years (when Moore revised the estimate to doubling every two years). Convinced of the future of silicon chips, and frustrated by the company's response to their work, in 1968 Moore and Noyce quit Fairchild to start Intel.

Moore's career illustrates a key characteristic: the willingness to make a commitment even when results are unknown. Although all decisions involve some risk, they should not be feared. After all, Moore says, "If everything you try works, then you are not trying hard enough."

For more information about Gordon Moore, visit the Discovering Computers 2004 People Web page (**scsite.com/dc2004/people**) and click Gordon Moore.

CHAPTER 4 | # CHAPTER REVIEW | ◄● Previous | Next ●►

The Chapter Review section summarizes the concepts presented in this chapter.

**QUIZZES AND
LEARNING GAMES**

Computer Genius

Crossword Puzzle

Interactive Labs

Practice Test

Quiz Yourself

Wheel of Terms

EXERCISES

Chapter Review

Checkpoint

Key Terms

Lab Exercises

Learn It Online

Web Research

BEYOND THE BOOK

Apply It

Career Corner

Companies

FAQ

High-Tech Talk

Issues

Looking Ahead

Trailblazers

Web Links

FEATURES

Guide to Web Sites

Making Use of the Web

Tech News

Timeline 2004

 WEB INSTRUCTIONS

To display this page from the Web, start your browser and enter the Web address **scsite.com/dc2004/ch4/review**. Click the links for current and additional information. To listen to an audio version of this Chapter Review, click the Audio button.

1 How Are Various Styles of System Units Different?

The **system unit** is a case that contains electronic components of the computer used to process data. On desktop personal computers, most storage devices also are part of the system unit. On notebook computers, the keyboard and pointing device often occupy the area on top of the system unit, and the display attaches to the system unit by hinges. On mobile devices, the display frequently is part of the system unit.

2 What Are Chips, Adapter Cards, and Other Components of the Motherboard?

The **motherboard** is the main circuit board of the system unit. The motherboard contains many electronic components including a processor chip, memory chips, expansion slots, and adapter cards. A **chip** is a small piece of semiconducting material, usually silicon, on which integrated circuits are etched. Expansion slots hold adapter cards that provide connections and functions not built into the motherboard.

3 What Are the Components of a Processor and How Do They Complete a Machine Cycle?

The **processor** interprets and carries out the basic instructions that operate a computer. Processors contain a **control unit** that directs and coordinates most of the operations in the computer and an **arithmetic logic unit** (*ALU*) that performs arithmetic, comparison, and logical operations. The *machine cycle* is a set of four basic operations — *fetching, decoding, executing,* and *storing* — that the processor repeats for every instruction. The control unit fetches program instructions and data from memory and decodes the instructions into commands the computer can execute. The ALU executes the commands, and the results are stored in memory.

4 What Are the Characteristics of Various Personal Computer Processors?

Intel produces the **Pentium**® processor for high-performance PCs, the **Celeron**® processor for basic PCs, and the **Xeon**™ and **Itanium**® processors for workstations and low-end servers. AMD manufactures **Intel-compatible processors**, which have a similar internal design as Intel processors. Motorola produces the *Motorola processor*, with a design different from the Intel-style processor, for Apple computers. Some devices have a *system on a chip* processor that integrates the functions of a processor, memory, and a video card on a single chip.

 Visit **scsite.com/dc2004/quiz** or click the Quiz Yourself button. Click Objectives 1 – 4 below Chapter 4.

5 What Is a Bit and How Does a Series of Bits Represent Data?

Most computers are **digital** and recognize only two discrete states: off and on. To represent these states, computers use the **binary system**, which is a number system that has just two unique digits – 0 (for off) and 1 (for on) – called bits. A **bit** is the smallest unit of data a computer can process. Grouped together as a unit, 8 bits form a **byte**, which provides enough different combinations of 0s and 1s to represent 256 individual characters. The combinations are defined by patterns, called coding schemes, such as *ASCII, EBCDIC,* and *Unicode*.

6 How Do Programs Transfer In and Out of Memory?

When an application program starts, the program's instructions load into memory from the hard disk. The program and operating system instructions are in memory and the program's window displays on the screen. When you quit the program, the program instructions are removed from memory and the program no longer displays on the screen.

CHAPTER REVIEW — CHAPTER 4

7 What Are the Various Types of Memory?

The system unit contains volatile and nonvolatile memory. *Volatile memory* loses its contents when the computer's power is turned off. *Nonvolatile memory* does not lose its contents when the computer's power is turned off. RAM is the most common type of volatile memory. ROM, flash memory, and CMOS are examples of nonvolatile memory. **RAM** consists of memory chips that can be read from and written to by the processor and other devices. **ROM** refers to memory chips storing permanent data and instructions that usually cannot be modified. **Flash memory** can be erased electronically and reprogrammed. **CMOS** technology uses battery power to retain information even when the power to the computer is turned off.

 Visit **scsite.com/dc2004/quiz** or click the Quiz Yourself button. Click Objectives 5 – 7 below Chapter 4.

8 What Are the Types of Expansion Slots and Adapter Cards?

An **expansion slot** is a socket on the motherboard that can hold an adapter card. An **adapter card** is a circuit board that enhances functions of a component of the system unit and/or provides a connection to a **peripheral** such as a modem, disk drive, printer, scanner, or keyboard. Several types of adapter cards exist. A **sound card** enhances the sound-generating capabilities of a personal computer. A **video card** converts computer output into a video signal that displays an image on the screen. A **modem card** enables computers to communicate. A **network card** allows a computer to access a network.

9 How Are a Serial Port, a Parallel Port, a USB Port, and Other Ports Different?

A **port** is the point at which a peripheral attaches to a system unit so it can send data to or receive information from the computer. A **serial port**, which transmits data 1 bit at a time, usually connects devices that do not require fast data transmission, such as a mouse, keyboard, or modem. A **parallel port**, which transfers more than 1 bit at a time, often connects a printer to

the system unit. A **USB port** can connect up to 127 different peripherals together with a single connector type. Five special-purpose ports are FireWire, MIDI, SCSI, IrDA, and Bluetooth. A **FireWire port** can connect multiple types of devices that require faster data transmission speeds. A **MIDI port** connects the system unit to a musical instrument. A **SCSI port** attaches the system unit to SCSI peripherals, such as disk drives. An **IrDA port** and **Bluetooth**™ technology allow wireless devices to transmit signals to a computer via infrared light waves or radio waves.

10 How Do Buses Contribute to a Computer's Processing Speed?

A **bus** is an electrical channel along which bits transfer within the circuitry of a computer, allowing devices both inside and attached to the system unit to communicate. The size of a bus, called the *bus width*, determines the number of bits that the computer can transmit at one time. The larger the bus width, the faster the computer transfers data.

11 What Are the Components in Mobile Computers and Mobile Devices?

In addition to the motherboard, processor, memory, sound card, PC Card slot, and drive bay, a mobile computer's system unit also houses devices such as the keyboard, pointing device, speakers, and display. The system unit for a typical notebook computer often has a keyboard/mouse, IrDA, serial, parallel, video, and USB ports. Tablet PCs usually include several slots and ports. PDAs often have an IrDA port or are Bluetooth enabled so users can communicate wirelessly.

 Visit **scsite.com/dc2004/quiz** or click the Quiz Yourself button. Click Objectives 8 – 11 below Chapter 4.

CHAPTER 4 KEY TERMS

‹● Previous | Next ●›

You should know the Primary Terms and be familiar with the Secondary Terms.

■ WEB INSTRUCTIONS:

To display this page from the Web, start your browser and enter the Web address **scsite.com/dc2004/ch4/terms**. Click a term to display its definition and a picture. When the picture displays, click the more info button for current and additional information about the term from the Web.

>> Primary Terms
(shown in bold-black characters in the chapter)

AC adapter (4.33)
access time (4.22)
adapter card (4.23)
analog (4.13)
arithmetic logic unit (4.06)
bay (4.32)
binary system (4.13)
bit (4.13)
Bluetooth™ (4.30)
bus (4.30)
byte (4.13)
cache (4.20)
Celeron® (4.08)
central processing unit (CPU) (4.05)
chip (4.04)
clock speed (4.08)
complementary metal-oxide semiconductor (CMOS) (4.22)
connector (4.25)
control unit (4.06)
digital (4.13)
drive bays (4.32)
expansion slot (4.23)
FireWire port (4.28)
firmware (4.20)
flash memory (4.21)
flash memory card (4.24)
gigabyte (GB) (4.16)
gigahertz (GHz) (4.08)
Intel-compatible processors (4.09)
IrDA port (4.29)
Itanium® (4.08)

kilobyte (KB or K) (4.16)
megabyte (MB) (4.16)
memory (4.15)
memory cache (4.20)
memory module (4.18)
memory slots (4.18)
MIDI port (4.29)
modem card (4.23)
motherboard (4.04)
nanosecond (4.22)
network card (4.23)
parallel port (4.27)
PC Card (4.24)
PC Card slot (4.24)
Pentium® (4.08)
peripheral (4.23)
Plug and Play (4.24)
port (4.25)
power supply (4.33)
processor (4.05)
RAM (4.17)
read-only memory (ROM) (4.20)
SCSI port (4.29)
serial port (4.27)
sound card (4.23)
system clock (4.07)
system unit (4.02)
USB hub (4.28)
USB port (4.28)
video card (4.23)
word size (4.31)
Xeon™ (4.08)

>> Secondary Terms
(shown in italic characters in the chapter)

Accelerated Graphics Port (AGP) (4.32)
address (4.16)
address bus (4.30)
advanced transfer cache (4.20)
ALU (4.06)
American Standard Code for Information Interchange (ASCII) (4.14)
arithmetic operations (4.06)
binary digit (4.13)
bus width (4.30)
Centronics interface (4.28)
chassis (4.02)
chip-for-chip upgrade (4.10)
clock cycle (4.07)
COM port (4.27)
comparison operations (4.06)
coprocessor (4.12)
daisy chain (4.28)
data bus (4.30)
daughterboard upgrade (4.10)
decoding (4.06)
DIMM (dual inline memory module) (4.18)
DIP (dual inline package) (4.05)
Double Data Rate SDRAM (DDR SDRAM) (4.18)
dynamic RAM (DRAM) (4.18)
EEPROM (electrically erasable programmable read-only memory) (4.20)
executing (4.06)
expansion bus (4.31)
expansion card (4.23)
Extended Binary Coded Decimal Interchange Code (EBCDIC) (4.14)
external drive bay (4.32)
fast infrared port (4.30)
female connectors (4.25)
fetching (4.06)
FireWire bus (4.32)
flip chip-PGA (FC-PGA) (4.05)
floating-point coprocessor (4.12)
gender changer (4.26)
graphics card (4.23)
heat pipe (4.12)
heat sink (4.12)
hertz (4.08)
hot plugging (4.24)
IEEE 1394 port (4.28)
integrated circuit (4.04)
internal drive bay (4.32)
internal modem (4.23)
IrDA (Infrared Data Association) (4.29)
ISA bus (Industry Standard Architecture bus) (4.32)
jack (4.25)
L1 cache (4.20)

L2 cache (4.20)
L3 cache (4.20)
local bus (4.32)
logical operations (4.06)
machine cycle (4.06)
main memory (4.17)
male connectors (4.25)
microcode (4.20)
microprocessor (4.05)
MIPS (millions of instructions per second) (4.08)
Motorola processor (4.09)
Musical Instrument Digital Interface (4.29)
nonvolatile memory (4.16)
ns (4.22)
parallel processing (4.12)
PC Card bus (4.32)
PCI bus (Peripheral Component Interconnect bus) (4.32)
PCMIA cards (4.24)
Personal Computer Memory Card International Association (4.24)
PGA (pin grid array) (4.05)
piggyback upgrade (4.10)
pipelining (4.07)
primary storage (4.17)
PROM (programmable read-only memory) (4.20)
Rambus® DRAM (RDRAM®) (4.18)
random access memory (4.17)
registers (4.07)
RIMM (Rambus® inline memory module) (4.18)
SCSI (4.29)
SIMM (single inline memory module) (4.18)
small computer system interface (4.29)
socket (4.11)
static RAM (SRAM) (4.18)
stored program concept (4.16)
storing (4.06)
superscalar (4.07)
synchronous DRAM (SDRAM) (4.18)
synthesizer (4.29)
system board (4.04)
system bus (4.31)
system on a chip (4.09)
transistor (4.04)
Unicode (4.14)
universal serial bus port (4.28)
USB 2.0 (4.28)
VESA local bus (Video Electronics Standards Association local bus) (4.32)
volatile memory (4.16)
zero-insertion force (ZIF) (4.11)

CHECKPOINT CHAPTER 4

Use the Checkpoint exercises to check your knowledge level of the chapter.

WEB INSTRUCTIONS:

To display this page from the Web, start your browser and enter the Web address **scsite.com/dc2004/ch4/check**. Click the links for current and additional information.

LABEL THE FIGURE — Identify these components of the motherboard.

a. expansion slots
b. memory chips
c. memory slots
d. adapter cards
e. processor chip

TRUE/FALSE — Mark T for True and F for False. (See page numbers in parentheses.)

_____ 1. On desktop personal computers, the electronic components and most of the <u>storage devices</u> normally occupy space outside of the system unit. (4.02)

_____ 2. The <u>motherboard</u> is the main circuit board of the system unit. (4.04)

_____ 3. <u>Pipelining</u> is when the processor begins fetching a second instruction before it completes the machine cycle for the first instruction. (4.07)

_____ 4. With a <u>piggyback upgrade</u>, you stack the new processor chip on top of the old one. (4.10)

_____ 5. A <u>bit</u> is the smallest unit of data the computer can process. (4.13)

_____ 6. A <u>gigabyte</u> equals approximately 1 million bytes. (4.16)

_____ 7. <u>RAM chips</u> usually reside on a memory module. (4.18)

_____ 8. Read-only memory (<u>ROM</u>) refers to memory chips storing permanent data and instructions. (4.20)

_____ 9. You cannot change a <u>flash memory</u> card without having to open the system unit or restart the computer. (4.24)

_____ 10. The <u>FireWire port</u> does not support Plug and Play. (4.28)

_____ 11. A <u>bay</u> is an opening inside the system unit in which you can install additional equipment. (4.32)

CHAPTER 4 CHECKPOINT

QUIZZES AND LEARNING GAMES

Computer Genius

Crossword Puzzle

Interactive Labs

Practice Test

Quiz Yourself

Wheel of Terms

EXERCISES

Chapter Review

Checkpoint

Key Terms

Lab Exercises

Learn It Online

Web Research

BEYOND THE BOOK

Apply It

Career Corner

Companies

FAQ

High-Tech Talk

Issues

Looking Ahead

Trailblazers

Web Links

FEATURES

Guide to Web Sites

Making Use of the Web

Tech News

Timeline 2004

MULTIPLE CHOICE Select the best answer. (See page numbers in parentheses.)

1. On _____, the display often is part of the system unit. (4.02)
   a. desktop personal computers
   b. notebook computers
   c. mobile devices
   d. all of the above

2. An integrated circuit _____. (4.04)
   a. contains microscopic pathways capable of carrying electrical current
   b. acts as an electronic switch that opens or closes a circuit for electrical charges
   c. cools the processor in notebook computers
   d. speeds the processes of a computer by storing frequently used instructions

3. _____ include conditions along with operators such as AND, OR, and NOT. (4.06)
   a. Arithmetic operations
   b. Logical operations
   c. Comparison operations
   d. All of the above

4. Processors that use _____ are faster because they do not have to wait for one instruction to complete the machine cycle before fetching the next. (4.07)
   a. registering   b. hot plugging
   c. pipelining   d. daisy chaining

5. The higher the clock speed, the _____ the computer. (4.08)
   a. slower the processor, and more expensive
   b. faster the processor, and more expensive
   c. slower the processor, and less expensive
   d. faster the processor, and less expensive

6. _____ is the most widely used coding scheme and is used by most personal computers and mid-range servers. (4.14)
   a. ASCII
   b. Unicode
   c. EBCDIC
   d. Microcode

7. Memory stores _____. (4.16)
   a. the operating system and other system software
   b. application programs that carry out specific tasks
   c. the data being processed by the application programs
   d. all of the above

8. A _____ of memory is equal to exactly 1,024 bytes, but often is rounded down to 1,000 bytes. (4.16)
   a. kilobyte (KB)
   b. megabyte (MB)
   c. gigabyte (GB)
   d. terabyte (TB)

9. A _____ is a type of memory module with pins on opposite sides of the circuit board that connect together to form a single set of contacts. (4.18)
   a. RIMM (Rambus® inline memory module)
   b. SIMM (single inline memory module)
   c. ROMM (Rambus® online memory module)
   d. DIMM (dual inline memory module)

10. Many of today's computers support _____, which means the computer automatically can configure adapter cards and other peripherals as you install them. (4.24)
    a. Pack and Go
    b. Park and Ride
    c. Pick and Choose
    d. Plug and Play

11. A _____ sometimes is called a Centronics interface, after the company that first defined the standard for communications between the system unit and a printer. (4.28)
    a. serial port
    b. USB port
    c. parallel port
    d. MIDI port

12. Word size is the _____. (4.31)
    a. pace of the system clock
    b. size of the bus
    c. amount of time it takes the processor to read instructions from memory
    d. number of bits the processor can interpret and execute at a given time

13. The most common and slowest expansion bus is the _____. (4.32)
    a. ISA bus (Industry Standard Architecture bus)
    b. VESA local bus (Video Electronics Standards Association local bus)
    c. PCI bus (Peripheral Component Interconnect bus)
    d. AGP (Accelerated Graphics Port)

14. _____ usually are installed in internal bays. (4.32)
    a. Floppy disk drives
    b. DVD drives
    c. Zip drives
    d. Hard disk drives

CHECKPOINT CHAPTER 4

☒ MATCHING Match the terms with their definitions. (See page numbers in parentheses.)

_____ 1. chassis (4.02)

_____ 2. microprocessor (4.05)

_____ 3. superscalar (4.07)

_____ 4. coprocessor (4.12)

_____ 5. address (4.16)

_____ 6. memory module (4.18)

_____ 7. microcode (4.20)

_____ 8. synthesizer (4.29)

_____ 9. expansion bus (4.31)

_____ 10. bay (4.32)

a. processors that can execute more than one instruction per clock cycle

b. integrates the functions of a processor, memory, and video card on a single chip

c. small circuit board on which RAM chips usually reside

d. additional processor chip or circuit board that assists in performing specific tasks

e. metal or plastic case that protects the internal components of the system unit

f. allows the processor to communicate with peripherals

g. type of instructions used to program a PROM chip

h. term used by some manufacturers to refer to a personal computer processor chip

i. unique number that identifies the location of a byte in memory

j. peripheral or chip that creates sound from digital instructions

k. opening inside the system unit in which additional equipment can be installed

l. small ceramic or metal component that absorbs and ventilates heat

☒ SHORT ANSWER Write a brief answer to each of the following questions.

1. What is the system clock? _____ How does clock speed affect a computer's speed? _____

2. How are a chip-for-chip upgrade, a piggyback upgrade, and a daughterboard upgrade different? _____ What is a zero-insertion force (ZIF) socket? _____

3. How is dynamic RAM different from static RAM? _____ Why are synchronous DRAM, Double Data Rate SDRAM, and Rambus® DRAM chips faster than basic DRAM? _____

4. What is memory cache? _____ How are the three types of cache (L1 cache, L2 cache, and L3 cache) different? _____

5. How are male connectors different from female connectors? _____ What is a gender changer and when would it be used? _____

☒ WORKING TOGETHER Working with a group of your classmates, complete the following team exercises.

1. Prepare a report on the different types of ports and the way you connect peripheral devices to a computer. As part of your report, include the following subheadings and an overview of each subheading topic: (1) What is a port? (2) What is a connector? (3) What is a serial port and how does it work? (4) What is a parallel port and how does it work? (5) What is a USB port and how does it work? Expand your report so that it includes information beyond that in your textbook. Create a PowerPoint presentation from your report. Share your presentation with your class.

2. Choose one Issue in this chapter: from page 4.07, 4.08, 4.23, or 4.35. Use the Web and/or print media to research the issue. Then, present a debate for the class, with different members of your team supporting different responses to the questions that accompany the issue.

3. Notebook computers comprise almost 40 percent of personal computer sales. How do notebook computers compare with desktop models? Have each member of your team use a catalogue, access a manufacturer's Web site, or visit a retailer and find a notebook compuer and a desktop computer with comparable system units. What is the price of each computer? How are the system units similar? How are they different? Contrast the peripheral devices (displays, keyboards, and so on) and the software included. Meet with the members of your team to discuss results of your investigations. Which computer is the better buy? Why? Use PowerPoint to create a group presentation and share your findings with the class.

CHAPTER 4   LEARN IT ONLINE

◀● Previous | Next ●▶

Use the Learn It Online exercises to reinforce your understanding of the chapter concepts.

☐ **WEB INSTRUCTIONS:**

To display this page from the Web, start your browser and enter the Web address **scsite.com/dc2004/ch4/learn**.

1 At The Movies – Andrew Grove

To view the Andrew Grove movie, click the number 1 button. Watch the movie and then complete the exercise by answering the question below. Intel is the leading manufacturer of processors, including the Pentium, Celeron, Itanium, and Xeon processors. Intel grew to its present size with more than 60,000 employees because of the outstanding leadership of Andrew Grove. Based on the personal information you learned about Mr. Grove in the movie, describe how his early life struggles, his strong work ethic, and his vision of capitalizing on business trends have been the foundation for Intel's worldwide processor empire. How might Andrew Grove's forward-growth visions for Intel continue to drive the company toward even greater success in the future?

2 Shelly Cashman Series Understanding the Motherboard Lab

Follow the instructions in Learn It Online 2 on page 1.46 to start and use the Shelly Cashman Series Understanding the Motherboard Lab. If you are running from the Web, enter the Web address **scsite.com/sclabs/menu** or display the Learn It Online page (see instructions at the top of this page) and then click the number 2 button.

3 How a Processor Works

After reading about what a processor does and the way it interacts with other system unit components, it still can be difficult to understand how a processor performs even a simple task such as adding two plus three. Click the number 3 button, and complete this exercise to learn what a processor does to find the answer.

4 Practice Test

Click the number 4 button. Answer each question. When completed, enter your name and click the Grade Test button to submit the quiz for grading. Make a note of any missed questions. If required, print a copy to submit to your instructor.

5 Web Guide

Click the number 5 button to display the Guide to Web Sites and Searching Techniques Web page. Click Computers and Computing and then click Virtual Museum of Computing. Scroll down the page, locate and click On-line exhibits and information. Click a link of your choice. Use your word processing program to prepare a brief report on your selection and submit the assignment to your instructor.

6 Scavenger Hunt

Click the number 6 button. Print a copy of the Scavenger Hunt page; use this page to write down your answers as you search the Web. Submit your completed page to your instructor.

7 Who Wants to Be a Computer Genius?

Click the number 7 button to find out if you are a computer genius. Directions on how to play the game will display. When you are ready to play, click the Play button. Submit your score to your instructor.

Go To | TOC | Chapter 1 | 2 | 3 | 4 | 5 | 6 | 7 | 8 | 9 | 10 | 11 | 12 | 13 | 14 | 15 | Home |

SHELLY
CASHMAN
SERIES.

4.47

LEARN IT ONLINE CHAPTER 4

8 Wheel of Terms

Click the number 8 button to reinforce important terms you learned in this chapter by playing the Shelly Cashman Series version of this popular game. Directions on how to play the game will display. When you are ready to play, click the Play button. Submit your score to your instructor.

9 Career Corner

Click the number 9 button to display the Penn State's Career Services Web page. Click a link of your choice. Write a brief report on the information you found. Submit the report to your instructor.

10 Search Sleuth

Click the number 10 button to learn search techniques that will help make you a research expert. Submit the completed assignment to your instructor.

11 Crossword Puzzle Challenge

Click the number 11 button. Complete the puzzle to reinforce skills you learned in this chapter. Directions on how to play the game will display. When you are ready to play, click the Play button. Submit the completed puzzle to your instructor.

12 Newsgroups

Would you like more information about a special interest? Maybe you would like to share opinions and advice with people who have the same interests. If so, you might be interested in newsgroups, also called discussion groups or forums. A newsgroup offers the opportunity to read articles about a specific subject, respond to the articles, and even post your own articles. Click the number 12 button to find out more about newsgroups. What is lurking? What is Usenet? Click the how do I find a newsgroup? link at the bottom of the page. Read and print the how do I find a newsgroup? Web page. How can you locate a newsgroup on a particular topic?

13 In the News

In February 2006, the forerunner of the modern computer will have its 60th anniversary. By today's standards for electronic computers, the ENIAC (Electronic Numerical Integrator And Computer) was a grotesque monster. It had 30 separate units, plus a power supply and forced-air cooling, and it weighed more than 30 tons. Its 19,000 vacuum tubes, 1,500 relays, and hundreds of thousands of resistors, capacitors, and inductors consumed almost 200 kilowatts of electrical power. The ENIAC performed fewer than 1,000 calculations per minute; today, personal computers can process more than 300 million instructions per second. The rapid development of computing power and capabilities is astonishing, and the rate of that development is accelerating. Click the number 13 button and read a news article about the introduction of a new or improved computer component. What is the component? Who is introducing it? Will the component change the way people use computers? If so, how?

CHAPTER 4 **LAB EXERCISES**

◄● Previous | Next ●►

Use the Lab Exercises to gain hands-on computer experience.

■ WEB INSTRUCTIONS:

To display this page from the Web, start your browser and enter the Web address **scsite.com/dc2004/ch4/lab**.

1 Installing New Hardware

This exercise uses Windows XP procedures. Plug and Play technology allows users to install new devices without having to reconfigure the system manually. To learn how to install a new device with Plug and Play technology, click the Start button on the taskbar, and then click Help and Support on the Start menu. When the Help and Support Center window displays, click the Hardware link in the Pick a Help topic list. Click Installing and configuring new hardware. Click the Install a device link in the Pick a task list.

- What are the two steps in installing a Plug and Play device?
- When would Windows not detect a Plug and Play device?
- How is a device that is not Plug and Play installed?

Close the Help and Support Center window.

2 Setting the System Clock

This exercise uses Windows XP procedures. Click the Start button on the taskbar and then click Control Panel on the Start menu. If necessary, switch to Category view. Click the Date, Time, Language, and Regional Options link in the Pick a category list. Click the Date and Time icon. Click the Question Mark button on the title bar of the Date and Time Properties dialog box, and then click the picture of the calendar. Read the information in the pop-up window and then click it to close it. Repeat this process for other areas of the dialog box. Answer these questions:

- What is the purpose of the calendar?
- How do you change the time zone?
- What is the difference between the OK and the Apply buttons?

Close the Date and Time Properties dialog box. Close the Date, Time, Language, and Regional Options window.

3 Using Calculator to Perform Number System Conversion

This exercise uses Windows XP/2000/98 procedures. Instead of the decimal (base 10) number system that people use, computers use the binary (base 2) or hexadecimal (base 16) number systems. It is not necessary to understand these number systems to use a computer, but it is interesting to see how decimal numbers look when in binary or hexadecimal form. Click the Start button on the taskbar, point to All Programs (Programs in Windows 2000/98) on the Start menu, point to Accessories on the All Programs submenu (Programs submenu in Windows 2000/98), and then click Calculator. Click Scientific on the View menu to display the scientific calculator. Perform the following tasks:

- Click Dec (decimal). Enter 35 by clicking the numeric buttons or using the numeric keypad. Click Bin (binary). What number displays? Click Hex (hexadecimal). What number displays? Click the C (Clear) button.
- Convert the following decimal numbers to binary and hexadecimal: 7,256 and 3,421.
- What decimal number is equal to 10010 in the binary system? What decimal number is equal to 2DA9 in the hexadecimal system?

Close the Calculator window.

4 Power Management

This exercise uses Windows XP procedures. Environmental and financial considerations make it important to manage the amount of power a computer uses. Click the Start button on the taskbar, click Control Panel on the Start menu. Click the Performance and Maintenance icon in the Control Panel window. Click the Power Options icon in the Performance and Maintenance window. If necessary, click the Power Schemes tab in the Power Options Properties dialog box.

- What is a power scheme?
- What power scheme currently is being used on your computer?
- After how many minutes of inactivity is the monitor turned off?
- After how many minutes of inactivity are the hard disks turned off?

Close the Power Options Properties dialog box and the Performance and Maintenance window.

WEB RESEARCH
CHAPTER 4

Use the Web Research exercises to learn more about the special features in this chapter.

WEB INSTRUCTIONS:

Use the link in each exercise or a search engine such as Google (google.com) to research the topic. Then, write a one-page, double-spaced report or create a presentation, unless otherwise directed below. Page numbers on which information can be found are in parentheses.

1   **Issue**   Choose one <u>Issue</u> from the following issues in this chapter: Do People Perform the Machine Cycle? (4.07), Perfection at What Price? (4.08), Does Lower Price Mean Less Value? (4.23), or Do You Want Air Conditioning? Power Windows? A Car Computer? (4.35). Use the Web to research the issue. Discuss the issue with classmates, instructors, and friends. Address the questions that accompany the issue in a report or presentation.

2   **Apply It**   Choose one of the following <u>Apply It</u> features in this chapter: Chip Identifies Pets and Valuables (4.04) or Computers at Work While You Sleep (4.13). Use the Web to gather additional information about the topic. Print two Web pages that relate to the Apply It. Detail in a report or presentation what you learned.

3   **Career Corner**   Read the <u>Career Corner</u> article in this chapter (4.36). Use the Web to find out more about the career. Describe the career in a report or presentation.

4   **Companies on the Cutting Edge**   Choose one of the <u>Companies on the Cutting Edge</u> in this chapter (4.38). Use the Web to research the company further. Explain in a report or presentation how this company has contributed to computer technology.

5   **Technology Trailblazers**   Choose one of the <u>Technology Trailblazers</u> in this chapter (4.39). Use the Web to research the person further. Explain in a report or presentation how this individual has affected the way people use, or think about, computers.

6   **Picture Yourself Upgrading a Computer**   Read the Picture Yourself Upgrading a Computer story at the beginning of this chapter (4.00). Use the Web to research upgrading your computer further. Describe in a report or presentation the ways in which you might upgrade your computer.

7   **High-Tech Talk**   Read the <u>High-Tech Talk</u> feature in this chapter (4.37). Use the Web to find out more about the topic. Summarize in a report or presentation what you learned.

8   **Web Links**   Review the <u>Web Link</u> boxes found in the margins of this chapter. Visit five of the Web Link sites. Print the main Web page for each site you visit. Choose one of the Web pages and then summarize in one paragraph the content of the Web page.

9   **Looking Ahead**   Choose one of the <u>Looking Ahead</u> articles in this chapter: Next-Generation Computers and Chips: Faster and Smaller (4.21) or Robotic Rats May Perform Rescue Missions (4.36). Use the Web to find out more about the topic. Detail in a report or presentation what you learned.

10   **FAQ**   Choose one <u>FAQ</u> found in this chapter. Use the Web to find out more about the topic. Summarize in one paragraph what you learned.

11   **Making Use of the Web**   Read the Resources section of <u>Making Use of the Web</u> in Appendix A (A.08). Complete the Resources Web Exercises at the end of the section (A.09). Answer the questions posed in each exercise.

Input

Picture Yourself Using a PDA

What a great birthday! Everyone pitched in and bought you a color Web-enabled PDA. No more writing class notes on paper. You will be taking notes by writing with a stylus onto the PDA's screen. Even more convenient, all your appointments and addresses always will be just a tap away.

Your second present is a gift certificate for a software memory card and two of the following accessories: a combination stylus/writing pen, a mini keyboard, a snap-on voice recorder, a snap-on digital camera, or a telephone conversion kit. Which accessories are the most important?

The only easy decision is which software memory card to choose ... you need the Merriam-Webster's Collegiate® Dictionary for schoolwork. Choosing two accessories is a much more difficult decision. The combination pen/stylus would be handy. The mini keyboard would make entering data a lot faster, especially school notes. Leaving yourself voice messages is a neat idea. Taking digital pictures of friends and family and saving them on the PDA would be real cool. With the telephone conversion kit, you could cancel your current cellular telephone service. You have many viable options.

You opt to be practical and select the mini keyboard. Then, you decide to have fun and choose the digital camera as the second accessory.

As you read Chapter 5, you will learn about input devices for PDAs and discover other types of input.

☑ DICT...
☐ TELEPH...
☑ MINI KEYBOARD
☐ VOICE RECORDER
☑ DIGITAL CAMERA
☐ PEN/STYLUS

OBJECTIVES

After completing this chapter, you will be able to:

1. Define input

2. List the characteristics of a keyboard

3. Describe different mouse types and how they work

4. Summarize how pointing devices work

5. Explain how voice recognition works

6. Describe various input devices for mobile users

7. Explain how a digital camera works

8. Describe the uses of PC video cameras, Web cams, and video conferencing

9. Discuss various scanners and reading devices and how they work

10. Explain the types of terminals

11. Summarize the various biometric devices

12. Identify alternative input devices for physically challenged users

CONTENTS

WHAT IS INPUT?

Input is any data or instructions entered into the memory of a computer. People have a variety of options available to input data and instructions into a computer. As shown in Figure 5-1, users can type characters on a keyboard; click a button or roll a wheel on a mouse; press a finger on a touch screen; write, draw on, or tap a device's screen with a stylus or digital pen; speak into a microphone; send images from a digital camera; transmit live images with a PC video camera; or scan a bar code or an image.

As discussed in Chapter 1, *data* is a collection of unprocessed text, numbers, images, audio, and video. Once data is in memory, the computer interprets and executes instructions to process the data into information. *Instructions* are the steps that tell the computer how to perform a particular task.

Input to a computer consists of either data or instructions (Figure 5-2). Instructions entered into the computer can be in the form of programs, commands, and user responses.

• A *program* is a series of instructions that tells a computer what to do and how to do it. When a programmer writes a program, he or

FIGURE 5-1 Users input data into a computer in a variety of ways.

she inputs the program into the computer by using a keyboard, mouse, or other input device. The programmer then stores the program in a file that a user can execute (run). When a user runs a program, the computer loads the program from a storage medium to memory. Thus, a program is input into a computer's memory.

• Programs respond to commands that a user issues. A *command* is an instruction that causes a program to perform a specific action. Users issue commands by typing or pressing keys on the keyboard, clicking a mouse button, speaking into a microphone, or touching an area on a screen.

• A *user response* is an instruction a user issues by replying to a question displayed by a program. A response to the question instructs the program to perform certain actions. Assume the program asks the question, Is the time card correct? If you answer Yes, the program processes the time card. If you answer No, the program gives you the opportunity to modify the time card entries.

touch screen

digital pen

voice input

FIGURE 5-2 Two types of input are data and instructions. Instructions entered into the computer can be in the form of programs, commands, and user responses.

WHAT ARE INPUT DEVICES?

An **input device** is any hardware component that allows users to enter data or instructions (programs, commands, and user responses) into a computer. Depending on the application and your particular requirements, the input device selected may vary. Popular input devices include the keyboard, mouse, stylus, digital pen, microphone, digital camera, and scanner. The following pages discuss these and other input devices.

Storage devices, such as disk drives, serve as both input and output devices. Chapter 7 discusses storage devices.

THE KEYBOARD

Many people use a keyboard as one of their input devices. A **keyboard** is an input device that contains keys users press to enter data into a computer (Figure 5-3).

Desktop computer keyboards typically have from 101 to 105 keys. Keyboards for smaller computers such as notebook computers contain fewer keys. All computer keyboards have a typing area that includes the letters of the alphabet, numbers, punctuation marks, and other basic keys. Many desktop computer keyboards also have a numeric keypad on the right side of the keyboard. A keyboard also contains other keys that allow users to enter data and instructions into the computer. Read Issue 5-1 for a related discussion.

ISSUE 5-1

What Is Happening on Your Computer?

Do you question your employees' work on company computers? Are you curious about your spouse's long e-mail messages? Do you have concerns about your teenager's conversations in Internet chat rooms? Keyboard monitoring software can dispel your doubts. When installed on a computer, *keyboard monitoring software* records every keystroke in a file, which you later access by supplying the correct password. With keyboard monitoring software, you see everything that was typed on the computer keyboard, including documents, e-mail, and other messages. You could catch a disgruntled employee preparing a resume on company time, discover that your spouse is e-mailing gardening tips to a distant friend, or keep your teenager from a potentially dangerous contact in a chat room. Many maintain, however, that keyboard monitoring software is an invasion of privacy. Should keyboard monitoring software ever be used? If so, when? Some marketers of keyboard monitoring software recommend that computer users should be informed that the software is installed. Is this a good idea? Why or why not?

For more information about keyboard monitoring, visit the Discovering Computers 2004 Issues Web page (**scsite.com/dc2004/issues**). Click Issue #1 below Chapter 5.

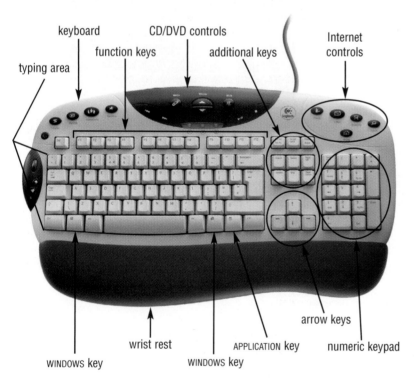

FIGURE 5-3 On a desktop computer keyboard, you type using keys in the typing area and on the numeric keypad.

Across the top of most keyboards are function keys, which are labeled with the letter F followed by a number (Figure 5-3). *Function keys* are special keys programmed to issue commands to a computer. The command associated with a function key depends on the program. To issue commands, users often press a function key in combination with other special keys (SHIFT, CTRL, ALT, and others). Many programs enable users to press key combinations, select a menu command, or click a button to obtain the same result (Figure 5-4).

MICROSOFT WORD KEY COMBINATION EQUIVALENTS

Command	Key Combination	Menu | Command	Button
Copy	SHIFT+F2 or CTRL+C	Edit | Copy	
Open	CTRL+F12	File | Open	
Paste	CTRL+V	Edit | Paste	

FIGURE 5-4 Many programs allow you to use key combinations, a menu, or a button on a toolbar to obtain the same result, as shown by these examples from Microsoft Word.

Keyboards also contain keys that allow you to position the insertion point, also known as a *cursor* in some applications. The **insertion point** is a symbol on the screen, usually a blinking vertical bar, that indicates where the next character you type will display (Figure 5-5). Users can move the insertion point left, right, up, or down by pressing the arrow keys and other keys on the keyboard.

Nearly all keyboards have toggle keys. A *toggle key* is a key that switches between two states each time a user presses the key. When you press the NUM LOCK key, for example, it locks the numeric keypad so you can use the keypad to type numbers. When you press the NUM LOCK key again, the numeric keypad unlocks so the same keys function as keys that move the insertion point. Many keyboards have status lights that light up when you activate a toggle key.

Most of today's desktop computer keyboards are enhanced keyboards. An *enhanced keyboard* has twelve function keys along the top, two CTRL keys, two ALT keys, and a set of arrow and additional keys between the typing area and the numeric keypad (Figure 5-3). Many keyboards also have a WINDOWS key(s) and an APPLICATION key. When pressed, the WINDOWS key displays the Start menu, and the APPLICATION key displays an item's shortcut menu.

Newer keyboards also include buttons that allow you to access the computer's CD/DVD drive, adjust speaker volume, open an e-mail program, start a Web browser, and search the Internet. Some keyboards even have USB ports so a user can plug a USB device directly into the keyboard instead of into the system unit.

❓ FAQ 5-1

What is the rationale for the arrangement of keys in the typing area?

The keys are arranged to reduce the frequency of key jams in a mechanical typewriter. Called a *QWERTY keyboard*, the first letters on the top alphabetic line spell QWERTY. A *Dvorak keyboard*, by contrast, places frequently typed letters in the middle of the typing area. Despite the Dvorak keyboard's logical design, the QWERTY keyboard is more widely used.

For more information about keyboards, visit the Discovering Computers 2004 FAQ Web page (**scsite.com/dc2004/faq**). Click Keyboards below Chapter 5.

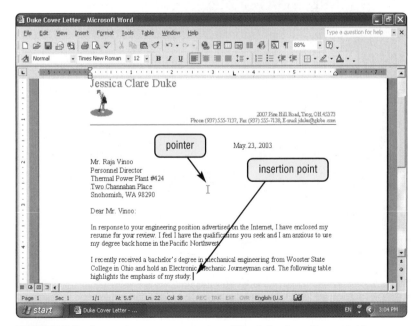

FIGURE 5-5 In most programs, such as Word, the insertion point is a blinking vertical bar. You use the keyboard or other input device to move the insertion point. The pointer, another symbol that displays on the screen, is controlled using a pointing device such as a mouse.

Keyboard Connections

Desktop computer keyboards often attach via a cable to a serial port, a keyboard port, or a USB port on the system unit. Some keyboards, however, do not use wires at all. A *cordless keyboard* is a battery-powered device that transmits data using wireless technology, such as radio waves or infrared light waves. Cordless keyboards communicate with a receiver attached to a port on the system unit. The port type varies depending on the type of wireless technology. For example, a Bluetooth-enabled keyboard communicates via radio waves with a Bluetooth receiver plugged into a serial, parallel, or USB port.

On notebook and many handheld computers, the keyboard is built into the top of the system unit (Figure 5-6). To fit in these smaller computers, the keyboards usually are smaller and have fewer keys. Most desktop computer keyboards have at least 101 keys. A typical notebook computer keyboard, by contrast, usually has about 85 keys. To provide all of the functionality of a desktop computer keyboard, manufacturers design many of the keys to serve two or three different purposes.

Keyboard Ergonomics

Regardless of size, many keyboards have a rectangular shape with the keys aligned in straight, horizontal rows. Users who spend a lot of time typing on these keyboards sometimes experience repetitive strain injuries (RSI) of their wrists and hands. For this reason, some manufacturers offer ergonomic keyboards. An **ergonomic keyboard** has a design that reduces the chance of the wrist and hand injuries (Figure 5-7). Even keyboards that are not ergonomically designed attempt to offer a user more comfort. For example, many keyboards today include a wrist rest or palm rest to reduce strain on the wrist while typing (Figure 5-3 on page 5.04).

The goal of **ergonomics** is to incorporate comfort, efficiency, and safety into the design of items in the workplace. Employees can be injured or develop disorders of the muscles, nerves, tendons, ligaments, and joints from working in an area that is not ergonomically designed.

❓FAQ 5-2

What can I do to reduce chances of experiencing repetitive strain injuries?

Do not rest your wrist on the edge of a desk; use a wrist rest. Keep your forearm and wrist level so your wrist does not bend. Do hand exercises every fifteen minutes. Keep your shoulders, arms, hands, and wrists relaxed while you work. Maintain good posture. Keep feet flat on the floor, with one foot slightly in front of the other.

For more information about repetitive strain injuries, visit the Discovering Computers 2004 FAQ Web page (**scsite.com/dc2004/faq**). Click Repetitive Strain Injuries below Chapter 5.

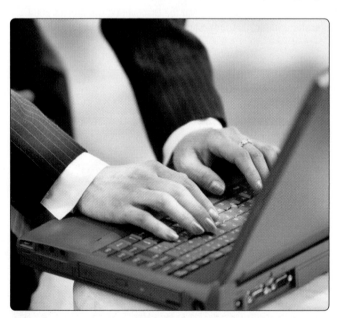

FIGURE 5-6   On notebook computers and many handheld computers, the keyboard is built into the top of the system unit.

FIGURE 5-7   An ergonomic keyboard is designed to minimize strain on your hands and wrists.

POINTING DEVICES

A **pointing device** is an input device that allows a user to control a pointer on the screen. In a graphical user interface, a **pointer** is a small symbol on the screen (Figure 5-5 on page 5.05) whose location and shape change as a user moves a pointing device. For example, a pointing device can move the insertion point; select text, graphics, and other objects; and click buttons, icons, links, and menu commands. The following sections discuss the mouse and other pointing devices.

MOUSE

A **mouse** is a pointing device that fits comfortably under the palm of your hand. The mouse is the most widely used pointing device on desktop computers.

With a mouse, users control the movement of the pointer, often called a *mouse pointer* in this case. The top and sides of a mouse have one to four buttons; some also have a small wheel. The bottom of a mouse is flat and contains a mechanism that detects movement of the mouse.

Mouse Types

A *mechanical mouse* has a rubber or metal ball on its underside (Figure 5-8). When the ball rolls in a certain direction, electronic circuits in the mouse translate the movement of the mouse into signals the computer can process.

You should place a mechanical mouse on a mouse pad. A **mouse pad** is a rectangular rubber or foam pad that provides better traction than the top of a desk. The mouse pad also protects the ball in the mouse from a build-up of dust and dirt, which could cause it to malfunction.

An optical mouse, by contrast, has no moving mechanical parts inside. Instead, an *optical mouse* uses devices that emit and sense light to detect the mouse's movement (Figure 5-9). Some use optical sensors, others use a laser. You can place an optical mouse that uses optical sensors on nearly all types of surfaces, eliminating the need for a mouse pad. An optical mouse that uses a laser usually requires a special mouse pad. An optical mouse is more precise than a mechanical mouse and does not require cleaning as does a mechanical mouse, but it also is more expensive.

A mouse connects to a computer in several ways. Many types connect with a cable that attaches to a serial port, mouse port, or USB port on the system unit. A *cordless mouse* is a battery-powered device that transmits data using wireless technology, such as radio waves or infrared light waves. The wireless technology used for a cordless mouse is very similar to that of a cordless keyboard discussed earlier. Some users prefer a cordless mouse because it frees up desk space and eliminates the clutter of a cord. For a more technical discussion about the wireless keyboard and mouse, read the High-Tech Talk article on page 5.37 at the end of this chapter.

FIGURE 5-8 A mechanical mouse contains a small ball.

FIGURE 5-9 This optical mouse uses an optical sensor. It also includes buttons to push with your thumb that enable forward and backward navigation through Web pages.

Using a Mouse

As you move a mouse, the pointer on the screen also moves (Figure 5-10). If you have never worked with a mouse, you might find it awkward at first. With a little practice, however, you will discover that a mouse is quite easy to use. Read Issue 5-2 for a related discussion.

Generally, you use the mouse to move the pointer on the screen to an object such as a button, a menu, an icon, a link, or text. Then, you press a mouse button to perform a certain action on that object. Windows users work with a mouse that has at least two buttons. For a right-handed user, the left button usually is the primary mouse button and the right mouse button is the secondary mouse button. Left-handed people, however, can reverse the function of these buttons. Read Apply It 5-1 for more information.

FIGURE 5-10   HOW TO MOVE THE POINTER WITH A MOUSE

Step 1:
Place the mouse toward the right of the mouse pad.

Step 2:
Move the mouse diagonally toward the left until the pointer is positioned on the Microsoft Outlook icon.

ISSUE 5-2

A Mouse Did What?

When you consider the causes of workplace injuries, you might not put clicking a mouse in the same category with lifting a bag of concrete, but perhaps you should. According to the chairman of a National Academy of Sciences panel that investigated workplace injuries, every year a million Americans lose workdays because of repetitive strain injuries. These injuries, which often result from prolonged use of a computer mouse and keyboard, are the largest job-related injury and illness problem in the United States today. OSHA proposed standards whereby employers would have to establish programs to prevent workplace injuries with respect to computer use. Yet, Congress rejected the standards, accepting the argument that the cost to employers would be prohibitive and unfair, because no proof exists that the injuries are caused exclusively by office work. Should standards for computer use be established by the government? Why or why not? Who is responsible for this type of workplace injury? Why?

For more information about workplace injuries, visit the Discovering Computers 2004 Issues Web page (**scsite.com/dc2004/issues**). Click Issue #2 below Chapter 5.

In addition to pointing, you can perform several operations using the mouse. These operations include click, right-click, double-click, triple-click, drag, right-drag, rotate wheel, and press wheel button. The table in Figure 5-11 explains how to perform these mouse operations. Some programs also use keys in combination with the mouse to perform certain actions. The function of the mouse buttons and the wheel varies depending on the program.

APPLY IT 5-1

Configuring the Mouse to Suit Your Preferences

Ten percent of the population is left-handed, according to some estimates. If they also are computer users, they may feel awkward using a mouse because this device is configured for a right-handed user. They can, however, configure the mouse to fit their needs. In fact, all mouse users can customize their mouse-usage preferences in a few simple steps.

Using Windows XP, click the Start button on the taskbar, click Control Panel, and then in Classic View double-click the Mouse icon in the Control Panel box. Windows displays the Mouse Properties dialog box, which contains a variety of options.

For example, on the Buttons tab you can configure the mouse for right- or left-handed use by choosing the primary and secondary buttons, adjust the double-click speed, and turn on ClickLock, which allows you to highlight or drag without holding down the mouse button.

On the Pointers tab, you can select a scheme of predefined mouse pointers, customize the pointers, and select whether you want a shadow to display under the pointer.

The Pointer Options tab includes options to select the pointer speed, automatically move the pointer to a default button in a dialog box, make the mouse pointer leave a trail, hide the mouse pointer while you type, and show the mouse pointer's location when the CTRL key is pressed.

If the Mouse Properties dialog box has a Wheel tab, you also can specify the number of lines the screen should scroll when you roll the wheel one notch.

For more information about configuring a mouse, visit the Discovering Computers 2004 Apply It Web page (**scsite.com/dc2004/apply**). Click Apply It #1 below Chapter 5.

FAQ 5-3

What is the purpose of a wheel on a mouse?

To scroll and zoom. Roll it forward or backward to scroll up or down. Hold down the CTRL key while rolling the wheel to make the text on the screen bigger or smaller. These scrolling and zooming functions work with most software and also on the Web.

For more information about using a mouse, visit the Discovering Computers 2004 FAQ Web page (**scsite.com/dc2004/faq**). Click Using a Mouse below Chapter 5.

WEB LINK 5-1

Mouse
Visit the Discovering Computers 2004 WEB LINK page (**scsite.com/dc2004/weblink**). Click Mouse below Chapter 5.

MOUSE OPERATIONS

Operation	Mouse Action	Example
Point	Move the mouse across a flat surface until the pointer on the desktop is positioned on the item of choice.	Position the pointer on the screen.
Click	Press and release the primary mouse button, which usually is the left mouse button.	Select or deselect items on the screen or start a program or program feature.
Right-click	Press and release the secondary mouse button, which usually is the right mouse button.	Display a shortcut menu.
Double-click	Quickly press and release the left mouse button twice without moving the mouse.	Start a program or program feature.
Triple-click	Quickly press and release the left mouse button three times without moving the mouse.	Select a paragraph.
Drag	Point to an item, hold down the left mouse button, move the item to the desired location on the screen, and then release the left mouse button.	Move an object from one location to another or draw pictures.
Right-drag	Point to an item, hold down the right mouse button, move the item to the desired location on the screen, and then release the right mouse button.	Display a shortcut menu after moving an object from one location to another.
Rotate wheel	Roll the wheel forward or backward.	Scroll up or down a few lines.
Press wheel button	Press the wheel button while moving the mouse on the desktop.	Scroll continuously.

FIGURE 5-11 The more common mouse operations.

OTHER POINTING DEVICES

The mouse is the most widely used pointing device today. Some users, however, work with other pointing devices. These include the trackball, touchpad, pointing stick, joystick, wheel, light pen, touch screen, stylus, and digital pen. The following sections discuss each of these pointing devices.

Trackball

Similar to a mechanical mouse that has a ball on the bottom, a **trackball** is a stationary pointing device with a ball on its top (Figure 5-12). The ball in most trackballs is about the size of a Ping-Pong ball.

To move the pointer using a trackball, you rotate the ball with your thumb, fingers, or the palm of your hand. In addition to the ball, a trackball usually has one or more buttons that work just like mouse buttons.

A trackball requires frequent cleaning because it picks up oils from fingers and dust from the environment. For users who have limited desk space, however, a trackball is a good alternative to a mouse because the device is stationary.

Touchpad

A **touchpad** is a small, flat, rectangular pointing device that is sensitive to pressure and motion (Figure 5-13). To move the pointer using a touchpad, slide your fingertip across the surface of the pad. Some touchpads have one or more buttons around the edge of the pad that work like mouse buttons. On many touchpads, you also can tap the pad's surface to imitate mouse operations such as clicking.

Although you can attach a stand-alone touchpad to any personal computer, touchpads are found most often on notebook computers.

FIGURE 5-13 Many notebook computers have a touchpad that allows users to control the movement of the pointer.

Pointing Stick

A **pointing stick** is a pressure-sensitive pointing device shaped like a pencil eraser that is positioned between keys on a keyboard (Figure 5-14). To move the pointer using a pointing stick, you push the pointing stick

FIGURE 5-14 Some notebook computers include a pointing stick to allow a user to control the movement of the pointer.

WEB LINK 5-2

Touchpad

Visit the Discovering Computers 2004 WEB LINK page (**scsite .com/dc2004/weblink**). Click Touchpad below Chapter 5.

WEB LINK 5-3

Pointing Stick

Visit the Discovering Computers 2004 WEB LINK page (**scsite .com/dc2004/weblink**). Click Pointing Stick below Chapter 5.

FIGURE 5-12 A trackball is like an upside-down mouse.

with a finger. The pointer on the screen moves in the direction you push the pointing stick. By pressing buttons below the keyboard, users can click and perform other mouse-type operations with a pointing stick.

A pointing stick does not require any additional desk space. In addition, it does not require cleaning like a mechanical mouse or trackball. IBM developed the pointing stick for its notebook computers.

Whether you select a notebook computer that has a touchpad or pointing stick is a matter of personal preference. Some notebook computers have both a touchpad and a pointing stick.

Joystick and Wheel

Users running game software or flight and driving simulation software often use a joystick or wheel as a pointing device (Figure 5-15). A **joystick** is a vertical lever mounted on a base. You move the lever in different directions to control the actions of the simulated vehicle or player. The lever usually includes buttons called triggers you press to activate certain events. Some joysticks also have additional buttons you set to perform other actions.

A **wheel** is a steering-wheel-type input device. Users turn the wheel to simulate driving a car, truck, or other vehicle. Most wheels also include foot pedals for acceleration and braking actions. A joystick and wheel typically attach via a cable to the game port on a sound card or game card or to a USB port.

Light Pen

A **light pen** is a handheld input device that can detect the presence of light. Some light pens require a specially designed monitor, while others work with a standard monitor (Figure 5-16). To select objects on the screen, a user presses the light pen against the surface of the screen or points the light pen at the screen and then presses a button on the pen.

Health care professionals, such as doctors and dentists, use light pens because they can slide a protective sleeve over the pen — keeping their fingers free of contaminants. Light pens also are ideal for areas where employees' hands might contain food, dirt, grease, or other chemicals that could damage the computer. Applications with limited desktop space such as industrial or manufacturing environments find light pens convenient, as well.

joystick

wheel

pedal

FIGURE 5-15 Joysticks and wheels help a user control the actions of players and vehicles in game and simulation software.

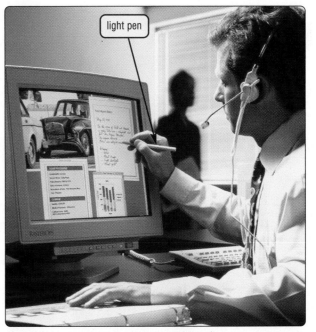

light pen

FIGURE 5-16 To make selections on the screen while processing an insurance claim, this insurance agent uses a light pen.

Touch Screen

A **touch screen** is a touch-sensitive display device. Users interact with these devices by touching areas of the screen with a finger. Because they require a lot of arm movements, you do not enter large amounts of data into touch screens. Instead, you touch words, pictures, numbers, or locations identified on the screen.

Kiosks often have touch screens. Travelers use kiosks in airports to print tickets ordered online, and they use kiosks in hotels for easy check in and check out (Figure 5-17). Store kiosks allow customers to order items not in stock at the store. Museum kiosks give visitors information. To allow easy access of your bank account from a car, many ATM machines have touch screens. Computers in restaurants, cafeterias, gift shops, and resorts also have touch screens. Most PDAs and Tablet PCs have touch screens, and some notebook computers even have touch screens.

WEB LINK 5-4

Touch Screen

Visit the Discovering Computers 2004 WEB LINK page (**scsite .com/dc2004/weblink**). Click Touch Screen below Chapter 5.

Stylus, Digital Pen, and Cursor

A **stylus** or **digital pen** looks like a ballpoint pen, but uses pressure, instead of ink, to write text and draw lines. Both allow a user to write, draw, and tap on a flat surface for input. A digital pen typically provides more functionality than a stylus. Originally called an electronic pen, this device was used primarily in professional graphical applications such as computer-aided design and drafting. These pens are quite sophisticated, featuring erasers and programmable buttons.

Architects, mapmakers, artists, and designers create drawings and sketches by using a pen or a cursor on a graphics tablet (Figure 5-18). A **graphics tablet** is a flat, rectangular, electronic plastic board. Large-scale applications sometimes refer to this device as a *digitizer*. A *cursor* looks similar to a mouse, except it has a window with crosshairs, so the user can see through to the tablet. Each location on the graphics tablet corresponds to a specific location on the screen. When drawing on the tablet with a pen or cursor, the tablet detects and converts the movements into digital signals that are sent into the computer.

Figure 5-18a (artist using pen)

Figure 5-18b (civil engineer using cursor)

FIGURE 5-17 A traveler uses a kiosk touch screen to check out of the hotel.

FIGURE 5-18 Artists, designers, and engineers use pens and cursors with graphics tablets or digitizers.

Pens used for handwriting recognition have grown in popularity. Using special software along with a pen and graphics tablet, a user sends handwritten notes via e-mail or signs his or her name electronically. Upon receipt, the receiver sees the handwritten note or signature in its original form. Businesses save time using *electronic signatures*, which now are just as legal as an ink signature.

Some desktop computer monitors and many mobile computers and devices have touch screens that allow you to input data using a pen or stylus (Figure 5-19). Instead of using a keyboard, you write or make selections on the computer screen with the stylus or pen. PDAs use a stylus, and Tablet PCs typically use a digital pen. These computers and mobile devices use *handwriting recognition software* that translates handwritten letters and symbols into characters that the computer can process. The stylus and digital pen are discussed in more depth later in this chapter. Read Looking Ahead 5-1 for a look at the next generation of pointing devices.

WEB LINK 5-5

Stylus and Pen

Visit the Discovering Computers 2004 WEB LINK page (**scsite.com/dc2004/weblink**). Click Stylus and Pen below Chapter 5.

LOOKING AHEAD 5-1

Wireless Pens Revolutionize Input Devices

The typewriter is regarded as the first significant everyday business tool. Patented in 1868, it had one major flaw: the keys jammed easily. To solve this problem, the keyboard was redesigned to reduce the frequency of jammed keys.

Most computer users have learned to memorize this keyboard and use it, along with a mouse, to gather and edit text, play games, draw images, and research the Internet. But a new generation of input devices is gathering support to facilitate entering data.

Intel's Human Computer Interface Devices project is exploring new hardware to replace the keyboard and mouse. One of the key products from its Microcomputer Research Labs (MRL) is the digital wireless pen. A similar device, the VPen™, is being developed at OTM Technologies to perform the same functions as a keyboard and mouse.

The digital pen resembles the stylus PDA owners use to enter and retrieve data. A tiny optical laser reader at the point interfaces with handwriting recognition software to convert handwriting to text. It also can be used as a joystick for games and to draw graphical images. The pen tip can be used on any surface, including the palm of a hand.

For a look at the next generation of pointing devices, visit the Discovering Computers 2004 Looking Ahead Web page (**scsite.com/dc2004/looking**). Click Looking Ahead #1 below Chapter 5.

pen for computer monitor

digital pen for Tablet PC

stylus for PDA

QUIZ YOURSELF 5-1

To check your knowledge of input techniques, the keyboard, the mouse, and other pointing devices, visit the Discovering Computers 2004 Quiz Yourself Web page (**scsite.com/dc2004/quiz**). Click Objectives 1 – 4 below Chapter 5.

FIGURE 5-19 All sizes of computers and mobile devices support handwriting input through a pen or stylus.

VOICE INPUT

As an alternative to using a keyboard to input data, some users are talking to their computers. **Voice input** is the process of entering data by speaking into a microphone. The microphone may be a stand-alone peripheral that sits on top of a desk, or is built into the computer or device, or is in a headset. Some external microphones have a cable that attaches to a port on the sound card on the computer. Others communicate using wireless technology such as IrDA or Bluetooth.

Voice recognition, also called *speech recognition*, is the computer's capability of distinguishing spoken words (Figure 5-20). Voice recognition programs do not understand speech. They recognize a vocabulary of pre-programmed words. The vocabulary of voice recognition programs can range from two words to millions of words. The automated telephone system at your bank may ask you to answer questions by speaking the words Yes or No into the telephone. A voice recognition program on your computer, by contrast, may recognize up to two million words.

In the past, voice recognition systems were found only in specialized applications in which a user's hands were occupied or disabled. Today, voice recognition applications are affordable and easy to use, providing all types of users with a convenient form of input. Users can search the Web, participate in chat rooms, and send and receive e-mail and instant messages — all by speaking into a microphone on a desktop computer, mobile computer, or mobile device. Some business software, such as word processing and spreadsheet, include voice recognition as part of the program. For example, users can dictate memos and letters into a word processing program instead of typing them.

The first voice recognition programs were speaker dependent. Today, most are a combination of speaker dependent and speaker independent. With *speaker-dependent software*, the

WEB LINK 5-6

Voice Input

Visit the Discovering Computers 2004 WEB LINK page (**scsite .com/dc2004/weblink**). Click Voice Input below Chapter 5.

FIGURE 5-20 HOW VOICE RECOGNITION WORKS

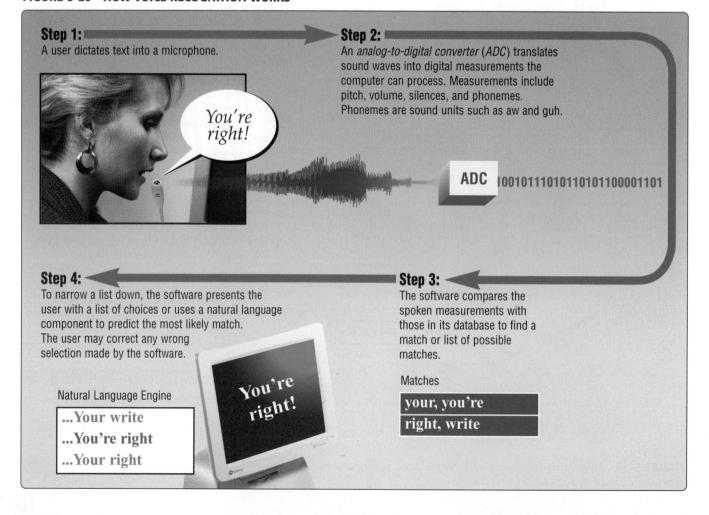

computer makes a profile of your voice, which means you have to train the computer to recognize your voice. To train the computer, you must speak each of the words in the vocabulary into the computer repeatedly. After hearing the spoken word repetitively, the program develops and stores a digital pattern for the word. When you later speak a word, the program compares the spoken word with those stored. *Speaker-independent software* has a built-in set of word patterns. That is, you do not have to train a computer to recognize your voice. Many products today include a built-in set of words that grows as the software learns your words.

Some voice recognition software requires *discrete speech*, which means you have to speak slowly and separate each word with a short pause. Most of today's products, however, allow you to speak in a flowing conversational tone, called *continuous speech*.

Keep in mind that the best voice recognition programs are 90 to 95 percent accurate, which means the software may interpret as many as one in ten words incorrectly. Experts agree voice recognition capability represents the future of software.

?FAQ 5-4

Which type of microphone is best?

For voice recognition software, headsets that have a microphone provide the highest quality because they typically do not pick up background noises. For group discussions, however, where multiple people will use the same microphone at the same time, you need a stand-alone or built-in microphone.

For more information about microphones, visit the Discovering Computers 2004 FAQ Web page (**scsite.com/dc2004/faq**). Click Microphones below Chapter 5.

Audio Input

Voice input is part of a larger category of input called audio input. **Audio input** is the process of entering any sound into the computer such as speech, music, and sound effects. To input high-quality sound, a personal computer must have a sound card. Users input sound via devices such as microphones, tape players, CD/DVD players, or radios, each of which plugs into a port on the sound card.

Some users also input music and other sound effects using external MIDI devices such as an electronic piano keyboard (Figure 5-21). As discussed in the previous chapter, in addition to being a port, *MIDI* (*musical instrument digital interface*) is the electronic music industry's standard that defines how digital musical devices represent sounds electronically. These devices connect to the sound card on a computer. Software programs that conform to the MIDI standard allow users to compose and edit music and many other sounds. For example, you can change the speed, add notes, or rearrange the score to produce an entirely new sound.

FIGURE 5-21 An electronic piano keyboard is an external MIDI device that allows users to record music, which can be stored in the computer.

INPUT DEVICES FOR MOBILE USERS

Mobile devices, such as the PDA and smart phone, and mobile computers such as the Tablet PC offer convenience for the mobile user. A variety of input alternatives are available for these devices and computers.

PDAs

A user inputs data into a PDA in many ways (Figure 5-22). PDAs ship with a basic stylus, which is the primary input device.

Users often purchase a more elaborate stylus that has a ballpoint pen at one end and a stylus at the other. With the stylus, you enter data in two ways: using an on-screen keyboard or using handwriting recognition software. PDAs typically use their own handwriting recognition software. For example, Palm PDAs include Graffiti®, that allows users to draw characters on the device's screen. For example, drawing a straight vertical line in a downward motion displays the number 1 on the PDA.

FIGURE 5-22   Users input data into a PDA using a variety of techniques.

For users who prefer typing to handwriting, some PDAs have a built-in keyboard. For those without a keyboard, users can purchase a mini keyboard that snaps onto the bottom of the device. Other users type onto a desktop computer or notebook computer and transfer the data into the PDA. As an alternative to typing, some PDAs support voice input that allows users to speak data and instructions into the device. To take photographs and view them on a PDA, simply attach a digital camera directly to the PDA. A telephone kit (along with a service package) allows users to make voice calls and send faxes on the PDA.

Instead of using a mini keyboard, some users prefer to enter data into a PDA using a full-sized keyboard. Two options are the portable keyboard and virtual keyboard. A *portable keyboard* is a full-sized keyboard you conveniently attach and remove from a PDA. Figure 5-23 shows a pocket-sized portable keyboard that unfolds into a full-sized keyboard.

A *virtual keyboard* projects an infrared image of a keyboard onto any flat surface. As the user types on the surface, the typed data transmits via a receiver to a PDA or other mobile device (Figure 5-24). The virtual keyboard is ideal for the mobile user.

For information about software for PDAs, read the PDA feature that follows this chapter.

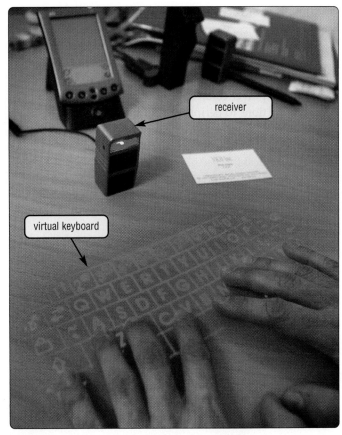

FIGURE 5-24 A virtual keyboard enables a user to enter data into a mobile device such as a PDA by typing on any flat surface.

FIGURE 5-23 This convenient portable keyboard unfolds into a full-sized keyboard, to which you can attach a PDA.

Tablet PCs

The primary input device for a Tablet PC is a digital pen, which allows users to write on the device's screen. A Tablet PC's handwriting recognition software works similarly to that of a PDA. The computer converts the handwriting into characters it can process. Read Issue 5-3 for a related discussion.

To access peripherals at their home or office, users have the option to slide their Tablet PC into a docking station. A *docking station*, which is an external device that holds a mobile computer, contains a power connection and provides connections to peripherals. In the docking station, Tablet PC users can work with a full-sized keyboard, mouse, and other desktop peripherals. In essence, a docking station converts a notebook computer or Tablet PC (Figure 5-25) into a desktop computer.

Smart Phones

Voice is the traditional method of input for

ISSUE 5-3

Can I Borrow Your Notes?

Bill Gates, cofounder of Microsoft, believes one of the next great innovations in the classroom will be the Tablet PC. The Tablet PC is a compact notebook computer that, according to Gates, combines "the simplicity of paper with the power of the PC." With a digital pen, students use the Tablet PC to run Windows-based applications. They also write notes on the Tablet PC screen and then sort, search, and save those notes and even convert them into typed documents. With wireless connectivity, students use a Tablet PC to access Web pages or communicate with classmates. The Tablet PC could enhance a classroom experience, but some fear that for most students it would be more of a distraction than a learning aid. How would the Tablet PC benefit students? What might be disadvantages of the Tablet PC in the classroom? With the benefits and disadvantages in mind, would you be better off in the classroom with a Tablet PC or with pencil and paper? Why?

For more information about the Tablet PC, visit the Discovering Computers 2004 Issues Web page (**scsite.com/dc2004/issues**). Click Issue #3 below Chapter 5.

smart phones. That is, a user speaks into the phone. Today, however, short message service has become a popular means of inputting data. Instead of calling someone's smart phone or cellular telephone, users input and send text messages using *SMS* (*short message service*). To send an SMS message, users type text messages, typically up to 150 characters, by pressing buttons on the telephone's keypad. As with chat rooms, SMS uses abbreviations and emoticons to minimize the amount of typing required. For example, instead of typing the text, I have just graduated, a user can type the emoticon, L:-), where the L stands for the tassel on the graduation cap.

FIGURE 5-25 To use a Tablet PC while working at a desk, simply insert the Tablet PC into a docking station. Devices such as a keyboard and mouse attach to the docking station.

FAQ 5-5

Can a mobile computer or device get a virus?

Yes. Mobile computers and devices can get a virus from downloading a Web page. A virus can transfer from a desktop computer to a mobile device when users connect the two together to synchronize data. Viruses also can transmit via wireless data transfer when two wireless devices communicate with one another, such as when receiving an SMS text message.

For more information about viruses and mobile devices, visit the Discovering Computers 2004 FAQ Web page (**scsite.com/dc2004/faq**). Click Viruses and Mobile Devices below Chapter 5.

DIGITAL CAMERAS

A **digital camera** allows users to take pictures and store the photographed images digitally, instead of on traditional film (Figure 5-26). Mobile users such as real estate agents, insurance agents, general contractors, and photojournalists use digital cameras so they immediately can view photographed images right on the camera. Home and business users have digital cameras to save the expense of film developing, duplication, and postage. With photo editing software, users add dazzling special effects to digital images. Many users share their digital images with family, friends, coworkers, and clients by posting the photographs on a Web site, e-mailing them, or simply printing copies of the images from a home or office printer.

Digital cameras use a variety of miniature mobile storage media to store images, including a floppy disk, flash memory card, memory stick, and mini-disc. Chapter 7 discusses these and other storage media in depth. Generally, higher-capacity storage devices can hold more pictures.

Digital cameras typically allow users to review, and sometimes edit, images while they are in the camera. Some digital cameras connect or communicate directly to a printer or television. This feature eliminates the need to copy images to a computer's hard disk. Instead, users print or view images directly from the camera.

Often users prefer to *download*, or transfer a copy of, the images from the digital camera to the computer's hard disk. With some digital cameras, images download through a cable that connects between the digital camera and a USB port or a FireWire port on the system unit. For cameras that store images on miniature mobile storage media, simply insert the media into a reading device that communicates wirelessly or attaches to a parallel port or USB port on the system unit. Copying images from the miniature media to the computer's hard disk is just like copying files from any other disk drive. Some cameras store images on a floppy disk. In this case, insert the floppy disk into the computer's disk drive and then copy the pictures to the computer's hard disk.

Some users prefer copying images to the hard disk in a computer, where the images are available for editing with photo editing software, printing, faxing, sending via e-mail, including in another document, or posting to a Web site or photo community for everyone to see. Many users add pictures to greeting cards, a computerized photo album, a family newsletter, certificates, and awards.

FIGURE 5-26 With a digital camera, users can view photographed images immediately through a small screen on the camera to see if the picture is worth keeping.

Figure 5-27 illustrates how one type of digital camera transforms the captured image into a screen display and printout.

The three basic types of digital cameras are studio cameras, field cameras, and point-and-shoot cameras. The most expensive and highest quality of the three is a *studio camera*, which is a stationary camera used for professional studio work. Often used by photojournalists, a *field camera* is a portable camera that has many lenses and other attachments. As with the studio camera, a field camera can be quite expensive. A *point-and-shoot camera* is much more affordable and lightweight and provides acceptable quality photographic images for the home or small business user.

A point-and-shoot camera often features flash, zoom, automatic focus, and special effects. Some allow users to record short audio narrations for photographed images. Others even record short video clips in addition to still images. Point-and-shoot digital cameras

FIGURE 5-27 HOW A DIGITAL CAMERA MIGHT WORK

Step 1:
Point to the image to photograph and take the picture. Light passes into the lens of the camera.

Step 2:
The image is focused on a chip called a *charge-coupled device* (*CCD*).

Step 3:
The CCD generates an analog signal that represents the image.

Step 4:
The analog signal is converted to a digital signal by an analog-to-digital converter (ADC).

Step 5:
A *digital signal processor* (*DSP*) adjusts the quality of the image and usually stores the digital image on miniature mobile storage media in the camera.

Step 6:
Images are transferred to a computer's hard disk by plugging one end of the cable into a camera and the other end of the cable into a computer; or the images are copied to the hard disk from storage media used in the camera.

Step 7:
Using software supplied with the camera, the images are viewed on the screen, incorporated into documents, edited, and printed.

often have a built-in TV out port, allowing users to display photographed images or play recorded video clips directly on a television. Read Apply It 5-2 for more information.

For additional information about digital cameras, read the Digital Imaging and Video Technology feature that follows Chapter 6.

Digital Camera Quality

One factor that affects the quality of a digital camera is its resolution. **Resolution** describes the sharpness and clearness of an image. A digital camera's resolution is defined in pixels. A *pixel* (short for picture element) is the smallest element in an electronic image (Figure 5-28). The greater the number of pixels the camera uses to capture an image, the better the quality of the image. Thus, the higher the resolution, the better the image quality, but the more expensive the camera.

pixel

FIGURE 5-28 A pixel is a single point in an electronic image.

Digital camera resolutions range from approximately 1 million to more than 6 million pixels (*MP*). A camera with a 4.2-megapixel (4,200,000 pixels) resolution will provide a better quality than one with a 2.2-megapixel resolution. As a rule, a 1-megapixel camera is fine for screen displays such as photo communities, Web pages, and e-mail attachments. These low-end cameras cost less than $200. Users planning to print photographs larger than 5 x 7 inches should have at least a 2-megapixel camera. For images as good as film-based cameras, use a 3-megapixel or higher camera. High-end point-and-shoot cameras cost less than $1,000.

Manufacturers often use pixels per inch to represent a digital camera's resolution. *Pixels per inch (ppi)* is the number of pixels in one inch of screen display. For example, a 1600 x 1200 (pronounced 1600 by 1200) ppi camera has 1,600 pixels per vertical inch and 1,200 pixels per horizontal inch. Multiplying these two numbers together will give you an approximate number of megapixels. For example, 1600 times 1200 equals approximately 2 million, or 2 megapixels. If just one number is stated, such as 1200 ppi, then both the vertical and horizontal numbers are the same.

Digital cameras for the consumer range from 640 x 480 ppi to 2280 x 1720 ppi. Some cameras provide a means to adjust the ppi to the desired resolution. With a lower ppi, you can capture and store more images in the camera. For example, a camera set at 800 x 600 ppi might capture and store 61 images, if it has sufficient storage capacity. The number of

---

☑ APPLY IT 5-2

Share Digital Photos with Friends and Family

If you have not made the switch to digital photography, it is likely you might think that the cameras are complicated and expensive. After all, the mere thought of setting shutter speeds and making aperture adjustments can be overwhelming. As digital cameras have become easier to use and less costly, however, more people are making the leap to this technology.

Taking photos with digital cameras now can be easy and fun. With prices for feature-rich cameras less than $200 and with many automatic settings, nearly everyone can capture the moment almost instantly after unpacking the camera.

When choosing a camera, consider the capacity of its storage media, resolution, and price. A higher resolution increases price, so choose the model that fits your budget and lifestyle. In addition, consider the type of lens. For example, if you take close-up shots of flowers, you will want a camera with macro capability or a macro lens. By contrast, if you take pictures of birds roosting in tall trees, you will need a camera with zoom capability or a zoom lens.

Sharing these photos with friends and family can be accomplished easily with features found on some cameras. With the push of a button, these cameras send the images to printers or to designated e-mail recipients when the camera connects to a computer or docking station. These individuals should use antivirus programs to safeguard their computers from viruses that may be imbedded in these picture files.

For more information about digital cameras, visit the Discovering Computers 2004 Apply It Web page (**scsite.com/dc2004/apply**). Click Apply It #2 below Chapter 5.

images may reduce to 24 on the same camera set at 1600 × 1200 ppi, because each image consumes more storage space.

The actual photographed resolution is known as the *optical resolution*. Some manufacturers state *enhanced resolution*, instead of, or in addition to, optical resolution. Optical resolution is different from enhanced resolution. The enhanced resolution usually is higher because it uses a special formula to add pixels between those generated by the optical resolution. Be aware that some manufacturers compute a digital camera's megapixels from the enhanced resolution, instead of optical resolution.

Another measure of a digital camera's quality is the number of bits it stores in a pixel. Each pixel consists of 1 or more bits of data. The more bits used to represent a pixel, the more colors and shades of gray that can be represented. One bit per pixel is enough for simple one-color images. For multiple colors and shades of gray, each pixel requires more than 1 bit of data. A point-and-shoot camera should be at least 24 bit.

❓ FAQ 5-6

What is dpi?

Some advertisements incorrectly use dpi to mean the same as ppi. The acronym *dpi*, which stands for *dots per inch*, is a measure of a print resolution. For screen resolution, the proper measurement term is ppi (pixels per inch).

For more information about resolution, visit the Discovering Computers 2004 FAQ Web page (**scsite.com/dc2004/faq**). Click Resolution below Chapter 5.

VIDEO INPUT

Video input is the process of capturing full-motion images into a computer and storing them on a storage medium such as a hard disk or DVD. Some video devices use analog video signals. Computers, by contrast, use digital signals. To input video from these analog devices, the analog signal must be converted to a digital signal. To do this, plug a video camera, VCR, or other analog video device into a video capture port on the system unit. One type of adapter card that has a video capture

port is a **video capture card**, which converts an analog video signal into a digital signal that a computer can use. (Most new computers are not equipped with a video capture card because not all users have the need for this type of adapter card.)

The new generation of video camera (camcorder), called a **digital video (DV) camera**, records video as digital signals instead of analog signals. Many DV cameras have the capability of capturing still frames, as well as motion. To transfer recorded images to a hard disk or CD or DVD, users connect DV cameras directly to a USB port or a FireWire port on the system unit. Thus, the computer does not need a video capture card. Simply connect the video device to the computer and begin transferring images. After saving the video on a storage medium, such as a hard disk or DVD, you can play it or edit it using video editing software on a computer (Figure 5-29).

video displays on television and on notebook computer

video camera

FIGURE 5-29 This sports fan transferred video of a volleyball game to his notebook computer, where he uses video editing software to edit the game.

PC Video Cameras

A **PC video camera**, or **PC camera**, is a type of digital video camera that enables a home or small business user to capture video and still images, send e-mail messages with video attachments, add live images to instant messages, broadcast live images over the Internet, and make video telephone calls. During a

video telephone call, both parties see each other as they talk over the Internet (Figure 5-30). The cost of PC video cameras usually is less than $100.

Attached to the computer's USB port or FireWire port, a PC video camera usually sits on top of your monitor. For more flexibility, some PC video cameras are portable. That is, you can detach them from the computer and use them anywhere.

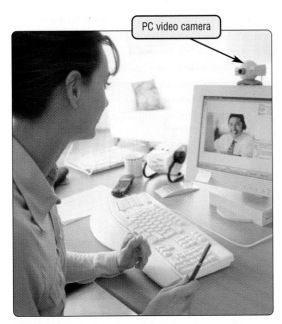

PC video camera

FIGURE 5-30 Using a PC video camera, these business associates communicate via video telephone calls on the Internet.

Web Cams

A **Web cam** is a video camera that displays its output on a Web page. A Web cam attracts Web site visitors by showing images that change regularly. Home or small business users might use Web cams to show a work in progress, weather and traffic information, employees at work, photographs of a vacation, and countless other images.

Some Web sites have live Web cams that display still pictures and update the displayed image at a specified time or time intervals, such as 15 seconds. Another type of Web cam, called a *streaming cam*, has the illusion of moving images because it sends a continual stream of still images.

Video Conferencing

A **video conference** is a meeting between two or more geographically separated people who use a network or the Internet to transmit audio and video data (Figure 5-31). To participate in a video conference, you need video conferencing software along with a microphone, speakers, and a video camera attached to a computer.

As you speak, members of the meeting hear your voice on their speakers. Any image in front of the video camera, such as a person's face, displays in a window on each participant's screen. A *whiteboard* is another window on the screen that displays notes and drawings simultaneously on all participants' screens. This window provides multiple users with an area on which they can write or draw.

Users with higher-speed broadband Internet connections experience much better video performance. As the costs of video conferencing hardware and software decrease, increasingly more business meetings, corporate training, and educational classes will be conducted as video conferences.

WEB LINK 5-7

PC Video Cameras

Visit the Discovering Computers 2004 WEB LINK page (**scsite .com/dc2004/weblink**). Click PC Video Cameras below Chapter 5.

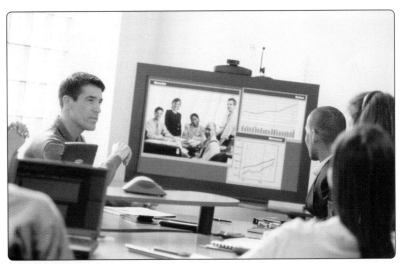

FIGURE 5-31 To save on travel expenses, many large businesses are turning to video conferencing.

QUIZ YOURSELF 5-2

To check your knowledge of voice recognition, input for mobile computers and devices, digital cameras, and video input, visit the Discovering Computers 2004 Quiz Yourself Web page (**scsite.com/dc2004/quiz**). Click Objectives 5 – 8 below Chapter 5.

SCANNERS AND READING DEVICES

Some input devices save users time by eliminating manual data entry. With these devices, users do not type or speak into the computer. Instead, these devices capture data from a *source document*, which is the original form of the data. Examples of source documents are time cards, order forms, invoices, paychecks, advertisements, brochures, photographs, inventory tags, or any other document that contains data to be processed.

Devices that can capture data directly from a source document include optical scanners, optical readers, bar code scanners, and magnetic-ink character recognition readers. The following pages discuss each of these devices.

Optical Scanner

An *optical scanner*, usually called a **scanner**, is a light-sensing input device that reads printed text and graphics and then translates the results into a form the computer can process. Four types of scanners are flatbed, pen, sheet-fed, and drum (Figure 5-32).

TYPES OF SCANNERS

Scanner	Method of Scanning and Use	Scannable Items
Flatbed	• Similar to a copy machine • Scanning mechanism passes under the item to be scanned, which is placed on a glass surface	• Single-sheet documents • Bound material • Photographs • Some models include trays for slides, transparencies, and negatives
Pen or Handheld	• Move pen over text to be scanned, then transfer data to computer • Ideal for mobile users, students, and researchers • Some connect to a PDA	• Any printed text
Sheet-fed	• Item to be scanned is pulled into a stationary scanning mechanism • Smaller than a flatbed scanner • Some models designed specifically for photographs are called a *photo scanner*	• Single-sheet documents • Photographs • Slides (with an adapter) • Negatives
Drum	• Item to be scanned rotates around stationary scanning mechanism • Very expensive • Used in publishing industry	• Single-sheet documents • Photographs • Slides • Negatives

FIGURE 5-32 This table describes the various types of scanners.

A **flatbed scanner** works in a manner similar to a copy machine except it creates a file of the document in memory instead of a paper copy (Figure 5-33). For example, you scan a picture and then include the picture when creating a brochure. A user can display a scanned object on the screen, store it on a storage medium, print it, fax it, attach it to an e-mail message, include it in another document, or post it to a Web site or photo community for everyone to see.

FIGURE 5-33 HOW A FLATBED SCANNER WORKS

Step 1:
The document to be scanned is placed face down on the glass window.

Step 2:
A bright light moves underneath the scanned document.

Step 3:
An image of the document is reflected into a series of mirrors.

Step 4:
The light is converted to an analog electrical current that is converted to a digital signal by an analog-to-digital converter (ADC).

Step 5:
The digital information is sent to memory in the computer to be used by the illustration, desktop publishing, or other software; or it is stored on disk.

Step 6:
Users can print the image, e-mail it, include it in a document, or place it on a Web page.

WEB LINK 5-8

Scanners

Visit the Discovering Computers 2004 WEB LINK page (**scsite .com/dc2004/weblink**). Click Scanners below Chapter 5.

As with a digital camera, the quality of a scanner is measured by the number of bits it stores in a pixel and the number of pixels per inch, or resolution. The higher each number, the better the quality, but the more expensive the scanner. Most of today's affordable color desktop scanners for the home or small business range from 30 to 48 bit and have an optical resolution ranging from 600 to 3,000 ppi. Commercial scanners designed for power users range from 4,000 to 12,500 ppi.

Many scanners include *OCR (optical character recognition) software*, which can read and convert text documents into electronic files. Suppose users need to modify a business report but do not have the original word processing file. If they scan the document with a flatbed scanner, they would not be able to edit the report. The scanner, which does not differentiate between text and graphics, saves the report as an image. OCR software converts a scanned image into a text file that can be edited, for example, with a word processing program. OCR software typically places any graphics in the scanned image into a separate file.

Current OCR software has a very high success rate and usually can identify more than 99 percent of scanned material. OCR software also marks text it cannot read, allowing users to make corrections easily.

Businesses often use scanners for *image processing*, which consists of capturing, storing, analyzing, displaying, printing, and manipulating images. Image processing allows users to convert paper documents such as reports, memos, and procedure manuals into electronic images. Users distribute and publish these electronic documents on networks and the Internet.

Business users typically store and index electronic documents with an image processing system. An *image processing system* is similar to an electronic filing cabinet that provides access to exact reproductions of the original documents. Local governments, for example, use image processing systems to store property deeds and titles to provide the public and professionals, such as lawyers and loan officers, quick access to electronic documents.

FAQ 5-7

How can I improve the quality of scanned documents?

Place a blank sheet of paper behind translucent papers, newspapers, and other see-through types of paper. If the original image is crooked, draw a line on the back at the bottom of the image. Use that mark to align the original on the scanner. Using photo editing software, editing the scanned image is easy.

For more information about scanning, visit the Discovering Computers 2004 FAQ Web page (**scsite.com/dc2004/faq**). Click Scanning below Chapter 5.

Optical Readers

An *optical reader* is a device that uses a light source to read characters, marks, and codes and then converts them into digital data that a computer can process. Two technologies used by optical readers are optical character recognition and optical mark recognition.

OPTICAL CHARACTER RECOGNITION

Optical character recognition (OCR) is a technology that involves reading typewritten, computer-printed, or hand-printed characters from ordinary documents and translating the images into a form that the computer can process. Most **OCR devices** include a small optical scanner for reading characters and sophisticated software to analyze what is read.

OCR devices range from large machines that can read thousands of documents per minute to handheld wands that read one document at a time. OCR devices read printed characters in an OCR font. A widely used OCR font is called OCR-A (Figure 5-34). During the scan of a document, an OCR device determines the shapes of characters by detecting patterns of light and dark. OCR software then compares these shapes with predefined shapes stored in memory and converts the shapes into characters the computer can process.

FIGURE 5-34 A portion of the characters in the OCR-A font. Notice how characters such as the number 0 and the letter O are shaped differently so the reading device easily can distinguish between them.

Many companies use OCR characters on turnaround documents. A **turnaround document** is a document that you return (turn around) to the company that creates and sends it. For example, when consumers receive a bill, they tear off a portion of the bill and send it back to the company with their payment (Figure 5-35). The portion of the bill they return usually has their payment amount, account number, and other information printed in OCR characters.

OPTICAL MARK RECOGNITION Optical **mark recognition** (OMR) is a technology that reads hand-drawn marks such as small circles or rectangles. A person places these marks on a form, such as a test, survey, or questionnaire answer sheet. With a test, the OMR device first scans the answer key sheet to record correct answers based on patterns of light. The OMR device then scans the remaining documents and matches their patterns of light against the answer key sheet.

Bar Code Scanner

A **bar code scanner** is an optical reader that uses laser beams to read bar codes (Figure 5-36). A **bar code** is an identification code that consists of a set of vertical lines and spaces of different widths. The bar code represents data that identifies the manufacturer and the item.

Manufacturers print a bar code either on a product's package or on a label that is affixed to a product. A bar code scanner reads a bar code by using light patterns that pass through the bar code lines.

FIGURE 5-35 OCR characters frequently are used with turnaround documents. With this bill, you tear off the bottom portion and return it with a payment.

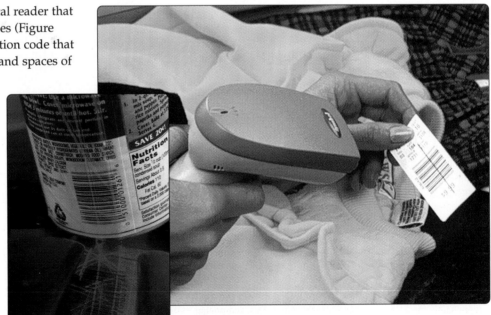

FIGURE 5-36 A bar code scanner uses laser beams to read bar codes on products such as clothing, groceries, pharmacy supplies, vehicles, mail, books, and packages.

A variety of products such as groceries, pharmacy supplies, vehicles, mail, magazines, and books have bar codes. Each industry uses its own type of bar code. Retail and grocery stores use the *UPC* (*Universal Product Code*) bar code (Figure 5-37). Read Issue 5-4 for a related discussion. The United States Postal Service (USPS) uses a POSTNET® bar code. The table in Figure 5-38 summarizes some of the more widely used bar codes.

number system character identifies type of product

manufacturer identification number (KODAK in this case)

item number (box of 4 rolls of film)

check character verifies accuracy of scanned UPC symbol

FIGURE 5-37 This UPC identifies a box of Kodak film.

ISSUE 5-4

What Is the Price of That Item?

Have you ever taken an item to a store's checkout and discovered that the price displayed when the item's bar code was scanned was different from the price shown on a shelf tag, sign, or advertisement? If you have, you are not alone. A government survey found that eight percent of the time, an item's scanned price is different from the price presented elsewhere. When an item is scanned at a store's checkout counter, a computer finds the item's price in the store's database. Store owners claim that discrepancies between the scanned price and a listed price are the result of human error; either failure to update the store's price database or incorrect shelf tags, signs, or advertisements. Yet, some consumer advocates insist that the discrepancy is intentional. They accuse stores of *scanner fraud*, insisting that some stores advertise one price and then charge another, hoping consumers will not recognize the difference. Who do you think is responsible for differences between scanned prices and posted costs? Why? Should stores be responsible for pricing errors? Why or why not?

For more information about bar code scanners, visit the Discovering Computers 2004 Issues Web page (**scsite.com/dc2004/issues**). Click Issue #4 below Chapter 5.

Bar Code Name/Sample	Primary Market
Codabar	Libraries, blood banks, and air parcel carriers
Code 39	Nonretail applications such as manufacturing, inventory, military, and health applications requiring numbers and letters in the bar code
EAN – European Article Numbering	Similar to UPC, only used internationally except the U.S. and Canada; variation of EAN is used for bar codes on books
Interleaved 2 of 5	Nonretail applications, such as game tickets, requiring only numbers in the bar code
POSTNET® – Postal Numeric Encoding Technique	United States Postal Service (USPS), used to represent a postal code or delivery point code
UPC – Universal Product Code	Supermarkets, convenience stores, and specialty stores use to identify manufacturers and products

FIGURE 5-38 Some of the more widely used types of bar codes.

MICR Reader

MICR (*magnetic-ink character recognition*) is a technology that reads text printed with magnetized ink. An **MICR reader** converts MICR characters into a form the computer can process. The banking industry almost exclusively uses MICR for check processing. Each check in your checkbook has precoded MICR characters beginning at the lower-left edge (Figure 5-39). The MICR characters represent the bank number, the customer account number, and the check number. These numbers may appear in a different order than the ones shown in the sample in Figure 5-39.

When a bank receives a check for payment, it uses an MICR inscriber to print the amount of the check in MICR characters in the lower-right corner. The check then is sorted or routed to the customer's bank, along with thousands of others. Each check is inserted into an MICR reader, which sends the check information — including the amount of the check — to a computer for processing. When you balance your checkbook, verify that the amount printed in the lower-right corner is the same as the amount written on the check; otherwise, your statement will not balance.

The banking industry has established an international standard not only for bank numbers, but also for the font of the MICR characters. This standardization makes it possible for people to write checks in other countries.

Data Collection Devices

Instead of reading or scanning data from a source document, a *data collection device* obtains data directly at the location where the transaction or event takes place. For example, employees use bar code scanners, PDAs, handheld computers, or other mobile devices to collect data wirelessly (Figure 5-40). These types of data collection devices are used in factories, warehouses, the outdoors, or other locations where heat, humidity, and cleanliness are not easy to control.

Data collection devices and many mobile computers and devices such as PDAs and smart phones have the capability of wirelessly transmitting data over a network or the Internet. Increasingly more users today send data wirelessly to central office computers using these devices.

FIGURE 5-40 Sales representatives use this rugged mobile device to take on-site orders from customers. The device, which is a combination PDA/bar code reader, wirelessly transmits the orders to the company's order and routing system. Upon delivery to the customer, the route driver uses the mobile device to record deliveries and print customer receipts wirelessly. Then, the device wirelessly transmits route information and updates inventory in the company's system.

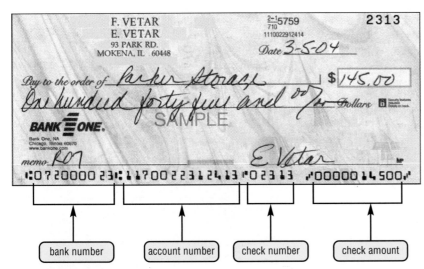

| bank number | account number | check number | check amount |

FIGURE 5-39 The MICR characters preprinted on the check represent the bank number, the customer account number, and the check number. The amount of the check in the lower-right corner is added after the check is cashed.

TERMINALS

A *terminal* consists of a keyboard, a monitor, a video card, and memory. Often, these components are housed in a single unit.

Terminals fall into three basic categories: dumb terminals, smart terminals, and special-purpose terminals. A *dumb terminal* has no processing power, thus, cannot function as an independent device. Users enter data into a dumb terminal and then transmit the data to a host computer over a network. The host computer processes the data and then, if necessary, sends information back to the dumb terminal. The host computer usually is a midrange server or mainframe. A *smart terminal* has a processor, giving it the capability of performing some functions independent of the host computer. In recent years, personal computers have replaced most smart terminals.

Special-purpose terminals perform specific tasks and contain features uniquely designed for use in a particular industry. Three special-purpose terminals are point-of-sale terminals, automated teller machines, and smart displays. The following sections discuss these types of terminals.

Point-of-Sale Terminals

The location in a retail or grocery store where a consumer pays for goods or services is the **point of sale (POS)**. Most retail stores use a **POS terminal** to record purchases, process credit or debit cards, and update inventory.

In a grocery store, the POS terminal is a combination of an electronic cash register, bar code reader, and printer. When the checkout clerk scans the bar code on the food product, the computer uses the manufacturer and item numbers to look up the price of the item and the complete product name in a database. Then, the price of the item in the database shows on the display device, the name of the item and its price print on a receipt, and the item being sold is recorded so the inventory can be updated. Thus, the output from a POS

terminal serves as input to other computers to maintain sales records, update inventory, verify credit, and perform other activities associated with the sales transactions that are critical to running the business. Some POS terminals are Web-enabled, allowing them to update inventory at geographically dispersed locations.

Many POS terminals handle credit card or debit card payments. Consumers simply swipe a credit or debit card through a **card reader**, which reads the customer's personal data from the magnetic strip on the card. Once the transaction is approved, the terminal prints a receipt for the customer.

A self-service POS terminal allows consumers to perform all checkout related activities (Figure 5-41). That is, they scan the items, bag the items, and pay for the items themselves. Consumers find the new self-service POS terminals very convenient because they often eliminate the hassle of waiting in long lines.

touch screen with graphical user interface

card reader scans credit, debit, or store saver card

bar code scanner reads UPC labels

FIGURE 5-41 Some grocery stores offer self-serve checkouts, where the consumers themselves use the POS terminals to scan purchases, scan their store saver card and coupons, and then pay for the goods. This POS terminal prints a receipt for the customer.

Automated Teller Machines

An **automated teller machine (ATM)** is a self-service banking machine that connects to a host computer through a network (Figure 5-42). Banks place ATMs in convenient locations, including grocery stores, convenience stores, retail outlets, shopping malls, and gas stations, so customers conveniently can access their bank accounts.

Using an ATM, people withdraw cash, deposit money, transfer funds, or inquire about an account balance. Some ATMs have a touch screen; others have special buttons or keypads for input. To access a bank account, you insert a plastic bankcard into the ATM's card reader, which reads personal data on the bankcard's magnetic strip. The ATM asks you to enter a password, called a *personal identification number* (*PIN*), which verifies that you are the holder of the bankcard. When your transaction is complete, the ATM prints a receipt for your records.

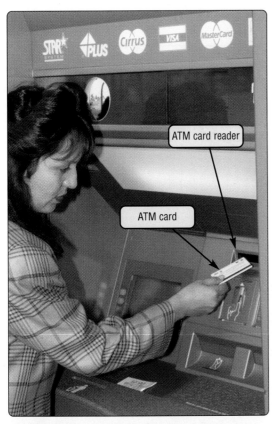

FIGURE 5-42 An ATM is a self-service banking terminal that allows customers to access their bank accounts.

Smart Displays

A **smart display** is a thin desktop monitor that detaches from the computer to function as a portable wireless touch screen, which can access the computer remotely (Figure 5-43). The intent of the smart display is to provide home users with the convenience of accessing their personal computers from anywhere in the house, using the portable monitor. For example, instead of writing down a home inventory list and then sitting down to enter the list into the computer, the smart display allows the home user to detach the monitor and walk from room to room — entering the items as he or she moves through the house.

As a user enters data into the smart display, it communicates with the computer through a wireless network. That is, from the wireless smart display, a user can access programs or data on his or her computer, browse the Web, send e-mail, and perform other functions, just as if he or she is sitting at the computer.

At the computer, a user interacts with the smart display using a standard keyboard, mouse, or any other personal computer input device. When detached from the computer, a user enters data and instructions into the smart display with a digital pen or through an on-screen keyboard.

The outward appearance of a smart display resembles that of a Tablet PC. The processor of the smart display, however, is less powerful and it contains a smaller amount of RAM than a Tablet PC. Another major difference is that smart displays usually do not contain a hard disk. Thus, the cost of a smart display is about one-third that of the Tablet PC.

FIGURE 5-43 A smart display allows home users to access their computer wirelessly from anywhere in the house.

BIOMETRIC INPUT

Biometrics is the technology of authenticating a person's identity by verifying a personal characteristic. Biometric devices grant users access to programs, systems, or rooms by analyzing some biometric identifier. A *biometric identifier* is a physical or behavioral characteristic. Examples include fingerprints, hand geometry, facial features, voice, signatures, and eye patterns.

A *biometric device* translates a personal characteristic (the input) into a digital code that is compared with a digital code stored in the computer. If the digital code in the computer does not match the personal characteristic's code, the computer denies access to the individual.

The most widely used biometric device today is a fingerprint scanner. A **fingerprint scanner** captures curves and indentations of a fingerprint. With the cost of fingerprint scanners dropping to less than $100, many believe this technology will become the home user's authentication device for e-commerce transactions. To make a credit-card transaction, the Web site would require you to hold your finger on the scanner. Businesses use fingerprint scanners to authenticate users before they can access a personal computer. Grade schools use fingerprint scanners as an alternative to lunch money. Their account balance adjusts for each lunch purchased. External fingerprint scanners usually plug into a parallel or USB port. To save on desk space, some newer keyboards and notebook computers have a fingerprint scanner built into them (Figure 5-44).

A *face recognition system* captures a live face image and compares it with a stored image to determine if the person is a legitimate user. Buildings secure rooms with face recognition systems. Law enforcement, surveillance systems, and airports use face recognition to protect the public. Some notebook computers use this security technique to safeguard a computer. The computer will not start unless the user is legitimate. These programs are becoming more sophisticated and can recognize people with or without glasses, makeup, or jewelry, and with new hairstyles. Read Issue 5-5 for a related discussion.

Biometric devices measure the shape and size of a person's hand using a *hand geometry system* (Figure 5-45). Because their cost is more than $1,000, larger companies typically use these systems as time and attendance devices or as security devices. One university cafeteria uses a hand geometry system to verify students when they use their meal card. A daycare center uses a hand geometry system to verify parents who pick up their children.

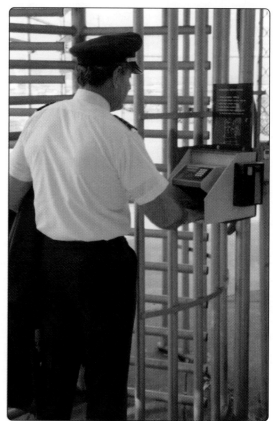

FIGURE 5-45 A hand geometry system verifies a pilot's identity before he is allowed access to the airplane.

FIGURE 5-44 This user has access to a computer only if her fingerprint matches one in a database.

A *voice verification system* compares a person's live speech with their stored voice pattern. Larger organizations sometimes use voice verification systems as time and attendance devices. Many companies also use this technology for access to sensitive files and networks. Some financial services use voice verification systems to secure telephone banking transactions. These systems use speaker-dependent voice recognition software. That is, users train the computer to recognize their inflection patterns.

A *signature verification system* recognizes the shape of your handwritten signature, as well as measuring the pressure exerted and the motion used to write the signature. Signature verification systems use a specialized pen and tablet.

Very high security areas use iris recognition systems. The camera in an *iris recognition system* uses iris recognition technology to read patterns in the iris of the eye (Figure 5-46). These patterns are as unique as a fingerprint. Iris recognition systems are very expensive and are used by government security organizations, the military, and financial institutions that deal with highly sensitive data.

ISSUE 5-5

Have You Seen This Face Before?

In the wake of terrorist attacks, biometric security has become a prominent part of national security. According to the International Biometric Group, the biometric industry approached $730 million in sales in 2002. Face recognition systems represented 15 percent of the sales. These systems calculate up to 60 facial characteristics, such as the distance between the eyes or cheekbone height, and convert the measurements into a mathematical formula that is checked against a database. At a recent Super Bowl, ticket buyers were scanned as they passed security cameras coming through the turnstiles. Using face recognition technology, the images gathered were compared against a database of known criminals and militants. Advocates of facial scanners say these systems help identify potential terrorists, but opponents maintain that the systems represent an unnecessary invasion of privacy and sometimes produce false identifications. At what events, if any, should facial scanners be used? Why? Are opponents of facial scanners justified in saying that the technology represents an unjustified invasion of privacy? Why or why not?

For more information about facial scanners, visit the Discovering Computers 2004 Issues Web page (**scsite.com/dc2004/issues**). Click Issue #5 below Chapter 5.

Sometimes, fingerprint, iris, and other biometric data are stored on a smart card. A **smart card**, which is comparable in size to a credit card or ATM card, stores the personal data on a thin microprocessor embedded in the card (Figure 5-47). Smart cards add an extra layer of protection. For example, when a user places a smart card through a card reader, the computer compares a fingerprint stored on the card with the one read by the fingerprint scanner.

WEB LINK 5-9

Biometric Input

Visit the Discovering Computers 2004 WEB LINK page (**scsite.com/dc2004/weblink**). Click Biometric Input below Chapter 5.

FIGURE 5-46   An iris recognition system.

microprocessor on smart card

smart card reader

FIGURE 5-47   A smart card reader reads data stored on a smart card's microprocessor.

PUTTING IT ALL TOGETHER

When you purchase a computer, you should have an understanding of the input devices included with the computer, as well as those you may need that are not included. Many factors influence the type of input devices you may use: the type of input desired, the hardware and software in use, and the desired cost. The type of input devices you require depends on your intended use. Figure 5-48 outlines several suggested input devices for specific computer users.

SUGGESTED INPUT DEVICES BY USER

User	Input Device
Home	• Enhanced keyboard or ergonomic keyboard • Mouse • Stylus for PDA • Joystick or wheel • 30-bit 600 x 1200 ppi color scanner • 1- or 2-megapixel digital camera • Headset that includes a microphone • PC video camera • Smart display
Small Office/Home Office	• Enhanced keyboard or ergonomic keyboard • Mouse • Stylus and portable keyboard for PDA or digital pen for Tablet PC • 36-bit 600 x 1200 ppi color scanner • 1- or 2-megapixel digital camera • Headset that includes a microphone • PC video camera
Mobile	• Wireless mouse for notebook computer • Trackball, touchpad, or pointing stick on notebook computer • Stylus and portable keyboard for PDA or digital pen for Tablet PC • 2- or 3-megapixel digital camera • Headset that includes a microphone • Fingerprint scanner for notebook computer
Large Business	• Enhanced keyboard or ergonomic keyboard • Mouse • Stylus and portable keyboard for PDA or digital pen for Tablet PC • Touch screen • Light pen • 42-bit 1200 x 1200 ppi color scanner • OCR/OMR readers, bar code scanners, MICR reader, or data collection devices • Microphone • Video camera for video conferences • Fingerprint scanner or other biometric device
Power	• Enhanced keyboard or ergonomic keyboard • Mouse • Stylus and portable keyboard for PDA • Pen for graphics tablet • 48-bit 1200 x 1200 ppi color scanner • 5- or 6-megapixel digital camera • Headset that includes a microphone • PC video camera

FIGURE 5-48   This table recommends suggested input devices.

INPUT DEVICES FOR PHYSICALLY CHALLENGED USERS

The ever-increasing presence of computers in everyone's lives has generated an awareness of the need to address computing requirements for those who have or may develop physical limitations. The **Americans with Disabilities Act (ADA)** requires any company with 15 or more employees to make reasonable attempts to accommodate the needs of physically challenged workers. Whether at work or at home, you may find it necessary to acquire input devices that address physical limitations. Besides voice recognition, which is ideal for blind or visually impaired users, several other input devices are available.

Users with limited hand mobility who want to use a keyboard have several options. A *keyguard* is a metal or plastic plate placed over the keyboard that allows users to rest their hands on the keyboard without accidentally pressing any keys. A keyguard also guides a finger or pointing device so a user presses only one key at a time (Figure 5-49).

Keyboards with larger keys also are available. Still another option is the *on-screen keyboard*, in which a graphic of a standard keyboard is displayed on the user's screen (Figure 5-50).

FIGURE 5-50 As you click letters on the on-screen keyboard, they display in the document at the location of the insertion point.

Various pointing devices are available for users with motor disabilities. Small trackballs that the user controls with a thumb or one finger can be attached to a table, mounted to a wheelchair, or held in the user's hand. Another option for people with limited hand movement is a *head-mounted pointer* to control the pointer or insertion point (Figure 5-51). To simulate the functions of a mouse button, a user works with switches that control the pointer. The switch might be a hand pad, a foot pedal, a receptor that detects facial motions, or a pneumatic instrument controlled by puffs of air.

Two exciting developments in this area are gesture recognition and computerized implant devices. Both in the prototype stage, they attempt to provide users with a natural computer interface. With *gesture recognition*, the computer will detect human motions.

FIGURE 5-49 A keyguard.

FIGURE 5-51 A camera/receiver mounted on the monitor tracks the position of the silver dot on this user's forehead. As the user moves his head, the pointer on the screen also moves.

LOOKING AHEAD 5-2

Brain Implants Help Physically Challenged

The phrase, "Monkey see, monkey do" may need revision to "Monkey think, monkey do" after analyzing the latest research.

Scientists implanted small chips in rhesus monkeys' brains and then trained the animals to move a joystick with their hands and chase a red dot moving around a monitor display. The implant, which is the size of a small pea, recorded the signals sent from the motor cortex area of the brain, which controls movement, to the hands. These signals were analyzed and then translated to computer instructions that repeated the same movement.

In the next step, the joystick was disconnected. One monkey was able to repeat the cursor action merely by thinking about the joystick motion.

The researchers are hoping their work will help paralyzed individuals use their minds to control computers and other devices within the decade. Some humans already have a similar device implanted, but the newest hardware is smaller, has thinner wires, and uses fewer neurons to function. Applications could include allowing paralyzed individuals to read e-mail, surf the Internet, control remote robotic devices, and move artificial limbs. The researchers are hopeful that this technology will help physically challenged individuals better interact with their environments.

Chip implants may raise ethical questions, such as determining who will receive the first implants, how chips will be updated, whether insurance companies will cover the costs, the number of applications to include on each chip, and whether monitoring patients' thoughts invades their privacy.

For a look at the next generation of brain implants, visit the Discovering Computers 2004 Looking Ahead Web page (**scsite.com/dc2004/looking**). Click Looking Ahead #2 below Chapter 5.

Computers with this capability have the potential to recognize sign language, read lips, track facial movements, or follow eye gazes. For paralyzed or speech impaired individuals, a doctor will implant a computerized device into the brain. This device will contain a transmitter. As the user thinks thoughts, the transmitter will send signals to the computer. Read Looking Ahead 5-2 for a look at the next generation of brain implants.

QUIZ YOURSELF 5-3

To check your knowledge of scanners and reading devices, terminals, biometric devices, and input for physically challenged users, visit the Discovering Computers 2004 Quiz Yourself Web page (**scsite.com/dc2004/quiz**). Click Objectives 9 – 12 below Chapter 5.

CHAPTER SUMMARY

Input is any data or instructions you enter into the memory of a computer. This chapter described the various techniques of input and several commonly used input devices. Topics presented included the keyboard, mouse and other pointing devices, voice input, input devices for mobile users, digital cameras, video input, scanners and reading devices, terminals, biometric input, and input devices for physically challenged users.

Career Corner

Data Entry Clerk

Data entry clerks have an essential role in today's information-producing industry. A *data entry clerk* inputs information into documents, databases, and other applications using computer keyboards and visual display devices. Duties can include manipulating, editing, and maintaining data to ensure that it is accurate and up to date, and researching information.

Some data entry clerks telecommute. Although they generally use keyboards, they also work with other input from scanners or electronically transmitted files. These systems require that they enter only data that cannot be identified by machines. Because of the nature of their job, data entry clerks often sit for hours typing in front of monitors. They can be susceptible to repetitive stress injuries and neck, back, and eye strain. To prevent these injuries, many offices use ergonomically designed input devices and incorporate regularly scheduled exercise breaks.

Data entry clerks usually are high school graduates with keyboarding skills. Some employers require an associate's degree or at least two years of post high school education plus two years of office experience. Data entry training, basic language skills, and familiarity with word processing, spreadsheet, and database programs are important. Data entry often serves as a stepping-stone to other administrative positions. The average annual salary for data entry clerks is around $21,000. Salaries start at about $15,000 and, with experience, can extend to more than $31,000.

To learn more about the field of Data Entry Clerk as a career, visit the Discovering Computers 2004 Careers Web page (**scsite.com/dc2004/careers**). Click Data Entry Clerk.

HIGH-TECH TALK

Input without Wires

On any given day, you encounter wireless technologies being used for a wide range of communications. Television remote controls, baby monitors, remote garage door openers, and cellular telephones, for example, all use wireless technologies to communicate with other devices. Wireless technologies also allow input devices, such as the keyboard (Figure 5-52) and mouse, to communicate with a computer.

A wireless keyboard and wireless mouse communicate with a computer using one of two wireless technologies: infrared or radio frequency technology. *Infrared* (*IR*) technology uses light waves to transmit signals to other infrared-enabled devices. Infrared-enabled devices, such as a notebook computer or PDA, have a small, red plastic-covered IrDA (Infrared Data Association) port that transmits and receives signals. Infrared technology, however, only can transmit signals approximately three feet, and the two IrDA ports must be in a direct line with each other to communicate. Given the clutter on most people's desks and the constant movement of a mouse, infrared technology is not the ideal solution for wireless input devices.

With *radio frequency* (*RF*) technology, devices transmit signals at least six feet, without a clear line of sight. Even piles of paper, books, and other desktop items will not degrade the communications among the wireless keyboard and mouse and the computer. Given these advantages, most users prefer a wireless keyboard and mouse that use radio frequency technology instead of infrared.

Standard connections are easy to grasp. To connect a keyboard or mouse with a computer, you simply plug the keyboard and mouse cables into ports on the computer. The computer's BIOS and operating system detect the devices (either when you start the computer or through Plug-and-Play technology) and then accept input from the keyboard and mouse.

You may be wondering how to connect a wireless keyboard and mouse to a computer without cables. Connecting a wireless keyboard and mouse using RF technology requires two key parts: a transmitter and a receiver. The radio *transmitter* is inside the input device — either the keyboard or mouse. The radio *receiver* plugs into a keyboard port, a mouse port, or a USB port. Once the receivers are plugged in, the BIOS and operating system detect the radio receivers and use the input as if the devices were connected directly by a cable.

When you press a key on a wireless keyboard or move a wireless mouse, the device creates a digital signal, just like a standard keyboard or mouse. That digital signal translates the keystroke or movement into the binary code that the computer can process. The radio transmitter in the wireless keyboard or mouse then uses digital-to-analog conversion (read High-Tech Talk on page 1.40) to convert the digital signal to analog radio waves, which it transmits along a specific frequency (usually 27 MHz).

The radio receiver monitors for signals along that same frequency. When it receives a signal, it uses analog-to-digital conversion to convert the radio frequency wave back into a digital signal. It then sends that signal to the computer through the BIOS and operating system. The computer then acts on the signal — for example, moving the mouse pointer to click a button or typing the letter, K, in a document.

A newer wireless mouse — especially one designed for use in large conference rooms — transmits signals to a computer more than fifty feet away. Some keyboards and mouse devices also allow users to select from one or more radio frequency channels, to eliminate possible interference with other RF-based equipment in a home, office, or computer lab.

In addition, to ensure that the signal transmitted from a wireless keyboard or mouse does not interfere with a neighbor's wireless keyboard or mouse, a unique 12-digit identifier is assigned to each device and its accompanying receiver. The receiver only accepts signals from devices with that identifier and ignores signals from any other wireless keyboard or mouse.

Keep in mind that a wireless keyboard and mouse require batteries to operate (usually two to three AA or AAA batteries). You need not worry that the batteries suddenly will run out: the software included with the keyboard or mouse monitors battery level and alerts you when battery power is low. The LEDs on the radio receivers also light up if the batteries need to be replaced.

For more information about the wireless keyboard and mouse, visit the Discovering Computers 2004 High-Tech Talk Web page (**scsite.com/dc2004/tech**) and click Wireless Keyboard and Mouse.

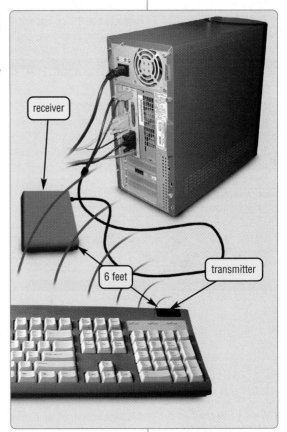

FIGURE 5-52
Wireless keyboard.

COMPANIES ON THE CUTTING EDGE

Logitech
Mice Are Welcome Here

Thinking about a room full of mice can send chills down your spine. But Logitech employees are not bothered by all the mice in their offices; in fact, they smile when they think of these creatures.

As a market leader in human interface devices and software, Logitech joins people and computers in an intuitive and natural way. Two engineering students from Stanford University, Italian-born Pierluigi Zappacosta and Swiss-born Daniel Borel, confident in the future of the newly born mouse, launched Logitech in Switzerland in 1981. Today, *Logitech* is the world's largest manufacturer of the mouse, having generated more than 300 million since the company's founding. The company also designs, produces, and markets a variety of other input devices, including keyboards, optical trackballs, joysticks, game controllers, multimedia speakers, and PC video cameras. Logitech innovates across its product line, with technologies such as cordless pointing devices and keyboards, game controllers that combine force feedback and motion sensing, and video cameras with new software. Cordless products account for more than one-third of the devices sold. Logitech also manufactures products that assist and enhance Internet use. By combining software, hardware, and Web applications, Logitech has transformed the mouse and the keyboard into hardware portals that offer a variety of Internet services. In the future, Logitech plans to progress from being a leading vendor of input devices to being a leading provider of information interfaces by expanding its place on the computer desktop, providing additional Internet services and devices, and moving beyond the personal computer to wherever people access information.

Logitech employs more than 4,800 people worldwide. More than one-half of Logitech's engineers are software engineers, and they have used their pioneering design and technological expertise to help the company win more than 50 worldwide awards. Among their 40 industry firsts are the cordless and optomechanical mouse devices, the color handheld scanner, and the digital still camera.

For more information about Logitech, visit the Discovering Computers 2004 Companies Web page (**scsite.com/dc2004/companies**) and click Logitech.

Nokia
Mobile Communications Leader

Have you heard of Nokia? If not, it would be a surprise. Every day, Nokia is the subject of more than 100 stories in media around the globe. With 18 production facilities in 10 countries, and sales in more than 130 countries, *Nokia* is the world leader in mobile communications. About 300 million people use Nokia telephones for business and for pleasure.

In 1967, Nokia Corporation was formed by a merger among producers of communications-related products: Nokia Company, a manufacturer of paper, and the Finnish Rubber Works and Finnish Cable Works, a maker of cables for telegraphs and telephones. In 1981, the company entered the mobile communications market, producing the first car phones for the world's first international cellular mobile telephone network, NMT. Nokia introduced the original hand-portable telephone in 1987. When the digital communications standard GSM, which carried data in addition to voice, was instituted in Europe in 1991, it became possible to connect a mobile telephone to a computer to access files and read e-mail. Nokia divested itself of other operations and focused on telecommunications. As the size of portable telephones shrank, Nokia's place in the market grew.

Today, Nokia contains two business groups. Nokia Mobile Phone, the world's largest producer of mobile telephones, represents about 76 percent of the company's sales. Nokia Networks, a provider of mobile, broadband, and IP networks and related services, makes up about 22 percent of sales. In addition, a separate Nokia Ventures Organization focuses on creating business opportunities outside the current path or focus of a company's activities. In response to a fast-changing market, around 35 percent of Nokia's 54,000 employees work in research and development.

For more information about Nokia, visit the Discovering Computers 2004 Companies Web page (**scsite.com/dc2004/companies**) and click Nokia.

TECHNOLOGY TRAILBLAZERS

Douglas Engelbart
Creator of the Mouse

Without *Douglas Engelbart*, the phrase "point and click" might not be part of every computer user's vocabulary. Engelbart created the computer mouse.

At the Stanford Research Institute in the 1960s, Engelbart led a team that worked on augmenting human intellect — finding ways to enhance people's ability to solve complex problems. Part of the project was to develop a device that made it easier to move a cursor around a computer screen. Engelbart's team combined the desirable characteristics of several existing pointing devices into a new, more efficient design consisting of a wooden shell covering two wheels mounted perpendicularly. Engelbart could tilt or rock the prototype to draw straight lines, or push it and lift it off the desk to spin the wheels and move the cursor across the screen. Initially, the cord that attached the prototype to a computer was in the front, but later Engelbart switched it to the rear to move it out of the way. Engelbart patented the device as an "X-Y position indicator for a display system." Because the cord resembled a tail, however, team members called it a mouse, and the name stuck.

Like much of Engelbart's thinking, the mouse was ahead of its time. Ten years later, engineers at Xerox's Palo Alto refined Engelbart's prototype and showed the redesigned product to Apple's Steve Jobs, who applied the concept to his graphical Macintosh computer. The mouse was mass produced in the mid-1980s, and today it is the most widely used pointing device.

Engelbart's creativity has not been limited to the mouse. He has 20 patents and has written more than 25 publications. In 2000, the president presented Engelbart with the National Medal of Technology, the nation's highest award for technological achievement.

For more information about Douglas Engelbart, visit the Discovering Computers 2004 People Web page (**scsite.com/dc2004/people**) and click Douglas Engelbart.

Don Wetzel
Developer of the ATM

Riddle: What do automated teller machines (ATMs) have in common with professional baseball players? Answer: They both have a lot of money. Riddle: What do ATMs have in common with semi-professional base-ball players? Answer: *Don Wetzel*, developer of the ATM, once was a semiprofes-sional baseball player.

After graduating from the University of Loyola, Wetzel played baseball with a farm team of the New York Giants. When he realized his future was not in professional baseball, however, he accepted a job with IBM. He enjoyed the work, but the hours were long and the conditions were difficult for his family — in twelve years, they moved five times. In 1968, IBM offered Wetzel a promotion that involved another move and a staff job, which Wetzel did not think he would like. Deciding the job was not for him, Wetzel accepted a position as vice president of product planning at Docutel, a Dallas-based company that developed automated equipment.

One day, while waiting in line at a bank, Wetzel realized that a machine could be built to perform most of a bank teller's work. He took his idea for an automated teller machine to Docutel, where it was well received, with some reservations. Would banks buy the machines? Would people use them? Would the machines be secure? Studies answered yes to the first two questions. In answer to the third question, Wetzel and engineers Tom Barnes and George Chastain created a machine that read specially produced ATM cards with magnetic strips to encode account information.

In 1973, Docutel patented the ATM. The first ATM, installed at Chemical Bank in New York, essentially just dispensed cash. Today, ATMs are available at locations around the world and can be used to perform almost any bank-related function.

For more information about Don Wetzel, visit the Discovering Computers 2004 People Web page (**scsite.com/dc2004/people**) and click Don Wetzel.

CHAPTER 5 CHAPTER REVIEW

◆● Previous | Next ●◆

The Chapter Review section summarizes the concepts presented in this chapter.

■WEB INSTRUCTIONS:

To display this page from the Web, start your browser and enter the Web address **scsite.com/dc2004/ch5/review**. Click the links for current and additional information. To listen to an audio version of this Chapter Review, click the Audio button.

1 What Is Input?

Input is any *data* or *instructions* entered into the memory of a computer. An <u>input device</u> is any hardware component that allows users to enter data or instructions.

2 What Are the Characteristics of a Keyboard?

A **keyboard** is an input device that contains keys users press to enter data into a computer. Computer keyboards have a typing area that includes letters of the alphabet, numbers, punctuation marks, and other basic keys. Most keyboards also have *function keys* programmed to issue commands; keys used to move the **insertion point**, usually a blinking vertical bar, on the screen; and toggle keys that switch between two states when pressed.

3 What Are Different Mouse Types and How Do They Work?

A **pointing device** is an input device that allows users to control a small graphical symbol, called a **pointer**, on the computer screen. A **mouse** is a pointing device that fits under the palm of your hand. As you move a mouse, the pointer on the screen also moves. A *mechanical mouse* translates the movement of a ball on its underside into signals the computer can process. An *optical mouse* uses devices that emit and sense light to detect the mouse's movement. A *cordless mouse* transmits data using wireless technology.

4 How Do Pointing Devices Work?

A **trackball** is a stationary device with a ball that you rotate to move the pointer. A **touchpad** is a flat, pressure-sensitive device that you slide your finger across to move the pointer. A <u>pointing stick</u> is a device positioned on the keyboard that you push to move the pointer. A **joystick** is a vertical lever that you move to control a simulated vehicle or player. A **wheel** is a steering-wheel-type device that you turn to simulate

driving a vehicle. A **light pen** is a light-sensitive device that you press against or point at the screen to select objects. A **touch screen** is a touch-sensitive display device that you interact with by touching areas of the screen. A **stylus** or digital **pen** uses pressure to write text and draw lines.

■ Visit **scsite.com/dc2004/quiz** or click the Quiz Yourself button. Click Objectives 1 – 4 below Chapter 5.

5 How Does Voice Recognition Work?

Voice recognition is the computer's capability of distinguishing spoken words. Voice recognition programs recognize a vocabulary of preprogrammed words. Most voice recognition programs are a combination of *speaker-dependent software*, which makes a profile of your voice, and *speaker-independent software*, which has a built-in set of word patterns.

6 What Are Input Devices for Mobile Users?

A primary input device for a PDA is a basic stylus. Some PDAs have a built-in keyboard or support voice input. You can attach a mini keyboard or a full-sized *portable keyboard* to a PDA, or type on the image projected by a *virtual keyboard*. The primary input device for a Tablet PC is a digital pen, with which you can write on the device's screen. If you slide a Tablet PC into a *docking station*, you can use a full-sized keyboard and mouse. Voice is the traditional input method for smart phones. With *SMS (short message service)*, you can type and send text messages using the telephone's keypad.

7 How Does a Digital Camera Work?

A **digital camera** allows users to take pictures and store the photographed images digitally. When you take a picture, light passes into the

CHAPTER REVIEW   CHAPTER 5

camera lens, which focuses the image on a *charge-coupled device (CCD)*. The CCD generates an analog signal that represents the image. An analog-to-digital converter (ADC) converts the analog signal to a digital signal. A *digital signal processor (DSP)* stores the digital image on the camera's storage media. The image is downloaded to a computer's hard disk via cable or copied from the camera's storage media.

8 How Are PC Video Cameras, Web Cams, and Video Conferencing Used?

A **PC video camera** is a digital video camera that enables users to capture video and still images and then send or broadcast the images over the Internet. A **Web cam** is a video camera that displays its output on a Web page. A **video conference** is a meeting between geographically separated people who use a network or the Internet to transmit audio and video data.

> 📷 Visit **scsite.com/dc2004/quiz** or click the Quiz Yourself button. Click Objectives 5 – 8 below Chapter 5.

9 What Are Various Types of Scanners and Reading Devices and How Do They Work?

A **scanner** is a light-sensing input device that reads printed text and graphics and translates the results into a form the computer can process. A **flatbed scanner** works in a manner similar to a copy machine except it creates a file of the document. An *optical reader* uses a light source to read characters, marks, and codes and converts them into digital data. **Optical character recognition (OCR)** reads characters from ordinary documents. **Optical mark recognition (OMR)** reads hand-drawn marks such as small circles. A **bar code scanner** is an optical reader that uses laser beams to read a **bar code**, or identification code. **MICR** (*magnetic-ink character recognition*) reads text printed with magnetized ink.

10 What Are Types of Terminals?

A *terminal* consists of a keyboard, a monitor, a video card, and memory. A *dumb terminal* has no processing power and relies on a host computer for processing. A *smart terminal*

has a processor and can perform some functions independent of the host computer. POS terminals, ATMs, and smart displays are special-purpose terminals. A **POS (point-of-sale) terminal** records purchases, processes credit cards or debit cards, and updates delivery at a consumer's location. Many POS terminals have a **card reader**, which reads personal data from the magnetic strip on a credit or debit card. An **automated teller machine (ATM)** is a self-service banking machine that connects to a host computer. To access a bank account, you insert a bankcard into the ATM's card reader and enter a *personal identification number (PIN)*. A **smart display** is a thin monitor that detaches from a computer to function as a wireless touch screen.

11 What Are Various Biometric Devices?

A *biometric device* translates a personal characteristic into digital code that is compared with a digital code stored in the computer to identify an individual. A **fingerprint scanner** captures curves and indentations of a fingerprint. A *face recognition system* captures a live face image. A *hand geometry system* measures the shape and size of a hand. A *voice verification system* compares live speech with a stored voice pattern. A *signature verification system* recognizes the shape of a signature. An *iris recognition system* reads patterns in the iris of the eye.

12 What Are Alternative Input Devices for Physically Challenged Users?

Voice recognition is ideal for visually impaired users. A *keyguard* is a plate placed over the keyboard that allows users with limited hand mobility to rest their hands and press only one key at a time. Keyboards with larger keys or an *on-screen keyboard* displayed on a user's screen also are available. A small trackball or a *head-mounted pointer* helps users with limited hand movement to control the pointer. Two developments in the prototype stage are *gesture recognition* and computerized implant devices.

> 📷 Visit **scsite.com/dc2004/quiz** or click the Quiz Yourself button. Click Objectives 9 – 12 below Chapter 5.

CHAPTER 5 — KEY TERMS

◄● Previous | Next ●►

You should know the Primary Terms and be familiar with the Secondary Terms.

WEB INSTRUCTIONS:

To display this page from the Web, start your browser and enter the Web address **scsite.com/dc2004/ch5/terms**. Click a term to display its definition and a picture. When the picture displays, click the more info button for current and additional information about the term from the Web.

>> Primary Terms
(shown in bold-black characters in the chapter)

Americans with Disabilities Act (ADA) (5.35)
audio input (5.15)
automated teller machine (ATM) (5.31)
bar code (5.27)
bar code scanner (5.27)
card reader (5.30)
digital camera (5.19)
digital pen (5.12)
digital video (DV) camera (5.22)
ergonomic keyboard (5.06)
ergonomics (5.06)
fingerprint scanner (5.32)
flatbed scanner (5.25)
graphics tablet (5.12)
input (5.02)
input device (5.04)
insertion point (5.05)
joystick (5.11)
keyboard (5.04)
light pen (5.11)
MICR (5.29)
MICR reader (5.29)
mouse (5.07)
mouse pad (5.07)
OCR devices (5.26)
optical character recognition (OCR) (5.26)

optical mark recognition (OMR) (5.27)
PC camera (5.22)
PC video camera (5.22)
point of sale (POS) (5.30)
pointer (5.07)
pointing device (5.07)
pointing stick (5.10)
POS terminal (5.30)
resolution (5.21)
scanner (5.24)
smart card (5.33)
smart display (5.31)
stylus (5.12)
touch screen (5.12)
touchpad (5.10)
trackball (5.10)
turnaround document (5.27)
video capture card (5.22)
video conference (5.23)
video input (5.22)
video telephone call (5.23)
voice input (5.14)
voice recognition (5.14)
Web cam (5.23)
wheel (5.11)

>> Secondary Terms
(shown in italic characters in the chapter)

analog-to-digital converter (ADC) (5.14)
biometric device (5.32)
biometric identifier (5.32)
biometrics (5.32)
charge-coupled device (CCD) (5.20)
command (5.03)
continuous speech (5.15)
cordless keyboard (5.06)
cordless mouse (5.07)
cursor (application program) (5.05)
cursor (graphics tablet) (5.12)
data (5.02)
data collection device (5.29)
digital signal processor (DSP) (5.20)
digitizer (5.12)
discrete speech (5.15)
docking station (5.18)
download (5.19)
dumb terminal (5.30)
electronic signatures (5.13)
enhanced keyboard (5.05)
enhanced resolution (5.22)
face recognition system (5.32)
field camera (5.20)
function keys (5.05)
gesture recognition (5.35)
hand geometry system (5.32)
handwriting recognition software (5.13)
head-mounted pointer (5.35)
image processing (5.26)
image processing system (5.26)
instructions (5.02)
iris recognition system (5.33)
keyguard (5.35)

magnetic-ink character recognition (5.29)
mechanical mouse (5.07)
MIDI (musical instrument digital interface) (5.15)
mouse pointer (5.07)
MP (5.21)
OCR (optical character recognition) software (5.26)
on-screen keyboard (5.35)
optical mouse (5.07)
optical reader (5.26)
optical resolution (5.22)
optical scanner (5.24)
personal identification number (PIN) (5.31)
pixel (5.21)
pixels per inch (ppi) (5.21)
point-and-shoot camera (5.20)
portable keyboard (5.17)
program (5.02)
signature verification system (5.33)
smart terminal (5.30)
SMS (short message service) (5.18)
source document (5.24)
speaker-dependent software (5.14)
speaker-independent software (5.15)
speech recognition (5.14)
streaming cam (5.23)
studio camera (5.20)
terminal (5.30)
toggle key (5.05)
UPC (Universal Product Code) (5.28)
user response (5.03)
virtual keyboard (5.17)
voice verification system (5.33)
whiteboard (5.23)

CHECKPOINT CHAPTER 5

Use the Checkpoint exercises to check your knowledge level of the chapter.

WEB INSTRUCTIONS:

To display this page from the Web, start your browser and enter the Web address **scsite.com/dc2004/ch5/check**. Click the links for current and additional information.

LABEL THE FIGURE   Identify these areas and keys on a desktop computer keyboard.

a. additional keys

b. APPLICATION key

c. arrow keys

d. CD/DVD controls

e. function keys

f. Internet controls

g. numeric keypad

h. typing area

i. WINDOWS key

j. wrist rest

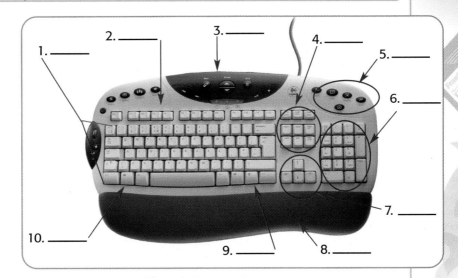

TRUE/FALSE   Mark T for True and F for False. (See page numbers in parentheses.)

_____ 1. Input is any data or instructions entered into the <u>memory</u> of a computer. (5.02)

_____ 2. An input device is any hardware component that allows users to enter <u>data</u> or instructions into a computer. (5.04)

_____ 3. The goal of <u>ergonomics</u> is to incorporate comfort, efficiency, and safety into the design of items in the workplace. (5.06)

_____ 4. A <u>trackball</u> is a stationary pointing device with a ball on its top. (5.10)

_____ 5. Audio input is the process of entering data by speaking into a <u>microphone</u>. (5.15)

_____ 6. A portable keyboard is a miniature-sized keyboard you conveniently attach and remove from a <u>PDA</u>. (5.17)

_____ 7. Digital cameras typically allow users to review, and sometimes edit, <u>images</u> while they are in the camera. (5.19)

_____ 8. A video conference is a meeting between two or more geographically separated people who use a <u>network</u> or the Internet to transmit audio and video data. (5.23)

_____ 9. An optical reader is a device that uses a light source to read characters, marks, and codes and then converts them into <u>digital data</u> that a computer can process. (5.26)

_____ 10. <u>Optical mark recognition (OMR)</u> is a technology that reads typewritten, computer-printed, or hand-printed characters from ordinary documents and translates the images into a form the computer can process. (5.27)

_____ 11. <u>Biometrics</u> is the technology of authenticating a person's identity by verifying a personal characteristic. (5.32)

_____ 12. No <u>pointing devices</u> currently are available for users with motor limitations. (5.35)

CHAPTER 5 CHECKPOINT

◄● Previous | Next ●►

MULTIPLE CHOICE Select the best answer. (See page numbers in parentheses.)

1. _____ is a series of instructions that tells a computer what to do and how to do it. (5.02)
   a. Data
   b. A program
   c. A command
   d. A user response

2. The NUM LOCK key, which locks and unlocks the numeric keypad, is an example of a(n) _____ key. (5.05)
   a. function
   b. WINDOWS
   c. toggle
   d. APPLICATION

3. A(n) _____ is a battery-powered device that transmits data using wireless technology, such as radio waves or infrared light waves. (5.06)
   a. enhanced keyboard
   b. ergonomic keyboard
   c. portable keyboard
   d. cordless keyboard

4. _____ is a common mouse operation in which you press and release the secondary mouse button. (5.09)
   a. Click
   b. Right-click
   c. Double-click
   d. Right-drag

5. To allow easy access of your bank account from a car, many ATMs have _____. (5.12)
   a. touch screens
   b. joy sticks
   c. touchpads
   d. pointing sticks

6. Voice input is the process of _____. (5.14)
   a. entering data by speaking into a microphone
   b. entering any sound into the computer such as speech, music, and sound effects
   c. capturing full-motion images into a computer and storing them on a storage medium
   d. all of the above

7. A portable keyboard _____. (5.17)
   a. is an infrared image of a keyboard projected on a flat surface
   b. has twelve function keys along the top, two CTRL keys, two ALT keys, and a set of arrow and additional keys between the typing area and the numeric keypad
   c. has a design that reduces the chance of wrist and hand injuries
   d. is a full-sized keyboard you conveniently attach and remove from a PDA

8. A _____ is an affordable and lightweight type of digital camera that provides acceptable quality photographic images for the home or small business user. (5.20)
   a. studio camera
   b. field camera
   c. point-and-shoot camera
   d. PC camera

9. A digital video (DV) camera _____. (5.22)
   a. records video as analog signals instead of digital signals
   b. is a stationary camera used for professional studio work
   c. records video as digital signals instead of analog signals
   d. is a mobile camera used for amateur studio work

10. Scanners capture data from a _____, which is the original form of the data. (5.24)
    a. duplicate document
    b. secondary document
    c. derivative document
    d. source document

11. The UPC (Universal Product Code) bar code is used by _____. (5.28)
    a. retail and grocery stores
    b. libraries, blood banks, and air parcel carriers
    c. the United States Postal Service (USPS)
    d. nonretail applications such as game tickets

12. Point-of-sale terminals, automated teller machines, and smart displays are types of _____ that perform specific tasks and contain features uniquely designed for use in a particular industry. (5.30)
    a. smart terminals
    b. dumb terminals
    c. general-purpose terminals
    d. special-purpose terminals

13. The most widely used biometric device is the _____. (5.32)
    a. face recognition system
    b. fingerprint scanner
    c. hand geometry system
    d. iris recognition system

14. _____ is an ideal form of input for visually impaired users. (5.35)
    a. A keyguard
    b. Voice recognition
    c. A head-mounted pointer
    d. Keyboard recognition

CHECKPOINT   CHAPTER 5

MATCHING   Match the terms with their definitions. (See page numbers in parentheses.)

_____ 1. insertion point (5.05)

_____ 2. ergonomic keyboard (5.06)

_____ 3. pointer (5.07)

_____ 4. mouse pad (5.07)

_____ 5. graphics tablet (5.12)

_____ 6. video capture card (5.22)

_____ 7. video telephone call (5.23)

_____ 8. bar code (5.27)

_____ 9. data collection device (5.29)

_____ 10. smart card (5.33)

a. symbol on the screen that indicates where the next character typed will display

b. designed to reduce the chance of wrist and hand injuries

c. stores personal data on a thin, embedded microprocessor

d. obtains data directly at the location where a transaction or event takes place

e. graphical symbol whose location changes with the movement of a pointing device

f. rectangular pad that provides better traction than the top of a desk

g. identification code that consists of vertical lines and spaces of different widths

h. allows both parties to see each other as they talk over the Internet

i. flat, rectangular, electronic plastic board sometimes called a digitizer

j. self-service banking machine that connects to a host computer

k. projects an infrared image of a keyboard on any flat surface

l. converts an analog video signal into a digital signal a computer can use

SHORT ANSWER   Write a brief answer to each of the following questions.

1. How does voice recognition work? _____ How is discrete speech different from continuous speech? _____

2. What is needed to participate in a video conference? _____ What is a whiteboard? _____

3. What is OCR (optical character recognition) software? _____ What is an image processing system? _____

4. What is optical character recognition (OCR), optical mark recognition (OMR), and MICR (magnetic-ink character recognition)? _____ How is each technology used? _____

5. What is the Americans with Disabilities Act (ADA)? _____ How might gesture recognition and computerized implant devices help physically challenged users in the future? _____

WORKING TOGETHER   Working with a group of your classmates, complete the following team exercises.

1. Carpal tunnel syndrome is the most well-known of a series of musculoskeletal disorders that fall under the umbrella of repetitive strain injuries (RSIs). Prepare a report and PowerPoint presentation on RSIs. Include information about RSI warning signs and risk factors and suggestions about proper workstation ergonomics. Share your report and presentation with your class.

2. Choose one Issue in this chapter: 5.04, 5.08, 5.18, 5.28, or 5.33. Use the Web and/or print media to research the issue. Then, present a debate for the class, with different members of your team supporting different responses to the questions that accompany the issue.

3. Stores, libraries, parcel carriers, and other organizations use optical codes. Some people mistakenly believe that an optical code contains the name of a product or its price, but the codes are only a link to a database in which this information, and more, is stored. Have each member of your team visit an organization that uses optical codes. How are the optical codes read? What information is obtained when the code is read? What information is recorded? How is the information used? Meet with the members of your team to discuss the results of your investigations. Then, use PowerPoint to create a group presentation and share your findings with the class.

CHAPTER 5 LEARN IT ONLINE

◀● Previous | Next ●▶

Use the Learn It Online exercises to reinforce your understanding of the chapter concepts.

WEB INSTRUCTIONS:

To display this page from the Web, start your browser and enter the Web address **scsite.com/dc2004/ch5/learn**.

1 At The Movies – Web Cam Virtual World

To view the Web Cam Virtual World movie, click the number 1 button. Watch the movie and then complete the exercise by answering the questions below. The Internet is where the curious meet the pretentious. With the availability of mobile cameras, Web cams, and PC video cameras, images reach millions of people. From around the globe, you can watch gorillas from Namibia, the miracle of birth at a hospital, or a toddler's birthday party next door. Some of this Web cam virtual world is informative, some serves a useful purpose, some of it is just entertainment, and some of it is intrusive. A more open society sounds like a good thing, but what about the privacy issues? Should limitations be placed on the type of content that is put on the Web, or should limitations exist only for those who have access to the Web? Is access to this virtual world too easy or distracting? Will it help or hinder efforts to solve the problems of the real world?

2 Shelly Cashman Series Scanning Documents Lab

Follow the instructions in Learn It Online 2 on page 1.46 to start and use the Shelly Cashman Series Scanning Documents Lab. If you are running from the Web, enter the Web address **scsite.com/sclabs/menu** or display the Learn It Online page (see instructions at the top of this page) and then click the number 2 button.

3 Sending E-Mail

It is estimated that 75 percent of all workers and 45 percent of all consumers, which represents a total of 58 percent of the U.S. population, use e-mail. E-mail allows you to send messages anywhere in the world. Use the e-mail account you set up in Learn It Online 12 in Chapter 3 on page 3.45 to send a message. Click the number 3 button to display your e-mail service. Log in to your e-mail service and then follow the instructions for composing a message. The subject of the message should be input devices. Type the e-mail address of one of your classmates. In the message itself, type something your classmate should know about input devices, and then send the message. Next, follow the instructions to read and reply to any messages you have received. When you are finished, quit your e-mail service.

4 Practice Test

Click the number 4 button. Answer each question. When completed, enter your name and click the Grade Test button to submit the quiz for grading. Make a note of any missed questions. If required, print a copy to submit to your instructor.

LEARN IT ONLINE   CHAPTER 5

5 Web Guide

Click the number 5 button to display the Guide to Web Sites and Searching Techniques Web page. Click Computers and Computing and then click ZDNet. In the Search text box, type `Web camera`. Scroll through the results and then click a link of your choice. Use your word processing program to prepare a brief report on your findings and submit your assignment to your instructor.

6 Scavenger Hunt

Click the number 6 button. Print a copy of the Scavenger Hunt page; use this page to write down your answers as you search the Web. Submit your completed page to your instructor.

7 Who Wants to Be a Computer Genius?

Click the number 7 button to find out if you are a computer genius. Directions on how to play the game will display. When you are ready to play, click the Play button. Submit your score to your instructor.

8 Wheel of Terms

Click the number 8 button to reinforce important terms you learned in this chapter by playing the Shelly Cashman Series version of this popular game. Directions on how to play the game will display. When you are ready to play, click the Play button. Submit your score to your instructor.

9 Career Corner

Click the number 9 button to display the Penn State's Career Services Web page. Click a link of your choice. Write a brief report on the information you found. Submit the report to your instructor.

10 Search Sleuth

Click the number 10 button to learn search techniques that will help make you a research expert. Submit the completed assignment to your instructor.

11 Crossword Puzzle Challenge

Click the number 11 button. Complete the puzzle to reinforce skills you learned in this chapter. Directions on how to play the game will display. When you are ready to play, click the Play button. Submit the completed puzzle to your instructor.

12 In the News

Many people spend a lot of time jotting notes on scratch pads, napkins, or little yellow Post-it® notes. This may be fine for the occasional thought; however, in a situation where you would rather concentrate on the substance of the ideas being expressed, you may need a more sophisticated method for taking notes. Tape recorders have long been the mainstay for recording lectures, interviews, or one's thoughts, but they are restricted by the fact that the tapes last only so long before they have to be flipped over or switched altogether. One new development is the voice pen, which is a flash-memory-based recording device. It records digitally, which offers higher quality over standard tapes, easy indexing, and instant erasure. It is approximately the size of a small cellular telephone or remote control unit, and can record up to 500 minutes on long play settings. Click the number 12 button and read a news article about a new or improved input device, an input device being used in a new way, or an input device being made more available. What is the device? Who is promoting it? How will it be used? Will the input device change the number, or effectiveness, of potential users? If so, why?

CHAPTER 5   LAB EXERCISES

◀● Previous | Next ●▶

Use the Lab Exercises to gain hands-on computer experience.

■ WEB INSTRUCTIONS:

To display this page from the Web, start your browser and enter the Web address **scsite.com/dc2004/ch5p/lab**.

1 About Your Computer

This exercise uses Windows XP procedures. Your computer probably has more than one input device. To learn about the input devices on your computer, click the Start button on the Windows taskbar, and then right-click My Computer on the Start menu. Click Properties on the shortcut menu. When the System Properties dialog box displays, click the Hardware tab. Click the Device Manager button. If necessary, click the plus sign next to the label for your computer in the Device Manager window to display a list of hardware device categories. What input devices appear in the list? Click the plus sign next to each category that contains an input device. What specific input devices in each category are connected to your computer? Close the Device Manager window. Click the Cancel button in the System Properties dialog box.

2 Customizing the Keyboard

This exercise uses Windows XP procedures. The Windows operating system provides several ways to customize the keyboard for people with physical limitations. Some of these options are StickyKeys, FilterKeys, and ToggleKeys. To discover more about each option, click the Start button on the Windows taskbar, and then click Control Panel on the Start menu. If necessary, switch to Category View. Click the Accessibility Options icon in the Control Panel window. Click the Accessibility Options icon in the Accessibility Options window. If necessary, click the Keyboard tab in the Accessibility Options dialog box. Click the Question Mark button on the title bar, click the StickyKeys area, read the information in the pop-up window, and then click the pop-up window to close it. Repeat this process for FilterKeys and ToggleKeys. What is the purpose of each option? How might each option benefit someone with a physical limitation? Click the Cancel button in the Accessibility Options dialog box and then click the Close button in the Accessibility Options window.

3 Using the Mouse and Keyboard to Interact with an Online Program

This exercise uses Windows XP/2000/98 procedures. Insert the Discover Data Disk into

drive A or see your instructor for the location of the Loan Payment Calculator program. Click the Start button on the Windows taskbar, and then click Run on the Start menu to display the Run dialog box. In the Open text box, type the path and file name of the program. For example, type `a:loancalc.exe` and then press the ENTER key to display the Loan Payment Calculator window. Type `12500` in the LOAN AMOUNT text box. Click the YEARS right scroll arrow or drag the scroll box until YEARS equals 15. Click the APR right scroll arrow or drag the scroll box until APR equals 8.5. Click the Calculate button. Write down the monthly payment and sum of payments. Click the Clear button. What are the monthly payment and sum of payments for each of these loan amounts, years, and APRs: (1) 28000, 5, 7.25; (2) 98750, 30, 9; (3) 6000, 3, 8.75; (4) 62500, 15, 9.25. Close the Loan Payment Calculator.

4 MouseKeys

This exercise uses Windows XP procedures. A graphical user interface allows you to perform many tasks simply by pointing the mouse and clicking a mouse button. Yet, what if you do not have, or cannot use, a mouse? The Windows XP operating system covers this possibility with an option called MouseKeys. When the MouseKeys option is turned on, you can use numeric keypad keys to move the mouse pointer, click, right-click, double-click, and drag. To find out how, click the Start button on the Windows taskbar and then click Help and Support on the Start menu. Type `MouseKeys` in the Search text box and then click the Start searching button. To answer each of the following questions, click an appropriate link in the Search Results box and then read the Help information. To display a different result in the right pane, click a different link in the Search Results box.

- How do you turn on MouseKeys?
- How do you change MouseKeys options?
- How do you click using MouseKeys?
- How do you drag using MouseKeys?

Click the Close button to close the Help and Support Center window.

WEB RESEARCH CHAPTER 5

Use the Web Research exercises to learn more about the special features in this chapter.

WEB INSTRUCTIONS:

Use the link in each exercise or a search engine such as Google (google.com) to research the topic. Then, write a one-page, double-spaced report or create a presentation, unless otherwise directed below. Page numbers on which information can be found are in parentheses.

1. **Issue** Choose one Issue from the following issues in this chapter: What Is Happening on Your Computer? (5.04), A Mouse Did What? (5.08), Can I Borrow Your Notes? (5.18), What Is the Price of That Item? (5.28), or Have You Seen This Face? (5.33). Use the Web to research the issue. Discuss the issue with classmates, instructors, and friends. Address the questions that accompany the issue in a report or presentation.

2. **Apply It** Choose one of the following Apply It features in this chapter: Configuring the Mouse to Suit Your Preferences (5.09) or Share Digital Photos with Friends and Family (5.21). Use the Web to gather additional information about the topic. Print two Web pages that relate to the Apply It. Detail in a report or presentation what you learned.

3. **Career Corner** Read the Career Corner article in this chapter (5.36). Use the Web to find out more about the career. Describe the career in a report or presentation.

4. **Companies on the Cutting Edge** Choose one of the Companies on the Cutting Edge in this chapter (5.38). Use the Web to research the company further. Explain in a report or presentation how this company has contributed to computer technology.

5. **Technology Trailblazers** Choose one of the Technology Trailblazers in this chapter (5.39). Use the Web to research the person further. Explain in a report or presentation how this individual has affected the way people use, or think about, computers.

6. **Picture Yourself Using a PDA** Read the Picture Yourself Using a PDA story at the beginning of this chapter (5.00). Use the Web to research PDAs further. Describe in a report or presentation the ways in which you might use a PDA.

7. **High-Tech Talk** Read the High-Tech Talk feature in this chapter (5.37). Use the Web to find out more about the topic. Summarize in a report or presentation what you learned.

8. **Web Links** Review the Web Link boxes found in the margins of this chapter. Visit five of the Web Link sites. Print the main Web page for each site you visit. Choose one of the Web pages and then summarize in one paragraph the content of the Web page.

9. **Looking Ahead** Choose one of the Looking Ahead articles in this chapter: Wireless Pens Revolutionize Input Devices (5.13) or Brain Implants Help Physically Challenged (5.36). Use the Web to find out more about the topic. Detail in a report or presentation what you learned.

10. **FAQ** Choose one FAQ found in this chapter. Use the Web to find out more about the topic. Summarize in one paragraph what you learned.

11. **PDA Application Software** Read the PDA Application Software Special Feature that follows this chapter (5.50–5.61). Select a field that uses PDA software. Use the Web to learn more about your selection. Describe in a report or presentation how PDA software is used in the field you selected.

12. **Making Use of the Web** Read the Auctions section of Making Use of the Web in Appendix A (A.10). Complete the Auctions Web Exercises at the end of the section. (A.11) Answer the questions posed in each exercise.

SPECIAL FEATURE

PDA Application Software

Not long ago, **PDA** (personal digital assistant) software consisted of a few programs, such as a to-do list and an address book. PDAs previously contained embedded software, meaning that a user could not change the software or add additional programs to the PDA. Today's PDAs allow for as much choice and versatility in their software as a typical personal computer. Most PDAs come equipped with a rich set of programs. In some cases, a user may want to use enhanced versions of the included software, such as an enhanced calculator program, or install additional software, such as a game.

Address Book/Contacts

To-Do List

Memos/Notepad

Calculator

Datebook/Calendar

FIGURE 1 PDAs usually are equipped with standard software. PDA software is available on the Web and at retail stores and sometimes is packaged with other personal computer software.

PDA Operating Systems

As with personal computers, PDAs run an operating system. A PDA runs software made only for the operating system of the PDA. PDAs can be categorized by the operating system on which each runs. Figure 2 lists the common PDA operating systems, the manufacturer, and a brief description of the operating system.

PDA Operating Systems

Operating System	Manufacturer	Description
Palm OS (versions 5 and later)	PalmSource™	The latest version of the operating system for Palm OS-based PDAs supports faster processors, multimedia, and more memory.
Palm OS (earlier versions)	PalmSource	Several PDA manufacturers continue to use earlier versions of the Palm OS operating system because of the simplicity and lower power requirements, resulting in longer usage between recharges.
PocketPC	Microsoft®	The PocketPC operating system tightly integrates with Microsoft's Windows operating systems and includes scaled down versions of many of Microsoft's popular programs, including Word, Outlook, Excel, and MSN Messenger.
Symbian OS	Symbian	Symbian OS is a popular PDA operating system commonly used on cellular telephones. Symbian OS is more popular in Europe and with business users.
Linux	Open source	Some PDAs use a scaled down version of the free Linux operating system.

FIGURE 2 PDA capabilities depend on the operating system that they run.

BUILT-IN PDA SOFTWARE

All PDAs include several programs that give the PDA its name, such as an **address book** and **date book**. Figure 3 lists the types of software that usually are preinstalled on a PDA.

BUILT-IN PDA SOFTWARE

Application	Description
Address book/Contacts	Maintains a list of acquaintances, including names, addresses, telephone numbers, e-mail addresses, and notes.
To-Do list	Maintains a list of tasks. Tasks can be categorized and assigned a priority.
Calculator	Offers functionality of standard desktop calculators.
Datebook/Calendar	Maintains appointments and important dates, such as birthdays and holidays. A user also sets audio or visual alarms to trigger when appointments are due.
Memos/Notepad	Keeps track of notes.
Launcher	The interface that allows a user to execute, or launch, programs, shown on the PDA screen in the center of Figure 1.

FIGURE 3 PDAs typically come preinstalled with this built-in software.

SYNCHRONIZATION SOFTWARE

Most PDAs allow a user to share data and information between his or her personal computer and the PDA. The software that enables the sharing is called **synchronization software**. A PDA may synchronize, or synch (pronounced sink), with a personal computer or a server on a network. Corporations often standardize on synchronization software so that employees share data across the corporate network, and so the data is backed up properly on a server. Figure 4 lists popular synchronization software for PDAs.

SYNCHRONIZATION SOFTWARE FOR PDAS

Application	Description	Samples
Built-in	Most PDAs include software that the user loads on a personal computer that allows the computer to communicate with the PDA and share data and information.	• The Palm OS® includes HotSync software • PocketPC PDAs include ActiveSync® software
Synching many sources	Some PDA users have data and information stored in may places. For example, users may want to have their address books on the Web, on their personal computers, on their cellular telephones, and on their PDAs. Special synchronization software allows users to keep all of the address books up to date.	• Starfish TrueSync® • PocketMirror® • XTNDConnect Server
SyncML	**SyncML** is a standard that is being adopted by many companies that create PDAs. SyncML is based on the XML data standard and allows for common information stored on a PDA to be shared among many devices, such as cellular telephones, other PDAs, and personal computers.	• IBM WebSphere® • Everyplace Access • Pumatech Intellisync® • Starfish TrueSync SynchML • fusionOne SynchML Server
iSync	Apple's iSync software allows a user to keep a calendar and contact information synchronized up to the minute between a cellular telephone, an Apple iPod, a Palm OS device, or multiple Macs.	• Apple iSync

FIGURE 4 PDAs use synchronization software to share data and information with a personal computer or server.

PRODUCTIVITY/BUSINESS SOFTWARE

Most programs used on a PDA have some counterpart program on a desktop computer. For example, both a personal computer and a PDA may include a word-processing program. Many productivity/business programs have counterparts on PDAs. The PDA versions of these programs generally have fewer features and options. For example, a word processing program on a PDA may not have a spelling checker and a spreadsheet program may not include all of the built-in calculations of its desktop computer counterpart. Figure 5 lists productivity/business software for PDAs.

PRODUCTIVITY/BUSINESS SOFTWARE FOR PDAS

Application	Description	Samples
Word processing	Allows for simple creation, editing, and viewing of documents.	• Documents To Go • WordSmith • PocketWord
Spreadsheet	Allows a user to create, edit, and view worksheets on a PDA.	• Pocket Excel • TinySheet™ • Quickoffice™
Readers	Allows read-only (view only) access to word processing documents, spreadsheets, or databases that a user downloads to a PDA from a personal computer. Readers are useful for taking large documents on the road to read them without the ability to modify them. Some readers allow the user to view all of these types of documents, while others are targeted to specific desktop program counterparts, such as presentation viewers or word processing document viewers.	• Pocket SlideShow • TealDoc™ • iSilo™ • Microsoft Reader
Database/List management	Allows creation, editing, and viewing of databases or lists. List management is a very popular use of PDAs. Some examples of lists that are handy to store on a PDA include shopping lists, to-do lists, exercise logs, and automobile maintenance logs.	• HanDBase® • thinkDB • SmartList To Go • JFile • ListPro®
Financial	Financial software includes programs to manage a bank account, track expenses during a trip, manage a budget, or track an investment portfolio. Many personal computer financial programs include PDA companion software that keeps the information on a PDA synchronized with the financial information on a personal computer or the Web.	• Microsoft Money for PocketPC • Pocket Quicken® • BankBook • Ultrasoft® Money

FIGURE 5 General-purpose software allows users to use scaled down versions of common desktop programs.

COMMUNICATIONS SOFTWARE

Most of the software used to interact with the Internet using a personal computer has a counterpart on the PDA. Some PDAs come equipped with e-mail software or a Web browser. Often, special servers allow the PDA to communicate securely with corporate databases or Web sites. For PDAs that do not include wireless Internet connectivity, a special PDA modem connects the PDA to the Internet. Web content and e-mail also synchronize to the PDA from a personal computer and the information may be browsed offline while using the PDA. Figure 6 provides a list of popular communications software for PDAs.

COMMUNICATIONS SOFTWARE FOR PDAS

Application	Description	Samples
E-mail	Used for composing and reading e-mail.	• Pocket Outlook • riteMail® • Mail+
Web browsers Explorer	Allows Web browsing. Some browsers use an **intermediate server** to make the pages smaller by stripping out images or making images smaller. Others attempt to display the full Web page on the PDA.	• Pocket Internet • Handspring Blazer • AvantGo
Clipping	**Web clippings** are programs that gather and display only the critical elements, or clips, of a Web page.	• Travelocity.com • The Weather Channel • Moviefone.com
Instant messaging	Instant messaging programs usually allow the user to use the same instant messaging ID as that used on a personal computer.	• MSN® Messenger • AIM for Palm OS

FIGURE 6 Communications software allows a PDA to access the Internet and other data sources while away from the classroom or office.

CORPORATE/GOVERNMENT SOFTWARE

Large organizations, such as corporations and government agencies, take advantage of the PDA's capability of keeping current information in the hands of their personnel. The organization's central employee telephone book is kept up to date and synchronized to each employee's PDA on a regular basis. Executives synchronize key corporate information. Traveling sales personnel and field technicians synchronize appointments, e-mail, notes about contact with customers, product lists, and sales information. Corporate/government software for PDAs is listed in Figure 7.

CORPORATE/GOVERNMENT SOFTWARE FOR PDAS

Application	Description	Samples
Executive	Executives keep up-to-date corporate information on their PDAs. Executives may keep current sales information, financial information, and inventory information available to make informed decisions.	• mySAP.com • Siebel 7 Mobile Solutions
Sales	Sales people working out of the office are perhaps the largest group of PDA users. PDAs are useful for keeping product information handy, keeping scheduled appointments, and maintaining customer information.	• Siebel 7 Mobile Solutions • Salesforce.com • ActionNames
Field technicians and mobile workers	Field technicians visit customer locations to troubleshoot problems. PDAs help technicians keep track of customer information, maintain up-to-date information on replacement parts, and log troubleshooting information.	• UPS and FedEx use specialized PDAs and software for their drivers to track package pickups and drop offs.
Military/Law enforcement	The military and law enforcement agencies deploy PDAs to manage the special needs of the military and law enforcement.	• Most software of this nature is custom made for the needs of particular agencies. Such programs help track cases or serve as legal references.
Connecting/Synchronizing with corporate data sources	Several solutions exist for synchronizing corporate data with PDAs. Special software keeps track of user permissions and making certain that the right people get the data they require on a day-to-day basis.	• Pumatech Intellisync
Large organization management issues	In organizations with thousands of PDA users, the support of those PDAs becomes tedious, especially when users install unsupported software on the PDAs that may interfere with the corporate software and data for which the PDA was intended. PDA management software may detect these conflicts when the user synchronizes with the corporate server and deletes or reports the offending software.	• Much of the software of this nature is custom built for each enterprise, as needs and infrastructure of each organization are different.

FIGURE 7 Large organizations utilize special software to keep their employees synchronized.

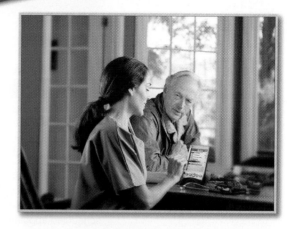

MEDICAL SOFTWARE

One of the largest communities to adopt PDA software in significant numbers is the medical community (Figure 8). Physicians and other medical workers routinely use specialized software to track patient charts, check information on drugs, and browse electronic versions of large reference books. The end result is a savings in time and money, and an increase in the level of care for the patient.

MEDICAL SOFTWARE FOR PDAS

Application	Description	Samples
Patient/Case management	Patient and case management programs allow medical workers to enter information as they interact with the patient. This eliminates transcription errors or the need for the worker to find a workstation to do his or her work.	• MedLogs • PatientKeeper Personal • Handy Patients
Drug information and drug interactions	Allows for fast access to critical drug information, such as dosages and drug interactions.	• Epocrates Rx • eDrugsDatabase • Dr Drugs
Reference books	Medical workers often rely on a large collection of references to do their job. Electronic versions of many popular references, such as the *Physicians' Desk Reference*, are available in electronic format and are kept up to date easily through regular downloads.	• PDRDrugs™ • eDrugs Database • DiagnosisPro for PocketPC • MedRules
Prescriptions	With electronic prescribing, physicians write prescriptions electronically. Physicians print legible prescriptions and hand the prescriptions to the patient. If the PDA is connected to the Internet or hospital network, the physician checks the patient's medication or medical history.	• iScribe™ • Rx Medicine
Medical calculations	Medical workers often make quick calculations for medication dosages or patient status. PDA programs assist many of these calculations and target the worker's specialty.	• MedMath • Pocket MedCalc • Medical MathPad

FIGURE 8 The medical community quickly has become one of the larger users of specialized PDA software.

SCIENTIFIC SOFTWARE

The mobility of PDAs makes them valuable tools for scientific use. Researchers use PDAs to gather and record data in the field, and later download the data to a personal computer or server. Scientists also use specialized software targeted to their specific field of interest, such as astronomy or meteorology, as a replacement for bulky reference manuals, or observation notes (Figure 9).

SCIENTIFIC SOFTWARE FOR PDAS

Application	Description	Samples
Data gathering	Scientists can input observations quickly into a PDA. These programs often are used in the field for gathering research statistics.	• Survey-It • CollectorPlus
Calculations/Conversions	Users can perform specialized calculations or data conversions. Many fields of science, such as astronomy, require special calculations that are useful to have available on a PDA.	• ME Tools • CoolCalc for the PocketPC • Convert It! • APCalc Converter
Reference	Scientists can look up information quickly, rather than using cumbersome manuals or textbooks.	• ChemRef Basic • PTE (Periodic Table of the Elements) • Gene • A B C's of Science • Astronomical Inform
Astronomy	Observers can follow the stars. With the large number of amateur astronomers in the world, programs specific to astronomy are some of the more popular scientific titles.	• Pocket Universe • Planetarium • Star Pilot • Pocket Stars
Weather	Meteorologists' specific needs are addressed because these programs allow quick calculations or data gathering in a changing environment. Some programs are linked to add-on PDA hardware that measure temperature, humidity, and other meteorological data.	• Weather Manager • WorldMate • Weather Calculator for Palm OS

FIGURE 9 Scientific programs help scientists manage complex information.

TRAVEL SOFTWARE

The mobile nature of PDAs makes them ideal for the business or leisure traveler. Even a night on the town can be enhanced by an on-the-go list of popular hot spots. The user keeps his or her itinerary handy along with maps and directions while traveling to new places. A GPS-enabled PDA tracks a user's route and keeps the user on course. Wireless connectivity allows the user to book flights and hotels from the back of a taxi cab. Figure 10 lists travel software for PDAs.

TRAVEL SOFTWARE FOR PDAS

Application	Description	Samples
Itinerary consolidation	Manages travel itineraries, including flights, hotels, and car rental. The software may keep track of travel preferences and make suggestions about travel and accommodations when planning a new trip.	• Traveler (PocketPC edition) • TravelPacker • Travel Pal
Mapping	Mapping software may download maps from the Web or a personal computer. Or, the software may include maps. The software may suggest travel routes from point to point, or simply serve as a reference.	• Vindigo® for Palm OS or PocketPC • Pocket Streets • HandMap
City guides	City guides are one of the more popular PDA programs. The user installs city guides for specific cities or an entire country. Guides include restaurant listings and ratings, hotels, direction, popular attractions, and local customs.	• Weissmann City Profiles • Vindigo for Palm OS or PocketPC • Frommer's Port@ble Guide • WorldMate
Hotel/Flight information	Users can view current hotel and flight information while planning a trip. Some of these programs require the PDA to connect to the Internet. Others occasionally allow downloading the information to a PDA from a personal computer. Some programs link to booking systems on the Internet, so the user makes reservations directly from a PDA.	• OAG Club • SkyGuide®
GPS	Usually requires additional GPS hardware connected to the PDA. Some software includes mapping data or only displays and saves GPS information, such as location and speed.	• GPS Port@ble Navigator - Travelers Edition • GPS Wireless Navigation System • GPS Atlas

FIGURE 10 Travel software acts as a personal concierge for the business or leisure traveler.

EDUCATIONAL SOFTWARE

With so much to organize, students and instructors greatly benefit from PDA software geared for educational uses (Figure 11). Students load textbook chapters or entire textbooks onto expansion cards and use special software to read the books and highlight key material. Instructors distribute electronic versions of the class syllabus, automatically updating each student's calendar on the students' PDAs. Some schools even acquire PDAs for the entire student body and require their use in the classroom.

EDUCATIONAL SOFTWARE FOR PDAS

Application	Description	Samples
eBooks and references	eBooks are electronic versions of books. eBooks are specially formatted files that may be viewed using Reader software, as noted in Figure 5 on page SF5.53. Many eBooks are available free, and many authors and publishing companies make eBooks available to those who have purchased a hard copy of a particular book.	• Dictionary ToGo • PocketLingo Pro • Formulas for Palm OS® • Speed Reader Plus • The collected works of William Shakespeare for Microsoft Reader
Class schedules and course management	Helps instructors and students manage their respective schedules. The information may include syllabus information distributed in electronic format by an instructor. The software may link to a central data repository of a school as well. The software helps track grading, assignments, to-do lists, instructor office hours, and notes.	• 4.0Student by Handmark • Pocket ClassPro for PocketPC • MyClasses
Roster	Manages grading, rosters, attendance, and contact information for students.	• Teachers P. E. T. • Head Start • Teach File
Review	Includes programs for quizzing students and reviewing coursework. Students often train the application to help the student review troublesome material.	• Math Classic • Mental Arithmetic • Quizzler

FIGURE 11 Educational software benefits both students and instructors.

MULTIMEDIA SOFTWARE

Most PDAs include the capability of viewing images and some are powerful enough to view short video clips. Some PDAs also double as audio players, allowing the user to take his or her favorite music anywhere. PDAs that are more recent contain, or allow the user to attach, a camera or recording device to capture video or audio, and then download the captured media to a personal computer. Some image viewers allow the user to use a PDA as an electronic picture frame while the PDA rests in its cradle on the user's desk. Popular multimedia software for PDAs is listed in Figure 12.

MULTIMEDIA SOFTWARE FOR PDAS

Application	Description	Samples
Picture viewer	Allows a user to view images uploaded to the PDA using software on a personal computer. Some viewers have a slide show mode that rotates through a list of images automatically.	• SplashPhoto • PocketPhoto • Palbum Picture Viewer
Video player	Allows the user to watch video clips on a PDA.	• FireViewer • Windows Media Player for PocketPC • PocketTV for PocketPC
Audio player	Permits a user to listen to his or her favorite music or record and playback voice recordings for meetings or personal audio notes. Some PDAs are equipped with additional hardware such as microphones, headphones, or audio controls to enhance the audio experience.	• AudioPlus • Windows Media Player for PocketPC • Replay Radio

FIGURE 12 Multimedia PDA software gives the user the ability to view images, watch video, and listen to audio.

ENTERTAINMENT SOFTWARE

While on the train ride into work or waiting at the airport, a PDA user can enjoy his or her favorite games on a PDA. The infrared port or wireless connectivity of a PDA allows a user to play some games against other players. Most PDAs include buttons to control games. Figure 13 lists popular entertainment software for PDAs.

ENTERTAINMENT SOFTWARE FOR PDAS

Application	Description	Samples
Strategy	Includes classic board games such as chess, backgammon, and Monopoly™.	• PocketChess • ChessGenius • Handmark Monopoly® • SimCity™
Card	Includes casino games, solitaire games, and other card games.	• AcidSolitaire • BlackJack++ • Pocket Cribbage
Action	Comprised of games that require quick reflexes, including many arcade-style games.	• Tomb Raider • Bejeweled
Puzzle	Thought-provoking puzzles to pass time and sharpen the mind, such as crossword puzzles, mazes, and word games.	• Handmark SCRABBLE® • Crossword

FIGURE 13 Entertainment software allows a user to relax with a PDA and enjoy his or her favorite games.

OBTAINING AND INSTALLING PDA SOFTWARE

PDA software often is available at a computer or electronics store. A significant number of programs are available as shareware, freeware, or trial editions at a number of Web sites. Most of the software listed in the previous figures are accessible on the Web sites listed in Figure 14. Because PDA software usually is smaller than the personal computer counterparts, downloading the software from the Web to your personal computer and then uploading it to your PDA often is the best alternative when you want to try something new. PDA software downloaded from the Web to a personal computer requires that the software be installed using the PDA's synchronization software. Additionally, some personal computer application software includes accompanying PDA software that corresponds with the personal computer software.

PDA software sold in a retail location usually is supplied on a CD-ROM. The CD-ROM first installs the PDA software on a personal computer. The PDA's synchronization software then is used to load the software onto the PDA while the PDA is connected to the personal computer. Depending on the type of software installed, this process may be automatic. Some PDA software is packaged as an add-on card that the user inserts into the PDA's expansion slot. Some Web sites allow the user to browse a software catalog from the PDA's Web browser and download the software directly to the PDA. When synchronizing a PDA on a corporate network, some companies automatically install software to the employees' PDAs with no interaction required from the employee.

WHERE TO GET PDA SOFTWARE

Application	Description	Samples
Web sites	Software publishers make their products available at their Web sites. Several Web sites also exist specifically to distribute PDA software. Tens of thousands of titles are available and most can be downloaded on a trial basis.	www.palmgear.com www.handandgo.com www.pdamd.com
Retail	Many popular software titles can be purchased at electronic and computer stores. The most popular titles at these locations include productivity and entertainment software.	www.bestbuy.com
Develop in-house	Many corporations develop their own PDA software to use internally to meet specific needs. These programs usually tap into existing corporate databases of product and customer information. The companies that produce PDA operating systems often make the development tools for such software available at no cost or a minimal cost.	www.palmsource.com www.microsoft.com/mobile/developer

FIGURE 14 PDA software is available from a number of sources.

Output

Picture Yourself Printing Pictures

A friend of yours, who is a computer guru and always has the latest digital equipment, just sold his *old* digital camera to you for $50. You know it was a great deal! What he considers old equipment actually still is state of the art. This one is a 2-megapixel digital camera that saves pictures on a memory card. You do not have a card reader so you purchase one for about $30 from a local electronics store. At the store, you also buy some high-gloss photo paper.

No more film to purchase or develop ever again! Now you have all the equipment and supplies necessary to take and print high-quality pictures. You immediately take photographs with the digital camera. As soon as the memory card is full, you remove it from the camera and insert it into the card reader. After transferring images from the memory card to the computer's hard disk, you insert the photo paper in your ink-jet printer and print the pictures in a variety of sizes — wallet, 4 x 6, 5 x 7, and 8 x 10. Although the larger prints are a little grainy, the quality of the smaller sizes is great. In the future, you plan to invest in a photo printer so you can print high-quality enlargements, too.

As you read Chapter 6, you will learn about printers and discover other types of output.

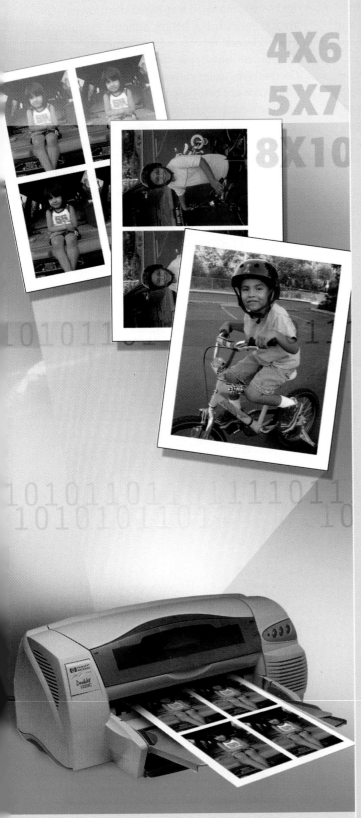

OBJECTIVES

After completing this chapter, you will be able to:

1. Describe the four categories of output

2. Describe the characteristics of a CRT monitor and factors that affect its quality

3. Explain the relationship between a video card and CRT monitor

4. Summarize the characteristics of flat panel monitors, LCD screens, gas plasma displays, and HDTV displays

5. Differentiate between an impact printer and a nonimpact printer

6. Summarize the characteristics of ink-jet printers, photo printers, laser printers, thermal printers, portable printers, label and postage printers, and plotters and large-format printers

7. Describe the methods used for wireless printing

8. Describe the uses of speakers and headsets

9. Identify the output characteristics of fax machines and fax modems, multifunction peripherals, data projectors, joysticks, and wheels

10. Identify output options for physically challenged users

CONTENTS

WHAT IS OUTPUT?

Output is data that has been processed into a useful form. That is, computers process input (data) into output (information). A computer generates several types of output, depending on the hardware and software being used and the requirements of the user.

Users view output on a screen, print it, or hear it though speakers or headsets. Monitors, notebook computers, Tablet PCs, PDAs, and smart phones have screens that allow users to view documents, Web sites, e-mail messages, and other types of output. Some printers produce black-and-white documents, and others produce brilliant colors, enabling users to print color documents, photographs, and transparencies. Through the computer's speakers or a headset, users listen to sounds, music, and voice messages.

While working with a computer, a user encounters four basic categories of output: text, graphics, audio, and video (Figure 6-1). Very often, a single form of output, such as a Web site, includes more than one of these categories.

- Text — Examples of text-based documents are memorandums, letters, announcements, press releases, reports, advertisements, newsletters, envelopes, and mailing labels. On the Web, users view and print many other types of text-based documents. These include newspapers, magazines, books, play or television show transcripts, stock quotes, famous speeches, and historical lectures.

- Graphics — Documents often include graphics to enhance their visual appeal and convey information. Business letters have logos. Reports include charts. Newsletters use drawings, clip art, and photographs. Users print high-quality photographs taken

FIGURE 6-1 Four categories of output are text, graphics, audio, and video.

with a digital camera, eliminating the need for film or film developers. Many Web sites use animated graphics, such as blinking icons, scrolling messages, or simulations.

- Audio — Users insert their favorite music CD in a CD or DVD drive and listen to the music while working on the computer. Software programs such as games, encyclopedias, and simulations often have musical accompaniments for entertainment and audio clips, such as narrations and speeches, to enhance understanding. On the Web, users tune into radio and television stations and listen to audio clips or live broadcasts of interviews, talk shows, sporting events, news, music, and concerts. They also use the Internet to have real-time conversations with friends, coworkers, or family members, just as if they were speaking on the telephone.

- Video — As with audio, software and Web sites often include video clips to enhance understanding. Users watch a live or prerecorded news report, view a movie, see a doctor perform a life-saving surgery, observe a hurricane in action, or enjoy a live performance of their favorite jazz band on the computer.

Attaching a video camera to the computer allows users to watch home movies on the computer. They also can attach a television's antenna or cable to the computer and watch a television program on the computer screen.

An **output device** is any hardware component that conveys information to one or more people. Commonly used output devices include display devices, printers, speakers and headsets, fax machines and fax modems, multifunction peripherals, data projectors, and force-feedback joysticks and wheels. This chapter discusses each of these output devices.

DISPLAY DEVICES

A **display device**, or simply *display*, is an output device that visually conveys text, graphics, and video information. Information on a display device, sometimes called *soft copy*, exists electronically and displays for a temporary period.

Display devices consist of a screen and the components that produce the information on the screen. Desktop computers typically use a monitor as their display device. A **monitor** is a plastic or metal case that houses a display device as a separate peripheral (Figure 6-2). Most mobile computers and devices, by contrast, integrate the display and other components into the same physical case. For example, the display on a notebook computer attaches with hinges. Some PDA displays also attach with a hinge to the device; with others, the display is part of the PDA case.

Most display devices show text, graphics, and video information in color. Some, however, are monochrome. *Monochrome* means the information displays in one color (such as white,

amber, green, black, blue, or gray) on a different color background, for example, black or grayish-white. Some PDAs and other mobile devices use monochrome displays to save battery power. To enhance the quality of their graphics, monochrome displays often use gray scaling. *Gray scaling* involves using many shades of gray from white to black, which provides better contrast on the images.

Two types of display devices are CRT monitors and flat-panel displays. The following sections discuss each of these display devices.

CRT MONITORS

A **CRT monitor** is a desktop monitor that is similar to a standard television because it contains a cathode-ray tube (Figure 6-3). A *cathode-ray tube (CRT)* is a large, sealed glass tube. The front of the tube is the screen. Tiny dots of phosphor material coat the screen on a CRT. Each dot consists of a red, a green, and a blue phosphor. The three dots combine to make up each pixel. Recall from Chapter 5 that a *pixel* (short for picture element) is a single point in an electronic image. Inside the CRT, an electron beam moves back and forth across the back of the screen. This causes the dots on the front of the screen to glow, which produces an image on the screen.

FIGURE 6-2 Most desktop monitors have color displays.

cathode ray tube

CRT monitor

screen

FIGURE 6-3 The core of most desktop monitors is a cathode-ray tube.

CRT monitors for desktop computers are available in various sizes, with the more common being 15, 17, 19, 21, and 22 inches. You measure a monitor the same way as you measure a television, that is, diagonally from one corner of the casing to the other. In addition to monitor size, advertisements also list a monitor's viewable size. The *viewable size* is the diagonal measurement of the actual viewing area provided by the screen in the monitor. A 21-inch monitor, for example, may have a viewable size of 20 inches.

Determining what size monitor to purchase depends on your intended use. A large monitor allows you to view more information on the screen at once, but usually is more expensive. You may want to invest in a 19-inch monitor if you use multiple applications at one time or do a lot of research on the Web. Users working with intense graphics applications, such as desktop publishing and engineering, typically have even larger monitors. Some use two monitors side by side at once — with one monitor showing the left half of a document and the other showing the right half.

CRT Monitor Ergonomics

CRT monitors usually include features to address ergonomic issues. Most monitors have a tilt-and-swivel base that allows users to adjust the angle of the screen to minimize neck strain and reduce glare from overhead lighting. Monitor controls permit users to adjust the brightness, contrast, positioning, height, and width of images. These controls usually are on the front of the monitor for easy access. Newer monitors have digital controls that allow fine-tuning of the display in small increments. An advantage of digital controls is that they allow users quickly to return to the default settings by pressing a reset button.

To help reduce the amount of electricity used by monitors and other computer components, the United States Department of Energy (DOE) and the United States Environmental Protection Agency (EPA) developed the **ENERGY STAR program**. This program encourages manufacturers to create energy-efficient devices that require little power when they are not in use. Monitors and devices that meet ENERGY STAR guidelines display an ENERGY STAR® label (Figure 6-4).

FIGURE 6-4 Products with an ENERGY STAR® label are energy efficient as defined by the Environmental Protection Agency (EPA).

In the past, CRT monitor screens were curved slightly. Many current models have flat screens. A flat screen reduces glare, reflection, and distortion of images. With a flat screen, users do not notice as much eyestrain and fatigue. Thus, a flat screen is an ergonomic screen.

FAQ 6-1

What can I do to ease eyestrain while using my computer?

Blink your eyes every five seconds. Use a glare screen. Adjust the room lighting. Use larger fonts or zoom a display. Take an eye break every 10 to 15 minutes: look into the distance and focus on an object for 20 to 30 seconds; roll your eyes in a complete circle; and then close your eyes for at least 30 seconds. If you wear glasses, ask your doctor about computer glasses.

For more information about computer eye strain, visit the Discovering Computers 2004 FAQ Web page (**scsite.com/dc2004/faq**). Click Eye Strain below Chapter 6.

Quality of a CRT Monitor

The quality of a CRT monitor depends largely on its resolution, dot pitch, and refresh rate. As mentioned in Chapter 5, **resolution** describes the sharpness and clearness of an image. Manufacturers state the resolution of a monitor in pixels. For example, a monitor set at an 800 x 600 resolution displays up to 800 pixels per horizontal inch and 600 pixels per vertical inch, for a total of 480,000 pixels to create a screen image.

Most monitors support a variety of screen resolutions. Standard CRT monitors today usually display up to a maximum of 1600 x 1200 pixels, with 800 x 600 often the norm. High-end CRT monitors (for the power user) can display up to a maximum of 2048 x 1536 pixels.

WEB LINK 6-1

CRT Monitors

Visit the Discovering Computers 2004 WEB LINK page (**scsite .com/dc2004/weblink**). Click CRT Monitors below Chapter 6.

Setting a monitor to display a higher resolution uses a greater number of pixels and thus provides a smoother image. As the resolution increases, however, some items on the screen appear smaller, such as menu bars, toolbars, and rulers (Figure 6-5). For this reason, you would not use a high resolution on a small display, such as a 15-inch monitor, because the small characters would be difficult to read. The display resolution you choose is a matter of preference. Larger monitors typically look best at a higher resolution, and smaller monitors look best at a lower resolution. For example, a 21-inch monitor may be set at a 1600 x 1200 resolution, while a 17-inch monitor may be set at a resolution of 800 x 600. A higher resolution also is desirable for graphics applications. A lower resolution usually is satisfactory for business applications such as word processing.

Dot pitch is another measurement of image clarity on a CRT monitor. *Dot pitch*, sometimes called *pixel pitch*, is the distance in millimeters between each like-colored pixel on a display. The smaller the distance between the pixels, the sharper the image. Text created with a smaller dot pitch is easier to read. To minimize eye fatigue, use a monitor with a dot pitch of .29 millimeters or lower. Advertisements normally specify a monitor's dot pitch.

Refresh rate is yet another measure of a CRT monitor's quality. *Refresh rate*, also called *scan rate*, is the speed that a monitor redraws the images on the screen. Ideally, a CRT monitor's refresh rate should be fast enough to maintain a constant, flicker-free image. A slower refresh rate causes the image to fade and then flicker as it is redrawn. This flicker can lead to eye fatigue and cause headaches for some users. Refresh rate is the number of times per second the screen is redrawn and is expressed in hertz (Hz). Although most people can tolerate a vertical refresh rate of 60 Hz, a high-quality CRT monitor will provide a vertical refresh rate of at least 75 Hz. This means the image on the screen redraws itself vertically 75 times in a second.

CRT monitors produce a small amount of electromagnetic radiation. *Electromagnetic radiation (EMR)* is a magnetic field that travels at the speed of light. Excessive amounts of EMR can pose a health risk. To be safe, all high-quality CRT monitors comply with MPR II standards. *MPR II* is a set of standards that defines acceptable levels of EMR for a monitor. To protect yourself even further, sit at arm's length from the CRT monitor because EMR only travels a short distance. In addition, EMR is greatest on the sides and back of the CRT monitor. Read Issue 6-1 for a related discussion.

Figure 6-5a (screen resolution at 800 x 600)

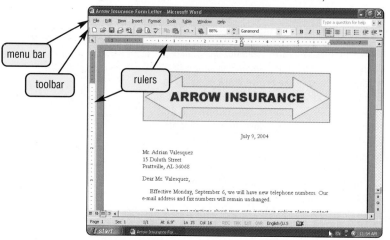

Figure 6-5b (screen resolution at 1600 x 1200)

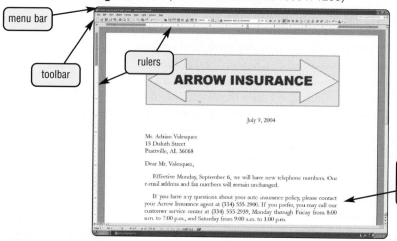

FIGURE 6-5 This comparison illustrates that some elements on the screen become smaller when the resolution is increased from 800 x 600 to 1600 x 1200. The higher resolution also displays more text on the screen.

ISSUE 6-1

Who Is Responsible for Disposing of an Old Monitor?

Studies conducted by the National Recycling Coalition forecast that by the year 2007, up to 500 million computers will become obsolete. According to environmentalists, disposing of old CRT monitors will be a major problem. CRT monitors can contain as much as eight pounds of lead, which protects users from radiation. When monitors are discarded in a landfill, however, the lead pollutes the environment and can cause developmental problems in children exposed to it. In the United States, several states already have proposed, or passed, laws prohibiting the dumping of old monitors in landfills. Other countries have taken a more extreme approach. In Germany, for example, because the computer makers are responsible for the eventual disposal of computer components, the price of every computer includes a fee for the cost of recycling. Should laws be enacted on the federal level barring the disposal of old monitors in landfills? Why or why not? Should manufacturers be made responsible for disposal of computer components? Why?

For more information about disposing of monitors, visit the Discovering Computers 2004 Issues Web page (**scsite.com/dc2004/issues**). Click Issue #1 below Chapter 6.

Video Cards and CRT Monitors

Many CRT monitors use an analog signal to produce an image. To display high-quality color on this type of CRT monitor, a desktop computer sends a signal through a video card on the motherboard. A cable on the CRT monitor plugs into a port on the video card. A **video card**, also called a *graphics card*, converts digital output from the computer into an analog video signal and sends the signal through the cable to the monitor, which displays output on the screen (Figure 6-6).

The number of colors a video card displays is determined by its bit depth. The video card's *bit depth*, also called the *color depth*, is the number of bits it uses to store information about each pixel. For example, an 8-bit video card (also called 8-bit color) uses 8 bits to store information about each pixel. Thus, this video card can display 256 different colors (computed as 2^8 or $2 \times 2 \times 2 \times 2 \times 2 \times 2 \times 2 \times 2$). A 24-bit video card uses 24 bits to store information about each pixel and can display 2^{24} or 16.7 million colors. The greater the number of bits, the better the resulting image.

FIGURE 6-6   HOW VIDEO TRAVELS FROM THE PROCESSOR TO A CRT MONITOR

Step 1: The processor sends digital video data to the video card.

processor

0010011011010101101

Step 2: The video card's digital-to-analog converter (DAC) converts the digital video data to an analog signal.

Step 3: The analog signal is sent through a cable to the CRT monitor.

Step 4: The CRT monitor separates the analog signal into red, green, and blue signals.

Step 5: Electron guns fire the three color signals to the front of the CRT.

Step 6: An image is displayed on the screen when the electrons hit phosphor dots on the back of the screen.

WEB LINK 6-2

Video Memory

Visit the Discovering Computers 2004 WEB LINK page (**scsite.com/dc2004/weblink**). Click Video Memory below Chapter 6.

Over the years, several video standards have been developed to define the resolution, number of colors, and other display properties. Today, *VESA* (*Video Electronics Standards Association*), which consists of video card and monitor manufacturers, develops video standards. Most current video cards support the *SVGA* (*super video graphics array*) standard, which also supports resolutions and colors in the VGA standard. The table in Figure 6-7 outlines the suggested resolution and number of displayed colors in the MDA, VGA, XGA, SVGA, and beyond SVGA standards.

For a monitor to display images using the resolution and number of colors defined by a video standard, the monitor must support the same video standard, and the video card must be capable of communicating appropriate signals to the monitor. Both the video card and the monitor must support the video standard to generate the desired resolution and number of colors.

A video card also must have enough memory to generate the resolution and number of colors you want to display. The memory in a video card stores information about each pixel. Video cards use many types of video memory: VRAM (video RAM), WRAM (window RAM), SGRAM (synchronous graphics RAM), or SDRAM (synchronous DRAM).

Manufacturers state video memory in megabytes. The table in Figure 6-8 outlines the amount of video memory required for various screen resolutions and color depth configurations. For example, if you want a 1600 x 1200 resolution with 32-bit color, then your video card should have at least 8 MB of video memory. Most video cards have 16 MB to 128 MB of video memory.

In addition to memory chips, the video card contains a processor chip, sometimes called a *graphics processing unit* (*GPU*) because it performs calculations used to display images on the screen. A video card's processor and memory chips generate a lot of heat. Thus, video cards usually contain a fan or heat sink to keep the chips from overheating.

VIDEO STANDARDS

Standard	Suggested Resolution	Maximum Possible Colors
Monochrome Display Adapter (MDA)	720 x 350	1 for text
Video Graphics Array (VGA)	640 x 480	16
	320 x 200	256
Extended Graphics Array (XGA)	1024 x 768	256
	640 x 480	65,536
Super Video Graphics Array (SVGA)	800 x 600	16.7 million
	1024 x 768	16.7 million
	1280 x 1024	16.7 million
	1600 x 1200	16.7 million
Beyond SVGA	1920 x 1440	16.7 million
	2048 x 1536	16.7 million

FIGURE 6-7 Various video standards are available.

VARIOUS VIDEO CARD CONFIGURATIONS

Video Memory	Color Depth	Number of Colors	Maximum Resolution
1 MB	8-bit	256	1024 x 768
	16-bit	65,536	800 x 600
2 MB	8-bit	256	1024 x 768
	16-bit	65,536	1280 x 1024
	24-bit	16.7 million	800 x 600
4 MB	24-bit	16.7 million	1024 x 768
6 MB	24-bit	16.7 million	1280 x 1024
8 MB	32-bit	16.7 million	1600 x 1200
16 MB	32-bit	16.7 million	1920 x 1440
32 MB	32-bit	16.7 million	2048 x 1536
64 MB	32-bit	16.7 million	2048 x 1536
128 MB	32-bit	16.7 million	2048 x 1536

FIGURE 6-8 Video memory requirements vary for a range of screen resolutions.

FLAT-PANEL DISPLAYS

A *flat-panel display* is a display with a shallow depth that does not use CRT technology. Flat panel monitors, LCD displays, gas plasma displays, and many HDTV displays are types of flat-panel displays. The following sections discuss various types of flat-panel displays.

Flat Panel Monitors

A **flat panel monitor**, also called an *LCD monitor*, is a desktop monitor that uses a liquid crystal display instead of a cathode-ray tube to produce images on a screen (Figure 6-9). These monitors produce sharp, flicker-free displays.

Flat panel monitors have a much smaller *footprint* than do CRT monitors; that is, they take up less desk space. For additional space savings, some flat panel monitors are wall mountable. A flat panel monitor also uses less than one-third the power consumed by a CRT monitor, produces less heat, and does not produce electromagnetic radiation. Flat panel monitors are available in a variety of sizes, with the more common being 15, 17, 18, 20, 21, and 23 inches. Read Issue 6-2 for a related discussion.

Mobile computers, such as notebook computers and Tablet PCs, and mobile devices, such as PDAs and smart phones, have LCD screens (Figure 6-10). Notebook computer screens are available in a variety of sizes, with the more common being 14.1, 15, and 16 inches. Tablet PC screens range from 8 inches to 15 inches. PDA screens average 3 inches wide by 4 inches tall. On smart phones, users see approximately five lines of text at a time on the display.

FIGURE 6-9 A flat panel monitor is much thinner and weighs less than a CRT monitor.

ISSUE 6-2

Are Thin Flat Panel Monitors In?

Home and business users currently spend a substantial amount of time working on computers. To reduce eyestrain and other types of monitor-related health conditions, it is important users have high-quality monitors that produce crisp, bright images. Until recently, CRT (cathode-ray tube) technology dominated the monitor industry. Today, however, flat panel monitors are transforming the way people look at their computers. The space-saving, brighter flat panel monitor, that uses LCD technology, has emerged as a key competitor in the monitor market. Although the goal of the flat panel monitor industry is to replace the CRT monitor as the dominant desktop monitor, some industry experts predict that flat panel monitors will appear on only one-half of users' desktops in the coming years. Can flat panel monitors compete against CRT monitors for desktop applications? Will price issues affect flat panel monitor sales? If so, how? Will health-related concerns influence the sales of flat panel monitors?

For more information about flat panel monitors, visit the Discovering Computers 2004 Issues Web page (**scsite.com/dc2004/issues**). Click Issue #2 below Chapter 6.

FIGURE 6-10 Notebook computers and Tablet PCs have color LCD screens. Some PDAs have color displays and a few smart phones even have color displays.

E-books are another mobile device that use an LCD screen. An **e-book** (*electronic book*) is a small, book-sized computer that allows users to read, save, highlight, bookmark, and add notes to online text (Figure 6-11). You download new book content to an e-book, mobile device, or computer from the Web. Some e-book vendors sell time-based permits, in which the e-book content disappears after the amount of time purchased has expired. To obtain the same functionality as an e-book device, some users install a program called *Microsoft Reader* onto a PDA, notebook computer, or desktop computer.

Microsoft developed a technology called ClearType® to improve the quality of reading material on LCD screens, such as an e-book. *ClearType* changes the brightness and contrast of pixels surrounding each letter to give the letter more of a printed appearance. The goal of ClearType is to make on-screen reading as natural as reading from printed material.

LCD Technology

Similar to LCDs in watches and calculators, a **liquid crystal display (LCD)** uses a liquid compound to present information on a screen. Computer LCDs typically have fluorescent tubes that emit light waves toward the liquid-crystal cells, which are sandwiched between two sheets of material (Figure 6-12). When an electrical charge passes through the cells, the cells twist. This twisting causes some light waves to be blocked and allows others to pass through, creating images on the screen.

FIGURE 6-11   E-books, which are about the size of a paperback book, use an LCD display. Users download new book content from Web sites to their e-books or other mobile devices.

FIGURE 6-12   HOW LCD WORKS

Step 1:
A panel of fluorescent tubes emits light waves through a polarizing glass filter, which guides the light toward the layer of liquid crystal cells.

Step 2:
As the light passes through the liquid crystal, an electrical charge causes some of the cells to twist — making the light waves bend as they pass through a color filter.

Step 3:
When the light reaches the second polarizing glass filter, light is allowed to pass through any cells that line up at the same angle as the first polarizing glass filter. The absence and presence of colored light cause the image to display on the screen.

liquid crystal cells
transparent electrodes
alignment layer
color filter
polarizing glass filter
fluorescent tube panel

Flat panel monitors and LCD screens produce color using either passive-matrix or active-matrix technology. An *active-matrix display*, also known as a *TFT (thin-film transistor) display*, uses a separate transistor for each liquid crystal cell and thus displays high-quality color that is viewable from all angles. A newer type of TFT, called *organic LED (OLED)*, uses organic molecules that produce an even brighter, easier-to-read display than standard TFT displays. Also, OLEDs are less expensive to produce, consume less power, and can be fabricated on flexible surfaces.

A *passive-matrix display* uses fewer transistors and requires less power than an active-matrix display. The color on a passive-matrix display often is not as bright as an active-matrix display. Users view images on a passive-matrix display best when working directly in front of it. The latest passive-matrix displays use *high-performance addressing* (HPA), which provides image quality near that of TFT displays. Passive-matrix displays are less expensive than active-matrix displays.

LCD Quality

The quality of a flat panel monitor or LCD screen depends primarily on its resolution, which generally is proportional to the size of a monitor or screen. That is, the resolution increases for larger monitors and devices. For example, a 15-inch flat panel monitor typically has a resolution of 1024 x 768, while a 17-inch has a resolution of 1280 x 1024. Unlike CRT monitors that can display a variety of resolutions, LCDs usually are geared for a specific resolution. When set at other resolutions, the quality often is not as good as the manufacturer's original resolution.

For most business applications, refresh rates usually are not an issue with flat panel monitors or LCD displays because the images either are on or off. If you intend to watch videos, movies, or play graphic-intensive games, however, slower refresh rates may be distracting. Thus, users of these applications often opt for a higher hertz or a CRT monitor.

An important measure of LCD displays is the *response time*, which is the time in milliseconds (ms) that it takes to turn a pixel on or off. Flat panel monitors' response times average 25 ms. The lower the number, the faster the response time.

Brightness of a flat panel monitor or LCD screen is measured in nits. A *nit* is a unit of visible light intensity equal to one candela (formerly called candlepower) per square meter. The *candela* is the standard unit of luminous intensity. Flat panel monitors today range from 200 to 350 nits. The higher the nits, the brighter the display.

Video Cards and Flat Panel Monitors

Flat panel monitors use a digital signal to produce a picture. When you plug a flat panel monitor into a video card that delivers analog signals, the flat panel monitor converts the analog signal from the video card back to a digital signal. This is one reason why flat panel monitors are more expensive than CRT monitors, sometimes costing two to three times as much as a comparable CRT monitor.

Ideally, a flat panel monitor should plug into a *DVI (Digital Video Interface)* port on the computer. Developed by the *Digital Display Working Group (DDWG)*, a *DVI port* accepts digital signals directly, eliminating the need for the analog to digital conversion. Newer video cards have DVI ports, some of which send both digital and analog signals to a monitor (Figure 6-13). These video cards usually also have a standard monitor port and an *S-video port*, allowing users to connect external devices such as a television, DVD player, or video recorder, to the computer.

WEB LINK 6-3

LCD Technology

Visit the Discovering Computers 2004 WEB LINK page (**scsite .com/dc2004/weblink**). Click LCD Technology below Chapter 6.

FAQ 6-2

Is a flat display the same as a flat-panel display?

No. A *flat display* refers to a CRT monitor that has a flat screen. A flat-panel display, by contrast, has a shallow depth and uses LCD, gas plasma, or some technology other than CRT.

For more information about flat-panel displays, visit the Discovering Computers 2004 FAQ Web page (**scsite.com/dc2004/faq**). Click Flat-Panel Displays below Chapter 6.

standard monitor port

S-video port

DVI port

FIGURE 6-13 Ports on a video card.

Gas Plasma Displays

Large business users or power users sometimes have gas plasma displays, which often measure more than 50 inches wide (Figure 6-14). A **gas plasma display** is a display that uses gas plasma technology, which substitutes a layer of gas for the liquid crystal material in a flat panel monitor. When voltage is applied, the gas releases ultraviolet (UV) light. This UV light causes the pixels on the screen to glow and form an image.

Gas plasma displays offer larger screen sizes and higher display quality than flat panel monitors but are much more expensive. These displays also can hang directly on a wall.

FIGURE 6-14   Large gas plasma displays can measure more than 50 inches wide.

Televisions and HDTV Displays

Home users who have a set-top box may have a television as a display device. Connecting a computer to an analog television requires an *NTSC converter*, which converts the digital signal from the computer into an analog signal that the television can display. NTSC stands for *National Television Standards Committee* and consists of industry members who have technical expertise about television-related issues. The best analog televisions have a resolution of only 520 x 400 pixels. Thus, users are turning to *digital television* (*DTV*) for crisper, higher-quality output.

Although televisions can use either CRT or flat-panel display technology, the trend in newer digital models is the flat-panel display.

Digital television signals provide two major advantages over analog signals. First, digital signals produce a higher-quality picture. Second, many programs can be broadcast on a single digital channel, whereas only one program can be broadcast on an analog channel. Currently, a limited number of U.S. television stations broadcast digital signals. By 2006, all stations must be broadcasting digital signals, as mandated by the FCC.

HDTV (*high-definition television*) is the most advanced form of digital television, working with digital broadcast signals, transmitting digital sound, supporting wide screens, and providing resolutions up to 1920 x 1080 pixels. With HDTV, the broadcast signals are digitized when they are sent via either satellite or cable. A decoder in your home receives the signal and sends it into the HDTV display.

As the cost of HDTV displays becomes more reasonable, home users will begin to use it as their computer's display device. HDTV also is ideal for presenting material to a large group. HDTV technology makes the use of interactive TV more widespread. **Interactive TV** is a two-way communications technology in which users interact with television programming. Instead of adding special equipment to an analog television, HDTV works directly with interactive TV. Uses of interactive TV include selecting a movie from a central library of movies, voting or responding to network questionnaires, banking and shopping, playing games, and video conferencing.

FAQ 6-3

Can I watch digital television broadcasts on my analog television?

Yes, if you buy a device that converts the digital signal to an analog signal. The image on your analog television, however, will not have HDTV resolution.

For more information about HDTV, visit the Discovering Computers 2004 FAQ Web page (**scsite.com/dc2004/faq**). Click HDTV below Chapter 6.

QUIZ YOURSELF 6-1

To check your knowledge of categories of output, CRT monitors, and flat-panel displays, visit the Discovering Computers 2004 Quiz Yourself Web page (**scsite.com/dc2004/quiz**). Click Objectives 1 – 4 below Chapter 6.

PRINTERS

A **printer** is an output device that produces text and graphics on a physical medium such as paper or transparency film. Printed information, called *hard copy*, exists physically and is a more permanent form of output than that presented on a display device (soft copy).

A hard copy, also called a *printout*, is either in portrait or landscape orientation (Figure 6-15). A printout in *portrait orientation* is taller than it is wide, with information printed across the shorter width of the paper. A printout in *landscape orientation* is wider than it is tall, with information printed across the widest part of the paper. Letters, reports, and books typically use portrait orientation. Spreadsheets, slide shows, and graphics often use landscape orientation.

Home computer users might print less than a hundred pages a week. Small business computer users might print several hundred pages a day. Users of mainframe computers, such as large utility companies that send printed statements to hundreds of thousands of customers each month, require printers that are capable of printing thousands of pages per hour.

To meet this range of printing needs, many different printers exist with varying speeds, capabilities, and printing methods. Figure 6-16 presents a list of questions to help you decide on the printer best suited to your needs. Read Looking Ahead 6-1 for a look at the next generation of paper.

1. What is my budget?
2. How fast must my printer print?
3. Do I need a color printer?
4. What is the cost per page for printing?
5. Do I need multiple copies of documents?
6. Will I print graphics?
7. Do I want to print photographs?
8. Do I want to print directly from a memory card or other type of miniature storage media?
9. What types of paper does the printer use?
10. What sizes of paper does the printer accept?
11. Do I want to print on both sides of the paper?
12. How much paper can the printer tray hold?
13. Will the printer work with my computer and software?
14. How much do supplies such as ink and paper cost?
15. Can the printer print on envelopes and transparencies?
16. How many envelopes can the printer print at a time?
17. How much printing do I print now, and what will I be printing in a year or two?
18. Will the printer be connected to a network?
19. Do I want wireless printing capability?

FIGURE 6-16   Questions to ask when purchasing a printer.

Figure 6-15a   (portrait orientation)

Figure 6-15b (landscape orientation)

FIGURE 6-15   Portrait orientation is taller than it is wide. Landscape orientation is wider than it is tall.

LOOKING AHEAD 6-1

Electronic Paper Writes a New Page

Magic wands often are found in fairy tales and in magicians' hands, but they may be finding the way to your home or office. The wands could be used to create images and text on electronic reusable paper.

Engineers at Xerox PARC (Palo Alto Research Center) and the Massachusetts Institute of Technology Media Laboratory are leaders in this technology. The Xerox inventors named their product Gyricon, which is the Greek word for rotating image. Each sheet has millions of beads randomly dispersed in oil between thin, transparent, plastic sheets. A bead is smaller than a grain of sand and has two contrasting colors, such as black and white or red and white; it rotates to display one of these colors when a voltage is applied to the sheet's surface. The various color patterns form letters and images that remain until a new voltage pattern changes the display.

The Xerox researchers envision waving a wand over the reusable paper, so the sheets can function as an all-in-one printer, copier, fax machine, and scanner. The technology also has possibilities in the advertising field, where in-store signs and prices can be updated regularly, and for electronic newspapers and magazines.

For a look at the next generation of electronic paper, visit the Discovering Computers 2004 Looking Ahead Web page (**scsite.com/dc2004/looking**). Click Looking Ahead #1 below Chapter 6.

A printer often connects by a cable to a parallel port or a USB port. Two categories of printers are impact and nonimpact. The following pages discuss various types of impact and nonimpact printers.

Impact Printers

An **impact printer** forms characters and graphics on a piece of paper by striking a mechanism against an inked ribbon that physically contacts the paper. Impact printers characteristically are noisy because of this striking activity. These printers commonly produce *near letter quality (NLQ)* output, which is print quality slightly less clear than what is acceptable for business letters.

Companies may use impact printers for routine jobs such as printing mailing labels, envelopes, and invoices. Impact printers also are ideal for printing multipart forms because they easily print through many layers of paper. Factories and retail counters use impact printers because these printers withstand dusty environments, vibrations, and extreme temperatures.

Two commonly used types of impact printers are dot-matrix printers and line printers. The following paragraphs discuss each of these printers.

DOT-MATRIX PRINTERS   A **dot-matrix printer** is an impact printer that produces printed images when tiny wire pins on a print head mechanism strike an inked ribbon (Figure 6-17). When the ribbon presses against the paper, it creates dots that form characters and graphics.

Most dot-matrix printers use *continuous-form paper*, in which thousands of sheets of paper are connected together end to end. The pages have holes along the sides to help feed the paper through the printer. Perforations along the inside of the holes and at each fold allow users to separate the sheets into standard-sized sheets of paper, such as 8½-by-11 inches. Many dot-matrix printers can print pages in either portrait or landscape orientation.

The print head mechanism on a dot-matrix printer contains 9 to 24 pins, depending on the manufacturer and the printer model. A higher number of pins means the printer prints more dots per character, which results in higher print quality.

The speed of a dot-matrix printer is measured by the number of characters per second (cps) it can print. The speed of most dot-matrix printers ranges from 300 to 1100 characters per second (cps), depending on the desired print quality.

LINE PRINTERS   A **line printer** is a high-speed impact printer that prints an entire line at a time (Figure 6-18). The speed of a line printer is measured by the number of lines per minute (lpm) it can print. Some line printers print as many as 3,000 lpm. Mainframes, midrange servers, or networked applications, such as manufacturing, distribution, or shipping, often use line printers. These printers typically use 11-by-17-inch continuous-form paper.

continuous-form paper

FIGURE 6-17   A dot-matrix printer produces printed images when tiny pins strike an inked ribbon.

FIGURE 6-18   A line printer is a high-speed printer often connected to a mainframe, midrange server, or network.

Two popular types of line printers used for high-volume output are band and shuttle-matrix. A *band printer* prints fully formed characters when hammers strike a horizontal, rotating band that contains shapes of numbers, letters of the alphabet, and other characters. A *shuttle-matrix printer* functions more like a dot-matrix printer. The difference is the shuttle-matrix printer moves a series of print hammers back and forth horizontally at incredibly high speeds, as compared with standard line printers. Unlike a band printer, a shuttle-matrix printer prints characters in various fonts and font sizes.

Nonimpact Printers

A **nonimpact printer** forms characters and graphics on a piece of paper without actually striking the paper. Some spray ink, while others use heat or pressure to create images. These printers are much quieter than the previously discussed impact printers because nonimpact printers do not strike the paper.

Commonly used nonimpact printers are ink-jet printers, photo printers, laser printers, thermal printers, portable printers, label and postage printers, plotters, and large-format printers. The following sections discuss each of these printers.

Ink-Jet Printers

An **ink-jet printer** is a type of nonimpact printer that forms characters and graphics by spraying tiny drops of liquid ink onto a piece of paper. Ink-jet printers have become the most popular type of color printer for use in the home because of their lower cost and *letter-quality (LQ)* print, which is an acceptable quality of print for business letters (Figure 6-19). A reasonable quality ink-jet printer costs less than a hundred dollars.

Ink-jet printers produce text and graphics in both black-and-white and color on a variety of paper types. Ink-jet printers normally use individual sheets of paper stored in one or two removable or stationary trays. Available paper types include plain paper, ink-jet paper, photo paper, glossy paper, and perhaps banner paper. Some ink-jet printers can print photographic-quality images on any of these types of paper. Others require heavier weight ink-jet paper for better-looking color documents.

FIGURE 6-19 Ink-jet printers are the most popular type of color printer used in the home.

Ink-jet printers also print on other materials such as envelopes, labels, index cards, greeting card paper, transparencies, and iron-on T-shirt transfers. Many ink-jet printers include software for creating greeting cards, banners, business cards, letterheads, and transparencies. Read Issue 6-3 for a related discussion.

As with many other input and output devices, one factor that determines the quality of an ink-jet printer is its resolution, or sharpness and clarity. Printer resolution is measured by the number of *dots per inch* (*dpi*) a printer can output. With an ink-jet printer, a dot is a drop of ink. A higher dpi means the drops of ink are smaller. Most ink-jet printers range from 300 to 2400 dpi. Printers with a higher dpi usually are more expensive.

As shown in Figure 6-20, the higher the dpi, the better the print quality. The difference in quality becomes noticeable when the size of the printed image increases. That is, a wallet-sized image printed at 300 dpi may look similar in quality to one printed at 1200 dpi. When you increase the size of the image, to 5 x 7 for example, the printout of the 300 dpi resolution looks grainier than the one printed using a 1200 dpi resolution.

The speed of an ink-jet printer is measured by the number of pages per minute (ppm) it can print. Most ink-jet printers print from 3 to 19 ppm. Graphics and colors print at a slower rate. For example, an ink-jet printer may print 17 ppm for black text and only 13 ppm for color and/or graphics.

FIGURE 6-20 You will notice a higher quality output with printers that can print at a higher dpi.

The print head mechanism in an ink-jet printer contains ink-filled print cartridges. Each cartridge has fifty to several hundred small ink holes, or nozzles. The steps in Figure 6-21 illustrate how a drop of ink appears on a page. Each nozzle in the print cartridge is similar to an individual pin on a dot-matrix printer. Just as any combination of dot-matrix pins can be activated, the ink propels through any combination of the nozzles to form a character or image on the paper. A *bubble-jet printer* is a printer that uses a technology very similar to the ink-jet, that is, propelling ink through tiny nozzles.

When the print cartridge runs out of ink, you simply replace the cartridge. Most ink-jet printers have at least two print cartridges: one containing black ink and the other(s) containing colors. These cartridges cost approximately $30 each. The number of pages a single cartridge can print varies by manufacturer and the type of documents you print. In some cases, a single cartridge might print as many as 300 pages.

On average, it costs from $.03 to $.05 per page for black ink and $.10 to $.15 per page for color ink. When coupled with premium photo paper, the cost for a high-quality photograph increases to about $1.00 per page.

ISSUE 6-3

Short of Cash?

Some college students found a solution to their money problems: they made their own. With a scanner, personal computer, and color printer, they produced bogus bills and passed more than $1,000 in counterfeit currency before they were caught. As printer quality improves, an estimated $1 million in counterfeit currency is passed every week. Police have arrested counterfeiters ranging from high school students to senior citizens. Spotting fake money is not that difficult, but most people never look that closely. Counterfeiting does not stop with money. With templates for diplomas, degrees, transcripts, Social Security cards, driver's licenses, birth certificates, and Green Cards available on the Web, almost any document can be produced. As one federal agent points out, counterfeiting has gone from a high-skill, low-tech job to a high-tech, low-skill job. Should printer manufacturers take responsibility for this problem? Why or why not? What, if anything, could printer makers do? Can you offer any other possible solutions? What should be the penalty for selling counterfeit documents online?

For more information about counterfeit cash, visit the Discovering Computers 2004 Issues Web page (**scsite.com/dc2004/issues**). Click Issue #3 below Chapter 6.

FIGURE 6-21   HOW AN INK-JET PRINTER WORKS

print cartridge

print head   nozzle

resistor

firing
chamber

bubble   nozzle   ink   paper   ink   ink dot

Step 1:
A small resistor heats
the ink, causing the ink
to boil and form a
vapor bubble.

Step 2:
The vapor bubble forces
the ink through the
nozzle.

Step 3:
Ink drops onto the paper.

Step 4:
As the vapor bubble
collapses, fresh ink is
drawn into the firing
chamber.

WEB LINK 6-4

Ink-Jet Printers
Visit the Discovering
Computers 2004 WEB
LINK page (**scsite
.com/dc2004/weblink**).
Click Ink-Jet Printers
below Chapter 6.

FAQ 6-4

Can ink-jet cartridges be refilled?

Yes. An ink-jet refill kit costs about one-half the
price of a new cartridge. Keep a spare refill kit on
hand, so you can refill an empty cartridge immediately. Once an empty cartridge dries, its ink jets
may clog. While refilling, wear the latex gloves
supplied with the kit and be careful not to squeeze
the cartridge — which may cause it to ooze ink
onto hands, clothing, furniture, or equipment.

For more information about ink-jet refill kits, visit
the Discovering Computers 2004 FAQ Web page
(**scsite.com/dc2004/faq**). Click Ink-Jet Refill Kits
below Chapter 6.

Photo Printers

A **photo printer** is a color printer that
produces photo-lab-quality pictures. Some
photo printers print just one or two sizes of
images, for example, 3 x 5 inches and 4 x 6
inches. Others print up to letter size, legal size,
or even as large as 13 x 19 inches. Some even
print panoramic photographs. Read Apply It
6-1 for more information.

APPLY IT 6-1

Picture This: Printing Digital Photographs

Seeing is believing. When you are ready to share printed copies of images you
took with your digital camera, the right paper can help you get the best results.

Many photo papers are available, so you need to look at the specifications
printed on the cartons and then match the products to your needs and budget.
To start, consider the surface finishes: high gloss, soft gloss, satin, or matte.

Next, look at the paper weight, which is measured in pounds. Professional
papers have the highest quality and are the heaviest, with weights ranging from
44 to 58 pounds. Price per sheet is about 50 cents. Premium papers have
weights from 24 to 32 pounds and cost about 15 cents per sheet. Everyday presentation and document papers are best for reports and generally weigh 20 to 24
pounds. Each sheet costs approximately 2 cents.

Another factor is paper brightness. The higher the brightness rating, the more
brilliant the whiteness. Brightness ranges from 84 to 113+.

Acid-free paper will not crumble or yellow over time, so it is good to use for
important photos that you will keep for a long time. Other considerations are
using recycled paper and the option of two-sided printing.

For more information about photo papers, visit the Discovering Computers
2004 Apply It Web page (**scsite.com/dc2004/apply**). Click Apply It #1 below
Chapter 6.

WEB LINK 6-5

Photo Printers

Visit the Discovering
Computers 2004 WEB
LINK page (**scsite
.com/dc2004/weblink**).
Click Photo Printers
below Chapter 6.

Many inexpensive photo printers use ink-jet technology. With models that can print letter-sized documents, users connect the photo printer to their computer and use it for all their printing needs. For a few hundred dollars, this type of photo printer is ideal for the home or small business user. Other photo printer technologies are discussed later in the chapter.

Many photo printers have a built-in card slot so the printer can print digital photographs directly from a media card (Figure 6-22).

That is, you do not need to transfer the images from the media card to the computer to print them. Simply remove the media card from the digital camera and insert it into the printer's card slot. Then, push buttons on the printer to select the desired photo, specify the number of copies, and indicate the size of the printed image. Some photo printers have built-in LCD color screens, allowing users to view and enhance the pictures before printing them.

FIGURE 6-22   HOW A PHOTO PRINTER PRINTS DIRECTLY FROM A MEDIA CARD

Step 1:
Take the photograph with the digital camera and store it on the media card in the camera. Remove the media card.

media card

photo printer

Step 2:
Insert the media card into the card reader on the photo printer.

media cards

Step 4:
Remove the printed photo from the printer.

Step 3:
Use the menu to select the desired image to print, view it on the LCD screen, edit it if necessary, choose the number of copies to print, select the size of the print, and then print the image.

Laser Printers

A **laser printer** is a high-speed, high-quality nonimpact printer (Figure 6-23). Laser printers for personal computers ordinarily use individual sheets of paper stored in one or more removable trays that slide into the printer case. Some laser printers have built-in trays that accommodate different sizes of paper, while others require separate trays for letter- and legal-sized paper. Most laser printers have a manual feed slot where you can insert individual sheets and envelopes. You also can print transparencies on a laser printer.

Laser printers print text and graphics in very high quality resolutions, usually ranging from 600 to 2400 dpi. While laser printers usually cost more than ink-jet printers, they also are much faster. A laser printer for the home and small office user typically prints text at speeds of 9 to 30 ppm. Laser printers for large business users print more than 150 ppm.

Depending on the quality and speed of the printer, the cost of a black-and-white laser printer ranges from a few hundred to several thousand dollars for the home and small office user, and several hundred thousand dollars for the large business user. The higher the resolution and speed, the more expensive the printer. Although color laser printers are available, they are relatively expensive, with prices for the home and small business user starting at about $2,000.

When printing a document, laser printers process and store the entire page before they actually print it. For this reason, laser printers sometimes are called page printers. Storing a page before printing requires that the laser printer has a certain amount of memory in the device.

Depending on the amount of graphics you intend to print, a laser printer for the home or small business user can have up to 384 MB of memory. To print a full-page 600-dpi picture, for instance, you might need 16 MB of memory in the printer. If the printer does not have enough memory to print the picture, either it will print as much of the picture as its memory will allow, or it will display an error message and not print any of the picture. If the printer memory is expandable, inserting a memory module into the printer's expansion slot(s) increases the memory.

Laser printers use software that enables them to interpret a *page description language* (*PDL*), which tells the printer how to lay out the contents of a printed page. When you purchase a laser printer, it comes with at least one of two common page description languages: PCL or PostScript. Developed by Hewlett-Packard, a leading printer manufacturer, *PCL* (*Printer Control Language*) is a standard printer language that supports the fonts and layout used in standard office documents. Professionals in the desktop publishing and graphic art fields commonly use *PostScript* because it is designed for complex documents with intense graphics and colors.

WEB LINK 6-6

Laser Printers

Visit the Discovering Computers 2004 WEB LINK page (**scsite .com/dc2004/weblink**). Click Laser Printers below Chapter 6.

FIGURE 6-23 Laser printers are used with personal computers, as well as larger computers.

Operating in a manner similar to a copy machine, a laser printer creates images using a laser beam and powdered ink, called *toner*. The laser beam produces an image on a special drum inside the printer. The light of the laser alters the electrical charge on the drum wherever it hits. When this occurs, the toner sticks to the drum and then transfers to the paper through a combination of pressure and heat (Figure 6-24).

When the toner runs out, you replace the toner cartridge. Toner cartridge prices range from $50 to $100 for about 5,000 printed pages. On average, the cost per printed page on a black-and-white laser printer is $.02 to $.03.

? FAQ 6-5

How do I dispose of toner cartridges?

Do not throw them in the garbage. The housing contains iron, metal, and aluminum that is not biodegradable. The ink toner inside the cartridges contains toxic chemicals that pollute water and soil if disposed in dumps. Instead, recycle empty toner cartridges. Contact your printer manufacturer to see if it has a recycling program.

For more information about recycling toner cartridges, visit the Discovering Computers 2004 FAQ Web page (**scsite.com/dc2004/faq**). Click Recycling Toner Cartridges below Chapter 6.

Thermal Printers

A **thermal printer** generates images by pushing electrically heated pins against heat-sensitive paper. Basic thermal printers are inexpensive, but the print quality is <u>low</u> and the images tend to fade over time. Self-service gas pumps often print gas receipts using a built-in lower-quality thermal printer.

Two special types of thermal printers have very high print quality. A *thermal wax-transfer printer* generates rich, nonsmearing images by using heat to melt colored wax onto heat-sensitive paper. Thermal wax-transfer printers are more expensive than ink-jet printers, but less expensive than many color laser printers.

A *dye-sublimation printer*, sometimes called a *digital photo printer*, uses heat to transfer colored dye to specially coated paper. Dye-sublimation printers create images that are of photographic quality (Figure 6-25). Professional applications requiring very high image quality, such as photography studios, medical labs, and security identification systems, use dye-sublimation printers. These high-end printers cost thousands of dollars and print images in a wide range of sizes. Dye-sublimation printers for the home or small business user, by contrast, typically print images in only one or two sizes and are much slower than their professional counterparts. These lower-end dye-sublimation printers cost more than a photo printer based on ink-jet technology, but usually less than $1,000. Some are small enough for the mobile user to carry the printer in a briefcase.

FIGURE 6-24   HOW A LASER PRINTER WORKS

Step 1:
After the user sends an instruction to print a document, the drum rotates as gears and rollers feed a sheet of paper into the printer.

Step 2:
A rotating mirror deflects a low-powered laser beam across the surface of a drum.

Step 3:
The laser beam creates a charge that causes toner to stick to the drum.

Step 4:
As the drum continues to rotate and press against the paper, the toner transfers from the drum to the paper.

Step 5:
A set of rollers uses heat and pressure to fuse the toner permanently to the paper.

Figure 6-25a (dye-sublimation printer for the professional)

Figure 6-25b (dye-sublimation printer for the home or small office user)

FIGURE 6-25 The printers shown in this figure use dye-sublimation technology to create photographic-quality output.

Portable Printers

A **portable printer** is a small, lightweight, battery-powered printer that allows a mobile user to print from a notebook computer, Tablet PC, or PDA while traveling (Figure 6-26). Barely wider than the paper on which they print, portable printers fit easily in a briefcase alongside a notebook computer.

Portable printers mainly use ink-jet, thermal, thermal wax-transfer, or dye-sublimation technology. Many of these printers connect to a parallel port or USB port. Others have a built-in wireless port through which they communicate with the computer wirelessly. Wireless printing is discussed later in this chapter.

Label and Postage Printers

A **label printer** is a small printer that prints on an adhesive-type material that can be placed on a variety of items such as envelopes, packages, floppy disks, CDs, DVDs, audio-cassettes, photographs, file folders, and toys. Most label printers also print bar codes.

A *postage printer* is a special type of label printer that has a built-in digital scale and prints postage stamps (Figure 6-27). Postage printers allow users to buy and print digital postage, called *Internet postage*, right from their personal computer. That is, you purchase an amount of postage from an authorized postal service Web site. As you need a stamp, you print it on the postage printer. Each time a postage stamp prints, your postage account is updated.

FIGURE 6-26 A portable printer is a compact printer that allows the mobile user to print from a notebook computer or mobile device.

FIGURE 6-27 Postage printers are a type of label printer with a built-in digital scale that prints postage.

Plotters and Large-Format Printers

Plotters are sophisticated printers used to produce high-quality drawings such as blueprints, maps, and circuit diagrams. These printers are used in specialized fields such as engineering and drafting and usually are very costly. Current plotters use a row of charged wires (called styli) to draw an electrostatic pattern on specially coated paper and then fuse toner to the pattern. The printed image consists of a series of very small dots, which provides high-quality output.

Using ink-jet printer technology, but on a much larger scale, a **large-format printer** creates photo-realistic-quality color prints. Graphic artists use these high-cost, high-performance printers for signs, posters, and other professional quality displays (Figure 6-28).

Plotters and large-format printers handle paper with widths up to 60 inches because blueprints, maps, signs, posters and other such drawings and displays can be quite large. Some plotters and large-format printers use individual sheets of paper, while others take large rolls.

Wireless Printing

Until a few years ago, users had to connect computers and devices to printers with a cable if they wanted to print. Today, wireless printing technology makes the task of printing from a notebook computer, Tablet PC, PDA, or digital camera much easier. As discussed in Chapter 4, two wireless technologies for printing are infrared and Bluetooth™.

With *infrared printing*, a printer communicates with a device using infrared light waves. Each device must have an IrDA port. To print from a PDA, for example, a user lines up the IrDA port on the PDA with the IrDA port on the printer. With *Bluetooth™ printing*, a device transmits output to a printer via radio waves (Figure 6-29). Bluetooth printing is more convenient than infrared printing because Bluetooth devices do not have to be aligned with each other, rather, they need to be within an approximate 30-foot range. Users can convert existing printers and devices into Bluetooth devices with a Bluetooth wireless port adapter or a Bluetooth card, which plugs into a USB port or parallel port.

FIGURE 6-28 Graphic artists use large-format printers to print signs, posters, and other professional quality displays.

WEB LINK 6-7

Wireless Printing

Visit the Discovering Computers 2004 WEB LINK page (**scsite .com/dc2004/weblink**). Click Wireless Printing below Chapter 6.

FIGURE 6-29 Bluetooth™ technology allows computers and devices to transmit to a printer wirelessly, as long as each is Bluetooth enabled or has a Bluetooth adapter or card.

FAQ 6-6

Where did the name Bluetooth originate?

Harald Blatand was king of Denmark circa 950. This king, whose last name they say roughly translates to blue tooth, was able to unite Denmark and Norway despite their differences. When Ericsson, Intel, IBM, Nokia, and Toshiba collectively were able to develop a new wireless communications standard, they named it Bluetooth — after the Danish leader.

For more information about Bluetooth, visit the Discovering Computers 2004 FAQ Web page (**scsite.com/dc2004/faq**). Click Bluetooth below Chapter 6.

QUIZ YOURSELF 6-2

To check your knowledge of various types of printers and wireless printing, visit the Discovering Computers 2004 Quiz Yourself Web page (**scsite.com/dc2004/quiz**). Click Objectives 5 – 7 below Chapter 6.

SPEAKERS AND HEADSETS

An **audio output device** is a component of a computer that produces music, speech, or other sounds, such as beeps. Two commonly used audio output devices are speakers and headsets.

Most personal computers have a small internal speaker that usually outputs only low-quality sound. Thus, many personal computer users add stereo **speakers** to their computers to generate a higher-quality sound (Figure 6-30). Some monitors even have larger speakers built into the sides of the monitor. Most speakers have tone and volume controls, allowing users to adjust settings. To boost the low bass sounds, some users add a *woofer* (also called a *subwoofer*). Users connect the stereo speakers and subwoofer to ports on the sound card. For a more technical discussion about how sound cards produce sound, read the High-Tech Talk article on page 6.31.

FIGURE 6-30 Most personal computer users add high-quality stereo speakers and a subwoofer to their computers.

When using speakers, anyone within listening distance can hear the output. In a computer laboratory or some other crowded environment, speakers might not be practical. Instead, users can plug a headset into a port on the sound card, into a speaker, or even into the front of the system unit. With the **headset**, only the individual wearing the headset hears the sound from the computer (Figure 6-31).

FIGURE 6-31 In a crowded environment where speakers are not practical, users wear a headset to hear audio output.

WEB LINK 6-8

Speakers and Headsets

Visit the Discovering Computers 2004 WEB LINK page (**scsite.com/dc2004/weblink**). Click Speakers and Headsets below Chapter 6.

Electronically produced voice output is growing in popularity. **Voice output** occurs when you hear a person's voice or when the computer talks to you through the speakers on the computer. In some software applications, the computer can speak the contents of a document through voice output. On the Web, you can listen to (or download and then listen to) interviews, talk shows, sporting events, news, recorded music, and live concerts from many radio and television stations (read Issue 6-4 for a related discussion). Some Web sites dedicate themselves to providing voice output, where you can hear songs, quotes, historical lectures, speeches, and books (Figure 6-32). Read Apply It 6-2 for more information.

FIGURE 6-32   Users can listen to book contents from the Web. Shown here is a sample audio broadcast of the book titled *A Beautiful Mind*. For users desiring to hear the entire book, they can purchase and download the entire audio file.

ISSUE 6-4

Wearing the Web?

A Hewlett-Packard executive predicts that someday the boundary between people and the Internet may disappear. The reason for its dissolution is a concept called "Internet wearables," which consist of portable, wireless output devices that people can wear to access the Web. On the surface, these devices may appear as innocuous as eyeglasses, a hearing aid, or a tooth filling. But, when a wearer speaks into a tiny microphone attached to the device, information from a remote computer or a Web site is seen on a lens of the eyeglasses or heard through a speaker in the hearing aid. Advocates say Internet wearables will make people more efficient by providing immediate material to those who need it. Critics argue, however, that people could become over-dependent on, or easily distracted by, the devices. Will Internet wearables help people be more productive? Why or why not? When would Internet wearables be a good idea? When would they not be a good idea? Why?

For more information about Internet wearables, visit the Discovering Computers 2004 Issues Web page (**scsite.com/dc2004/issues**). Click Issue #4 below Chapter 6.

APPLY IT 6-2

Audio Books Tell a Good Story

Many students' fondest memories are recalling their teachers and parents reading favorite books aloud. You can relive these times with audio books that you hear while relaxing at the end of a hectic day, while traveling in the car or on an airplane, or while exercising on a treadmill at the gym.

Audio books are available from several sources. You can purchase CD and cassette versions at retail stores or online. One newer method is downloading from several sources, including a service called Audible and Web sites.

These suppliers may have more than 5,000 selections in the fiction, nonfiction, business, history, science, and comedy categories. For less than $20 per month, you can make several selections, download the files, and then listen to the text using a headset or speakers and a PDA, MP3 player, or computer. File sizes range from a few to more than 100 megabytes; the greater the file size, the better the sound quality.

You can burn many of the files onto a CD and then listen conveniently in your car or on a portable CD player. While some people question the ethics of making copies of these files, others say the practice really is no different from lending books to friends. Another option is listening to the texts as audio streams over the Internet, but this technique works best with a high-speed Internet connection.

For more information about audio books, visit the Discovering Computers 2004 Apply It Web page (**scsite.com/dc2004/apply**). Click Apply It #2 below Chapter 6.

Very often, voice output works with voice input. For example, when you call an airline to check the status of gates, terminals, and arrival times, your voice interacts with a computer-generated voice output. *Internet telephony* allows users to have conversations over the Web, just as if they were on the telephone.

Sophisticated programs enable the computer to converse with you. Talk into the microphone and say, "I'd like today's weather report." The computer replies, "For which city?" You reply, "Chicago." The computer says, "Sunny and 80 degrees."

OTHER OUTPUT DEVICES

In addition to monitors, printers, and speakers, many other output devices are available for specific uses and applications. These include fax machines and fax modems, multifunction peripherals, data projectors, and force-feedback joysticks and wheels. The following pages discuss these devices.

Fax Machines and Fax Modems

A **fax machine**, short for *facsimile machine*, is a device that transmits and receives documents over telephone lines. The documents can contain text, drawings, or photographs, or can be handwritten. The term *fax* refers to a document that you send or receive via a fax machine.

A stand-alone fax machine scans an original document, converts the image into digitized data, and transmits the digitized image (Figure 6-33). A fax machine at the receiving end reads the incoming data, converts the digitized data back into an image, and prints or stores a copy of the original image.

Many computers include fax capability by using a fax modem. A *fax modem* is a modem that also allows you to send (and sometimes receive) electronic documents as faxes (Figure 6-34). A fax modem transmits computer-prepared documents, such as a word processing letter, or documents that have been digitized with a scanner or digital camera. A fax modem transmits these faxes to a fax machine or to another fax modem.

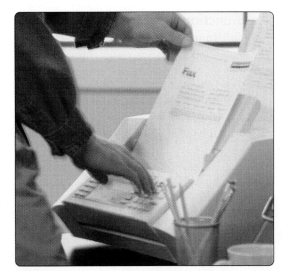

WEB LINK 6-9

Fax Modems

Visit the Discovering Computers 2004 WEB LINK page (**scsite .com/dc2004/weblink**). Click Fax Modems below Chapter 6.

FIGURE 6-33   A stand-alone fax machine.

external fax modem

internal fax modem card in system unit

fax machine

FIGURE 6-34   A fax modem allows users to send (and sometimes receive) electronic documents as faxes to a fax machine or another computer.

When a computer (instead of a fax machine) receives a fax, users can view the fax on the screen, saving the time and expense of printing it. If necessary, you also can print the fax using special fax software. The quality of a viewed or printed fax is less than that of a word processing document because the fax actually is an image. Optical character recognition (OCR) software, which was discussed in Chapter 5, enables you to convert the image to text and then edit it.

A fax modem can be an external device that plugs into a port on the back of the system unit or an internal adapter card inserted into an expansion slot on the motherboard.

Multifunction Peripherals

A **multifunction peripheral** is a single device that looks like a copy machine but provides the functionality of a printer, scanner, copy machine, and perhaps a fax machine (Figure 6-35). The features of these devices, which sometimes are called *all-in-one devices*, vary widely. For example, some use color ink-jet printer technology, while others include a black-and-white laser printer.

WEB LINK 6-10

Multifunction Peripherals

Visit the Discovering Computers 2004 WEB LINK page (**scsite .com/dc2004/weblink**). Click Multifunction Peripherals below Chapter 6.

Small offices and home offices (SOHOs) use multifunction peripherals because they require less space than having a separate printer, scanner, copy machine, and fax machine. Another advantage of these devices is that it is significantly less expensive than if you purchase each device separately. If the device breaks down, however, you lose all four functions, which is the primary disadvantage. Despite this disadvantage, increasingly more users are bringing multifunction peripherals into their offices and homes.

Data Projectors

A **data projector** is a device that takes the image from a computer screen and projects it onto a larger screen so an audience of people can see the image clearly. For example, many classrooms use data projectors so all students easily can see an instructor's presentation on the screen.

Some data projectors are large devices that attach to a ceiling or wall in an auditorium. Others are small portable devices. Two types of smaller, lower-cost units are LCD projectors and DLP projectors.

An *LCD projector*, which uses liquid crystal display technology, attaches directly to a computer, and uses its own light source to display the information shown on the computer screen. Because LCD projectors tend to produce lower-quality images, users often prefer DLP projectors for their sharper, brighter images.

A *digital light processing (DLP) projector* uses tiny mirrors to reflect light, which produces crisp, bright, colorful images that remain in focus and can be seen clearly even in a well-lit room (Figure 6-36). Read Looking Ahead 6-2 for a look at the next generation of movie projectors.

FIGURE 6-35   This multifunction peripheral is a color printer, scanner, copy machine, and fax machine all in one device.

FIGURE 6-36 DLP projectors produce sharp, bright images.

Force-Feedback Joysticks and Wheels

As discussed in Chapter 5, joysticks and wheels are input devices used to control actions of a player or movements of a vehicle. Today's joysticks and wheels also include *force feedback*, which is a technology that sends resistance to the device in response to actions of the user (Figure 6-37). For example, as you use the simulation software to drive from a smooth road onto a gravel alley, the steering wheel jars itself — to make the driving experience as realistic as possible. In addition to games, these devices are used in practical training applications such as in the military and aviation.

WEB LINK 6-11

Force Feedback Devices

Visit the Discovering Computers 2004 WEB LINK page (**scsite .com/dc2004/weblink**). Click Force Feedback Devices below Chapter 6.

LOOKING AHEAD 6-2

Digital Movies Project New Image

George Eastman experimented in his mother's kitchen and developed the flexible transparent base for film in the late 1800s. More than 100 years later, George Lucas experimented in a computer laboratory and developed the highest-profile movie entirely shot and shown in a digital format, *Star Wars, Episode 2: Attack of the Clones.*

Movie industry experts predict digital technology will replace film by 2007, with some of these individuals forecasting that the movie projector will be obsolete by 2005. Seven of the bigger Hollywood studios are collaborating to develop digital technical standards, and leading equipment manufacturers, including Kodak and Texas Instruments, are developing projection hardware.

The Boeing Company is one of the project's major investors. Being the largest satellite manufacturer, this corporation desires to help transmit full-length digital movies throughout the world and supply movie theaters with digital equipment.

While digital movies offer superior visual and sound clarity, they also are susceptible to piracy. Hundreds of thousands of copies of *Attack of the Clones* were downloaded from the Internet before the film's release. The Motion Picture Association of America predicts that more than 1 million movies will be downloaded illegally daily, resulting in billions of dollars of lost profits. This organization and other groups are wrestling with convincing the public that this piracy is unethical and ultimately leads to increased ticket prices at the box office.

For a look at the next generation of digital movies, visit the Discovering Computers 2004 Looking Ahead Web page (**scsite.com/dc2004/looking**). Click Looking Ahead #2 below Chapter 6.

FIGURE 6-37 Joysticks, wheels, and other gaming devices often provide force feedback, giving the user a realistic experience.

PUTTING IT ALL TOGETHER

Many factors influence the type of output devices you should use: the type of output desired, the hardware and software in use, and the anticipated cost. Figure 6-38 outlines several suggested monitors, printers, and other output devices for various types of computer users.

SUGGESTED OUTPUT DEVICES BY USER

User	Monitor	Printer	Other
Home	• 17- or 19-inch color CRT monitor or flat panel monitor	• Ink-jet color printer • Photo printer	• Speakers • Headset • Force-feedback joystick and wheel
Small Office/Home Office	• 19- or 21-inch color CRT monitor or flat panel monitor • Color LCD display on Tablet PC or PDA	• Multifunction peripheral; or • Ink-jet color printer; or • Laser printer, black and white • Label printer • Postage printer	• Fax machine • Speakers
Mobile	• 15.7-inch color LCD display on notebook computer • Color LCD display on PDA	• Portable color printer • Ink-jet color printer; or • Laser printer, black and white, for in-office use • Photo printer	• Fax modem • Headset • DLP data projector
Large Business	• 19- or 21-inch color CRT monitor or flat panel monitor • Color LCD display on Tablet PC and PDA	• High-speed laser printer • Laser printer, color • Line printer (for large reports from a mainframe) • Label printer	• Fax machine or fax modem • Speakers • Headset • DLP data projector
Power	• 23-inch color flat panel monitor	• Laser printer, black and white • Plotter or large-format printer; or • Photo printer; or • Dye-sublimation printer	• Fax machine or fax modem • Speakers • Headset

FIGURE 6-38 This table recommends suggested output devices for various types of users.

OUTPUT DEVICES FOR PHYSICALLY CHALLENGED USERS

As discussed in Chapter 5, the growing presence of computers has generated an awareness of the need to address computing requirements for those with physical limitations. Read Issue 6-5 for a related discussion.

For users with mobility, hearing, or vision disabilities, many different types of output devices are available. Hearing-impaired users, for example, can instruct programs to display words instead of sounds. With the Windows XP operating system, users also can set options to make programs easier to use. For example, the Magnifier command enlarges text and other items in a window on the screen (Figure 6-39).

ISSUE 6-5

How Should Employers Accommodate Employees with Disabilities?

Section 508 of the Workforce Investment Act (Rehabilitation Act Amendments) requires that electronics and information technology in federal agencies accommodate the needs of all end users — including people with disabilities. Computers used in federal agencies must be compatible with assistive technologies, such as screen readers that translate what appears on a computer screen into audible output and refreshable Braille displays for people who are visually impaired. To date, Section 508 does not apply to the private sector. Some believe, however, that the same standards should apply to private companies and organizations. Opponents insist that applying such standards to private companies would place an undue burden on employers. Should private companies be forced to make their computers accessible to physically challenged employees? Why or why not? Should such regulations apply only to companies with a minimum number of employees? If so, how many? What relatively inexpensive measures could employers take to accommodate employees with disabilities?

For more information about accommodating employees with disabilities, visit the Discovering Computers 2004 Issues Web page (**scsite.com/ dc2004/issues**). Click Issue #5 below Chapter 6.

Text on the line that contains the mouse pointer is magnified at the top of the screen.

FIGURE 6-39 The Magnifier command in Windows XP enlarges text and other on-screen items for individuals with vision disabilities.

Visually impaired users can change Windows XP settings, such as increasing the size or changing the color of the text to make the words easier to read. Instead of using a monitor, blind users can work with voice output. That is, the computer reads the information that displays on the screen. Another alternative is a *Braille printer*, which outputs information in Braille onto paper (Figure 6-40).

QUIZ YOURSELF 6-3

To check your knowledge of speakers and headsets, other output devices, and output for physically challenged users, visit the Discovering Computers 2004 Quiz Yourself Web page (**scsite.com/dc2004/quiz**). Click Objectives 8 – 10 below Chapter 6.

CHAPTER SUMMARY

Computers process and organize input into output. This chapter described the various methods of output and several commonly used output devices. Output devices presented included CRT monitors, flat-panel displays, printers, speakers and headsets, fax machines and fax modems, multifunction peripherals, data projectors, and force-feedback joysticks and wheels.

FIGURE 6-40   A Braille printer.

Graphic Designer/Illustrator

Career Corner

Graphic designers and *graphic illustrators* are artists, but many do not create original works. Instead, they portray visually the ideas of their clients. Illustrators create pictures for books and other publications and sometimes for commercial products, such as greeting cards. They work in fields such as fashion, technology, medicine, animation, or even cartoons. Illustrators often prepare their images on a computer. Designers combine practical skills with artistic talent to convert abstract concepts into designs for products and advertisements. Many use computer-aided design (CAD) tools to create, visualize, and modify designs. Designer careers usually are specialized in particular areas, such as:
- Graphic designers — book covers, stationery, and CD covers
- Commercial and industrial designers — products and equipment
- Costume and theater designers — costumes and settings for theater and television
- Interior designers — layout, decor, and furnishings of homes and buildings
- Merchandise displayers — commercial displays
- Fashion designers — clothing, shoes, and other fashion accessories

Certificate, two-year, four-year, and masters-level educational programs are available within design areas. About 30 percent of graphic illustrators/designers choose to freelance, while others work with advertising agencies, publishing companies, design studios, or specialized departments within large companies. Salaries range from $25,000 to $75,000-plus, based on experience and educational background.

To learn more about the field of Graphic Designer/Illustrator as a career, visit the Discovering Computers 2004 Careers Web page (**scsite.com/dc2004/careers**). Click Graphic Designer/Illustrator.

HIGH-TECH TALK

Sound Cards: Creating Music to Your Ears

Speakers, headsets, and other audio output devices rely on sound cards to produce sounds such as music, voice, beeps, and chimes. Sound cards contain the chips and circuitry to record and play back a wide range of sounds using analog-to-digital conversion and digital-to-analog conversion, as described in the Chapter 1 High-Tech Talk on page 1.37.

To record a sound, the sound card must be connected to an input device, such as a microphone or audio CD player. The input device sends the sound to the sound card as an analog signal. The analog signal flows to the sound card's analog-to-digital-converter (ADC). The ADC converts the signal into digital (binary) data of 1s and 0s by sampling the signal at set intervals.

The analog sound is a continuous waveform, with a range of frequencies and volumes. To represent the waveform in a recording, the computer would have to store the waveform's value at every instant in time. Because this is not possible, the sound is recorded using a sampling process. *Sampling* involves breaking up the waveform into set intervals and representing all values during that interval with a single value.

Several factors in the sampling process — sampling rate, audio resolution, and mono or stereo recording — affect the quality of the recorded sound during playback.

- *Sampling rate*, also called sampling frequency, refers to the number of times per second the sound is recorded (Figure 6-41). The more frequently a sound is recorded, the smaller the intervals and the better the quality. The sampling frequency used for audio CDs, for example, is 44,100 times per second, which is expressed in hertz (Hz) as 44,100 Hz. Cassette tape-quality multimedia files use a sampling rate of 22,050 Hz; and basic Windows sounds use a sampling rate of 11,025 Hz.
- *Audio resolution* — defined as a bit rate such as 8-bit, 16-bit, or 24-bit — refers to the number of bytes used to represent the sound at any one interval. A sound card using 8-bit resolution, for example, represents a sound with any 1 of 256 values (2^8). A 16-bit sound card uses any 1 of 65,536 values (2^{16}) for each interval. Using a higher resolution provides a finer measurement scale, which results in a more accurate representation of the value of each sample and better sound quality. With 8-bit resolution, the sound quality is like that of an AM radio; 16-bit resolution gives CD quality sound, and a 24-bit resolution is used for high-quality digital audio editing.
- Mono or stereo recording refers to the number of channels used during recording. *Mono* means that the same sound emits from both the left and right speaker during playback; *stereo* means that two separate channels exist in the recording: one each for the right and left speakers. Most sound cards support stereo recording for better playback.

After the ADC converts the analog sound through sampling, the digital data flows to the digital signal processor (DSP) on the sound card. The DSP then requests instructions from the sound card's memory chip on how to process the digital data. Typically, the DSP then compresses the digital data to save space. Finally, the DSP sends the compressed data to the computer's main processor, which stores the data in .WAV, .MP3, or other audio file format.

To play a recorded sound, such as a WAV, an MP3, or a CD track, the main processor retrieves the sound file from a hard disk, CD, or other storage device. The processor then sends the digital data to the DSP, which decompresses the data and looks to the memory chip to determine how to recreate the sound.

The DSP then sends the digital signals to the sound card's digital-to-analog converter (DAC), which converts the digital data back to an analog electrical voltage. An output device, such as a speaker, uses an amplifier to strengthen the electrical voltage. This causes the speaker's cone to vibrate, recreating the sound.

All of this happens in an instant. The next time your computer beeps or chirps, consider the complex process required to make that simple sound. Then, insert your favorite CD and enjoy the sweet music provided courtesy of the sound card.

For more information about sound cards, visit the Discovering Computers 2004 High-Tech Talk Web page (**scsite.com/dc2004/tech**) and click Sound Cards.

Figure 6-41a (recording made using low sampling rate and resolution causes significant sampling error; results in recorded sound with poor sound quality)

Figure 6-41b (recording made using higher sampling rate and resolution reduces sampling error; results in recorded sound with better sound quality)

FIGURE 6-41 Comparison of low versus high sampling rates.

COMPANIES ON THE CUTTING EDGE

Hewlett-Packard
Printers and More

In a one-car garage, two 26-year-old engineers started a company with a collection of simple tools and $538 in working capital. They decided to use their last names to identify the company, but whose name would be first? William Hewlett and David Packard tossed a coin, and Hewlett won. That one-car garage where *Hewlett-Packard* (*HP*) was born now is a California State Historical Landmark.

HP's first product was an audio oscillator, an instrument used to test sound equipment. In 1939, the Walt Disney Studios bought eight oscillators to use in developing sound effects for the movie, Fantasia. Soon after, HP constructed its first building, but the founders designed the new facility so it easily could be converted into a grocery store if the electronics business failed.

Instead of failing, HP grew. The company's initial products were test and measurement equipment, but in the 1960s, its product line expanded to include calculators. In the 1980s, HP turned toward the computer and printer markets. By 1993, HP had sold 20 million printers. Today, market analysts estimate that 60 percent of printers sold bear the HP logo. HP is noted for a range of high-quality, computer-related products including personal computers, notebook computers, scanners, and ink-jet and laser printers. In 2002, HP enlarged its presence in the computer market with a $25 billion buyout of Compaq Computer Corporation.

In addition to new products, HP spearheaded changes in corporate culture. In 1957, HP created the first set of corporate objectives, which became known as the HP Way. This philosophy embraced the free exchange of information, trust and respect, integrity, teamwork, and what HP calls Management by Walking Around.

For more information about HP, visit the Discovering Computers 2004 Companies Web page (**scsite.com/dc2004/companies**) and click Hewlett-Packard.

RealNetworks
Delivering Multimedia Content

Imagine having hundreds of thousands of new users visit your home page each day. That is the success RealNetworks has experienced with its RealOne Player (formerly RealPlayer), amounting to a 300 percent growth since 1998. The RealNetworks family of Web sites is one of the 20 most popular Internet destinations. No wonder *PC Magazine* ranks the company on its list of the 100 most influential companies in the world.

RealNetworks develops technology that allows people to create, send, and receive multimedia over the Internet. More than 400,000 companies rely on RealNetworks software to deliver audio, video, and multimedia services to personal computers and other electronic devices. RealNetworks technology is used to broadcast more than 350,000 hours of live music, sports, news, and entertainment every week.

One year after leaving Microsoft in 1994, RealNetworks founder Rob Glaser introduced the first version of RealAudio, and the company set the standard for sending multimedia content across the Internet. Today, the company's two more popular products are RealPlayer and RealJukebox. RealPlayer, the second most popular Internet-based software application, uses streaming-media technology to deliver a song when you click its title. According to RealNetworks, RealPlayer is installed on 90 percent of America's home computers. RealJukebox stores and plays downloadable files such as MP3s, a popular digital music format. RealOne Player integrates RealPlayer and RealJukebox functions and allows subscribers to download and stream premium digital music, sports, entertainment, and news. With its RealSystem iQ, RealNetworks continues to lead the way in delivering the highest quality Internet media experience from any point of origin to any person on any Web-enabled device anywhere in the world.

For more information about RealNetworks, visit the Discovering Computers 2004 Companies Web page (**scsite.com/dc2004/companies**) and click RealNetworks.

TECHNOLOGY TRAILBLAZERS

Donna Dubinsky
Cofounder of Handspring

For most people, being the president and CEO of 3Com's Palm Computing Division, the world's leading producer of PDAs, would be enough of a challenge. Yet, in 1998 Palm's CEO, *Donna Dubinsky*, left to found Handspring with Jeff Hawkins and revolutionize the PDA market.

Dubinsky always has been independent. After graduating from Harvard Business School, instead of following her classmates to high-paying jobs in established firms, Dubinsky took an unassuming position in customer service at Apple Computer. There, she worked her way up to director of distribution and international vice president at Claris, the company's software unit. When Apple failed to spin off Claris as a separate firm, Dubinsky left and traveled to Paris, where she learned French, studied painting, and taught school. When she returned to Silicon Valley, California, Dubinsky met Jeff Hawkins, an engineer who was developing a user-friendly electronic organizer. The pair introduced the PalmPilot in 1996, and sales of more than two million units made it the most-rapidly adopted new computing product ever manufactured. To learn how consumers actually used the PalmPilot, Dubinsky even took some technical support calls to hear the questions they asked.

When Dubinsky and Hawkins left 3Com to form Handspring, they introduced another innovative product, the Handspring Visor™. Dubinsky believes the Visor "marks the next step in the evolution of handhelds." The Visor uses the same operating system as the PalmPilot and supports many of the same applications, but it is less expensive and includes an expansion slot that allows users to add modules with various functions, including pagers, music players, game cartridges, and modems. Already, the Handspring Visor has claimed more than 15 percent of the PDA market.

For more information about Donna Dubinsky, visit the Discovering Computers 2004 People Web page (**scsite.com/dc2004/people**) and click Donna Dubinsky.

Heidi Van Arnem
Advocate for the Physically Challenged

In 1983, 16-year old *Heidi Van Arnem* accidentally was shot in the neck. The shooting left her paralyzed, but not defeated. As a law student at the University of Detroit, Van Arnem taught herself to type using the knuckle of her little finger. "That's when I realized," Van Arnem recalled, "I could have some value in my life, some control." Throughout her life, Van Arnem worked to enhance the lives of people with disabilities and help the individuals and organizations that support them.

For eight years, Van Arnem owned and operated a Birmingham travel agency, specializing in making arrangements for travelers with disabilities. In 1998, she sold the travel agency and started iCan!, Inc., a company that provides an online forum for the physically challenged community. The iCan! Web site is designed for people with disabilities and helps businesses better address their needs. As chairman and CEO of iCan!, Van Arnem brought together businesses, the medical industry, government-led efforts, and non-profit organizations. To assist people with special needs, iCan! works in the travel industry, the automotive industry, and computer technology. "With this," Van Arnem once said, indicating her notebook computer, "I'm just as productive as the next person."

As a successful businesswoman, entrepreneur, and inventor, Van Arnem was recognized as one of the Top 25 Women on the Web. She was the first recipient of the Evan Kemp Entrepreneur of the Year award by the President's Committee on Employment of People with Disabilities and received numerous awards for her business achievements and community outreach by organizations such as the U.S. Chamber of Commerce. In addition, Van Arnem's Spend a Day in a Wheelchair program received national acclaim for helping sensitize students to the difficulties wheelchair users face.

For more information about Heidi Van Arnem, visit the Discovering Computers 2004 People Web page (**scsite.com/dc2004/people**) and click Heidi Van Arnem.

CHAPTER 6 — CHAPTER REVIEW

◀● Previous | Next ●▶

The Chapter Review section summarizes the concepts presented in this chapter.

■ WEB INSTRUCTIONS:

To display this page from the Web, start your browser and enter the Web address **scsite.com/dc2004/ch6/review**. Click the links for current and additional information. To listen to an audio version of this Chapter Review, click the Audio button.

1 What Are the Four Categories of Output?

Output is data that has been processed into a useful form. Four categories of output are text, graphics, audio, and video. An <u>output device</u> is any hardware component that conveys information to one or more people.

2 What Is a CRT Monitor and What Factors Affect Its Quality?

A **CRT monitor** is a desktop monitor that is similar to a standard television set because it contains a *cathode ray tube (CRT)*. The screen on the front of the CRT is coated with tiny dots of red, green, and blue phosphor that combine to make up each *pixel*, which is a single element in an electronic image. As an electron beam inside the CRT moves back and forth across the back of the screen, the dots glow, which produces an image. The quality of a CRT monitor depends largely on its resolution, dot pitch, and refresh rate. **Resolution** describes the sharpness and clearness of an image. *Dot pitch*, sometimes called <u>pixel pitch</u>, is the distance in millimeters between each like-colored pixel on the screen. *Refresh rate* is the speed that a monitor redraws the images on the screen.

3 How Are a Video Card and CRT Monitor Related?

Many CRT monitors use an analog signal to produce an image. A **video card**, also called a <u>graphics card</u>, converts digital output from the computer into an analog video signal and sends the signal through a cable to the CRT monitor, which displays output on the screen.

4 What Are Flat Panel Monitors, LCD Screens, Gas Plasma Displays, and HDTV Displays?

Flat panel monitors, LCD displays, gas plasma displays, and many types of HDTV displays are types of flat-panel displays. A *flat-panel display* is a display with a shallow depth that does not use CRT technology. A **flat panel monitor** is a desktop monitor that uses a liquid crystal display instead of a cathode-ray tube. A <u>liquid crystal display (LCD)</u> uses a liquid compound to present information on a screen. A **gas plasma display** is a display that uses gas plasma technology, which substitutes a layer of gas for the liquid crystal material in a flat panel monitor. **HDTV** (*high-definition television*) is the most advanced form of digital television, working with digital broadcasting signals, transmitting digital sound, supporting wide screens, and providing resolutions up to 1920 x 1080 pixels.

⬛ Visit **scsite.com/dc2004/quiz** or click the Quiz Yourself button. Click Objectives 1 – 4 below Chapter 6.

5 How Is an Impact Printer Different From a Nonimpact Printer?

A **printer** is an output device that produces text and graphics on a physical medium, such as paper or transparency film. An **impact printer** forms characters and graphics on a piece of paper by striking a mechanism against an inked ribbon that physically contacts the paper. Two commonly used types of impact printers are the **dot-matrix printer** and the **line printer**. A **nonimpact printer** forms characters and graphics on a piece of paper without actually striking the paper. Commonly used nonimpact printers are ink-jet printers, photo printers, laser printers, thermal printers, portable printers, label and postage printers, plotters, and <u>large-format printers</u>.

CHAPTER REVIEW   CHAPTER 6

6 What Are Ink-Jet Printers, Photo Printers, Laser Printers, Thermal Printers, Portable Printers, Label and Postage Printers, and Plotters and Large-Format Printers?

An ink-jet printer is a type of nonimpact printer that forms characters and graphics by spraying tiny drops of liquid ink onto a piece of paper. A **photo printer** is a color printer that produces photo-lab-quality pictures. A **laser printer** is a high-speed, high-quality nonimpact printer that operates in a manner similar to a copy machine, creating images using a laser beam and powdered ink, called *toner*. A **thermal printer** generates images by pushing electronically heated pins against heat-sensitive paper. A **portable printer** is a small, lightweight, battery-powered printer that allows a mobile user to print from a notebook computer. A **label printer** is a small printer that prints on an adhesive-type material that can be placed on a variety of items. A *postage printer* is a special type of label printer that has a built-in scale and prints postage stamps. **Plotters** are sophisticated printers used to produce high-quality drawings. A **large-format printer** uses ink-jet technology on a large scale to create photo-realistic-quality color prints.

7 What Methods Are Used for Wireless Printing?

Two wireless technologies for printing are infrared and Bluetooth™. With *infrared printing*, a printer communicates with a device using infrared light waves. With *Bluetooth™ printing*, a device transmits output to a printer via radio waves.

> Visit **scsite.com/dc2004/quiz** or click the Quiz Yourself button. Click Objectives 5 – 7 below Chapter 6.

8 How Are Speakers and Headsets Used?

Speakers and headsets are two commonly used audio output devices. An audio output device is a component of a computer that produces sound. Many personal computer users add stereo **speakers** to their computers to generate a higher-quality sound. With a **headset**, only the individual wearing the headset hears the sound from the computer.

9 What Are Fax Machines and Fax Modems, Multifunction Peripherals, Data Projectors, Joysticks, and Wheels?

A **fax machine**, short for *facsimile machine*, is a device that transmits and receives documents over telephone lines. A document sent or received via a fax machine is a *fax*. Many computers include fax capability using a *fax modem*, which is a modem that allows you to send (and sometimes receive) electronic documents as faxes. A **multifunction peripheral** is a single device that looks like a copy machine but provides the functionality of a printer, scanner, copy machine, and perhaps a fax machine. A **data projector** is a device that takes the image from a computer screen and projects it onto a larger screen so an audience of people can see the image clearly. Joysticks and wheels are input devices used to control actions of a player or vehicle. Today's joysticks and wheels also include *force feedback*, which is a technology that sends resistance to the device in response to actions of the user.

10 What Output Options Are Available for Physically Challenged Users?

Hearing-impaired users can instruct programs to display words instead of sound. With the Windows XP operating system, visually impaired users can enlarge items on the screen and change other settings, such as increasing the size or changing the color of text to make words easier to read. Blind users can work with voice output instead of a monitor. Another alternative is a *Braille printer*, which outputs information in Braille onto paper.

> Visit **scsite.com/dc2004/quiz** or click the Quiz Yourself button. Click Objectives 8 – 10 below Chapter 6.

CHAPTER 6 KEY TERMS

You should know the Primary Terms and be familiar with the Secondary Terms.

WEB INSTRUCTIONS:

To display this page from the Web, start your browser and enter the Web address **scsite.com/dc2004/ch6/terms**. Click a term to display its definition and a picture. When the picture displays, click the more info button for current and additional information about the term from the Web.

QUIZZES AND
LEARNING GAMES

Computer Genius

Crossword Puzzle

Interactive Labs

Practice Test

Quiz Yourself

Wheel of Terms

EXERCISES

Chapter Review

Checkpoint

Key Terms

Lab Exercises

Learn It Online

Web Research

BEYOND THE BOOK

Apply It

Career Corner

Companies

FAQ

High-Tech Talk

Issues

Looking Ahead

Trailblazers

Web Links

FEATURES

Guide to Web Sites

Making Use of the Web

Tech News

Timeline 2004

>> Primary Terms
(shown in bold-black characters in the chapter)

audio output device (6.23)
CRT monitor (6.04)
data projector (6.26)
display device (6.04)
dot-matrix printer (6.14)
e-book (6.10)
ENERGY STAR program (6.05)
fax machine (6.25)
flat panel monitor (6.09)
gas plasma display (6.12)
HDTV (6.12)
headset (6.23)
impact printer (6.14)
ink-jet printer (6.15)
interactive TV (6.12)
label printer (6.21)
large-format printer (6.22)
laser printer (6.19)

line printer (6.14)
liquid crystal display (LCD) (6.10)
monitor (6.04)
multifunction peripheral (6.26)
nonimpact printer (6.15)
output (6.02)
output device (6.04)
photo printer (6.17)
plotters (6.22)
portable printer (6.21)
printer (6.13)
resolution (6.05)
speakers (6.23)
thermal printer (6.20)
video card (6.07)
voice output (6.24)

>> Secondary Terms
(shown in italic characters in the chapter)

active-matrix display (6.11)
all-in-one devices (6.26)
band printer (6.15)
bit depth (6.07)
Bluetooth™ printing (6.22)
Braille printer (6.30)
bubble-jet printer (6.16)
candela (6.11)
cathode-ray tube (CRT) (6.04)
ClearType (6.10)
color depth (6.07)
continuous-form paper (6.14)
Digital Display Working Group (DDWG) (6.11)
digital light processing (DLP) projector (6.26)
digital photo printer (6.20)
digital television (DTV) (6.12)
display (6.04)
dot pitch (6.06)
dots per inch (dpi) (6.16)
DVI (Digital Video Interface) (6.11)
DVI port (6.11)
dye-sublimation printer (6.20)
electromagnetic radiation (EMR) (6.06)
electronic book (6.10)
facsimile machine (6.25)
fax (6.25)
fax modem (6.25)
flat-panel display (6.09)
footprint (6.09)
force feedback (6.27)
graphics card (6.07)
graphics processing unit (GPU) (6.08)
gray scaling (6.04)
hard copy (6.13)
high-definition television (6.12)
high-performance addressing (HPA) (6.11)
infrared printing (6.22)

Internet postage (6.21)
Internet telephony (6.25)
landscape orientation (6.13)
LCD monitor (6.09)
LCD projector (6.26)
letter-quality (LQ) (6.15)
Microsoft Reader (6.10)
monochrome (6.04)
MPR II (6.06)
National Television Standards Committee (6.12)
near letter quality (NLQ) (6.14)
nit (6.11)
NTSC converter (6.12)
organic LED (OLED) (6.11)
page description language (PDL) (6.19)
passive-matrix display (6.11)
PCL (Printer Control Language) (6.19)
pixel (6.04)
pixel pitch (6.06)
portrait orientation (6.13)
postage printer (6.21)
PostScript (6.19)
printout (6.13)
refresh rate (6.06)
response time (6.11)
scan rate (6.06)
shuttle-matrix printer (6.15)
soft copy (6.04)
subwoofer (6.23)
SVGA (super video graphics array) (6.08)
S-video port (6.11)
TFT (thin-film transistor) display (6.11)
thermal wax-transfer printer (6.20)
toner (6.20)
VESA (Video Electronics Standards Association) (6.08)
viewable size (6.05)
woofer (6.23)

CHECKPOINT CHAPTER 6

Use the Checkpoint exercises to check your knowledge level of the chapter.

WEB INSTRUCTIONS:

To display this page from the Web, start your browser and enter the Web address **scsite.com/dc2004/ch6/check**. Click the links for current and additional information.

LABEL THE FIGURE   Identify the ports on a video card.

a. DVI port

b. standard monitor port

c. S-video port

1._____   2._____   3._____

TRUE/FALSE   Mark T for True and F for False. (See page numbers in parentheses.)

_____ 1. <u>Output</u> is data that has been processed into a useful form. (6.02)

_____ 2. Information on a <u>display device</u> is sometimes called hard copy. (6.04)

_____ 3. A <u>video card</u> converts digital output from the computer into an analog video signal. (6.07)

_____ 4. A flat-panel display is a display with a shallow depth that uses <u>CRT technology</u>. (6.09)

_____ 5. A <u>pixel</u> is a unit of visible light intensity equal to one candela per square meter. (6.11)

_____ 6. A <u>line printer</u> is a high-speed impact printer that prints an entire line at a time. (6.14)

_____ 7. A <u>photo printer</u> is a color printer that produces photo-lab-quality pictures. (6.17)

_____ 8. A thermal printer is a high-speed, high-quality <u>nonimpact printer</u>. (6.20)

_____ 9. With <u>Bluetooth™ printing</u>, a device transmits output to a printer via radio waves. (6.22)

_____ 10. A <u>fax modem</u> transmits computer-prepared documents or documents that have been digitized with a scanner or digital camera. (6.25)

_____ 11. A multifunction peripheral is a single device that looks like a copy machine but provides the functionality of a printer, scanner, copy machine, and perhaps a <u>fax machine</u>. (6.26)

_____ 12. <u>Force feedback</u> is a technology that sends resistance to the device in response to actions of the user. (6.27)

CHAPTER 6 CHECKPOINT

QUIZZES AND LEARNING GAMES

Computer Genius

Crossword Puzzle

Interactive Labs

Practice Test

Quiz Yourself

Wheel of Terms

EXERCISES

Chapter Review

Checkpoint

Key Terms

Lab Exercises

Learn It Online

Web Research

BEYOND THE BOOK

Apply It

Career Corner

Companies

FAQ

High-Tech Talk

Issues

Looking Ahead

Trailblazers

Web Links

FEATURES

Guide to Web Sites

Making Use of the Web

Tech News

Timeline 2004

▨ **MULTIPLE CHOICE** Select the best answer. (See page numbers in parentheses.)

1. Many Web sites use animated _____, such as blinking icons, scrolling messages, or simulations. (6.03)
   a. text
   b. graphics
   c. audio
   d. video

2. The viewable size of a monitor is the _____ measurement of the actual viewing area provided by the screen in the monitor. (6.05)
   a. horizontal
   b. vertical
   c. diagonal
   d. three-dimensional

3. The number of colors a video card displays is determined by its _____. (6.07)
   a. dot pitch
   b. refresh rate
   c. bit depth
   d. viewable size

4. To generate the desired resolution and number of colors, _____ must support the required video standard. (6.08)
   a. only the video card
   b. only the monitor
   c. neither the video card nor the monitor
   d. both the video card and the monitor

5. A passive matrix display _____ an active matrix display. (6.11)
   a. uses more transistors than
   b. requires more power than
   c. often is not as bright as
   d. is more expensive than

6. Gas plasma displays offer larger screens _____. (6.12)
   a. but lower display quality than flat panel monitors and are less expensive
   b. but lower display quality than flat panel monitors and are more expensive
   c. and higher display quality than flat panel monitors but are less expensive
   d. and higher display quality than flat panel monitors but are more expensive

7. A(n) _____ is an impact printer that produces printed images when tiny wire pins on a print head mechanism strike an inked ribbon. (6.14)
   a. dot-matrix printer
   b. ink-jet printer
   c. laser printer
   d. thermal printer

8. Printer resolution is measured by the number of _____ a printer can output. (6.16)
   a. pages per minute (ppm)
   b. dots per inch (dpi)
   c. lines per minute (lpm)
   d. pixels per inch (ppi)

9. Laser printers usually cost _____. (6.19)
   a. more than ink-jet printers and are faster
   b. less than ink-jet printers and are faster
   c. more than ink-jet printers and are slower
   d. less than ink-jet printers and are slower

10. With Bluetooth printing, Bluetooth devices _____ an approximate 30-foot range. (6.22)
    a. have to be aligned with each other but can be outside
    b. have to be aligned with each other and need to be within
    c. do not have to be aligned with each other and can be outside
    d. do not have to be aligned with each other but need to be within

11. _____ allows users to have conversations over the Web. (6.25)
    a. An electronic book
    b. Internet postage
    c. Force feedback
    d. Internet telephony

12. When a computer receives a fax, _____ software enables the user to convert the image to text and then edit it. (6.26)
    a. optical character recognition (OCR)
    b. magnetic-ink character recognition (MICR)
    c. optical mark recognition (OMR)
    d. bar code recognition (BCR)

13. The disadvantage of multifunction peripherals is that _____. (6.26)
    a. they require more space than having separate devices
    b. they are significantly more expensive than purchasing each device separately
    c. if the multifunction peripheral breaks down, all functions are lost
    d. all of the above

14. The _____ command in Windows XP enlarges text and other on-screen items for individuals with vision disabilities. (6.29)
    a. Magnifier
    b. On-Screen Keyboard
    c. Narrator
    d. Utility Manager

CHECKPOINT CHAPTER 6

MATCHING Match the terms with their definitions. (See page numbers in parentheses.)

_____ 1. soft copy (6.04)

_____ 2. monochrome (6.04)

_____ 3. gray scaling (6.04)

_____ 4. nit (6.11)

_____ 5. hard copy (6.13)

_____ 6. near letter quality (NLQ) (6.14)

_____ 7. letter quality (LQ) (6.15)

_____ 8. woofer (6.23)

_____ 9. LCD projector (6.26)

_____ 10. DLP projector (6.26)

a. added to boost low bass sounds

b. printed information that exists physically and is a more permanent form of output

c. uses many shades of gray from white to black to enhance the quality of graphics

d. changes the brightness and contrast of pixels surrounding each letter

e. acceptable print quality for business letters

f. information on a display device that exists electronically and displays for a temporary period

g. uses tiny mirrors to reflect light, which produces crisp, bright, colorful images

h. unit of visible light intensity equal to one candela

i. magnetic field that travels at the speed of light

j. print quality slightly less clear than what is acceptable for business letters

k. attaches directly to a computer and uses its own light source to display information

l. information displays in one color on a different background color

SHORT ANSWER Write a brief answer to each of the following questions.

1. What features do CRT monitors usually include to address ergonomic issues? _____ What is the ENERGY STAR program? _____

2. How is an active-matrix display different from a passive-matrix display? _____ What is organic LED (OLED)? _____

3. What advantages do digital television signals provide over analog signals? _____ What is interactive TV? _____

4. How is portrait orientation different from landscape orientation? _____ What is continuous form paper? _____

5. What is a page description language? _____ How is PCL different from PostScript? _____

WORKING TOGETHER Working with a group of your classmates, complete the following team exercises.

1. A group of business employees would like to set up a small accounting office, with 10 to 12 employees. They have hired your group as consultants to help with the setup. Your primary responsibility is to determine the type of output devices you think they will need within the office. Consider the types and number of printers, types and number of display devices, audio and video devices, and whether fax machines, fax modems, and/or multifunction peripherals are needed. Use the Internet to research information. Prepare a report to share with the class. Include a table listing the pros and cons of the various devices and a short explanation of why you selected each device.

2. Choose one Issue in this chapter from page 6.07, 6.09, 6.16, 6.24, or 6.29. Use the Web and/or print media to research the issue. Present a debate for the class, with different members of your team supporting different responses to the questions that accompany the issue.

3. Plotters can draw on any part of a page at random, and then move on to any other part. This capability and their capacity to use large sheets of paper make plotters invaluable to engineers, electrical contractors, architects, home builders, and city planners. Have each member of your team interview someone in an organization that uses plotters. What type of plotter is used? Why? For what purpose is the plotter used? What is the advantage (or disadvantage) of using a plotter compared with simply creating a drawing by hand? Discuss the results of your interviews in the group. Use PowerPoint to create a group presentation and share your findings with the class.

CHAPTER 6 LEARN IT ONLINE

◄● Previous | Next ●►

Use the Learn It Online exercises to reinforce your understanding of the chapter concepts.

WEB INSTRUCTIONS:

To display this page from the Web, start your browser and enter the Web address **scsite.com/dc2004/ch6/learn**.

1 At The Movies – E-Books

To view the E-Books movie, click the number 1 button. Watch the movie and then complete the exercise by answering the questions below. Electronic books are here. Holding half-a-dozen novels, a semester's worth of textbooks, or a library of sales and service manuals, they promise a new world of portability, access, and convenience. Book files can be downloaded easily from the Internet. Prices range from $150 to $500 for the e-book itself, with thousands of titles currently available for $5 to $25 each. The technology and the market for e-books continue to improve in parallel. Better screens and voice recognition already are in the works. What other features might you suggest? What, if anything, do you think inhibits consumer acceptance of this technology?

2 Shelly Cashman Series Setting Up to Print Lab

Follow the instructions in Learn It Online 2 on page 1.46 to start and use the Shelly Cashman Series Setting Up to Print Lab. If you are running from the Web, enter the Web address **scsite.com/sclabs/menu** or display the Learn It Online page (see instructions at the top of this page) and then click the number 2 button.

3 Shelly Cashman Series Configuring Your Display Lab

Follow the instructions in Learn It Online 2 on page 1.46 to start and use the Shelly Cashman Series Configuring Your Display Lab. If you are running from the Web, enter the Web address **scsite.com/sclabs/menu** or display the Learn It Online page (see instructions at the top of this page) and then click the number 3 button.

4 Practice Test

Click the number 4 button. Answer each question. When completed, enter your name and click the Grade Test button to submit the quiz for grading. Make a note of any missed questions. If required, print a copy to submit to your instructor.

5 Web Guide

Click the number 5 button to display the Guide to Web Sites and Searching Techniques Web page. Click Computers and Computing. Click ZDNet and then type `audio devices` in the Search text box. Click the Go button and then review the information. Use your word processing program to prepare a brief report about your findings and submit your assignment to your instructor.

6 Scavenger Hunt

Click the number 6 button. Print a copy of the Scavenger Hunt page; use this page to write down your answers as you search the Web. Submit your completed page to your instructor.

7 Who Wants to Be a Computer Genius?

Click the number 7 button to find out if you are a computer genius. Directions on how to play the game will display. When you are ready to play, click the Play button. Submit your score to your instructor.

LEARN IT ONLINE CHAPTER 6

8 Wheel of Terms

Click the number 8 button to reinforce important terms you learned in this chapter by playing the Shelly Cashman Series version of this popular game. Directions on how to play the game will display. When you are ready to play, click the Play button. Submit your score to your instructor.

9 Career Corner

Click the number 9 button to display the Penn State's Career Services Web page. Click a link of your choice. Write a brief report on the information you found. Submit the report to your instructor.

10 Search Sleuth

Click the number 10 button to learn search techniques that will help make you a research expert. Submit the completed assignment to your instructor.

11 Crossword Puzzle Challenge

Click the number 11 button. Complete the puzzle to reinforce skills you learned in this chapter. Directions on how to play the game will display. When you are ready to play, click the Play button. Submit the completed puzzle to your instructor.

12 Choosing a Printer

The printer is a key component of any new personal computer that you purchase. Whether you are printing black and white reports or producing photo-lab-quality pictures, determining which printer is best for your individual needs requires some research. Printers are available in a range of speeds and capabilities. Click the number 12 button for a tutorial on how to select the printer that is best for your particular requirements.

13 In the News

Display device technology continues to advance. Not long ago, computer users would have considered connecting their $1,000 computers to a color television instead of paying outrageous prices for a color monitor. Today, you can purchase a 20-inch monitor that is faster and sharper than that color television for less than $300. Yet, as prices fall, consumers surely will purchase the display devices for HDTV and crystal-clear Internet access. Click the number 13 button and then read a news article about a new or improved output device. What is the device? Who manufactures it? How is the output device better than, or different from, earlier devices? Who do you think is most likely to use the device? Why?

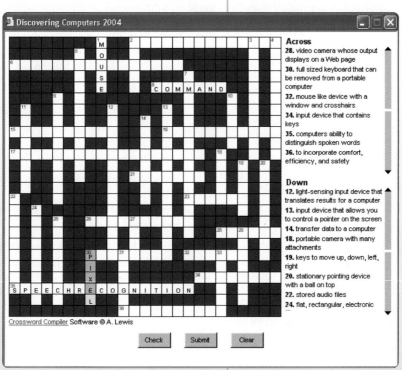

Discovering Computers 2004

Across
28. video camera whose output displays on a Web page
30. full sized keyboard that can be removed from a portable computer
32. mouse like device with a window and crosshairs
34. input device that contains keys
35. computers ability to distinguish spoken words
36. to incorporate comfort, efficiency, and safety

Down
12. light-sensing input device that translates results for a computer
13. input device that allows you to control a pointer on the screen
14. transfer data to a computer
18. portable camera with many attachments
19. keys to move up, down, left, right
20. stationary pointing device with a ball on top
22. stored audio files
24. flat, rectangular, electronic

Crossword Compiler Software © A. Lewis

Check   Submit   Clear

CHAPTER 6 LAB EXERCISES

Use the Lab Exercises to gain hands-on computer experience.

■ WEB INSTRUCTIONS:

To display this page from the Web, start your browser and enter the Web address **scsite.com/dc2004/ch6/lab**.

1 About Your Computer

This exercise uses Windows XP procedures. To learn about the output devices on your computer, click the Start button on the taskbar, and then right-click the My Computer icon on the Start menu. Click Properties on the shortcut menu. When the System Properties dialog box displays, click the Hardware tab. Click the Device Manager button. Click the plus sign next to Computer. Below Computer, a list of hardware device categories displays. What output devices are listed? Click the plus sign next to each category. What specific output devices in each category are connected to your computer? Close the Device Manager window. Click the Cancel button in the System Properties dialog box.

2 Accessibility Options

This exercise uses Windows XP procedures. The Windows operating system offers several output options for people with hearing or visual impairments. Three of these options are SoundSentry, ShowSounds, and High Contrast. To find out more about each option, click the Start button on the taskbar and then click Control Panel on the Start menu. In Category View, click the Accessibility Options icon in the Control Panel window, and then click the Accessibility Options icon in the Accessibility Options window. Click the Sound tab in the Accessibility Options dialog box. Click the Question Mark button on the title bar, click SoundSentry, read the information in the pop-up window, and then click the pop-up window to close it. Repeat this process for ShowSounds. Click the Display tab. Click the Question Mark button on the title bar and then click High Contrast. Read the information in the pop-up window, and then click the pop-up window to close it. What is the purpose of each option? Click the Cancel button. Click the Close button to close the Accessibility Options window.

3 Self-Portrait

This exercise uses Windows XP/2000/98 procedures. Windows includes a drawing program called Paint. The quality of graphics

produced with this program depends on a variety of factors, including the quality of your printer, your understanding of the software, and (to some extent) your artistic talent. In this exercise, you use Paint to create a self-portrait. To access Paint, click the Start button on the taskbar, point to All Programs (Programs in Windows 2000/98) on the Start menu, point to Accessories on the All Programs submenu (Programs submenu in Windows 2000/98), and then click Paint on the Accessories submenu. When the untitled - Paint window is displayed, you will see the Paint toolbar on the left side of the window. Point to a toolbar button to see a tool's name; click a button to use that tool. Use the tools and colors available in Paint to draw a picture of yourself. If you make a mistake, you can click Undo on the Edit menu to undo your most recent action, you can erase part of your picture using the Eraser/Color Eraser tool, or you can clear the entire picture by clicking Clear Image on the Image menu. When your self-portrait is finished, print it by clicking Print on the File menu. Close Paint. Do not save your changes.

4 Magnifier

This exercise uses Windows 2000 procedures. Magnifier is a Windows utility for the visually impaired. To find out about the Magnifier capabilities, click the Start button on the taskbar and then click Help on the Start menu. Click the Index tab in the Windows 2000 window and then type `magnifier` in the Type in the keyword to find text box. Click the overview subentry below the Magnifier entry in the list of topics and then click the Display button. Click Magnifier overview in the Topics Found dialog box and then click the Display button. Read the Help information in the right pane of the Windows 2000 window and answer the following questions:

- How does Magnifier make the screen more readable for the visually impaired?
- What viewing options does Magnifier have?
- What tracking options does Magnifier have?

Click the Close button to close the Windows 2000 window.

WEB RESEARCH CHAPTER 6

Use the Web Research exercises to learn more about the special features in this chapter.

WEB INSTRUCTIONS:

Use the link in each exercise or a search engine such as Google (google.com) to research the topic. Then, write a one-page, double-spaced report or create a presentation, unless otherwise directed below. Page numbers on which information can be found are in parentheses.

1. **Issue** Choose one Issue from the following issues in this chapter: Who Is Responsible for Disposing of an Old Monitor? (6.07), Are Thin Flat Panel Monitors In? (6.09), Short of Cash? (6.16), Wearing the Web? (6.24), or How Should Employers Accommodate Employees with Disabilities? (6.29). Use the Web to research the issue. Discuss the issue with classmates, instructors, and friends. Address the questions that accompany the issue in a report or presentation.

2. **Apply It** Choose one of the following Apply It features in this chapter: Picture This: Printing Digital Photographs (6.17) or Audio Books Tell a Good Story (6.24). Use the Web to gather additional information about the topic. Print two Web pages that relate to the Apply It. Detail in a report or presentation what you learned.

3. **Career Corner** Read the Career Corner article in this chapter (6.30). Use the Web to find out more about the career. Describe the career in a report or presentation.

4. **Companies on the Cutting Edge** Choose one of the Companies on the Cutting Edge in this chapter (6.32). Use the Web to research the company further. Explain in a report or presentation how this company has contributed to computer technology.

5. **Technology Trailblazers** Choose one of the Technology Trailblazers in this chapter (6.33). Use the Web to research the person further. Explain in a report or presentation how this individual has affected the way people use, or think about, computers.

6. **Picture Yourself Printing Pictures** Read the Picture Yourself Printing Pictures story at the beginning of this chapter (6.00). Use the Web to research printing pictures further. Describe in a report or presentation the ways in which you might print pictures.

7. **High-Tech Talk** Read the High-Tech Talk feature in this chapter (6.31). Use the Web to find out more about the topic. Summarize in a report or presentation what you learned.

8. **Web Links** Review the Web Link boxes found in the margins of this chapter. Visit five of the Web Link sites. Print the main Web page for each site you visit. Choose one of the Web pages and then summarize in one paragraph the content of the Web page.

9. **Looking Ahead** Choose one of the Looking Ahead articles in this chapter: Electronic Paper Writes a New Page (6.13) or Digital Movies Project New Image (6.27). Use the Web to find out more about the topic. Detail in a report or presentation what you learned.

10. **FAQ** Choose one FAQ found in this chapter. Use the Web to find out more about the topic. Summarize in one paragraph what you learned.

11. **Digital Imaging and Video Technology** Read the Digital Imaging and Video Technology Special Feature that follows this chapter (6.44–6.55). Select the technology in which you are most interested (digital imaging or video). Use the Web to learn more about your selection. Explain in a report or presentation the entire process, from capturing a digital image or video to distributing it.

12. **Making Use of the Web** Read the Government section of Making Use of the Web Appendix A (A.12). Complete the Government Web Exercises at the end of the section. Answer the questions posed in each exercise.

Digital Imaging and Video Technology

Everywhere you look, people are capturing moments they want to remember. They take pictures or make movies of their vacations, birthday parties, activities, accomplishments, sporting events, weddings, and more. Because of the popularity of digital cameras and digital video cameras, increasingly more people desire to capture their memories digitally, instead of on film. With digital technology, picture takers have the ability to modify and share the digital images and videos they create. When you use special hardware and/or software, you can copy, manipulate, print, and distribute digital images and videos using your personal computer and the Internet. Amateurs can create professional quality results by using more sophisticated hardware and software.

Home Digital Imaging Technology

digital camera (input)

USB

personal computer

FireWire or USB 2.0

digital video camera (input)

S-video

television (output)

Home Video Editing Technology

FIGURE 1 The top portion of the figure shows a typical home digital imaging setup and the lower portion of the figure shows a typical home setup for editing personal video.

Digital photography and recordings deliver significant benefits over film-based photography and movie making. With digital cameras, no developing is needed. Instead, the images reside on storage media such as a hard disk, DVD, or flash memory card. Unlike film, storage media can be reused, which reduces costs, saves time, and provides immediate results. Digital technology allows greater control over the creative process, both while taking pictures and video and in the editing process. You can check results immediately after capturing a picture or video to determine whether it meets your expectations. If you are dissatisfied with a picture or video, you can erase it and recapture it, again and again.

As shown in the top portion of Figure 1, a digital camera functions as an input device when it transmits pictures through a cable to a personal computer via a USB port or FireWire port. Using a digital camera in this way allows you to edit the pictures, save them on storage media, and print them on a photographic-quality printer via a parallel port or USB port.

The lower portion of Figure 1 illustrates how you might use a digital video camera with a personal computer. The process typically is the same for most digital video cameras. You capture the images or video with the video camera. Next, you connect the video camera to your personal computer using a FireWire or USB 2.0 port, or you place the storage media used on the camera in the computer. The video then is copied or downloaded to the computer's hard disk. Then, you can edit the video using video editing software. If desired, you can preview the video during the editing process on a television. Finally, you save the finished result to the desired media, such as a VHS tape or DVD+RW or, perhaps, e-mail the edited video. In this example, a VCR and a DVD player also can be used to input video from a VHS tape or a DVD.

USB

photographic-quality printer (output)

DVD recorder (input, output, storage)

VCR (input, output, storage)

S-video-in

S-video-out

DIGITAL IMAGING TECHNOLOGY

Digital imaging technology involves capturing and manipulating still photographic images in an electronic format. The following sections outline the steps involved in the process of using digital imaging technology.

 Select a Digital Camera

A **digital camera** is a type of camera that stores photographed images electronically instead of on traditional film. Digital cameras are divided into three categories (Figure 2) based mainly on image resolution, features, and of course, price. The image resolution is measured in pixels (short for picture element). The image quality increases with the number of pixels. The image resolution usually is measured in **megapixels** (million of pixels), often abbreviated as **MP**. Features of digital cameras include red-eye reduction, zoom, autofocus, flash, self-timer, and manual mode for fine-tuning settings. Figure 3 summarizes the three categories of digital cameras.

TYPES OF DIGITAL CAMERAS

Type	Maximum Resolution	Comment	Price
Low-end point and shoot	Less than 2 MP	Fully automatic; fits in your pocket; usually limited to 4-by-6-inch printed output; ideal for Web pages, e-mail attachments, and newsletters	Less than $200
High-end point and shoot	Greater than 2 MP and less than 5 MP	Includes more advanced features that allow for creative control of the camera's settings; makes up to 8-by-10-inch printed pictures; capable of taking pictures at lower resolutions	$200 to $1,000
Professional	Greater than 5 MP	Based on 35mm and APS SLR cameras; includes three image sensors for capturing great color and resolution; has much greater control over exposure and lenses	$1,000 and up

FIGURE 3 Digital cameras often are categorized by image resolution, features, and price.

(a) low-end point and shoot

(b) high-end point and shoot

(c) professional

FIGURE 2 The low-end point and shoot digital camera (a) requires no adjustments before shooting. The high-end point and shoot digital camera (b) offers improved quality and features that allow you to make manual adjustments before shooting. The professional digital camera (c) offers better color and resolution and greater control over exposure and lenses.

 Take Pictures

Digital cameras provide you with several options that are set before a picture is taken. Three of the more important options are the resolution, compression, and image file format in which the camera should save the picture. While a camera may allow for a very high resolution for a large print, you may choose to take a picture at a lower resolution if the image does not require great detail or must be a small size. For example, you may want to use the image on a Web page where smaller image file sizes are beneficial.

Compression results in smaller image file sizes. Figure 4 illustrates the image file sizes for varying resolutions and compressions under standard photographing conditions using a 4 megapixel digital camera. Figure 4 also shows the average picture size for a given resolution. The camera may take more time to save an image at lower compression, resulting in a longer delay before the camera is ready to take another picture. A higher compression, however, may result in loss of some image quality. If a camera has a 16 MB flash memory card, you can determine the number of pictures the card can hold by dividing 16 MB by the file size. Flash memory cards are available in sizes from 16 MB to 1 GB.

IMAGE FILE SIZE WITH A FOUR MEGAPIXEL DIGITAL CAMERA

Resolution in Pixels	COMPRESSION			Picture Size in Inches
	Low	Medium	High	
2272 x 1704	2 MB	1.1 MB	556 KB	11 by 17
1600 x 1200	1 MB	558 KB	278 KB	8 by 10
1024 x 768	570 KB	320 KB	170 KB	4 by 6
640 x 480	249 KB	150 KB	84 KB	3 by 5

FIGURE 4 Image file sizes for varying resolutions and compressions under standard shooting conditions using a 4 megapixel digital camera.

Most digital cameras also allow you to choose an image file format. Two popular file formats are TIFF and JPEG. The TIFF file format saves the image uncompressed. All of the image detail is captured and stored, but the file sizes can be large. The JPEG file format is compressed. The resolution of the image may be the same as a TIFF file, but some detail may be lost in the image.

Finally, before you take the photograph, you should choose the type of media on which to store the resulting image file. Some cameras allow for a choice of locations, such as a CompactFlash card or Memory Stick, while others allow for only one type of storage media. One major advantage of a digital camera is that you easily can erase pictures from its media, freeing up space for new pictures.

 Transfer and Manage Image Files

The method of transferring images from the camera to the personal computer differs greatly depending on the capabilities of both. Digital cameras use a variety of storage media (Figure 5). If your camera uses a flash memory card such as a CompactFlash, SmartMedia, Secure Digital (SD), or Memory Stick, then, you can remove the media from the camera and place it in a slot on the personal computer or in a device connected to the personal computer for reading the cards. Your camera also may connect to the personal computer using a USB, USB 2.0, or FireWire port (Figure 6). When you insert the memory card or connect the camera,

software on the personal computer guides you through the process of transferring the images to the hard disk. Some operating systems and software recognize a memory card or camera as though it is another hard disk on the computer. This feature allows you to access the files, navigate them, and then copy, delete, or rename the files while the media still is in the camera.

Microdrive

SD Card   Memory Stick

FIGURE 5 Microdrives, SD Cards, and Memory Sticks are popular storage devices for digital cameras.

FIGURE 6 Using a USB or FireWire connection, you can add a card reader to your personal computer.

Figure 7 shows some of the effects available in Jasc's Paint Shop Pro on the Enhance Photo submenu.

After you transfer the files to the hard disk on your personal computer, you should organize the files by sorting them or renaming them so that information, such as the subject, date, time, and purpose, is saved along with the image. Finally, before altering the images digitally, or using the images for other purposes, you should back up the images to another location, such as a CD or DVD, so the original image is recoverable.

FIGURE 7 The ability to use effects separates digital photography from film photography.

⑤ Print Images

Once an image is digitally altered, it is ready to be printed. You can print images on a personal color printer, or send them to a professional service that specializes in digital photo printing.

When printing the images yourself, make sure that the resolution used to create the image was high enough for the size of the print you want to create. For example, if the camera used a resolution of 640 x 480 pixels, then the ideal print size is a wallet size. If you print such an image at a size of 8-by-10 inches, then the image will appear **pixilated**, or blurry. Use high-quality photo paper for the best results. A photo printer gives the best results when printing digital photography.

Many services print digital images, either over the Internet or through traditional photo developing locations and kiosks (Figure 8), such as those found in drug stores or shopping marts. Some services allow you to e-mail or upload the files to the service, specify the size, quality, and quantity of print, and then they send the prints to you via the postal service. Other services allow you drop off flash memory cards, CD-ROMs, or floppy disks at a photo shop and allow you to pick up the prints, just as you do with traditional photo developing shops.

④ Edit Images

Image editing software allows you to edit digital images. The following list summarizes the more common image enhancements or alterations:

- Adjust the contrast and brightness; correct lighting problems; or help give the photograph a particular feeling; such as warm or stark

- Remove red-eye

- Crop an image to remove unnecessary elements and resize it

- Rotate the image to change its orientation

- Add elements to the image, such as descriptive text, a date, a logo, or decorative items; create collages or add missing elements

- Replace individual colors with a new color

- Add special effects, such as texture or motion blurring to enhance the image

FIGURE 8 A Kodak EasyShare™ kiosk allows you to print digital images in high resolution on photo paper.

⑥ Distribute Images Electronically

Rather than printing images, you often need to use the images electronically. Depending on the electronic use of the image, the image may require additional processing. If you use the images on a Web site or want to e-mail a photo, you probably want to send a lower-resolution image. Image editing software allows you to lower the resolution of the image, resulting in a smaller file size. You also should use standard file formats when distributing an electronic photo. The JPEG format is viewable using most personal computers or Web browsers.

You can store very high resolution photos on a DVD or a CD. **DVD and CD mastering software** (Figure 9) allows you to create slide show presentations on a recordable DVD or CD that can play in many home DVD players or personal computer DVD drives.

FIGURE 9 Photo2VCD and similar software applications allow you to create your own photo slide shows on DVD or CD.

Finally, you should back up and store images that you distribute electronically with the same care as you store your traditional film negatives.

DIGITAL VIDEO TECHNOLOGY

Digital video technology allows you to input, edit, manage, publish, and share your videos using a personal computer. With digital video technology, you can transform home videos into Hollywood-style movies by enhancing the videos with scrolling titles and transitions, cutting out or adding scenes, and adding background music and voice-over narration. The following sections outline the steps involved in the process of using digital video technology.

 Select a Video Camera

Video cameras record in either analog or digital format. **Analog formats** include 8mm, Hi8, VHS, VHS-C, and Super VHS-C. The latter three formats use the types of tapes similar to those used in a standard VCR. **Digital formats** include Mini-DV, MICROMV, Digital8, and DVD. Consumer digital video cameras are by far the most popular type among consumers. They fall into three general categories, high-end consumer, consumer, and webcasting and monitoring (Figure 10). Digital video cameras provide more features than analog video cameras, such as a higher level of zoom, better sound, or more control over color and lighting.

 Record a Video

Video cameras are easier to use than digital cameras. Video cameras, for example, do not require you to set the resolution, compression, or file format before recording. Most video cameras do, however, provide you with a choice of recording programs sometimes called automatic settings. Each recording program includes a different combination of camera settings, so you can adjust the exposure and other functions to match the recording environment. Usually, several different programs are available, such as point and shoot, point and shoot with manual adjustment, sports, portrait, spot lit scenes, and low light. You also have the ability to select special digital effects, such as fade, wipe, and black and white. If you are shooting outside on a windy day, then you can enable the wind screen to prevent wind noise. If you are shooting home videos, then the point-and-shoot recording program is sufficient.

 Transfer and Manage Videos

After recording the video, the next step is to transfer the video to your personal computer. Most video cameras connect directly to a USB 2.0 or FireWire port on your personal computer (Figure 11). Transferring video with a digital camera is easy, because the video already is in a digital format that the computer can understand.

An analog camcorder or VCR requires additional hardware to convert the analog signals into a digital counterpart before the video can be manipulated on a personal computer. The additional hardware includes a special video capture card using a standard RCA video cable or an S-video cable (Figure 12). *S-video* cables provide greater quality. When you use video capture hardware with an analog video, be sure to close all open programs on your computer because capturing video requires a great deal of processing power.

(a) high-end consumer

(b) consumer

(c) webcasting and monitoring

FIGURE 10 The high-end consumer digital video camera (a) can produce professional-grade results. The consumer digital video camera (b) produces amateur-grade results. The webcasting and monitoring digital video camera (c) is appropriate for webcasting and security monitoring.

When transferring video, plan to use approximately 15 to 30 gigabytes of hard disk storage space per hour of digital video. A typical video project requires about four times the amount of raw footage as the final product. Therefore, at the high end, a video that lasts an hour may require up to 120 gigabytes of storage for the raw footage, editing process, and final video. This storage requirement can vary depending on the software you use to copy the video from the video camera to the hard disk and the format you select to save the video. For example, Microsoft claims that the latest version of its Windows Movie Maker can save 15 hours of video in 10 gigabytes when creating video for playback on a computer but saves only 1 hour of video in 10 gigabytes when creating video for playback on a DVD or VCR.

personal computer

USB 2.0 or FireWire

digital video camera

FIGURE 11 A digital video camera is connected to the personal computer via a FireWire or USB 2.0 port and the video. No additional hardware is needed.

video capture card

personal computer

S-video

S-video

VCR

analog camera

FIGURE 12 An analog camcorder or VCR is connected to the personal computer via an s-video port on a video capture card.

The video transfer requires application software on the personal computer. Windows XP includes the Windows Movie Maker software (Figure 13) that allows you to transfer the video from your video camera. Depending on the length of video and the type of connection used, the video may take a long time to download. Make certain that no other programs are running on your personal computer while transferring the video.

File formats support codecs to encode the audio and video into the file formats. A particular file format may be able to store audio and video in a number of different codecs. A **codec** specifies how the audio and video is compressed and stored within the file. Figure 15 shows some options available for specifying a file format and codec in the Microsoft Windows Movie Maker. The file format and codec you choose often is based on what you plan to do with the movie. For example, if you plan to stream video over the Web using RealNetworks software, the best choice for the file format is the RealMedia format, which uses the RealVideo codec.

FIGURE 13   Some video editing software, such as Microsoft Windows Movie Maker, allows you to transfer your video from any video source to a hard disk.

When transferring video, the software may allow you to choose a file format and a codec to store the video. A video **file format** holds the video information in a manner specified by a vendor, such as Apple or Microsoft. Some of the more popular file formats are listed in Figure 14.

POPULAR VIDEO FILE FORMATS

File Format	File Extensions
Apple QuickTime	.MOV or .QT
Microsoft Windows Media Video	.WMV or .ASF
RealNetworks RealMedia	.RM or .RAM

FIGURE 14   Apple, Microsoft, and RealNetworks offer the more popular video file formats.

FIGURE 15   Video editing software applications allow you to specify a combination of file format and codec when saving a video.

After transferring the video to a personal computer, and before manipulating the video, you should store the video files in appropriate folders, named correctly, and backed up. Most video transfer application software helps manage these tasks.

 Edit a Video

Once the video is stored on your hard disk, the next step is to edit, or manipulate, the video. If you used a video capture card to transfer analog video to your computer (Figure 12), the files may require extra initial processing. When you use a video capture card, some of the video frames may be lost in the transfer process. Some video editing programs allow you to fix this problem with **frame rate correction** tools.

The first step in the editing process is to split the video into smaller pieces, or *scenes*, that you can manipulate more easily. This process is called splitting. Most video software automatically splits the video into scenes, thus saving you the time. After *splitting*, you should cut out unwanted scenes or portions of scenes. This process is called *pruning*.

After you create the scenes you want to use in your final production, you edit each individual scene. You can crop, or change the size of, scenes. That is, you may want to cut out the top or a side of a scene that is irrelevant. You also can resize the scene. For example, you may be creating a video that will display in a Web browser. Making a smaller video, such as 320 x 200 pixels instead of 640 x 480 pixels, results in a smaller file that transmits faster over the Internet.

If video has been recorded over a long period, using different cameras or under different lighting conditions, the video may need color correction. *Color correction* (Figure 16) tools analyze your video and match brightness, colors, and other attributes of video clips to create a smooth look to the video.

FIGURE 16 Color correction tools in video editing software allow a great deal of control over the mood of your video creation.

You can add logos, special effects, or titles to scenes. You can place a company logo or personal logo in a video to identify yourself or the company producing the video. Logos often are added on the lower-right corner of a video and remain for the duration of the video. Special effects include warping, changing from color to black and white, morphing, or zoom motion. *Morphing* is a special effect in which one video image is transformed into another image over the course of several frames of video, creating the illusion of metamorphosis. You usually add titles at the beginning and end of a video to give the video context. A training video may have titles throughout the video to label a particular scene, or each scene may begin with a title.

The next step in editing a video is to add audio effects, including voice-over narration and background music. Many video editing programs allow you to add additional tracks, or *layers*, of sound to a video in addition to the sound that was recorded on the video camera. You also can add special audio effects.

The final step in editing a video is to combine the scenes into a complete video (Figure 17). This process involves ordering scenes and adding transition effects between scenes (Figure 18). Video editing software allows you to combine scenes and separate each scene with a transition. *Transitions* include fading, wiping, blurry, bursts, ruptures, erosions, and more.

FIGURE 17 Scenes, shown on the right, are combined into a sequence on the bottom of the screen.

FIGURE 18 Smooth and dynamic transitions eliminate the hard cuts between scenes typically found in raw footage.

5 Distribute the Video

After editing the video, the final step is to distribute it or save it on a desired media. You can save video in a variety of formats. Using special hardware, you can save the video on standard video tape. *A digital-to-analog converter* is necessary to allow your personal computer to transmit video to a VCR. A digital-to-analog converter may be an external device that connects to both the computer and input device, or may be a video capture card inside the computer.

Video also can be stored in digital formats in any of several DVD formats, on CD-R, or on video CD (VCD). *DVD* or *CD creation software*, which often is packaged with video editing software, allows you to create, or *master*, DVDs and CDs. You can add interactivity to your DVDs. For example, you can allow viewers to jump to certain scenes using a menu (Figure 19). A *video CD (VCD)* is a CD format that stores video on a CD-R that can be played in many DVD players.

You also can save your video creation in electronic format, for distribution over the Web or via e-mail. Your video editing software must support the file format and codec you want to use. For example, RealNetworks's Helix media delivery system allows you to save media files in the RealVideo file formats.

After creating your final video for distribution or your personal video collection, you should backup the final video file. You can save your scenes for inclusion in other video creations or create new masters using different effects, transitions, and ordering of scenes.

FIGURE 19 DVD mastering software allows you to create interactive menus on your DVD.

Professionals use hardware and software that allow them to create a film version of digital video that can be played in movie theaters. This technology is becoming increasingly popular and has been used in such movies as the recent *Star Wars* movies. Some Hollywood directors believe that eventually, all movies will be recorded and edited digitally.

Storage

Picture Yourself Using a Picture CD

At your family reunion this weekend, you took several rolls of film. While filling out the film-processing envelope, you notice it has a check box for a Kodak Picture CD. "What's a Picture CD?" you ask the clerk. He explains that in addition to prints and negatives, you receive a CD that contains digital images of all your pictures. Picture CDs can last longer and take up less storage space than printed pictures. Some users also print additional pictures from the Picture CD.

You mention that you do not have a high-quality printer. He says you can print pictures on the Picture CD using the Kodak Picture Maker, which is an in-store kiosk that offers the capabilities of enlarging, cropping, eliminating red eye, and adding text to pictures before you print them. You also could e-mail the images from the Picture CD or post them on a photo community (usually without cost).

After thanking the clerk for his great explanation, you mark the Kodak Picture CD box on the film-processing envelope. With the Picture CD, you will be able to send images of the family reunion to everyone. Using the Kodak Picture Maker, you can make printed copies of the great pictures to hang on your wall.

As you read Chapter 7, you will learn about Picture CDs and discover other types of storage.

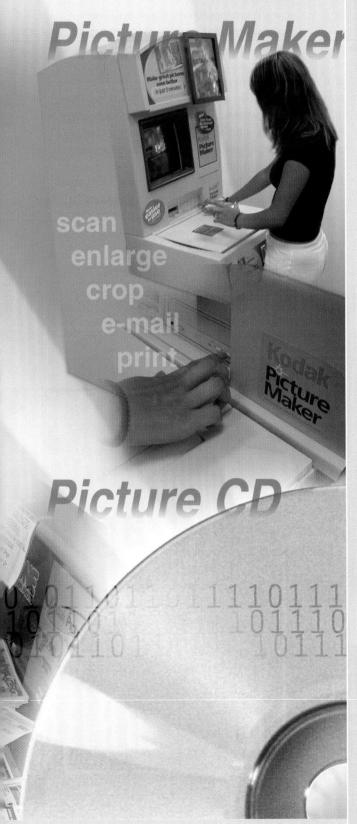

scan
enlarge
crop
e-mail
print

OBJECTIVES

CONTENTS

STORAGE

Storage holds data, instructions, and information for future use. Every computer uses storage to hold software, specifically, system software and application software. To start up, a computer locates an operating system (system software) in storage and loads it into memory. When a user issues a command to start application software, such as word processing or a Web browser, the operating system locates the program in storage and loads it into memory.

In addition to programs, users store a variety of data and information on mainframe computers, servers, desktop computers, notebook computers, handheld computers, Tablet PCs, PDAs, and smart phones:

• The home user might store letters, budgets, bank statements, a household inventory, records of stock purchases, tax data, addresses of friends and relatives, daily schedules, e-mail messages, homework assignments, recipes, digital photographs, music, and videos.

• The small office/home office user often stores correspondence, faxes, business reports, financial records, tax data, travel records, appointments, contact information, e-mail messages, customer orders, payroll records, inventory records, and Web pages.

• The mobile user usually stores letters, faxes, presentations, appointments, travel records, contacts and addresses, homework assignments, quotations, e-mail messages, and digital photographs.

• The large business user accesses many stored items, including customer orders and invoices, vendor payments, payroll records, tax data, inventory records, presentations, contracts, marketing literature, contacts,

floppy disk

Zip disk

microfiche

Storage

miniature mobile storage media

PC Card

FIGURE 7-1 Data, instructions, and information are stored on a variety of storage media.

appointments, schedules, e-mail messages, and Web pages. The large business user accesses hundreds or thousands of employee, customer, and vendor records, whereas the small office/home office user may access less than one hundred of these types of records.

- The power user stores diagrams, drawings, blueprints, designs, marketing literature, corporate newsletters, product catalogs, videos, audio recordings, multimedia presentations, digital photographs, Web pages, letters, contacts, appointments, schedules, and e-mail messages.

Storage requirements among these users vary greatly. Home users, small office/home office users, and mobile users typically have much smaller storage requirements than the large business user or power user. For example, a home user may need 80 billion bytes of storage, while the large business user may require 50 trillion bytes of storage.

A **storage medium** (media is the plural), also called *secondary storage*, is the physical material on which a computer keeps data, instructions, and information. Examples of storage media are floppy disks, Zip disks, hard disks, CDs and DVDs, tape, PC Cards, miniature mobile storage media such as memory sticks or cards, and microfiche (Figure 7-1). Memory, by contrast, typically consists of one or more chips on the motherboard or some other circuit board in the computer.

internal hard disk

external hard disk

tape

CD or DVD

removable hard disk

Capacity is the number of bytes (characters) a storage medium can hold. Figure 7-2 identifies the terms manufacturers use to define the capacity of storage media. For example, a typical floppy disk can store up to 1.44 MB of data (approximately 1.4 million bytes) and a typical hard disk has 80 GB (approximately 80 billion bytes) of storage capacity.

Items on a storage medium remain intact even when power is removed from the computer. Thus, a storage medium is nonvolatile. Most memory, by contrast, holds data and instructions temporarily and thus is volatile. Figure 7-3 illustrates the concept of volatility.

For an analogy, think of a filing cabinet that holds file folders as a storage medium, and the top of your desk as memory. When you want to work with a file, you remove it from the filing cabinet (storage medium) and place it on your desk (memory). When you are finished with the file, you remove it from your desk (memory) and return it to the filing cabinet (storage medium).

A **storage device** is the computer hardware that records and/or retrieves items to and from storage media. **Writing** is the process of transferring data, instructions, and information from memory to a storage medium. **Reading** is the process of transferring these items from a storage medium into memory. When storage devices write data on storage media, they are creating output. Similarly, when storage devices read from storage media, they function as a source of input. Nevertheless, they are categorized as storage devices, not as input or output devices.

The speed of storage devices and memory is defined by access time. **Access time** measures (1) the amount of time it takes a storage device to locate an item on a storage medium or (2) the time required to deliver an item from memory to the processor. The access time of storage devices is slow, compared with the access time of memory. Memory (chips) accesses items in billionths of a second (nanoseconds). Storage devices, by contrast, access items in thousandths of a second (milliseconds).

STORAGE TERMS

Storage Term	Approximate Number of Bytes	Exact Number of Bytes
Kilobyte (KB)	1 thousand	2^{10} or 1,024
Megabyte (MB)	1 million	2^{20} or 1,048,576
Gigabyte (GB)	1 billion	2^{30} or 1,073,741,824
Terabyte (TB)	1 trillion	2^{40} or 1,099,511,627,776
Petabyte (PB)	1 quadrillion	2^{50} or 1,125,899,906,842,624
Exabyte (EB)	1 quintillion	2^{60} or 1,152,921,504,606,846,976

FIGURE 7-2 The capacity of storage media is measured by the amount of bytes it can hold.

AN ILLUSTRATION OF VOLATILITY

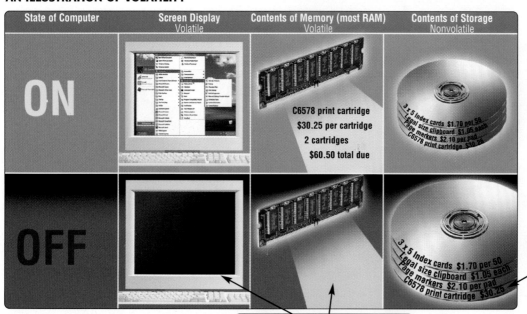

FIGURE 7-3 A screen display is considered volatile because its contents disappear when power is removed. Likewise, most RAM chips are volatile. That is, their contents are erased when power is removed from the computer. Storage, by contrast, is nonvolatile. Its contents remain when power is off.

Instead of, or in addition to access time, some manufacturers state a storage device's transfer rate because it affects access time. *Transfer rate* is the speed with which data, instructions, and information transfer to and from a device. Transfer rates for disks are stated in *KBps* (kilobytes per second) and *MBps* (megabytes per second).

Numerous types of storage media and storage devices exist to meet a variety of users' needs. Figure 7-4 shows how different types of storage media and memory compare in terms of transfer rates and uses. This chapter discusses these storage media, as well as other media.

FIGURE 7-4 A comparison of different types of storage media and memory in terms of relative speed and uses. Memory is faster than storage, but is expensive and not practical for all storage requirements. Storage is less expensive but is slower than memory.

FLOPPY DISKS

A **floppy disk**, also called a *diskette*, is a portable, inexpensive storage medium that consists of a thin, circular, flexible plastic Mylar film with a magnetic coating enclosed in a square-shaped plastic shell (Figure 7-5).

A typical floppy disk can store up to 500 double-spaced pages of text, several digital photographs, or a small audio file. Floppy disks are not as widely used as they were ten years ago because of their low storage capacity. They are used, however, for specific applications. Some digital cameras store pictures on a floppy disk. Users work with floppy disks to transport small files to and from non-networked personal computers, such as from school or work to home. If your personal computer malfunctions, you could use a floppy disk to boot it up (or start it). Chapter 8 discusses booting up a computer.

When IBM first introduced the floppy disk as a new type of storage in the early 1970s, these 8-inch-wide disks were known as floppies because they had flexible plastic covers. The next generation of floppies looked much the same, but they were only 5.25 inches wide. Today, the standard floppy disk is 3.5 inches wide and has a rigid plastic outer cover. Although the exterior of the 3.5-inch disk is not floppy, users still refer to this storage medium as a floppy disk because of the flexible Mylar film inside the plastic outer cover.

FIGURE 7-5 In a 3.5-inch floppy disk, a thin, circular, flexible Mylar film is enclosed between two liners. A piece of metal called a shutter covers an opening to the recording surface in the rigid plastic shell.

A floppy disk is a portable storage medium. With respect to a storage medium, the term *portable* means you can remove the medium from one computer and carry it to another computer.

Floppy Disk Drives

A **floppy disk drive** is a device that reads from and writes on a floppy disk. A user inserts a floppy disk into and removes it from a floppy disk drive. Desktop personal computers and many notebook computers have a floppy disk drive installed inside the system unit (Figure 7-6a). Some notebook computers allow you to remove the floppy disk drive and replace it with another type of drive.

Some computers use an *external floppy disk drive*, in which the drive is a separate device with a cable that plugs into a port on the system unit (Figure 7-6b). These external drives are attached to the computer only when the user needs to access items on a floppy disk. Users who seldom work with floppy disks purchase their computers without an internal floppy disk drive and opt for the external floppy disk drive instead. A mobile user who seldom uses floppy disks, for example, may purchase a notebook computer without an internal floppy disk drive to eliminate the extra weight.

If a personal computer has one floppy disk drive, it is named drive A. Computers with two floppy disk drives designate the second one as drive B.

To read from or write on a floppy disk, a floppy disk drive must support that floppy disk's density. *Density* is the number of bits in an area on a storage medium. A disk with a higher density has more bits in an area and thus has a larger storage capacity. Most standard floppy disks today are high density (*HD*). To access a high-density floppy disk, you must have a high-density floppy disk drive.

Floppy disk drives usually are *downward compatible*, which means they recognize and can use earlier media. Floppy disk drives are not *upward compatible*, and thus cannot recognize newer media. For example, a lower-density floppy disk drive cannot read from or write on a high-density floppy disk.

When you insert a 3.5-inch floppy disk into a floppy disk drive, the drive slides a piece of metal on the disk called the *shutter* to the side, exposing a portion of both sides of the disk's recording surface. The *read/write head* in the drive is the mechanism that reads items or writes items as it barely touches the disk's recording surface. Most floppy disk drives have an external light emitting diode (LED) that lights up when the drive is accessing the floppy disk. You should not remove a floppy disk when the LED is lit.

Figure 7-7 illustrates how a floppy disk drive reads from and writes on a floppy disk. The average time it takes a current floppy disk drive to locate an item on a disk (access time) is 84 milliseconds, or approximately 1/12 of a second. The transfer rates range from 250 to 500 KBps.

Figure 7-6a (floppy disk drive built into a desktop computer)

Figure 7-6b (external floppy disk drive attaches to computer with a cable)

FIGURE 7-6 On a personal computer, you insert and remove a floppy disk from a floppy disk drive.

FIGURE 7-7   HOW A FLOPPY DISK DRIVE WORKS

Step 1:
When you insert the floppy disk into the drive, the shutter moves to the side to expose the recording surface on the disk.

Step 2:
When you initiate a disk access, the circuit board on the drive that contains electronics sends signals to control movement of the read/write heads until they barely touch the surface (film) inside the floppy disk's shell.

Step 6:
The read/write heads read data from and write data on the floppy disk.

Step 5:
A motor positions the read/write heads over the correct location on the recording surface of the disk.

Step 4:
A motor spins a shaft, which causes the surface inside the floppy disk's shell to spin.

Step 3:
For write instructions, the circuit board verifies whether the disk can be written on or not.

❓FAQ 7-1

What is the problem when the floppy disk drive will not read a disk?

The disk may be corrupt, which is why it is important to keep backup copies of all data. If the problem repeats with multiple floppy disks, the read/write heads in the floppy disk drive may have a buildup of dust or dirt. Try cleaning the read/write heads with a floppy disk cleaning kit. If the drive still malfunctions, you usually can replace it for less than $50.

For more information about backing up, read Chapter 8. For more information about floppy disk drives, visit the Discovering Computers 2004 FAQ Web page (**scsite.com/dc2004/faq**). Click Floppy Disk Drives below Chapter 7.

Characteristics of a Floppy Disk

A floppy disk is a type of magnetic media that allows users to read from and write on a disk any number of times. *Magnetic media* use magnetic particles to store items such as data, instructions, and information on a disk's surface. Depending on how the magnetic particles are aligned, they represent either a zero (0) bit or a one (1) bit. Recall from Chapter 4 that a bit (binary digit) is the smallest unit of data a computer can process. Thus, the alignment of the magnetic particles represents the data.

A floppy disk stores data in tracks and sectors (Figure 7-8). A *track* is a narrow recording band that forms a full circle on the surface of the disk. The disk's storage locations consist of pie-shaped sections, which break the tracks into small arcs called *sectors*. A sector stores up to 512 bytes of data. A typical floppy disk stores data on both sides of the disk, has 80 tracks on each side of the recording surface, and has 18 sectors per track.

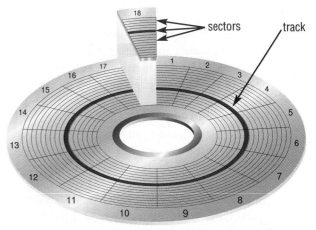

FIGURE 7-8   Tracks form circles on the surface of a disk. The disk's storage locations are divided into pie-shaped sections, which break the tracks into small arcs called sectors.

To compute a disk's storage capacity, you multiply the number of sides on the disk, the number of tracks on the disk, the number of sectors per track, and the number of bytes in a sector. For example, the following is the formula for a high-density 3.5-inch floppy disk: 2 (sides) x 80 (tracks) x 18 (sectors per track) x 512 (bytes per sector) = 1,474,560 bytes (Figure 7-9). Disks often store system files in some tracks, which means the available capacity on a disk may be less than the total possible capacity.

The actual number of available bytes on a floppy disk is 1,474,560, yet manufacturers call them 1.44 MB disks. The 1.44 MB is not a rounding of the 1,474,560. Instead, it is a result of dividing the number of bytes in the disk (1,474,560) by the number of bytes in a kilobyte (1,024).

For reading and writing purposes, sectors are grouped into clusters. A *cluster* is the smallest unit of disk space that stores data. Each cluster, also called an *allocation unit*, consists of two to eight sectors (the number varies depending on the operating system). Even if a file consists of only a few bytes, it uses an entire cluster. Each cluster holds data from only one file. One file, however, can span many clusters.

Sometimes, a sector has a flaw and cannot store data. When you format a disk, the operating system marks these bad sectors as unusable. **Formatting** is the process of preparing a disk for reading and writing. For a technical discussion about formatting, read the High-Tech Talk article on page 7.31.

Care of Floppy Disks

Disk manufacturers state that a floppy disk can last at least seven years, with reasonable care. In many cases, the disks do not have that long of a life span. A floppy disk drive may malfunction and ruin the disk. More commonly, the disk itself is damaged from improper care.

When you handle a floppy disk, avoid exposing it to heat, cold, magnetic fields, magnets, and contaminants such as dust, smoke, or salt air. Exposure to any of these elements could damage or destroy the data, instructions, and information stored on the floppy disk. Never open the disk's shutter and touch its recording surface. When you are not using disks, keep them in a storage tray or some other container that allows them to stand vertically.

To protect a floppy disk from accidentally being erased, the plastic outer shell on the disk contains a write-protect notch in its corner. A **write-protect notch** is a small opening that has a tab you slide to cover or expose the notch (Figure 7-10). The write-protect notch works much like the recording tab on a VHS tape: if you remove the recording tab, a VCR cannot record onto the VHS tape.

On a floppy disk, if the write-protect notch is open, the drive cannot write on the floppy disk. If the write-protect notch is covered, or closed, the drive can write on the floppy disk. A floppy disk drive can read from a floppy disk whether the write-protect notch is open or closed. On the opposite corner, some floppy disks have a second opening without a small tab. This opening identifies the disk as a high-density floppy disk (Figure 7-10).

CHARACTERISTICS OF A 3.5-INCH HIGH-DENSITY FLOPPY DISK

Capacity	1.44 MB
Sides	2
Tracks	80
Sectors per track	18
Bytes per sector	512
Sectors per disk	2880

FIGURE 7-9 Most of today's personal computers use high-density disks.

WEB LINK 7-1

Floppy Disks

Visit the Discovering Computers 2004 WEB LINK page (**scsite .com/dc2004/weblink**). Click Floppy Disks below Chapter 7.

notch open means you cannot write on the disk

write-protected

notch closed means you can write on the disk

not write-protected

hole on this side means disk is high density

FIGURE 7-10 To protect data from being erased accidentally, floppy disks have a write-protect notch. By sliding a small tab, you either can cover or expose the notch.

ZIP® DISKS

A **Zip disk** is a type of portable magnetic media that can store from 100 MB to 750 MB of data. The larger capacity Zip disks hold about 500 times more than a standard floppy disk. These large capacities make it easy to transport many files or large items such as graphics, audio, or video files. Another popular use of Zip disks is to back up important data and information. A **backup** is a duplicate of a file, program, or disk that you can use in case the original is lost, damaged, or destroyed. Chapter 8 discusses backup utilities.

Zip disks are slightly larger than and about twice as thick as a 3.5-inch floppy disk. A **Zip drive** is a high-capacity disk drive developed by Iomega Corporation that reads from and writes on a Zip disk (Figure 7-11). These drives cannot read standard 3.5-inch floppy disks.

Many users prefer to purchase an external Zip drive, which connects to a USB port, FireWire port, or parallel port on the system unit. The external Zip drive is convenient for users with multiple computers, because it allows them to move the drive from computer to computer as needed. As an alternative, some users prefer to order a computer with a built-in Zip drive.

QUIZ YOURSELF 7-1

To check your knowledge of items users store, storage devices and storage media, floppy disks, and Zip disks, visit the Discovering Computers 2004 Quiz Yourself Web page (**scsite.com/dc2004/ quiz**). Click Objectives 1 – 4 below Chapter 7.

HARD DISKS

A **hard disk**, also called a *hard disk drive*, is a storage device that contains one or more inflexible, circular platters that store data, instructions, and information. Today's hard disks have enough storage capacity for the most complex multimedia software. People use hard disks to store all types of documents, spreadsheets, presentations, databases, e-mail messages, Web pages, digital photographs, music, videos, and software.

The system unit on most desktop and notebook computers contains at least one hard disk. The hard disk inside the system unit sometimes is called a *fixed disk* because it is mounted in a drive bay and usually is not portable (Figure 7-12). The entire device is enclosed in an airtight, sealed case to protect it from contamination. Two other types of hard disks, external and removable, are discussed later in this chapter.

WEB LINK 7-2

Zip® Disks

Visit the Discovering Computers 2004 WEB LINK page (**scsite .com/dc2004/weblink**). Click Zip Disks below Chapter 7.

FIGURE 7-11 An external Zip drive.

FIGURE 7-12 The hard disk in a desktop computer is enclosed inside an airtight, sealed case inside the system unit.

Current personal computer hard disks have storage capacities from 40 to 160 GB and more. The storage capacity of the average hard disk is more than 40,000 times that of a standard floppy disk. Like floppy disks and Zip disks, hard disks store data magnetically. Hard disks also are read/write storage media. That is, you can read from and write on a hard disk any number of times. A recently developed hard disk, called an *optically assisted hard drive*, combines optic technologies with the magnetic media. These optically assisted hard drives have potential storage capacities up to 400 GB.

If the computer contains only one hard disk, the operating system designates it as drive C. Additional hard disks are assigned the next available drive letter. Read Issue 7-1 for a discussion about how some merchants use a hard disk.

ISSUE 7-1

Do You Use a Shoppers Card?

Grocery stores, pharmacies, hotel chains, and other merchants are offering shoppers cards to customers. With these cards, sometimes called names such as saver card, buyers card, or club card, consumers earn reduced prices when they make purchases. In return, sellers track consumer acquisitions, preferences, and buying habits and store the information on their computer's hard disk. Merchants claim that these cards reward loyal customers. Yet, not everyone agrees. One study found that, on average, shoppers card customers spent more money on each store visit than customers who do not use shoppers cards. CASPIAN (Consumers Against Supermarket Privacy Invasion and Numbering), a consumers group opposed to the use of club cards, argues that the shoppers cards give artificial discounts on inflated prices. Additionally, consumers have no guarantee that information gained by a merchant will remain private. In a recent divorce case, a lawyer used information from a merchant about an alcohol purchase against a spouse. Are shoppers cards a good idea? Why or why not? Should the buying information remain private? Would you or do you use a shoppers card? Why or why not?

For more information about shoppers cards, visit the Discovering Computers 2004 Issues Web page (**scsite.com/dc2004/issues**). Click Issue #1 below Chapter 7.

Characteristics of a Hard Disk

Characteristics of a hard disk include its capacity, platters, read/write heads, cylinders, sectors and tracks, revolutions per minute, and transfer rate. Figure 7-13 shows sample characteristics of a 40 GB hard disk. The following paragraphs discuss each of these characteristics.

The capacity of a hard disk is determined from the number of platters it contains, together with composition of the magnetic coating on the platters. A *platter* is made of aluminum, glass, or ceramic and is coated with an alloy material that allows items to be recorded magnetically on its surface. The coating usually is three millionths of an inch thick.

SAMPLE HARD DISK CHARACTERISTICS

Advertised capacity	40 GB
Platters	2
Read/write heads	4
Cylinders	16,383
Bytes per sector	512
Sectors per track	63
Sectors per drive	78,165,360
Revolutions per minute	7,200
Transfer rate	100 MB per second
Access time	9 ms

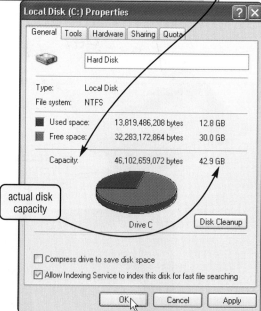

FIGURE 7-13 Characteristics of a sample 40 GB hard disk. The actual disk's capacity often is greater than the advertised capacity, to allow for bad sectors on the disk.

On desktop computers, platters have a *form factor*, or size, of approximately 5.25 inches or more commonly 3.5 inches in diameter. A typical hard disk has multiple platters stacked on top of one another. Each platter has two read/write heads, one for each side. The hard disk has arms that move the read/write heads to the proper location on the platter (Figure 7-14).

The location of the read/write heads often is referred to by its cylinder. A *cylinder* is the vertical section of a track that passes through all platters (Figure 7-15). A single movement of the read/write head arms accesses all the platters in a cylinder. If a hard disk has two platters (four sides), each with 1,000 tracks, then it will have 1,000 cylinders with each cylinder consisting of 4 tracks (2 tracks for each platter).

While the computer is running, the platters in the hard disk rotate at a high rate of speed. This spinning, which usually is 5,400 to 7,200 *revolutions per minute* (*rpm*), allows nearly instant access to all tracks and sectors on the platters. The platters typically continue to spin until power is removed from the computer. (On some computers, the hard disk stops spinning after a specified time to save power.) The spinning motion creates a cushion of air between the platter and its read/write head. This cushion ensures that the read/write head floats above the platter instead of making direct contact with the platter surface. The distance between the read/write head and the platter is about two millionths of one inch.

FIGURE 7-14   HOW A HARD DISK WORKS

Step 1:
The circuit board controls the movement of the head actuator and a small motor.

Step 2:
A small motor spins the platters while the computer is running.

Step 3:
When software requests a disk access, the read/write heads determine the current or new location of the data.

Step 4:
The head actuator positions the read/write head arms over the correct location on the platters to read or write data.

FIGURE 7-15   A cylinder is the vertical section of a track through all platters on a hard disk.

As shown in Figure 7-16, this close clearance leaves no room for any type of contamination. Dirt, hair, dust, smoke, and other particles could cause the hard disk to have a head crash. A *head crash* occurs when a read/write head touches the surface of a platter, usually resulting in a loss of data or sometimes loss of the entire drive. Although current internal hard disks are built to withstand shocks and are sealed tightly to keep out contaminants, head crashes do occasionally still occur. Thus, it is crucial that you back up your hard disk regularly. Chapter 8 discusses backup techniques. Read Apply It 7-1 for more information.

Depending on the type of hard disk, transfer rates normally range from 15 MBps to 160 MBps. Access time for today's hard disks ranges from approximately 5 to 12 ms (milliseconds). The average hard disk access time is at least seven times faster than the average floppy disk drive. This is because a hard disk spins much faster than a floppy disk and a hard disk usually spins constantly, while a floppy disk starts spinning only when it receives a read or write command.

Some computers improve hard disk access time by using disk caching. *Disk cache* (pronounced cash) is a portion of memory that the processor uses to store frequently accessed items (Figure 7-17). Disk cache and memory cache work in a similar way. When a program needs data, instructions, or information, the processor checks the disk cache. If the item is in disk cache, the processor uses that item. If the processor does not find the requested item in the disk cache, then the processor must wait for the hard disk to locate and transfer the item from the disk to the processor.

FIGURE 7-16 The clearance between a disk read/write head and the platter is about two millionths of an inch. A smoke particle, dust particle, human hair, or other contaminant could render the drive unusable.

FIGURE 7-17 When a program needs an item such as data, instructions, or information, the processor checks the disk cache. If the item is located, the processor uses it. If the processor does not find the item in the disk cache, then the processor must wait for the disk drive to locate and transfer the item from the disk.

☑ **APPLY IT 7-1**

Save Data Now for Safekeeping

"A penny saved is a penny earned," according to Benjamin Franklin. From an early age, individuals are taught the value of saving. Whether it is a bank account or mementoes from grade school, these saved treasures provide comfort and peace of mind when they are tucked away safely.

But something happens when it comes to saving computer files. For some reason, many people fail to save precious data for safekeeping. And when disaster strikes, such as when a head crash occurs or the data on the hard disk is destroyed by a virus or worm, the loss can be devastating.

The best advice is to save important files regularly on two storage media. Floppy disks are good for small files, while Zip disks are better for large files and programs. CDs, DVDs, tape, PC Cards, and miniature storage media all have value for saving computer files.

An entire hard disk also can be backed up. This process is accomplished by using software included with Microsoft Windows or using special backup software. Whenever you install new computer components, such as a motherboard or memory, it is advisable to back up the hard disk in case the upgrade goes awry and to save the second copy offsite.

For more information about backing up your computer, visit the Discovering Computers 2004 Apply It Web page (**scsite.com/dc2004/apply**). Click Apply It #1 below Chapter 7.

A *cache controller* manages cache and thus determines which items cache should store. On newer processors, the cache controller is part of the processor. Some disk caching systems also attempt to predict what data, instructions, or information might be needed and place them into cache before the processor requests them. Almost all current disk drives work with some amount of disk cache because it significantly improves disk access times.

External and Removable Hard Disks

Two types of portable hard disks are external hard disks and removable hard disks (Figure 7-18). An **external hard disk** is a separate free-standing hard disk that connects with a cable to a USB port, FireWire port, or other port on the system unit. As with the internal hard disk, the entire hard disk is enclosed in an airtight, sealed case. External hard disks have storage capacities up to 120 GB or higher.

Figure 7-18a
(external hard disk)

removable hard disk

Figure 7-18b
(removable hard disk)

FIGURE 7-18 Examples of portable hard disk drives.

A **removable hard disk**, also called a *disk cartridge*, is a hard disk that you insert and remove from a hard disk drive. Sometimes the hard disk drive is built into the system unit. Others are external devices that connect with a cable to a USB port, FireWire port, or other port on the system unit. The hard disk drive operates in a manner similar to a floppy disk drive, reading from and writing on the removable hard disk. A plastic or metal case surrounds the hard disk to protect it from damage. Removable hard disks have storage capacities up to 60 GB or higher.

External hard disks and removable hard disks offer the following advantages over internal hard disks (fixed disks):

- Transport a large number of files
- Back up important files or an entire internal hard disk
- Easily store large audio and video files
- Secure your data; for example, at the end of a work session, remove the hard disk and lock it up, leaving no data in the computer
- Add storage space to a notebook computer
- Add storage space to a desktop computer without having to open the system unit
- Share a drive with multiple computers

As the prices of portable hard disks drop, increasingly more users will purchase one to supplement a home or office internal hard disk. Keep in mind though that internal hard disks transfer data at much faster rates than external or removable hard disks.

Hard Disk Controllers

A *disk controller* consists of a special-purpose chip and electronic circuits that control the transfer of data, instructions, and information from a disk to and from the system bus and other components in the computer. Some users refer to the disk controller as an interface.

A disk controller for a hard disk, called the hard disk controller, may be part of a hard disk or may be a separate adapter card inside in the system unit. Many external hard disks use a USB port or FireWire port as their interface.

Vendors usually state the type of hard disk controller in their personal computer advertisements. Thus, you should understand the types of available hard disk controllers. In addition to USB and FireWire, two other types of hard disk controllers for personal computers are EIDE and SCSI.

WEB LINK 7-3

Hard Disks

Visit the Discovering Computers 2004 WEB LINK page (**scsite .com/dc2004/weblink**). Click Hard Disks below Chapter 7.

EIDE   One of the more widely used controllers for hard disks is the *EIDE* (*Enhanced Integrated Drive Electronics*) controller. EIDE controllers can support up to four hard disks at 137 GB per disk. They transfer data, instructions, and information to and from the disk at rates up to 66 MBps. This interface also provides connections for CD and DVD drives and tape drives.

Some manufacturers market their EIDE controllers as Fast ATA. EIDE controllers are downward compatible with earlier IDE and ATA controllers.

SCSI   Depending on the type of *SCSI controller*, it can support up to eight or fifteen peripheral devices, including hard disks, CD and DVD drives, tape drives, printers, scanners, network cards, and much more. Recall from Chapter 4 that SCSI is an acronym for Small Computer System Interface. Some computers have a built-in SCSI controller, while others use an adapter card to add a SCSI controller.

SCSI controllers are faster than EIDE controllers, providing up to 160 MBps transfer rates. Newer versions of SCSI controllers generally are downward compatible with earlier SCSI devices.

?FAQ 7-2

What are the transfer rates of USB and FireWire?

USB 1.1 has a transfer rate of 12 *Mbps* (megabits per second). USB 2.0 is much faster with transfer rates up to 480 Mbps. FireWire is even faster, with transfer rates up to 3,200 Mbps. When performance has a higher priority than cost, choose FireWire. For example, FireWire is the better choice for high-quality video streaming.

For more information about USB and FireWire controllers, visit the Discovering Computers 2004 FAQ Web page (**scsite.com/dc2004/faq**). Click USB and FireWire Controllers below Chapter 7.

Maintaining Data Stored on a Hard Disk

Most manufacturers guarantee their hard disks to last approximately three to five years. Many last much longer with proper care. To prevent the loss of items stored on a hard disk, you regularly should perform preventive maintenance such as defragmenting or scanning the disk for errors. Chapter 8 discusses these and other utilities in depth.

Internet Hard Drives

Instead of storing data locally on a hard disk, some users choose to store data on an Internet hard drive. An **Internet hard drive**, sometimes called **online storage**, is a service on the Web that provides storage to computer users, usually for a minimal monthly fee (Figure 7-19). Fee arrangements vary. For example, one online storage service charge is as low as $4.95 per month for 75 MB of storage.

Users store data and information on an Internet hard drive for a variety of reasons:

- To access files on the Internet hard drive from any computer or device that has Internet access.
- To save time by storing large audio, video, and graphics files on an Internet hard drive instantaneously, instead of downloading to a local hard disk.
- To allow others to access files on your Internet hard drive to play an audio file, watch a video clip, or view a picture — instead of e-mailing the file to them.
- To view time-critical data and images immediately while away from the main office or location. For example, doctors can view x-ray images from another hospital, home, or office, or while on vacation.
- To store offsite backups of data. Chapter 8 presents this and other backup strategies.

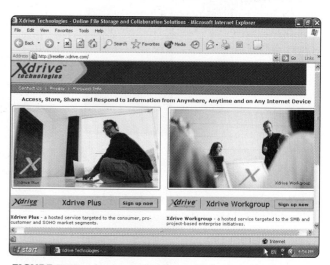

FIGURE 7-19   An example of one Web site advertising its Internet hard drive service.

In addition to storage space, these Web sites offer other services. These services often include e-mail, calendar, address book, and task list applications. As with other files on the Internet hard drive, you can share your calendars, address books, and tasks lists with others who have Web access.

Some operating systems support access to Internet hard drives. Once users subscribe to the Internet hard drive service, they can save on the Internet hard drive in the same manner they save on a floppy disk, their hard disk, or any other drive.

CDs AND DVDs

CDs and DVDs are a type of optical storage media that consists of a flat, round, portable, metal disc with a protective plastic coating. These discs usually are 4.75 inches in diameter and less than one-twentieth of an inch thick. (Recall from Chapter 1 that the term disk is used for magnetic media, and disc is used for optical media.)

CDs and DVDs primarily store software, digital photographs, movies, and music. Some CD and DVD formats are read only, meaning you cannot write (save) on the media. Others are read/write, which allows users to save on the disc just as they save on a hard disk. The specifics of various CD and DVD formats are discussed later in this chapter.

Just about every personal computer today includes some type of CD or DVD drive installed in a drive bay. These drives read CDs and DVDs, and in many cases, will play audio CDs. On these drives, you push a button to slide out a tray, insert the disc with the label side up, and then push the same button to close the tray (Figure 7-20). Other convenient features on most of these drives include a volume control button and a headphone port (or jack) so you can use stereo headphones to listen to audio without disturbing others nearby.

Push the button to slide out the tray.

Insert the disc, label side up.

Push the same button to close the tray.

FIGURE 7-20 On CD and DVD drives, you push a button to slide out a tray, insert the disc with the label side up, and then push the same button to close the tray.

WEB LINK 7-4

Internet Hard Drives
Visit the Discovering Computers 2004 WEB LINK page (**scsite .com/dc2004/weblink**). Click Internet Hard Drives below Chapter 7.

Characteristics of CDs and DVDs
Recall that a floppy disk drive is designated as drive A. The drive designation of a CD or DVD drive usually follows alphabetically after that of all the hard disks and portable disks. For example, if the computer has one hard disk (drive C), a Zip disk drive (drive D), and an external hard disk (drive E), then the first CD or DVD drive is drive F. A second CD or DVD drive would be drive G.

CDs and DVDs are not magnetic media. Instead, they are optical media that store items such as data, instructions, and information by using microscopic pits (indentations) and lands (flat areas) that are in the middle layer of the disc (Figure 7-21). (Most manufacturers place a silk-screened label on the top layer of the disc so users can identify the disc.) A high-powered laser light creates the pits. A lower-powered laser light reads items from the disc by reflecting light through the bottom of the disc, which usually is either solid gold or silver in color. The reflected light is converted into a series of bits the computer can process. A land causes light to reflect, which is read as binary digit 1. Pits absorb the light; this absence of light is read as binary digit 0.

CDs and DVDs commonly store items in a single track that spirals from the center of the disc to the edge of the disc. As with a hard disk, this single track is divided into evenly sized sectors in which items are stored (Figure 7-22).

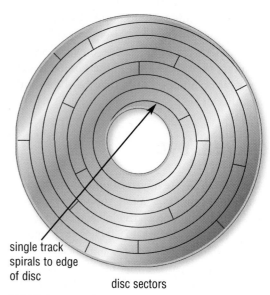

single track spirals to edge of disc

disc sectors

FIGURE 7-22 CDs and DVDs typically store data, instructions, and information in a single track that spirals from the center of the disc to the edge of the disc.

FIGURE 7-21   HOW A LASER READS DATA ON A CD OR DVD

disc label

lens — pit — land — lens

0

1

Step 2: If light strikes a pit, it scatters. If light strikes a land, it is reflected back toward the laser diode.

prism — light-sensing diode — laser diode — prism — light-sensing diode — laser diode

Step 1: A laser diode shines a light beam toward the disc.

Step 3: Reflected light is deflected to a light-sensing diode, which sends a digital signal of 1 to the computer. Absence of reflected light is read as a digital signal of 0.

Care of CDs and DVDs

Manufacturers guarantee that a properly cared for CD or DVD will last 5 years, but could last up to 100 years. Figure 7-23 outlines some guidelines for the proper care of CDs and DVDs. Never bend a disc; it may break. If a disc becomes warped or if its surface is scratched, data on the disc may be unreadable. Exposing these discs to extreme temperatures or humidity could cause them to warp. The ideal temperature range for disc storage is 50 to 70 degrees Fahrenheit. Stacking discs, touching the underside of discs, or exposing them to any type of contaminant may scratch a disc. Thus, place a CD or DVD in its protective case, called a *jewel box*, when you are finished using it.

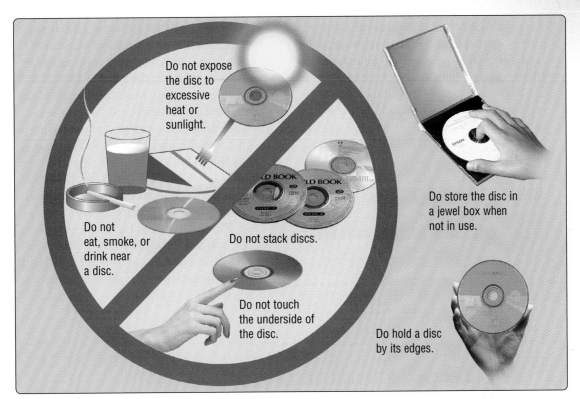

FIGURE 7-23 Some guidelines for the proper care of CDs and DVDs.

? FAQ 7-3

Can I clean a CD or DVD?

Yes, you can remove dust, dirt, smudges, and fingerprints from the bottom surface of a CD or DVD. Moisten a soft cloth with warm water or window cleaner and then wipe the disc in straight lines from the center outward. You also can repair scratches on the bottom surface with a specialized disc repair kit.

For more information about cleaning and repairing CDs and DVDs, visit the Discovering Computers 2004 FAQ Web page (**scsite.com/dc2004/faq**). Click Cleaning and Repairing CDs and DVDs below Chapter 7.

■ QUIZ YOURSELF 7-2

To check your knowledge of hard disks, Internet hard drives, and CDs and DVDs, visit the Discovering Computers 2004 Quiz Yourself Web page (**scsite.com/dc2004/quiz**). Click Objectives 5 – 7 below Chapter 7.

CD-ROMs

A **CD-ROM** (pronounced SEE-DEE-rom), or *compact disc read-only memory*, is a type of optical disc that uses laser technology to store data, instructions, and information. In addition to audio, a CD-ROM can contain text, graphics, and video.

Manufacturers write, or record, the contents of standard CD-ROMs. Users only can read the contents of these discs. That is, you cannot erase or modify their contents — hence, the name read-only. A standard CD-ROM is called a *single-session disc* because manufacturers write all items on the disc at one time.

To read items stored on a CD-ROM, insert the disc into a **CD-ROM drive** or a CD-ROM player. Because audio CDs and CD-ROMs use the same laser technology, you may be able to use a CD-ROM drive to listen to an audio CD while you are working on the computer. Some music companies, however, configure their CDs so the music will not play on a computer. They do this to protect themselves from customers illegally copying and sharing the music.

● WEB LINK 7-5

CD-ROMs

Visit the Discovering Computers 2004 WEB LINK page (**scsite .com/dc2004/weblink**). Click CD-ROMs below Chapter 7.

A typical CD-ROM holds from 650 MB to 1 GB of data, instructions, and information. This is equivalent to about 450 high-density 3.5-inch floppy disks. Manufacturers use CD-ROMs to store and distribute today's multimedia and other complex software because these discs have such high storage capacities (Figure 7-24). Read Issue 7-2 for a related discussion.

The speed of a CD-ROM drive determines how fast it installs programs and accesses the disc. Original CD-ROM drives were single-speed drives with transfer rates of 150 KBps (kilobytes per second). Manufacturers measure all CD-ROM drives relative to this original CD-ROM drive. They use an X to denote the original transfer rate of 150 KBps. For example, a 48X CD-ROM drive has a data transfer rate of 7,200 (48 x 150) KBps, or 7.2 MBps. Current CD-ROM drives have transfer rates, or speeds, ranging from 48X to 75X or faster. The higher the number, the faster the CD-ROM drive. Faster CD-ROM drives, however, are more expensive than slower drives.

FIGURE 7-24 Encyclopedias, games, and many other programs are distributed on CD-ROM.

ISSUE 7-2

Promotions on CD-ROM?

Instead of printed brochures, many companies now offer marketing CD-ROMs to potential customers. CD-ROMs are more expensive than conventional advertisements, but companies feel that the storage medium's interactivity is worth the cost. Some automobile manufacturers, for example, offer a CD-ROM that introduces new vehicles to prospective buyers. The CD-ROM shows photographs, statistics, option packages, and pricing information. Using a mouse, automobile shoppers can "walk around and kick the tires" by viewing the car from different angles, seeing close-ups of special features, and even enjoying a simulated test drive. But, not everyone is convinced that marketing on CD-ROM is worthwhile. Despite their cost, some believe that consumers do not use most publicity CD-ROMs; they insist that potential customers are more likely to page through a brochure than to use a promotional CD-ROM. In general, is advertising on CD-ROM worth the cost? Why or why not? What products are best suited to promotion on CD-ROM? Why? What products are least suited? Why? Will marketing CD-ROMs ever replace printed advertising materials? Why or why not?

For more information about advertising on CD-ROM, visit the Discovering Computers 2004 Issues Web page (**scsite.com/dc2004/issues**). Click Issue #2 below Chapter 7.

Picture CDs and PhotoCDs

A Kodak **Picture CD** is a type of compact disc that stores digital versions of a single roll of film using a jpg file format. Many film developers offer Picture CD service for consumers when they drop off film to be developed. That is, in addition to printed photographs and negatives, you also receive a Picture CD containing the film's pictures. The resolution of images on a Picture CD usually is 1024 x 1536 pixels. The additional cost for a Picture CD is about $10 per roll of film.

A standard CD-ROM drive can read a Picture CD. Using photo editing software and the photographs on the Picture CD, you can remove red eye, crop the photograph, enhance colors, trim away edges, adjust the lighting, and edit just about any aspect of a photograph. In addition, a Picture CD allows you to print copies of the photographs on glossy paper with an ink-jet printer. If you do not have a printer to print the images, many stores have kiosks at which you can print pictures from a Picture CD (Figure 7-25).

Another type of compact disc that stores digital photographic images is the PhotoCD™. A single *PhotoCD* stores images from multiple rolls of film using the Image Pac, or PCD, file format, which is a file format developed by Eastman Kodak. Designed for commercial and professional users, images on a PhotoCD are available in many resolutions, ranging from 128 x 192 to 4096 x 6144 pixels. Film developers and professional photography businesses store images from 35mm pictures, negatives, slides, and scanned items on PhotoCDs for users. Most professional desktop publishing software reads the PhotoCD format. PhotoCDs can be read by most standard CD-ROM drives.

A PhotoCD is a *multisession disc*, which means users can save additional photos on the disc at a later time. That is, as users capture more photographs, they can save them to the PhotoCD. The next section discusses recordable discs.

⁇ FAQ 7-4

How do I share my digital pictures with others?

You can send them as e-mail attachments or post them on an Internet hard drive, a personal Web page, or a photo community. At a *photo community*, users can create online photo albums and share their digital photographs on the Web. Some photo communities provide free, unlimited storage space; others charge a nominal fee.

For more information about photo communities, read Making Use of the Web in Appendix B at the back of the book or visit the Discovering Computers 2004 FAQ Web page (**scsite.com/dc2004/faq**). Click Photo Communities below Chapter 7.

👆 WEB LINK 7-6

Picture CDs

Visit the Discovering Computers 2004 WEB LINK page (**scsite .com/dc2004/weblink**). Click Picture CDs below Chapter 7.

FIGURE 7-25   HOW A PICTURE CD WORKS

Step 1:
Drop off the film to be developed. Mark the Picture CD box on the film-processing envelope.

Step 2:
When you pick up prints and negatives, a Picture CD contains digital images of each photograph.

Step 3:
At home, print images from the Picture CD on your ink-jet or photo printer. At a store, print images from the Picture CD at a kiosk.

CD-Rs and CD-RWs

Many personal computers today include either a CD-R or CD-RW drive as a standard feature. Others offer one or more of these drives as an option. Unlike standard CD-ROM drives, users record, or write, their own data onto a disc with a CD-R or CD-RW drive. The process of writing on an optical disc is called *burning*. Some operating systems, such as Windows XP, include the capability of burning discs.

A **CD-R** (*compact disc-recordable*) is a multi-session CD onto which users record their own items such as text, graphics, and audio. With a CD-R, you can write on part of the disc at one time and another part at a later time. Once recorded, a CD-R can be read from as many times as necessary. Each part of a CD-R can be written on only one time, and the disc's contents cannot be erased. Most current CD-ROM drives can read a CD-R.

Writing on the CD-R requires a *CD recorder* or a **CD-R drive**. A CD-R drive usually can read both audio CDs and standard CD-ROMs. These drives read at speeds of 48X or more and write at speeds of 40X or more. Manufacturers often list the write speed first, for example, as 40/48. CD-R drives are slightly more expensive than standard CD-ROM drives.

Instead of using a CD-R drive, many users opt for a CD-RW drive. A **CD-RW** (*compact disc-rewritable*) is an erasable disc you can write on multiple times. Originally called an *erasable CD (CD-E)*, a CD-RW overcomes the major disadvantage of CD-R disks, which is being able to write on them only once. With CD-RW, the disc acts like a floppy disk or hard disk, allowing users to write and rewrite data, instructions, and information onto it multiple times. Reliability of the disc tends to drop, however, with each successive rewrite.

To write on a CD-RW disc, you must have CD-RW software and a **CD-RW drive**. These drives have write speeds of 40X or more, rewrite speeds of 10X or more, and read speeds of 40X or more. Manufacturers state the speeds in this order; that is, write speed, rewrite speed, and read speed as 40/10/40.

Multiread CD drives are the only drives that can read CD-RW discs. A *multiread CD drive* is a drive that reads audio CDs, data CDs, CD-Rs, and CD-RWs. Most current CD drives are multiread.

Using a CD-RW disc, users easily back up large files from a hard disk. They also share data and information with other users who have a multiread CD drive.

A popular use of CD-RW and CD-R discs is to create audio CDs. For example, users can record their own music and save it on a CD, purchase and download MP3 songs from the Web, or rearrange tracks on a purchased music CD. The process of copying an individual song from a purchased audio CD and converting it to a digital format is called *ripping*. The steps in Figure 7-26 illustrate techniques for copying the song(s) from an existing audio CD or downloading the song(s) from the Web, in most cases for a fee. Read Issue 7-3 for a related discussion.

WEB LINK 7-7

CD-Rs and CD-RWs

Visit the Discovering Computers 2004 WEB LINK page (**scsite .com/dc2004/weblink**). Click CD-Rs and CD-RWs below Chapter 7.

ISSUE 7-3

Is It Ethical to Copy CDs?

A musician's recent release quickly became the second most-played CD in computer CD drives — before the CD even appeared on store shelves. CD-R and CD-RW technology makes copying music easy and affordable. People use CD-R and CD-RW technology to copy CDs they have purchased, CDs they have borrowed, or CDs they have pirated on the Web. At some campuses, students use college servers to create music Web sites, download copyrighted music, and then record and distribute unauthorized copies. The recording industry claims this practice is unfair to the industry and, in essence, steals from the recording artists. But, others insist bootlegged music actually is a marketing vehicle, influencing listeners who pay to attend concerts eventually to purchase the CD. Is it ethical to download and copy portions of a music CD, or an entire music CD, from the Web? Why? If you purchase a CD, is it ethical to make copies for yourself? For a friend? Why? Should recording or movie companies be able to use formatting techniques to keep people from copying CDs or DVDs?

For more information about copying music, visit the Discovering Computers 2004 Issues Web page (**scsite.com/dc2004/issues**). Click Issue #3 below Chapter 7.

FIGURE 7-26 HOW TO CREATE AN AUDIO CD

Step 1:
The artist composes a song.

Step 2:
The song is stored on an audio CD and purchased by the user.

Step 2:
The song is compressed and stored on the Internet.

Step 3:
The user inserts the audio CD into the CD drive, plays the song, and rips the desired track onto the hard disk.

Step 5:
The user listens to the song on a personal computer or removes the CD and listens to the song on a portable CD player.

Step 3:
The user pays for and downloads a song as an audio file onto a hard disk.

Step 4:
The user copies the file to a CD-RW disc.

⁇ FAQ 7-5

Is it legal to copy songs onto a CD?

It is legal to copy songs from an audio CD that you obtained legally, if you use the copied music for your own personal use. If you share the copy with a friend, however, you are violating copyright law. It is legal to download copyrighted music if the song's copyright holder has granted permission for users to download and play the song. In most cases, you pay a fee for the song.

For more information about copying music, visit the Discovering Computers 2004 FAQ Web page (**scsite.com/dc2004/faq**). Click Copying Music below Chapter 7.

DVD-ROMs and DVD+RWs

A **DVD-ROM** (*digital versatile disc-ROM* or *digital video disc-ROM*) is an extremely high capacity optical disc capable of storing 4.7 GB to 17 GB (Figure 7-27). The storage capacity of a DVD-ROM is more than enough to hold a telephone book containing every resident in the United States. Not only is the storage capacity of a DVD-ROM greater than that of a CD-ROM, a DVD-ROM's quality also far surpasses that of a CD-ROM because images are stored at higher resolution.

The goal of DVD technology is to meet the needs of home entertainment, computer usage, and business data and information storage with a single medium (read Apply It 7-2 for more information). DVDs store huge databases, music, complex software, and movies. When you rent or buy a DVD movie, it uses the *DVD-video format* to store the motion picture digitally.

To read a DVD-ROM, you must have a **DVD-ROM drive** or DVD player. These drives can read at speeds of 48X or more. Newer DVD-ROM drives also can read audio CDs, CD-ROMs, CD-Rs, and CD-RWs. Manufacturers advertise this multifunctional drive as a *CD-RW/DVD*.

At a glance, a DVD-ROM looks like a CD-ROM. Although the size and shape are similar, a DVD-ROM stores data, instructions, and information in a slightly different manner and thus achieves a higher storage capacity.

A DVD-ROM uses one of three storage techniques. The first involves making the disc denser by packing the pits closer together. The second involves using two layers of pits. For this technique to work, the lower layer of pits is semitransparent so the laser can read through it to the upper layer. This technique doubles the capacity of the disc. Finally, some DVD-ROMs are double-sided, which means you must remove the DVD-ROM and turn it over to read the other side. The storage capacities of various types of DVD-ROMs are shown in the table in Figure 7-28.

FIGURE 7-27 A DVD-ROM is an extremely high-capacity optical disc.

DVD

DVD drive

☑ **APPLY IT 7-2**

Turn Your Computer into a Home Theater System

Do you dream about the day when surround sound and an awesome entertainment system will be at your fingertips? That day can be today with a good set of speakers and a few inexpensive add-ons that turn your computer into a full-functioning home entertainment system.

Several companies have developed hardware priced at less than $300 that transforms a computer into a home theater with five- or six-speaker surround sound from DVDs and MP3s. Some of these products install in minutes and do not require opening the system unit because they plug into a computer's USB port. Other products require a bit more work by inserting sound cards into an expansion slot on the computer's motherboard.

Microsoft is collaborating with Hewlett-Packard, NEC, and Samsung to create the *e-Home initiative*, which is a system that will interface computers with televisions. Consumers will be able to download and store television programs on their computers and then play these files on their televisions. In addition, they will use their computers to control playing music and videos and also show digital photos on their big-screen televisions.

For more information about home entertainment system add-ons, visit the Discovering Computers 2004 Apply It Web page (**scsite.com/dc2004/apply**). Click Apply It #2 below Chapter 7.

DVD-ROM STORAGE CAPACITIES

Sides	Layers	Storage Capacity
1	1	4.7 GB
1	2	8.5 GB
2	1	9.4 GB
2	2	17 GB

FIGURE 7-28 Storage capacities of DVD-ROMs.

DVD+RW and Other DVD Variations

DVDs are available in a variety of formats, one of which stores digital motion pictures. To view a movie on a DVD, insert the DVD movie disc into a DVD player connected to a television or into a DVD-ROM drive to view the movie on a computer screen. Movies on DVD have near-studio-quality video, which far surpasses VHS tapes. When music is stored on a DVD, it includes surround sound and has a much better quality than that of an audio CD.

Recordable and rewritable versions of DVD also are available. A *DVD-R* (*DVD-recordable*) allows users to write on the disc once and read (play) it many times. A DVD-R is similar to a CD-R.

Instead of DVD-R, most users work with DVD+RW or DVD+RAM media. With **DVD+RW** (*DVD-rewriteable*) discs, a user can erase and record more than 1,000 times. A DVD+RW is similar to a CD-RW, except it has storage capacities up to 3.0 GB per side. These drives have rewrite speeds of 12X or more, and read speeds of 24X or more. DVD+RW drives usually can read DVD-ROM, DVD-R, and all CD media, and they can write on DVD+RW, DVD-R, CD-R, and CD-RW media. To write on DVD+RW discs, you must have a *DVD+RW drive* or a *DVD writer*.

A competing technology to DVD+RW is *DVD+RAM* (*DVD+random access memory*), which allows users to erase and record on a DVD+RAM disc more than 100,000 times. DVD+RAM discs have storage capacities up to 4.7 GB per side. These discs can be read by DVD+RAM drives and some DVD-ROM drives and players.

As the cost of DVD technologies becomes more reasonable, many industry professionals expect that DVD eventually will replace all CD media. For a look at the next generation of disc storage, read Looking Ahead 7-1.

LOOKING AHEAD 7-1

Holographic Storage Expands Capacity

Like an overstuffed suitcase, current storage media are being squeezed to store every possible byte of data. They physically are nearing their density capacity. Engineers are scrambling to develop new storage systems, and holographic storage appears to fit the bill.

Microsoft Chairman Bill Gates considers holographic storage an impressive improvement. Major technology corporations, including IBM, Lucent, and Samsung, have spent millions of dollars researching this innovative storage system. And one day you may be using *holographic storage* to save 100 movie, photo, or music files on one disc holding one terabyte of data.

The rush to develop this system is being driven by several factors. First, high-definition video files are 10 times larger than today's DVD movie files. Virtual reality video games and multimedia content delivered by broadband connections also demand massive storage. Today's holographic drives and light-sensitive recording media are extremely expensive and fragile.

The increased storage capacity is based on how images are saved. Current storage media save each bit of data individually, which accounts for slow data transfer rates. The holographic process, by contrast, stores approximately 1 million bits simultaneously on the disc. Multiple pages can be stacked on top of each other.

For a look at the next generation of holographic storage, visit the Discovering Computers 2004 Looking Ahead Web page (**scsite.com/dc2004/looking**). Click Looking Ahead #1 below Chapter 7.

FAQ 7-6

Do any digital video cameras record movies on DVD?

Yes. Video cameras that store at least 120 minutes of recording on *mini-DVD media* (three-inch diameter) are available, but they are quite expensive. Once recorded, users can view the DVD media in a standard computer DVD drive or a DVD player. Many video cameras include the capability of editing the video right in the camera.

For more information about DVD recorders, visit the Discovering Computers 2004 FAQ Web page (**scsite.com/dc2004/faq**). Click DVD Recorders below Chapter 7.

WEB LINK 7-8

DVDs

Visit the Discovering Computers 2004 WEB LINK page (**scsite .com/dc2004/weblink**). Click DVDs below Chapter 7.

WEB LINK 7-9

Tape

Visit the Discovering Computers 2004 WEB LINK page (**scsite .com/dc2004/weblink**). Click Tape below Chapter 7.

TAPE

One of the first storage media used with mainframe computers was tape. **Tape** is a magnetically coated ribbon of plastic capable of storing large amounts of data and information at a low cost. Tape no longer is used as a primary method of storage. Instead, business and home users utilize tape most often for long-term storage and backup.

Comparable to a tape recorder, a **tape drive** reads and writes data and information on a tape. Although older computers used reel-to-reel tape drives, today's tape drives use tape cartridges. A *tape cartridge* is a small, rectangular, plastic housing for tape (Figure 7-29). Tape cartridges that contain quarter-inch-wide tape are slightly larger than audio-cassette tapes. Business and home users sometimes back up personal computer hard disks onto tape.

Some personal computers have external tape units. Others have the tape drive built into the system unit. On larger computers, tape cartridges are mounted in a separate cabinet called a *tape library*.

Common types of tape drives are digital audio tape (also called digital data storage), digital linear tape, linear tape-open, quarter-inch cartridge, and Travan. The table in Figure 7-30 compares the storage capacities of each of these types of tape. Transfer rates of tape drives range from 500 KBps to 1 MBps.

FIGURE 7-29 A tape cartridge and a tape drive.

Tape storage requires *sequential access*, which refers to reading or writing data consecutively. As with a music tape, you must forward or rewind the tape to a specific point to access a specific piece of data. For example, to access item W requires passing through points A through V sequentially.

Floppy disks, Zip disks, hard disks, CDs and DVDs all use direct access. *Direct access*, also called *random access*, means that the device can locate a particular data item or file immediately, without having to move consecutively through items stored in front of the desired data item or file. When writing or reading specific data, direct access is much faster than sequential access.

PC CARDs

As discussed in Chapter 4, a **PC Card** is a thin, credit-card-sized device that fits into a PC Card slot. Different types and sizes of PC Cards add storage, additional memory, fax/modem, networking, sound, and other capabilities to a desktop or notebook computer. PC Cards commonly are used in notebook computers (Figure 7-31).

FIGURE 7-31 A PC Card in a notebook computer.

POPULAR TYPES OF TAPE

Name	Abbreviation	Storage Capacity
Digital audio tape (also called digital data storage)	DAT (also called DDS)	2 GB to 240 GB
Digital linear tape	DLT	20 GB to 220 GB
Linear tape-open	LTO	100 GB to 200 GB
Quarter-inch cartridge	QIC	40 MB to 25 GB
Travan	TR	8 GB to 40 GB

FIGURE 7-30 Common types of tape.

Originally, PC Cards were called PCMCIA cards. They are available in three kinds: Type I, Type II, and Type III (Figure 7-32). The only difference in size among the three types is their thickness. Some digital cameras use a Type II or Type III PC Card to store photographs. PC Cards that house a hard disk have storage capacities up to 5 GB. The advantage of a PC Card for storage is portability. You easily can transport large amounts of data, instructions, and information from one computer to another using a Type II or Type III PC Card.

PC CARDS

Category	Thickness	Use
Type I	3.3 mm	RAM, SRAM, flash memory
Type II	5.0 mm	Modem, LAN, SCSI, sound, TV tuner, hard disk, or other storage
Type III	10.5 mm	Rotating storage such as a hard disk

FIGURE 7-32   Various uses of PC Cards.

MINIATURE MOBILE STORAGE MEDIA

PDAs, digital cameras, music players, and smart phones are convenient devices that provide the mobile user with instant access to technology. These devices do not have much internal storage. Thus, they use some form of miniature mobile storage media to store digital images, music, or documents (Figure 7-33).

Users store digital photographs, contact lists, names and addresses, music, and small files on miniature mobile storage media. Many types of miniature storage media are available, with capacities ranging from 16 MB to 2 GB. Most miniature storage media are no bigger than a postage stamp.

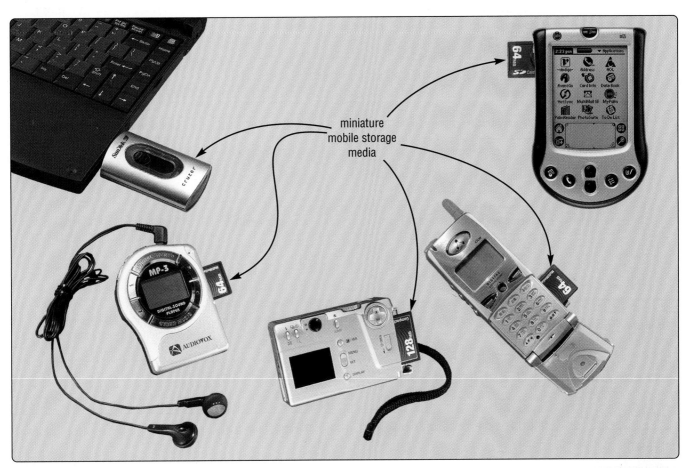

miniature mobile storage media

FIGURE 7-33   Digital cameras, music players, PDAs, smart phones, and notebook computers use miniature mobile storage media.

Common types of miniature mobile storage media include *CompactFlash* (*CF*), *Smart Media*, *Secure Digital* (*SD*), *Memory Stick®*, *Microdrive™*, and *USBDrive™*. The table in Figure 7-34 compares storage capacities and uses of these miniature storage media.

These miniature, rewritable media usually are in the form of flash memory cards or miniature hard disks. Flash memory cards are sometimes called *solid-state devices*, which

means they consist entirely of electronics (chips, wires, etc.) and contain no moving parts. Miniature hard disks are magnetic media and operate like their desktop-sized counterparts — just on a smaller scale.

Depending on the device, manufacturers claim miniature mobile storage media can last from 10 to 100 years. Transfer rates range from about 1 MBps to 3 MBps or more, depending on the device. Miniature storage media are

MINIATURE MOBILE STORAGE MEDIA

Device Name	Storage Capacity	Type	Use
CompactFlash	16 MB to 1 GB	Flash memory card	Digital cameras, PDAs, notebook computers, printers, music players, cellular telephones
Smart Media	16 MB to 128 MB	Flash memory card	Digital cameras, PDAs, photo printers, cellular telephones
Secure Digital	16 MB to 256 MB	Flash memory card	Digital cameras, PDAs, music players, cellular telephones, digital video cameras, car navigation systems, e-books
Memory Stick®	16 MB to 128 MB	Flash memory card	Digital cameras, notebook computers, photo printers
Microdrive™	1 GB	Magnetic media	Digital cameras, PDAs, music players, notebook computers, video cameras
USBDrive™	32 MB to 2 GB	Flash memory card	Plugs into any USB port to function as a mini hard disk

FIGURE 7-34 A variety of miniature mobile storage media.

 WEB LINK 7-10

Flash Memory Cards
Visit the Discovering Computers 2004 WEB LINK page (**scsite .com/dc2004/weblink**). Click Flash Memory Cards below Chapter 7.

much smaller, lighter in weight, and more portable than other storage media such as hard disks. They are, however, much more expensive. For example, a 192 MB flash memory card costs more than a 40 GB hard disk. For the next generation of miniature storage, read Looking Ahead 7-2.

LOOKING AHEAD 7-2

Millipede Reinvents Punch Card Storage Concept

In the 1880s, Herman Hollerith invented the punch card to store data gathered in the 1890 U.S. Census. Operators sat at machines and punched as many as 80 holes — each representing one character of data — in the dollar-bill-sized cards. Hollerith's company became International Business Machines (IBM) in 1923 and held a monopoly on using punch cards for storage.

Today, IBM has reinvented the punch card with *Millipede*, a postage-size storage device that can hold as much as 1 terabit of data per square inch. In fact, 3 billion bits of Millipede data will fit in an area the size of one hole punched in Hollerith's card. This capacity is the equivalent of 25 million printed textbook pages, which is more than 20 times larger than any of today's storage devices.

Unlike magnetic storage media, Millipede uses more than 4,000 sharp tips to indent a thin, reusable plastic film. The indentations are 10 nanometers apart.

Although IBM has no current plans to market its Millipede device, company engineers believe the prototype can be used as a basis for developing storage media to replace the flash memory cards currently used in digital cameras, PDAs, and cellular telephones.

For a look at the next generation of storage, visit the Discovering Computers 2004 Looking Ahead Web page (**scsite.com/dc2004/looking**). Click Looking Ahead #2 below Chapter 7.

To view, edit, or print images and information stored on miniature mobile storage media, you transfer the contents to your desktop computer or other device. Some printers also have slots to read PC Cards and other miniature mobile storage media. If your computer or printer does not have a built-in slot, card readers are available. A **card reader** is a device that reads data, instructions, and information stored on PC Cards or memory cards (Figure 7-35). Card readers usually connect to the USB port, FireWire port, or parallel port on the system unit. The type of card you have will determine the type of card reader needed.

FIGURE 7-35 A card reader.

Smart Cards

A **smart card**, which is similar in size to a credit card or ATM card (Figure 7-36), stores data on a thin microprocessor embedded in the card. Smart cards contain a processor and have input, process, output, and storage capabilities. Thus, some people refer to these cards as intelligent smart cards to differentiate them from a flash memory card, which has only storage capabilities.

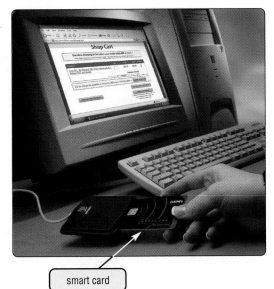

FIGURE 7-36 A sample smart card.

When you insert the smart card into a specialized card reader, the information on the smart card is read and, if necessary, updated. One popular use of smart cards is to store a prepaid dollar amount, as in a prepaid telephone calling card. You receive the card with a specific dollar amount stored in the microprocessor. Each time you use the card, it reduces the available amount of money. Using these cards provides convenience to the caller, eliminates the telephone company's need to collect coins from telephones, and reduces vandalism of pay telephones. Other uses of smart cards include storing medical records, vaccination data, and other health-care information; tracking information such as customer purchases or employee attendance; and storing a prepaid amount such as electronic money. Read Issue 7-4 for a related discussion.

WEB LINK 7-11

Smart Cards

Visit the Discovering Computers 2004 WEB LINK page (**scsite .com/dc2004/weblink**). Click Smart Cards below Chapter 7.

E-money (electronic money), also called *digital cash*, is a means of paying for goods and services over the Internet. A bank issues unique digital cash numbers that represent an amount of money. When you purchase digital cash, the amount of money is withdrawn from your bank account. One implementation of e-money places the digital cash on a smart card. To use the card, you swipe it through a card reader on your computer or a card reader that is attached to your computer.

MICROFILM AND MICROFICHE

Microfilm and microfiche store microscopic images of documents on roll or sheet film (Figure 7-37). **Microfilm** is a 100- to 215-foot roll of film. **Microfiche** is a small sheet of film, usually about 4 inches by 6 inches.

FAQ 7-7

Are some credit cards smart cards?

Yes. More than 42 million people around the world have the smart Visa card, which contains a microchip filled with their personal information. Credit card smart cards offer the consumer the convenience of using the card to make purchases in stores and online. In both cases, users simply swipe the card in a card reader. At home, the card reader is attached to the home computer.

For more information about credit card smart cards, visit the Discovering Computers 2004 FAQ Web page (**scsite.com/dc2004/faq**). Click Credit Card Smart Cards below Chapter 7.

ISSUE 7-4

Should the World Become a Cashless Society?

Who is pictured on the $10 bill? Futurists predict that someday most Americans will have as much trouble answering this question (Alexander Hamilton) as they do today recognizing the man pictured on the $10,000 bill (Salmon P. Chase). Some forecasters say that the world is moving toward a cashless society. One form of payment that could end the need for cash is the smart card, which can store a dollar amount on a thin microprocessor and update the amount whenever a transaction is made. Advocates claim that smart cards would eliminate muggings and robberies, make it difficult to purchase illegal goods, and reduce taxes by identifying tax cheats. Smart cards already are common in Europe, but many Americans cite privacy concerns. A cash purchase is anonymous. Yet, a smart card purchase preserves a record of the transaction that could become available to other merchants, advertisers, or government agencies. Considering the advantages and disadvantages, should the world become a cashless society? Why or why not? Would you be comfortable using a smart card instead of cash? Why?

For more information about a cashless society, visit the Discovering Computers 2004 Issues Web page (**scsite.com/dc2004/issues**). Click Issue #4 below Chapter 7.

FIGURE 7-37 Microfilm and microfiche store microscopic images of documents on roll or sheet film.

A *computer output microfilm recorder* is the device that records the images on the film. The stored images are so small that you can read them only with a microfilm or microfiche reader.

Applications of microfilm and microfiche are widespread. Libraries use these media to store back issues of newspapers, magazines, and genealogy records. Large organizations use microfilm and microfiche to archive inactive files. Banks use them to store transactions and canceled checks. The U.S. Army uses them to store personnel records.

The use of microfilm and microfiche provides a number of advantages. They greatly reduce the amount of paper firms must handle. They are inexpensive and have the longest life of any storage media (Figure 7-38).

PUTTING IT ALL TOGETHER

Many factors influence the type of storage devices you should use: the amount of data, instructions, and information to be stored; the hardware and software in use; and the desired cost. The table in Figure 7-39 outlines several suggested storage devices for various types of computer users.

MEDIA LIFE EXPECTANCIES

Media Type	Guaranteed Life Expectancy	Potential Life Expectancy
Magnetic disks	3 to 5 years	20 to 30 years
CDs and DVDs	5 to 10 years	50 to 100 years
Microfilm	100 years	500 years

FIGURE 7-38 Microfilm is the medium with the longest life.

CATEGORIES OF USERS

User	Typical Storage Devices
Home	• 3.5-inch high-density floppy disk drive • 250 MB Zip drive • 60 GB hard disk • Internet hard drive • CD or DVD drive • Card reader
Small Office/Home Office	• 3.5-inch high-density floppy disk drive • 250 MB Zip drive • 100 GB hard disk • Internet hard drive • CD or DVD drive • External hard drive for backup
Mobile 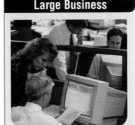	• 3.5-inch high-density floppy disk drive • 2 GB PC Card hard disk or USBDrive™ • 40 GB hard disk • Internet hard drive • CD or DVD drive • Card reader • External or removable hard disk for backup
Large Business	• 3.5-inch high-density floppy disk drive • 160 GB hard disk • CD or DVD drive • Microfilm or microfiche • Smart card reader • Tape drive
Power	• 3.5-inch high-density floppy disk drive • CD or DVD drive • 160 GB hard disk • Internet hard drive • External or removable hard disk for backup

FIGURE 7-39 Recommended storage devices for various users.

QUIZ YOURSELF 7-3

To check your knowledge of types of CDs and DVDs, tape, PC Cards, miniature mobile storage media, and microfilm and microfiche, visit the Discovering Computers 2004 Quiz Yourself Web page (**scsite.com/dc2004/quiz**). Click Objectives 8 – 11 below Chapter 7.

CHAPTER SUMMARY

Storage holds data, instructions, and information for future use. Users depend on storage devices to provide access to their storage media for years and decades to come. Read Issue 7-5 for a discussion about the future of storage.

This chapter identified and discussed various storage media and storage devices. Storage media covered included floppy disks, Zip disks, internal hard disks, external hard disks, removable hard disks, CD-ROMs, CD-RWs, DVD-ROMs, DVD+RWs, tape, PC Cards, flash memory cards and other miniature mobile storage media, and microfilm and microfiche.

ISSUE 7-5

Can You Read It Tomorrow?

Up to 75 percent of today's data is created digitally and has never existed on paper. Although written documents can be read hundreds of years after they are created, rapid changes in computer technology can make digital records almost inaccessible in just one decade. For most computer users, hardware changes have made data stored on once-popular 5-inch floppy disks, or on the 8-inch floppy disks used in the early '70s, unavailable today. Software changes also take a toll. One computer expert claims that trying to read material written with an obsolete word processing program is like trying to interpret Egyptian hieroglyphics without the Rosetta Stone. Pennsylvania State University recently admitted that almost 3,000 student and school files could not be accessed due to lost or outdated software. Is the potential unavailability of digital data a problem? Why or why not? What can be done to keep today's digital information available in the future?

For more information about digital data, visit the Discovering Computers 2004 Issues Web page (**scsite.com/dc2004/issues**). Click Issue #5 below Chapter 7.

Computer Technician

Career Corner

Computer technicians are in great demand in every organization and industry. For many, this is the entry point for a career in the computer/information technology field. The responsibilities of a *computer technician*, also called a computer service technician, include a variety of duties. Most companies that employ someone with this title expect the technician to have basic across-the-board knowledge of concepts in the computer electronics field. Some of the tasks are hardware repair and installation; software installation, upgrade, and configuration; and troubleshooting client and/or server problems. Because computers are a rapidly changing field, technicians must work to remain abreast of current technology and become aware of future developments. Computer technicians generally work with a variety of users, which requires expert people skills, especially the ability to work with groups of nontechnical users.

Most entry-level computer technicians possess the *A+ certification*. This certification attests that a computer technician has demonstrated knowledge of computer setup, maintenance, and software that meets industry standards and has at least six months of experience in the field. The Electronics Technicians Association also provides a Computer Service Technician (CST) certification program.

Because this is an entry-level position, the pay scale is not as high as other more demanding and skilled positions. Individuals can expect an average annual starting salary of around $25,000 to $35,000. Companies pay more for computer technicians with experience and certification.

To learn more about the field of computer technician as a career, visit the Discovering Computers 2004 Careers Web page (**scsite.com/dc2004/careers**). Click Computer Technician.

HIGH-TECH TALK

Disk Formatting and File Systems

Formatting a disk can be compared to starting a library. Before any books can be put in place, you must install the bookshelves and a catalog system. Similarly, a disk must have a file system set up to make it ready to receive data. This is true of many different storage media — including floppy disks, hard disks, removable hard disks such as the Peerless™ disk, and CD-ROMs — all of which must be formatted, to allow a way to organize and find files saved on the disk.

This discussion focuses on the formatting process required to take a hard disk from its newly manufactured state to a fully functional storage medium. Three main steps are involved in the process of formatting a hard disk: (1) low-level (physical) formatting; (2) partitioning; and (3) high-level (logical) formatting.

A hard disk must be formatted physically before it can be formatted logically. A hard drive physically formats a hard disk by writing a pattern of 1s and 0s on the surface of the disk. The pattern of 1s and 0s serves as small electronic markers, which divide the hard disk platter into its basic physical elements: tracks, sectors, and cylinders.

These elements define the way data is written on and read from the disk physically. As the read/write head moves over the spinning disks, it reads the electronic markers that define the tracks, sectors, and cylinders to determine where it is in relation to the data on the disk's surface. The hard disk manufacturer usually performs a hard disk's physical, or *low-level*, *formatting*.

Once a hard disk has been formatted physically, it can be partitioned. *Partitioning* is the process of dividing the hard disk into regions called partitions. Each partition occupies a group of adjacent cylinders. Partitioning allows you to organize a hard disk into segments and lets you run multiple operating systems on a single computer. You also can keep the entire hard disk as one partition. After a disk partition has been formatted, it is referred to as a *volume*.

After a hard drive has been formatted physically and partitioned, it must be formatted logically. Logical, or *high-level*, *formatting* places a file system on the disk. A *file system* allows an operating system, such as DOS or Windows XP, to use the space available on a hard disk to store and retrieve files. The operating system uses the file system to store information about the disk's directory, or folder, structure.

The file system also defines the size of the clusters used to store data on the hard disk. A cluster, or *block*, is made up of two or more sectors on a single track on a hard disk. A cluster is the minimum unit the operating system uses to store information. Even if a file has a size of 1 byte, a cluster as large as 64 KB might be used to store the file on large drives. The number of sectors and tracks and, therefore, the number of clusters that a drive can create on a disk's surface, determine the capacity of the disk.

While creating the file system during logical formatting, the drive creates a special table in the disk's first sector, sector 0. This table stores entries that the operating system uses to locate files on a disk. Each entry in the table takes up a certain number of bits, which is why file systems often are referred to as 12-bit, 16-bit, or 32-bit. The content of each entry consists of a whole number, which identifies one or more clusters where the file is stored.

Depending on the operating system used to format the disk, the file system can be one of several types, as shown in the table in Figure 7-40. Whatever file system is used, the file system is the interface between the operating system and drives.

For more information about formatting a hard disk, visit the Discovering Computers 2004 High-Tech Talk Web page (**scsite.com/dc2004/tech**) and click Disk Formatting.

File System	Description	Key Features
FAT (also called FAT12 and FAT16)	The standard file system for DOS and Windows. Because of its widespread use, FAT also is accessible by most other operating systems.	• FAT12 is used for floppy disk drives and very small hard disks (up to 16 MB) • FAT16 is used for small to moderate-sized hard disk volumes (up to 2 GB)
VFAT (Virtual FAT)	A newer protected-mode version of the FAT file system, introduced with Windows 95.	• Supports long file names up to 255 characters long • Faster than FAT because the computer can read files at least 32 bits at a time
FAT32	A 32-bit version of FAT, introduced with Windows 95.	• Same key features as VFAT • Used for medium-sized to very large hard disk volumes (up to 2 terabytes)
NTFS (NT File System)	The 32-bit file system currently used for Windows NT, Windows 2000, and Windows XP.	• 32- or 64-bit entries in file system table • Fully recoverable file system, designed to restore consistency after a system crash • Used for medium-sized to very large hard disk volumes (up to 16 billion GB)

FIGURE 7-40 Comparison of various file systems.

COMPANIES ON THE CUTTING EDGE

Kingston
Memory in the Making

Have you ever sat down to take a test and have your mind go blank, and then wonder if you were losing your memory?

The computer industry also thought it was losing its memory in 1987. At that time, memory for personal computers was scarce. John Tu and David Sun knew they could help solve the problem. They founded *Kingston Technology* and designed a standard single inline memory module (SIMM) using a readily available alternative chip.

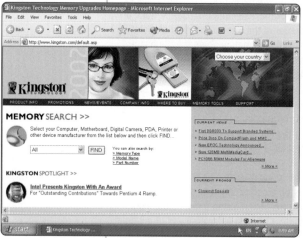

As the memory shortage problem eased a few years later, Kingston branched into manufacturing processor upgrades, storage subsystems, and networking solutions. Today, Kingston is the world's leading independent manufacturer of memory products for computers, servers, digital cameras, and other electronic devices. Headquartered in Fountain Valley, California, Kingston has manufacturing facilities in the United States, Taiwan, Malaysia, and China to meet memory market needs on a global scale. Kingston sells more than 2,000 products and enjoys annual sales of more than $1.6 billion.

Kingston's success results from an emphasis on reliability. This emphasis contributes to the trust between Kingston and its customers. Kingston uses some of the most rigorous testing procedures in the memory industry. The company exceeds industry standards for product quality and product dependability. To ensure memory reliability, Kingston screens components thoroughly and uses only the highest quality components. In addition, Kingston tests modules at all stages of production. Kingston's manufacturing process is so effective that the mean time between failure rating, a measure of product reliability, exceeds 500 years!

Fortune magazine has honored Kingston as one of the 100 Best Companies to Work for in the United States. Part of this honor is due to Kingston's company philosophy of treating all employees as family members and of displaying such traits as courtesy, honesty, and compassion.

For more information about Kingston Technology, visit the Discovering Computers 2004 Companies Web page (**scsite.com/dc2004/companies**) and click Kingston.

EMC
Big-Time Storage Solutions

When your closet gets too small for your wardrobe, one solution is to find a larger closet. When the world's larger corporations run out of space to store their data, they, too, can look for additional storage space. Chances are that when they do, they consider EMC Corporation, a provider of storage systems.

EMC Corporation supplies storage capabilities to large companies. EMC is a world leader in providing systems that store, safeguard, and control information resources, allowing companies to combine their information resources into a single asset. Richard Egan and Roger Marino (the "E" and "M" in EMC) founded EMC in 1979 to fill a demand for add-on memory boards in the minicomputer market. In 1981, EMC introduced its first computer product, a 64 KB chip memory board. By 1984, sales approached $20 million. In the late 1980s, EMC moved from a supplier of memory products to a provider of storage solutions. Soon, the company expanded to provide small disk drives for mainframe computers, which is the industry standard for storage systems today.

In 1990, EMC introduced Symmetrix, a 24 GB storage system with speeds significantly faster than other available products but uses less than a quarter of the floor space. The Symmetrix line of information storage won numerous awards for performance and innovation in helping customers protect and share data. By 1993, EMC had abandoned its memory products to focus entirely on disk storage. EMC improved its Symmetrix systems with intelligent software programs that added special data management, business protection, and features.

EMC recently was named by *Fortune* as one of the 100 Best Companies to Work for in America.

For more information about EMC Corporation, visit the Discovering Computers 2004 Companies Web page (**scsite.com/dc2004/companies**) and click EMC.

TECHNOLOGY TRAILBLAZERS

Al Shugart
Storage Expert

The day after receiving his Bachelor of Science degree in Engineering and Physics from the University of Redlands in 1951, *Al Shugart* joined IBM as a customer engineer. He got into it because he liked fixing things and went to work for IBM as a broken machine repairman. He was intrigued with being faced with a problem and then having to fix it. When he felt he had fixed all the problems, he was going to quit, but instead IBM made him part of a product development program that would have a profound impact on the computer industry. Shugart supervised the development of a removable, portable data storage device, an effort that led to the construction of the first removable rigid read/write disk drive. Shugart left IBM in 1969 and went to work as vice president of product development for Memorex. In 1973, he started Shugart Associates, a pioneer in the manufacture of floppy disks. Because of internal problems, the following year Shugart left the company bearing his name. He spent the next few years as a bar-owner, a salmon fisherman, and a private consultant to the technology industry.

In 1979, Shugart and some associates founded Seagate Technology, Inc. Today, Shugart is chairman of the board, president, and CEO of Seagate, which is a leader in the design and marketing of storage products. Seagate has more than 100,000 employees worldwide and the largest revenue share in the hard disk industry.

Despite his success, Shugart feels that life has more important things to offer. He has said, "Your priority has to be on being nice, not on being successful. If you're a nice person and you're talented, then success will follow. If you're a nice person and you're not talented, success won't follow, but at least you're a nice person and you'll enjoy life."

For more information about Al Shugart, visit the Discovering Computers 2004 People Web page (**scsite.com/dc2004/people**) and click Al Shugart.

Mark Dean
Inventor

Not many first graders can handle algebra problems. But, Mark Dean was no ordinary first grader. Along with solving math equations in his first year of school, he also tutored older students, surprising some of his classmates with his scholastic ability.

As one of the few African-Americans in his high school, and a straight-A student and star athlete, Dean spent hours inventing new products. Together with his dad, he built a tractor from scratch. After graduating at the top of his class from the University of Tennessee in 1979, he joined IBM and helped design improvements in architecture that allow components, such as modems and printers, to communicate with personal computers. This technology is used in more than 40 million personal computers manufactured each year. Dean earned his Ph.D. degree at Stanford, and he headed a team at IBM that invented the first CMOS microprocessor chip to operate at 1 gigahertz (1,000 MHz). As an IBM idea man and Vice President of Systems in IBM Research, Dean is responsible today for developing future-generation hardware and software. Currently, he is developing an electronic tablet that functions as an e-book, DVD player, radio, wireless telephone, and Web-enabled device. "If you can talk about it," Dean says, "that means it's possible."

Dean is the first African-American to receive an IBM Fellowship, the company's highest technical ranking. He has received numerous awards including the National Society of Black Engineers Distinguished Engineer Award, the Black Engineer of the Year President's Award, and the Ronald H. Brown American Innovators Award. Dean was inducted into the National Inventor's Hall of Fame, an honor he shares with fewer than 150 other people. Dean has more than 30 patents or patents pending, three of which are for the internal architecture of the original personal computer.

For more information about Mark Dean, visit the Discovering Computers 2004 People Web page (**scsite.com/dc2004/people**) and click Mark Dean.

CHAPTER 7 # CHAPTER REVIEW   ◀● Previous | Next ●▶

The Chapter Review section summarizes the concepts presented in this chapter.

■ WEB INSTRUCTIONS:

To display this page from the Web, start your browser and enter the Web address **scsite.com/dc2004/ch7/review**. Click the links for current and additional information. To listen to an audio version of this Chapter Review, click the Audio button.

1 What Types of Items Do Users Store on Computer Media?

Storage holds <u>data</u>, instructions, and information for future use. Every computer uses storage to hold software. In addition to programs, users store a variety of data and information including correspondence, reports, records, digital photographs, music, video, Web pages, drawings, and multimedia presentations. Home users, small office/home office users, and mobile users typically have much smaller storage requirements than the large business or power user.

2 How Are Storage Devices Different from Storage Media?

A **storage medium** (media is the plural) is the physical material on which a computer keeps data, instructions, and information. The number of bytes (characters) a storage medium can hold is its <u>capacity</u>. A **storage device** is the computer hardware that records and/or retrieves items to and from storage media. **Writing** is the process of transferring items from memory to a storage medium, and **reading** is the process of transferring these items from a storage medium into memory.

3 What Are the Characteristics of a Floppy Disk Drive?

A **floppy disk** is a portable, inexpensive storage medium that consists of a thin, circular, flexible plastic Mylar film enclosed in a square-shaped plastic shell. Floppy disks are a *magnetic media* that uses magnetic particles to store items in tracks and sectors. A *track* is a narrow recording band that forms a full circle on the surface of the disk. Each track is broken into small, arc-shaped storage locations called *sectors*. A <u>floppy disk drive</u> is a device that reads from and writes on a floppy disk. A mechanism in the drive called the *read/write head* reads items or writes items as it barely touches the disk's recording surface.

4 How Are Zip Disks Used?

A **Zip disk** is a type of portable magnetic media that can store up to 500 times more than a standard floppy disk. These large capacities make it easy to transport many files or large items. Another popular use of Zip disks is to make a <u>backup</u>, or duplicate, of a file, program, or disk that you can use in case the original is lost, damaged, or destroyed.

▣ Visit **scsite.com/dc2004/quiz** or click the Quiz Yourself button. Click Objectives 1 – 4 below Chapter 7.

5 What Are the Characteristics of a Hard Disk?

A **hard disk**, also called a *hard disk drive*, is a storage device that contains one or more inflexible, circular platters that store data, instructions, and information. A *platter* is made of aluminum, glass, or ceramic and is coated with a material that allows items to be recorded magnetically on its surface. Each platter has two read/write heads, one for each side. The location of a read/write head often is referred to by its cylinder. A *cylinder* is the vertical section of a track that passes through all platters. While the computer is running, the platters rotate at 5,400 to 7,200 *revolutions per minute (rpm)*, which allows nearly instant access to all tracks and sectors on the platters. The spinning creates a cushion of air between the platters and the read/write heads. A *head crash* occurs when a read/write head touches the surface of a platter, usually resulting in a loss of data.

6 What Are the Advantages of Using an Internet Hard Drive?

An **Internet hard drive** is a service on the Web that provides storage to computer users, usually for a minimal fee. An Internet hard drive allows users to access files from any computer or device that has <u>Internet access</u>, save time by storing large files instantaneously instead of downloading them to a local hard disk, permit others to access files,

CHAPTER REVIEW   CHAPTER 7

view time-critical data and images immediately while away from the main computer location, and store offsite backups of data.

7 | What Are the Characteristics of CDs and DVDs?

CDs and DVDs are a type of storage media that consists of a flat, round, portable metal disc with a protective plastic coating. CDs and DVDs are optical media that store items by using microscopic pits (indentations) and lands (flat areas). A high-powered laser light creates the pits, and a lower-powered laser light reads items by reflecting light through the bottom of the disc. CDs and DVDs commonly store items in a single track that spirals from the center to the edge of the disc.

> 📷 Visit **scsite.com/dc2004/quiz** or click the Quiz Yourself button. Click Objectives 5 – 7 below Chapter 7.

8 | How Are CD-ROMs, CD-RWs, DVD-ROMs, and DVD+RWs Different?

A **CD-ROM** is a type of optical disc that uses laser technology to store items. A typical CD-ROM holds from 650 MB to 1 GB of data, instructions, and information. Users can read the contents of standard CD-ROMs but cannot erase or modify their contents. A **CD-R** (*compact disc-recordable*) is a *multisession disc* onto which users record their own items. Each part of a CD-R can be written on only one time, and the disc's contents cannot be erased. A CD-RW (*compact disc-rewritable*) is an erasable disc that can be written on multiple times. A **DVD-ROM** (*digital versatile disc-ROM* or *digital video disc-ROM*) is an extremely high capacity optical disk capable of storing from 4.7 GB to 17 GB. Not only is the storage capacity of a DVD-ROM greater than that of a CD-ROM, a DVD-ROM's quality also far surpasses that of a CD-ROM. A **DVD+RW** disc is a recordable version of DVD that allows users to erase and record more than 1,000 times.

9 | How Is Tape Used?

Tape is a magnetically coated ribbon of plastic capable of storing large amounts of data and information at a low cost. A tape drive reads and writes data and information on tape. Businesses and home users sometimes back up personal computer hard disks on tape.

10 | What Are PC Cards and Other Types of Miniature Storage Media?

A PC Card is a thin, credit-card-sized device that fits into a PC Card slot to add storage or other capabilities to a desktop or notebook computer. PDAs, digital cameras, music players, and smart phones use some form of miniature storage media to store digital images, music, or documents. Common types of miniature mobile storage media include *CompactFlash* (*CF*), *Smart Media*, *Secure Digital* (*SD*), *Memory Stick*, *Microdrive*, and *USBDrive*. A **smart card**, which is similar in size to a credit card, stores data on a thin microprocessor embedded in the card.

11 | How Are Microfilm and Microfiche Used?

Microfilm is a 100- to 215-foot roll of film. **Microfiche** is a small sheet of film, usually about 4 inches by 6 inches. Libraries use microfilm and microfiche to store back issues of newspapers, magazines, and records; large organizations use them to archive inactive files; banks use them to store transactions and canceled checks; and the U.S. Army uses them to store personnel records.

> 📷 Visit **scsite.com/dc2004/quiz** or click the Quiz Yourself button. Click Objectives 8 – 11 below Chapter 7.

CHAPTER 7 KEY TERMS

◄● Previous | Next ●►

You should know the Primary Terms and be familiar with the Secondary Terms.

WEB INSTRUCTIONS:

To display this page from the Web, start your browser and enter the Web address **scsite.com/dc2004/ch7/terms**. Click a term to display its definition and a picture. When the picture displays, click the more info button for current and additional information about the term from the Web.

>> Primary Terms
(shown in bold-black characters in the chapter)

access time (7.04)
backup (7.09)
capacity (7.04)
card reader (7.27)
CD-R (7.20)
CD-R drive (7.20)
CD-ROM (7.17)
CD-ROM drive (7.17)
CD-RW (7.20)
CD-RW drive (7.20)
DVD+RW (7.23)
DVD-ROM (7.22)
DVD-ROM drive (7.22)
external hard disk (7.13)
floppy disk (7.05)
floppy disk drive (7.06)
formatting (7.08)
hard disk (7.09)

Internet hard drive (7.14)
microfiche (7.28)
microfilm (7.28)
online storage (7.14)
PC Card (7.24)
Picture CD (7.19)
reading (7.04)
removable hard disk (7.13)
smart card (7.27)
storage device (7.04)
storage medium (7.03)
tape (7.24)
tape drive (7.24)
write-protect notch (7.08)
writing (7.04)
Zip disk (7.09)
Zip drive (7.09)

>> Secondary Terms
(shown in italic characters in the chapter)

allocation unit (7.08)
burning (7.20)
cache controller (7.13)
CD recorder (7.20)
CD-RW/DVD (7.22)
cluster (7.08)
compact disc read-only memory (7.17)
compact disc-recordable (7.20)
compact disc-rewritable (7.20)
CompactFlash (CF) (7.26)
computer output microfilm recorder (7.29)
cylinder (7.11)
density (7.06)
digital cash (7.28)
digital versatile disc-ROM (7.22)
digital video disc-ROM (7.22)
direct access (7.24)
disk cache (7.12)
disk cartridge (7.13)
disk controller (7.13)
diskette (7.05)
downward compatible (7.06)
DVD writer (7.23)
DVD+RAM (DVD+random access memory) (7.23)
DVD+RW drive (7.23)
DVD-R (DVD-recordable) (7.23)
DVD-rewriteable (7.23)
DVD-video format (7.22)
EIDE (Enhanced Integrated Drive Electronics) (7.14)
e-money (7.28)
erasable CD (CD-E) (7.20)

external floppy disk drive (7.06)
fixed disk (7.09)
form factor (7.11)
hard disk drive (7.09)
head crash (7.12)
HD (7.06)
jewel box (7.16)
KBps (7.05)
magnetic media (7.07)
MBps (7.05)
Memory Stick® (7.26)
Microdrive™ (7.26)
multiread CD drive (7.20)
multisession disc (7.19)
optically assisted hard drive (7.10)
PhotoCD (7.19)
platter (7.10)
portable (7.06)
random access (7.24)
read/write head (7.06)
revolutions per minute (rpm) (7.11)
ripping (7.20)
SCSI controller (7.14)
secondary storage (7.03)
sectors (7.07)
Secure Digital (SD) (7.26)
sequential access (7.24)
shutter (7.06)
single-session disc (7.17)
Smart Media (7.26)
solid-state devices (7.26)
storage (7.02)
tape cartridge (7.24)
tape library (7.24)
track (7.07)
transfer rate (7.05)
upward compatible (7.06)
USBDrive™ (7.26)

CHECKPOINT CHAPTER 7

Use the Checkpoint exercises to check your knowledge level of the chapter.

◼ WEB INSTRUCTIONS:

To display this page from the Web, start your browser and enter the Web address **scsite.com/dc2004/ch7/check**. Click the links for current and additional information.

🔲 LABEL THE FIGURE   Identify each part of this disassembled 3.5-inch floppy disk.

a. flexible thin film
b. liner
c. magnetic coating
d. metal hub
e. shell
f. shutter

1. _____
2. _____
3. _____
4. _____
5. _____
6. _____

🔲 TRUE/FALSE   Mark T for True and F for False. (See page numbers in parentheses.)

_____ 1. <u>Storage</u> holds data, instructions, and information for future use. (7.02)

_____ 2. A <u>storage medium is</u> the physical material on which a computer keeps data, instructions, and information. (7.03)

_____ 3. <u>Density</u> is the number of bits in an area on a storage medium. (7.06)

_____ 4. A <u>sector</u> is a narrow recording band that forms a full circle on the surface of the disk. (7.07)

_____ 5. A <u>cluster</u> can hold data from many files. (7.08)

_____ 6. A typical hard drive contains only one <u>platter</u>. (7.11)

_____ 7. An external hard disk is a separate, free-standing hard disk that connects with a cable to a <u>port</u> on the system unit. (7.13)

_____ 8. CDs and <u>DVDs</u> are magnetic media. (7.16)

_____ 9. <u>Ripping</u> is the process of copying a song from an audio CD and converting it to a digital format. (7.20)

_____ 10. <u>Direct access</u> means that the device can locate a particular data item by moving consecutively through the items stored. (7.24)

_____ 11. <u>Solid-state devices</u> consist entirely of electronics and contain no moving parts. (7.26)

_____ 12. <u>E-money</u> is a means of paying for goods and services over the Internet. (7.28)

CHAPTER 7   CHECKPOINT

QUIZZES AND LEARNING GAMES

Computer Genius

Crossword Puzzle

Interactive Labs

Practice Test

Quiz Yourself

Wheel of Terms

EXERCISES

Chapter Review

Checkpoint

Key Terms

Lab Exercises

Learn It Online

Web Research

BEYOND THE BOOK

Apply It

Career Corner

Companies

FAQ

High-Tech Talk

Issues

Looking Ahead

Trailblazers

Web Links

FEATURES

Guide to Web Sites

Making Use of the Web

Tech News

Timeline 2004

☒ MULTIPLE CHOICE   Select the best answer. (See page numbers in parentheses.)

1. Examples of storage media include all of the following, except _____. (7.03)
   a. monitors and printers
   b. floppy disks and hard disks
   c. CDs and DVDs
   d. tape and PC Cards

2. A _____ is the smallest unit of disk space that stores data. (7.08)
   a. cluster   b. track
   c. shutter   d. sector

3. On a floppy disk, if the write-protect notch is closed, the floppy disk drive _____. (7.08)
   a. can write on but cannot read from the floppy disk
   b. can write on and read from the floppy disk
   c. can read from but cannot write on the floppy disk
   d. cannot read from or write on the floppy disk

4. A Zip disk can store from _____ of data. (7.09)
   a. 10 MB to 75 MB
   b. 100 MB to 750 MB
   c. 10 GB to 75 GB
   d. 100 GB to 750 GB

5. The storage capacity of the average hard disk is _____ that of a standard floppy disk. (7.10)
   a. less than half
   b. about the same as
   c. more than 40,000 times
   d. more than 400,000 times

6. External hard disks and removable hard disks offer all of the following advantages over internal hard disks, except _____. (7.13)
   a. they can transport a large number of files
   b. they can add storage space to a notebook computer
   c. they can be shared with multiple computers
   d. they can transfer data at much faster rates

7. Users store data and information on an Internet hard drive to _____. (7.14)
   a. save time by storing large files instantaneously
   b. allow others to access files
   c. store offsite backups of data
   d. all of the above

8. When a laser light reads CDs or DVDs, a land _____. (7.16)
   a. causes light to reflect, which is read as binary digit 0
   b. causes light to reflect, which is read as binary digit 1
   c. absorbs the light, which is read as binary digit 0
   d. absorbs the light, which is read as binary digit 1

9. To maintain an optical disc, place it in its protective case, called a _____, when you are finished using it. (7.16)
   a. music box
   b. boom box
   c. jewel box
   d. sentry box

10. The process of writing on an optical disc is called _____. (7.20)
    a. formatting   b. ripping
    c. burning   d. reading

11. A storage technique that a DVD-ROM uses to achieve a higher storage capacity than a CD-ROM is _____. (7.22)
    a. making the disc denser by packing the pits closer together
    b. using two layers of pits
    c. using both sides of the disc
    d. all of the above

12. _____ storage requires sequential access. (7.24)
    a. Hard disk   b. Tape
    c. Floppy disk   d. CD

13. _____ is a type of magnetic miniature storage media used in digital cameras, PDAs, music players, notebook computers, and video cameras. (7.26)
    a. CompactFlash
    b. Smart Media
    c. Memory Stick
    d. Microdrive

14. Microfilm and microfiche _____. (7.29)
    a. greatly increase the amount of paper firms must handle
    b. are expensive
    c. have the longest life of any storage media
    d. all of the above

CHECKPOINT   CHAPTER 7

MATCHING   Match the terms with their definitions. (See page numbers in parentheses.)

_____ 1. transfer rate (7.05)

_____ 2. shutter (7.06)

_____ 3. formatting (7.08)

_____ 4. form factor (7.11)

_____ 5. disk cache (7.12)

_____ 6. disk controller (7.13)

_____ 7. Picture CD (7.19)

_____ 8. DVD-video format (7.22)

_____ 9. tape library (7.24)

_____ 10. e-money (7.28)

a. speed with which data, instructions, and information move to and from a device

b. portion of memory that the processor uses to store frequently accessed items

c. used to store a motion picture digitally

d. combines optic technologies with magnetic media

e. piece of metal on a floppy disk that slides to expose the surface of the disk

f. size of hard disk platters on desktop computers

g. compact disc that stores digital versions of a single roll of film

h. number of bytes a storage medium can hold

i. means of paying for goods and services over the Internet

j. process of preparing a disk for reading and writing

k. special-purpose chip and electronic circuits that control the transfer of items to and from the system bus

l. separate cabinet on which tape cartridges are mounted on larger computers

SHORT ANSWER   Write a brief answer to each of the following questions.

1. What is access time? _____ Why is the average hard disk access time faster than the average floppy disk access time? _____

2. What is density? _____ What does it mean to say that floppy disk drives usually are downward compatible but not upward compatible? _____

3. Why is a hard disk inside the system unit sometimes called a fixed disk? _____ How is an external hard disk different from a removable hard disk? _____

4. How is a single-session disc different from a multisession disc? _____ What is a multiread CD drive? _____

5. How is sequential access different from direct access? _____ When reading or writing specific data, which type of access is faster? _____

WORKING TOGETHER   Working with a group of your classmates, complete the following team exercises.

1. Data and information backup is as important for people with personal computers as it is for companies. Develop a report detailing what your group would consider to be the ideal backup system and required devices for the following scenarios: (1) a home computer for personal use, (2) a computer used in a home-based business, (3) a small business with 6 to 8 computers, (4) a business or organization with up to 100 computers, and (5) a business or organization with more than 100 computers. Include information that supports why you selected the particular options. Develop a PowerPoint presentation to share the information with your class.

2. Choose one Issue from the following issues in this chapter: Do You Use a Shoppers Card? (7.10), Promotions on CD-ROM? (7.18), Is It Ethical to Copy CDs? (7.20), Should the World Become a Cashless Society? (7.28), or Can You Read It Tomorrow? (7.30). Use the Web and/or print media to research the issue. Then, present a debate for the class, with different members of your team supporting different responses to the questions that accompany the issue.

3. Some organizations, such as insurance companies, banks, and libraries, are information intensive, meaning that they must keep track of and manipulate large amounts of data. For these organizations, choosing a suitable storage medium is a crucial decision. Have each member of your team visit an information intensive organization and interview someone responsible for maintaining data. What are the storage requirements? What type of storage medium is used? Why? What backup procedures are employed? Meet with the members of your team to discuss the results of your interviews. Then, use PowerPoint to create a group presentation and share your findings with the class.

CHAPTER 7 LEARN IT ONLINE

◀● Previous | Next ●▶

Use the Learn It Online exercises to reinforce your understanding of the chapter concepts.

WEB INSTRUCTIONS:

To display this page from the Web, start your browser and enter the Web address **scsite.com/dc2004/ch7/learn**.

1 At The Movies – Pocket Card

To view the Pocket Card movie, click the number 1 button. Watch the movie, and then complete the exercise by answering the questions below. The dangers of too-easy credit are all too obvious, and often personally painful. Addressing these dangers, the pocket card (actually a debit card) was developed to provide access to a fixed-dollar limit, corresponding to a predeposited amount. In emergencies (or perhaps with a heartrending story to one's parent) it is possible to increase the amount with a deposit or transfer, either online or using a Touch-Tone telephone. Pocket cards also offer monitoring and accountability, because purchases trigger e-mail notification to the card's owner. The budgeting and monitoring features have attracted two prime markets: parents of out-of-town students and employers of salespeople. Why these two markets? What other target opportunities can you see?

2 Shelly Cashman Series Maintaining Your Hard Drive Lab

Follow the instructions in Learn It Online 2 on page 1.46 to start and use the Shelly Cashman Series Maintaining Your Hard Drive Lab. If you are running from the Web, enter the Web address **scsite.com/sclabs/menu** or display the Learn It Online page (see instructions at the top of this page) and then click the number 2 button.

3 DVD

A DVD can hold almost 25 times more data than a CD. This translates into richer sound and images than ever seen or heard before. The quality of DVD storage is having a major impact on the market. Some industry professionals expect that the sales of DVD drives soon will approach the $10 billion mark. Click the number 3 button and complete this exercise to learn more about DVDs.

4 Practice Test

Click the number 4 button. Answer each question. When completed, enter your name and click the Grade Test button to submit the quiz for grading. Make a note of any missed questions. If required, print a copy to submit to your instructor.

5 Web Guide

Click the number 5 button to display the Guide to Web Sites and Searching Techniques Web page. Click Reference and then click Webopedia. Search for DVD. Click one of the DVD links. Use your word processing program to prepare a brief report on your findings and submit your assignment to your instructor.

6 Scavenger Hunt

Click the number 6 button. Print a copy of the Scavenger Hunt page; use this page to write down your answers as you search the Web. Submit your completed page to your instructor.

7 Who Wants to Be a Computer Genius?

Click the number 7 button to find out if you are a computer genius. Directions on how to play the game will display. When you are ready to play, click the Play button. Submit your score to your instructor.

LEARN IT ONLINE   CHAPTER 7

8 Wheel of Terms

Click the number 8 button to reinforce important terms you learned in this chapter by playing the Shelly Cashman Series version of this popular game. Directions on how to play the game will display. When you are ready to play, click the Play button. Submit your score to your instructor.

9 Career Corner

Click the number 9 button to display the Campus Career Center page. Click a link of an area of interest and review the information. Write a brief report describing what you discovered. Submit the report to your instructor.

10 Search Sleuth

Click the number 10 button to learn search techniques that will help make you a research expert. Submit the completed assignment to your instructor.

11 Crossword Puzzle Challenge

Click the number 11 button. Complete the puzzle to reinforce skills you learned in this chapter. Directions on how to play the game will display. When you are ready to play, click the Play button. Submit the completed puzzle to your instructor.

12 Personal Information Management

Are you tired of forgetting birthdays, missing meetings, overlooking appointments, or neglecting to complete important tasks? If so, then personal information management software may be perfect for you. Click the number 12 button to find out about a free, Internet-based calendar. How could this calendar help you organize your life? How might the calendar help you have more fun? After reading the information, you may sign up to create your own Internet-based calendar.

13 In the News

IBM sells a small disk drive, about the size of a quarter, which is capable of storing 1 GB of information, as much as 690 floppy disks. The drive will be used in devices such as digital cameras. What other storage devices are on the horizon? Click the number 13 button and read a news article about a new or improved storage device. What is the device? Who manufactures it? How is the storage device better than, or different from, earlier devices? How will the device be used? Why?

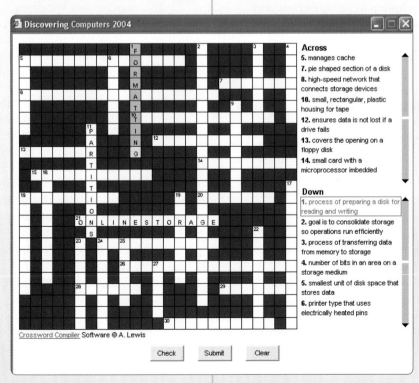

Discovering Computers 2004

Across
5. manages cache
7. pie shaped section of a disk
8. high-speed network that connects storage devices
10. small, rectangular, plastic housing for tape
12. ensures data is not lost if a drive fails
13. covers the opening on a floppy disk
14. small card with a microprocessor imbedded

Down
1. process of preparing a disk for reading and writing
2. goal is to consolidate storage so operations run efficiently
3. process of transferring data from memory to storage
4. number of bits in an area on a storage medium
5. smallest unit of disk space that stores data
6. printer type that uses electrically heated pins

Crossword Compiler Software © A. Lewis

Check   Submit   Clear

CHAPTER 7 LAB EXERCISES

◄● Previous | Next ●►

Use the Lab Exercises to gain hands-on computer experience.

WEB INSTRUCTIONS:

To display this page from the Web, start your browser and enter the Web address **scsite.com/dc2004/ch7/lab**.

1 Recycle Bin

This exercise uses Windows XP procedures. The Recycle Bin, which is located on the desktop, provides a safety net when deleting files or folders. When you send an item to the Recycle Bin, it remains there until it is deleted permanently. Use the Recycle Bin to retrieve files you deleted in error, or empty the Recycle Bin to create more disk space. Windows XP provides one Recycle Bin for each hard disk. To find out more about the Recycle Bin, click the Start button on the taskbar and then click Help and Support on the Start menu. Type recycle bin in the Search text box and then click the Start searching button. To answer each of the following questions, click an appropriate result link in the Search Results box and then read the Help information. To display a different result, click another result link.

- How do you delete a file or folder?
- How do you restore a file?
- How can you change the storage capacity of the Recycle Bin?
- How do you empty the Recycle Bin?

Click the Close button to close the Help and Support Center window.

2 Working with Files

This exercise uses Windows XP/2000/98 procedures. To complete this exercise, you first must complete Lab Exercises 2 in Chapter 3 on page 3.46. Insert your floppy disk into drive A. Click the Start button on the taskbar. Click My Computer on the Start menu (double-click the My Computer icon on the desktop in Windows 2000/98). When the My Computer window is displayed, right-click the 3½ Floppy (A:) icon. Click Open on the shortcut menu. Click View on the menu bar and then click Icons (Large Icons in Windows 2000/98). Right-click the lab3-2 icon. Click Copy on the shortcut menu. Click Edit on the menu bar and then click Paste. How has the 3½ Floppy (A:) window changed? Right-click the new icon (Copy of lab3-2) and then click Rename on the shortcut menu. Type

lab7-2 and then press the ENTER key. Right-click the lab7-2 icon and then click Print on the shortcut menu. Close the 3½ Floppy (A:) window. Close the My Computer window.

3 Learning About the Hard Disk

This exercise uses Windows 2000/98 procedures. What are the characteristics of your hard disk? To find out, right-click the My Computer icon on the desktop. Click Open on the shortcut menu. Right-click the Hard disk (C:) icon in the My Computer window. Click Properties on the shortcut menu. If necessary, click the General tab and then answer the following questions:

- What Label is on the disk?
- What Type of disk is it?
- How much of the hard disk is Used space?
- How much of the hard disk is Free space?
- What is the total Capacity of the hard disk?

Close the Hard disk (C:) Properties dialog box and the My Computer window.

4 Disk Cleanup

This exercise uses Windows XP procedures. Just as people maintain they never can have too much money, computer users insist that you never can have too much hard disk space. Fortunately, Windows includes a utility program called Disk Cleanup that can increase available hard disk space. To find out more about Disk Cleanup, click the Start button on the taskbar and then click Help and Support on the Start menu. Type disk cleanup in the Search text box and then click the Start searching button. Click the Using Disk Cleanup link in the Search Results box. Read the information in the right pane of the Help and Support Center window and answer the following questions:

- How does Disk Cleanup help to free up space on the hard disk?
- How do you start Disk Cleanup using the Start button?

Click the Close button to close the Help and Support Center window.

WEB RESEARCH　CHAPTER 7

Use the Web Research exercises to learn more about the special features in this chapter.

WEB INSTRUCTIONS:

Use the link in each exercise or a search engine such as Google (google.com) to research the topic. Then, write a one-page, double-spaced report or create a presentation, unless otherwise directed below. Page numbers on which information can be found are in parentheses.

1   **Issue**   Choose one Issue from the following issues in this chapter: Do You Use a Shoppers Card? (7.10), Promotions on CD-ROM? (7.18), Is It Ethical to Copy CDs? (7.20), Should the World Become a Cashless Society? (7.28), or Can You Read It Tomorrow? (7.30). Use the Web to research the issue. Discuss the issue with classmates, instructors, and friends. Address the questions that accompany the issue in a report or presentation.

2   **Apply It**   Choose one of the following Apply It features in this chapter: Save Data Now for Safekeeping (7.12) or Turn Your Computer into a Home Theater System (7.22). Use the Web to gather additional information about the topic. Print two Web pages that relate to the Apply It. Detail in a report or presentation what you learned.

3   **Career Corner**   Read the Career Corner article in this chapter (7.30). Use the Web to find out more about the career. Describe the career in a report or presentation.

4   **Companies on the Cutting Edge**   Choose one of the Companies on the Cutting Edge in this chapter (7.32). Use the Web to research the company further. Explain in a report or presentation how this company has contributed to computer technology.

5   **Technology Trailblazers**   Choose one of the Technology Trailblazers in this chapter (7.33). Use the Web to research the person further. Explain in a report or presentation how this individual has affected the way people use, or think about, computers.

6   **Picture Yourself Using a Picture CD**   Read the Picture Yourself Using a Picture CD story at the beginning of this chapter (7.00). Use the Web to research Picture CDs further. Describe in a report or presentation the ways in which you might use a Picture CD.

7   **High-Tech Talk**   Read the High-Tech Talk feature in this chapter (7.31). Use the Web to find out more about the topic. Summarize in a report or presentation what you learned.

8   **Web Links**   Review the Web Link boxes found in the margins of this chapter. Visit five of the Web Link sites. Print the main Web page for each site you visit. Choose one of the Web pages and then summarize in one paragraph the content of the Web page.

9   **Looking Ahead**   Choose one of the Looking Ahead articles in this chapter: Holographic Storage Expands Capacity (7.23) or Millipede Reinvents Punch Card Storage Concept (7.27). Use the Web to find out more about the topic. Detail in a report or presentation what you learned.

10   **FAQ**   Choose one FAQ found in this chapter. Use the Web to find out more about the topic. Summarize in one paragraph what you learned.

11   **Making Use of the Web**   Read the Shopping section of Making Use of the Web in Appendix A (A.14). Complete the Shopping Web Exercises at the end of the section (A.15). Answer the questions posed in each exercise.

Operating Systems and Utility Programs

Picture Yourself with a Virus-Infected Computer

While reading your new e-mail messages, you see one that congratulates you on winning a weekend getaway. As soon as you open the attachment in the message, the computer freezes and then displays the word, Gotcha. You click the mouse button. Nothing happens. You press a key on the keyboard. The computer beeps. You click the mouse again. Still no response. You restart the computer. By now, you expect to see the Windows XP desktop, but it does not appear. Something is wrong.

You call a friend of yours, who works as a computer technician, for help. After explaining the situation to her, she says the computer probably has a virus that was hidden in the attachment that you opened. She asks you several questions, and you answer: Did you have antivirus software installed on the computer? No. Did you have firewall software installed on the computer? No. Do you have a backup of the computer's hard disk? No. After explaining the importance of antivirus software, firewall software, and backups, she tells you the first step in solving this problem is to start the computer again — this time with the recovery disk in the floppy disk drive. Now you know you are in trouble… what's a recovery disk?

As you read Chapter 8, you will learn about recovery disks and antivirus, firewall, and backup utilities, and discover features common to most operating systems and utility programs.

OBJECTIVES

After completing this chapter, you will be able to:

1. Identify the types of system software

2. Summarize the startup process on a personal computer

3. Describe the functions of an operating system

4. Discuss ways that some operating systems help administrators control a network and administer security

5. Explain the purpose of the utilities included with most operating systems

6. Summarize the features of several stand-alone operating systems

7. Identify various network operating systems

8. Identify devices that use several embedded operating systems

9. Explain the purpose of several stand-alone utility programs

CONTENTS

SYSTEM SOFTWARE

System software consists of the programs that control or maintain the operations of the computer and its devices. System software serves as the interface between the user, the application software, and the computer's hardware.

Two types of system software are operating systems and utility programs. Several types of utility programs are provided with an operating system. Other utility programs are available as programs separate from the operating system. This chapter discusses the operating system and its functions, as well as several types of utility programs for personal computers.

OPERATING SYSTEMS

An **operating system (OS)** is a set of programs containing instructions that coordinate all the activities among computer hardware resources. Most operating systems perform similar functions that include starting a computer, providing a user interface, managing programs, managing memory, scheduling jobs, configuring devices, establishing an Internet connection, monitoring performance, and providing file management and other utilities. Some operating systems also allow users to control a network and administer security (Figure 8-1).

FIGURE 8-1 Most operating systems perform the functions illustrated in this figure.

In most cases, the operating system is installed and resides on the computer's hard disk. On smaller handheld computers and PDAs, however, the operating system may reside on a ROM chip.

Different sizes of computers typically use different operating systems. For example, a mainframe computer does not use the same operating system as a personal computer. Even the same types of computers, such as desktop computers, may not use the same operating system. Furthermore, the application software for these various operating systems often is not compatible with each other. For example, PCs use Windows XP, and iMacs use Mac OS X. When purchasing application software, you must ensure that it works with the operating system installed on your computer.

The operating system that a computer uses sometimes is called the *platform*. On purchased application software, the package identifies the required platform (operating system). A *cross-platform* program is one that has multiple versions, and each version runs identically on multiple operating systems.

provide a user interface

manage programs

manage memory

schedule jobs and configure devices

establish an internet connection

OPERATING SYSTEM FUNCTIONS

Many different operating systems exist, designed for all types of computers. Regardless of the size of the computer, however, most operating systems provide similar functions. The following sections discuss functions common to most operating systems. The operating system handles many of these functions automatically, without requiring any input from a user.

Starting a Computer

Booting is the process of starting or restarting a computer. When turning on a computer that has been powered off completely, you are performing a **cold boot**. A **warm boot**, by contrast, is the process of restarting a computer that already is powered on. With Windows XP, for example, you can perform a warm boot by pressing a combination of keyboard keys (CTRL+ALT+DEL), selecting a button or an option from a list in a dialog box, or pressing the reset button on the computer (Figure 8-2).

When you install new software, often an on-screen prompt instructs you to restart the computer. In this case, a warm boot is appropriate. If your computer stops responding, try to restart it with a warm boot first. If it does not respond to the warm boot, then restart the computer with a cold boot; that is, push the power button.

Each time you boot a computer, the kernel and other frequently used operating system instructions are loaded, or copied, from the hard disk (storage) to the computer's memory (RAM). The *kernel* is the core of an operating system that manages memory and devices, maintains the computer's clock, starts applications, and assigns the computer's resources, such as devices, programs, data, and information. The kernel is *memory resident*, which means it remains in memory while the computer is running. Other parts of the operating system are *nonresident*, that is, these instructions remain on the hard disk until they are needed.

When you boot a computer, a series of messages may be displayed on the screen (Figure 8-3). The actual information displayed varies depending on the make and type of the computer and the equipment installed. The boot process, however, is similar for large and small computers.

Figure 8-2a (warm boot from Windows desktop)

puts computer in low-power consumption state

performs a warm boot

Figure 8-2b (warm boot from system unit)

power button

reset button

FIGURE 8-2 To perform a warm boot, click the Restart button in the dialog box or press the reset button on the system unit.

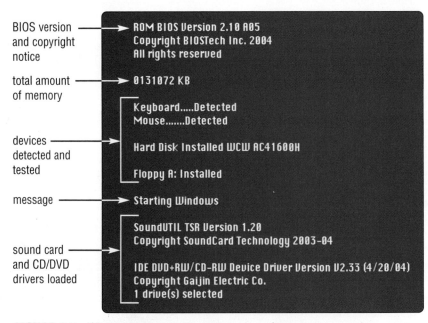

BIOS version and copyright notice

total amount of memory

devices detected and tested

message

sound card and CD/DVD drivers loaded

FIGURE 8-3 When you boot a computer, a set of messages may be displayed on the screen. The actual information displayed varies depending on the make of the computer and the devices installed.

The following steps explain what occurs during a cold boot on a personal computer using the Windows XP operating system. Figure 8-4 illustrates and briefly summarizes these steps.

1. When you turn on the computer, the power supply sends an electrical signal to the components in the system unit.

2. The charge of electricity causes the processor chip to reset itself and find the ROM chip(s) that contains the BIOS. The **BIOS** (pronounced BYE-ose), which stands for *basic input/output system*, is firmware that contains the computer's startup instructions.

FIGURE 8-4 HOW A PC BOOTS UP

Step 1:
The power supply sends a signal to the components in the system unit.

Step 2:
The processor finds the ROM chip(s) that contains the BIOS (basic input/output system).

Step 3:
The BIOS performs the POST (power-on self test), which checks components, such as the mouse, keyboard, and adapter cards.

Step 4:
The results of the POST are compared with data in a CMOS chip.

Step 5:
The BIOS looks for the system files in drive A (floppy disk drive), sometimes a CD or DVD drive, and then drive C (hard disk).

Step 6:
The system files and the kernel of the operating system load into memory (RAM) from storage (hard disk).

Step 7:
The operating system loads configuration information, may request user information, and displays the desktop on the screen.

system unit

floppy disk drive

CD/DVD drive

CMOS

hard disk

Pentium® 4 processor

(RAM) memory modules

ROM BIOS ROM BIOS ROM BIOS

SCSI CARD

VIDEO CARD

3. The BIOS executes a series of tests to make sure the computer hardware is connected properly and operating correctly. The tests, collectively called the *power-on self test* (*POST*), check the various system components including the buses, system clock, adapter cards, RAM chips, mouse, keyboard, and drives. As the POST executes, LEDs (tiny lights) flicker on devices such as the disk drives and keyboard. Several beeps also sound, and messages are displayed on the screen.

4. The POST results are compared with data in a CMOS chip. As discussed in Chapter 4, CMOS is a technology that uses battery power to retain information when the computer is off. The CMOS chip stores configuration information about the computer, such as the amount of memory; type of disk drives, keyboard, and monitor; the current date and time; and other startup information. It also detects any new devices connected to the computer. If any problems are identified, the computer may beep, display error messages, or cease operating — depending on the severity of the problem.

5. If the POST completes successfully, the BIOS searches for specific operating system files called *system files*. Usually, the operating system looks first to see if a disk is in drive A (the designation for a floppy disk drive). If drive A contains a disk, the BIOS checks the disk for system files. If drive A does not contain a disk or if the system files are not on a disk in drive A, the BIOS looks in drive C (the designation usually given to the first hard disk). Some computers also look in a CD or DVD drive for system files.

6. Once located, the system files load into memory (RAM) from storage (usually the hard disk) and execute. Next, the kernel of the operating system loads into memory. Then, the operating system in memory takes control of the computer.

7. The operating system loads system configuration information. In Windows XP, the *registry* consists of several files that contain the system configuration information. Windows XP constantly accesses the registry during the computer's operation for information such as installed hardware and software devices and individual user preferences for mouse speed, passwords, and other user-specific information.

Necessary operating system files are loaded into memory. On some computers, the operating system verifies that the person attempting to use the computer is a legitimate user. Finally, the Windows XP desktop and icons are displayed on the screen. The operating system executes programs in the *Startup folder*, which contains a list of programs that open automatically when you boot the computer. Read Apply It 8-1 for more information.

☑ APPLY IT 8-1

Customizing the Startup Folder

Some people start their day by drinking a cup of coffee. Your computer, likewise, starts to run by loading the operating system kernel into memory from the hard disk. The kernel contains instructions that control components, memory, peripheral devices, and the system clock. It also automatically loads the programs found in the Startup folder, which is located on the All Programs submenu on the Start menu.

One program frequently found in the Startup folder is antivirus software, such as Norton AntiVirus or McAfee VirusScan. Most computer users desire this software to run at all times to protect against documents and e-mail messages infected with viruses. Most computers also have an e-mail program or Web browser added to the Startup folder because this software is used so frequently.

Some programs are installed automatically in the Startup folder, so it is a good idea to check the folder periodically if you have added or removed software. The programs listed in the Startup folder are shortcuts, meaning they are not actually stored in this folder. You can, consequently, delete or add a program in the Startup folder without modifying or damaging the existing program.

For more information about starting Windows XP, visit the Discovering Computers 2004 Apply It Web page (**scsite.com/dc2004/apply**). Click Apply It #1 below Chapter 8.

⊛ WEB LINK 8-1

BIOS

Visit the Discovering Computers 2004 WEB LINK page (**scsite .com/dc2004/weblink**). Click BIOS below Chapter 8.

RECOVERY DISK A **boot drive** is the drive from which your personal computer boots (starts). In most cases, drive C (the hard disk) is the boot drive. Sometimes a hard disk becomes damaged and the computer cannot boot from the hard disk. In this case, you can boot from a special disk. A **recovery disk**, also called a **boot disk**, is a floppy disk, Zip disk, CD, or DVD that contains a few system files that will start the computer. For this reason, it is crucial you have a recovery disk available and ready for use — in case of computer failure.

When a user installs an operating system, one of the installation steps often involves creating a recovery disk. Most users, however, do not install an operating system because the manufacturer preinstalls it on their computer. Thus, you may not have a recovery disk. In this case, you should create one and keep it in a safe place. The steps in Figure 8-5 show how to create a recovery disk in Windows XP.

FAQ 8-1

When I am finished using the computer, can I simply turn it off?

No! You must use the operating system's shut-down procedure so various processes are closed in sequence and items in memory released properly. Depending on the computer, several shut-down options exist. The Turn Off command removes power from the computer. Restart does a warm boot. *Hibernate* saves all documents in memory and then turns off the computer. *Stand By* places the entire computer in a low-power state but does not turn it off. With Hibernate and Stand By, the next time you resume work on the computer, the desktop is restored to exactly how you left it.

For more information about shut-down options, visit the Discovering Computers 2004 FAQ Web page (**scsite.com/dc2004/faq**). Click Shut-Down Options below Chapter 8.

FIGURE 8-5   HOW TO CREATE A RECOVERY DISK IN WINDOWS XP

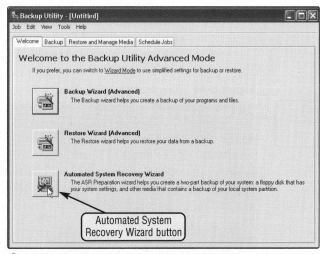

Automated System Recovery Wizard button

Step 1:
Click the Start button on the taskbar, point to All Programs on the Start menu, point to Accessories on the All Programs submenu, point to System Tools on the Accessories submenu, and then point to Backup.

Step 2:
Click Backup on the System Tools submenu to open the Backup Utility window. (If the Backup or Restore Wizard displays, click the Advanced Mode link.) Point to the Automated System Recovery Wizard button.

Step 3:
Click the Automated System Recovery Wizard button to create the recovery disk. Follow the on-screen instructions and insert a disk into the disk drive when prompted.

Providing a User Interface

You interact with software through its user interface (Figure 8-6). That is, a **user interface** controls how you enter data and instructions and how information is displayed on the screen. Three types of user interfaces are command-line, menu-driven, and graphical. Operating systems often use a combination of these interfaces to define how a user interacts with a computer.

COMMAND-LINE INTERFACE To configure devices, manage system resources, and troubleshoot network connections, network administrators and other advanced users work with a command-line interface. In a *command-line interface*, a user types commands or presses special keys on the keyboard (such as function keys or key combinations) to enter data and instructions. When working with a command-line interface, the set of commands entered into the computer is called the *command language*. Command-line interfaces often are

difficult to use because they require exact spelling, grammar, and punctuation. Minor errors, such as a missing period, generate an error message. Command-line interfaces, however, give a user more control over setting details. For a technical discussion about a command-line interface, read the High-Tech Talk article on page 8.31 at the end of this chapter.

MENU-DRIVEN INTERFACE A *menu-driven interface* provides menus as a means of entering commands. Menu-driven interfaces are easier to learn than command-line interfaces because users do not have to learn the rules of entering commands.

GRAPHICAL USER INTERFACE Most users today work with a graphical user interface. With a *graphical user interface* (GUI), you interact with menus and visual images such as icons, buttons, and other graphical objects to issue commands. Many current GUI operating systems incorporate features similar to those of a Web browser. The Help and Support Center window in Windows XP shown in Figure 8-7, for example, contains links and navigation buttons such as the Back button and the Forward button.

Figure 8-6a (command-line interface)

Figure 8-6b (graphical user interface)

FIGURE 8-6 Examples of command-line and graphical user interfaces.

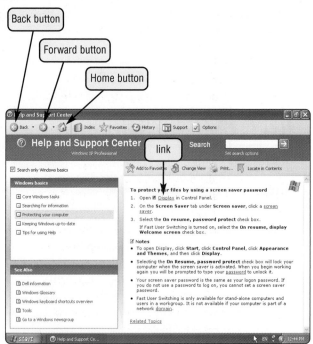

FIGURE 8-7 This GUI operating system window incorporates links and navigation buttons.

Managing Programs

Some operating systems support a single user and only one running program at a time. Others support thousands of users running multiple programs. How an operating system handles programs directly affects your productivity.

A *single user/single tasking* operating system allows only one user to run one program at a time. Suppose, for example, you are creating a poster in a graphics program and then decide to check your e-mail messages. With a single tasking operating system, you must quit the graphics program before you can run the e-mail program. You then must close the e-mail program and restart the graphics program to finish the poster. Early systems were single user/single tasking. Most of today's operating systems are multitasking. PDAs and other small computing devices, however, often use a single user/single tasking operating system.

A *single user/multitasking* operating system allows a single user to work on two or more programs that reside in memory at the same time. Using the example just cited, if you are working with a single user/multitasking operating system, you do not have to quit the graphics program to run the e-mail program. Both programs can run concurrently. Users today typically run multiple programs concurrently. It is common to have an e-mail program and Web browser open at all times, while working in applications such as word processing or graphics.

When a computer is running multiple programs concurrently, one program is in the foreground and the others are in the background. The one in the *foreground* is the active program; that is, the one you currently are using. The other applications running but not in use are in the *background*. In Figure 8-8a, the National Geographic Web page is in the foreground, and three other programs are running in the background (Microsoft Outlook, Microsoft Word, and Jasc Paint Shop Pro). Background programs can continue to execute when another program is in the foreground. For example, Outlook can be receiving e-mail messages while you are browsing the Web.

Notice in Figure 8-8a that you can see the foreground program, but not the background programs. You easily can switch between foreground and background programs. To make a program active (in the foreground) in

Windows XP, click its program button on the taskbar. This causes the operating system to place all other programs in the background.

In addition to application programs, an operating system manages other processes. These processes include utilities or routines that provide support to other programs or hardware. Some are memory resident. Others run as they are required. Figure 8-8b shows a list of all processes running on a Windows XP computer. The list contains the programs running, as well as other processes.

Figure 8-8a (multiple programs running)

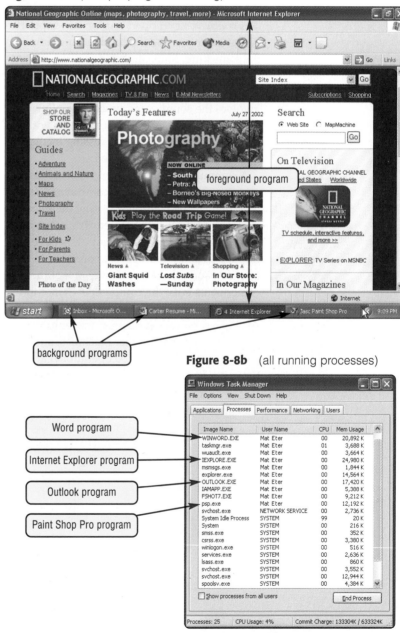

Figure 8-8b (all running processes)

FIGURE 8-8 Windows XP manages multiple programs and processes while you use the computer.

Some operating systems use preemptive multitasking to prevent any one process from monopolizing the computer's resources. With *preemptive multitasking*, the operating system interrupts a program that is executing and passes control to another program waiting to be executed. An advantage of preemptive multitasking is the operating system regains control if one program stops operating properly.

A *multiuser* operating system enables two or more users to run programs simultaneously. Networks, midrange servers, mainframes, and supercomputers allow hundreds to thousands of users to connect at the same time, and thus are multiuser.

A *multiprocessing* operating system supports two or more processors running programs at the same time. Multiprocessing works in a manner similar to parallel processing, which was discussed in Chapter 4. Multiprocessing involves the coordinated processing of programs by more than one processor. As with parallel processing, multiprocessing increases a computer's processing speed.

A computer with separate processors also can serve as a fault-tolerant computer. A *fault-tolerant computer* continues to operate when one of its components fails, ensuring that no data is lost. Fault-tolerant computers have duplicate components such as processors, memory, and disk drives. If any one of these components fails, the computer switches to the duplicate component and continues to operate. Airline reservation systems, communications networks, automated teller machines, and other systems that must be operational at all times use fault-tolerant computers.

Managing Memory

The purpose of **memory management** is to optimize the use of random access memory (RAM). As discussed in Chapter 4, RAM consists of one or more chips on the motherboard that hold items such as data and instructions while the processor interprets and executes them. The operating system allocates, or assigns, data and instructions to an area of memory while they are being processed. Then, it carefully monitors the contents of memory. Finally, the operating system releases these items from being monitored in memory when the processor no longer requires them.

If you are working on multiple programs simultaneously, it is possible to run out of RAM. For example, assume an operating system requires 128 MB of RAM, a Web browser — 32 MB of RAM, a business software suite — 40 MB of RAM, and a photo editing program — 32 MB of RAM. With all these programs running simultaneously, the total RAM required would be 232 MB of RAM (128 + 32 + 40 + 32). If the computer has only 128 MB of RAM, the operating system may have to use virtual memory to solve the problem.

With **virtual memory**, the operating system allocates a portion of a storage medium, usually the hard disk, to function as additional RAM (Figure 8-9). As you interact with a program, part of it may be in physical RAM, while the rest of the program is on the hard disk as virtual memory. Because virtual memory is slower than RAM, users may notice the computer slowing down while it uses virtual memory.

Step 1:
The operating system transfers the least recently used data and program instructions to disk because memory is needed for other functions.

Step 2:
The operating system transfers data and program instructions from disk to memory when they are needed.

page swapped out →

disk (virtual memory)

swap file

RAM (physical memory)

← page swapped in

FIGURE 8-9 With virtual memory (VM), the operating system allocates a portion of a storage medium, usually the hard disk, to function as additional RAM.

The area of the hard disk used for virtual memory is called a *swap file* because it swaps (exchanges) data, information, and instructions between memory and storage. A *page* is the amount of data and program instructions that can swap at a given time. The technique of swapping items between memory and storage, called *paging*, is a time consuming process for the computer.

When an operating system spends much of its time paging, instead of executing application software, it is said to be *thrashing*. If application software, such as a Web browser, has stopped responding and the hard disk's LED blinks repeatedly, the operating system probably is thrashing.

⁇ FAQ 8-2

How can I stop a computer from thrashing?

Try to quit the program that stopped responding. If the computer does not respond and continues to thrash, do a warm boot. When the computer reboots, check whether the available hard disk space is less than 200 MB. If it is, remove unnecessary files from the hard disk and if necessary uninstall seldom used programs. Defragment the hard disk (discussed later in this chapter). If thrashing continues to occur, you may need to install more RAM in the computer.

For more information about optimizing memory, visit the Discovering Computers 2004 FAQ Web page (**scsite.com/dc2004/faq**). Click Optimizing Memory below Chapter 8.

Scheduling Jobs

The operating system determines the order in which jobs are processed. A **job** is an operation the processor manages. Jobs include receiving data from an input device, processing instructions, sending information to an output device, and transferring items from storage to memory and from memory to storage.

A mulituser operating system does not always process jobs on a first-come, first-served basis. Sometimes, one user may have a higher priority than other users. In this case, the operating system adjusts the schedule of jobs.

Sometimes, a device already may be busy processing one job when it receives a second job. This occurs because the processor operates at a much faster rate of speed than peripheral devices. For example, if the processor sends five print jobs to a printer, the printer can print only one document at a time.

While waiting for devices to become idle, the operating system places items in buffers. A **buffer** is a segment of memory or storage in which items are placed while waiting to be transferred from an input device or to an output device.

The operating system commonly uses buffers with print jobs. This process, called **spooling**, sends print jobs to a buffer instead of sending them immediately to the printer. The buffer holds the information waiting to print while the printer prints from the buffer at its own rate of speed. By spooling print jobs to a buffer, the processor can continue interpreting and executing instructions while the printer prints. This allows users to work on the computer for other tasks while a printer is printing. Multiple print jobs line up in a **queue** (pronounced Q) within the buffer. A program, called a *print spooler*, intercepts print jobs from the operating system and places them in the queue (Figure 8-10).

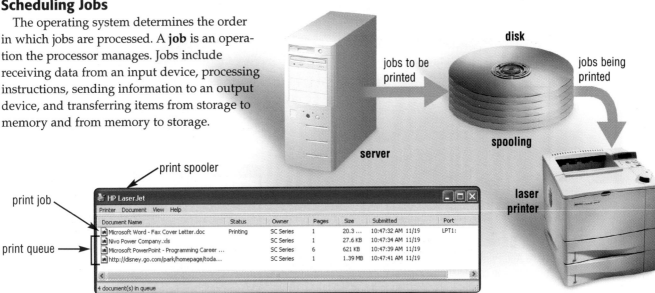

FIGURE 8-10 Spooling increases both processor and printer efficiency by placing print jobs in a buffer on disk before they are printed. This figure illustrates three jobs in the queue and one job printing.

Configuring Devices

A **driver**, short for *device driver*, is a small program that tells the operating system how to communicate with a specific device. Each device on a computer, such as the mouse, keyboard, monitor, printer, card reader, and scanner, has its own specialized set of commands and thus requires its own specific driver. When you boot a computer, the operating system loads each device's driver. These devices will not function without their correct drivers.

If you attach a new device to a computer, such as a printer or scanner, its driver must be installed before you can use the device. Windows XP provides a wizard to guide users through the installation steps. Figure 8-11 shows how to install a driver for a printer. You follow the same general steps to install drivers for any type of hardware. For many devices, the computer's operating system already may include the necessary drivers. If it does not, you can install the drivers from the CD or disk provided with the purchased device.

FIGURE 8-11 HOW TO INSTALL DRIVERS FOR NEW HARDWARE IN WINDOWS XP

Step 1:
Open the Control Panel window. Point to the Printers and Other Hardware link.

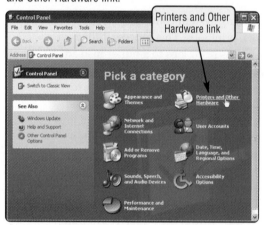

Step 2:
Click the Printers and Other Hardware link. Point to the Add a printer link.

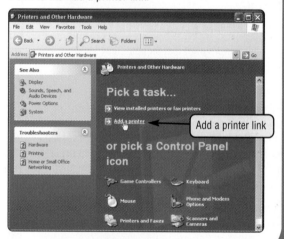

Step 4:
The Add Printer Wizard searches for Plug and Play printers on your computer. If it finds any such printers, it installs them.

Step 3:
Click the Add a printer link. Follow the on-screen instructions.

Step 5:
If the Add Printer Wizard cannot find any Plug and Play printers, you can select the type of printer you want to install. An on-screen prompt may ask you to insert the floppy disk, CD-ROM, or DVD-ROM that contains the necessary driver files to complete the installation of the printer.

In the past, installing a new hardware device often required setting switches and other elements on the motherboard. Today, installation is easier because most devices and operating systems support Plug and Play. As discussed in Chapter 4, **Plug and Play** means the operating system automatically configures new devices as you install them. Specifically, it assists you in the device's installation by loading the necessary drivers automatically and checking for conflicts with other devices. With Plug and Play, a user plugs in a device, turns on the computer, and then uses (plays) the device without having to configure the system manually.

When installing devices in the past, users sometimes needed to tell the operating system which interrupt request line the device should use for communications. An *interrupt request line* (*IRQ*) is a communications line between a device and the processor. Most computers have 16 IRQs.

With Plug and Play, the operating system determines an appropriate IRQ to use for these communications. If the operating system uses an IRQ that already is assigned to another device, an IRQ conflict may occur and the computer may not work properly. If an IRQ conflict occurs, you will have to obtain the correct IRQ for the device. This information typically is located in the installation directions that accompany the device.

Establishing an Internet Connection

Operating systems typically provide a means to establish Internet connections. For example, Windows XP includes a New Connection Wizard that guides users through the process of setting up a connection between a computer and an Internet service provider (Figure 8-12).

Some operating systems also include a Web browser and an e-mail program, enabling you to begin using the Web and communicate with others as soon as you set up the Internet connections. This feature eliminates the expense of purchasing extra software and saves the time of installing additional programs to use Internet services. Read Issue 8-1 for a related discussion.

FIGURE 8-12 To display the New Connection Wizard in WindowsXP, click the Start button, point to All Programs, point to Accessories, point to Communications, and then click New Connection Wizard on the Communications submenu.

WEB LINK 8-2

Plug and Play

Visit the Discovering Computers 2004 WEB LINK page (**scsite .com/dc2004/weblink**). Click Plug and Play below Chapter 8.

? FAQ 8-3

What if I do not have the driver for a device?

When reinstalling an operating system, you may have to supply a device's driver. If you do not have the original driver disk, visit the manufacturer's Web site. Most post drivers for download at no cost, or they may suggest a similar driver that will work. If you do not have Internet access, call the manufacturer and request a new disk via the postal service.

For more information about drivers, visit the Discovering Computers 2004 FAQ Web page (**scsite.com/dc2004/faq**). Click Drivers below Chapter 8.

ISSUE 8-1

Should Manufacturers Bundle Applications?

Microsoft includes a Web browser, a paint program, a word processing program, plug-ins, and other applications and features with its Windows operating system. Apple bundles QuickTime, CD burning software, and other programs and features into Mac OS X. Manufacturers say that combining additional features and programs with their operating systems is a convenience for consumers and sometimes integral to the operating systems' performance. Yet, because other developers create programs and features similar to those included with operating systems, some consumer advocates argue that bundling applications is unfair and leads to monopolies. (Microsoft's bundling of its Web browser with its Windows operating system was the proximate cause of an antitrust action against the software giant.) Critics also insist that bundling applications with an operating system forces consumers to pay for programs they may never use. Is bundling applications with an operating system fair, or is it a monopolistic practice? Why? Who should decide what an operating system should include? The manufacturer? The government? The marketplace? Why?

For more information about bundling applications, visit the Discovering Computers 2004 Issues Web page (**scsite.com/dc2004/issues**). Click Issue #1 below Chapter 8.

Monitoring Performance

Operating systems typically contain a performance monitor. A **performance monitor** is a program that assesses and reports information about various computer resources and devices (Figure 8-13). For example, users can monitor the processor, disks, memory, and network usage. A performance monitor also can check the number of reads and writes to a disk.

The information in performance reports helps users identify a problem with resources so they can try to resolve any problems. If your computer is running extremely slow, for example, the performance monitor may determine that the computer's memory is being used to its maximum. Thus, you might consider installing additional memory in the computer.

FIGURE 8-13 A performance monitor is a program that assesses and reports information about various system resources and devices. The System Monitor above is tracking the kernel usage and the amount of unused physical memory.

Providing File Management and Other Utilities

Operating systems often provide users with the capability of managing files, viewing graphics files, uninstalling programs, scanning disks, defragmenting disks, diagnosing problems, backing up files and disks, and setting up screen savers. A later section in the chapter discusses these utilities in depth.

Controlling a Network

Some operating systems are network operating systems. A **network operating system**, or *network OS*, is an operating system that organizes and coordinates how multiple users access and share resources on a network. Resources include hardware, software, data, and information. For example, a network OS allows multiple users to share a printer, Internet access, files, and programs.

Some operating systems have network features built into them. In other cases, the network OS is a set of programs separate from the operating system on the client computers that access the network. When not connected to the network, the client computers use their own operating system. When connected to the network, the network OS may assume some of the operating system functions.

The *network administrator*, the person overseeing network operations, uses the network OS to add and remove users, computers, and other devices to and from the network. The network administrator also uses the network operating system to install software and administer network security.

Administering Security

The network administrator uses the network OS to establish permissions to resources. These permissions define who can access certain resources and when they can access those resources.

For each user, the network administrator establishes a user account, which enables a user to access, or **log on** to, a computer or a network. Each user account typically consists of a user name and password (Figure 8-14). A **user name**, or **user ID**, is a unique combination of characters, such as letters of the alphabet or numbers, that identifies one specific user. Many users select a combination of their first and last names as their user name. A user named Katy Bollini might choose K Bollini as her user name.

FIGURE 8-14 Most multiuser operating systems allow each user to log on, which is the process of entering a user name and password into the computer.

A **password** is a private combination of characters associated with the user name that allows access to certain computer resources. Some operating systems allow the network administrator to assign passwords to files and commands, restricting access to only authorized users. Read Issue 8-2 for a related discussion.

ISSUE 8-2

Would You Share Your Password?

If your school uses a network, you probably must enter a user name and password to access the system. User names and passwords, however, do not guarantee network security. A recent survey by the Computer Security Institute reported that 70 percent of the organizations polled said that their network defenses had been breached. Sometimes, people outside the organization invade a network by guessing the necessary password. But in a school environment, unauthorized access often results from students sharing their passwords with nonstudents. Although students who share passwords usually believe that it is no worse than sharing a locker combination, sharing passwords with unauthorized users can drain network resources and even provide access to private information. Should sharing a password be considered a crime? Why or why not? What can be done to eliminate password sharing? One security expert suggests that password sharing could be reduced by mandating that passwords be changed every 30 to 60 days. Is this a good idea? Why?

For more information about sharing passwords, visit the Discovering Computers 2004 Issues Web page (**scsite.com/dc2004/issues**). Click Issue #2 below Chapter 8.

To prevent unauthorized users from accessing computer resources, keep your password confidential. While entering your password, most computers hide the actual password characters by displaying some other characters, such as asterisks (*) or dots. After entering a user name and password, the operating system compares the user's entry with a list of authorized user names and passwords. If the entry matches the user name and password kept on file, the operating system grants the user access. If the entry does not match, the operating system denies access to the user.

The operating system records successful and unsuccessful logon attempts in a file. This allows the network administrator to review who is using or attempting to use the computer. Network administrators also use these files to monitor computer usage.

To protect sensitive data and information further as it travels over the network, a network operating system often encrypts it. *Encryption* is the process of encoding data and information into an unreadable form. Network administrators usually set up a network to encrypt data as it travels over the network to prevent unauthorized users from reading the data. When an authorized user attempts to read the data, it automatically is decrypted, or converted back into a readable form.

QUIZ YOURSELF 8-1

To check your knowledge of types of system software and features common to most operating systems, visit the Discovering Computers 2004 Quiz Yourself Web page (**scsite.com/dc2004/quiz**). Click Objectives 1 – 4 below Chapter 8.

OPERATING SYSTEM UTILITY PROGRAMS

A **utility program**, also called a **utility**, is a type of system software that allows a user to perform maintenance-type tasks, usually related to managing a computer, its devices, or its programs. Most operating systems include several utility programs (Figure 8-15).

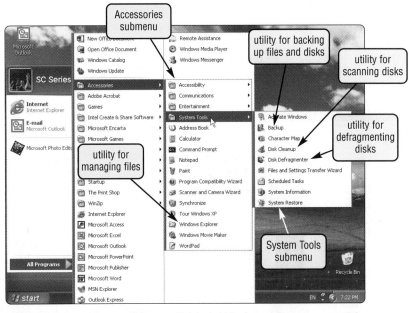

FIGURE 8-15 Many utilities available in Windows XP are accessible through the Accessories and System Tools submenus.

Users often buy stand-alone utilities, however, because they offer improvements over those included with the operating system.

Utility programs included with most operating systems provide the following functions: managing files, viewing graphics files, uninstalling programs, scanning disks, defragmenting disks, diagnosing problems, backing up files and disks, and setting up screen savers. The following paragraphs briefly discuss each of these utilities.

File Manager

A **file manager** is a utility that performs functions related to file management. Windows XP includes a file manager called *Windows Explorer*. Some of the file management functions that a file manager performs are formatting and copying disks; displaying a list of files on a storage medium (Figure 8-16); checking the amount of used or free space on a storage medium; organizing, copying, renaming, deleting, moving, and sorting files; and creating shortcuts. A *shortcut* is an icon on the desktop that provides a user with immediate access to a program or file.

Formatting is the process of preparing a disk for reading and writing. Most floppy and hard disk manufacturers preformat their disks. If you must format a floppy disk, do so by issuing the operating system's format command.

Various operating systems format disks differently. Thus, you may not be able to use a disk formatted in one operating system in a computer that has a different operating system.

For example, you cannot use a Mac OS X floppy disk in a computer that uses Windows XP — without special hardware and software. For a technical discussion about formatting, read the High-Tech Talk article on page 7.31 in Chapter 7.

FAQ 8-4

Can I use the file manager to delete a program?

No! If you remove software from a computer by deleting the files and folders associated with the program without running the uninstaller, the system file entries are not updated. This may cause the operating system to display error messages when you start the computer. If the program has an uninstaller, always use it to remove software.

For more information about uninstalling programs, visit the Discovering Computers 2004 FAQ Web page (**scsite.com/dc2004/faq**). Click Uninstalling Programs below Chapter 8.

Image Viewer

An **image viewer** is a utility that allows users to display and copy the contents of a graphics file. With an image viewer, users can see images without having to open them in a paint or image editing program. Windows XP includes an image viewer called *Windows Picture and Fax Viewer* (Figure 8-17). To display a file in this image viewer, simply double-click the thumbnail of the image in the file manager, in this case, Windows Explorer shown in Figure 8-16.

FIGURE 8-16 Windows Explorer, which is the file manager included with Windows XP, allows users to perform functions related to file management.

FIGURE 8-17 Windows Picture and Fax Viewer allows users to see the contents of a graphics file.

Uninstaller

An **uninstaller** is a utility that removes a program, as well as any associated entries in the system files. In Windows XP, the uninstaller is available through the Add/Remove Programs command in the Control Panel.

When you install an application, the operating system records the information it uses to run the software in the system files. The uninstaller deletes files and folders from the hard disk, as well as removes program entries from the system files.

Disk Scanner

A **disk scanner** is a utility that (1) detects and corrects both physical and logical problems on a hard disk or floppy disk and (2) searches for and removes unnecessary files. A physical disk problem is a problem with the media such as a scratch on the surface of the disk. A logical disk problem is a problem with the data, such as a corrupt file. Windows XP includes two disk scanner utilities. One detects problems and the other searches for and removes unnecessary files such as temporary files (Figure 8-18).

FIGURE 8-18   Disk Cleanup searches for and removes unnecessary files.

Disk Defragmenter

A **disk defragmenter** is a utility that reorganizes the files and unused space on a computer's hard disk so the operating system accesses data more quickly and programs run faster. When an operating system stores data on a disk, it places the data in the first available sector on the disk. It attempts to place data in sectors that are contiguous (next to each other), but this is not always possible. When the contents of a file are scattered across two or more noncontiguous sectors, the file is *fragmented*.

Fragmentation slows down disk access and thus the performance of the entire computer. **Defragmenting** the disk, or reorganizing it, so the files are stored in contiguous sectors, solves this problem (Figure 8-19). Windows XP includes a disk defragmenter, called Disk Defragmenter, available on the System Tools submenu. Read Apply It 8-2 for more information.

disk after defragmentation process

FIGURE 8-19   A fragmented disk has many files stored in noncontiguous sectors. Defragmenting reorganizes the files, so they are located in contiguous sectors, which speeds access time.

✓ APPLY IT 8-2

Tune Up Your Computer for Optimum Performance

Your toolbox likely contains a hammer, pliers, screwdrivers, a measuring tape, and other gadgets. Having the right tool can help you save money and time while making home improvements and repairs. Your computer also has a toolbox containing a hard disk defragmenter, scanner, compressor, uninstaller, and other programs. These system tools can help your computer run quickly and smoothly.

While you might keep your toolbox in your garage or the trunk of your car, Windows XP keeps its tools in the Accessories folder on the All Programs submenu on the Start menu. One of these tools is Disk Defragmenter, which rearranges files and unused space on your hard disk. You should run Disk Defragmenter monthly and more frequently if you add and delete files from the hard disk regularly.

You already may be familiar with the ScanDisk tool if you have turned off your computer without shutting down Windows properly. The next time you start your computer ScanDisk may check the hard disk for errors and then repair damaged areas or delete unnecessary files.

The Maintenance Wizard performs specific tasks on a regular basis, including checks to see if programs are running at optimum speed, whether the hard disk has errors, and if extra hard disk space is available.

For more information about system tools, visit the Discovering Computers 2004 Apply It Web page (**scsite.com/dc2004/apply**). Click Apply It #2 below Chapter 8.

Diagnostic Utility

A **diagnostic utility** compiles technical information about your computer's hardware and certain system software programs and then prepares a report outlining any identified problems. For example, Windows XP includes the diagnostic utility, *Dr. Watson*, which diagnoses problems as well as suggests courses of action (Figure 8-20). Information in the report assists technical support staff in remedying any problems.

problems detected with these programs

FIGURE 8-20 Dr. Watson is a diagnostic utility included with Windows.

Backup Utility

A **backup utility** allows users to copy, or *back up*, selected files or an entire hard disk onto another disk or tape. During the backup process, the backup utility monitors progress and alerts you if it needs additional disks or tapes. Many backup programs *compress*, or shrink the size of, files during the backup process. By compressing the files, the backup program requires less storage space for the backup files than for the original files.

Because they are compressed, you usually cannot use backup files in their backed up form. In the event you need to use a backup

file, a **restore program** reverses the process and returns backed up files to their original form. Backup utilities include restore programs.

You should back up files and disks regularly in the event your originals are lost, damaged, or destroyed. Windows XP includes a backup utility (Figure 8-21). Instead of backing up to a local disk storage device, some users opt to back up their files to an Internet hard drive. As described in Chapter 7, an Internet hard drive is a service on the Web that provides online storage for a fee to computer users.

FIGURE 8-21 A backup utility allows users to copy files or an entire hard disk to another disk or tape.

Screen Saver

A **screen saver** is a utility that causes a monitor's screen to display a moving image or blank screen if no keyboard or mouse activity occurs for a specified time (Figure 8-22). When you press a key on the keyboard or move the mouse, the screen saver disappears and the screen returns to the previous state.

FIGURE 8-22 A Windows XP screen saver.

WEB LINK 8-3

Screen Savers

Visit the Discovering Computers 2004 WEB LINK page (**scsite .com/dc2004/weblink**). Click Screen Savers below Chapter 8.

Screen savers originally were developed to prevent a problem called *ghosting*, in which images could be permanently etched on a monitor's screen. Ghosting is not a problem with today's monitors. Still, screen savers are popular for security, business, and entertainment purposes. To secure a computer, users configure their screen saver to require a password to deactivate. In addition to those included with the operating system, many screen savers are available for a minimal fee in stores and on the Web.

TYPES OF OPERATING SYSTEMS

Many of the first operating systems were device dependent and proprietary. A *device-dependent* program is one that runs only on a specific type or make of computer. *Proprietary software* is privately owned and limited to a specific vendor or computer model. Historically, when manufacturers introduced a new computer or model, they often produced an improved and different proprietary operating system. Problems arose when a user wanted to switch computer models or manufacturers. The user's application software often would not work on the new computer because the programs were designed to work with a specific operating system.

Some operating systems still are device dependent. The trend today, however, is toward *device-independent* operating systems that run on computers provided by a variety of manufacturers. The advantage of device-independent operating systems is you can retain existing application software and data files even if you change computer models or vendors. This feature usually represents a sizable savings in time and money.

When you purchase a new computer, it typically has an operating system preinstalled (read Issue 8-3 for a related discussion). As new versions of the operating system are released, users upgrade their existing computers to incorporate features of the new version. An upgrade usually costs less than purchasing the entire operating system.

New versions of an operating system usually are downward compatible. That is, they recognize and work with application software written for an earlier version of the operating system (or platform). The application software, by contrast, is said to be upward compatible, meaning it will run on new versions of the operating system.

The three basic categories of operating systems that exist today are stand-alone, network, and embedded. The table in Figure 8-23 lists names of operating systems in each category. The following pages discuss the operating systems listed in the table.

CATEGORIES OF OPERATING SYSTEMS

Category	Operating System Name
Stand-alone	• DOS • Early Windows versions (Windows 3.x, Windows 95, Windows NT Workstation, Windows 98, Windows 2000 Professional, Windows Millennium Edition) • Windows XP • Mac OS X • OS/2 Warp Client • UNIX • Linux
Network	• NetWare • Early Windows Server versions (Windows NT Server, Windows 2000 Server) • Windows Server 2003 • OS/2 Warp Server for e-business • UNIX • Linux • Solaris
Embedded	• Windows CE .NET • Pocket PC 2002 • Palm OS • Symbian OS

FIGURE 8-23 Examples of stand-alone, network, and embedded operating systems. Some stand-alone operating systems include the capability of configuring small home or office networks.

ISSUE 8-3

Would You Like an Operating System with That?

When Windows 98 was introduced, one retailer offered customers the chance to buy a limited number of new computers, with Windows 98 installed, for $98. The promotion worked. A buyer waited in line 11 hours for a chance to buy a discounted computer with the new operating system. When asked if he would have come out simply for Windows 98, he replied, "Not a chance." Most computers you buy come with an operating system and applications installed on the hard disk. Some buyers consider this a convenience, but others feel it forces them to accept an operating system, and other programs, they may not want. These buyers argue that merchants should sell hardware without installed software so consumers can, for example, install Linux instead of Windows if that is what they want. Should computers be sold without installed operating systems and application programs? Why or why not? Should pricing for hardware be separate from pricing for software? Why? Should computers without installed software cost more, or less, than computers with installed software? Why?

For more information about preinstalled operating systems, visit the Discovering Computers 2004 Issues Web page (**scsite.com/dc2004/issues**). Click Issue #3 below Chapter 8.

STAND-ALONE OPERATING SYSTEMS

A **stand-alone operating system** is a complete operating system that works on a desktop computer, notebook computer, or mobile computing device. Some stand-alone operating systems are called *client operating systems* because they also work in conjunction with a network operating system. Client operating systems can operate with or without a network. Other stand-alone operating systems include networking capabilities, allowing the home and small business user to set up a small network.

Examples of stand-alone operating systems are DOS, Windows XP, Mac OS X, OS/2 Warp Client, UNIX, and Linux. The following paragraphs briefly discuss these operating systems.

DOS

The term **DOS** (*Disk Operating System*) refers to several single user operating systems developed in the early 1980s for personal computers. The two more widely used versions of DOS were PC-DOS and MS-DOS. Microsoft Corporation developed both PC-DOS and MS-DOS. The functionality of these two operating systems was essentially the same. The basic difference between PC-DOS and MS-DOS was the type of computer on which each was installed. Microsoft developed PC-DOS (Personal Computer DOS) for IBM, which in turn installed and sold PC-DOS on its computers. At the same time, Microsoft marketed and sold MS-DOS (Microsoft DOS) to makers of IBM-compatible PCs.

DOS used a command-line interface when Microsoft first developed it. Later versions included both command-line and menu-driven user interfaces. At its peak, DOS was a widely used operating system, with an estimated 70 million computers running it. DOS hardly is used today because it does not offer a graphical user interface and it cannot take full advantage of modern 32-bit personal computer processors.

Windows XP

Since 1990, Microsoft has continually updated its Windows operating system, incorporating new features and functions with each subsequent version (Figure 8-24). **Windows XP** is Microsoft's fastest, most reliable Windows operating system yet, providing quicker startup, better performance, and a new, simplified visual look (Figure 8-25).

COMPARISON OF WINDOWS VERSIONS

Windows Version	Year Released	Highlights
Windows 3.x	1990	• Provided a GUI • An operating environment only — worked in combination with DOS
Windows NT 3.1	1993	• Client OS that connected to a Windows NT Advanced Server • Interface similar to Windows 3.x
Windows 95	1995	• True multitasking operating system • Improved GUI • Included support for networking, Plug and Play technology, longer file names, and e-mail
Windows NT Workstation 4.0	1996	• Client OS that connected to a Windows NT Server • Interface similar to Windows 95 • Network integration
Windows 98	1998	• Upgrade to Windows 95 • More integrated with the Internet; included *Internet Explorer* (a Web browser) • Faster system startup and shutdown, better file management, support for multimedia technologies (e.g., DVDs), and USB connectivity
Windows Millennium Edition	2000	• Upgrade to Windows 98 • Designed for the home user who wanted music playing, video editing, and networking capabilities
Windows 2000 Professional	2000	• Upgrade to Windows NT Workstation 4.0 • Complete multitasking client OS designed for business personal computers • Certified device drivers, faster performance, adaptive Start menu, image viewer, enhanced for mobile users
Windows XP	2001	• Upgrade to Windows Millennium Edition called Windows XP Home Edition • Upgrade to Windows 2000 Professional called Windows XP Professional • Windows XP Tablet PC Edition designed for Tablet PC users • Improved interface and increased performance in all editions

FIGURE 8-24   Microsoft had many versions of Windows before Windows XP.

FIGURE 8-25 Windows XP, with its simplified look, is the fastest and most reliable Windows operating system to date.

Windows XP is available in three editions: Home Edition, Professional, and Tablet PC Edition. The table in Figure 8-26 highlights features in all editions of Windows XP. The next page identifies the differences. Read Looking Ahead 8-1 for a look at the next generation of the Windows operating system.

WINDOWS XP FEATURES

Appearance and Performance
- New look and feel to the user interface
- Increased reliability and security
- Increased performance to run programs faster
- Redesigned Start menu and Control Panel
- Minimized clutter on the taskbar with multiple open windows organized into groups
- Crisper display of images on LCD screens with ClearType

Administration
- Improved interface for creating multiple user accounts and switching among accounts
- Enhanced system recovery from failure with System Restore, without causing loss of data
- Easy-to-install home or small office network
- Internet Connection Firewall to protect a home or small office network from hackers
- Improved wireless network support
- Improved battery-life management for notebook computers

Help and Support
- Comprehensive Help and Support system
- Remote Assistance that allows another person (with your permission) to control your computer remotely to demonstrate a process or solve a problem

Communications and the Web
- New version of Windows Messenger to send instant messages; communicate in real time using text, graphics, video, and voice to other online users; and a whiteboard available for use in video conferences
- New version of Internet Explorer with improved look
- Remote Desktop to access data and applications on your desktop computer while away from the computer using another Windows-based computer with a network or Internet connection
- Publish, store, and share text, graphics, photographs, and other items on the Web

Digital Media
- New version of Windows Media Player to listen to more than 3,000 Internet radio stations, play MP3 and Microsoft's WMA music format, copy music and data onto blank CDs, and watch DVD movies
- New version of Movie Maker
- Transfer images from a digital camera or scanner to your computer

FIGURE 8-26 Some features of Windows XP.

LOOKING AHEAD 8-1

Trustworthy Computing — Heart of Windows Upgrade

The ancient Greeks believed that the city of Troy would be safe as long as the statue of Pallas Athena, the Greek goddess of wisdom, was preserved. Microsoft is taking that safety concept one step further by naming its new security initiative, *Palladium*.

Microsoft Chairman and Chief Software Architect Bill Gates promises this Trustworthy Computing will be used for both software and hardware. Palladium, for example, will help keep passwords secure and encrypt keystrokes and video display signals transmitted through wires. The company is collaborating with Intel and Advanced Micro Devices (AMD) to develop these security measures.

Most likely, Palladium will be featured in the next version of the Windows operating system, currently code-named *Longhorn*. Overall, Longhorn is being developed as a consumer-friendly product with a completely object-oriented interface. When the software is released in 2004 or later, it will recognize users and tailor the systems for their specific needs by storing personal data in encrypted folders. It also will filter junk e-mail messages and prevent viruses from attacking systems. One major feature will be incorporating *DRM* (*Digital Rights Management*) technologies, which protects files from unauthorized access.

For a look at the next generation of the Windows operating system, visit the Discovering Computers 2004 Looking Ahead Web page (scsite.com/dc2004/looking). Click Looking Ahead #1 below Chapter 8.

WINDOWS XP HOME EDITION The *Windows XP Home Edition* is an upgrade to Windows Millennium Edition. In addition to providing the capabilities of Windows Millennium Edition, Windows XP Home Edition offers features and functionality that allow users to perform the following tasks:

- Acquire, organize, and share digital pictures
- Download, store, and play back high-quality music through Windows Media Player
- Create, edit, and share videos with Windows Movie Maker
- Easily network and share multiple home computers
- Use built-in instant messaging and video conferencing with Windows Messenger
- Recover from problems with easy-to-use tools

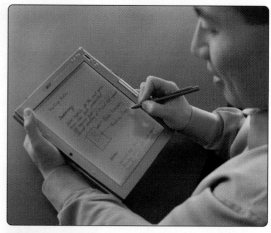

FIGURE 8-27 With Windows XP Tablet PC Edition, users write and save handwritten notes directly on the Tablet PC.

WINDOWS XP PROFESSIONAL *Windows XP Professional* is an upgrade to Windows 2000 Professional. In addition to providing the capabilities of Windows 2000 Professional, Windows XP Professional includes all the capabilities of Windows XP Home Edition and offers the following features and functionality:

- Greater data security through encryption of files and folders
- Remote access to a computer, its data, and its files from any other computer anywhere
- Simpler administration of groups of users or computers
- Multiple language user interface
- Support for secured wireless network access

WINDOWS XP TABLET PC EDITION The *Windows XP Tablet PC Edition* includes all the features of Windows XP Professional and provides the following additional features that are designed to make users more productive while working on their Tablet PCs:

- Write on screen or issue instructions to the Tablet PC using a digital pen (Figure 8-27)
- Save documents in handwritten form or convert them into typewritten text for use in other application software
- Add handwritten notes to documents created in other application software
- Enter text and instructions by speaking into the Tablet PC
- Grab-and-go: Take the Tablet PC wherever/ whenever you need the convenience of a notebook computer, but the portability of a computer the size of a spiral-bound notebook

Mac OS X

Since it was released with Macintosh computers in 1984, Apple's **Macintosh operating system** has set the standard for operating system ease of use and has been the model for most of the new GUIs developed for non-Macintosh systems. The latest version, **Mac OS X**, is a multitasking operating system available only for computers manufactured by Apple (Figure 8-28).

Mac OS X includes features from previous versions of the Macintosh operating system such as large photo-quality icons, built-in networking support, e-mail, online shopping, enhanced speech recognition, CD burning, and enhanced multimedia capabilities. In addition, Mac OS X includes these features:

- Built-in AOL-compatible instant messenger
- Filter to eliminate junk e-mail messages
- Contact lists synchronized with PDA or Bluetooth-enabled smart phone
- Web search without a browser
- Latest version of QuickTime to listen to music and view videos on the Internet
- Easy networking of computers and devices
- Conversion of handwritten text into typewritten text
- Windows network connection and shared Windows documents

WEB LINK 8-4

Windows XP

Visit the Discovering Computers 2004 WEB LINK page (**scsite .com/dc2004/weblink**). Click Windows XP below Chapter 8.

WEB LINK 8-5

Mac OS X

Visit the Discovering Computers 2004 WEB LINK page (**scsite .com/dc2004/weblink**). Click Mac OS X below Chapter 8.

FIGURE 8-28 Mac OS X is the operating system used with Apple Macintosh computers.

OS/2 Warp Client

OS/2 Warp Client is IBM's GUI multitasking client operating system that supports networking, Java, the Internet, and speech recognition (Figure 8-29). In addition to running programs written specifically for OS/2 (pronounced OH-ESS-two), the operating system also runs DOS and most Windows programs.

OS/2 has been used by businesses because of IBM's long association with business computing and OS/2's strong networking support.

UNIX

UNIX (pronounced YOU-nix) is a multitasking operating system developed in the early 1970s by scientists at Bell Laboratories. Bell Labs (a subsidiary of AT&T) was prohibited from actively promoting UNIX in the commercial marketplace because of federal regulations. Bell Labs instead licensed UNIX for a low fee to numerous colleges and universities, where UNIX obtained a wide following. UNIX was implemented on many different types of computers. After deregulation of the telephone companies in the 1980s, UNIX was licensed to many hardware and software companies.

Several versions of this operating system exist, each slightly different. When programmers move application software from one UNIX version to another, they sometimes have to rewrite some of the programs. Although some versions of UNIX have a command-line interface, most versions of UNIX offer a graphical user interface (Figure 8-30).

Today, a version of UNIX is available for most computers of all sizes. Power users often work with UNIX because of its flexibility and power.

WEB LINK 8-6

UNIX

Visit the Discovering Computers 2004 WEB LINK page (**scsite .com/dc2004/weblink**). Click UNIX below Chapter 8.

FIGURE 8-29 OS/2 is IBM's multitasking GUI operating system designed to work with 32-bit personal computer processors.

FIGURE 8-30 Some versions of UNIX have a graphical user interface.

Linux

Linux is one of the faster growing operating systems. **Linux** (pronounced LINN-uks) is a popular, multitasking UNIX-type operating system. One reason users choose Linux is because it is free. In addition to the basic operating system, Linux also includes many free programming languages and utility programs.

Linux is not proprietary software like the operating systems discussed thus far. Instead, Linux is *open source software*, which means its code is available to the public. Many programmers have donated time to make Linux the best possible version of UNIX. Promoters of open source state two main advantages: users who modify the software share their improvements with others, and customers can personalize the software to meet their needs. Read Issue 8-4 for a related discussion.

Some versions of Linux are command-line. Others are GUI. The two most popular GUIs available for Linux are GNOME and KDE. Some companies market software applications that run on their own version of Linux. Figure 8-31 shows a Red Hat Linux graphical user interface.

Users obtain Linux in a variety of ways. Many people download it free from the Web. Linux CD-ROMs are included in many Linux books and also are available for purchase from vendors. For purchasers of new personal computers, some retailers will preinstall Linux on the hard disk on request.

⬛ ISSUE 8-4

Is Open Source Software a Good Idea?

Linux is a fast-growing, innovative new operating system. One of the things that make it different from other operating systems is that Linux is open source and its source code, along with any changes, remains public. Since its introduction in 1991, Linux has been altered, adapted, and improved by hundreds of programmers. Unlike Linux, most operating systems are proprietary, and their program code often is a zealously guarded secret. At one large software developer, an employee reported that application programmers had little opportunity to contribute to operating system programs because they had no access to the operating system program source code. Supporters of open source maintain that source code should be open to the public so that it can be scrutinized, corrected, and enhanced. In light of concerns about security and fears of possible virus problems, however, some people are not sure open source software is a good idea. Besides, they argue, developers should be able to control, and profit from, the operating systems they create. Is open source software a good idea? Why or why not? Can the concerns about open source software be addressed? How?

For more information about open source software, visit the Discovering Computers 2004 Issues Web page (**scsite.com/dc2004/ issues**). Click Issue #4 below Chapter 8.

🛑 QUIZ YOURSELF 8-2

To check your knowledge of utilities included with most operating systems and stand-alone operating systems, visit the Discovering Computers 2004 Quiz Yourself Web page (**scsite.com/dc2004/quiz**). Click Objectives 5 – 6 below Chapter 8.

FIGURE 8-31   Red Hat provides a version of Linux called Red Hat Linux.

NETWORK OPERATING SYSTEMS

As discussed earlier in this chapter, a network operating system is an operating system that is designed specifically to support a network. A network operating system typically resides on a server. The client computers on the network rely on the server(s) for resources. Many of the client operating systems discussed in the previous section work in conjunction with a network operating system.

Some of the stand-alone operating systems discussed in the previous section include networking capability. The difference between those and the network operating systems discussed in this section is these are designed specifically to support all sizes of networks, including medium to large-sized businesses and Web servers.

Examples of network operating systems include NetWare, Windows Server 2003, OS/2 Warp Server for e-business, UNIX, Linux, and Solaris. The following pages briefly discuss these operating systems.

NetWare

Novell's *NetWare* is a network operating system designed for client/server networks. NetWare has a server portion that resides on the network server and a client portion that resides on each client computer connected to the network. The server portion of NetWare allows users to share hardware devices attached to the server (such as a printer), as well as any files or application software stored on the server. The client portion of NetWare communicates with the server. Client computers also can have their own stand-alone operating system such as Windows XP Professional or Mac OS X.

Windows Server 2003

Windows Server 2003 is an upgrade to Windows 2000 Server, which was an upgrade to Windows NT Server. Windows Server 2003, which includes features of previous server versions, offers the following capabilities:

- Web site management and hosting
- Easy application development tool across platforms with Windows Distributed interNet Applications (DNA) Architecture
- Delivery and management of multimedia across intranets and the Internet

- Document storage in Web folders
- Information management about network users and resources with *Active Directory*
- Client support using Windows XP and earlier versions of Windows, Mac OS X, and UNIX

In addition, Windows Server 2003 provides developers with dynamic tools that allow businesses and customers to connect and communicate easily via the Internet. Through Windows Server 2003, programmers have the ability to use *Web services*, which are Web applications created with any programming language or any operating system to communicate and share data seamlessly.

To meet the needs of all sizes of businesses, the **Windows Server 2003 family** includes four products:

- *Windows Server 2003, Standard Edition* for the typical small- to medium-sized business network
- *Windows Server 2003, Enterprise Edition* for medium- to large-sized businesses, including those with e-commerce operations
- *Windows Server 2003, Datacenter Edition* for businesses with huge volumes of transactions and large-scale databases
- *Windows Server 2003, Web Edition* for Web server and Web hosting businesses

OS/2 Warp Server for e-business

OS/2 Warp Server for e-business is IBM's network operating system designed for all sizes of businesses. Many e-commerce applications use OS/2 Warp Server for e-business. The Web browser and e-mail program in OS/2 Warp Server for e-business is similar to Netscape. Clients use OS/2 Warp Client or some version of Windows.

UNIX

In addition to being a stand-alone operating system, UNIX also is a network operating system. That is, UNIX is capable of handling a high volume of transactions in a multiuser environment and working with multiple processors using multiprocessing. For this reason, some computer professionals call UNIX a *multipurpose operating system* because it is both a stand-alone and network operating system.

WEB LINK 8-7

NetWare

Visit the Discovering Computers 2004 WEB LINK page (**scsite .com/dc2004/weblink**). Click NetWare below Chapter 8.

Linux

Some network servers use Linux as their operating system. Thus, Linux also is a multipurpose operating system. With Linux, a network administrator can configure the network, administer security, run a Web server, and process e-mail. Clients on the network can run Linux, UNIX, or Windows. Versions of Linux include both the Netscape and Mozilla Web browsers.

Solaris

Solaris, a version of UNIX developed by Sun Microsystems, is a network operating system designed specifically for e-commerce applications. Solaris manages high-traffic accounts and incorporates security necessary for Web transactions. Client computers use a GNOME-based version of Solaris.

EMBEDDED OPERATING SYSTEMS

The operating system on most PDAs and small devices, called an **embedded operating system**, resides on a ROM chip. Popular embedded operating systems include Windows CE .NET, Pocket PC 2002, Palm OS, and Symbian OS. The following pages discuss these operating systems. Read Looking Ahead 8-2 for a look at the current and next generation of entertainment devices with operating systems.

Windows CE .NET

Windows CE .NET is a scaled-down Windows operating system designed for use on communications, entertainment, and mobile devices, and small handheld computers. Devices that use Windows CE .NET include PDAs, smart phones, set-top boxes, digital cameras, DVD players, printers, in-vehicle devices, and smart displays (Figure 8-32).

Windows CE .NET is a GUI that supports color, sound, multitasking, multimedia, e-mail, Internet access, and Web browsing. Many applications, such as Microsoft Word and Microsoft Excel, have scaled-down versions that run with Windows CE .NET.

FIGURE 8-32   Many smart displays, which are thin desktop monitors that detach from the computer to function as portable wireless touch screens, use Windows CE .NET as their operating system.

LOOKING AHEAD 8-2

Freon Possible Xbox Successor

For years, the fluorocarbon Freon was used as a refrigerant in air conditioners and as a propellant in aerosol cans. Microsoft is banking that its latest Xbox project, Freon, will be the cool device that propels the company over its hot video-game rival, Sony.

Economics is part of the reason behind Microsoft's Xbox redesign. Its current console is more expensive to produce than Sony's PlayStation because the Xbox includes a version of the Microsoft Windows operating system and is a complete computer, with a hard disk and motherboard. Experts predict that game boxes eventually will become the primary in-home computer with access to the Internet, so Microsoft wants to add this product to the marketplace to compete with Sony and Nintendo and to take part in all levels of computing — from large systems to the Pocket PC.

The Xbox's hard disk also provides the technology to provide gaming extras, such as hearing voice commentary and also recording gamers' moves to replay at different speeds. The proposed Freon console would record television programs onto the hard disk.

New video-game systems release approximately every five years. But Microsoft is looking to beat Sony to the punch by releasing the Freon Xbox version before Sony releases its new PlayStation.

For a look at the next generation of the Xbox, visit the Discovering Computers 2004 Looking Ahead Web page (**scsite.com/dc2004/ looking**). Click Looking Ahead #2 below Chapter 8.

Devices equipped with Windows CE .NET can communicate wirelessly with computers and other devices using Bluetooth or other wireless technologies, as long as the device is equipped with the necessary communications hardware.

Pocket PC 2002

Pocket PC 2002 is a scaled-down operating system developed by Microsoft that works on a specific type of PDA, called a **Pocket PC** (Figure 8-33). With this operating system and a Pocket PC device, users have access to all the basic PIM (personal information manager) functions such as contact lists, schedules, tasks, calendars, and notes.

The Pocket PC 2002 operating system, which has a Windows XP look, also provides numerous additional features that allow users to check e-mail, browse the Web, listen to music, watch a video, send and receive instant messages, record a voice message, manage finances, read an e-book, or create a word processing document or spreadsheet. Some devices with the Pocket PC 2002 operating system also support handwriting and sometimes voice input. With the Pocket PC 2002 Phone Edition, users can make telephone calls and send text messages using the PDA.

FIGURE 8-33 Pocket PC 2002 runs on any Pocket PC device, such as the Bluetooth-enabled PDA in this figure.

WEB LINK 8-8

Pocket PC 2002

Visit the Discovering Computers 2004 WEB LINK page (**scsite .com/dc2004/weblink**). Click Pocket PC 2002 below Chapter 8.

Palm OS

A competing operating system to the Pocket PC 2002 is the *Palm OS*. Palm-powered PDAs, that use the Palm OS as their operating system, include the Palm, Visor, and CLIE (Figure 8-34).

With the Palm OS and a compatible PDA, users manage schedules and contacts, telephone messages, project notes, reminders, task and address lists, and important dates and appointments. Information on the PDA easily synchronizes with a personal computer using a cable or a wireless technology such as IrDA or Bluetooth. Palm OS supports handwriting recognition software, called Graffiti. Some Palm-powered PDAs allow users to connect wirelessly to the Internet; browse the Web; and send and receive e-mail messages, instant messages, and text messages.

The latest version of Palm OS includes improved security for data transmission, allows for biometric identification, and supports the use of smart cards.

Symbian OS

Symbian OS is an open source multitasking operating system designed for smart phones (Figure 8-35). In addition to making telephone calls, users of Symbian OS can maintain contact lists; save appointments; browse the Web; and send and receive text messages, e-mail messages, and faxes using a smart phone. Users input data by pressing keys on the keypad or keyboard, touching the screen, writing on the screen with a stylus, or speaking into the smart phone. Symbian OS allows users to communicate wirelessly using a variety of technologies including Bluetooth and IrDA.

Symbian OS has been extremely popular in Europe and has the support from major companies such as Motorola and Nokia. Industry analysts expect the popularity of Symbian OS in the United States to grow as increasingly more people use smart phones for data access.

FIGURE 8-34 The Sony CLIE uses the Palm OS.

WEB LINK 8-9

Palm OS

Visit the Discovering Computers 2004 WEB LINK page (**scsite .com/dc2004/weblink**). Click Palm OS below Chapter 8.

FIGURE 8-35 This smart phone, called the Nokia Communicator, uses the Symbian OS.

STAND-ALONE UTILITY PROGRAMS

Although operating systems typically include some built-in utilities, many stand-alone utility programs are available for purchase. For example, you can purchase backup utilities and screen savers. These stand-alone utilities typically offer improvements over those features built-in to the operating system or provide features not included in an operating system.

Other functions provided by stand-alone utilities include protecting against viruses, securing a computer from unauthorized access, compressing files, and maintaining a personal computer. The following sections discuss each of these utilities.

Antivirus Programs

The term, computer **virus**, describes a potentially damaging computer program that affects, or infects, a computer negatively by altering the way the computer works without the user's knowledge or permission. More specifically, a computer virus is a segment of program code from some outside source that implants itself in a computer. Once the virus is in a computer, it can spread throughout and may damage your files and operating system.

Currently, more than 61,000 known virus programs exist with an estimated 6 new virus programs discovered each day. Computer viruses do not generate by chance. The programmer of a virus, known as a *virus author*, intentionally writes a virus program. Some virus authors find writing viruses a challenge. Others write them to cause destruction. Writing a virus program usually requires significant programming skills.

Some viruses are harmless pranks that simply freeze a computer temporarily or display sounds or messages. The Music Bug virus, for example, instructs the computer to play a few chords of music. Other viruses destroy or corrupt data stored on the hard disk of the infected computer. If you notice any unusual changes in your computer's performance, it may be infected with a virus. Figure 8-36 outlines some common symptoms of virus infection.

WEB LINK 8-10

Antivirus Programs
Visit the Discovering Computers 2004 WEB LINK page (**scsite .com/dc2004/weblink**). Click Antivirus Programs below Chapter 8.

SIGNS OF VIRUS INFECTION

- An unusual message or image is displayed on the computer screen
- An unusual sound or music plays randomly
- The available memory is less than what should be available
- A program or file suddenly is missing
- An unknown program or file mysteriously appears
- The size of a file changes without explanation
- A file becomes corrupted
- A program or file does not work properly
- System properties change

FIGURE 8-36 Viruses attack computers in a variety of ways. This list indicates some of the more common signs of virus infection.

Viruses are just one type of malicious-logic program. A *malicious-logic program* is a program that acts without a user's knowledge and deliberately alters the computer's operations. In addition to viruses, other types of malicious-logic programs are worms and Trojan horses.

A **worm**, such as CodeRed, copies itself repeatedly, for example in memory or over a network, using up system resources and possibly shutting the system down. A **Trojan horse** (named after the Greek myth) hides within or looks like a legitimate program such as a screen saver. A certain condition or action usually triggers the Trojan horse. Unlike a virus or worm, a Trojan horse does not replicate itself to other computers. For a more technical discussion about computer viruses, read the High-Tech Talk article in Chapter 3 on page 3.35.

To protect a computer from virus attacks, install an antivirus program and update it frequently. An **antivirus program** protects a computer against viruses by identifying and removing any computer viruses found in memory, on storage media, or on incoming files (Figure 8-37). Most antivirus programs also protect against worms and Trojan horses. When you purchase a new computer, it often includes antivirus software.

The two more popular antivirus programs are McAfee VirusScan and Norton AntiVirus. As an alternative to purchasing these products on CD, both McAfee and Norton offer Web-based antivirus programs. That is, during your paid subscription period, the program continuously protects the computer against viruses.

FIGURE 8-37 An antivirus program scans memory, disks, and incoming e-mail messages and attachments for viruses and attempts to remove any viruses it finds.

❓ FAQ 8-5

Should I take any other steps to prevent virus infections on my computer?

Set up the antivirus software to scan on a regular basis. Never open an e-mail attachment unless you are expecting the attachment and it is from a trusted source. Never start a computer with a floppy disk in drive A. Set macro security in programs such as word processing and spreadsheet so you can enable or disable macros. Write-protect your recovery disk. Back up files regularly.

For more information about preventing virus infections, visit the Discovering Computers 2004 FAQ Web page (**scsite.com/dc2004/faq**). Click Preventing Virus Infections below Chapter 8.

Personal Firewalls

A **personal firewall** is a utility program that detects and protects a personal computer from unauthorized intrusions. Personal firewalls constantly monitor all transmissions to and from a computer.

When connected to the Internet, your computer is vulnerable to attacks from a hacker. A *hacker* is someone who tries to access a computer or network illegally. Users with broadband Internet connections, such as through DSL and Internet cable television, are even more susceptible than those with dial-up access because the Internet connection is always on.

Personal firewall programs often are sold as part of an Internet utility suite (Figure 8-38). In addition to including a personal firewall, Internet utility suites consist of utilities that protect against viruses, secure your data, block advertisements from Web pages, and enable parents to restrict access to certain Web sites.

🌐 WEB LINK 8-11

Personal Firewalls

Visit the Discovering Computers 2004 WEB LINK page (**scsite .com/dc2004/weblink**). Click Personal Firewalls below Chapter 8.

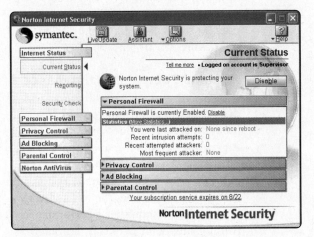

FIGURE 8-38 Internet security suites often include a variety of utilities including a personal firewall and antivirus program.

File Compression

A **file compression utility** shrinks the size of a file(s). A compressed file takes up less storage space than the original file (Figure 8-39). Compressing files frees up room on the storage media and improves system performance. Attaching a compressed file to an e-mail message, for example, reduces the time needed for file transmission. Uploading and downloading compressed files to and from the Internet reduces the file transmission time.

zip extension

compressed files

percent compressed

FIGURE 8-39 This file (Chemistry Lecture #1) contains five compressed files. Without being compressed, these files consume 478 KB. Compressing them reduces the amount of storage by about 80 percent.

Compressed files, sometimes called **zipped files**, usually have a .zip extension. When you receive or download a compressed file, you must uncompress it. To **uncompress**, or *unzip*, a file, you restore it to its original form. Some operating systems such as Windows XP include uncompress capabilities. To compress a file, however, you need a stand-alone file compression utility. Two popular stand-alone file compression utilities are PKZIP™ and WinZip®.

Personal Computer Maintenance

Operating systems typically include a diagnostic utility that diagnoses computer problems but does not repair them. A **personal computer maintenance utility** identifies and fixes operating system problems, detects and repairs disk problems, and includes the capability of improving a computer's performance. Additionally, some personal computer maintenance utilities continuously monitor a computer while you use it to identify and repair problems before they occur. Norton Utilities is a popular personal computer maintenance utility designed for Windows operating systems (Figure 8-40).

FIGURE 8-40   Norton Utilities is a popular maintenance program for users of Windows.

QUIZ YOURSELF 8-3

To check your knowledge of network operating systems, embedded operating systems, and stand-alone utility programs, visit the Discovering Computers 2004 Quiz Yourself Web page (**scsite.com/dc2004/quiz**). Click Objectives 7 – 9 below Chapter 8.

CHAPTER SUMMARY

This chapter defined an operating system and then discussed the functions common to most operating systems. Next, it introduced several utility programs commonly found in operating systems. The chapter discussed a variety of stand-alone operating systems, network operating systems, and embedded operating systems. Finally, the chapter described several stand-alone utility programs.

Career Corner

Systems Programmer

System software is a key component in any computer system. A *systems programmer* evaluates, installs, and maintains system software and provides technical support to the programming staff.

Systems programmers work with the programs that control computers, such as operating systems, network operating systems, and database systems. They identify current and future processing needs and then recommend the software and hardware necessary to meet those needs. In addition to selecting and installing system software, systems programmers must be able to adapt system software to the requirements of an organization, provide regular maintenance, measure system performance, determine the impact of new or updated software on the system, design and implement special software, and provide documentation. Because they are familiar with the entire system, systems programmers often help application programmers to diagnose technical problems.

Systems programmers must be thoroughly acquainted with a variety of operating systems. They must be able to think logically, pay attention to detail, work with abstract concepts, and devise solutions to complex problems. Systems programmers often work in teams and interact with programmers and nontechnical users, so communication skills are important.

Most systems programmers have a four-year B.S. degree in Computer Science or Information Technology. Depending on responsibilities and experience, salaries range from $40,000 to as much as $97,000.

To learn more about the field of Systems Programmer as a career, visit the Discovering Computers 2004 Careers Web page (**scsite.com/dc2004/careers**). Click Systems Programmer.

HIGH-TECH TALK

Windows XP: Taking Control with the Command Prompt

When Microsoft developed the Windows XP operating system, it gave it a fresh, new graphical user interface. However, you still can complete many important tasks using the command-line interface. Microsoft's first operating system, MS-DOS, was based entirely on a command-line interface. Today, Windows XP supports many of the original MS-DOS commands — and many new commands that help you complete tasks.

With Windows XP, you enter commands via a command shell. A *command shell* is a software program with a nongraphical, command-line interface that provides an environment to run text-based application software and utility programs. The Windows XP command shell is called *Command Prompt*; the file name for the Command Prompt application is cmd.exe.

To open the Command Prompt window, click the Start button and point to All Programs, point to Accessories, and then click Command Prompt. Clicking Run on the Start menu and then typing cmd in the Run dialog box also opens the Command Prompt window. To execute a command, type one command per line and then press the ENTER key. Many commands allow you to enter one or more *options*, or *arguments*, which are additions to a command that change or refine the command in a specified manner. To close the Command Prompt window, type `exit` and then press the ENTER key or click the Close button in the Command Prompt window.

The Command Prompt window allows you to complete a wide range of tasks, including troubleshooting network connections. The ping command, for example, allows you to test TCP/IP connectivity for network and Internet connections (Figure 8-6a on page 8.08). When you enter the ping command with an IP address, your computer sends a special packet called ICMP Echo to that address. If everything is working, a reply comes back; if not, the ping times out. You also can use TRACERT (traceroute), a command-line utility that traces a data packet's path to its destination. When you enter tracert course.com, for example, the tracert utility traces the path from your computer to the Course Technology Web server.

You also can use the Windows XP Command Prompt to help manage your computer. When you enter the systeminfo command, Command Prompt queries your computer for basic system information, including operating system configuration and hardware properties, such as RAM and disk space. If you enter the tasklist command, the Command Prompt window returns a list of processes running on a computer, with each process identified by a process ID (PID) (Figure 8-41). You can terminate any process by entering the taskkill command and the PID as the argument. For example, if you enter taskkill /pid 5168, the process with PID 516 ends.

Network administrators can use this command to fix problems on networked computers by closing applications.

The Windows XP Command Prompt also supports commands used to manage the files and file system on your hard disk. The *chkdsk command* checks for and corrects errors on the disk. You also can defragment your hard disk by entering the *defrag command*, with an argument specifying the drive to defragment (for example, defrag c:). When you are done working, you can use the *shutdown command* to shut down or restart your local or a remote computer.

In most cases, the command-line tools perform functions similar to the GUI application. The Disk Defragmenter utility and the defrag command, for example, provide similar functionality. In others, the command-line tools provide additional functionality. For instance, the *diskpart command* starts the command-line version of the DiskPart utility and gives you access to advanced features not available in the GUI version.

The commands discussed here are just some of the wide range of commands supported by Windows XP. For more information about the Windows XP Command Prompt, visit the Discovering Computers 2004 High-Tech Talk Web page (**scsite.com/dc2004/tech**) and click Windows XP Command Prompt.

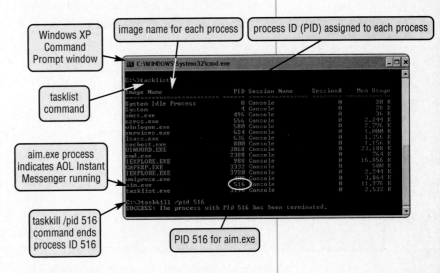

FIGURE 8-41 An example of the tasklist command.

COMPANIES ON THE CUTTING EDGE

Red Hat
Open Source Software Provider

Red Hat markets disruptive technology. According to Red Hat, disruptive technologies change the way people relate to the world. The telephone was a disruptive technology because it changed the way people communicate. The automobile was a disruptive technology because it changed the way people travel. Red Hat's disruptive technology is open source — a fundamental shift in the way software is created.

Most software is proprietary. The software code, or instructions, is known only to the companies that produce the software. Red Hat is the largest supplier of open source technology. Open source is software whose code is available to the public. Open source software allows buyers to modify, and perhaps improve, the software. Red Hat claims that the collaboration between sellers and buyers of open source software leads to rapid innovation and better software. Red Hat delivers software improvements to customers through the Red Hat Network, the company's Internet service.

Red Hat's most well-known product is Red Hat Linux. Linus Torvalds, a Finnish college student, wrote the first version of Linux in 1991 and made the operating system, together with its source code, available on the Internet. With each new version, demand for the operating system grew. In 1994, Bob Young and Marc Ewing founded Red Hat and started selling a packaged

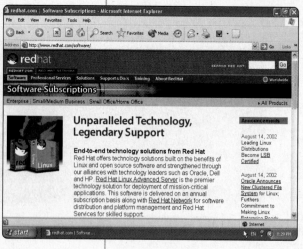

version of the operating system, called Red Hat Linux, complete with documentation and support. Today, Red Hat Linux is the most popular, and most trusted, version of Linux with a 52 percent market share among Linux users and partnerships with technology companies such as Dell, IBM, and Intel. Red Hat attributes the success of Red Hat Linux to the software's reliable performance, exceptional flexibility, and low cost. Red Hat also offers a training and certification program that has become an industry standard. A recent study voted the Red Hat Certified Engineer (RHCE) program the best for overall quality.

For more information about Red Hat, visit the Discovering Computers 2004 Companies Web page (**scsite.com/dc2004/companies**) and click Red Hat.

Network Associates
Security Provider

Some people take megadoses of zinc to fight a cold. Others rely on homemade chicken soup to combat viruses. But how can you protect your computer from viral attacks? The best approach is to use a combination of an antivirus program and a personal firewall, such as McAfee VirusScan and Firewall, developed by Network Associates.

Founded in 1989, *Network Associates* is a leading supplier of network security. Network Associates consists of three businesses:

*   McAfee Security develops products to protect companies from security breaks and virus attacks.
*   Sniffer Technologies offers products to keep networks and applications running at optimum levels.
*   Magic Solutions delivers products that provide a unique, Internet-based solution for information technology resource management.

Network Associates also is the majority owner of McAfee.com, a primary source of managed online security services for consumers and small businesses. More than 61,000 strains of viruses, Trojan horses, and worms are on the rampage to infect your computer. But, the Network Associates cybersleuths are on the lookout for these malicious programs, sometimes finding as many as six new viruses each day. These cyber-investigators are part of the company's 3,200 employees, making Network Associates the world's largest independent network security and management software corporation.

MacAfee's VirusScan has been named the top antivirus product in independent testing performed by the University of Hamburg's Virus Test Center and by the West Coast Labs for Secure Computing. This software, along with other Network Associates e-business products, is used by more than 60 million people worldwide.

For more information about Network Associates, visit the Discovering Computers 2004 Companies Web page (**scsite.com/dc2004/companies**) and click Network Associates.

TECHNOLOGY TRAILBLAZERS

Linus Torvalds
Creator of Linux

Imagine creating an operating system that compares favorably with Windows and is backed by a technical support group one-million strong. Now, imagine giving that operating system away free. Unimaginable? Well, that is what happened when *Linus Torvalds* created Linux.

In 1991, Torvalds was a computer-science student in Finland. Frustrated with current operating systems, he decided to create his own. This might seem a daunting task, but the young programmer was confident. "I knew I was the best programmer in the world," Torvalds recalls. "Every 21-year-old programmer knows that. How hard can it be? It's just an operating system." He announced his project in an Internet newsgroup: "I'm doing a (free) operating system … Any suggestions are welcome, but I won't promise I'll implement them. :-)."

Torvalds soon posted the first version of the operating system. He incorporated suggestions and adopted a proposed name, Linux. As he posted new versions, the process was repeated and the number of reviewers grew. When Linux was released in 1994, the operating system had networking capability and more than 100,000 users. Torvalds eventually copyrighted Linux under a GPL (General Public License), allowing versions to be sold as long as the source code, and any alterations, remain public.

Today, Linus Torvalds works for Transmeta (a small company that develops and sells software-based microprocessors) and lives in a modest California house. He still considers himself Linux's lead technical developer. Due to Linux's popularity, however, he has to delegate some tasks and spend time answering e-mail messages and coordinating work efforts. A celebrity among programmers, Torvalds has no regrets about making the operating system available free. "A big part of personal satisfaction," Torvalds points out, "is having your work recognized by your peers."

For more information about Linus Torvalds, visit the Discovering Computers 2004 People Web page (**scsite.com/dc2004/people**) and click Linus Torvalds.

Steve Jobs
Cofounder of Apple Computer

Before he was thirty-five, *Steve Jobs* helped build the first desktop personal computer, cofounded Apple Computer Corporation, marketed a revolutionary operating system, and became a multimillionaire. Not bad.

In 1972, Jobs graduated from high school and attended Reed College for a semester. He took classes in philosophy, embraced the contemporary counterculture, and eventually journeyed to India in search of enlightenment. When he returned, he joined Steve Wozniak's Homebrew Computer Club. "Woz[niak] was the first person I met who knew more about electronics than I did," Jobs recalls. When Wozniak designed a simple small computer, Jobs suggested they start a company and make the PC boards. The founders of Apple Computer sold their most valuable possessions — Jobs, his Volkswagen minibus and Wozniak, his scientific calculator — for capital and built a prototype. The computer, marketed in 1976 as the Apple I, was an immediate success, earning almost $775,000 from sales. The Apple II, introduced the next year, earned much more. Suddenly, Wozniak and Jobs had a very prosperous company.

As Apple grew, Jobs showed an uncompromising drive for perfection. Jobs also was a brilliant motivator, getting the best from the people around him. Employees joked about his "reality-distortion field" that allowed him to make seemingly unreasonable ideas appear reasonable. The Macintosh computer, announced in 1984, incorporated one of these ideas: a graphical interface controlled by a mouse. The Macintosh was a hit.

Jobs left Apple in 1985. He later would cofound NeXT Software and become CEO of Pixar, the computer animation studio that developed the feature film, *Toy Story*. Apple eventually acquired both companies. In 1997, Jobs returned to a troubled Apple as CEO. Under his leadership, the company continues to manufacture innovative products and improve its bottom line.

For more information about Steve Jobs, visit the Discovering Computers 2004 People Web page (**scsite.com/dc2004/people**) and click Steve Jobs.

CHAPTER 8 **CHAPTER REVIEW**

◄● Previous | Next ●►

The Chapter Review section summarizes the concepts presented in this chapter.

■ WEB INSTRUCTIONS:

To display this page from the Web, start your browser and enter the Web address **scsite.com/dc2004/ch8/review.** Click the links for current and additional information. To listen to an audio version of this Chapter Review, click the Audio button.

1 What Are the Types of System Software?

System software consists of the programs that control or maintain the operations of a computer and its devices. Two types of system software are operating systems and utility programs. An **operating system (OS)** contains instructions that coordinate all the activities among computer hardware resources. A **utility program** performs maintenance-type tasks, usually related to managing a computer, its devices, or its programs.

2 What Is the Startup Process on a Personal Computer?

Booting is the process of starting or restarting a computer. When a user turns on a computer, the power supply sends a signal to the system unit. The processor chip finds the ROM chip(s) that contains the **BIOS**, which is firmware with the computer's startup instructions. The BIOS performs the _power-on self test (POST)_ to check system components and compares the results with data in a CMOS chip. If the POST completes successfully, the BIOS searches for the _system files_ and the _kernel_ of the operating system, which manages memory and devices, and loads them into memory from storage. Finally, the operating system loads configuration information, requests any necessary user information, and displays the desktop on the screen.

3 What Are the Functions of an Operating System?

The operating system provides a user interface, manages programs, manages memory, schedules jobs, configures devices, establishes an Internet connection, and monitors performance. The **user interface** controls how data and instructions are entered and how information is displayed. Three types of user interfaces are a _command-line interface_, a _menu-driven interface_, and a _graphical user interface_. Managing programs refers to how many users, and how many programs, an operating system can support at one time. An operating system can be _single user/single tasking, single user/multitasking, multiuser,_ or _multiprocessing_.

Memory management optimizes the use of random access memory (RAM). If memory is insufficient, the operating system may use **virtual memory**, which allocates a portion of a storage medium to function as additional RAM. Scheduling jobs determines the order in which jobs are processed. A **job** is an operation the processor manages. Configuring devices involves loading each device's driver when a user boots the computer. A **driver** is a program that tells the operating system how to communicate with a specific device. Establishing an Internet connection sets up a connection between a computer and an Internet service provider. A **performance monitor** is an operating system program that assesses and reports information about computer resources and devices.

4 How Can Operating Systems Help Administrators Control a Network and Manage Security?

A network operating system, or _network OS_, is an operating system that organizes and coordinates how multiple users access and share network resources. A _network administrator_ uses the network OS to add and remove users, computers, and other devices to and from the network. A network administrator also uses the network OS to administer network security. For each user, the network administrator establishes a user account that enables the user to **log on**, or access, the network by supplying the correct **user name** and **password**.

Visit **scsite.com/dc2004/quiz** or click the Quiz Yourself button. Click Objectives 1 – 4 below Chapter 8.

5 What Is the Purpose of the Utilities Included with Most Operating Systems?

Most operating systems include several utility programs. A **file manager** performs functions related to file management. An **image viewer** displays and copies the contents of a graphics file. An **uninstaller** removes a program and any associated entries in the system files. A **disk**

CHAPTER REVIEW   CHAPTER 8

scanner detects and corrects problems on a disk and searches for and removes unnecessary files. A **disk defragmenter** reorganizes the files and unused space on a computer's hard disk. A <u>diagnostic utility</u> compiles and reports technical information about a computer's hardware and certain system software programs. A **backup utility** is used to copy, or *back up*, selected files or an entire hard disk. A **screen saver** displays a moving image or blank screen if no keyboard or mouse activity occurs for a specified time.

6 What Are Features of Several Stand-Alone Operating Systems?

A **stand-alone operating system** is a complete operating system that works on a desktop computer, notebook computer, or mobile computing device. Stand-alone operating systems include DOS, Windows XP, Mac OS X, OS/2 Warp Client, UNIX, and Linux. **DOS** (*Disk Operating System*) refers to several single user, command-line operating systems developed for personal computers. <u>Windows XP</u> is Microsoft's fastest, most reliable Windows operating system, providing better performance and a new GUI with a simplified look. **Mac OS X** is a multitasking GUI operating system available only for Apple computers. *OS/2 Warp Client* is IBM's GUI multitasking client operating system that supports networking, Java, the Internet, and speech recognition. **UNIX** is a multitasking operating system developed at Bell Laboratories. **Linux** is a popular, multitasking UNIX-type operating system that is *open source software*, which means its code is available to the public.

> [STOP] Visit **scsite.com/dc2004/quiz** or click the Quiz Yourself button. Click Objectives 5 – 6 below Chapter 8.

7 What Are Various Network Operating Systems?

Network operating systems include NetWare, Windows Server 2003, OS/2 Warp Server for e-business, UNIX, Linux, and Solaris. Novell's *NetWare* is a network OS designed for client/server networks. **Windows Server 2003** is an upgrade to Windows 2000 Server and

includes features of previous server versions. *OS/2 Warp Server for e-business* is IBM's network OS designed for business. Linux, like UNIX, is a <u>multipurpose operating system</u> because it is both a stand-alone and network operating system. *Solaris*, a version of UNIX developed by Sun Microsystems, is a network OS designed for e-commerce applications.

8 What Devices Use Embedded Operating Systems?

Most PDAs and small devices have an **embedded operating system** that resides on a ROM chip. Popular embedded operating systems include Windows CE .NET, Pocket PC 2002, Palm OS, and Symbian OS. **Windows CE .NET** is a scaled-down Windows operating system designed for use on communications, entertainment, and mobile devices and on handheld computers. **Pocket PC 2002** is a scaled-down operating system from Microsoft that works on a specific type of PDA, called the **Pocket PC**. The *Palm OS* is an operating system used on Palm-powered PDAs. *Symbian OS* is an open source multitasking operating system designed for smart phones.

9 What Is the Purpose of Several Stand-Alone Utility Programs?

Stand-alone utility programs offer improvements over features built into the operating system or provide features not included in the operating system. An <u>antivirus program</u> protects computers against a **virus**, or potentially damaging computer program, by identifying and removing any computer viruses. A **personal firewall** detects and protects a personal computer from unauthorized intrusions. A **file compression utility** shrinks the size of a file so that it takes up less storage space. A **personal computer maintenance utility** identifies and repairs operating system problems or disk problems, and improves a computer's performance.

> [STOP] Visit **scsite.com/dc2004/quiz** or click the Quiz Yourself button. Click Objectives 7 – 9 below Chapter 8.

CHAPTER 8 # KEY TERMS

◄● Previous | Next ●►

You should know the Primary Terms and be familiar with the Secondary Terms.

■ **WEB INSTRUCTIONS:**

To display this page from the Web, start your browser and enter the Web address **scsite.com/dc2004/ch8/terms**. Click a term to display its definition and a picture. When the picture displays, click the more info button for current and additional information about the term from the Web.

>> Primary Terms
(shown in bold-black characters in the chapter)

antivirus program (8.28)
backup utility (8.18)
BIOS (8.05)
boot disk (8.07)
boot drive (8.07)
booting (8.04)
buffer (8.11)
cold boot (8.04)
defragmenting (8.17)
diagnostic utility (8.18)
disk defragmenter (8.17)
disk scanner (8.17)
DOS (8.20)
driver (8.12)
embedded operating
  system (8.26)
file compression utility
  (8.29)
file manager (8.16)
image viewer (8.16)
job (8.11)
Linux (8.24)
log on (8.14)
Mac OS X (8.22)
Macintosh operating
  system (8.22)
memory management
  (8.10)
network operating
  system (8.14)
operating system (OS)
  (8.02)
password (8.15)
performance monitor
  (8.14)

personal computer
  maintenance utility
  (8.30)
personal firewall (8.29)
Plug and Play (8.13)
Pocket PC (8.27)
Pocket PC 2002 (8.27)
queue (8.11)
recovery disk (8.07)
restore program (8.18)
screen saver (8.18)
spooling (8.11)
stand-alone operating
  system (8.20)
system software (8.02)
Trojan horse (8.28)
uncompress (8.30)
uninstaller (8.17)
UNIX (8.23)
user ID (8.14)
user interface (8.08)
user name (8.14)
utility (8.15)
utility program (8.15)
virtual memory (8.10)
virus (8.28)
warm boot (8.04)
Windows Server 2003
  (8.25)
Windows Server 2003
  family (8.25)
Windows CE .NET (8.26)
Windows XP (8.20)
worm (8.28)
zipped files (8.30)

>> Secondary Terms
(shown in italic characters in the chapter)

Active Directory (8.25)
back up (8.18)
background (8.09)
*basic input/output system
  (8.05)*
*client operating systems
  (8.20)*
command language (8.08)
*command-line interface
  (8.08)*
compress (8.18)
cross-platform (8.03)
device driver (8.12)
device-dependent (8.19)
device-independent (8.19)
*Disk Operating System
  (8.20)*
Dr. Watson (8.18)
encryption (8.15)
*fault-tolerant computer
  (8.10)*
foreground (8.09)
formatting (8.16)
fragmented (8.17)
ghosting (8.19)
*graphical user interface
  (GUI) (8.08)*
hacker (8.29)
*interrupt request line (IRQ)
  (8.13)*
kernel (8.04)
*malicious-logic program
  (8.28)*
memory resident (8.04)
menu-driven interface (8.08)
multiprocessing (8.10)
*multipurpose operating
  system (8.25)*
multiuser (8.10)
NetWare (8.25)
*network administrator
  (8.14)*
network OS (8.14)
nonresident (8.04)
open source software (8.24)

OS/2 Warp Client (8.23)
*OS/2 Warp Server for
  e-business (8.25)*
page (8.11)
paging (8.11)
Palm OS (8.27)
platform (8.03)
*power-on self test (POST)
  (8.06)*
*preemptive multitasking
  (8.10)*
print spooler (8.11)
proprietary software (8.19)
registry (8.06)
shortcut (8.16)
*single user/multitasking
  (8.09)*
*single user/single tasking
  (8.09)*
Solaris (8.26)
Startup folder (8.06)
swap file (8.11)
Symbian OS (8.20)
system files (8.06)
thrashing (8.11)
unzip (8.30)
virus author (8.28)
Web services (8.25)
*Windows Server 2003,
  Datacenter Edition (8.25)*
*Windows Server 2003,
  Enterprise Edition (8.25)*
*Windows Server 2003,
  Standard Edition (8.25)*
*Windows Server 2003,
  Web Edition (8.25)*
Windows Explorer (8.16)
*Windows Picture and Fax
  Viewer (8.16)*
*Windows XP Home Edition
  (8.22)*
*Windows XP Professional
  (8.22)*
*Windows XP Tablet PC
  Edition (8.22)*

CHECKPOINT CHAPTER 8

Use the Checkpoint exercises to check your knowledge level of the chapter.

WEB INSTRUCTIONS:

To display this page from the Web, start your browser and enter the Web address **scsite.com/dc2004/ch8/check**. Click the links for current and additional information.

LABEL THE FIGURE   Identify each part of virtual memory.

a. disk (virtual memory)
b. page swapped in
c. swap file
d. page swapped out
e. RAM (physical memory)

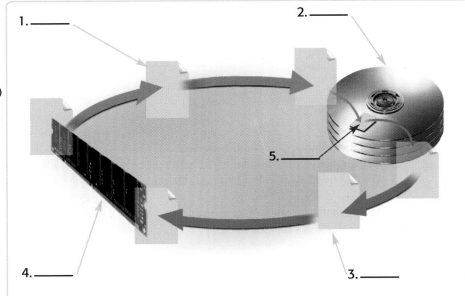

TRUE/FALSE   Mark T for True and F for False. (See page numbers in parentheses.)

_____ 1. The <u>operating system</u> that a system uses sometimes is called the level. (8.03)

_____ 2. <u>Booting</u> is the process of starting or restarting a computer. (8.04)

_____ 3. A <u>user interface</u> controls how you enter data and instructions and how information is displayed on the screen. (8.08)

_____ 4. A buffer is a segment of memory or storage in which items are placed while waiting to be transferred from an <u>input device</u> or to an output device. (8.11)

_____ 5. A <u>utility program</u> is a program that assesses and reports information about various computer resources and devices. (8.15)

_____ 6. A disk defragmenter is a <u>utility</u> that reorganizes the files and unused space on a computer's hard disk so the operating system accesses data more quickly and programs run faster. (8.17)

_____ 7. A stand-alone operating system is a complete operating system that works on a desktop computer, notebook computer, or <u>mobile computing device</u>. (8.20)

_____ 8. Linux is IBM's GUI multitasking client operating system that supports networking, Java, the Internet, and <u>speech recognition</u>. (8.24)

_____ 9. Most antivirus programs do not protect against worms or <u>Trojan horses</u>. (8.28)

_____ 10. A personal firewall is a <u>utility program</u> that detects and protects a personal computer from unauthorized intrusions. (8.29)

CHAPTER 8 **CHECKPOINT** ◀ Previous | Next ▶

MULTIPLE CHOICE Select the best answer. (See page numbers in parentheses.)

1. The _____ chip, which uses battery power, stores configuration information about the computer. (8.06)
   a. BIOS
   b. POST
   c. CMOS
   d. RAM

2. In most cases, drive _____ (the hard disk) is the boot drive from which a personal computer starts. (8.07)
   a. A
   b. B
   c. C
   d. D

3. Many current _____ operating systems incorporate features similar to those of a Web browser, such as links and navigation buttons. (8.08)
   a. command-line interface
   b. menu-driven interface
   c. graphical user interface
   d. all of the above

4. When an operating system spends much of its time paging, instead of executing application software, it is said to be _____. (8.11)
   a. booting
   b. thrashing
   c. spooling
   d. formatting

5. Encryption is the process of _____. (8.15)
   a. encoding data and information into an unreadable form
   b. recording successful and unsuccessful logon attempts in a file
   c. establishing a user account that allows a user to log on to a network
   d. entering a user name and password

6. Windows XP includes a(n) _____ called Windows Explorer. (8.16)
   a. image viewer
   b. disk scanner
   c. uninstaller
   d. file manager

7. Defragmenting reorganizes the files on a disk so they are located in _____ access time. (8.17)
   a. noncontiguous sectors, which slows
   b. noncontiguous sectors, which speeds
   c. contiguous sectors, which slows
   d. contiguous sectors, which speeds

8. _____ hardly is used today because it does not offer a GUI and it cannot take full advantage of modern 32-bit personal computer processors. (8.20)
   a. DOS
   b. Windows XP
   c. Mac OS X
   d. UNIX

9. Apple's _____ has set the standard for operating system ease of use and has been the model for most of the new GUIs. (8.22)
   a. OS/2 Warp Client operating system
   b. Macintosh operating system
   c. Windows XP operating system
   d. Linux operating system

10. In addition to being a stand-alone operating system, _____ also is a network operating system. (8.25)
    a. DOS
    b. UNIX
    c. NetWare
    d. Windows XP

11. _____, developed by Sun Microsystems, manages high-traffic accounts and incorporates security necessary for Web transactions. (8.26)
    a. Solaris
    b. Linux
    c. Windows Server 2003
    d. OS/2 Warp Server for e-business

12. Palm OS is an embedded operating system used with _____. (8.27)
    a. a specific type of PDA called a Pocket PC
    b. digital cameras, DVD players, and smart displays
    c. PDAs such as Visor and CLIE
    d. smart phones

13. A _____ is a malicious-logic program that does not replicate itself to other computers. (8.28)
    a. virus
    b. Trojan horse
    c. worm
    d. all of the above

14. Two popular stand-alone _____ are PKZIP and WinZip. (8.30)
    a. antivirus programs
    b. personal computer maintenance utilities
    c. personal firewalls
    d. file compression utilities

CHECKPOINT CHAPTER 8

MATCHING   Match the terms with their definitions. (See page numbers in parentheses.)

_____ 1. recovery disk (8.07)

_____ 2. fault-tolerant computer (8.10)

_____ 3. page (8.11)

_____ 4. buffer (8.11)

_____ 5. interrupt request line (IRQ) (8.13)

_____ 6. password (8.15)

_____ 7. shortcut (8.16)

_____ 8. restore program (8.18)

_____ 9. proprietary software (8.19)

_____ 10. uncompress (8.30)

a. program that tells the operating system how to communicate with a device

b. communications line between a device and the processor

c. continues to operate when one of its components fails

d. private combination of characters associated with a user name

e. contains a few system files that will start the computer

f. reverses the backup process and restores backed up files

g. restore a zipped file to its original form

h. with virtual memory, the amount of data and program instructions that can be swapped at a given time

i. icon on the desktop that provides immediate access to a program or file

j. segment of memory or storage in which items are placed while waiting to be transferred

k. privately owned and limited to a specific vendor or computer model

l. contains a list of programs that open when a computer boots up

SHORT ANSWER   Write a brief answer to each of the following questions.

1. How is a cold boot different from a warm boot? _____ How is a memory-resident part of an operating system different from a nonresident part of an operating system? _____

2. What is a user interface? _____ How are a command-line interface, a menu-driven interface, and a graphical user interface different? _____

3. How is a single user/single tasking operating system different from a single user/multitasking operating system? _____ What is preemptive multitasking? _____

4. What are Web services? _____ What four products are included in the Windows Server 2003 family? _____

5. What is a malicious-logic program? _____ How is a worm different from a Trojan horse? _____

WORKING TOGETHER   Working with a group of your classmates, complete the following team exercises.

1. Most application programs are designed to be used with specific operating systems. When you purchase software, you should read the packaging to determine whether it is compatible with your computer's operating system. Have each member of your team visit a computer software vendor and find four application programs of interest. What operating system is required for each application? What is the earliest version of the operating system that can be used? Meet with the members of your team and compare your findings. Based on your results, what operating system would you choose? Use PowerPoint to create a group presentation and share your findings with the class.

2. Choose one Issue from the following issues in this chapter: Should Manufacturers Bundle Applications? (8.13), Would You Share Your Password? (8.15), Would You Like an Operating System with That? (8.19), or Is Open Source Software a Good Idea? (8.24). Use the Web and/or print media to research the issue. Then, present a debate for the class, with different members of your team supporting different responses to the questions that accompany the issue.

3. The Buyer's Guide on page 8.44 offers tips on buying a computer. Have each member of your team answer the four questions presented in the Buyer's Guide to determine the type of computer he or she needs. Then, each team member should visit one or more computer vendors and, using the guidelines and tools presented in the Buyer's Guide, find the "perfect" computer. Later, meet with the members of your team and compare your results. How are the computers similar? How are they different? Use PowerPoint to create a group presentation and share your findings with the class.

CHAPTER 8   LEARN IT ONLINE

◄● Previous | Next ●►

Use the Learn It Online exercises to reinforce your understanding of the chapter concepts.

■ WEB INSTRUCTIONS:

To display this page from the Web, start your browser and enter the Web address **scsite.com/dc2004/ch8/learn**.

1 At The Movies – Linux Gets Personal

To view the Linux Gets Personal movie, click the number 1 button. Watch the movie, and then complete the exercise by answering the question below. It looks like Microsoft Windows has some meaningful competition. The Linux operating system has shown itself to be easy to transition to from Windows, apparently more reliable in networking situations, and, at the price of free, it decidedly is less expensive. Though Linux is free, aligned companies make their money by providing customization services and selling new applications. Major companies, including IBM, and HP, have formed an alliance to develop desktop office software that competes with Microsoft. Is Linux a boon to, or will it just complicate things for, computer users?

2 Shelly Cashman Series Evaluating Operating Systems Lab

Follow the instructions in Learn It Online 2 on page 1.46 to start and use the Shelly Cashman Series Evaluating Operating Systems Lab. If you are running from the Web, enter the Web address **scsite.com/sclabs/menu** or display the Learn It Online page (see instructions at the top of this page) and then click the number 2 button.

3 Shelly Cashman Series Working at Your Computer Lab

Follow the instructions in Learn It Online 3 on page 1.46 to start and use the Shelly Cashman Series Working at Your Computer Lab. If you are running from the Web, enter the Web address **scsite.com/sclabs/menu** or display the Learn It Online page (see instructions at the top of this page) and then click the number 3 button.

4 Practice Test

Click the number 4 button. Answer each question. When completed, enter your name and click the Grade Test button to submit the quiz for grading. Make a note of any missed questions. If required, print a copy to submit to your instructor.

5 Web Guide

Click the number 5 button to display the Guide to Web Sites and Searching Techniques Web page. Click Reference and then click Webopedia. Search for operating system. Click one of the operating system links. Prepare a brief report on your findings and submit your assignment to your instructor.

6 Scavenger Hunt

Click the number 6 button. Print a copy of the Scavenger Hunt page; use this page to write down your answers as you search the Web. Submit your completed page to your instructor.

7 Who Wants to Be a Computer Genius?

Click the number 7 button to find out if you are a computer genius. Directions on how to play the game will display. When you are ready to play, click the Play button. Submit your score to your instructor.

LEARN IT ONLINE CHAPTER 8

8 Wheel of Terms

Click the number 8 button to reinforce important terms you learned in this chapter by playing the Shelly Cashman Series version of this popular game. Directions on how to play the game will display. When you are ready to play, click the Play button. Submit your score to your instructor.

9 Career Corner

Click the number 9 button to display the QuintEssential Careers page. Click one of the tutorial links and complete the tutorial. Prepare a brief report describing what you learned. Submit the report to your instructor.

10 Search Sleuth

Click the number 10 button to learn search techniques that will help make you a research expert. Submit the completed assignment to your instructor.

11 Crossword Puzzle Challenge

Click the number 11 button. Complete the puzzle to reinforce skills you learned in this chapter. Directions on how to play the game will display. When you are ready to play, click the Play button. Submit the completed puzzle to your instructor.

12 A Picture Is Worth a Thousand Words

Although she is not a programmer, Susan Kare's impact on the modern graphical user interface has been substantial. Kare is the person responsible for many of the icons you see in today's graphical interfaces. According to *Forbes* magazine, "When it comes to giving personality to what otherwise might be cold and uncaring office machines, Kare is the queen of look and feel." Click the number 11 button to learn more about Susan Kare and her approach to developing icons.

13 In the News

When Windows XP was launched in October 2001, hundreds queued up at computer outlets. It is unclear, however, whether the anticipation was caused by the new operating system or by the promotions many dealers offered. Click the number 12 button and read a news article about the impact, quality, or promotion of an operating system. What operating system was it? What was done to sell the operating system? Is the operating system recommended? Why or why not?

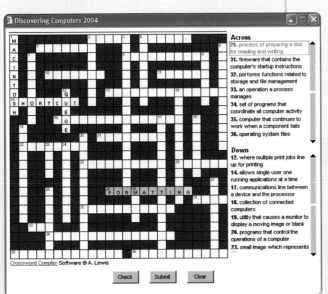

8.42

THOMSON
★
COURSE TECHNOLOGY™

Discovering Computers 2004 A Gateway to Information
Go To | TOC | Chapter 1 | 2 | 3 | 4 | 5 | 6 | 7 | 8 | 9 | 10 | 11 | 12 | 13 | 14 | 15 | Home |

CHAPTER 8 LAB EXERCISES

◀• Previous | Next •▶

Use the Lab Exercises to gain hands-on computer experience.

■ WEB INSTRUCTIONS:

To display this page from the Web, start your browser and enter the Web address **scsite.com/dc2004/ch8/lab**.

1 About Windows

This exercise uses Windows XP procedures. Click the Start button on the taskbar and then click My Computer on the Start menu. When the My Computer window is displayed, click Help on the menu bar and then click About Windows. Answer the following questions:

- What version of Windows is being used?
- To whom is Windows licensed?
- How much physical memory is available to Windows?

Click the OK button in the About Windows dialog box. Close the My Computer window.

2 Using a Screen Saver

This exercise uses Windows XP/2000/98 procedures. Right-click an empty area on the desktop and then click Properties on the shortcut menu. When the Display Properties dialog box is displayed (as shown in the figure below), click the Screen Saver tab. Click the Screen saver box arrow and then click any new screen saver. Click the Preview button to display the actual screen saver. Move the mouse to make the screen saver disappear. Answer the following questions:

- How many screen savers are available in your Screen saver list?
- How many minutes does your system wait before activating a screen saver?
- What other options are available?

Click the Cancel button in the Display Properties dialog box.

3 Changing Desktop Colors

This exercise uses Windows XP procedures. Right-click an empty area on the desktop and then click Properties on the shortcut menu. When the Display Properties dialog box is displayed, click the Appearance tab. Perform the following tasks: (1) Click the Question Mark button on the title bar and then click the Color scheme box. When the pop-up window displays, right-click it. Click Print Topic on the shortcut menu and then click the OK button in the Print dialog box. Click anywhere to remove the pop-up window. (2) Click the Color scheme box arrow and then click Silver to display the Silver color scheme. (3) Select a color scheme you like. Click the Cancel button in the Display Properties dialog box.

4 Customizing the Desktop for Multiple Users

This exercise uses Windows 2000/98 procedures. If more than one person uses a computer, how can you customize the desktop for each user? Click the Start button on the taskbar and then click Help on the Start menu. Click the Contents tab. Click the Exploring Your Computer book. Click The Windows Desktop book. Click the Customize Windows 2000/98 book. Click the Multiple Users book. Click an appropriate Help topic and read the information to answer each of the following questions:

- How can you display a list of users at startup?
- How can you add personalized settings for a new user?
- How do you log off the computer so someone else can use it?
- How can you change desktop settings for multiple users?

Click the Close button to close the Windows Help window.

WEB RESEARCH

CHAPTER 8

Use the Web Research exercises to learn more about the special features in this chapter.

WEB INSTRUCTIONS:

Use the link in each exercise or a search engine such as Google (google.com) to research the topic. Then, write a one-page, double-spaced report or create a presentation, unless otherwise directed below. Page numbers on which information can be found are in parentheses.

1   **Issue**   Choose one Issue from the following issues in this chapter: Should Manufacturers Bundle Applications? (8.13), Would You Share Your Password? (8.15), Would You Like an Operating System with That? (8.19), or Is Open Source Software a Good Idea? (8.24). Use the Web to research the issue. Discuss the issue with classmates, instructors, and friends. Address the questions that accompany the issue in a report or presentation.

2   **Apply It**   Choose one of the following Apply It features in this chapter: Customizing the Startup Folder (8.06) or Tune Up Your Computer for Optimum Performance (8.17). Use the Web to gather additional information about the topic. Print two Web pages that relate to the Apply It. Detail in a report or presentation what you learned.

3   **Career Corner**   Read the Career Corner article in this chapter (8.30). Use the Web to find out more about the career. Describe the career in a report or presentation.

4   **Companies on the Cutting Edge**   Choose one of the Companies on the Cutting Edge in this chapter (8.32). Use the Web to research the company further. Explain in a report or presentation how this company has contributed to computer technology.

5   **Technology Trailblazers**   Choose one of the Technology Trailblazers in this chapter (8.33). Use the Web to research the person further. Explain in a report or presentation how this individual has affected the way people use, or think about, computers.

6   **Picture Yourself with a Virus-Infected Computer**   Read the Picture Yourself with a Virus-Infected Computer story at the beginning of this chapter (8.00). Use the Web to research computer viruses further. Describe in a report or presentation the ways in which you might prevent, or respond to, a virus-infected computer.

7   **High-Tech Talk**   Read the High-Tech Talk feature in this chapter (8.31). Use the Web to find out more about the topic. Summarize in a report or presentation what you learned.

8   **Web Links**   Review the Web Link boxes found in the margins of this chapter. Visit five of the Web Link sites. Print the main Web page for each site you visit. Choose one of the Web pages and then summarize in one paragraph the content of the Web page.

9   **Looking Ahead**   Choose one of the Looking Ahead articles in this chapter: Trustworthy Computing — Heart of Windows Upgrade (8.21) or Freon Possible Xbox Successor (8.26). Use the Web to find out more about the topic. Detail in a report or presentation what you learned.

10   **FAQ**   Choose one FAQ found in this chapter. Use the Web to find out more about the topic. Summarize in one paragraph what you learned.

11   **Buyer's Guide**   Read the Buyer's Guide Special Feature that follows this chapter (8.44-8.66). Select the area (purchasing a desktop computer, purchasing a notebook computer, purchasing a handheld computer, installing a computer, or maintaining a computer) in which you are most interested. Visit at least three of the Web addresses given to learn more about your selection. Explain what you learn in a report or presentation.

12   **Making Use of the Web**   Read the Weather, Sports, News section of Making Use of the Web in Appendix A (A.16). Complete the Weather, Sports, News Web Exercises at the end of the section (A.17). Answer the questions posed in each exercise.

Buyer's Guide 2004

HOW TO PURCHASE, INSTALL, AND MAINTAIN A PERSONAL COMPUTER

(a) Desktop computer

(c) Tablet PC

(b) Notebook computer

(d) PDA

For what purposes will I use the computer?

Should I buy a desktop or mobile computer?

Should the computer I buy be compatible with the computers at school or work?

Should I buy a Mac or PC?

FIGURE 1

At some point, perhaps while you are taking this course, you may decide to buy a personal computer. The decision is an important one, which will require an investment of both time and money. As with many buyers, you may have little computer experience and find yourself unsure of how to proceed. You can get started by talking to your friends, coworkers, and instructors about their computers. What type of computers did they buy? Why? For what purposes do they use their computers? You also should answer the following four questions to help narrow your choices to a specific computer type, before reading the Buyer's Guide guidelines for purchasing a desktop computer, notebook computer, Tablet PC, or PDA.

1 **Do you want a desktop or mobile computer?**

A desktop computer (Figure 1a) is designed as a stationary device that sits on or below a desk or table in a location such as a home, office, or dormitory room. A desktop computer must be plugged into an electrical outlet to operate. A mobile computer or device, such as a notebook computer (Figure 1b), Tablet PC (Figure 1c), and PDA (Figure 1d), is smaller, more portable, and has a battery that allows you to operate it for a period without an electrical outlet.

Desktop computers are a good option if you work mostly in one place and have plenty of space in your work area. Desktop computers generally give you more performance for your money and are easier to upgrade than mobile computers.

Increasingly more desktop computer users are buying notebook computers to take advantage of their portability to work in the library, while traveling, and at home. The past disadvantages of notebook computers, such as lower processor speeds, poor-quality monitors, weight, short battery life, and significantly higher prices, have all but disappeared when compared with desktop computers.

If you are thinking of using a mobile computer to take notes in class or in business meetings, then consider a Tablet PC with handwriting and drawing capabilities. Typically, note-taking involves writing text notes and drawing charts, schematics, and other illustrations. By allowing you to write and draw directly on the screen with a digital pen, a Tablet PC eliminates the distracting sound of the notebook keyboard tapping and allows you to capture drawings. Some notebook computers can convert to Tablet PCs.

A PDA is a lightweight mobile device that easily fits in your pocket, which makes it ideal if you require a mobile computing device as you move from place to place. PDAs provide personal organizer functions, such as a calendar, appointment book, address book, and thousands of other applications. Some PDAs also function as a cellular telephone. The small size of the processor, screen, and keyboard, however, limit a PDA's capabilities when compared with a desktop or notebook computer. For this reason, most people who purchase PDAs also have a desktop or notebook computer to handle heavy-duty applications.

Drawbacks of mobile computers and devices are that they tend to have a shorter useful lifetime than desktop computers, cost more than desktop computers, and lack the high-end capabilities. Their portability makes them susceptible to vibrations, heat or cold, and accidental drops, which can cause components such as hard disks or monitors to fail. Also, because of their size and portability, they are easy to lose and are the prime targets of thieves.

2 **For what purposes will you use the computer?** Having a general idea of the purposes for which you want to use your computer will help you decide on the type of computer to buy. At this point in your research, it is not necessary to know the exact application software titles or version numbers you might want to use. Knowing that you plan to use the computer primarily to create word processing, spreadsheet, database, and presentation documents, however, will point you in the direction of a desktop or notebook computer. If you plan to use a mobile device to get organized, then a PDA may be your best choice. If you want the portability of a PDA, but need more computing power, then a Tablet PC may be the best alternative. You also must consider that some application software runs only on a Mac, while others run only on a PC with the Windows operating system. Still other software may run only on a PC running the UNIX or Linux operating system.

3 **Should the computer be compatible with the computers at school or work?** If you plan to bring work home, telecommute, or take distance education courses, then you should purchase a computer that is compatible

with those at school or work.

Compatibility is primarily a software issue. If your computer runs the same operating system version, such as Windows XP, and the same application software, such as Office XP, then your computer will be able to read documents created at school or work and vice versa. Incompatible hardware can become an issue if you plan to connect directly to a school or office network using a cable or wireless technology. You usually can obtain the minimum system requirements from the Information Technology department at your school or workplace.

4 **Should the computer be a Mac or PC?** If you ask a friend, coworker, or instructor, which is better — a Mac or a PC — you may be surprised by the strong opinion expressed in the response. No other topic in the computer industry causes more heated debate. The Mac has strengths, especially in the areas of graphics, movies, photos, and music. The PC, however, has become the industry standard with 95 percent of the market share. Figure 2 compares features of the Mac and PC in several different areas.

Area	Comparison
Cost and availability	A Mac has slightly higher prices than a PC. Mac peripherals also are more expensive. The PC offers more available models from a wide range of vendors. You can custom build, upgrade, and expand a PC for less money than a Mac.
Exterior design	The Mac has a more distinct and stylish appearance than most PCs.
Free software	Although free software for the Mac is available on the Internet, significantly more free software applications are available for the PC.
Market share	The PC dominates the personal computer market. While the Mac sells well in education, publishing, Web design, graphics, and music, the PC is the overwhelming favorite of businesses.
Operating system	Both Mac OS X and Windows XP are stable. Users claim that Mac OS X provides a better all-around user experience than Windows XP. The PC supports other operating systems, such as Linux and UNIX.
Program control	Both have simple and intuitive graphical user interfaces. The Mac relies more on the mouse and less on keyboard shortcuts than the PC. The mouse on the Mac has one button, whereas the mouse on a PC has a minimum of two buttons.
Software availability	The basic application software most users require, such as the Office suite, is available for both the Mac and PC. More specialized software, however, often is only available for PCs. Many programs are released for PCs long before they are released for Macs.
Speed	The PC has faster processors than the Mac to choose from.
Viruses	Dramatically fewer viruses attack Macs. Mac viruses also generally are less infectious than PC viruses.

FIGURE 2 Comparison of Mac and PC features.

Overall, the Mac and PC have more similarities than differences, and you should consider cost, compatibility, and other factors when choosing whether to purchase a Mac or PC.

After evaluating the answers to these four questions, you should have a general idea of how you plan to use your computer and the type of computer you want to buy. Once you have decided on the type of computer you want, you can follow the guidelines presented in this Buyer's Guide to help you purchase a specific computer of that type, along with software, peripherals, and other accessories.

This first set of guidelines will help you purchase, install, and maintain a desktop computer. Many of the guidelines presented also apply to the purchase of a mobile computer or device, such as a notebook computer, Tablet PC, and PDA. Later in this special feature, sections on purchasing a notebook computer, PDA, or Tablet PC address additional considerations specific to those computer types.

Type of Computers	Web Site	URL
PC	Computer Shopper	shopper.cnet.com
	PC World Magazine	pcworld.com
	BYTE Magazine	byte.com
	PC Magazine	zdnet.com/reviews
	Yahoo! Computers	computers.yahoo.com
	Microsoft Network	eshop.msn.com
	Dave's Guide to Buying a Home Computer	css.msu.edu/PC-Guide/
Mac	ZDNet News	zdnet.com/mac
	Macworld Magazine	macworld.com
	Apple	apple.com
	Switch to Mac Campaign	apple.com/switch

For an updated list of hardware and software reviews and their Web site addresses, visit scsite.com/dc2004/ch8/buyers.

FIGURE 3 Hardware and software reviews.

HOW TO PURCHASE A DESKTOP COMPUTER

Once you have decided that a desktop computer is most suited to your computing needs, the next step is to determine specific software, hardware, peripheral devices, and services to purchase, as well as with where to buy the computer.

1 **Determine the specific software you want to use on your computer.** Before deciding to purchase a particular program, be sure it contains the features necessary for the tasks you want to perform. Rely on the computer users in whom you have confidence to help you decide on the software to use. The minimum requirements of the application software you select may determine the operating system (Windows XP, Linux, UNIX, Mac OS X) you need. If you have decided to use a particular operating system that does not support application software you want to use, you may be able to purchase the similar application software from other manufacturers.

Many Web sites and trade magazines, such as those listed in Figure 3, provide reviews of software products. These Web sites frequently have articles that rate computers and software on cost, performance, and support.

Your hardware requirements depend on the minimum requirements of the application software you will run on your computer. Some application software requires more memory and disk space than others, as well as additional input, output, and storage devices. For example, suppose you want to run software that can copy one CD's or DVD's contents directly to another CD or DVD, without first copying the data to your hard disk. To support that, you should consider a desktop computer or a high-end notebook computer, because the computer will need two CD or DVD drives: one that reads from a CD or DVD, and one that reads from and writes on a CD or DVD. If you plan to run software that allows your computer to work as an entertainment system, then you will need a CD or DVD drive, quality speakers, and an upgraded sound card.

2 **Look for bundled software.** When you purchase a computer, it may come bundled with several programs. Some sellers even let you choose which application software you want. Remember, however, that bundled software has value only if you would have purchased the software even if it had not come with the computer. At the very least, you probably will want word processing software and a browser to access the Internet. If you need additional applications, such as a spreadsheet, a database, or presentation graphics, consider purchasing a software suite, such as Microsoft Works, Microsoft Office, or Sun StarOffice™, which include several programs at a reduced price.

3 **Avoid buying the least powerful computer available.** Once you know the application software you want to use, you then can consider the following important criteria about the computer's components: (1) processor speed, (2) size and types of memory (RAM) and storage, (3) types of input/output devices, (4) types of ports and adapter cards, and (5) types of communications devices.

The information in Figures 4 and 5 can help you determine what system components are best for you. Figure 4 outlines considerations for specific hardware components. Figure 5 (on page 8.07) provides a Base Components worksheet that lists PC recommendations for each category of user discussed in this book: Home User, Small Office/Home Office User, Mobile User, Large Business User, and Power User. In the worksheet, the Home User category is divided into two groups: Application Home User and Game Home User. The Mobile User recommendations list criteria for a notebook computer, but do not include the PDA or Tablet PC options.

Computer technology changes rapidly, meaning a computer that seems powerful enough today may not serve your computing needs in a few years. In fact, studies show that many users regret not buying a more powerful computer. To avoid this, plan to buy a computer that will last you for two to three years. You can help delay obsolescence by purchasing the fastest processor, the most memory, and the largest hard disk you can afford. If you must buy a less powerful computer, be sure you can upgrade it with additional memory, components, and peripheral devices as your computer requirements grow.

CD/DVD Drives: Most computers come with a 32X to 48X speed CD-ROM drive that can read CDs. If you plan to write music, audio files, and documents on a CD or DVD, then you should consider upgrading to a CD-RW. An even better alternative is to upgrade to a DVD+RW/CD-RW combination drive. It allows you to read DVDs and CDs and to write data on (burn) a DVD or CD. A DVD has a capacity of at least 4.7 GB versus the 650 MB capacity of a CD.

Card Reader: A card reader is useful for transferring data directly from a removable flash memory card, such as the ones used in your camera or music player. Make sure the card reader can read the flash memory cards that you use.

Digital Camera: Consider an inexpensive point-and-shoot digital camera. They are small enough to carry around, usually operate automatically in terms of lighting and focus, and contain storage cards for storing photographs. A 1.3- to 2.2-megapixel camera with an 8 MB or 16 MB storage card is fine for creating images for use on the Web or to send via e-mail.

Digital Video Capture Device: A digital video capture device allows you to connect your computer to a camcorder or VCR and record, edit, manage, and then write video back to a VCR tape, a CD, or a DVD. The digital video capture device can be an external device or an adapter card. To create quality video (true 30 frames per second, full-sized TV), the digital video capture device should have a USB 2.0 or FireWire port. You will find that a standard USB port is too slow to maintain video quality. You also will need sufficient storage: an hour of a data on VCR tape takes up about 5 GB of disk storage.

Floppy Disk Drive: Make sure the computer you purchase has a standard 3.5", 1.44 MB floppy disk drive. A floppy disk drive is useful for backing up and transferring files.

Hard Disk: It is recommended that you buy a computer with 40 to 60 GB if your primary interests are browsing the Web and using e-mail and Office suite-type applications; 60 to 80 GB if you also want to edit digital photographs; 80 to 100 GB if you plan to edit digital video or manipulate large audio files even occasionally; and 100 to 160 GB if you will edit digital video, movies, or photography often or store audio files and music or consider yourself to be a power user.

Joystick/Wheel: If you use your computer to play games, then you will want to purchase a joystick or a wheel. These devices, especially the more expensive ones, provide for realistic game play with force feedback, programmable buttons, and specialized levers and wheels.

Keyboard: The keyboard is one of the more important devices used to communicate with the computer. For this reason, make sure the keyboard you purchase has 101 to 105 keys, is comfortable, easy to use, and has a USB connection. A wireless keyboard should be considered, especially if you have a small desk area.

Microphone: If you plan to record audio or use speech recognition to enter text and commands, then purchase a close-talk headset with gain adjustment support.

Modem: Most computers come with a modem so that you can use your telephone line to dial out and access the Internet. Some modems also have fax capabilities. Your modem should be rated at 56 Kbps.

Monitor: The monitor is where you will view documents, read e-mail messages, and view pictures. A minimum of a 17" screen is recommended, but if you are planning to use your computer for graphic design or game playing, then you may want to purchase a 19" or 21" monitor. The LCD flat panel monitor should be considered, especially if space is an issue.

FIGURE 4 Hardware guidelines.

(Continued)

(Continued from previous page)

Mouse: As you work with your computer, you use the mouse constantly. For this reason, spend a few extra dollars, if necessary, and purchase a mouse with an optical sensor and USB connection. The optical sensor replaces the need for a mouse ball, which means you do not need a mouse pad. For a PC, make sure your mouse has a wheel, which acts as a third button in addition to the top two buttons on the left and right. An ergonomic design is also important because your hand is on the mouse most of the time when you are using your computer. A wireless mouse should be considered to eliminate the cord and allow you to work at short distances from your computer.

Network Card: If you plan to connect to a network or use broadband (cable or DSL) to connect to the Internet, then you will need to purchase a network card. Broadband connections require a 10/100 PCI Ethernet network card.

Printer: Your two basic printer choices are ink-jet and laser. Color ink-jet printers cost on average between $50 and $300. Laser printers cost from $300 to $2,000. In general, the cheaper the printer, the lower the resolution and speed, and the more often you are required to change the ink cartridge or toner. Laser printers print faster and with a higher quality than an ink-jet, and their toner on average costs less. If you want color, then go with a high-end ink-jet printer to ensure quality of print. Duty cycle (the number of pages you expect to print each month) also should be a determining factor. If your duty cycle is on the low end — hundreds of pages per month — then stay with a high-end ink-jet printer, rather than purchasing a laser printer. If you plan to print photographs taken with a digital camera, then you should purchase a photo printer. A photo printer is a dye-sublimation printer or an ink-jet printer with higher resolution and features that allow you to print quality photographs.

Processor: For a PC, a 2.0 GHz Intel or AMD processor is more than enough processor power for application home and small office/home office users. Game home, large business, and power users should upgrade to faster processors.

RAM: RAM plays a vital role in the speed of your computer. Make sure the computer you purchase has at least 256 MB of RAM. If you have extra money to invest in your computer, then consider increasing the RAM to 512 MB or more. The extra money for RAM will be well spent.

Scanner: The most popular scanner purchased with a computer today is the flatbed scanner. When evaluating a flatbed scanner, check the color depth and resolution. Do not buy anything less than a color depth of 48 bits and a resolution of 1200 x 2400 dpi. The higher the color depth, the more accurate the color. A higher resolution picks up the more subtle gradations of color.

Sound Card: Most sound cards today support the Sound Blaster and General MIDI standards and should be capable of recording and playing digital audio. If you plan to turn your computer into an entertainment system or are a game home user, then you will want to spend the extra money and upgrade from the standard sound card.

Speakers: Once you have a good sound card, quality speakers and a separate subwoofer that amplifies the bass frequencies of the speakers can turn your computer into a premium stereo system.

Video Graphics Card: Most standard video cards satisfy the monitor display needs of application home and small office users. If you are a game home user or a graphic designer, you will want to upgrade to a higher quality video card. The higher refresh rates will further enhance the display of games, graphics, and movies.

PC Video Camera: A PC video camera is a small camera used to capture and display live video (in some cases with sound), primarily on a Web page. You also can capture, edit, and share video and still photos. The camera sits on your monitor or desk. Recommended minimum specifications include 640 x 480 resolution, a video with a rate of 30 frames per second, and a USB 2.0 or FireWire connection.

Wireless LAN Access Point: A **Wireless LAN Access Point** allows you to network several computers, so they can share files and access the Internet through a single cable modem or DSL connection. Each device that you connect requires a wireless card. A Wireless LAN Access Point can offer a range of operation up to several hundred feet, so be sure the device has a high-powered antenna.

Zip® Drive: Consider purchasing a Zip® or Peerless® disk drive to back up important files. The Zip® drive, which has a capacity of up to 750 MB, is sufficient for most users. An alternative to purchasing a backup drive is to purchase a CD-RW or DVD+RW and burn backups of key files on a CD or DVD.

FIGURE 4 Hardware guidelines.

BASE COMPONENTS

	Application Home User	Game Home User	Small Office/Home Office User	Mobile User	Large Business User	Power User
HARDWARE						
Processor	Pentium®4 at 2.0 GHz	Pentium®4 at 3.0 GHz	Pentium®4 at 2.0 GHz	Pentium®4 at 1.8 GHz	Pentium®4 at 3.0 GHz	Multiple Itanium™ at 2.5 GHz
RAM	256 MB	512 MB	256 MB	256 MB	512 MB	1 GB
Cache	256 KB L2	512 KB L2	512 KB L2	512 KB L2	512 KB L2	2 MB L3
Hard Disk	60 GB	120 GB	100 GB	40 GB	160 GB	160 GB
Monitor/LCD Flat Panel	17" or 19"	23"	19" or 21"	16.1" SuperVGA+ TFT	19" or 21"	23"
Video Graphics Card	64 MB	128 MB	64 MB	16 MB	64 MB	128 MB
CD/DVD Bay 1	48x CD-ROM	48x CD-ROM	48x CD-ROM	24x CD-ROM	48x CD-ROM	48x CD-ROM
CD/DVD Bay 2	32x/10x/40x CD-RW/DVD	DVD+RW/CD-RW	32x/10x/40x CD-RW/DVD	24x CD-RW/DVD	DVD+RW/CD-RW	DVD+RW/CD-RW
Floppy Disk Drive	3.5"	3.5"	3.5"	3.5"	3.5"	3.5"
Printer	Color Ink-Jet	Color Ink-Jet	10 ppm Laser	Portable Ink-Jet	24 ppm Laser	10 ppm Laser
PC Video Camera	Yes	Yes	Yes	Yes	Yes	Yes
Fax/Modem	Yes	Yes	Yes	Yes	Yes	Yes
Microphone	Close-Talk Headset with Gain Adjustment	Close-Talk Headset with Gain Adjustment	Close-Talk Headset with Gain Adjustment	Close-Talk Headset with Gain Adjustment	Close-Talk Headset with Gain Adjustment	Close-Talk Headset with Gain Adjustment
Speakers	Stereo	Full-Dolby Surround	Stereo	Stereo	Stereo	Full-Dolby
Pointing Device	IntelliMouse or Optical Mouse	Optical Mouse and Joystick	IntelliMouse or Optical Mouse	Touchpad or Pointing Stick and Optical Mouse	IntelliMouse or Optical Mouse	IntelliMouse or Optical Mouse and Joystick
Keyboard	Yes	Yes	Yes	Built-In	Yes	Yes
Backup Disk/Tape Drive	750 MB Zip®	10 GB Peerless™	10 GB Peerless™	10 GB Peerless™	20 GB Peerless™	20 GB Peerless™
Sound Card	Sound Blaster Compatible	Sound Blaster Compatible	Sound Blaster Compatible	Built-In	Sound Blaster Compatible	Sound Blaster
Network Card	Yes	Yes	Yes	Yes	Yes	Yes
TV-Out Connector	Yes	Yes	Yes	Yes	Yes	Yes
USB Port	Yes	Yes	Yes	Yes	Yes	Yes
FireWire Port	Yes	Yes	Yes	Yes	Yes	Yes
SOFTWARE						
Operating System	Windows XP Home Edition	Windows XP Home Edition	Windows XP Professional	Windows XP Professional	Windows XP Professional	Windows XP Professional
Application Suite	Office XP Standard Edition	Office XP Standard Edition	Office XP Small Business Edition	Office XP Small Business Edition	Office XP Professional with FrontPage 2002	Office XP Professional with FrontPage 2002
AntiVirus	Yes, 12-Mo. Subscription	Yes, 12-Mo. Subscription	Yes, 12-Mo. Subscription	Yes, 12-Mo. Subscription	Yes, 12-Mo. Subscription	Yes, 12-Mo. Subscription
Internet Access	Cable, DSL, or Dial-up	Cable, DSL, or Dial-up	Cable, DSL, or Dial-up	Satellite or Cellular	LAN/WAN (T1/T3)	Cable or DSL
OTHER						
Surge Protector	Yes	Yes	Yes	Portable	Yes	Yes
Warranty	3-Year Limited, 1-Year Next Next Business Day On-Site Service	3-Year Limited, 1-Year Next Next Business Day On-Site Service	3-year On-Site Service	3-Year Limited, 1-Year Next Business Day On-Site Service	3-year On-Site Service	3-year On-Site Service
Other		Wheel	Postage Printer	Docking Station Carrying Case Fingerprint Scanner Portable Data Projector		Graphics Tablet Plotter or Large-Format Printer

Optional Components for all Categories	
802.11b Wireless Card	Graphics Tablet
Bluetooth™ Enabled	iPod Music Player
Biometric Input Device	IrDa Port
Card Reader	Mouse Pad/Wrist Rest
Digital Camera	Multifunction Peripheral
Digital Video Capture	Photo Printer
Digital Video Camera	Portable Data Projector
Dual-Monitor Support with Second Monitor	Scanner
Ergonomic Keyboard	TV/FM Tuner
External Hard Disk	Uninterruptible Power Supply
	USB Drive

FIGURE 5 Base computer components and optional components. A copy of the Base Components worksheet is on the Discover Data Disk. To obtain a copy of the Discover Data Disk, see the inside back cover of this book for instructions.

4 Consider upgrades to the mouse, keyboard, monitor, printer, microphone, and speakers.
You use these peripheral devices to interact with your computer, so you should make sure they are up to your standards. Review the peripheral devices listed in Figure 4 and then visit both local computer dealers and large retail stores to test the computers on display. Ask the salesperson what input and output devices would be best for you and whether you should upgrade beyond what comes standard. A few extra dollars spent on these components when you initially purchase a computer can extend its usefulness by years.

5 Determine whether you want to use telephone lines or broadband (cable or DSL) to access the Internet. If your computer has a modem, then you can access the Internet using a standard telephone line. Ordinarily, you call a local or toll-free 800 number to connect to an ISP (see Guideline 6 on the next page). Using a dial-up Internet connection is relatively inexpensive but slow.

DSL and cable connections provide much faster Internet connections, which are ideal if you want faster file download speeds for software, digital photos, and music. As you would expect, they also are more expensive. DSL, which is available through local telephone companies, also may require that you subscribe to an ISP. Cable is available through your local cable television provider and some online service providers (OSPs). If you get cable, then you would not use a separate Internet service provider or online service provider.

7 **Use a worksheet to compare computers, services, and other considerations.** You can use a separate sheet of paper to take notes on each vendor's computer and then summarize the information on a worksheet, such as the one shown in Figure 7. You can use Figure 7 to compare prices for either a PC or a MAC. Most companies advertise a price for a base computer that includes components housed in the system unit (processor, RAM, sound card, video card), disk drives (floppy disk, hard disk, CD-ROM, CD-RW, DVD-ROM, and DVD+RW), a keyboard, mouse, monitor, printer, speakers, and modem. Be aware, however, that some advertisements list prices for computers with only some of these components. Monitors and printers, for example, often are not included in a base computer's price. Depending on how you plan to use the computer, you may want to invest in additional or more powerful components. When you are comparing the prices of computers, make sure you are comparing identical or similar configurations.

Company	Service	URL
America Online	OSP	aol.com
AT&T WorldNet	ISP	www.att.net
CompuServe	OSP	compuserve.com
EarthLink®	ISP	earthlink.net
Juno®	OSP	juno.com
NetZero®	OSP	netzero.com
Prodigy™	ISP/OSP	www.prodigy.net
MSN	OSP	msn.com

For an updated list of national ISPs and OSPs and their Web site addresses, visit scsite.com/dc2004/ch8/buyers.

FIGURE 6 National ISPs and OSPs.

6 **If you are using a dial-up or wireless connection to connect to the Internet, then select an ISP or OSP.** You can access the Internet via telephone lines in one of two ways: via an ISP or an OSP. Both provide Internet access for a monthly fee that ranges from $6 to $25. If you are using DSL, you will have to pay additional costs for a residential DSL line. Local ISPs offer Internet access to users in a limited geographic region, through local telephone numbers. National ISPs provide access for users nationwide (including mobile users), through local and toll-free telephone numbers and cable. Because of their size, national ISPs generally offer more services and have a larger technical support staff than local ISPs. OSPs furnish Internet access as well as members-only features for users nationwide. Figure 6 lists several national ISPs and OSPs. Before you choose an ISP or OSP, compare such features as the number of access hours, monthly fees, available services (e-mail, Web page hosting, chat), and reliability.

PC or MAC Cost Comparison Worksheet

Dealers list prices for computers with most of these components (instead of listing individual component costs). Some dealers do not supply a monitor. Some dealers offer significant discounts, but you must subscribe to an Internet service for a specified period to receive the dicounted price. To compare computers, enter overall system price at top and enter a 0 (zero) for components included in the system cost. For any additional components not covered in the system price, enter the cost in the appropriate cells.

Items to Purchase	Desired System (PC)	Desired System (Mac)	Local Dealer #1	Local Dealer #2	Online Dealer #1	Online Dealer #2	Comments
					Price		
OVERALL SYSTEM							
Overall System Price	< $1,500	< $1,500					
HARDWARE							
Processor	Pentium® 4 at 2.0 GHz	PowerPC G4 at 800 MHz					
RAM	256 MB	256 MB					
Cache	256 KB L2	256 KB L2					
Hard Disk	80 GB	80 GB					
Monitor	17 Inch	17 Inch					
Video Graphics Card	64 MB	64 MB					
Floppy Disk Drive	3.5 Inch	3.5 Inch					
CD/DVD Bay 1	48x CD-ROM	32x/10x/40x CD-RW/DVD					
CD/DVD Bay 2	32x/10x/40x CD-RW/DVD	NA					
Speakers	Stereo	Stereo					
Sound Card	Sound Blaster Compatible	Sound Blaster Compatible					
USB Ports	2	2					
FireWire Port	2	2					
Network Card	Yes	Yes					
Fax/Modem	56 Kbps	56 Kbps					
Keyboard	Standard	Apple Pro Keyboard					
Pointing Device	IntelliMouse	Intellimouse or Apple Pro Mouse					
Microphone	Close-Talk Headset with Gain Adjustment	Close-Talk Headset with Gain Adjustment					
Printer	Color Ink-Jet	Color Ink-Jet					
Printer Cable	Yes	Yes					
Backup	250 MB Zip®	250 MB Zip®					
SOFTWARE							
Operating System	Windows XP Home Edition	Mac OS X					
Application Software	Office XP Small Business Edition	Office v.X for Mac					
Antivirus	Yes - 12 Mo. Subscription	Yes - 12 Mo. Subscription					
OTHER							
Card Reader	MemoryStick Dual	MemoryStick Dual					
Digital Camera	2-Megapixel	2-Megapixel					
Internet Connection	1-Year Subscription	1-Year Subscription					
Joystick	Yes	Yes					
PC Video Camera	With Microphone	With Microphone					
Scanner							
Surge Protector							
Warranty	3-Year On-Site Service	3-Year On-Site Service					
Wireless card	Internal	Internal					
Wireless LAN Access Point	LinkSys	Apple AirPort					
Total Cost			$.	$.	$.	$.	

FIGURE 7 A worksheet is an effective tool for summarizing and comparing the prices and components of different computer vendors. A copy of the Computer Cost Comparison Worksheet for the PC or Mac is on the Discover Data Disk. To obtain a copy of the Discover Data Disk, see the inside back cover of this book for instructions.

8 **If you are buying a new computer, you have several purchasing options: buying from your school bookstore, a local computer dealer, a local large retail store, or ordering by mail via telephone or the Web.** Each purchasing option has certain advantages. Many college bookstores, for example, sign exclusive pricing agreements with computer manufacturers and, thus, can offer student discounts. Local dealers and local large retail stores, however, more easily can provide hands-on support. Mail-order companies that sell computers by telephone or online via the Web (Figure 8) often provide the lowest prices, but extend less personal service. Some major mail-order companies, however, have started to provide next-business-day, on-site services. A credit card usually is required to buy from a mail-order company. Figure 9 lists some of the more popular mail-order companies and their Web site addresses.

Type of Computer	Company	URL
PC	Computer Shopper	shopper.cnet.com
	HP/Compaq	thenew.hp.com
	CompUSA	compusa.com
	dartek.com™	dartek.com
	Dell	dell.com
	Gateway	gateway.com
	Micron	micron.com
Macintosh	Apple Computer	store.apple.com
	Club Mac	clubmac.com
	MacConnection	macconnection.com
	MacExchange	macx.com

For an updated list of new computer mail-order companies and their Web site addresses, visit scsite.com/dc2004/ch8/buyers.

FIGURE 9 New computer mail-order companies.

FIGURE 8 Mail-order companies, such as Dell, sell computers online.

9 **If you are buying a used computer, stay with name brands such as Dell, Gateway, Hewlett-Packard, and Apple.** Although brand-name equipment can cost more, most brand-name computers have longer, more comprehensive warranties, are better supported, and have more authorized centers for repair services. As with new computers, you can purchase a used computer from local computer dealers, local large retail stores, or mail order via the telephone or the Web. Classified ads and used computer sellers offer additional outlets for purchasing used computers. Figure 10 lists several major used computer brokers and their Web site addresses.

Company	URL
Amazon.com	amazon.com
Off Lease Computer Supermarket	off-leasecomputers.com
American Computer Exchange	www.amcoex.com
U.S. Computer Exchange	uscomputerexchange.com
eBay	ebay.com

For an updated list of used computer mail-order companies and their Web site addresses, visit scsite.com/dc2004/ch8/buyers.

FIGURE 10 Used computer mail-order companies.

10 **If you have a computer and are upgrading to a new one, then consider selling or trading in the old one.** If you are a replacement buyer, your older computer still may have value. If you cannot sell the computer through the classified ads, via a Web site, or to a friend, then ask if the computer dealer will buy your old computer. An increasing number of companies are taking trade-ins, but do not expect too much money for your old computer.

11 **Be aware of hidden costs.** Before purchasing, be sure to consider any additional costs associated with buying a computer, such as an additional telephone line, a cable or DSL modem, an uninterruptible power supply (UPS), computer furniture, floppy disks and paper, and computer training classes you may want to take. Depending on where you buy your computer, the seller may be willing to include some or all of these in the computer purchase price.

12 **Consider more than just price.** The lowest-cost computer may not be the best long-term buy. Consider such intangibles as the vendor's time in business, the vendor's regard for quality, and the vendor's reputation for support. If you need to upgrade your computer often, you may want to consider a leasing arrangement, in which you pay monthly lease fees, but can upgrade or add on to your computer as your equipment needs change. No matter what type of buyer you are, insist on a 30-day, no-questions-asked return policy on your computer.

13 **Avoid restocking fees.** Some companies charge a restocking fee of 10 to 20 percent as part of their money-back return policy. In some cases, no restocking fee for hardware is applied, but it is applied for software. Ask about the existence and terms of any restocking policies before you buy.

14 **Consider purchasing an extended warranty or service plan.** If you use your computer for business or require fast resolution to major computer problems, consider purchasing an extended warranty or a service plan through a local dealer or third-party company. Most extended warranties cover the repair and replacement of computer components beyond the standard warranty. Most service plans ensure that your technical support calls receive priority response from technicians. You also can purchase an on-site service plan that states that a technician will come to your home, work, or school within 24 hours. If your computer includes a warranty and service agreement for a year or less, think about extending the service for two or three years when you buy the computer.

CENTURY COMPUTERS

Performance Guarantee

(See reverse for terms & conditions of this contract)

Invoice #: 1984409	Effective Date: 10/12/04
Invoice Date: 10/12/04	Expiration Date: 10/12/09

Customer Name: Leon, Richard	System & Serial Numbers
Date: 10/12/04	IMB computer
Address: 1123 Roxbury	S/N: US759290C
Sycamore, IL 60178	
Day phone: (815) 550-0303	
Evening Phone: (728) 550-0230	

John Smith
Print Name of Century's Authorized Signature

10/12/04
Date

---

15 **Use a credit card to purchase your new computer.** Many credit cards offer purchase protection and extended warranty benefits that cover you in case of loss of or damage to purchased goods. Paying by credit card also gives you time to install and use the computer before you have to pay for it. Finally, if you are dissatisfied with the computer and are unable to reach an agreement with the seller, paying by credit card gives you certain rights regarding withholding payment until the dispute is resolved. Check your credit card terms for specific details.

HOW TO PURCHASE A NOTEBOOK COMPUTER

If you need computing capability when you travel or to use in lecture or meetings, you may find a notebook computer to be an appropriate choice. The guidelines mentioned in the previous section also apply to the purchase of a notebook computer. The following are additional considerations unique to notebook computers.

1 Purchase a notebook computer with a sufficiently large active-matrix screen.
Active-matrix screens display high-quality color that is viewable from all angles. Less expensive, passive-matrix screens sometimes are difficult to see in low-light conditions and cannot be viewed from an angle. Notebook computers typically come with a 12.1-inch, 13.3-inch, 14.1-inch, 15-inch, or 16.1-inch display. For most users, a 14.1-inch display is satisfactory. If you intend to use your notebook computer as a desktop computer replacement, however, you may opt for a 15-inch or 16.1-inch display. Notebook computers with these larger displays weigh seven to ten pounds, however, so if you travel a lot and portability is essential, you might want a lighter computer with a smaller display. The lightest notebook computers, which weigh less than 3 pounds, are equipped with a 12.1-inch display. Regardless of size, the resolution of the display should be at least 1024 x 768 pixels. To compare the monitor size on various notebook computers, visit the company Web sites in Figure 11.

Type of Notebook	Company	URL
PC	Acer	acer.com
	Dell	dell.com
	Fujitsu	fujitsu.com
	Gateway	gateway.com
	HP	hp.com
	IBM	ibm.com
	NEC	nec.com
	Sony	sony.com
	Sharp	sharp.com
	Toshiba	toshiba.com
Mac	Apple	apple.com
For an updated list of companies and their Web site addresses, visit		

FIGURE 11 Companies that sell notebook computers.

2 Experiment with different keyboards and pointing devices. Notebook computer keyboards are far less standardized than those for desktop computers. Some notebook computers, for example, have wide wrist rests, while others have none. Notebook computers also use a range of pointing devices, including pointing sticks, touchpads, and trackballs. Before you purchase a notebook computer, try various types of keyboard and pointing devices to determine which is easiest for you to use. Regardless of the pointing device you select, you also may want to purchase a regular mouse to use when you are working at a desk or other large surface.

3 Make sure the notebook computer you purchase has a CD and/or DVD drive.
Loading and installing software, especially large Office suites, is much faster if done from a CD-ROM, CD-RW, DVD-ROM, or DVD+RW. Today, most notebook computers come with an internal or external CD-ROM drive. Some notebook computers even come with a CD-ROM drive and a CD-RW drive or a DVD-ROM drive and a CD-RW or DVD+RW/CD-RW drive. Although DVD drives are more expensive, they allow you to play CDs and DVD movies using your notebook computer and a headset.

4 **If necessary, upgrade the processor, memory, and disk storage at the time of purchase.**
As with a desktop computer, upgrading your notebook computer's memory and disk storage usually is less expensive at the time of initial purchase. Some disk storage is custom designed for notebook computer manufacturers, meaning an upgrade might not be available in the future. If you are purchasing a lightweight notebook computer, then it should include at least a 1.4 GHz processor, 256 MB RAM, and 40 GB of storage.

5 **The availability of built-in ports on a notebook computer is important.** A notebook computer does not have a lot of room to add adapter cards. If you know the purpose for which you plan to use your notebook computer, then you can determine the ports you will need. Most notebooks come with common ports, such as a mouse port, IrDA port, serial port, parallel port, video port, and USB port. If you plan to connect your notebook computer to a TV, however, then you will need a PC-toTV port. If you want to connect to networks at school or in various offices, make sure the notebook computer you purchase has a built-in network card. If your notebook computer does not come with a network card built-in, then you will have to purchase an external network card that slides into an expansion slot in your notebook computer, as well as a network cable. If you expect to connect an iPod portable digital music player to your notebook computer, then you will need a FireWire port.

6 **If you plan to use your notebook computer for note-taking at school or in meetings, consider a notebook computer that converts to a Tablet PC.** Some computer manufacturers have developed convertible notebook computers that allow the screen to rotate 180 degrees on a central hinge and then fold down to cover the keyboard and become a Tablet PC (Figure 12). You then can use a pencil-like device to input text or drawings into the computer by writing on the screen.

FIGURE 12 The Acer TravelMate 100 notebook computer converts to a Tablet PC.

7 **Consider purchasing a notebook computer with a built-in wireless card to connect to your home network.** Many users today are setting up wireless home networks. With a wireless home network, the desktop computer functions as the server and your notebook computer can access the desktop computer from any location in the house to share files and hardware, such as a printer, and browse the Web. If your notebook computer does not come with a built-in wireless card, you can purchase an external one that slides into your notebook computer. Most home wireless networks allow connections from distances of 150 to 800 feet.

8 **If you are going to use your notebook computer for long periods without access to an electrical outlet, purchase a second battery.** The trend among notebook computer users today is power and size over battery life, and notebook computer manufacturers have picked up on this. Many notebook computer users today are willing to give up longer battery life for a larger screen, faster processor, and bigger storage. For this reason, you need to be careful in choosing a notebook computer if you plan to use it without access to electrical outlets for long periods, such as an airplane flight. You also might want to purchase a second battery as a backup. If you anticipate running your notebook computer on batteries frequently, choose a computer that uses **lithium-ion batteries** (they last longer than nickel cadmium or nickel hydride batteries).

9 **Purchase a well-padded and well-designed carrying case.** An amply padded carrying case will protect your notebook computer from the bumps it will receive while traveling. A well-designed carrying case will have room for accessories such as spare floppy disks, CDs and DVDs, a user manual, pens, and paperwork (Figure 13).

FIGURE 13 Well-designed carrying case.

10 **If you travel overseas, obtain a set of electrical and telephone adapters.** Different countries use different outlets for electrical and telephone connections. Several manufacturers sell sets of adapters that will work in most countries (Figure 14).

FIGURE 14 Set of electrical and telephone adapters for travel abroad.

11 **If you plan to connect your notebook computer to a video projector, make sure the notebook computer is compatible with the video projector.** You should check, for example, to be sure that your notebook computer will allow you to display an image on the computer screen and projection device at the same time (Figure 15). Also, ensure that your notebook computer has the ports required to connect to the video projector.

FIGURE 15 A notebook computer connected to a video projector to project what displays on the screen.

12 **For improved security, consider a fingerprint scanner.** More than a quarter million notebook computers are stolen or lost each year. If you have critical information stored on your notebook computer, then consider purchasing one with a fingerprint scanner to protect the data if your computer is stolen or lost. Fingerprint security offers a level of protection that extends well beyond the standard password protection.

HOW TO PURCHASE A TABLET PC

The Tablet PC (Figure 16) combines the mobility features of a traditional notebook computer with the simplicity of pencil and paper, because you can create and save Office-type documents by writing and drawing directly on the screen with a digital pen. Tablet PCs use the Windows XP Tablet PC Edition operating system, which expands on Windows XP Professional by including digital pen and speech capabilities. A notebook computer and a Tablet PC have many similarities. For this reason, if you are considering purchasing a Tablet PC, review the guidelines for purchasing a notebook computer, as well as the guidelines below.

FIGURE 16 The lightweight Tablet PC, with its handwriting capabilities, is the latest addition to the family of mobile computers.

1 **Make sure the Tablet PC fits your mobile computing needs.** The Tablet PC is not for every mobile user. If you find yourself in need of a computer in class or you are spending more time in meetings than in your office, then the Tablet PC may be the answer. Before you invest money in a Tablet PC, however, determine the programs you plan to use it for. You should not buy a Tablet PC simply because it is a new and interesting type of computer. For additional information on

the Tablet PC, visit the Web sites listed in Figure 17. You may have to use the search capabilities on the home page of the companies listed to locate information about the Tablet PC.

Company	URL
Acer	acer.com/us
Fujitsu	fujitsu.com
Hewlett-Packard	hp.com
Microsoft	microsoft.com/windowsxp/tabletpc
ViewSonic	viewsonic.com
VIA Technologies	via.com

For an updated list of companies and their Web site addresses, visit scsite.com/dc2004/ch8/buyers.

FIGURE 17 Companies involved with Tablet PCs and their Web sites.

2 **Decide whether you want a convertible or pure Tablet PC.** **Convertible Tablet PCs** have an attached keyboard and look like a notebook computer. You rotate the screen and lay it flat against the computer for note-taking. The **pure Tablet PCs** are slim and lightweight, weighing less than four pounds. They have the capability of easily docking at a desktop to gain access to a large monitor, keyboard, and mouse. If you spend a lot of time attending lectures or meetings, than the pure Tablet PC is ideal. Acceptable specifications for a Tablet PC are shown in Figure 18.

3 **Be sure the weight and dimensions are conducive to portability.** The weight and dimensions of the Tablet PC are important because you carry it around like a notepad. The Tablet PC you buy should weigh in at four pounds or less. Its dimensions should be approximately 12 inches by 9 inches by 1.5 inches.

4 **Port availability, battery life, and durability are even more important with a Tablet PC than they are with a notebook computer.** Make sure the Tablet PC you purchase has the ports required for the applications you plan to run. As with any mobile computer, battery life is important especially if you plan to use your Tablet PC for long periods without access to an electrical outlet. A Tablet PC must be durable because if you use it for what it was built for, then you will be handling it much like you handle a pad of paper.

Tablet PC Specifications	
Dimensions	12" x 9" x 1.5"
Weight	Less than 4 Pounds
Processor	Pentium III at 2.0 GHz
RAM	128 MB
Hard Disk	20 GB
Display	10.4" XGA TFT 16-Bit Color
Digitizer	Electromagnetic Digitizer
Battery	4-Cell (3-Hour)
USB	2
FireWire	1
Docking Station	Grab and Go with CD-ROM, Keyboard, and Mouse
Bluetooth Port	Yes
802.11b Card	Yes
Network Card	10/100 Ethernet
Modem	56 Kbps
Speakers	Internal
Microphone	Internal
Operating System	Windows XP Tablet PC Edition
Application Software	Office XP Small Business Edition
Antivirus Software	Yes - 12 Month Subscription
Warranty	1-Year Limited Warranty Parts and Labor

FIGURE 18 Tablet PC specifications.

FIGURE 19 A Tablet PC lets you handwrite notes and draw on the screen using a digital pen.

Mouse Unit	Digital Pen
Point	Point
Click	Tap
Double-click	Double-tap
Right-click	Tap and hold
Click and drag	Drag

FIGURE 20 Standard point-and-click of a mouse unit compared with the gestures made with a digital pen.

5 **Experiment with different models of the Tablet PC to find the digital pen that works best for you.** The key to making use of the Tablet PC is to be comfortable with its handwriting capabilities and on-screen keyboard. Not only is the digital pen used to write on the screen (Figure 19), but you also use it to make gestures to complete tasks, in a manner similar to the way you use a mouse. Figure 20 compares the standard point-and-click of a mouse unit with the gestures made with a digital pen. Other gestures with the digital pen replicate some of the commonly used keys on a keyboard.

6 **Check out the comfort level of handwriting in different positions.** You should be able to handwrite on a Tablet PC with your hand resting on the screen. You also should be able to handwrite holding the Tablet PC in one hand, as well as with it sitting in your lap.

7 **Make sure the LCD display device has a resolution high enough to take advantage of Microsoft's ClearType technologies.** Tablet PCs use a digitizer under a standard 10.4-inch motion-sensitive LCD display to make the digital ink on the screen look like real ink on paper. The Tablet PC also uses ClearType technology that makes the characters crisper on the screen, so your notes are easier to read and cause less fatigue to the eyes. To ensure you get the maximum benefits from the new ClearType technology, make sure the LCD display has a resolution of 800 x 600 in landscape mode and a 600 x 800 in portrait mode.

8 Test the built-in Tablet PC microphone and speakers. With many application software packages recognizing human speech, such as the Microsoft Office XP, it is important that the Tablet PC's built-in microphone operates at an acceptable level. If the microphone is not to your liking, you may want to purchase a close-talk headset with your Tablet PC. Increasingly more users are sending information as audio files, rather than relying solely on text. For this reason, you also should check the speakers on the Tablet PC to make sure they meet your standards.

9 Consider a Tablet PC with a built-in PC video camera. A PC video camera adds streaming video and still photography capabilities to your Tablet PC, while still allowing you to take notes in lecture or in meetings.

10 Review the docking capabilities of the Tablet PC. The Windows XP Tablet PC Edition operating system supports a grab-and-go form of docking, so you can pick up and take a docked Tablet PC with you, just as you would pick up a notepad on your way to a meeting. Two basic types of docking stations are available. One type of docking station (Figure 21) changes the Tablet PC into a desktop computer. It uses the Tablet PC as a monitor. The station has a CD or DVD drive, full-size keyboard, mouse, and other accessories. Another type of docking station lets you dock your PC to your desktop computer and use Windows XP Dual Monitor support. **Windows XP Dual Monitor support** allows you to work on one monitor, while using the Tablet PC monitor to display often-used applications, such as your calendar or address book.

11 Wireless access to the Internet and your e-mail is essential with a Tablet PC. Make sure the Tablet PC has wireless networking, so you can access the Internet and your e-mail anytime and anywhere. Your Tablet PC also should include standard network connections, such as dial-up and Ethernet connections.

12 Review available accessories to purchase with your Tablet PC. Tablet PC accessories include docking stations, mouse units, keyboards, security cables, additional memory and storage, protective handgrips, screen protectors, and various types of digital pens. You should review the available accessories when you purchase a Tablet PC.

FIGURE 21 A Tablet PC docked to create a desktop computer with the Tablet PC as the monitor.

HOW TO PURCHASE A PDA

If you need to stay organized when you are on the go, then a lightweight, palm-sized or pocket-sized mobile device, called a PDA, may be the right choice. PDAs typically are categorized by the operating system they run. Although several are available, the two primary operating systems are Palm OS® (Figure 22) or a Windows-based operating systems, such as Pocket PC 2002 (Figure 23).

This section lists guidelines you will want to consider when purchasing a PDA. You also should visit the Web sites listed in Figure 24 to gather more information about the type of PDA that best suits your computing needs.

Web Site	URL
Compaq	compaq.com/products/handhelds
Computer Shopper	shopper.cnet.com
Handspring	handspring.com
Microsoft	pocketpc.com
Palm	palm.com
PDA Buyers Guide	pdabuyersguide.com
Sony	sonystyle.com
Wireless Developer Network	wirelessdevnet.com

For an updated list of reviews and information about PDAs and their Web site addresses, visit scsite.com/dc2004/ch8/buyers.

FIGURE 24 Reviews and information about PDAs.

FIGURE 22 Sony's NR70V PDA with Palm OS. The NR70V lets you take pictures with its digital camera, listen to MP3 files, display videos and images, plus keep your datebook and contact list organized.

FIGURE 23 Compaq's iPaq H3970 with Pocket PC 2002 includes Bluetooth™ wireless connectivity. The iPaq plays MP3 music or audio programs from the Web, as well as records and plays back voice notes or meeting notes.

1 **Determine the programs you plan to run on your PDA.** All PDAs can handle basic organizer-type software such as a calendar, address book, and notepad. The availability of other software depends on the operating system you choose. The depth and breadth of software for the Palm OS is significant, with more than 11,000 basic programs and over 600 wireless programs. PDAs that run Windows-based operating systems, such as Pocket PC 2002, may have fewer programs available, but the operating system and application software are similar to those with which you are familiar, such as Word and Excel.

2 **Consider how much you want to pay.** The price of a PDA can range from $100 to $800, depending on its capabilities. In general, Palm OS devices are at the lower end of the cost spectrum and Pocket PC and other Windows-based devices are at the higher end. For the latest PDA prices, capabilities, and accessories, visit the Web sites listed in Figure 24.

3 **Determine whether you need wireless access to the Internet and e-mail or mobile telephone capabilities with your PDA.** Some PDAs offer wireless access to the Internet, instant messaging, and e-mail for a monthly network connection fee. To run the wireless, the functionality of the PDAs often is stripped down to conserve battery power. Some wireless

PDAs, such as Handspring's Treo 270, come with a mobile telephone built-in (Figure 25). These features and services allow PDA users to access real-time information from anywhere to help make decisions while on the go.

FIGURE 25 The Handspring Treo 270 running Palm OS has a full-color display and can be used as a telephone, an organizer, or to access e-mail and the Web.

4 **Make sure your PDA has enough memory.** Memory (RAM) is not a major issue with low-end PDAs with monochrome displays and basic organizer functions. Memory is a major issue, however, for high-end PDAs that have color displays and wireless features. Without enough memory, the performance level of your PDA will drop dramatically. If you plan to purchase a high-end PDA running the Palm OS operating system, the PDA should have at least 16 MB of RAM. If you plan to purchase a high-end PDA running the Pocket PC 2002 operating system, the PDA should have at least 48 MB of RAM.

5 **Practice with the touch screen, handwriting recognition, and built-in keyboard before deciding on a model.** To enter data into a PDA, you use a pen-like stylus to handwrite on the screen or a keyboard. The keyboard either is mounted on the front of the PDA or it slides out. The Handspring Treo shown in Figure 25, comes with a small, built-in keyboard that works like a mobile telephone keypad. With handwriting recognition, the PDA translates the handwriting into a computerized font. You also can use the stylus as a pointing device to select items on the screen and enter data by tapping on an on-screen keyboard. By practicing data entry before buying a PDA, you can learn if one PDA may be easier for you to use than another. You also can buy third-party software to improve a PDA's handwriting recognition.

6 **Decide whether you want a color display.** Pocket PC devices usually come with a color display that supports as many as 65,536 colors.

Palm OS devices also have a color display, but the less expensive ones have a monochrome display in 4 to 16 shades of gray. Having a color display does result in greater on-screen detail, but it also requires more memory and uses more power. Resolution also influences the quality of the display.

7 **Compare battery life.** Any mobile device is good only if it has the power required to run. Palm OS devices with monochrome screens typically have a much longer battery life than Pocket PC devices with color screens. To help alleviate this problem, many Palm OS and Pocket PC devices have incorporated rechargeable batteries that can be recharged by placing the PDA in a cradle or connecting it to a charger.

8 **Even with PDAs, seriously consider the importance of ergonomics.** Will you put the PDA in your pocket, a carrying case, wear it on your belt? How does it feel in your hand? Will you use it indoors or outdoors? Many screens are unreadable outdoors. Do you need extra ruggedness, such as would be required in construction, in a plant, or a warehouse?

9 **Check out the accessories.** Determine which accessories you want for your PDA. PDA accessories include carrying cases, portable mini- and full-size keyboards, removable storage, modems, synchronization cradles and cables, car chargers, wireless communications, global positioning system modules, digital camera modules, expansion cards, dashboard mounts, replacement styli, and more.

10 **Decide whether you want additional functionality.** In general, off-the-shelf Pocket PC devices have broader functionality than Palm OS devices. For example, voice-recording capability, e-book players, MP3 players, and video players are standard on most Pocket PC devices. If you are leaning towards a Palm OS device and want these additional functions, you can purchase additional software or expansion modules to add them later.

11 **Determine whether synchronization of data with other PDAs or personal computers is important.** Most PDAs come with a cradle that connects to the USB or serial port on your computer so you can synchronize data on your PDA with your desktop or notebook computer. Increasingly more PDAs are Bluetooth and/or 802.11b enabled, which gives them the capability of synchronizing wirelessly. Most PDAs today also have an infrared port that allows you to synchronize data with any device that has a similar infrared port, including desktop and notebook computers or other PDAs.

HOW TO INSTALL A COMPUTER

It is important that you spend time planning for the installation of your computer. Follow these steps to ensure your installation experience will be a pleasant one and that your work area is safe, healthy, and efficient.

1 **Read the installation manuals before you start to install your equipment.** Many manufacturers include separate installation manuals that contain important information with their equipment. You can save a great deal of time and frustration if you make an effort to read the manuals before starting the installation process.

2 **Do some additional research.** To locate additional instructions or advice about installing your computer, review the computer magazines or Web sites listed in Figure 26 to search for articles about installing a computer.

Web Site	URL
Getting Started/Installation	
HelpTalk Online	www.helptalk.com
Ergonomics	
Ergonomic Computing	cobweb.creighton.edu/training/ergo.htm
HealthyComputing.com	healthycomputing.com
IBM Healthy Computing	www.pc.ibm.com/ww/healthycomputing
Apple Ergonomics	apple.com/about/ergonomics/
Healthy Choices for Computer Users	www-ehs.ucsd.edu/ergo/ergobk/ vdt.htm
Video Display Terminal Health and Safety Guidelines	uhs.berkeley.edu/Facstaff/Ergonomics
For an updated list of reference materials, visit scsite.com/dc2004/ ch8/buyers.	

FIGURE 26 Web references on setting up and using your personal computer.

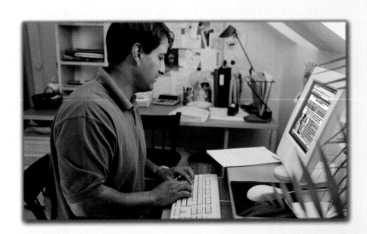

3 **Set up your computer in a well-designed work area and remain aware of health issues as you work.** Ergonomic studies have shown that using the correct type and configuration of chair, keyboard, monitor, and work surface will help you work comfortably and efficiently, and help protect your health. For your computer work space, experts recommend an area of at least two feet by four feet. You also should set up a document holder that keeps documents at the same height and distance as your computer screen to minimize neck and eye discomfort. Finally, use non-glare light bulbs that illuminate your entire work area to reduce eyestrain. Figure 27 illustrates additional guidelines for setting up your work area. Figure 28 provides computer user health guidelines.

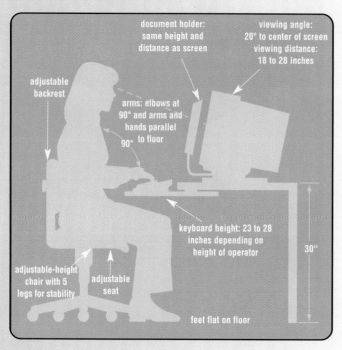

FIGURE 27 A well-designed work area should be flexible to allow adjustments to the height and build of different individuals. Good lighting and air quality also are important considerations.

1. Work in a well-designed work area, as shown in Figure 27.

2. Alternate work activities to prevent physical and mental fatigue. If possible, change the order of your work to provide some variety.

3. Take frequent breaks. Every 15 minutes, look away from the screen to give your eyes a break. At least once per hour, get out of your chair and move around. Every two hours, take at least a 15-minute break.

4. Incorporate hand, arm, and body stretching exercises into your breaks. During your lunch break, try to get outside and walk.

5. Make sure your computer monitor is designed to minimize electromagnetic radiation (EMR).

6. Try to eliminate or minimize surrounding noise that contributes to stress and tension.

7. If you frequently use the telephone and the computer at the same time, consider using a telephone headset. Cradling the telephone between your head and shoulder can cause muscle strain.

8. Be aware of symptoms of repetitive strain injuries: soreness, pain, numbness, or weakness in neck, shoulders, arms, wrists, and hands. Do not ignore early signs; seek medical advice.

FIGURE 28 Following these health guidelines can help computer users maintain their health.

4 **Install your computer in a work space where you can control the temperature and humidity.** You should keep the computer in an area with a constant temperature between 60°F and 80°F. High temperatures and humidity can damage electronic components. Be careful when using space heaters, for example, as the hot, dry air they generate can cause disk problems.

5 **Set up your work space near an available electrical outlet and set aside a proper location for the electrical wires.** Your computer and peripheral devices, such as the monitor and printer, require an electrical outlet. To maintain safety and simplify the connections, purchase a surge protector to connect the computer and peripheral devices to the electrical outlet. Place the electrical wires in a location where they are not a fire risk and you can avoid tripping on them. After you turn your computer off, turn the master switch on the surge protector to off.

7 **If you plan to set up a wireless network, choose an area that is free from potential signal interference.** Low-level basement areas, doors, trees, and walls, for example, can affect the signals between wireless devices. The signal pattern for most wireless antennae is circular, with the strongest signal closest to the antenna. The best advice is to give the antenna ample room and determine its placement by trial and error.

8 **Install bookshelves.** When you set up your work space, install bookshelves above and/or to the side of your computer area to keep manuals and other reference materials handy.

9 **Obtain a computer tool set.** Computer tool sets include any screwdrivers and other tools you might need to work on your computer. Computer dealers, office supply stores, and mail-order companies sell these tool sets. To keep all the tools together, get a tool set that comes in a zippered carrying case.

10 **Save all the paperwork that comes with your computer.** Keep the documents that come with your computer in an accessible place, along with the paperwork from your other computer-related purchases. To keep different-sized documents together, consider putting them in a manila file folder, large envelope, or sealable plastic bag.

11 **Record the serial numbers of all your equipment and software.** Write the serial numbers of your equipment and software on the outside of the manuals packaged with these items. As noted in the next section, you also should create a single, comprehensive list that contains the serial numbers of all your equipment and software.

12 **Complete and mail your equipment and software registration cards or register online.** When you register your equipment and software, the vendor usually enters you in its user database. Being a registered user not only can save you time when you call with a support question, it also makes you eligible for special pricing on software upgrades.

6 **Have a telephone outlet and telephone or cable connection near your work space so you can connect your modem and/or place calls while using your computer.** To plug in your modem to dial up and access the Internet, you will need a telephone outlet or cable connection close to your computer. Having a telephone nearby also helps if you need to place business or technical support calls while you are working on your computer. Often, if you call a vendor about a hardware or software problem, the support person can talk you through a correction while you are on the telephone. To avoid data loss, however, do not place floppy disks on the telephone or near any other electrical or electronic equipment.

13 **Keep the shipping containers and packing materials for all your equipment.** Shipping containers and packing materials will come in handy if you have to return your equipment for servicing or must move it to another location.

14 **Identify device connectors.** At the back or front of your computer, you will find a number of connectors for your printer, monitor, mouse, telephone line, and so forth (Figure 29). If the manufacturer has not identified them for you, use a marking pen to write the purpose of each connector on the back or front of the computer case, or photograph or draw the connectors and label them in a notebook.

15 **Keep your computer area clean.** Avoid eating and drinking around your computer. Also avoid smoking, because cigarette smoke can damage floppy disk drives and floppy disk surfaces.

16 **Check your home or renter's insurance policy.** Some renter's insurance policies have limits on the amount of computer equipment they cover. Other policies do not cover computer equipment at all if it is used for business. In this instance, you may want to obtain a separate insurance policy.

FIGURE 29 Adapter cards have a connector that is positioned in the back of the computer when the card is inserted in an expansion slot on the motherboard.

HOW TO MAINTAIN YOUR COMPUTER

Even with the most sophisticated hardware and software, you may need to do some type of maintenance to keep your computer working properly. You can simplify and minimize the maintenance by following the steps listed in this section.

(1) Start a notebook or file using a simple outline that includes information about your computer. Keep a notebook that provides a single source of information about your entire computer, both hardware and software and network connectivity. Each time you make a change to your computer, such as adding or removing hardware or software or altering computer parameters, record the change in your notebook. Include the following items in your notebook:

- Vendor support numbers from your user manuals

- Serial numbers of all equipment and software

- User IDs, passwords, and nicknames for your ISP or OSP, network access, Web sites, and so on

- Vendor and date of purchase for all software and equipment

- Trouble log that provides a chronological history of equipment or software problems

- Notes on any discussions with vendor support personnel

Figure 30 provides a suggested outline for the contents of your Computer Owner's Notebook.

OUTLINE FOR COMPUTER OWNER'S NOTEBOOK

1. List of Vendors
Vendor
Product(s)
City/State
URL
E-mail address
Telephone number
Technical support telephone
  number

2. Internet and online services information
Service provider name
URL
E-mail address
Logon telephone number
Alternate logon telephone
  number
Technical support telephone
  number
User ID
Password

3. Serial numbers
Product
Manufacturer
Serial number

4. Hardware purchase history
Date
Product
Manufacturer
Vendor
Cost
Warranty information

5. Software purchase history
Product
Manufacturer
Vendor
Cost
Date purchased
Date installed/uninstalled
Product keys/registration
  numbers

6. Trouble log
Date
Time
Problem
Resolution

7. Support calls
Date
Time
Company
Contact
Problem
Comments

8. Vendor paperwork

FIGURE 30 To keep important information about your computer on hand and organized, use an outline such as this sample outline.

(2) Before you work inside your computer, turn off the power and disconnect the equipment from the power source. Working inside your computer with the power on can affect both you and the computer adversely. In addition, before you touch anything inside the computer, you should touch an unpainted metal surface, such as the power supply. Doing so will help discharge any static electricity that could damage internal components. As an added protection, for less than $10 from an electronics or computer store, buy an antistatic wristband to prevent static electricity from damaging the computer's circuitry while you replace components. Do not twist, bend, or force components into place. Gently work around existing cables.

If your operating system does not provide the tools, you can purchase a stand-alone utility program to perform basic maintenance functions.

3 **Keep the area surrounding your computer dirt and dust free.** Reducing the dirt and dust around your computer will reduce the need to clean the inside of your computer. If dust builds up inside the computer, remove it carefully with compressed air and a small vacuum. Do not touch the components with the vacuum.

FIGURE 31 The Disk Defragmenter utility defragments the hard disk by reorganizing the files so they are in contiguous (adjacent) clusters, making disk operations faster.

4 **Back up important files and data.** Use a utility program included with the operating system or from a third-party to create a recovery or rescue disk to help you restart your computer if it crashes. Regularly copy important data files to disks, tape, or another computer.

5 **Protect your computer from viruses.** You can protect your computer from viruses by installing an antivirus program and then periodically updating the program by connecting to the manufacturer's Web site. Also, never open a file from an unknown user, particularly those received as e-mail attachments.

6 **Keep your computer tuned.** Most operating systems include several computer utilities that provide basic maintenance functions. In Windows, for example, these utilities are available via the System Tools submenu on the Accessories submenu. One important utility is the disk defragmenter, which allows you to reorganize files so they are in contiguous (adjacent) clusters, making disk operations faster (Figure 31). Some programs allow you to schedule maintenance tasks for times when you are not using your computer. If necessary, leave your computer on at night so it can run the required maintenance programs.

7 **Learn to use diagnostic tools.** Diagnostic tools help you identify and resolve problems, thereby helping to reduce your need for technical assistance. Diagnostic tools help you test components, monitor resources such as memory and processing power, undo changes made to files, and more. As with basic maintenance tools, most operating systems include diagnostic tools; you also can purchase or download many stand-alone diagnostic tools.

8 **Conserve energy wherever possible.** A simple way to conserve energy is to avoid animated screen savers, which use additional power and prevent your computer from going into hibernation. Fortunately, many of the recent computer, monitor, and printer models go into a very low power mode when not in use for a few minutes. If your printer does not go into a very low power mode, then keep it turned off until you need to print a document or report. Finally, shut your computer system down at night and turn off the main switch on your surge protector.

APPENDIX A

Making Use of the Web

A wealth of information is available on the World Wide Web. The riches are yours if you know where to find this material. Locating useful Web sites may be profitable for your educational and professional careers, as the resources may help you research class assignments and make your life more fulfilling and manageable.

Because the World Wide Web does not have an organizational structure to assist you in locating reliable material, you need additional resources to guide you in searching. To help you find useful Web sites, this feature describes specific information about a variety of Web pages, and it includes tables of Web addresses, so you can get started. The material is organized in several categories.

CATEGORIES

FUN AND ENTERTAINMENT	**LEARNING**
TRAVEL	**SCIENCE**
FINANCE	**ENVIRONMENT**
RESOURCES	**HEALTH**
AUCTIONS	**RESEARCH**
GOVERNMENT	**CAREERS**
SHOPPING	**ARTS AND LITERATURE**
WEATHER, SPORTS, AND NEWS	

Web Exercises at the end of each category will reinforce the material and help you discover Web sites that may add a treasure of wealth to your life.

Fun *and* Entertainment

THAT'S ENTERTAINMENT

Surf's Up for Fun Web Sites

Girls just want to have fun, according to singer Cyndi Lauper. The Internet abounds with fun sites for both gals and guys, with everything from the Rock and Roll Hall of Fame and Museum to the Rock of Gibraltar.

Do you want to see the attractions at Walt Disney World®? Or, how about wild animals at a game preserve in Africa, pandas at the San Diego Zoo, and landmarks in Yosemite Valley (Figure A-1)? Travel to the South Pole and hear the frigid wind blow, to Yellowstone Park to see the Old Faithful geyser, and to Loch Ness for a possible glimpse of the famous monster. Web cams take armchair travelers across the world for views of natural attractions, historical monuments, colleges, and cities. Some of the world's Web cams are listed in Figure A-2.

FIGURE A-1 Web cams provide a glimpse of locations throughout the world, including landmarks in Yosemite Valley.

FUN AND ENTERTAINMENT WEB SITES	URL
Web Cams	
Discovery Channel Cams	dsc.discovery.com/cams/cams.html
Iowa State Insect Zoo Live Camera	www.ent.iastate.edu/zoo/enhance14.html
Lochness Live	www.lochness.scotland.net/camera.cfm
Panda Cam San Diego Zoo	sandiegozoo.org/special/pandas/pandacam/index.html
The Automated Astrophysical Site-Testing Observatory (AASTD) (South Pole)	www.phys.unsw.edu.au/southpolediaries/webcam.html
Walt Disney World – Theme Park Live Camera	home.disney.com/DisneyWorld/cgi-bin/oneShot.cgi?type=st&park=ds
Weather and Webcams from OnlineWeather.com and CamVista	onlineweather.com/v4/webcams/index.html
Wild Birds Unlimited Bird FeederCam	wbu.com/feedercam_home.htm
World Map of Live Webcams	members.ozemail.com.au/~worldmap/World.html
World Surf Cameras	surfrock.com.br/surfcam.htm
Entertainment	
AMG All Music Guide	allmusic.com
E! Online	eonline.com
Entertainment Tonight	etonline.com
Entertainment Weekly's EW.com	ew.com/ew
Old Time Radio (OTR) – Radio Days: A Soundbite History	otr.com
Rock and Roll Hall of Fame and Museum	rockhall.com
Spinner	spinner.com
The Internet Movie Database (IMDb)	imdb.com
World Radio Network (WRN)	wrn.org

For an updated list of fun and entertainment Web sites, visit scsite.com/dc2004/web.

FIGURE A-2 When you visit Web sites offering fun and entertainment resources, you can be both amused and informed.

If you need an update on your favorite reality-based television program or a preview of the upcoming Halle Berry movie, the Web can satisfy your entertainment thirst. E! Online (Figure A-3) and Entertainment Tonight provide the latest features on television and movie stars. The Internet Movie Database contains credits and reviews of more than 323,000 titles.

If your passion is music and radio, the AMG All Music Guide provides backgrounds on new releases and top artists. See and hear the musicians inducted into the Rock and Roll Hall of Fame and Museum (Figure A-4). The World Radio Network features international public radio programs, such as the *Voice of Russia* and *United Nations Radio*.

For more information about fun and entertainment Web sites, visit the Discovering Computers 2004 Making Use of the Web page (scsite.com/dc2004/web) and click Fun and Entertainment.

FIGURE A-3 The entertainment Web sites feature celebrity news and profiles.

FIGURE A-4 Visitors exploring the Rock and Roll Hall of Fame and Museum Web site will find history, exhibitions, programs, and the names and particulars of the latest inductees.

Fun *and* Entertainment

WEB EXERCISES

1. Visit the World Map of Live Webcams site listed in Figure A-2. View two of the Web cams closest to your hometown, and describe the scenes. Then, visit the Discovery Channel Cams Web site and view two of the animal cams in the Featured Cams. What do you observe? Visit another Web site listed in Figure A-2 and describe the view. What are the benefits of having Web cams at these locations throughout the world?

2. What are your favorite movies? Use The Internet Movie Database Web site listed in Figure A-2 to search for information about two of these films, and write a brief description of the biographies of the major stars and director for each movie. Then, visit one of the entertainment Web sites and describe three of the featured stories. At the Rock and Roll Hall of Fame and Museum Web site, view the information on Elvis and one of your favorite musicians. Write a paragraph describing the information available about these rock stars.

Travel

GET PACKING!

Explore the World without Leaving Home

Balmy beaches. Majestic mountains. Exotic destinations. Just dreaming of experiencing these locales can lift your spirits. Researchers conclude that vacations are healthy for your mind and body because they help eliminate stress, offer opportunities to spend quality time with family and friends, and provide exercise. Whether you are ready to arrange your next travel adventure or just want to explore destination possibilities, the Internet provides ample resources to set your plans in motion.

Some good starting places are all-encompassing Web sites such as Travelocity.com, which is owned by Sabre, the electronic booking service travel agents use, Expedia Travel (Figure A-5), and Trip.com (Figure A-6). These general travel Web sites have tools to help you find the lowest prices and details on flights, car rentals, cruises, and hotels, and they include such features as airplane seating maps, local weather, popular restaurants, and photos. Each of the major airlines and cruise lines also has a Web site where you can check prices, purchase tickets and tour packages, and sign up for weekly e-mail alerts about specials and new services.

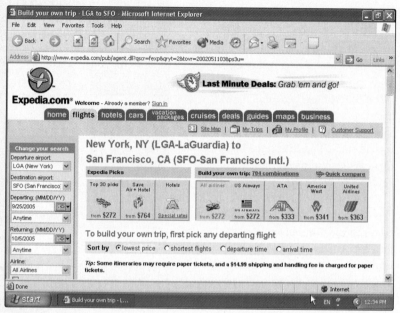

FIGURE A-5 Book flights, cruises, and ski trips with all-encompassing travel resources.

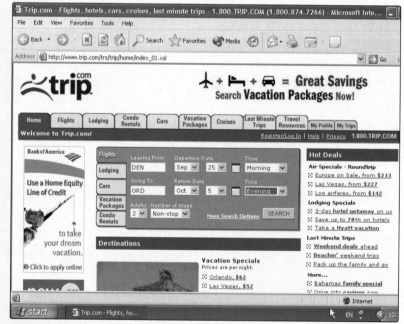

FIGURE A-6 General travel Web sites allow users to check fares to their favorite

FIGURE A-7 Cartography Web sites such as MapQuest provide directions, traffic reports, maps, and more.

TRAVEL WEB SITES	URL
General Travel	
Expedia.com	expedia.com
Orbitz	orbitz.com
Travelocity.com	travelocity.com
Trip.com	trip.com
Yahoo! Travel	travel.yahoo.com
Cartography	
MapQuest	mapquest.com
Maps.com	maps.com
Rand McNally	randmcnally.com
Travel and City Guides	
All the Largest Cities of the World	greatestcities.com
Frommers.com	frommers.com
U.S.-Parks.com – US National Parks Adventure Travel Guide	us-parks.com

For an updated list of travel Web sites, visit scsite.com/dc2004/web.

To discover exactly where your destination is on this planet, cartography Web sites, including MapQuest (Figure A-7), Maps.com, and Rand McNally, allow you to pinpoint your destination. These Web pages generally are divided into geographical areas, such as North America and Europe. When you choose an area, you see a subject-based index that lists helpful tools such as route planners, subway maps, entertainment, and ski trails.

For more information about travel Web sites, visit the Discovering Computers 2004 Making Use of the Web page (scsite.com/dc2004/web) and click Travel.

FIGURE A-8 These travel resources Web sites offer travel information to exciting destinations throughout the world.

Travel

WEB EXERCISES

1. Visit one of the cartography Web sites listed in Figure A-8 and print directions from your campus to one of these destinations: the White House in Washington, D.C.; Elvis's home in Memphis, Tennessee; Walt Disney World in Orlando, Florida; or the Grand Old Opry in Nashville, Tennessee. How many miles is it to your destination? What is the estimated driving time? Then, visit one of the general travel Web sites listed in the table and plan a flight from the nearest major airport to one of the four destinations for the week after finals and a return trip one week later. What is the lowest economy coach fare for this round-trip flight? What airline, flight numbers, and departure and arrival times did you select? Finally, explore car rental rates for a subcompact car for this one-week vacation. What rental agency and rate did you choose?

2. Visit one of the travel and city guide Web sites listed in Figure A-8, and choose a destination for a getaway this coming weekend. Write a one-page paper giving details about this location, such as popular hotels and lodging, expected weather, population, local colleges and universities, parks and recreation, ancient and modern history, and tours. Print a map of this place. Why did you select this destination? How would you travel there and back? What is the breakdown of expected costs for this weekend, including travel expenditures, meals, lodging, and tickets to events and activities? What URLs did you use to complete this exercise?

Finance

KA-CHING, KA-CHING

Cashing In on Financial Advice

"Money makes the world go 'round," according to Liza Minnelli and her friends in the 1972 hit musical, *Cabaret*. If that musical were written today, the lyrics would be updated to "Money makes the World Wide Web go 'round," based on the volume of financial Web sites available to Internet users.

When Doug Lebda became thoroughly disgusted with all the red tape he encountered trying to apply for a home mortgage, he took matters into his own hands. He started LendingTree®, a Web site that helps consumers conveniently obtain mortgages, loans, and credit cards, as shown in Figure A-9. This Web site and a growing number of other Internet companies work with hundreds of national lenders to match consumers' needs with the marketplaces' lenders. One of the leading online banks is Wells Fargo (listed in Figure A-10), with a Web site that features online banking, tax help, personal finance, and small business and commercial services.

If you do not have a personal banker or a financial planner, consider a Web adviser to guide your investment decisions. Three highly recognized financial Web sites are MSN Money, Yahoo! Finance, and The Motley Fool (Figure A-11) for commentary and education on investing strategies, financial news, and taxes.

FIGURE A-9 Online lending Web sites can help consumers seeking assistance with financial matters, including obtaining loans or comparing mortgage rates.

FINANCE WEB SITES	URL
Advice and Education	
Bankrate.com	bankrate.com
LendingTree	lendingtree.com
Loan.com	loan.com
MSN Money	money.msn.com
The Motley Fool	fool.com
Wells Fargo	wellsfargo.com
Yahoo! Finance	finance.yahoo.com
Stock market	
E*TRADE Financial	us.etrade.com
Financial Engines	financialengines.com
FreeEDGAR®	www.freeedgar.com
Harris*direct*	harrisdirect.com
Merrill Lynch Direct	mldirect.ml.com
MVC Capital	www.mevc.com
Morningstar.com	www.morningstar.com
The Vanguard Group	vanguard.com
Taxes	
H&R Block	hrblock.com
Internal Revenue Service – The Digital Daily	www.irs.gov

For an updated list of finance Web sites, visit scsite.com/dc2004/web.

FIGURE A-10 Financial resources Web sites offer general information, stock market analyses, and tax advice, as well as guidance and tips.

FIGURE A-11 The Motley Fool Web site contains strategies and news stories related to personal financing and investing.

FIGURE A-12 Income tax forms, employment opportunities, and filing procedures and regulations are posted on the Internal Revenue Service The Digital Daily Web page.

You likely have heard stories of people who have made — and lost — their fortunes in the stock market. If you are ready to ride the ups and downs of the NASDAQ and the Dow, an abundance of Web sites can help you pick companies that fit your interests and financial needs. For example, FreeEDGAR allows you to read company filings with the SEC. Morningstar.com gives you research reports and the latest market news to help you reach your financial goals.

When April 15 rolls around, many taxpayers mutter the words, Internal Revenue Service. But the IRS can be a friend, too, when you visit Internal Revenue Service The Digital Daily (Figure A-12). Claiming to be the fastest, easiest tax publication on the planet, this Web page contains procedures for filing tax appeals, and contains IRS forms, publications, and legal regulations. H&R Block also offers tax information on its Taxes Web page.

For more information about financial Web sites, visit the Discovering Computers 2004 Making Use of the Web page (scsite.com/dc2004/web) and click Finance.

Finance

WEB EXERCISES

1. Visit three advice and education Web sites listed in Figure A-10 and read their top business world reports. Write a paragraph about each, summarizing these stories. Which stocks or mutual funds do these Web sites predict as being sound investments today? What are the current market indexes for the DJIA (Dow Jones Industrial Average), S&P 500, and NASDAQ, and how do these figures compare with the previous day's numbers?

2. Using two of the stock market Web sites listed in Figure A-10, search for information about Microsoft, Adobe Systems, and one other software vendor discussed in Chapter 3. Write a paragraph about each of these stocks describing the revenues, net incomes, total assets for the previous year, current stock price per share, highest and lowest prices of each stock during the past year, and other relevant investment information.

LOOK IT UP

Web Resources Ease Computer Concerns

Have you heard of a Diffie-Hellman or a mouse potato? If you do not know a JDK from an OSS, then an online computer technology dictionary may be the tool you need. From dictionaries and encyclopedias to online technical support, the Web is filled with a plethora of resources, including those listed in Figure A-13, to answer your computer questions and resolve specialized problems.

Chapter 4 describes the components of the system unit, including the different processors, various types of memory, and other devices associated with it, as well as the components of notebook and handheld computers. With the continual developments in technology and communications, new products reach the marketplace daily.

A way to keep up with the latest developments is to look to online dictionaries that add to their collections of computer and product terms on a regular basis and include thousands of descriptions and designations. An example is the whatis?com Web site listed in the table in Figure A-13 and shown in Figure A-14. The whatis?com Web site contains more than 3,000 cyberterms, with daily updates to the words and definitions. This Web site and many other reference Web pages feature a word of the day that identifies a new product or industry standard as well as highlight recently added or revised terms.

RESOURCES WEB SITES	URL
Dictionaries and Encyclopedias	
CDT's Guide to Online Privacy	cdt.org/privacy/guide/terms
ComputerUser High-Tech Dictionary	computeruser.com/resources/dictionary
TechWeb: The Business Technology Network	techweb.com/encyclopedia
Webopedia: Online Computer Dictionary for Computer and Internet Terms	webopedia.com
whatis?com	whatis.com
Computer Shopping Guides	
BizRate.com®	bizrate.com/marketplace
Online Computer Buying Guide™	grohol.com/computers
Shopforacomputer.com	shopforacomputer.com
The CPU Scorecard	cpuscorecard.com
ZDNet Shopper	zdnetshopper.cnet.com
Upgrading Guides	
CNET Shopper.com	shopper.cnet.com
eHow™	ehow.com
Focus on Mac Support	macsupport.about.com
PCWorld.com	pcworld.com/howto
Upgrade Source™	upgradesource.com
Online Technical Support	
Dux Computer Digest	duxcw.com
MSN Tech & Gadgets	computingcentral.msn.com
PC911	pcnineoneone.com
PC Pitstop	pcpitstop.com
Technical and Consumer Information	
CNET.com	cnet.com
CompInfo – The Computer Information Center	www.compinfo-center.com
NewsHub	newshub.com/tech
Wired News	wirednews.com
ZDNet	zdnet.com

For an updated list of resources Web sites, visit scsite.com/dc2004/web.

FIGURE A-13 A variety of Web resources can provide information about buying, repairing, and upgrading computers.

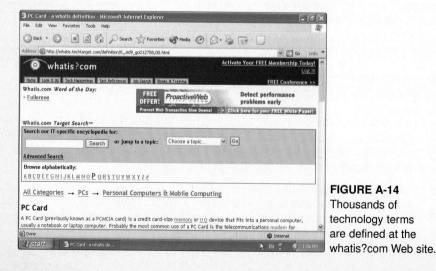

FIGURE A-14 Thousands of technology terms are defined at the whatis?com Web site.

FIGURE A-15 Buying and upgrading a computer is simplified with helpful Web sites such as PCWorld.com.

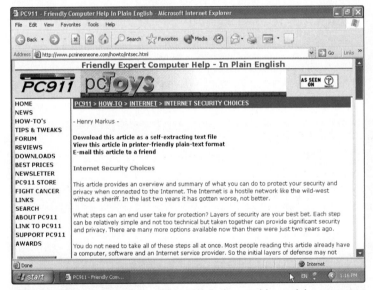

FIGURE A-16 Articles at the PC911 Web site provide useful technological information.

Shopping for a new computer can be a daunting experience, but many online guides can help you select the components that best fit your needs and budget. Most of these Web sites, including PCWorld.com (Figure A-15), feature the latest desktop and notebook computer prices, hardware and software reviews, bargains, and links to popular manufacturers' sale Web pages. If you want to upgrade your present computer, several online guides, such as CNET Shopper.com and Upgrade Source, give current prices for these components and list the more popular products.

If you are not confident in your ability to solve a problem alone, turn to online technical support. Such Web sites, including PC911 (Figure A-16), often provide streaming how-to video lessons, tutorials, and real-time chats with experienced technicians.

The Web offers a variety of technical and consumer information. Hardware and software reviews, price comparisons, shareware, technical questions and answers, and breaking technology news are found on comprehensive portals such as CNET and ZDNet.

For more information on Web resources sites, visit the Discovering Computers 2004 Making Use of the Web page (scsite.com/dc2004/web) and click Resources.

Resources

WEB EXERCISES

1. Visit the dictionaries and encyclopedias Web sites listed in Figure A-13. Search these resources for five terms. Create a table with two columns: one for the cyberterm and one for the Web definition. Then, create a second table listing five recently added or updated words and their definitions on these Web sites. Next, visit two of the listed computer shopping guides Web sites to choose the components you would buy if you were building a customized desktop computer and notebook computer. Create a table for both computers, listing the computer manufacturer, processor model name or number and manufacturer, clock speed, RAM, cache, number of expansion slots, and number of bays.

2. Visit three upgrading guides Web sites listed in Figure A-13. Write a paragraph describing available advice for buying a motherboard. Describe the strengths and weaknesses of these Web sites, focusing on such criteria as clarity of instructions, thoroughness, and ease of navigation. Would you use these Web sites as a resource to troubleshoot computer problems? Then, view two technical and consumer information Web sites listed in the table and write a paragraph about each one, describing the top two news stories of the day.

Auctions

GOING ONCE, GOING TWICE

Rare, Common Items Flood Web Sites

Getting a few personal golfing tips from Tiger Woods might be the key to a lower scorecard. An undisclosed winner of an eBay auction and three friends paid $425,000 to play a round of golf with Woods at his home course in Florida. The proceeds of the auction went to the charitable Tiger Woods Foundation, which initializes and supports community-based programs for disadvantaged children.

The golfing experience is among the high-profile items offered on online auction Web sites. George Lucas donated *Star Wars* props and memorabilia, including a light saber used in *The Phantom Menace* and a Darth Vader helmet, for eBay's Auction for America, which benefits families of the September 11 terrorist attacks. PepsiCo donated a replica of Jeff Gordon's NASCAR racecar.

eBay (Figure A-17) is one of thousands of Internet auction Web sites and is the world's largest personal online trading community. The company's assortment of auctioned items has ranged from the usual to the unusual. Among the unusual was the opportunity to become the 43rd president of the United States. Bidding opened at one penny and soared to $100 million in four hours before eBay officials canceled the offer.

FIGURE A-17 eBay is one of the world's more popular auction Web sites.

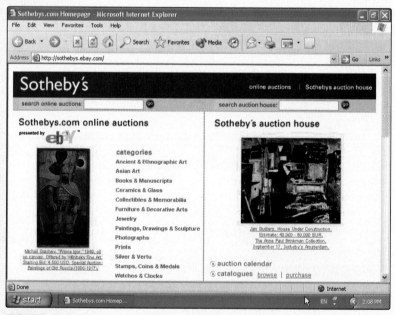

FIGURE A-18 Rare and valuable art, jewelry, and furniture are featured on Sotheby's Web pages.

Traditional auction powerhouses, such as Christie's in London and Sotheby's (Figure A-18) on Manhattan's Upper East Side, are known for their big-ticket items: selected pieces of Elton John's clothing sold for $615,000, a bottle of Italian red wine for $13,000, and a Tyrannosaurus rex fossil for $8.4 million.

If those prices are a bit out of your league, you can turn to a wealth of other auction Web sites to find just the items you need, and maybe some you really do not need, for as little as $1. Some of these auction Web sites are listed in Figure A-19. Categories include antiques and collectibles such as the fountain pen shown in Figure A-20, automotive, computers, electronics, music, sports, sports cards and memorabilia, and toys.

For more information about auction Web sites, visit the Discovering Computers 2004 Making Use of the Web page (scsite.com/dc2004/web) and click Auctions.

AUCTION WEB SITES	URL
Christie's	christies.com
CNET Auctions	auctions.cnet.com
eBay®	ebay.com
Midwest Auction Galleries	midwestauctiongalleries.com
musichotbid	musichotbid.com
Penbid.com	penbid.com
Sothebys.com	sothebys.com
uBid™	ubid.com
Yahoo! Auctions	auctions.yahoo.com

For an updated list of auction Web sites, visit scsite.com/dc2004/web.

FIGURE A-19 These auction Web sites feature a wide variety of items.

FIGURE A-20 Rare and unusual pens are featured on the Penbid auction Web site.

Auctions

WEB EXERCISES

1. Visit the Christie's and Sothebys.com Web sites and read about the items that have been sold recently. Find two unusual objects and write a paragraph about each one summarizing your discoveries. What were the opening and final bids on these objects? Then, review two of the upcoming auctions. When are the auctions' dates? What items are available? What are some of the opening bids? What are the advantages and disadvantages of bidding online?

2. Using one of the auction Web sites listed in Figure A-19, search for two objects pertaining to your hobbies. For example, if you are a baseball fan, you can search for a complete set of Topps cards. If you are a car buff, search for your dream car. Describe these two items. How many people have bid on these items? Who are the sellers? What are the opening and current bids?

Government

STAMP OF APPROVAL

Making a Federal Case for Useful Information

When it is time to buy stamps to mail your correspondence, you no longer need to wait in long lines at your local post office. Instead, log on to the Internet and download a stamp right to your personal computer.

The U.S. Postal Service has authorized several corporations to sell stamps online. Users can download software from a company's Web site, charge the postage fee to a credit card, and then print the postage on a label printer or directly onto envelopes and labels. Some of these Web sites, such as Stamps.com, shown in Figure A-21, charge a small percentage of each order as a convenience fee.

Although citizens may not be enthusiastic about paying income taxes, April 15 can be more tolerable knowing that some of their hard-earned dollars are spent subsidizing useful government Web sites.

You can recognize these Web sites on the Internet by their .gov top-level domain abbreviation. For example, The Library of Congress Web site is lcweb.loc.gov. As the oldest federal cultural institution in the United States and the largest library in the world, the mission of The Library of Congress is to serve the research needs of the U.S. Congress. Patrons can visit one of 22 reading rooms on Capitol Hill and access more than 119 million items written in 470 languages. The Library of Congress Web site, shown in Figure A-22, has forms

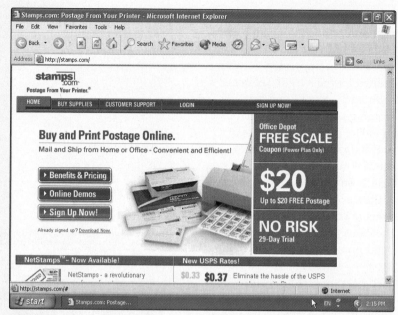

FIGURE A-21 Purchasing stamps on the Internet eliminates making a trip to the post office and waiting in long lines.

FIGURE A-22 The Library of Congress Web site contains more than 119 million items written in 470 languages.

and information from the Copyright Office, an online gallery, and links to a variety of topics, including the National Agricultural Library and the United States National Library of Medicine. These and other government resources Web sites are listed in Figure A-23.

Government and military Web sites offer a wide range of information. The Time Service Department Web site will provide you with the correct time. If you are looking for a federal document, FedWorld lists thousands of documents distributed by the government on its Web site. For access to the names of your congressional representatives, the president's cabinet members, and the Supreme Court justices, or to read portions of a federal statute or the U.S. Constitution, visit the extensive Hieros Gamos Web site, which is a governmental and legal portal with links to the legislative, judicial, and executive branches of government.

For more information about government resources Web sites, visit the Discovering Computers 2004 Making Use of the Web page (scsite.com/dc2004/web) and click Government.

GOVERNMENT WEB SITES	URL
Postage	
Pitney Bowes	pb.com
Neopost Online	simplypostage.com
Stamps.com	stamps.com
Government	
FedWorld	www.fedworld.gov
Hieros Gamos – Law and Legal Research Center	hg.org
NARA – United States National Archives and Records Administration	archives.gov
National Agricultural Library	www.nal.usda.gov
The Library of Congress	lcweb.loc.gov
THOMAS Legislative Information	thomas.loc.gov
Time Service Department	tycho.usno.navy.mil
United States Department of Education	ed.gov
United States Department of the Treasury	treas.gov
United States Government Printing Office	www.access.gpo.gov
United States National Library of Medicine	www.nlm.nih.gov
United States Patent and Trademark Office	www.uspto.gov
USAJOBS	www.usajobs.opm.gov
White House	whitehouse.gov

For an updated list of government Web sites, visit scsite.com/dc2004/web.

FIGURE A-23 These Web sites offer information about buying U.S.-approved postage online and researching federal agencies.

Government

WEB EXERCISES

1. View the three postage Web sites listed in Figure A-23. Compare and contrast the available services on each one. Consider postage cost, necessary equipment, shipping services, security techniques, and tracking capability. Explain why you would or would not like to use this service.

2. Visit the Hieros Gamos Web site listed in Figure A-23. What are the names, addresses, and telephone numbers of your two state senators and your local congressional representative? On what committees do they serve? Who is the chief justice of the Supreme Court, and what has been this justice's opinion on two recently decided cases? Who are the members of the president's cabinet? Then, visit two other Web sites listed in Figure A-23. Write a paragraph about each Web site describing its content and features.

Shopping

CYBERMALL MANIA

Let Your Mouse Do Your Shopping

From groceries to clothing to computers, you can buy just about everything you need with just a few clicks of your mouse. Electronic retailers (e-tailers), especially those listed in Figure A-24, are cashing in on cybershoppers' purchases. Books, computer software and hardware, and music are the hottest commodities. Online sales in the United States exceed $65 billion yearly. E-shoppers can browse for a variety of goods at these popular Web sites.

Holiday sales account for a large portion of Internet purchases with nearly nine million households doing some of their holiday shopping online. During the holiday season, some Web sites such as BestBuy.com (Figure A-25) receive thousands of hits per day. Macy's, Bloomingdale's, and other e-tailers ship more than 300,000 boxes daily out of warehouses the size of 20 football fields and stocked with five million items.

The two categories of Internet shopping Web sites are those with physical counterparts, such as Eddie Bauer (Figure A-26), Wal-Mart, and Tower Records, and those with only a Web presence, such as Amazon.com (Figure A-27).

Some e-shoppers, however, are finding online shopping even more frustrating than finding a convenient parking space at the neighborhood mall on Saturday afternoon.

SHOPPING WEB SITES	URL
Apparel	
Eddie Bauer Since 1920	eddiebauer.com
J.Crew	jcrew.com
Lands' End	landsend.com
Books and Music	
Amazon.com	amazon.com
Barnes & Noble.com	bn.com
Tower Records	towerrecords.com
Computers and Electronics	
Crutchfield.com	crutchfield.com
BestBuy.com	bestbuy.com
buy.com	buy.com
Miscellaneous	
1-800-flowers.com	1800flowers.com
drugstore.com	drugstore.com
The Sharper Image	sharperimage.com
Walmart.com	walmart.com

For an updated list of shopping Web sites, visit scsite.com/dc2004/web.

FIGURE A-24 Popular shopping Web sites.

FIGURE A-25 Shopping for popular computer equipment online eliminates waiting in lines in stores.

FIGURE A-26 Stores such as Eddie Bauer have both a physical and an Internet presence.

FIGURE A-27 Amazon.com is a business with only an Internet presence.

Delayed shipments, out-of-stock merchandise, poor customer service, and difficult return policies have left some savvy shoppers with a poor impression of their Internet experience. As e-tailers rush to set up an Internet site, they sometimes overlook important considerations, such as customer service telephone numbers and e-mail addresses, adequate staff to answer queries quickly and courteously, and sufficient in-stock merchandise.

Paying for the merchandise online causes concern for many e-shoppers. Although online merchants promise secure transactions, some users are wary of cyberthieves. One way of calming their fears may be through the use of e-money, which is a payment system that allows consumers to purchase goods and services anonymously. Several computer companies, Web merchants, and credit card companies are collaborating to develop a standard method of transferring money securely and quickly from electronic wallets, which verify a user's identity.

For more information about shopping Web sites, visit the Discovering Computers 2004 Making Use of the Web page (scsite.com/dc2004/web) and click Shopping.

Shopping

WEB EXERCISES

1. Visit two of the three apparel Web sites listed in the table in Figure A-24 and select a specific pair of jeans and a shirt from each one. Create a table with these headings: e-tailer, style, fabric, features, price, tax, and shipping fee. Enter details about your selections in the table. Then, visit two of the books and music Web sites and search for a CD you would consider purchasing. Create another table with the names of the Web site, artist, and CD, as well as the price, tax, and shipping fee.

2. Visit two of the computers and electronics and two of the miscellaneous Web sites listed in Figure A-24. Write a paragraph describing the features these Web sites offer compared with the same offerings from stores. In another paragraph, describe any disadvantages of shopping at these Web sites instead of actually seeing the merchandise. Then, describe their policies for returning unwanted merchandise and for handling complaints.

Weather, Sports, and News

WHAT'S NEWS?

Weather, Sports, and News Web Sites Score Big Hits

Rain or sun? Hot or cold? Do you toss a coin to determine tomorrow's forecast? Or, do you study weather maps displayed on television and Internet sites? The world seems neatly divided into these two camps, with Web sites such as The Weather Channel (Figure A-28) receiving more than 10 million hits each day. Weather is the leading online news item, with at least 10,000 Web sites devoted to this field. A few of the more popular Web sites are listed in Figure A-29. A multitude of weather, sports, and news Web sites resides on the Internet.

Baseball may be the national pastime, but sports aficionados yearn for major league football, basketball, and hockey along with everything from auto racing to cricket. Although television has four major networks and two live, 24-hour all-sports channels, these media outlets do not provide enough action to quench the thirst of fans across the globe. The Internet fills this void with such Web sites as CBS SportsLine.com (Figure A-30), with more than one million pages of multimedia sports news, entertainment, and merchandise, and Sports.com, which covers rugby, cricket, Formula One racing, tennis, and golf. CBS SportsLine.com creates the official Major League Football and the PGA Tour Web sites and provides content for America Online and Netscape.

Olympics fans are hungry for sports action, results, and athlete profiles. The biggest event ever delivered on the Internet was the 2000 Olympic Games in Sydney, Australia. The official Olympic

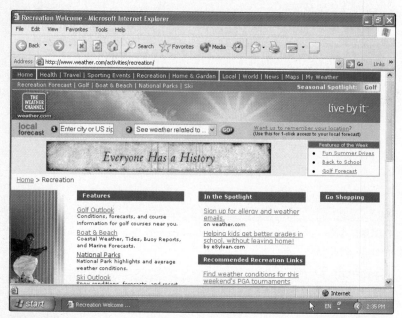

FIGURE A-28 Local, national, and international weather conditions and details about breaking weather stories are available on The Weather Channel Web pages. Various sections provide information about the affects and interactions of weather that influence a variety of activities and conditions, such as Recreation.

WEATHER, SPORTS, AND NEWS WEB SITES	URL
Weather	
Infoplease Weather	infoplease.com/weather.html
Intellicast.com	intellicast.com
STORMFAX®	stormfax.com
The Weather Channel	weather.com
WX.com	wx.com
Sports	
CBS SportsLine.com	cbs.sportsline.com
ESPN.com	espn.com
NCAA Online	ncaa.org
OFFICIAL WEBSITE OF THE OLYMPIC MOVEMENT	www.olympic.org
Sports.com	sports.com
Sporting News Radio	radio.sportingnews.com
SportServer.com	sportserver.com
News	
Google	news.google.com
MSNBC	msnbc.com
NYPOST.COM	nypost.com
onlinenewspapers.com	onlinenewspapers.com
SiliconValley.com	siliconvalley.com
Starting Page Best News Sites	startingpage.com/html/news.html
USATODAY.com	usatoday.com
washingtonpost.com	washingtonpost.com

For an updated list of weather, sports, and news Web sites, visit scsite.com/dc2004/web.

FIGURE A-29 Numerous weather, sports, and news Web sites reside on the Internet.

Games Web site received more than 6.5 billion hits during the 17-day event. That number is greater than the number of Internet visitors at the 2002 Salt Lake Winter Olympic Games Web site. The IBM-run Web site also permitted fans to send e-mail to the 10,500 competitors.

The Internet has emerged as a major source for news, with one-third of Americans going online at least once a week and 15 percent going online daily for reports of major news events. These viewers, who tend to be under the age of 50 and college graduates, are attracted to the Internet's flashy headline format, immediacy, and in-depth reports.

Users are attracted to Web news sites that have a corresponding print or television presence. MSNBC, CNN, ABC News, USA TODAY, FOX News, The Washington Post, and The New York Times are among the more popular Internet news destinations. The technology content in the SiliconValley.com Web site (Figure A-31) and crime, justice, and safety news in APBnews.com appeal to users.

For more information about weather, sports, and news Web sites, visit the Discovering Computers 2004 Making Use of the Web page (scsite.com/dc2004/web) and click Weather, Sports, and News.

FIGURE A-30 Sports fans can catch the latest scores and player profiles on sports Web sites.

FIGURE A-31 The SiliconValley.com Web site posts feature stories with details on the ever-changing world of technology.

Weather, Sports, and News

WEB EXERCISES

1. Visit two of the weather Web sites listed in the table in Figure A-29. Do they contain the same local and five-day forecasts for your city? What similarities and differences do they have in coverage of a national weather story? Next, visit two of the sports Web sites in the table and write a paragraph describing the content these Web sites provide concerning your favorite sport.

2. Visit the OnlineNewspapers.com and Starting Page Best News Sites Web sites listed in Figure A-29 and select two newspapers from each site. Write a paragraph describing the top national news story featured in each of these four Web pages. Then, write another paragraph describing the top international news story displayed at each Web site. In the third paragraph, discuss which of the four Web sites is the most interesting in terms of story selection, photographs, and Web page design.

Learning

YEARN TO LEARN

Discover New Worlds Online

"To try and fail is at least to learn. To fail to try is to suffer the loss of what might have been." Benjamin Franklin's words bring home the point that despite setbacks encountered along the way, learning nurtures the creative spirit and helps people grow.

While you may believe your education ends when you finally graduate from college, learning is a lifelong process. Although much of this learning may occur on the job and through personal experiences, the Internet can fuel much of your desire and need to expand your mind. Many Web sites use streaming media and graphic-intense applications, so the high-speed Internet connections such as cable modems and DSL, are ideal for these online learning tools.

Learning to enhance your culinary skills can be a rewarding endeavor. No matter if you are a gourmet chef or a weekend cook, you will be cooking in style with the help of online resources. At the Betty Crocker Web site (Figure A-32), you can learn how to prepare nutritious meals and bake for special occasions, almost as if Betty Crocker herself were guiding you along. If you find your kitchen familiar territory, the photographs from recipecenter.com can add flair and finesse to your style.

If you would rather sit in front of the computer than stand in front of the stove, you can learn to search the Internet skillfully and delve into its treasures by visiting several Web sites, including Learn the Net (Figure A-33) and NetLearn. These learning Web sites offer tutorials

FIGURE A-32 From soups to soufflés, cooking and baking will be a piece of cake with tips from the Betty Crocker and other culinary Web sites.

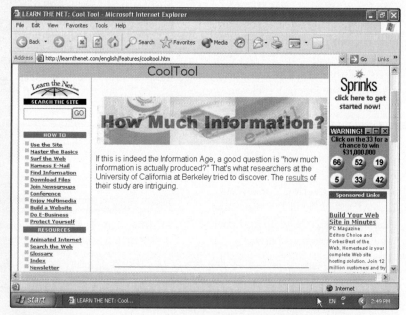

FIGURE A-33 Web sites such as Learn the Net make navigating the Web a more rewarding experience.

FIGURE A-34 The Internet has something for everyone with numerous Web sites that help you find information quickly and easily about how technology works, the principles of flight, or educational adventures.

LEARNING WEB SITES	URL
Cooking	
Betty Crocker	bettycrocker.com
recipecenter.com	recipecenter.com
Internet	
Learn the Net	learnthenet.com
NetLearn	www.rgu.ac.uk/~sim/research/netlearn/callist.htm
Wireguide™	www.wiredguide.com/
Technology and Science	
Global Online Adventure Learning Site	goals.com/homebody.asp
HowStuffWorks	howstuffworks.com
General Learning	
Bartleby.com: Great Books Online	bartleby.com
Blue Web'n	www.kn.pacbell.com/wired/bluewebn
MSN Learning & Research	encarta.msn.com

For an updated list of learning Web sites, visit scsite.com/dc2004/web.

FIGURE A-35 These Web sites contain a variety of topics that can help you learn about all aspects of life.

on building your own Web sites, the latest news about the Internet, and resources for visually impaired users.

Have you ever wondered how to fly an airplane? Take a look at the Global Online Adventure Learning Site. You might be interested in finding out about how your car's catalytic converter reduces pollution or how the Electoral College functions. Marshall Brain's HowStuffWorks Web site (Figure A-34) is filled with articles and animations.

The table in Figure A-35 lists some innovative and informative learning Web sites. Have a seat in this virtual classroom, and do not be afraid to fail along the way.

For more information about learning Web sites, visit the Discovering Computers 2004 Making Use of the Web page (scsite.com/dc2004/web) and click Learning.

Learning

WEB EXERCISES

1. Visit one of the cooking Web sites listed in Figure A-35 and find two recipes or cooking tips that you can use when preparing your next meal. Write a paragraph about each one, summarizing your discoveries. What are the advantages and disadvantages of accessing these Web sites on the new Web appliances that might someday be in your kitchen?

2. Using one of the technology and science Web sites and one of the other Web sites listed in Figure A-35, search for information about communications and networks. Write a paragraph about your findings. Then, review the material in the two general learning Web sites listed in Figure A-35, and write a paragraph describing the content on each Web site that is pertinent to your major.

Science

E = MC²

Rocket Science on the Web

For some people, space exploration is a hobby. Building and launching model rockets allow these scientists to participate in exploring the great frontier of space. For others, space exploration is their life. For National Aeronautics and Space Administration (NASA) engineers and scientists, rockets are their full-time job. These employees launch rockets at NASA's Cape Canaveral facility in Florida and direct them from the Johnson Space Center in Houston, Texas.

The NASA Liftoff Web site, shown in Figure A-36, contains information about rockets, the space shuttle, the International Space Station, space transportation, and communications. Other science resources explore space-related questions about astronomy, physics, the earth sciences, microgravity, and robotics. Information about training to become an astronaut and current astronaut biographies and photographs also are available.

Rockets and space are not the only areas to explore in the world of science. Where can you find the latest pictures taken with the *Hubble Space Telescope*? Do you know which cities experienced an earthquake today? Have you ever wondered what a 3-D model of the amino acid glutamine looks like? You can find the answer to these questions and many others through the Librarians' Index to the Internet (lii.org) shown in Figure A-37.

This index can take you to the National Hurricane Center so you can track a hurricane or fly through

FIGURE A-36 The NASA Liftoff Web site takes space exploration to new heights.

FIGURE A-37 Numerous science resources are organized clearly in the Librarians' Index to the Internet.

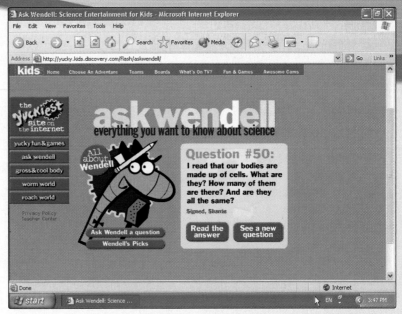

FIGURE A-38 The Yuckiest Site on the Internet Web site makes learning science fun for children.

the eye of a hurricane with the Hurricane Hunters. It also provides a link to the National Earthquake Information Center where you can learn the locations and the intensities of earthquakes that have occurred in the past few days.

The Yuckiest Site on the Internet Web site (Figure A-38) from Discovery Communications entertains as it teaches, especially when children are involved. Combined with Discovery Kids TV, the Web site features fun and games, crafts, recipes, and other activities that capture kids' imaginations as they learn science through adventure and experiments.

The Web offers a wide variety of science resources designed for all ages. Professional scientists, students, hobbyists, and children can find information with a few clicks of the mouse. The Web sites listed in Figure A-39 include up-to-date science resources, discuss the latest research, and can provide answers to technical questions, helping students or anyone who has a thirst for scientific knowledge.

For more information about science Web sites, visit the Discovering Computers 2004 Making Use of the Web page (scsite.com/dc2004/web) and click Science.

SCIENCE WEB SITES	URL
Periodicals	
Astronomy.com	astronomy.com
Archaeology Magazine	archaeology.org
NewScientist.com	newscientist.com
OceanLink	oceanlink.island.net
Science Magazine	sciencemag.org
SCIENTIFIC AMERICAN.com	sciam.com
Resources	
National Science Foundation (NSF)	nsf.gov
SOFWeb	www.sofweb.vic.edu.au
To Science Databases	www.internets.com/sscilink.htm
Science Community	
American Scientist, The Magazine of Sigma Xi, The Research Society	amsci.org
Federation of American Scientists	fas.org
Liftoff to Space Exploration	liftoff.msfc.nasa.gov
Sigma Xi, The Scientific Research Society	sigmaxi.org

For an updated list of science Web sites, visit scsite.com/dc2004/web.

FIGURE A-39 Resources available on the Internet offer a wide range of subjects for enthusiasts who want to delve into familiar and unknown territories in the world of science.

Science

WEB EXERCISES

1. Visit the Liftoff to Space Exploration Web site listed in the table in Figure A-39. View the links about spacecraft, the universe, or tracking satellites and spacecraft, and then write a summary of your findings.

2. Visit the Librarians' Index to the Internet shown in Figure A-37. Click the Science, Computers, & Technology link and then click the Inventions topic. View the Web site for the Greatest Engineering Achievements of the Twentieth Century. Pick two achievements, read their history, and write a paragraph summarizing each of these accomplishments. Then, view two of the science Web sites listed in Figure A-39 and write a paragraph about each of these Web sites describing the information each contains.

Environment

THE FATE OF THE ENVIRONMENT

Protecting the Planet's Ecosystem

The figures are startling: Each year Americans consume 1.4 trillion sheets of paper, an increase of 76 percent since the 1980s. In the past 50 years, people have consumed as many natural resources as every human who has ever lived. According to The Center for a New American Dream (Figure A-40), the U.S. Postal Service's letter carriers deliver an average of 17.8 tons of junk mail each year, which is the weight of four male elephants.

From the rain forests of Africa to the marine life in the Pacific Ocean, the fragile ecosystem is under extreme stress. Many environmental groups have developed Internet sites in attempts to educate world-wide populations and to increase resource conservation.

The U.S. federal government has a number of Web sites devoted to specific environmental concerns. For example, the Acid Rain Data and Reports Web site, developed by the U.S. Geological Survey, monitors the chemicals found in acid rain and conducts research to analyze the effects of these atmospheric deposits on aquatic and terrestrial ecosystems. Figure A-41 shows the home page for the Central African Regional Program for the Environment (CARPE). This continuing project of The United States Agency for International Development (USAID) protects the Congo Basin's tropical forests from population growth, deforestation,

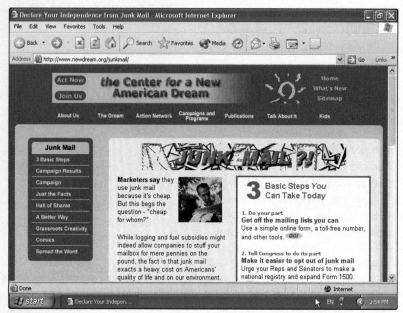

FIGURE A-40 The Center for a New American Dream Web site provides an area where you can declare your independence from junk mail and get your address removed from bulk mail lists.

FIGURE A-41 The Congo Basin's ecological, economic, and political issues are discussed in the CARPE Web site.

and other economic and political problems. In another Web site, the U.S. Environmental Protection Agency (EPA) provides pollution data, including ozone levels and air pollutants, for specific areas. Its AirData Web site, shown in Figure A-42, displays air pollution emissions and monitoring data from the entire United States and is the world's most extensive collection of air pollution data.

On an international scale, the Environmental Sites on the Internet Web page developed by the Royal Institute of Technology in Stockholm, Sweden, has been rated as one of the better ecological Web sites. Its comprehensive listing of environmental concerns range from aquatic ecology to wetlands. This Web site is among the environment Web sites listed in Figure A-43.

For more information about environment Web sites, visit the Discovering Computers 2004 Making Use of the Web page (scsite.com/dc2004/web) and click Environment.

FIGURE A-42 A visit to the EPA AirData Web site, with its extensive database, can assist you in checking your community's ozone and air pollutant levels.

ENVIRONMENT WEB SITES	URL
Central African Regional Program for the Environment (CARPE)	carpe.umd.edu
Earthjustice	www.earthjustice.org
Environmental Defense	edf.org
Environmental Sites on the Internet	www.lib.kth.se/~lg/envsite.htm
EPA AirData – Access to Air Pollution Data	epa.gov/air/data
Green Solitaire.org	greensolitaire.bizland.com
GreenNet	www.gn.apc.org
Environment News Service (ENS)	ens-news.com
The Center for a New American Dream	newdream.org
The Virtual Library of Ecology & Biodiversity	conbio.org/vl
USGS Acid rain data and reports	btdqs.usgs.gov/acidrain
UWM Environmental Health, Safety & Risk Management	www.uwm.edu/Dept/EHSRM/ EHSLINKS

For an updated list of environment Web sites, visit scsite.com/dc2004/web.

FIGURE A-43 Environment Web sites provide vast resources for ecological data and action groups.

Environment

WEB EXERCISES

1. The Center for a New American Dream Web site encourages consumers to reduce the amount of junk mail sent to their homes. Using the table in Figure A-43, visit the Web site and write a paragraph stating how many trees are leveled each year to provide paper for these mailings, how many garbage trucks are needed to haul this waste, and other statistics. Read the letters that you can use to eliminate your name from bulk mail lists. To whom would you mail these letters? How long does it take to stop these unsolicited letters?

2. Visit the EPA AirData Web site. What is the highest ozone level recorded in your state this past year? Where are the nearest air pollution monitoring Web sites, and what are their levels? Where are the nearest sources of air pollution? Read two reports about two different topics, such as acid rain and air quality, and summarize their findings. Include information on who sponsored the research, who conducted the studies, when the data was collected, and the impact of this pollution on the atmosphere, water, forests, and human health. Whom would you contact for further information regarding the data and studies?

Health

NO PAIN, ALL GAIN

Store Personal Health Records Online

Ouch! You stepped on a rusty nail with your bare foot and made your way to the local hospital's emergency room. The admitting nurse asks when you had your last tetanus shot. You give her a sheepish grin and shrug your shoulders.

You might have been able to eliminate the pain and expense of an immunization if you had tracked your shots using an online database management system. Figure A-44 lists a few of the more than 25 Internet health services and portals available online to store your personal health history, including prescriptions, lab test results, doctor visits, allergies, and immunizations. Web sites such as WellMed (Figure A-45) are free to consumers; revenue is generated in many ways, including charging insurance companies, physicians, and employers that offer this service.

In minutes, you can register with a health Web site by choosing a user name and password. Then you create a record to enter your medical history. You also can store data for your emergency contacts, primary care physicians, specialists, blood type, cholesterol levels, blood pressure, and insurance plan.

Similar to the records stored in a company or school database, you can access, retrieve, add, change, delete, and use these online records in a variety of ways. You can decide what data to include. You also can determine who can access this medical data under specific circumstances. No matter where you are in the world, you and medical personnel can obtain records such as the health record shown in Figure A-46 via the Internet or fax

HEALTH WEB SITES	URL
AboutMyHealth	aboutmyhealth.com
Aetna^{sm} IntelliHealth	intellihealth.com
GlobalMedic	globalmedic.com
PersonalMD	personalmd.com
WebMD®	my.webmd.com/my_health_record
WellMed	wellmed.com

For an updated list of health Web sites, visit scsite.com/dc2004/web.

FIGURE A-44 These Internet-based health database management systems Web sites allow you to organize your medical information and store it in an online database.

FIGURE A-45 You can store health records for you and your family in the WellMed database.

machine. Some Web sites offer an audit log that displays the names of people who have accessed your record and when this action occurred.

Some Web sites issue a wallet-sized emergency medical card with instructions for paramedics and other emergency medical personnel about how they can access your vital data (Figure A-47). Other Web sites can import data directly from pharmacies, hospitals, and physicians' offices.

More than 70 million consumers use the Internet yearly to search for health information, so using the Web to store personal medical data is a natural extension of the Internet's capabilities. Health-care reformers strongly support comprehensive online databases. They explain that using the Internet as a health-history database helps eliminate administrative inefficiencies by automatically transferring data among patients, doctors, and insurance providers. The net results are improved health care overall.

For more information about online health database management systems and for an updated list of health Web sites, visit the Discovering Computers 2004 Making Use of the Web page (scsite.com/dc2004/web) and click Health.

FIGURE A-46 The WellMed database allows you to create, store, and access secure online health information whenever the need arises.

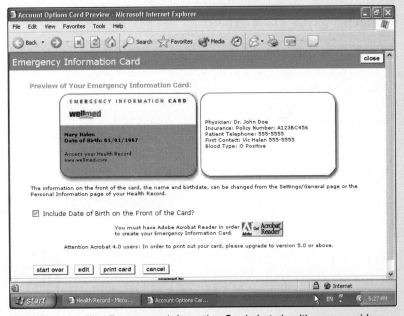

FIGURE A-47 The Emergency Information Card alerts health-care providers that your medical records are stored online.

Health

WEB EXERCISES

1. Access one of the health Web sites listed in Figure A-44. Register yourself or a family member, and then enter the full health history. Create an emergency medical card if the Web site provides the card option. Print this record and emergency card.

2. Visit three of the health Web sites listed in Figure A-44. Describe the features of each. Which of the three is the most user-friendly? Why? Describe the privacy policies of these three Web sites. Print your analysis of these Web sites.

Research

SEARCH AND YE SHALL FIND

Info on the Web

Just about everyone these days wants to know how to find information using the Internet. From students doing research, to teachers, to the general Web surfer, people are using search engines on the Web to get their answers.

Unlike the days when you used the Dewey Decimal Classification or the Library of Congress system to locate reference materials easily, you will not find Internet documents organized in any systematic manner. And no helpful, patient reference librarian is working behind a desk to assist you in your quest for information. Instead, you are on your own when you navigate the tangled Web. But you have some tools: search engines and subject directories.

Yahoo!, AltaVista, GO.com, Northern Light, Excite, FAST Search, and Google are some of the more popular search engines. They crawl through a Web page, and with the help of programs such as spiders and robots, they record each word in their enormous databases. When you enter a key term, search text, or query in their search boxes, the search engines scan the databases and list the Web sites that contain the specified search text. As shown in Figure A-48, the Yahoo! News search results for the phrase, DVD-ROM, lists 26 stories.

The key to effective searching on the Web is composing search queries that narrow the search results and place the most relevant Web sites at the top of the list. Think of major terms that describe the issue or item you are researching and use Boolean operators — and, or, and not — to help retrieve appropriate Web sites.

The GO.com search in Figure A-49 locates Web sites describing the Beatles platinum albums and eliminates Web sites describing platinum jewelry or Beatles memorabilia.

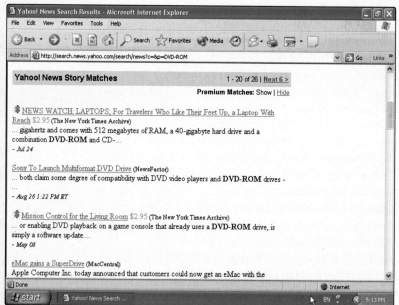

FIGURE A-48 Search the Yahoo! News Web site for information about computer products and technology issues.

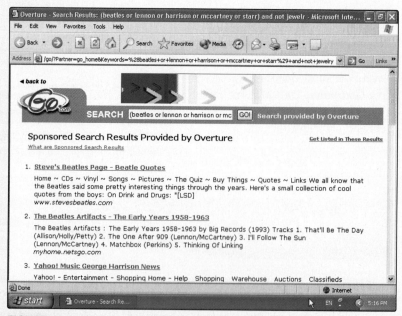

FIGURE A-49 The GO.com Web site features a search engine to locate information such as Beatles platinum albums.

Using the search terms beatles, or lennon, or harrison, or mccartney, or starr along with platinum and not jewelry helps narrow the list of results.

Even when using these searching techniques, one search engine can explore only 20 percent of the 5.5 billion Web pages. All the search engines combined can rummage through less than half of these Web sites.

Another search tool is a subject directory, which is a collection of related Web sites. Yahoo! and LookSmart have two of the more comprehensive subject directories on the Web. Their organized lists often are called trees because a few main categories, such as Entertainment, Computing, Lifestyle, and Work, branch out to more specific subtopics. Figure A-50 shows LookSmart's tree for buying or selling a used car. The list begins with the Buy or Sell a Used Car main category and branches to Auction Lots, Brokers & Services, Classifieds by State, Online Auctions, and finally Vintage Classifieds. A listing of search engines and subject directories are included in the table in Figure A-51.

For more information about searching on the Web and for an updated list of research Web sites, visit the Discovering Computers 2004 Making Use of the Web page (scsite.com/dc2004/web) and click Research.

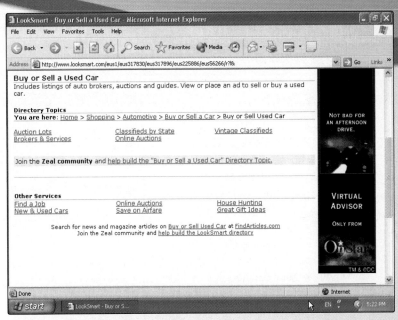

FIGURE A-50 Webrarians index millions of Web pages into more than 200,000 categories.

RESEARCH WEB SITES	URL
Search Engines	
AltaVista	altavista.com
Excite	excite.com
Fast Search & Transfer (FAST)	fastsearch.com
GO.com	go.com
Google	google.com
Northern Light®	northernlight.com
Yahoo!	yahoo.com
Subject Directories	
About	about.com
Librarians' Index to the Internet	lii.org
LookSmart	looksmart.com
The Internet Public Library	ipl.org
The WWW Virtual Library	vlib.org
Yahoo!	yahoo.com

For an updated list of research Web sites, visit scsite.com/dc2004/web.

FIGURE A-51 Web users can find information by using search engines and subject directories.

Research

WEB EXERCISES

1. Use two of the search engines listed in Figure A-51 to find three Web sites that review the latest digital cameras from Sony and Kodak. Make a table listing the search engines, Web site names, and the cameras' model numbers, suggested retail price, megapixels, memory, and features.

2. If money were no object, virtually everyone would have an exquisite car. On the other hand, drivers need a practical vehicle to drive around town daily. Use one of the subject directories listed in Figure A-51 to research your dream car and another directory to research your practical car. Write a paragraph about each car describing the particular subject directory tree you used, the MSRP of the car, standard and optional equipment, engine size, miles per gallon, and safety features.

Careers

IN SEARCH OF THE PERFECT JOB

Web Helps Career Hunt

If you choose a job you love, you never will have to work a day in your life, according to Confucius. Does that sound good? All you need to do is find that perfect job, but that is no easy feat.

While your teachers give you valuable training to prepare you for a career, they rarely teach you how to begin that career. On-campus interviews are a start, but you can broaden your horizons by searching the Internet for career information and job openings.

First, examine some of the job search Web sites. These resources list thousands of openings in hundreds of fields, companies, and locations. For example, the Monster Web site, shown in Figure A-52, allows you to choose a broad job area, such as programmer, narrow your search to specific fields within that area, and then search for specific salary ranges, locations, and job functions. Other job search Web sites are listed in Figure A-53.

Next, prepare your resume. Some Web sites have forms that allow you to type pertinent information into the blank form. Other Web sites want you to submit, or post, a document. If so, write your resume using nouns to describe your skills and experience, such as team player, Spanish, and Microsoft Word. Be sure to check spelling and scan the document for viruses.

FIGURE A-52 Monster's global online network connects companies with career-minded individuals.

CAREERS WEB SITES	URL
Job Search	
BestJobsUSA.com	bestjobsusa.com
CareerBuilder	careerbuilder.com
CareerExchange.com	careerexchange.com
Careermag.com	vertical.worklife.com/onlines/careermag
CareerNet	careernet.com
College Grad Job Hunter	collegegrad.com
EmploymentGuide.com	employmentguide.com
HotJobs.com	hotjobs.com
JobBankUSA.com	jobbankusa.com
JobOptions	joboptions.com
JobsOnline™	jobsonline.com
JobWeb.com	www.jobweb.com
Monster	monster.com
MonsterTRAK	www.jobtrak.com
VolunteerMatch	volunteermatch.com
Company/Industry Information	
AmericanCompanies.com	www.americancompanies.com
Career ResourceCenter.com	www.resourcecenter.com
FASTCOMPANY	fastcompany.com
FORTUNE	fortune.com
Hoover's Online	hoovers.com
Occupational Outlook Handbook	stats.bls.gov/oco

For an updated list of careers Web sites, visit scsite.com/dc2004/web.

FIGURE A-53 Careers Web sites provide a variety of job openings and information about major companies worldwide.

When you write your cover letter, use words the company incorporated in its job posting. Many companies use computer software applications, not humans, to find interviewees. The software searches for particular buzzwords, called keywords, in the files and then lists the documents that contain the most matches.

When a company contacts you for an interview, learn as much about it and the industry as possible before the interview. Many of the Web sites listed in Figure A-53 include detailed company profiles and links to their corporate Web sites. For instance, company information about Microsoft Corporation is displayed in the Hoover's Online Web site, as shown in Figure A-54. Also, look at Web sites for professional organizations and discussion groups for further insights.

For more information about using the Web for career information and for an updated list of career Web sites, visit the Discovering Computers 2004 Making Use of the Web page (scsite.com/dc2004/web) and click Careers.

FIGURE A-54 Company and industry information form the core of Hoover's Online Web site.

Careers

WEB EXERCISES

1. Use two of the job search Web sites listed in Figure A-53 to find three companies with job openings in your field. Make a table listing the Web site name, position available, description, salary, location, desired education, and desired experience.

2. It is a good idea to acquire information before graduation about the industry in which you would like to work. Are you interested in the automotive manufacturing industry, the restaurant service industry, or the financial industry? Use two of the company/industry information Web sites listed in Figure A-53 to research a particular career related to your major. Write a paragraph naming the Web sites and the specific information you found, such as the nature of the work, recommended training and qualifications, employment outlook, and earnings. Then, use two other Web sites to profile three companies with positions available in this field. Write a paragraph about each of these companies, describing the headquarters' location, sales and earnings for the previous year, total number of employees, working conditions, perks, and competitors.

Arts and Literature

FIND SOME CULTURE

Get Ready to Read, Paint, and Dance

Brush up your Shakespeare. Start quoting him now. Brush up your Shakespeare. And the women you will wow. This refrain to one of the songs in Broadway's hit musical, Cole Porter's *Kiss Me Kate*, emphasizes the value of knowing the Bard of Avon's words. You can expand your knowledge of Shakespeare and other literary greats with a little help from the Internet.

For example, Shakespeare.com provides in-depth reviews and news of the world's most famous playwright and his works. The Bartleby.com Web site features biographies, definitions, quotations, dictionaries, and indexes. At the Fantastic Fiction Bibliographies Web site, you can peruse an online bibliography database of science fiction authors and book titles. The Electronic Literature Directory allows you to search for genres, titles, authors, and publishers.

The full text of hundreds of books is available online from the Bibliomania (Figure A-55) and Project Gutenberg Web sites. If you are not keen on reading all of Dostoevsky's *Crime and Punishment* or Homer's *Iliad* on your desktop computer monitor, you can download these works to your e-book or PDA.

When you are ready to absorb more culture, you can turn to various art Web sites on the Internet. Many museums have images of their collections online. Among them are the Getty Museum in Los Angeles, the Montreal Museum of Fine Arts (Figure A-56), the

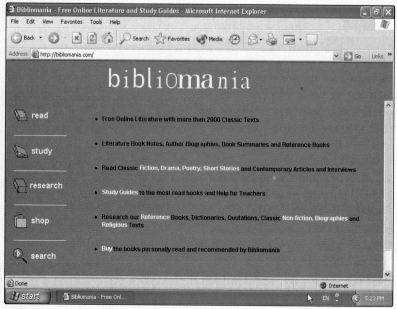

FIGURE A-55 Classic fiction, short stories, drama, poetry, and dictionaries are available for viewing or downloading from Bibliomania and other Web sites.

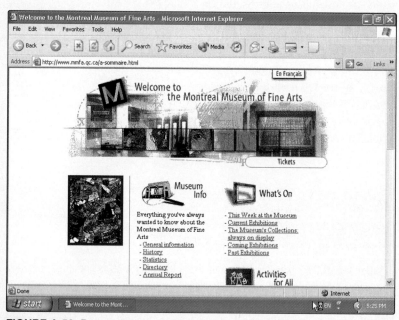

FIGURE A-56 Permanent, temporary, and virtual exhibitions, educational activities, a boutique, and a bookstore are featured on the Montreal Museum of Fine Arts Web site.

Children's Museum of Indianapolis, and the Louvre Museum in Paris (Figure A-57). Comprehensive glimpses of galleries, museums, and other cultural meccas throughout the world as well as paintings and sculptures are found on such Web sites as Art News – absolutearts.com and the GalleryGuide.org.

Access Place Arts and The New York Times Web sites focus on the arts and humanities and provide fascinating glimpses into the worlds of dance, music, performance, cinema, and other topics pertaining to creative expression.

So brush up your knowledge of Shakespeare, grab a canvas, and put on your dancing shoes. The visual arts and literature Web sites on the Internet (Figure A-58) are about to sweep you off your cyberfeet.

For more information about arts and literature Web sites, visit the Discovering Computers 2004 Making Use of the Web page (scsite.com/dc2004/web) and click Arts and Literature.

FIGURE A-57 Established in 1793 by the French Republic, the Louvre Museum is one of the earlier European museums. You can view its collections online.

ARTS AND LITERATURE WEB SITES	URL
Arts	
Access Place Arts	accessplace.com/arts.htm
Art News – absolutearts.com	absolutearts.com
GalleryGuide.org	galleryguide.org
Louvre Museum	www.louvre.fr
Montreal Museum of Fine Arts	www.mmfa.qc.ca
The Children's Museum of Indianapolis	childrensmuseum.org
The Getty	getty.edu
The New York Times: Arts	nytimes.com/pages/arts/index.html
Virtual Library museums pages (VLmp)	vlmp.museophile.com
Literature	
Bartleby.com	bartleby.com
Bibliomania	bibliomania.com
Electronic Literature Directory	directory.wordcircuits.com
Fantastic Fiction Bibliographies	fantasticfiction.co.uk
Project Gutenberg	promo.net/pg
shakespeare.com	shakespeare.com
The Modern Library eBook List	randomhouse.com/modernlibrary/ebookslist.html

For an updated list of arts and literature Web sites, visit scsite.com/dc2004/web.

FIGURE A-58 Discover culture throughout the world by visiting these arts and literature Web sites.

Arts *and* Literature

WEB EXERCISES

1. Visit The Modern Library eBook List Web site listed in Figure A-58 and view one book in the 20TH CENTURY NOVELS, 19TH CENTURY NOVELS, BRITISH LITERATURE, and HISTORY sections. Create a table with columns for the book name, author, cost, online store, local store, and description. Then, read the excerpt from each of the four books and write a paragraph describing which of these four books is the most interesting to you. What are the advantages and disadvantages of reading classic literature electronically?

2. Using the arts Web sites listed in Figure A-58, search for three temporary exhibitions in galleries throughout the world. Describe the venues, the artists, and the works. What permanent collections are found in these museums? Some people shop for gifts in the museums' stores. View and describe three items for sale.

APPENDIX B
Coding Schemes and Number Systems

CODING SCHEMES

As discussed in Chapter 4, a computer uses a coding scheme to represent characters. This section presents the ASCII, EBCDIC, and Unicode coding schemes and discusses parity.

ASCII and EBCDIC

Two widely used codes that represent characters in a computer are the ASCII and EBCDIC codes. The **American Standard Code for Information Interchange**, called ASCII (pronounced ASK-ee), is the most widely used coding system to represent data. Many personal computers and midrange servers use ASCII. The **Extended Binary Coded Decimal Interchange Code**, or EBCDIC (pronounced EB-see-dic), is used primarily on mainframe computers. Figure B-1 summarizes these codes. Notice how the combination of bits (0s and 1s) is unique for each character.

When the ASCII or EBCDIC code is used, each character that is represented is stored in one byte of memory. Other binary formats exist, however, that the computer sometimes uses to represent numeric data. For example, a computer may store, or pack, two numeric characters in one byte of memory. The computer uses these binary formats to increase storage and processing efficiency.

Unicode

The 256 characters and symbols that are represented by ASCII and EBCDIC codes are sufficient for English and western European languages but are not large enough for Asian and other languages that use different alphabets. Further compounding the problem is that many of these languages use symbols, called **ideograms**, to represent multiple words and ideas. One solution to this situation is Unicode. **Unicode** is a 16-bit code that has the capacity of representing more than 65,000 characters and symbols.

ASCII	SYMBOL	EBCDIC
00110000	0	11110000
00110001	1	11110001
00110010	2	11110010
00110011	3	11110011
00110100	4	11110100
00110101	5	11110101
00110110	6	11110110
00110111	7	11110111
00111000	8	11111000
00111001	9	11111001
01000001	A	11000001
01000010	B	11000010
01000011	C	11000011
01000100	D	11000100
01000101	E	11000101
01000110	F	11000110
01000111	G	11000111
01001000	H	11001000
01001001	I	11001001
01001010	J	11010001
01001011	K	11010010
01001100	L	11010011
01001101	M	11010100
01001110	N	11010101
01001111	O	11010110
01010000	P	11010111
01010001	Q	11011000
01010010	R	11011001
01010011	S	11100010
01010100	T	11100011
01010101	U	11100100
01010110	V	11100101
01010111	W	11100110
01011000	X	11100111
01011001	Y	11101000
01011010	Z	11101001
00100001	!	01011010
00100010	"	01111111
00100011	#	01111011
00100100	$	01011011
00100101	%	01101100
00100110	&	01010000
00101000	(	01001101
00101001	)	01011101
00101010	*	01011100
00101011	+	01001110

FIGURE B-1

Unicode represents all the world's current languages using more than 34,000 characters and symbols (Figure B-2). A code for a symbol in Figure B-2 is obtained by appending the symbol's corresponding digit in the left-most column to the symbol's corresponding three-digit code in the column heading. For example, the Unicode for the letter C in row 2 is 0421. In Unicode, 30,000 codes are reserved for future use, such as ancient languages,

and 6,000 codes are reserved for private use. Existing ASCII coded data is fully compatible with Unicode because the first 256 codes are the same. Unicode currently is implemented in several operating systems, including Windows XP.

Parity

Regardless of whether ASCII, EBCDIC, or other binary methods are used to represent characters in memory, it is important that the characters be stored accurately. For each byte of memory, most computers have at least one extra bit, called a **parity bit**, that is used by the computer for error checking. A parity bit can detect if one of the bits in a byte has been changed inadvertently. While such errors are extremely rare (most computers never have a parity error during their lifetime), they can occur because of voltage fluctuations, static electricity, or a memory failure.

Computers are either odd- or even-parity machines. In computers with odd-parity, the total number of on bits in the byte (including the parity bit) must be an odd number (Figure B-3). In computers with even parity, the total number of on bits must be an even number. The computer checks parity each time it uses a memory location. When the computer moves data from one location to another in memory, it compares the parity bits of both the sending and receiving locations to see if they are the same. If the system detects a difference or if the wrong number of bits is on (e.g., an odd number in a system with even parity), an error message is displayed. Many computers use multiple parity bits that enable them to detect and correct a single-bit error and detect multiple-bit errors.

NUMBER SYSTEMS

This section describes the number systems that are used with computers. Whereas thorough knowledge of this subject is required for technical computer personnel, a general understanding of number systems and how they relate to computers is all most users need.

	041	042	043	044	045	046	047
0	А	Р	а	р		ꙍ	ѱ
1	Б	С	б	с	ĕ	ѡ	҂
2	В	Т	в	т	ђ	ꙃ	ѳ
3	Г	У	г	у	ѓ	ꙅ	ѻ
4	Д	Ф	д	ф	є	Ꙁ	ѵ
5	Е	Х	е	х	ѕ	ю	ү
6	Ж	Ц	ж	ц	і	Ꙇ	ѷ
7	З	Ч	з	ч	ї	ꙁ	ҁ
8	И	Ш	и	ш	ј	Ꙗ	Оу
9	Й	Щ	й	щ	љ	ꙗ	оу
A	К	Ъ	к	ъ	њ	Ꙃ	Ꙩ
B	Л	Ы	л	ы	ћ	ꙃ	ꙩ
C	М	Ь	м	ь	ќ	Ꙉ	꙳
D	Н	Э	н	э		ꙉ	ꙣ
E	О	Ю	о	ю	ў	ꙓ	ꙭ
F	П	Я	п	я	џ	ꙥ	ꙫ

FIGURE B-2

4 bits on parity off

2 bits on parity off

3 bits on parity on

FIGURE B-3

The binary (base 2) number system is used to represent the electronic status of the bits in memory. It also is used for other purposes such as addressing the memory locations. Another number system that commonly is used with computers is **hexadecimal** (base 16). The computer uses the hexadecimal system to communicate with a programmer when a problem with a program exists, because it would be difficult for the programmer to understand the 0s and 1s of binary code. Figure B-4 shows how the decimal values 0 through 15 are represented in binary and hexadecimal.

The mathematical principles that apply to the binary and hexadecimal number systems are the same as those that apply to the decimal number system. To help you better understand these principles, this section starts with the familiar decimal system, then progresses to the binary and hexadecimal number systems.

The Decimal Number System

The decimal number system is a base 10 number system (deci means ten). The base of a number system indicates how many symbols are used in it. The decimal number system uses 10 symbols: 0 through 9. Each of the symbols in the number system has a value associated with it. For example, 3 represents a quantity of three and 5 represents a quantity of five.

The decimal number system also is a positional number system. This means that in a number such as 143, each position in the number has a value associated with it. When you look at the decimal number 143, the 3 is in the ones, or units, position and represents three ones or (3 x 1); the 4 is in the tens position and represents four tens or (4 x 10); and

DECIMAL	BINARY	HEXADECIMAL
0	0000	0
1	0001	1
2	0010	2
3	0011	3
4	0100	4
5	0101	5
6	0110	6
7	0111	7
8	1000	8
9	1001	9
10	1010	A
11	1011	B
12	1100	C
13	1101	D
14	1110	E
15	1111	F

FIGURE B-4

the 1 is in the hundreds position and represents one hundred or (1 x 100). The number 143 is the sum of the values in each position of the number (100 + 40 + 3 = 143). The chart in Figure B-5 shows how you can calculate the positional values (hundreds, tens, and units) for a number system. Starting on the right and working to the left, the base of the number system, in this case 10, is raised to consecutive powers (10^0, 10^1, 10^2). These calculations are a mathematical way of determining the place values in a number system.

When you use number systems other than decimal, the same principles apply. The base of the number system indicates the number of symbols that are used, and each position in a number system has a value associated with it. By raising the base of the number system to consecutive powers beginning with zero, you can calculate the positional value.

power of 10	10^2	10^1	10^0	1	4	3	=	
				(1×10^2) +	(4×10^1) +	(3×10^0)	=	
positional value	100	10	1	(1×100) +	(4×10) +	(3×1)	=	
number	1	4	3	100 +	40 +	3	=	143

FIGURE B-5

The Binary Number System

As previously discussed, binary is a base 2 number system (bi means two), and the symbols it uses are 0 and 1. Just as each position in a decimal number has a place value associated with it, so does each position in a binary number. In binary, the place values, moving from right to left, are successive powers of two (2^0, 2^1, 2^2, 2^3) or (1, 2, 4, 8). To construct a binary number, you place ones in the positions where the corresponding values add up to the quantity you want to represent; you place zeros in the other positions. For example, in a four-digit binary number, the binary place values are (from right to left) 1, 2, 4, and 8. The binary number 1001 has ones in the positions for the values 1 and 8 and zeros in the positions for 2 and 4. Therefore, the quantity represented by binary 1001 is 9 (8 + 0 + 0 + 1) (Figure B-6).

The Hexadecimal Number System

The hexadecimal number system uses 16 symbols to represent values (hex means six, deci means ten). These include the symbols 0 through 9 and A through F (Figure B-4 on the previous page). The mathematical principles previously discussed also apply to hexadecimal (Figure B-7).

The primary reason why the hexadecimal number system is used with computers is because it can represent binary values in a more compact and readable form and because the conversion between the binary and the hexadecimal number systems is very efficient.

An eight-digit binary number (a byte) can be represented by a two-digit hexadecimal number. For example, in the ASCII code, the character M is represented as 01001101. This value can be represented in hexadecimal as 4D. One way to convert this binary number (4D) to a hexadecimal number is to divide the binary number (from right to left) into groups of four digits; calculate the value of each group; and then change any two-digit values (10 through 15) into the symbols A through F that are used in hexadecimal (Figure B-8).

power of 2	2^3	2^2	2^1	2^0		1	0	0	1 =
						(1×2^3) + (0×2^2) + (0×2^1) + (1×2^0) =			
positional value	8	4	2	1		(1×8) + (0×4) + (0×2) + (1×1) =			
binary	1	0	0	1		8 + 0 + 0 + 1 = 9			

FIGURE B-6

power of 16	16^1	16^0		A	5	=
				(10×16^1) + (5×16^0) =		
positional value	16	1		(10×16) + (5×1) =		
hexadecimal	A	5		160 + 5 = 165		

FIGURE B-7

positional value	8421	8421
binary	0100	1101
decimal	4	13
hexadecimal	4	D

FIGURE B-8

APPENDIX C
Computer Acronyms

Acronym	Description	Page
AC	alternating current	4.32
ADA	Americans with Disabilities Act	5.35
ADC	analog-to-digital converter	1.37, 5.14
AGP	Accelerated Graphics Port	4.32
ALU	arithmetic logic unit	4.06
AMD	Advanced Micro Devices	4.38
AOL	America Online	2.38
ARPA	Advanced Research Projects Agency	2.02
ARPANET	Advanced Research Projects Agency network	2.03
ASCII	American Standard Code for Information Interchange	4.14
ASP	application service provider	3.32
ATM	automated teller machine	5.31
B2B	business-to-business	2.25
B2C	business-to-consumer	2.24
BIOS	basic input/output system	8.05
Bit	binary digit	4.13
BMP	bit map	2.19
C2C	consumer-to-consumer	2.25
CAD	computer-aided design	3.21
CAI	computer-aided instruction	3.28
CAM	computer-aided manufacturing	1.36
CBT	computer-based training	3.28
CCD	charge-coupled device	5.20
CD	compact disc	1.06, 1.07, 7.15-21
CD-E	compact disc-erasable	7.20
CD-R	compact disc-recordable	7.20
CD-ROM	compact disc read-only memory	7.17
CD-RW	compact disc-rewritable	7.20
CD-RW/DVD	compact disc-rewritable drive/digital video disc	7.22
CF	CompactFlash	7.26
CMOS	complementary metal-oxide semiconductor	4.22
COM port	communications port	4.27
CPU	central processing unit	1.06, 4.05-13
CRM	customer relationship management	1.29
CRT	cathode-ray tube	6.04
DAC	digital-to-analog converter	1.37, 6.31
DC	direct current	4.32
DDR SDRAM	double data rate synchronous dynamic random access memory	4.18, 4.22
DDWG	Digital Display Working Group	6.11
DHCP	Dynamic Host Configuration Protocol	2.37
DIMM	dual inline memory module	4.18
DIP	dual inline package	4.05
DL	distance learning	3.32
DLP projector	digital light processing projector	6.26
DNA	Windows Distributed interNet Applications	8.25
DNS	domain name system	2.08
DOS	Disk Operating System	8.20
Dpi	dots per inch	5.22, 6.16
DRAM	dynamic random access memory	4.18
DRM	Digital Rights Management	8.21
DSL	Digital Subscriber Line	2.05
DSP	digital signal processor	1.37, 5.20

Acronym	Description	Page
DTP	desktop publishing	3.21
DTV	digital television	6.12
DV camera	digital video camera	5.22
DVD	digital versatile disc or digital video disc	1.06, 7.15-17
DVD drive	digital versatile disc or digital video disc drive	1.07, 7.15
DVD writer	digital versatile disc or digital video disc writer	7.23
DVD-R	digital versatile disc or digital video disc recordable	7.23
DVD+RAM	digital versatile disc or digital video disc + random access memory	7.23
DVD-ROM	digital versatile disc or digital video disc read-only memory	1.07, 7.22
DVD+RW	digital versatile disc or digital video disc + rewriteable	7.23
DVD-video format	digital versatile disc or digital video disc-video format	7.22
DVI	Digital Video Interface	6.11
DVI port	Digital Video Interface port	6.11
EBCDIC	Extended Binary Coded Decimal Interchange	4.14
E-book	electronic book	6.10
E-commerce	electronic commerce	1.27, 2.24-25
EEPROM	electrically erasable programmable read-only memory	4.20
E-filing	electronic filing	3.26
EIDE	Enhanced Integrated Drive Electronics	7.14
E-mail	electronic mail	1.11, 2.25-28
E-money	electronic money	7.28
EMR	electromagnetic radiation	6.06, 8.62
FAQ	frequently asked questions	2.34, 3.33
Fax	facsimile	6.25-26
FC-PGA	flip chip-PGA	4.05
FTP	File Transfer Protocol	2.29
GB	gigabyte	4.16
GHz	gigahertz	4.08
GIF	Graphics Interchange Format	2.19, 2.20
GIGO	garbage in, garbage out	1.08
GPU	graphics processing unit	6.08
GUI	graphical user interface	1.12, 8.08
HD	high density	7.06
HDTV	high-definition television	6.12
HP	Hewlett-Packard	1.39, 6.32
HPA	high-performance addressing	6.11
http	Hypertext Transfer Protocol	2.11
Hz	hertz	4.08
IC	integrated circuit	4.04, 4.39
ICANN	Internet Corporation for Assigned Names and Numbers	2.08
IDE controllers	Integrated Device Electronics controllers	7.14
IM	instant messaging	2.32
IP address	Internet Protocol address	2.08, 2.37
IPng	Internet protocol Next Generation	2.37
IPv6	Internet Protocol version 6	2.37
IR	infrared	4.29
IrDA	Infrared Data Association	4.29
IRQ	interrupt request	8.13

Acronym	Description	Page
IS	information system	1.22
ISA bus	Industry Standard Architecture bus	4.32
ISDN	Integrated Services Digital Network	2.05
ISP	Internet service provider	2.06
IT department	information technology department	1.29
JPEG	Joint Photographic Experts Group	2.18, 7.19
K	kilobyte	4.16
KB	kilobyte	4.16
KBps	kilobytes per second	7.05, 7.18
L1 cache	Level 1 cache	4.20
L2 cache	Level 2 cache	4.20
L3 cache	Level 3 cache	4.20
LCD	liquid crystal display	6.10, 8.57
LQ	letter-quality	6.15
Mac OS	Macintosh Operating System	1.17, 3.03, 8.22
Mac OS X	Macintosh Operating System X	3.03, 3.05, 8.22
MB	megabyte	4.16
MBps	megabytes per second	7.05, 7.14
M-commerce	mobile commerce	2.24
MHz	megahertz	4.22
MICR	magnetic-ink character recognition	5.29
MIDI	Musical Instrument Digital Interface	4.29, 5.15
Mini-DVD	mini-digital video disc	7.23
MIPS	millions of instructions per second	4.08
MP	million pixels	5.21
MPEG	Moving Pictures Experts Group	2.22
MPEG-4	Moving Pictures Experts Group 4	2.22
MS-DOS	Microsoft Disk Operating System	8.20
MSN	Microsoft Network, The	2.06, 2.16, 2.27
Netiquette	Internet etiquette	2.34
NLQ	near letter quality	6.14
NOS	network operating system	8.14
Ns	nanosecond	4.22
NSF	National Science Foundation	2.03, 2.04
NTSC	National Television Standards Committee	6.12
OCR	optical character recognition	5.26
OLED	organic light emitting diode	6.11
OMR	optical mark recognition	5.27
OS	operating system	1.13, 8.02-27
OSP	online service provider	2.06
Palm OS	Palm operating system	8.27
PC	personal computer	1.16-17
PC Card	personal computer Card	4.24, 7.24-27
PC-compatible	personal computer compatible	1.17
PCD	photo compact disc file format	7.19
PC-DOS	personal computer Disk Operating System	8.20
PCI bus	Peripheral Component Interconnect bus	4.32
PCL	Printer Control Language	6.19
PCMCIA	Personal Computer Memory Card International Association	4.24
PC-to-TV port	personal computer-to-television port	8.54
PDA	personal digital assistant	1.19

Acronym	Description	Page
PDL	page description language	6.19
PGA	pin grid array	4.05
PhotoCD	photo compact disc	7.19
Picture CD	picture compact disc	7.19
PIM	personal information manager	3.18
PIN	personal identification number	5.31
Pixel	picture element	5.21, 6.04
PNG format	Portable Network Graphics format	2.19
POP	point of presence	2.05
POP	Post Office Protocol	2.27
POP3	Post Office Protocol 3	2.27
POS	point of sale	5.30
POST	power-on self test	8.06
ppi	pixels (picture elements) per inch	5.21, 5.22
PROM	programmable read-only memory	4.20
Pure Tablet PCs	Pure Tablet personal computers	8.56
RAM	random access memory	4.16, 4.17-19
RDRAM	Rambus® dynamic random access memory	4.18
RHCE	Red Hat Certified Engineer	8.32
RIMM	Rambus® inline memory module	4.18
ROM	read-only memory	4.20
Rpm	revolutions per minute	7.11
SCSI	small computer system interface	4.29
SD	Secure Digital	7.26
SDRAM	synchronous dynamic random access memory	4.18
SIMM	single inline memory module	4.18
SMS	short message service	5.18
SMTP	simple mail transfer protocol	2.27
SOHO	small office/home office	1.26
SRAM	static random access memory	4.18
SVGA	super video graphics array	6.08
Symbian OS	Symbian operating system	8.27
TFT display	thin-film transistor display	6.11
TIFF	Tagged Image File Format	2.19
TRACERT	traceroute	8.31
UPC	Universal Product Code	5.28
UPS	uninterruptible power supply	8.52
URL	Uniform Resource Locator	2.10
USB	universal serial bus	4.32
USB 2.0	universal serial bus 2.0	4.28
User ID	user identification	8.14
VESA	Video Electronics Standards Association	6.08
VR	virtual reality	2.22
W3C	World Wide Web Consortium	2.04, 2.39
WBT	Web-based training	3.32
Windows DNA	Windows Distributed interNet Applications	8.25
WSP	wireless service provider	2.06
WWW	World Wide Web	2.09
WYSIWYG	what you see is what you get	3.05
ZIF	zero-insertion force	4.11

INDEX

PHOTO CREDITS

Chapter 1: *Opener and End of Chapter margin: Photo 1* Courtesy of Ford Motor Company; *Photo 2* ©www.comstock.com; *Photo 3* Courtesy of Fujitsu Siemens Computers; *Photo 4* Courtesy of Handspring, Inc.; *Figure 1-1a* ©Barros & Barros/The Image Bank; *Upper left hand page folio* ©2002 PhotoDisc; *Upper right hand page folio* ©2002 PhotoDisc; *Figure 1-1b* ©2002 PhotoDisc; *Figure 1-1c* ©2002 PhotoDisc; *Figure 1-1d* ©2002 PhotoDisc; *Figure 1-1e* ©2002 PhotoDisc; *Figure 1-2* ©2002 EyeWire Collection; *Figure 1-3a* Courtesy of Dell Computer Corporation; *Figure 1-3b* Courtesy of Logitech, Inc.; *Figure 1-3c* Courtesy of Hewlett-Packard Company; *Figure 1-3d* Courtesy of Telex Communications, Inc.; *Figure 1-3e* Courtesy of SanDisk; *Figure 1-3f* Courtesy of SanDisk; *Figure 1-3g* Courtesy of Hewlett-Packard Company; *Figure 1-3h* Photo Courtesy of Linksys; *Figure 1-4* ©Royalty-Free/CORBIS; *Figure 1-5* Courtesy of Seagate Technology; *Figure 1-6* ©Scott Goodwin Photography; *Figure 1-11* Courtesy of William Vermaat; *Figure 1-12 Step 2* Courtesy of Kingston Technology Company, Inc.; *Figure 1-14* ©Scott Goodwin Photography; *Looking Ahead 1-1a* Courtesy of Xybernaut Corporation; *Looking Ahead 1-1b* Courtesy of Xybernaut Corporation; *Figure 1-17* Courtesy of International Business Machines Corporation; *Figure 1-18* Courtesy of Apple Computer Corporation; *Figure 1-19a* Courtesy of O'Sullivan Furniture; *Figure 1-19b* Courtesy of O'Sullivan Furniture; *Figure 1-20* Courtesy of Dell Computer Corporation; *Figure 1-21a,b* Courtesy of ViewSonic Corporation; *Figure 1-22* Courtesy of OQO, Inc.; *Figure 1-23a* Courtesy of Palm, Inc., Palm is a trademark of Palm, Inc.; *Figure 1-23b* Courtesy of Handspring, Inc.; *Figure 1-23b2* Courtesy of Microsoft® Corporation; *Figure 1-24* Courtesy of Microsoft® Corporation; *Figure 1-25* Courtesy of Hewlett-Packard Company; *Figure 1-26* Courtesy of International Business Machines Corporation; *Figure 1-27* ©Don Gonzalez/Lawrence Livermore National Laboratory; *Figure 1-28 Step 3* ©2002 EyeWire Collection; *Figure 1-29a* ©Larry Dale Gordon/The Image Bank; *Figure 1-29b* ©Ulf E. Wallin/The Image Bank; *Figure 1-29c* ©MICHAEL MALYSZKO/ Taxi; *Figure 1-29d* ©Terry Vine/Stone; *Figure 1-29e* ©Jeff Smith/The Image Bank; *Figure 1-30* ©Larry Dale Gordon/The Image Bank; *Figure 1-31* ©Xavier Bonghi/The Image Bank; *Figure 1-32* Courtesy of Microsoft® Corporation; *Figure 1-33* ©Ulf E. Wallin/The Image Bank; *Figure 1-35a* ©Michael Malyszko/Taxi; *Figure 1-35b* ©Steve Lewis/The Image Bank; *Figure 1-35c1* ©Royalty-Free/CORBIS; *Figure 1-35c2* ©2002 PhotoDisc; *Figure 1-36* ©Jon Feingersh/CORBIS; *Figure 1-37* ©Terry Vine/Stone; *Figure 1-39* Courtesy of NCR Corporation; *Figure 1-40* ©Royalty-Free/CORBIS; *Figure 1-41* ©Jeff Smith/The Image Bank; *Looking Ahead 1-2* ©AFP/CORBIS; *Figure 1-42* ©Loren Santow/Stone; *Figure 1-45* ©Royalty-Free/CORBIS; *Figure 1-46 Step 1* ©AP/WIDE WORLD PHOTOS; *Figure 1-46 Step 3* ©Allan H. Shoemake/Taxi; *Figure 1-48a* Courtesy of Saab Cars USA; *Figure 1-48b* Courtesy of OnStar; *Figure 1-48c* Courtesy of OnStar; *Figure 1-49* ©Luis Castaneda Inc./The Image Bank; *Career Corner* ©Jose Luis Pelaez, Inc./CORBIS; *Technology Trailblazer* ©Reuters NewMedia Inc./CORBIS; *Technology Trailblazer* ©Reuters NewMedia Inc./CORBIS; *Checkpoint: Figure 1* Courtesy of Dell Computer Corporation; *Figure 2* Courtesy of Logitech, Inc.; *Figure 3* Courtesy of Hewlett-Packard Company; *Figure 4* Courtesy of Telex Communications, Inc.; *Figure 5* Courtesy of SanDisk; *Figure 6* Courtesy of SanDisk; *Figure 7* Courtesy of Hewlett-Packard Company; *Figure 8* Photo Courtesy of Linksys. *Timeline: 1937* Courtesy of Iowa State University; *1943* Photo courtesy of The Computer History Museum; *1943* Photo courtesy of The Computer History Museum; *1945* Courtesy of the Archives of the Institute for Advanced Study; *1946* From the Collections of the University of Pennsylvania Archives; *1947* ©IBM Corporate Archives.; *1951* Courtesy Unisys Corporation; *1952* Courtesy of Hagley Museum and Library; *1953* ©IBM Corporate Archives.; *1957* ©IBM Corporate Archives.; *1957* Courtesy of the Department of the Navy; *1958* Courtesy of Texas Instruments; *1959* ©IBM Corporate Archives.; *1960* Courtesy of Hagley Museum and Library; *1964* ©IBM Corporate Archives.; *1965* Courtesy of Dartmouth College; *1965* Courtesy of Digital Equipment Corporation; *1970* ©IBM Corporate Archives.; *1971* Courtesy of Intel Corporation; *1975* Courtesy of InfoWorld; *1975* Photo courtesy of The Computer History Museum; *1976* Courtesy of Apple Computer Corporation; *1976* ©Bettmann/CORBIS; *1979* Photo courtesy of The Computer History Museum; *1980* ©IBM Corporate Archives.; *1980* Courtesy of Microsoft® Corporation; *1981* ©IBM Corporate Archives.; *1982* Courtesy of Zoom Telephonics, Inc.; *1983* ©IBM Corporate Archives; *1983* ©2002 Time Inc. reprinted by permission; *1984* Courtesy of Hewlett-Packard Company; *1984* Courtesy of Apple Computer Corporation; *1984* ©IBM Corporate Archives.; *1987* ©IBM Corporate Archives.; *1989* Courtesy of Intel Corporation; *1989* W3C©1994-2002 (MIT, INRIA, Keio), All Rights Reserved.; *1992* Courtesy of Microsoft® Corporation; *1993* Courtesy of Intel Corporation; *1993* ©Jim Clark/Getty Images; *1993* Courtesy of Netscape Communications Corporation; *1994* Courtesy of Netscape Communications Corporation; *1995* Box shot reprinted with permission from Microsoft Corporation; *1995* Courtesy of Sun Microsystems, Inc.; *1996* Box shot reprinted with permission from Microsoft Corporation.; *1996* ©Reuters/Rick T. Wilking/Archive Photos; *1996* Courtesy of Microsoft Corporation; *1997* ©IBM Corporate Archives.; *1997* I. Uiomonen/CORBIS Sygma; *1997* Courtesy of Intel Corporation; *1997* ©PhotoDisc; *1997* Motion Picture & Television Archives; *1997* Courtesy of Denon Electronics; *1998* Courtesy of Intel Corporation; *1998* Box shot reprinted with permission from Microsoft Corporation; *1998* Courtesy of Apple Computer Corporation; *1999* Box shot reprinted with permission from Microsoft Corporation; *2000* Box shots reprinted with permission from Microsoft Corporation; *2000* Courtesy of Intel Corporation; *2001* Box shots reprinted with permission from Microsoft Corporation; *2001* Courtesy of RCA/Thomson Consumer Electronics; *2001* Compaq Computer Corporation; *2002* Courtesy of Handspring, Inc.; *2002* Courtesy of Intel Corporation; *2002* ©Scott Goodwin Photography; *2002* ©2002 PhotoDisc; *2002* Courtesy of Sharp Electronics; *2003* Courtesy of Palm, Inc., Palm is a trademark of Palm, Inc.; *2003* ©ArtToday.com, Inc., an IMSI Company; *2003* Courtesy of Sony Electronic Inc.; *2003* Courtesy of PhotoDisc, Inc.; *2003* ©2003 Fujitsu Siemens computer. **Chapter 2:** *Figure 2-7a1* Courtesy of Microsoft® Corporation; *Figure 2-7a2* Courtesy of Hewlett-Packard Company; *Figure 2-7b1* Courtesy of AT&T Wireless; *Figure 2-7b2* Courtesy of Nokia. Copyright ©2002 Nokia. All rights reserved. Nokia and Nokia Connecting People are registered trademarks of Nokia Corporation; *Looking Ahead 2-1* ©2002

PhotoDisc; *Looking Ahead 2-2* ©2002 EyeWire Collection; *Figure 2-18 Step 2* Courtesy of International Business Machines Corporation; *Figure 2-18 Step 3* Courtesy of International Business Machines Corporation; *Figure 2-23a* ©RON CHAPPLE/Taxi; *Figure 2-24 Step 5* Courtesy of William Vermaat; *Figure 2-33 Step 1* ©Walter Hodges/CORBIS; *Figure 2-33 Step 2* ©Walter Hodges/CORBIS; *Figure 2-33 Steps 3,4,5* ©AJA Productions/The Image Bank; *Career Corner* ©Andreas Pollok/Taxi; *Technology Trailblazer* ©Sam Ogden / Photo Researchers, Inc.; *Technology Trailblazer* Courtesy of Anita Brown. **Guide to World Wide Web Sites and Searching Techniques:** *Page 2.50* Courtesy of PhotoDisc, Inc.; *Page 2.50* ©2003 Fujitsu Siemens computer; *Page 2.50* ©2002 Dynamic Graphics, Inc.; *Page 2.51* Earth, ©2002 Dynamic Graphics Inc.; *Page 2.51* Courtesy of PhotoDisc, Inc; *Page 2.52* Mouse, Courtesy of PhotoDisc Inc.; *Page 2.53* Earth and computer, ©2002 Dynamic Graphics Inc.; *Page 2.54* Hand, Courtesy of PhotoDisc Inc.; *Page 2.55* Father and Son, Courtesy of PhotoDisc Inc.; *Page 2.56* Girl and laptop, Courtesy of PhotoDisc Inc.; *Page 2.58* Courtesy of PhotoDisc Inc.; *Page 2.58* Earth, ©2002 Dynamic Graphics Inc.; *Page 2.60* ©2003 Fujitsu Siemens computer; *Page 2.61* Courtesy of PhotoDisc, Inc.; *Page 2.62* Courtesy of PhotoDisc, Inc.; *Page 2.63* Boy with computer, Courtesy of PhotoDisc Inc.; *Page 2.63* Background, ©2002 Dynamic Graphics Inc. **Chapter 3:** *Upper left hand page folio* ©2002 PhotoDisc; *Upper right hand page folio* ©2002 PhotoDisc; *Figure 3-3a* ©2002 EyeWire Collection; *Figure 3-3b* ©2002 EyeWire Collection; *Figure 3-9* ©2002 PhotoDisc; *Figure 3-17* Courtesy of Fujitsu Siemens Computers; *Looking Ahead 3-1* ©2002 PhotoDisc; *Figure 3-19* Courtesy of Intuit; *Figure 3-21* ©Greg Pease/Stone; *Figure 3-22* Courtesy of Adobe; *Figure 3-23* Courtesy of Adobe; *Figure 3-24* Courtesy of Adobe; *Figure 3-25* Courtesy of Macromedia, Inc.; *Figure 3-27* ©2002 PhotoDisc; *Figure 3-28* Courtesy of Cosmi Corporation; *Figure 3-29* Courtesy of Intuit; *Figure 3-31* Courtesy of Adobe; *Figure 3-33* Courtesy of Broderbund; *Figure 3-34* ©AFP/CORBIS; *Looking Ahead 3-2* ©2002 PhotoDisc; *Figure 3-36* Courtesy of Broderbund; *Figure 3-42* ©Scott Goodwin Photography; *Career Corner* ©2002 EyeWire Collection; *High-Tech Talk* ©Artville/Getty Images; *Technology Trailblazer* ©Louis Fabian Bachrach/Daniel Bricklin; *Technology Trailblazer* ©Reuters NewMedia Inc./CORBIS. **Chapter 4:** *Opener and End of Chapter margin: Photo 1* Courtesy of Intel Corporation; *Photo 2* Courtesy of Kingston Technology Company, Inc.; *Photo 3* Courtesy of Creative Labs, Inc.; *Photo 4* Courtesy of Matrox Graphics Inc.; *Photo 5* Courtesy of Creative Labs, Inc.; *Upper left hand page folio* ©Bruce Dale/National Geographic; *Upper right hand page folio* Courtesy of Scott Goodwin Photography; *Figure 4-1a* Courtesy of Gateway, Inc; *Figure 4-1b* Courtesy of Apple Computer Corporation; *Figure 4-1c* Courtesy of Dell Computer Corporation; *Figure 4-1d* Courtesy of Palm, Inc., Palm is a trademark of Palm, Inc.; *Figure 4-2a* ©Scott Goodwin Photography; *Figure 4-2b* Courtesy of Intel Corporation; *Figure 4-2c* Courtesy of Kingston Technology Company, Inc.; *Figure 4-2d* Courtesy of Creative Labs, Inc.; *Figure 4-2e* Courtesy of Matrox Graphics Inc.; *Figure 4-2f* Courtesy of Creative Labs, Inc.; *Figure 4-2g* Courtesy of 3Com Corporation; *Figure 4-3* ©Scott Goodwin Photography; *Figure 4-4a* ©James A. Sugar/CORBIS; *Figure 4-4b* ©2002 PhotoDisc; *Figure 4-4c* Courtesy of Intel Corporation; *Figure 4-4d* Courtesy of Intel Corporation; *Figure 4-9a,b* Courtesy of Intel Corporation; *Figure 4-9c* Courtesy of Intel Corporation; *Figure 4-9d* Courtesy of Intel Corporation; *Figure 4-10 Step 1, Step 2, Step 3* ©Scott Goodwin Photography; *Figure 4-11* Courtesy of HLS Systems, Inc.; *Figure 4-16, Step 2* ©Scott Goodwin Photography; *Figure 4-17a* Courtesy of Amtrak; *Figure 4-17b* ©2002 PhotoDisc; *Figure 4-19 hard disk* Courtesy of Seagate Technology; *Figure 4-19 RAM* Courtesy of Kingston Technology Company, Inc.; *Figure 4-20a* ©Scott Goodwin Photography; *Figure 4-20b* Courtesy of Kingston Technology Company, Inc.; *Figure 4-21* Courtesy of William Vermaat; *Figure 4-24 Step 2* Courtesy of SONICblue; *Looking Ahead Box 4-1* ©2000 IEEE; *Figure 4-26* ©Scott Goodwin Photography; *Figure 4-28* ©Scott Goodwin Photography; *Figure 4-29* ©Scott Goodwin Photography; *Figure 4-30* Courtesy of SanDisk; *Figure 4-31a* Courtesy of William Vermaat; *Figure 4-31b* ©Scott Goodwin Photography; *Figure 4-32* ©Scott Goodwin Photography; *Figure 4-37* Photo: courtesy of Nokia. Copyright ©2002 Nokia. All rights reserved. Nokia and Nokia Connecting People are registered trademarks of Nokia Corporation; *Figure 4-38* Courtesy of Intel Corporation; *Figure 4-39a* Courtesy of Intel Corporation; *Figure 4-39b* Courtesy of Kingston Technology Company, Inc.; *Figure 4-40* Courtesy of William Vermaat; *Figure 4-41a* ©Scott Goodwin Photography; *Figure 4-41b* Courtesy of Palm, Inc., Palm is a trademark of Palm, Inc.; *Figure 4-42a* ©Scott Goodwin Photography; *Figure 4-42b* ©Scott Goodwin Photography; *Figure 4-43* ©Scott Goodwin Photography; *Figure 4-44* Courtesy of Fujitsu Siemens Computers; *Figure 4-45a* ©Larry Dale Gordon/The Image Bank; *Figure 4-45b* ©Ulf E. Wallin/The Image Bank; *Figure 4-45c* ©MICHAEL MALYSZKO/ Taxi; *Figure 4-45d* ©Terry Vine/Stone; *Figure 4-45e* ©Jeff Smith/The Image Bank; *Looking Ahead 4-2* ©2001 Time Inc. reprinted by permission; *Career Corner* Courtesy of Intel Corporation; *Technology Trailblazer* ©AFP/CORBIS; *Technology Trailblazer* ©BORENSZTEIN, LEON/TimePix; *Checkpoint* ©Scott Goodwin Photography. **Chapter 5:** *Opener and End of Chapter margin: Photo 1* Morph Duo Ball-Point Pen with Stylus Courtesy of A. T. Cross Co.; *PDA and accessories photos* Courtesy of Handspring, Inc.; *Upper left hand page folio* Courtesy of 3M Touch Systems; *Upper right hand page folio* ©Bruce Avery/SuperStock; *Figure 5-1a* ©2002 EyeWire Collection; *Figure 5-1b* ©2002 EyeWire Collection; *Figure 5-1c* Courtesy of 3M Touch Systems; *Figure 5-1d* Courtesy of Fujitsu Siemens Computers; *Figure 5-1e* ©Bruce Ayres/Stone; *Figure 5-1f1* ©2002 Photodex Corporation; *Figure 5-1f2* Courtesy of Casio, Inc.; *Figure 5-1g* ©Jose Luis Pelaez, Inc./CORBIS; *Figure 5-1h* ©Mark Douet/Stone; *Figure 5-3* Courtesy of Logitech, Inc.; *Figure 5-6* ©2002 PhotoDisc; *Figure 5-7* Courtesy of Microsoft® Corporation; *Figure 5-9* Courtesy of Microsoft® Corporation; *Figure 5-12a* ©Scott Goodwin Photography; *Figure 5-12b* ©Scott Goodwin Photography; *Figure 5-13* ©Bruce Avery/SuperStock; *Figure 5-14a,b* Courtesy of International Business Machines Corporation; *Figure 5-15a* Courtesy of Logitech, Inc.; *Figure 15-15b* Courtesy of Logitech, Inc.; *Figure 15-15c* Courtesy of Logitech, Inc.; *Figure 5-16* ©Greg Pease/Stone; *Figure 5-17* Courtesy of NCR Corporation; *Figure 5-18a* ©David Young-Wolff/Photo Edit — All rights reserved.; *Figure 5-18b* Courtesy of GTCO Calcomp Corp.; *Figure 5-19a* Courtesy of Wacom Technology Corp.; *Figure 5-19b* Courtesy of Fujitsu Siemens Computers; *Figure 5-19c*

PHOTO CREDITS

©Michael Keller/CORBIS; *Looking Ahead 5-1* VPen Courtesy of OTM Technologies Ltd; *Figure 5-21* ©Michael Newman/Photo Edit—All right reserved.; *Figure 5-22a* Courtesy of Handspring, Inc.; *Figure 5-22 collage PDA accessories* Courtesy of Handspring, Inc.; *Figure 5-23a* Courtesy of Palm, Inc., Palm is a trademark of Palm, Inc.; *Figure 5-23b* Courtesy of Palm, Inc., Palm is a trademark of Palm, Inc.; *Figure 5-23c* Courtesy of Palm, Inc., Palm is a trademark of Palm, Inc.; *Figure 5-24* ©AP/WIDE WORLD PHOTOS; *Figure 5-25* Courtesy of Fujitsu Siemens Computers; *Figure 5-26a* Courtesy of Gary Herrington; *Figure 5-26b* Courtesy of Gary Herrington; *Figure 5-26c* Courtesy of Gary Herrington; *Figure 5-27* compact flash card Courtesy of Sandisk; *Figure 5-29* ©David Young-Wolff / Photo Edit — All rights reserved.; *Figure 5-30* ©Andreas Pollok/Stone *Figure 5-31* ©Jon Feingersh/CORBIS; *Figure 5-32a* Courtesy of Hewlett-Packard Company; *Figure 5-32b* Courtesy of C Technologies AB; *Figure 5-32c* Courtesy of Visioneer, Inc.; *Figure 5-32d* Howtek HiResolve 8000 Drum Scanner, image courtesy of Howtek, Inc.; *Figure 5-35* Courtesy of William Vermaat; *Figure 5-36a* Courtesy of Symbol Technologies, Inc.; *Figure 5-36b* ©Phil Degginger/Stone; *Figure 5-39* Courtesy of William Vermaat; *Figure 5-40* Courtesy of Symbol Technologies, Inc.; *Figure 5-41* Courtesy of NCR Corporation; *Figure 5-42* ©Tony Freeman/Photo Edit—All rights reserved.; *Figure 5-43* Courtesy of Microsoft® Corporation; *Figure 5-44* Courtesy of Fujitsu Siemens Computers; *Figure 5-45* Courtesy of IR Recognition Systems; *Figure 5-46* Courtesy of Iridian Technologies, Inc.; *Figure 5-47a* Courtesy of Fujitsu Siemens Computers; *Figure 5-47b* Courtesy of Fujitsu Siemens Computers; *Figure 5-48a* ©Larry Dale Gordon/The Image Bank; *Figure 5-48b* ©Ulf E. Wallin/The Image Bank; *Figure 5-48c* ©MICHAEL MALYSZKO/ Taxi; *Figure 5-48d* ©Terry Vine/Stone; *Figure 5-48e* ©Jeff Smith/The Image Bank; *Figure 5-49* Courtesy of www.keytools.com; *Figure 5-51* Courtesy of NaturalPoint; *Looking Ahead 5-2* ©International Stock; *Career Corner* Courtesy Superstock; *Technology Trailblazer* ©AP/WIDE WORLD PHOTOS; *Technology Trailblazer* ©John Harrington Photography; *Checkpoint photo* Courtesy of Logitech, Inc.; *Learn It Online photo* Courtesy of Logitech, Inc. **PDA Application Software:** *Page 5.50* Palm, Courtesy of Dell Computer Corporation; *Page 5.50* Woman, Courtesy of PhotoDisc, Inc.; *Page 5.50* Couple with Palm, ©2003 Fujitsu Siemens computer; *Page 5.51* Palm with memory stick, ©1999-2003 Handspring; *Page 5.52* Girl with Palm, ©2003 Fujitsu Siemens computer; *Page 5.53* Hand hold palm on, ©2003 Fujitsu Siemens computer; *Page 5.54* Three people, ©2003 Fujitsu Siemens computer; *Page 5.56* Doctor and patient, ©2003 Fujitsu Siemens computer; *Page 5.59* ©2003 Fujitsu Siemens computer; *Page 5.60* ©2002 Sony Electronic, Inc.; *Page 5.61* Chinese girl, Courtesy of PhotoDisc, Inc. **Chapter 6:** *Opener and End of Chapter margin: Photo1* Courtesy of Sandisk; *Photo 2* Courtesy of Hewlett-Packard Company; *Upper right hand page folio* ©Charles Gupton/CORBIS; *Figure 6-1a1* Courtesy of International Business Machines Corporation; *Figure 6-1a2* Palm, property of Genicom; *Figure 6-1a3* Courtesy of Handspring, Inc.; *Figure 6-1b1* Courtesy of Handspring, Inc.; *Figure 6-1b2* Courtesy of Hewlett-Packard Company; *Figure 6-1c1* Courtesy of Altec Lansing® Technologies, Inc.; *Figure 6-1c2* Courtesy of Fujitsu Siemens Computers; *Figure 6-1d1* Photo: courtesy of Nokia. Copyright ©2002 Nokia. All rights reserved. Nokia and Nokia Connecting People are registered trademarks of Nokia Corporation.; *Figure 6-1d2* Courtesy of Sony Electronics Inc.; *Figure 6-2* Courtesy of ViewSonic Corporation; *Figure 6-4* Courtesy of Environmental Protection Agency; *Figure 6-6, Step 1* Courtesy of Intel Corporation; *Figure 6-9* Courtesy of International Business Machines Corporation; *Figure 6-10a* Courtesy of Dell Computer Corporation; *Figure 6-10b* Courtesy of ViewSonic Corporation; *Figure 6-10c* Courtesy of Sony Electronics Inc.; *Figure 6-10d* Courtesy of Handspring, Inc.; *Figure 6-10e* Siemens press photo ©Siemens AG, Munich/Berlin; *Figure 6-11a* Image used with permission from Gemstar-eBook Group Limited, a subsidiary of Gemstar-TV Guide International, Inc. All Rights Reserved.; *Figure 6-11b* Courtesy of RCA/Thomson Consumer Electronics; *Figure 6-13* Courtesy of ATI Technologies, Inc.; *Figure 6-14* Courtesy of ViewSonic Corporation; *Looking Ahead 6-1* Photo Courtesy of Palo Alto Research Center (PARC); *Figure 6-17* Courtesy of Oki Data Americas, Inc.; *Figure 6-18* Courtesy of International Business Machines Corporation; *Figure 6-19 collage* Inkjet printer and output pictures provided by Epson America, Inc.; *Figure 6-19a* Courtesy of Gary Herrington; *Figure 6-21* Courtesy of Gary Herrington; *Figure 6-22, Step 1* Courtesy of SanDisk; *Figure 6-22* Courtesy of Gary Herrington; *Figure 6-23* Courtesy of Hewlett-Packard Company; *Figure 6-25b* Courtesy of Sony Electronics Inc.; *Figure 6-26* Courtesy of Canon U.S.A., Inc.; *Figure 6-27* Courtesy of Neopost, Inc.; *Figure 6-28* Courtesy of Encad, Inc.-A Kodak Company; *Figure 6-29a* Courtesy of Palm, Inc., Palm is a trademark of Palm, Inc.; *Figure 6-29a2* Courtesy of Palm, Inc., Palm is a trademark of Palm, Inc.; *Figure 6-29b* Courtesy of 3Com Corporation; *Figure 6-29b2* Courtesy of Hewlett-Packard Company; *Figure 6-29c* ©Copyright Socket Communications, Inc. All rights reserved.; *Figure 6-29c2* ©Copyright Socket Communications, Inc. All rights reserved.; *Figure 6-30* Courtesy of Dell Computer Corporation; *Figure 6-31* ©Charles Gupton/CORBIS; *Figure 6-33* ©LWA-Stephen Welstead/CORBIS; *Figure 6-35* Courtesy of Panasonic; *Figure 6-36a,b* Courtesy of InFocus; *Looking Ahead 6-2* ©2002 PhotoDisc; *Figure 6-37a* Courtesy of Microsoft® Corporation; *Figure 6-37b* Courtesy of Microsoft® Corporation; *Figure 6-38a* ©Larry Dale Gordon/The Image Bank; *Figure 6-38b* ©Ulf E. Wallin/The Image Bank; *Figure 6-38c* ©MICHAEL MALYSZKO/ Taxi; *Figure 6-38d* ©Terry Vine/Stone; *Figure 6-38e* ©Jeff Smith/The Image Bank; *Figure 6-40a* Courtesy of Freedom Scientific Inc.; *Figure 6-40b* ©Tony Freeman/Photo Edit—All rights reserved; *Career Corner* ©David Young-Wolff/Photo Edit—All rights reserved.; *Technology Trailblazer* Courtesy of Handspring, Inc.; *Technology Trailblazer* Heidi Van Arnem, founder of iCan! Inc. and iCan.com, an online community for people with disabilities, their families and friends; *Checkpoint* Courtesy of ATI Technologies, Inc. **Digital Imaging and Video Technology:** *Page 6.44* ©2002 Sony Electronic, Inc.; *Page 6.44* Family, ©2002 Sony Electronic, Inc.; *Page 6.45* Girl, Courtesy of PhotoDisc, Inc.; *Page 6.46* ©2002 Sony Electronic, Inc.; *Page 6.47* ©2002 Sony Electronic, Inc.; *Page 6.47* SD Card and card reader, ©CompactFlash, a registered trademark of SanDisk Corporation, and ImageMate and SanDisk Ultra are trademarks of SanDisk Corporation, SmartMedia is a trademark of Toshiba Corporation; *Page 6.47* ©IBM Corporation 1994-2003, All rights reserved; *Page 6.48* Woman, ©Eastman Kodak Company, 1994-2003; *Page 6.49* Kiosk, ©Eastman Kodak Company, 1994-2003; *Page 6.49* Camera phone,

©2003 Siemens AG; *Page 6.49* Photo2VCD, ©2001-2002 Photo2VCD Software, All rights reserved; *Page 6.50* Video Cameras, ©2002 Sony Electronic Inc.; *Page 6.51* Video camera, VCR, computers, ©2002 Sony Electronic Inc.; *Page 6.53* Man with tablet PC, ©2002 Sony Electronic Inc.; *Page 6.55* Man with camcorder, Courtesy of PhotoDisc, Inc. **Chapter 7:** *Upper left hand page folio* Courtesy of International Business Machines Corporation; *Figure 7-1a* ©2002 PhotoDisc; *Figure 7-1b* Photo courtesy of Iomega Corporation. Copyright ©2002 Iomega Corporation. All Rights Reserved. Iomega, the sylized "i" logo and product images are property of Iomega Corporation in the United States and/or other countries; *Figure 7-1c* Courtesy of International Business Machines Corporation; *Figure 7-1d* Photo courtesy of Iomega Corporation. Copyright ©2002 Iomega Corporation. All Rights Reserved. Iomega, the sylized "i" logo and product images are property of Iomega Corporation in the United States and/or other countries.; *Figure 7-1e* Photo courtesy of Iomega Corporation. Copyright ©2002 Iomega Corporation. All Rights Reserved. Iomega, the sylized "i" logo and product images are property of Iomega Corporation in the United States and/or other countries.; *Figure 7-1g* Courtesy of Imation Corp.; *Figure 7-1h* Courtesy of Kingston Technology Company, Inc.; *Figure 7-1i* Courtesy of Sony Electronics Inc.; *Figure 7-1j* Courtesy of Eastman Kodak Company; *Figure 7-6b* Courtesy of International Business Machines Corporation; *Figure 7-11a* Photo courtesy of Iomega Corporation. Copyright ©2002 Iomega Corporation. All Rights Reserved. Iomega, the sylized "i" logo and product images are property of Iomega Corporation in the United States and/or other countries.; *Figure 7-11b* Photo courtesy of Iomega Corporation. Copyright ©2002 Iomega Corporation. All Rights Reserved. Iomega, the sylized "i" logo and product images are property of Iomega Corporation in the United States and/or other countries.; *Figure 7-12a* Courtesy of International Business Machines Corporation; *Figure 7-12b* ©Scott Goodwin Photography; *Figure 7-13* ©Biondo Productions/Stone; *Figure 7-14* Courtesy of International Business Machines Corporation; *Figure 7-17a* Courtesy of Intel Corporation; *Figure 7-17c* Courtesy of International Business Machines Corporation; *Figure 7-18a* Photo courtesy of Iomega Corporation. Copyright ©2002 Iomega Corporation. All Rights Reserved. Iomega, the sylized "i" logo and product images are property of Iomega Corporation in the United States and/or other countries.; *Figure 7-18b* Photo courtesy of Iomega Corporation. Copyright ©2002 Iomega Corporation. All Rights Reserved. Iomega, the sylized "i" logo and product images are property of Iomega Corporation in the United States and/or other countries.; *Figure 7-25 Step 3b* ©Michael Newman/Photo Edit All rights reserved.; *Figure 7-27c* Courtesy of International Business Machines Corporation; *Looking Ahead 7-1* Courtesy of InPhase; *Figure 7-29* Courtesy of Seagate Removable Storage Solutions LLC; *Figure 7-31* Photo: courtesy of Nokia. Copyright ©2002 Nokia. All rights reserved. Nokia and Nokia Connecting People are registered trademarks of Nokia Corporation.; *Figure 7-33a* Courtesy of SanDisk; *Figure 7-33b* Courtesy of Palm, Inc., Palm is a trademark of Palm, Inc.; *Figure 7-33c* Courtesy of SanDisk; *Figure 7-33d* Courtesy of SanDisk; *Figure 7-33e* Courtesy of SanDisk; *Figure 7-34a* Courtesy of Kingston Technology Company, Inc.; *Figure 7-34b* Courtesy of Kingston Technology Company, Inc.; *Figure 7-34c* Courtesy of SanDisk; *Figure 7-34d* Courtesy of SanDisk; *Figure 7-34e* Courtesy of International Business Machines Corporation; *Figure 7-34f* Courtesy of JMTek, LLC.; *Figure 7-34f* Courtesy of SanDisk; *Looking Ahead 7-2* Courtesy of IBM Research; *Figure 7-35* Courtesy of SanDisk; *Figure 7-36* Courtesy of Datakey Inc.; *Figure 7-37* Courtesy of Eastman Kodak Company; *Figure 7-39a* ©Larry Dale Gordon/The Image Bank; *Figure 7-39b* ©Ulf E. Wallin/The Image Bank; *Figure 7-39c* ©MICHAEL MALYSZKO/ Taxi; *Figure 7-39d* ©Terry Vine/Stone; *Figure 7-39e* ©Jeff Smith/The Image Bank; *Career Corner* ©Royalty-Free/CORBIS; *Technology Trailblazer* ©AP/WIDE WORLD PHOTOS; *Technology Trailblazer* ©AP/WIDE WORLD PHOTOS. **Chapter 8:** *End of Chapter margin: Photo 1* Courtesy of Intel Corporation; *Photo 2* Courtesy of Kingston Technology Company, Inc.; *Photo 3* Courtesy of Creative Labs, Inc.; *Photo 4* Courtesy of Matrox Graphics Inc.; *Photo 5* Courtesy of Creative Labs, Inc.; *Upper left hand page folio* Courtesy of Microsoft® Corporation; *Figure 8-1h* Courtesy of Kingston Technology Company, Inc., *Figure 8-1c* Courtesy of International Business Machines Corporation; *Figure 8-1d* Courtesy of NEC Solutions (America), Inc.; *Figure 8-1d2* Courtesy of Altec Lansing® Technologies, Inc.; *Looking Ahead 8-1* ©Araldo de Luca/CORBIS; *Figure 8-27* Courtesy of Microsoft® Corporation; *Figure 8-28* Screen shot(s) reprinted by permission from Apple Computer, Inc.; *Figure 8-29* Reproduced by permission from OS/2 Warp Version 4 Copyright 1987, 1995 1996 by International Business Machines Corporation.; *Figure 8-30* Reproduced by permission from http://www.ibm.com Copyright 1994-2002 by International Business Machines Corporation.; *Figure 8-31* Courtesy of Red Hat, Inc.; *Figure 8-32* Courtesy of ViewSonic Corporation; *Looking Ahead 8-2* Microsoft, Xbox and the Xbox Logos are either registered trademarks or trademarks of Microsoft Corporation in the U.S. and/or in other countries.; *Figure 8-33* Courtesy of Fujitsu Siemens Computers; *Figure 8-34* Courtesy of Sony Electronics Inc.; *Figure 8-35* Courtesy of Symbian; *Career Corner* ©2002 PhotoDisc; *Technology Trailblazer* ©Reuters NewMedia Inc./CORBIS; *Technology Trailblazer* ©AP/WIDE WORLD PHOTOS. **Buyer's Guide:** *Figure 1a* Courtesy of International Business Machines Corporation; *Figure 1b* Courtesy of Dell Computer Corporation; *Figure 1c* Courtesy of ViewSonic Corporation; *Figure 1d* Courtesy Courtesy of Palm, Inc., Palm is a trademark of Palm, Inc.; *Figure 12* ©2002 Acer, Inc;* Figure 13* Courtesy of Toshiba America; *Figure 14* Courtesy of Toshiba America; *Figure 15* ©Jon Feingersh/ CORBIS; *Figure 16* ©2002 Acer Inc.; *Figure 19* Courtesy of Microsoft® Corporation; *Figure 21* Courtesy of Fujitsu Siemens Computers; *Figure 22* Courtesy of Sony Electronics, Inc.; *Figure 23* Courtesy of Compaq Computer Corporation; *Figure 25* Courtesy of Handspring, Inc.; *How to Install a Computer* ©Jiang Jin/SuperStock; *Figure 29a* ©Scott Goodwin Photography; *Figure 29b* Courtesy of Intel Corporation; *Figure 29c* Courtesy of Kingston Technologies; *Figure 29d,e* Courtesy of SMC; *Figure 31* Courtesy of Seagate Technology LLC; *How to Maintain Your Computer* ©E. Dygas/Getty Images/Taxi.